## Other Related Titles

| ISBN | AUTHOR | TITLE |
|------|--------|-------|
| 0-07-060360-X | Spohn | *Data Network Design* |
| 0-07-019022-4 | Edmunds | *SAA/LU6.2 Distributed Networks and Applications* |
| 0-07-054418-2 | Sackett | *IBM's Token-Ring Networking Handbook* |
| 0-07-004128-8 | Bates | *Disaster Recovery Planning: Networks, Telecommunications, and Data Communications* |
| 0-07-020346-6 | Feit | *TCP/IP: Architecture, Protocols, and Implementation* |
| 0-07-005076-7 | Berson | *Client/Server Architecture* |
| 0-07-012926-6 | Cooper | *Computer and Communications Security* |
| 0-07-016189-5 | Dayton | *Telecommunications* |
| 0-07-016196-8 | Dayton | *Multi-Vendor Networks: Planning, Selecting, and Maintenance* |
| 0-07-034243-1 | Kessler/Train | *Metropolitan Area Networks: Concepts, Standards, and Service* |
| 0-07-051144-6 | Ranade/Sackett | *Introduction to SNA Networking: A Guide for Using VTAM/NCP* |
| 0-07-051143-8 | Ranade/Sackett | *Advanced SNA Networking: A Professional's Guide to VTAM/NCP* |
| 0-07-033727-6 | Kapoor | *SNA: Architecture, Protocols, and Implementation* |
| 0-07-005553-X | Black | *TCP/IP and Related Protocols* |
| 0-07-005554-8 | Black | *Network Management Standards: SNMP, CMOT, and OSI* |
| 0-07-021625-8 | Fortier | *Handbook of LAN Technology* |
| 0-07-063636-2 | Terplan | *Effective Management of Local Area Networks: Functions, Instruments, and People* |
| 0-07-004563-1 | Baker | *Downsizing: How to Get Big Gains from Smaller Computer Systems* |
| 0-07-046321-2 | Nemzow | *The Token-Ring Management Guide* |
| 0-07-032385-2 | Jain/Agrawala | *Open Systems Interconnection: Its Architecture and Protocols* |
| 0-07-707778-4 | Perley | *Migrating to Open Systems: Taming the Tiger* |
| 0-07-033754-3 | Hebrawi | *OSI Upper Layer Standards and Practices* |
| 0-07-049309-X | Pelton | *Voice Processing* |
| 0-07-057442-1 | Simonds | *McGraw-Hill LAN Communications Handbook* |
| 0-07-060362-6 | McDysan/Spohn | *ATM: Theory and Applications* |
| 0-07-042591-4 | Minoli Vitella | *ATM and Cell Relay Service for Corporate Environments* |
| 0-07-067375-6 | Vaughn | *Client/Server System Design and Implementation* |
| 0-07-004674-3 | Bates | *Wireless Networked Communications: Concepts, Technology, and Implementation* |
| 0-07-042588-4 | Minoli | *Imaging in Corporate Environments* |
| 0-07-005089-9 | Baker | *Networking the Enterprise: How to Build Client/Server Systems That Work* |
| 0-07-004194-6 | Bates | *Disaster Recovery for LANs: A Planning and Action Guide* |
| 0-07-046461-8 | Naugle | *Network Protocol Handbook* |
| 0-07-046322-0 | Nemzow | *FDDI Networking: Planning, Installation, and Management* |
| 0-07-042586-8 | Minoli | *1st, 2nd, and Next Generation LANs* |
| 0-07-046321-2 | Nemzow | *The Token-Ring Management Guide* |

*To order or receive additional information on these or any other McGraw-Hill titles, in the United States please call 1-800-822-8158. In other countries, contact your local McGraw-Hill representative.*  **BC14BCZ**

# SNMP

A Guide to Network Management

## Dr. Sidnie M. Feit

**McGraw-Hill, Inc.**

New York   San Francisco   Washington, D.C.   Auckland   Bogotá
Caracas   Lisbon   London   Madrid   Mexico City   Milan
Montreal   New Delhi   San Juan   Singapore
Sydney   Tokyo   Toronto

**Library of Congress Cataloging-in-Publication Data**

Feit, Sidnie.
    SNMP : a guide to network management / Sidnie Feit.
      p.   cm. — (McGraw-Hill series on computer communications)
    Includes bibliographical references and index.
    ISBN 0-07-020359-8
    1. Simple Network Management Protocol (Computer network protocol)
    2. Computer networks—Management.   I. Title.  II. Series.
    TK5105.55.F45   1995
    004.6'2—dc20                                  94-20346
                                                      CIP

    4 5 6 7 8 9 0  DOC/DOC  9 0 9 8 7

ISBN 0-07-020359-8

*The sponsoring editor for this book was Jerry Papke; the production supervisor was Suzanne W. Babeuf. It was set in Century Schoolbook by North Market Street Graphics.*

*Printed and bound by R. R. Donnelley & Sons Company.*

This book is printed on acid-free paper.

# Trademarks

AIX and RISC System/6000 are trademarks of International Business Machines Corporation.

AppleTalk is a trademark of Apple Computer, Inc.

cisco is a trademark of cisco Systems, Inc.

DEC, VAX, VMS, ULTRIX, DIGITAL, and DECnet are trademarks of Digital Equipment Corporation.

Ethernet is a registered trademark of Xerox Corporation.

Hewlett-Packard and HP are registered trademarks of Hewlett-Packard Company.

HP OpenView is a trademark of Hewlett-Packard Company.

Hyperchannel is a trademark of Network Systems Corp.

IBM, MVS, and OS/2 are trademarks of International Business Machines Corporation.

IBM PC is a registered trademark of International Business Machines Corporation.

Intel is a trademark of Intel Corporation.

LANWatch, PC/TCP, and FTP Software are registered trademarks of FTP Software, Inc.

Microsoft and LAN Manager are registered trademarks of Microsoft Corporation.

MS-DOS is a registered trademark of Microsoft Corporation.

NetBlazer is a trademark of Telebit.

NetView/6000 is a trademark of International Business Machines Corporation.

NetWare and Novell are registered trademarks of Novell, Inc.

Network Computing System is a trademark of Hewlett-Packard Company.

OSF/1 is a trademark of the Open Software Foundation.

Performance Systems International, Inc. owns the copyright for snmplookup.

PC/TCP is a registered trademark of FTP Software, Inc.

Macintosh is a registered trademark of Apple Computer, Inc.

Sniffer is a registered trademark of Network General Corporation.

SunNet Manager is a trademark of SunConnect.

NFS, Network File System, Sun, and SunOS are trademarks of Sun Microsystems, Inc.

PC DOS is a trademark of International Business Machines Corporation.

TransLAN is a registered trademark of Vitalink Communications Corporation.

UNIX is a registered trademark of UNIX System Laboratories Inc.

Xerox is a trademark of Xerox Corporation.

X/Open is a trademark of X/Open Company Limited.

RSA Laboratories is a trademark of RSA Data Security, Inc.

*To Alexandra, Paul, and Walter, who make life interesting.*

# Contents

## Chapter 15.  Managing UDP                                               213

## Chapter 16.  Managing the Exterior Gateway Protocol                     219

## Chapter 17.  Reporting SNMP Traffic                                      229

## Chapter 24.  Managing a DS3/ES3 (T3 or E3) Interface                347

## Chapter 25.  Managing an X.25 Interface                            365

## ABOUT THE AUTHOR

Dr. Sidnie Feit is a systems architect, designer, lecturer, writer, and programmer with more than 20 years of experience working with systems and communications protocols. She is the author of McGraw-Hill's *TCP/IP: Architecture, Protocols, and Implementation.*

# Preface

This book introduces the Simple Network Management Protocol, and includes extensive network management reference materials. It also presents many real-world examples of network management dialogues, using a number of popular tools.

The first goal of the book is to explain the ideas and mechanisms of the simple network management frameworks for both version 1 and version 2 as clearly and plainly as possible.

The second goal is to make the Simple Network Management Protocol (SNMP) truly usable. Someone sitting at a network management console will see terminology, measurements, and error reports that relate to a large number of technologies. Each technology—Ethernet, Token-Ring, FDDI, X.25, Frame Relay, T1, T3, Transparent Bridge, Spanning Tree Bridge, and on and on—has its own language, set of critical measurements, and problems. There are many chapters in the book devoted to managing these different types of networking technologies. Each of these chapters includes a tutorial for the technology. There are descriptions of how the technology works, discussions of what goes wrong, and explanations of measurements and error reports. Theoretical material is supplemented by interactive sessions with real management and monitoring tools.

There are dozens of standards documents relating to SNMP, totaling thousands of pages. Obviously, it is impossible to present every nuance within the covers of a single book. However, this book will familiarize the reader with the style and organization of the source standards documents, and make these sources easy to use.

There are four chapters in this book that cover SNMP version 2 in detail, and explain how authentication, security, and access control are realized.

The reader will need some basic familiarity with TCP/IP in order to understand some of the technical details of this book.

## ACKNOWLEDGMENTS

Gary C. Kessler reviewed the draft for this book, and made many helpful, detailed comments. I want to thank Graham Yarbrough for reading through the manuscript and suggesting many improvements. And because of Graham, the final manuscript contains far fewer exclamation points!

H. Morrow Long, Manager of Development for the Yale Computer Science department, was as always a source of interesting insights into the real world of the Internet. Fredi Israel of OSS Corp. provided insights into the telephony switching world, and the point of view of implementors within that world.

Many RFC authors were courteous and thorough in their replies to questions about their work.

Several vendors contributed their products and their time. Thanks to Z. Bam of IBM for not only providing a copy of *NetView/6000,* but walking me through installation and providing tips on its use. Bob Berger of Network General provided a *"Sniffer"* network monitor that became an extremely valued helper. Sun Microsystems *SunNet Manager* and Hewlett-Packard's *Open View* completed the picture of today's leading management stations.

FTP Software provided the *PC/TCP* package that allowed me to run TCP/IP on a DOS/Windows desktop system and manage the DOS desktop station. FTP Software also provided the *LANWatch* program that captured some useful traces of LAN activity.

*Sidnie M. Feit*

# 1

# Introduction

## 1.1 NEED FOR SIMPLE NETWORK MANAGEMENT

The arrival of PCs, workstations, LANs, and servers changed the shape of networks forever. Where once there were dumb terminals and a handful of intelligent hosts, communities of intelligent systems clustered together and then reached out to communicate with one another.

The market responded with a cornucopia of new devices—local and remote bridges, multiprotocol routers, distributed hubs, and switching hubs. The higher bandwidth requirements of LAN-to-LAN networking brought in high-performance telecommunications equipment, such as T1 DSU/CSU units or frame relay interfaces. Figure 1.1 shows the composition of a modern network.

Customers began to buy systems and equipment from many different vendors. When customers demanded that the vendors supply the means to configure, monitor, and test network equipment, each vendor produced a console product that talked to its equipment using a hand-crafted secret language.

Every time a new product was introduced to the environment, a new user interface elbowed its way into the crowded Network Operations Center. Each user interface came complete with its own terminology, mysterious command phrases, and navigational logic. Every tool measured and counted according to different rules.

It seemed unlikely that the situation could do anything but get steadily more chaotic and more confusing.

But where are we today? There is a widely implemented protocol for network management—the Simple Network Management Protocol or SNMP. There has been rapid and effective cooperation in developing a common language and a common set of measurements for network

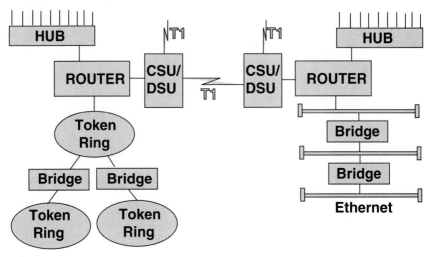

**Figure 1.1** The structure of a modern network.

equipment of all types. Devices ranging in sophistication from repeaters to supercomputers contain the standard software that they need in order to participate in network management.

In this book we shall explore how this happened, how simple network management works, and how to use it.

## 1.2 FEATURES OF THE MANAGEMENT FRAMEWORK

Some special features of the Simple Network Management framework have contributed to its astonishing growth:

- Any device that can support a very small amount of software can participate. Even modems and repeaters are network-manageable!

- Any software developer can use publicly available standard protocols and tools to build a Management Station and offer it as a product.

- A Management Station talks to all devices in the same way, and so potentially can manage any type of device.

- Extending the scope of management is easy. Gather a committee of interested vendor and technology experts, and let them write a set of definitions in a high-level language.

SNMP's very simple software got implementations into the field quickly. There is no faster way than hands-on use to find out what has been left out, what makes life inconvenient, what is never used, and what just does not work! And, fortunately, the framework was flexible enough to make room for corrections and improvements and to allow old and new implementations to work together.

SNMP originally was targeted at the TCP/IP environment, but its rapid adoption and easy extendibility have caused its use to spread into proprietary environments ranging from NetWare to DECnet and SNA.

## 1.3  SNMP VERSION 2

Currently, a second version of SNMP is making its way through the standards process and into implementations. There are many features in SNMP version 2 that are clearly needed and easy to incorporate.

However, many vendors and users are concerned that *some* aspects of version 2 of the Simple Network Management Protocol are not *simple* at all. These parts of version 2 will have to travel a rocky road to adoption and use. The reason is that version 2 tries to solve some very hard problems. Among the thorniest are:

- When I receive a network management message, how can I be sure of the identity of the originator?
- How can I protect my information from network eavesdroppers?
- How do I know that a new message is not just a replay of an old one?

There are many sophisticated application environments in daily use today that do not attempt to solve these problems. The SNMP version 2 developers felt that the problems had to be addressed. As computing becomes increasingly distributed, the integrity of the devices that hold the entire enterprise together has to be protected.

### 1.3.1  Treatment of Versions in This Book

Both SNMP version 1 and SNMP version 2 are presented in the text. The improvements provided by version 2 are described as we go along, and version 2 is described as a coherent whole in the final chapters of the book.

However, significant attention is devoted to version 1, since it can be expected that real implementations will continue to adhere to this version for quite a long transitional period. At the time of writing, version 2 has not yet attained standard status, and is still subject to revision.

## 1.4  TERMINOLOGY

Every time a new technology is introduced, the language of data communications gets reinvented! The terms "element," "device," "node," and "system" can refer to any kind of networking equipment. All of these terms will be used in the chapters that follow. Any device—from a repeater to a supercomputer—will be considered a node *if* it has been assigned a network address, and if it contains the software and instrumentation that allow a management station to sense it or talk to it in some way.

We have made an effort to select a fairly simple vocabulary and stick with it throughout the book. Some of the terminology will be described in the sections that follow.

In some cases, vendors within a particular technology will choose a word from the networking word-stock and use it for their own special purposes. When a chapter deals with a special technology, it will explain the language of that particular environment, and use it.

### 1.4.1  LANs and Stations

Authors who write about LAN equipment customarily use the term *station* for any addressable system on a LAN, no matter what its networking role may be. When discussing LANs, we will defer to common usage, and talk about "stations."

### 1.4.2  Bytes and Octets

To most of us, the word *byte* means an 8-bit quantity. However, the term *byte* also has been used by some computer vendors to refer to their addressable units of data in computer memory. Computer designers have created machines with many different *byte* sizes.

Standards writers avoid confusion by using the term *octet*. In this book, byte and octet will be used interchangeably.

### 1.4.3  Frames, Packets, and Protocol Data Units

Bits are sent across a data link or across a LAN in formatted units called *frames*. A frame has a header, usually carries some payload data, and ends with a trailer field used to detect transmission errors.

The term *packet* sometimes is used instead of frame. For example, vendors of network monitoring products talk about *packet capture* and *packet format*. The SNMP standards documents that deal with network monitors use the term *packet* in this way, and Chapter 28, which deals with network monitors, adopts this terminology in order to be consistent with the standards.

*Packet* also is used to label the unit of data that is transmitted by the network level, most notably for X.25.

The term *Protocol Data Unit* or PDU is a correct (if somewhat dry) term for the formatted unit of data created at any network level. A frame is a link-level PDU, while an X.400 electronic mail message is an application-level PDU.

### 1.4.4   Interfaces

A *network interface* is made up of the software and hardware required to construct frames and transmit them onto a medium. The management of LAN, Point-to-Point, and packet network interfaces will be discussed in detail in Chapters 17 to 26.

### 1.4.5   Ports

*Port* is a very popular word in networking. In TCP/IP, *application port numbers* are used to identify communicating clients and servers.

On the other hand, bridge vendors use the term *port* differently. Data flows into and out of a bridge through its *ports*. When a frame is sent out through a *port* on a bridge, it ends up on a LAN, a Point-to-Point line, or on a circuit across a packet switching net.

To add to the confusion, AppleTalk defines *logical ports* that correspond either to real hardware interfaces or to a software interface for some kind of backbone technology—e.g., a connection to an IP network used to tunnel traffic between two AppleTalk nets.

Throughout this text, a chapter devoted to a technology will explain the way that terms commonly are used within that technology, and then will switch to that common usage. For example, Chapter 27, "Managing Bridges," will use the term *port* in the way that bridge vendors normally do.

### 1.4.6   Multiprotocol Bridge/Routers

Enterprise networks that encompass multiple protocols are becoming commonplace. In order to tie together their heterogeneous networks, many organizations are turning to *multiprotocol bridge/routers.* Multiprotocol bridge/routers allow local and wide area media to be shared by all of the protocols in common use today: TCP/IP, DECnet, NetWare IPX/SPX, AppleTalk, Vines, NetBeui, and others. Some vendors also carry IBM SNA traffic.

### 1.4.7   Tunneling

Some organizations prefer to manage a single protocol across their wide area backbones. IP has become a popular choice. The way that this works is that traffic for any of the other protocols is wrapped up in an IP routing header and moved from a source LAN, onto the wide area backbone, across the backbone, and then onto a destination LAN. This procedure is called *tunneling,* and often is applied to proprietary LAN protocols such as AppleTalk or NetWare IPX/SPX. Figure 1.2 illustrates tunneling.

## 1.5   A BRIEF OVERVIEW OF TCP/IP

SNMP had management of TCP/IP networks as its first objective, and several of the chapters in this book deal with managing components of TCP/IP. We'll present a brief overview of the TCP/IP protocol suite here and save the details for later.

### 1.5.1   The ISO Model

The International Organization for Standardization (ISO) Open Systems Interconnect (OSI) model is a useful blueprint for identifying the major components of TCP/IP. Figure 1.3 compares TCP/IP and OSI layers.

### 1.5.2   The Physical Layer

As you might expect, the Physical Layer (layer 1) deals with the real world of communications hardware. Physical Layer standards include detailed descriptions of media, such as coaxial cable, twisted pair, or fiber. They specify physical attachments and signaling methods.

An SNMP management station can trigger tests that check the status of a medium or of the interfaces to the medium.

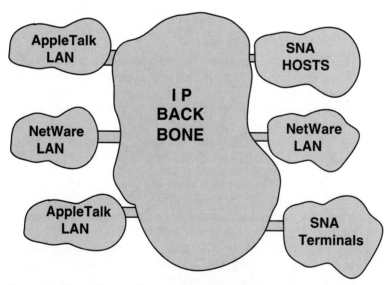

**Figure 1.2**  Tunneling traffic across an IP backbone.

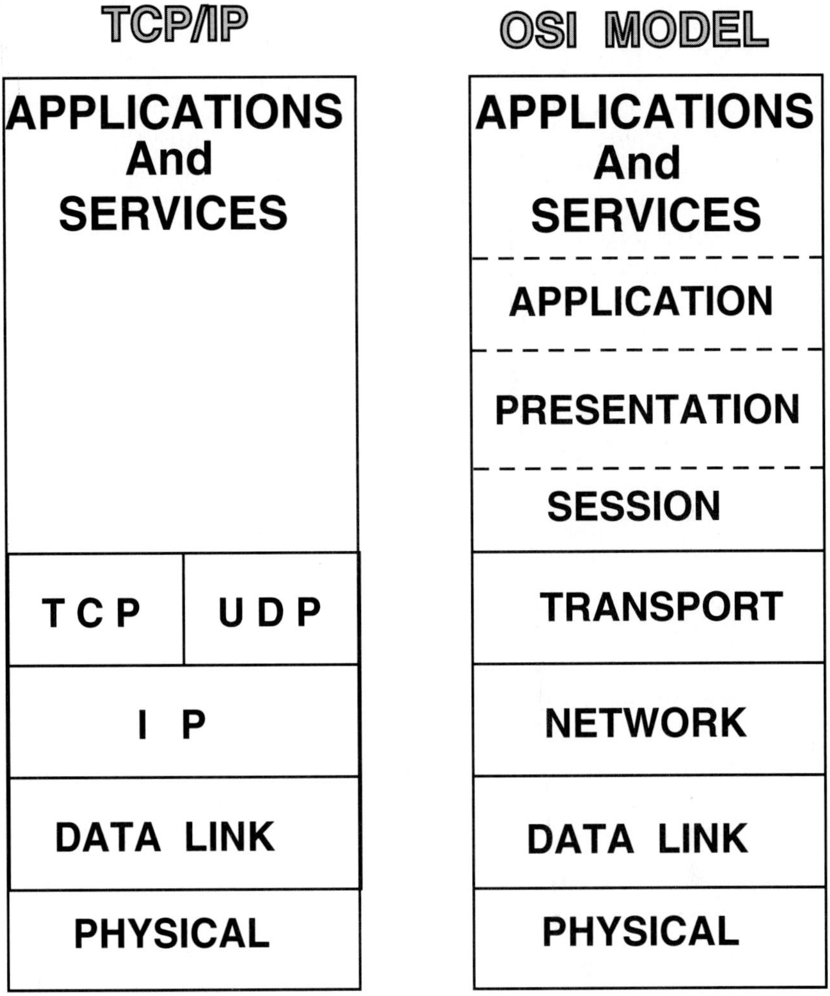

## TCP/IP

| | |
|---|---|
| APPLICATIONS<br>And<br>SERVICES | |
| T C P | U D P |
| I P | |
| DATA  LINK | |
| PHYSICAL | |

## OSI MODEL

| |
|---|
| APPLICATIONS<br>And<br>SERVICES |
| APPLICATION |
| PRESENTATION |
| SESSION |
| TRANSPORT |
| NETWORK |
| DATA  LINK |
| PHYSICAL |

**Figure 1.3**  TCP/IP and OSI layers.

### 1.5.3  The Data Link Layer

The Data Link Layer (layer 2) is concerned with moving information between two systems connected by a point-to-point link, a LAN, or a packet network (e.g., frame relay) circuit. The Data Link Layer:

- Packages information into frames.
- Provides physical address information identifying sources and destinations.

- Identifies the protocol type for the information—e.g., IP, Novell IPX, or Banyan Vines.

For LANs, the Data Link Layer is divided into two sublayers. The *Media Access Control* or MAC sublayer defines the rules that must be followed when using a medium. For example, Ethernet requires a station to listen to make sure that no data is currently on the medium before sending a frame. The Token-Ring MAC protocol requires that a station obtain a token before sending a frame.

An SNMP management station can be used to configure, activate, and deactivate interfaces. A management station can obtain incoming and outgoing frame, octet, and error counts for each interface.

### 1.5.4   The Network Layer

The Internet Protocol, IP, operates at layer 3, the Network Layer, and has the job of routing data across a network. Any network that is based on IP is called an *internet*. The correct operation of IP depends on:

- The unique assignment of IP network addresses.
- The ability to translate IP network addresses to physical addresses.
- Accurate entries in routing tables.

An SNMP management station can check up on IP address assignments, address translation tables, and routing tables. It can obtain counts of incoming and outgoing IP traffic and errors.

### 1.5.5   The Transport Layer

Two protocols, TCP and UDP, operate at layer 4, the Transport Layer. The Transmission Control Protocol, TCP, sets up connections and is responsible for the reliable transmission of data from one application to another.

The User Datagram Protocol, UDP, delivers simple stand-alone messages from one application to another.* UDP is the preferred protocol for carrying network management messages.

An SNMP management station can watch the number and duration of TCP connections at a system, and track who is talking to whom. It can obtain counts of TCP and UDP traffic and errors.

---

\* In other words, UDP is a *connectionless* protocol.

### 1.5.6 Applications

Standard TCP/IP applications include electronic mail, file transfer, and terminal access. Work on managing electronic mail is in progress at the time of writing.

### 1.5.7 Protocol Data Units (PDUs)

Any formatted message is called a *Protocol Data Unit* or PDU. As noted earlier, the layer 2 formatted Protocol Data Units are called *frames*. The IP layer 3 Protocol Data Units are called *datagrams*. TCP's layer 4 PDUs are called *segments,* while UDP's layer 4 PDUs are called *user datagrams.*

## 1.6 NOTATIONAL CONVENTIONS

Occasionally, parameters are expressed in hexadecimal notation. There are many different formats that are used for expressing hexadecimal numbers. The preferred notation for these parameters will be 'nn'H—for example '23A4'H. This is the display notation suggested in one of the SNMP standards. An exception is the presentation of physical addresses for Network Interface Cards. These will be written with octets separated by "-". For example, 09-00-09-00-00-01.

In the text, sometimes quotations or screen displays will contain hexadecimal numbers expressed in one of the many other formats for writing hexadecimal numbers, such as 0x'23A4, X'23A4, or 23:A4. The meaning will be made clear within each context.

There are many interactive dialogues in this text. They were generated using personal computers, Sun Microsystems workstations, an AIX computer, a NeXt system, and a Network General *Sniffer* monitor.

In dialogues, end-user input is represented in **bold** text, while computer prompts and responses appear without emphasis.

## 1.7 PRESENTATION OF MANAGEMENT INFORMATION

Many of the chapters present descriptions of the configuration, status, and measurement parameters defined in network management standards. These are presented in a concise tabular format, rather than in the more lengthy format of the standards documents.

The tabular format is intended for users of management systems. *An implementor or tester should consult the source standards for complete details.* The text contains many individual examples of definitions from the source standards documents, with the intention of making these documents easy to read.

Technologies evolve, and the methods of managing technologies are steadily improving due to experience gained in real implementations. The standards documents referenced in this text are updated on a regular basis, and issued with new numbers.

## 1.8   REFERENCE MATERIAL

Because so many technologies are discussed, this book contains a record-setting number of acronyms. Appendix A at the end of the book translates the acronyms, and a separate Glossary contains complete definitions.

# 2

# Where Does "Simple Network Management" Come From?

## 2.1 THE INTERNET-STANDARD MANAGEMENT FRAMEWORK

Open any trade magazine today, and every advertisement will proclaim that its hub, bridge, router, multiplexor, switch, or whatever can be managed by the Simple Network Management Protocol, SNMP. How did this happen?

"Support for SNMP" actually is a shorthand for the fact that these products conform to the *Internet-Standard Management Framework*. This framework is easy to implement, is powerful, and opens up like a big umbrella to take more and more technologies under its protection.

The elegant simplicity and amazing flexibility of the Simple Network Management framework is due to the work of a small corps of brilliant designers. At the center were Keith McCloghrie, Marshall Rose, Jeffrey D. Case, Mark Fedor, Martin Lee Schoffstall, and James R. Davin.

The insights of this team were sharpened and verified by means of the research and development methodology that is embedded in the Internet community. A spirit of cooperation and rapid implementation are characteristic of the Internet approach to networking. But sweetness and light do not build tough products. Internet protocol designers and developers work in a rough-and-tumble open forum, in which ideas are marched out, are challenged, defended, altered, and clarified.

## 2.2 THE INTERNET COMMUNITY

Internet standards are created by a community with a unique history. The Internet community has its roots in experimental work on packet switching and internetworking that was sponsored by the U.S. *Defense Advanced Research Projects Agency* (DARPA) in the late 1960s and 1970s. The *Internet Protocol* (IP) and the *Transmission Control Protocol* (TCP) were products of this experimental work. IP and TCP are the pure communications components of the TCP/IP *protocol suite,* which also includes:

- Applications such as file transfer, electronic mail, and terminal access.
- Utilities such as computer name-to-address translation, computer clock synchronization, and software downloads to bridges or routers.

The TCP/IP Protocol suite matured in an environment nurtured by academic research and government support. Initially, a small core of universities, research labs, and government agencies adopted the protocols and connected their networks together. TCP/IP proved to be a sturdy workhorse, and was adopted as an official government and Department of Defense networking standard.

Over the past few years, more and more organizations have plugged their networks into the world's largest and fastest-growing network— the Internet.* During this time, the Internet has doubled in size approximately every 13 months. Today, as illustrated in Figure 2.1, the Internet is made up of thousands of networks reaching dozens of countries.†

Development of many protocol improvements, new applications, and new utilities has been driven by urgent needs that have been voiced by managers and users in the Internet community.

In particular, as more and more people came to depend on the Internet in their daily work lives, the manageability of the network—the assurance of availability, satisfactory performance, and rapid solution of problems—assumed increasing importance.

## 2.3  COMMERCIAL REQUIREMENTS

The Internet TCP/IP protocol suite has been widely adopted for use within private commercial enterprise networks. Furthermore, some of these private networks are growing at a rate comparable to the rate of Internet growth.

---

* Recall that any network based on IP is called an *internet. The Internet* is a very special and very large internet!

† The job of connecting networks to the Internet is carried out by Service Provider companies such as Advanced Network and Services, Inc. (ANS), Performance Systems International, Inc. (PSI), Global Enterprise Service, Inc. (GES), and many others. These companies also provide general commercial wide-area IP networking services.

**Figure 2.1** Scope of the Internet.

Commercial use poses some special problems that need solutions. Increasingly, vendors and users have had to find ways for TCP/IP to coexist and interwork with popular proprietary protocols. Commercial enterprises cannot tolerate long network outages any more than they can tolerate long host downtimes. They are seriously concerned about network security and data confidentiality.

The Internet research community has responded quickly to these new demands. In this book, we shall examine several of the new technologies that have been offered to answer these needs.

## 2.4 THE INTERNET ARCHITECTURE BOARD (IAB)

How are protocols found that meet the requirements of the research and commercial communities? Who determines that a protocol solution is adequate? Who chooses between competing solutions?

From the late 1970s onward, the evolution of the TCP/IP protocol suite has been guided by a committee which, in 1983, was named the *Internet Activities Board* (IAB). In 1992, the name of the IAB was changed to the *Internet Architecture Board,* and its formal charter was updated. Neither the initials nor the fundamental functions of the group were altered, however.

The IAB oversees the Internet protocol development process, focusing effort on areas that need work and deciding if and when a protocol is ready to be admitted as an Internet standard. The IAB is in turn driven by the urgent requirements that spring from real, live operating networks comprising:

- Every known type of computer
- Bridges and routers purchased from dozens of vendors
- Serial links of all types
- Connectivity to commercial packet networks
- All popular LAN technologies

## 2.5   THE INTERNET ENGINEERING TASK FORCE (IETF)

The IAB sets general directions and decides which protocols will be standards. The grueling work of sifting through requirements and designing, implementing, and testing new standards is carried out by the Internet Engineering Task Force (IETF). The IETF is a loosely defined group of people with networking know-how: researchers, designers, people with operating experience, and equipment vendor engineers.

## 2.6   THE INTERNET ENGINEERING STEERING GROUP (IESG)

The Internet Engineering Steering Group (IESG) is made up of IETF chairpeople and others performing a leadership role in the IETF. The IESG performs an oversight and coordinating function for the IETF.

## 2.7   THE INTERNET RESEARCH TASK FORCE (IRTF)

Long-term architectural issues are considered by another group called the *Internet Research Task Force* (IRTF). Its steering group is the Internet Research Steering Group (IRSG).

## 2.8   REQUESTS FOR COMMENTS AND STANDARDS

Internet standards are published within a series documents called *Requests For Comments* (RFCs). Note, however, that there are RFCs on many topics, ranging from how to name your computer to experimental results in networking research.

An RFC under serious consideration for incorporation in the Internet protocol suite will be published as a proposed standard. If all goes well, it can be promoted to draft standard after at least six months. At this point there must be two or more implementations of the protocol. Finally, after a review period of at least four more months, if the IESG recommends adoption as a standard, the IAB makes the final decision on adoption.

The standards development process is an extremely open one. RFC documents are freely available to anyone who has file transfer or email access to the Internet. In fact, even early rough drafts are available online. Paper copies are available for a modest copying fee.

Master copies of RFCs and early rough drafts currently are kept at a special document services node (*ds.internic.net*) administered by AT&T. Copies of RFCs are kept at many other systems, including Network Information Centers run by service providers around the world.

Anyone can comment on these documents at any stage (well, they *are* called *Requests for Comments*!)—and lots of people do. If you have a better idea than the authors, you may find yourself put to work on a committee.

The standards track process is illustrated in Figure 2.2. Often a protocol will need to be modified substantially during this process. In this case, a new RFC will be published detailing the corrected protocol and obsoleting the old protocol.

All RFC documents are listed in a master index called *rfc-index.txt* which is stored in the */pub/rfc* directory at *ds.internic.net*. This document is updated when a new RFC is published.

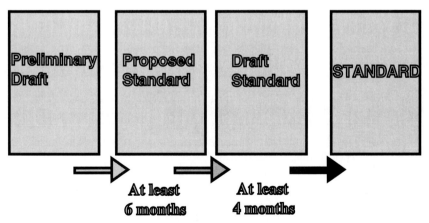

**Figure 2.2**  Moving along the standards track.

## 2.9  OFFICIAL PROTOCOL STANDARDS

It is important to keep in mind that publication of a protocol in an RFC does not make it a standard. The IAB periodically issues a very important RFC called *IAB Official Protocol Standards.* This document tracks the status of every protocol.

## 2.10  ASSIGNED NUMBERS

Another important document issued periodically is *Assigned Numbers.* This document tracks the current complete set of parameters used in the TCP/IP suite. A group called the *Internet Assigned Numbers Authority* (IANA) is responsible for keeping this information up to date.

## 2.11  THE IAB AND NETWORK MANAGEMENT

By 1988, the need for a common network management toolset for TCP/IP networks in general (and for the massively mushrooming Internet in particular) was clear and urgent.

After many meetings and deliberations, the IAB sounded the starting bell in *RFC 1052, IAB Recommendations for the Development of Internet Network Management Standards,* published in April of 1988.* Here the IAB called for the rapid development of the elements of Simple Network Management and made the frank statements:

> We still don't have a common understanding of what [Inter]Network Management really is.

> We will learn what [Inter]Network Management is by doing it.

> (*a*) in as large a scale as is possible
> (*b*) with as much diversity of implementation as possible
> (*c*) over as wide a range of protocol layers as possible
> (*d*) with as much administrative diversity as we can stand

Work on SNMP went forward quickly. Many of the ideas that are central to SNMP were borrowed from earlier work on monitoring Internet routers (historically called *gateways*), the *Simple Gateway Monitoring Protocol* (SGMP). The three landmark documents that ushered in SNMP were published in August of 1988:

---

* See *The Simple Book* by Marshall Rose for the full inside story of the early history of SNMP.

- RFC 1065: *Structure and Identification of Management Information for TCP/IP-based internets*
- RFC 1066: *Management Information Base for Network Management of TCP/IP-based internets*
- RFC 1067: *A Simple Network Management Protocol*

## 2.12 INFLUENCE OF ISO AND CCITT

The International Organization for Standardization (ISO) is an international body founded to promote international trade and cooperative progress in science and technology. Open Systems Interconnect (OSI) task forces within ISO have been very influential in the world of data communications. The ISO model is familiar to almost everyone involved with communications. Many new protocols have been published under the ISO banner.

The International Telegraph and Telephone Consultative Committee (CCITT) is an organization formed to facilitate connecting communications facilities into international networks. For several years, CCITT technical groups have worked cooperatively with ISO task forces. Many CCITT *Recommendations* are closely aligned with ISO standards.

Recently, due to reorganization by its parent organization, the International Telecommunications Union* (ITU), the CCITT has been renamed the *International Telecommunications Union—Telecommunications Standardization Sector* or ITU-T. We will use the old "CCITT" title in this text, since it is still prevalent, and many documents that will be referenced were published under CCITT sponsorship.

Ongoing ISO and CCITT work on network management was a very strong influence on SNMP. Initially, there was a desire to be as consistent with the ISO/CCITT architecture as was possible. The IAB believed that in the long run it would be desirable to make a transition to ISO *Common Management Information Service* (CMIS) and its corresponding *Common Management Information Protocol* (CMIP). The combination of CMIS services and the CMIP protocol with a TCP/IP transport was referred to as *CMOT.*

The IAB wished to structure the Internet framework so that this transition would be as painless as possible. The ideas emerging from ISO/CCITT work were simplified and reshaped so that implementations could be brought to market quickly. It also was important to

---

* The International Telecommunications Union is the organization responsible for international telephone, telegraph, and ship-to-shore communications.

respond promptly to market feedback on what worked, what did not work, and what was missing.

## 2.13  CMOT ABANDONED—SNMP MOVES FORWARD

It turned out to be very difficult to keep in step with the ISO standards. New ideas, fresh discoveries about what it was like to use the new tools in a real-world network, and urgent customer needs were reshaping SNMP. It became clear that it was impossible to maintain the alignment with ISO/CCITT while also nurturing the rapid evolution of protocol elements to meet immediate and explicit requirements springing from the network user and vendor communities. The plan to migrate to CMOT, which was CMIS/CMIP running over TCP/IP and managing TCP/IP nodes, was abandoned. The decision was made to let each protocol family go its own way.* SNMP designers were free to define whatever constructs were needed to get their job done.

After this decision, things began to move quickly. The RFC documents defining the Internet-standard management framework were rewritten, incorporating many improvements. The documents that defined the next SNMP generation† were RFC 1155, 1156, and 1157. RFC 1156 defined management variables, and was revised twice in fairly rapid succession in response to reports of experience in the field. Along the way, a better method of writing definitions of management variables was developed.

Finally, in May of 1991, a stable foundation for the rising SNMP version 1 edifice was complete, consisting of:

- RFC 1155: *Structure and Identification of Management Information for TCP/IP-based Internets* (May, 1990)

  —Describes how management information has been structured into a global tree.

  —Introduces the rules for assigning names to objects. For example, if you want to find out whether the third Ethernet interface on one of your routers is up and running, how do you ask for it?

  —Lays down some restrictions that force the Internet network management standards writers to keep it simple!

- RFC 1212: *Concise MIB Definitions* (March, 1991)

  —Improves on the definition techniques defined in RFC 1155.

---

* See RFC 1109.

† This was an upgrade of SNMP version 1, not a move to a new version.

- RFC 1213: *Management Information Base for Network Management of TCP/IP-based Internets: MIB-II* (March, 1991)
    - —Lists over 100 variables that hold the configuration, status, and statistical information that are most needed in order to manage a system that operates in a TCP/IP network.
- RFC 1157: *A Simple Network Management Protocol (SNMP)* (May, 1990)
    - —Defines the messages that can be exchanged between a management station and a system to read or update variable values.
    - —Defines trap (alarm) messages that are sent by a system whose status is changing in a serious way.
    - —Deals with the nitty-gritty details of message format and communications protocol specification.

## 2.14   EXPANDING THE SCOPE OF SNMP

The introduction of these baseline standards was just the beginning. Working groups of researchers and vendor engineering specialists rolled up their sleeves and hammered out specifications for managing:

- All sorts of equipment—bridges, repeaters, ASCII terminals.
- Many types of interface technology—Point-to-Point, DS1, DS3, X.25, Frame Relay, Ethernet, Token-Ring, FDDI, and others.
- Popular proprietary protocols such as DECnet Phase IV and AppleTalk.

## 2.15   INTEGRATING LAN MONITORS INTO SNMP

SNMP was strengthened in November of 1991 with the publication of specifications for integrating network monitoring stations into SNMP network management.

Monitors can watch LAN traffic, recording levels of activity and statistical breakdowns based on protocol, source, destination, or other criteria. Monitors can watch for incipient problems. A network manager can set thresholds in a monitor so that a dangerous combination of events causes an alert message to be sent to one or management stations.

Monitors also have the unique ability to capture traffic to be recorded for later problem analysis. Adding the power of network monitors to SNMP management was an important step forward.

## 2.16    MARCHING TOWARD SNMP VERSION 2

The simplicity of version 1 of SNMP contributed to its rapid implementation and acceptance. However, version 1 had some serious shortcomings. There was no reliable method of authenticating the source of network management messages. There was no way to secure the contents of network management messages from network eavesdroppers.

In April of 1993, SNMP version 2 was put onto the standards track. Version 2 addressed the authentication and security of management messages. It also contained useful protocol enhancements and improved the administrative framework for the maturing protocol suite.

Version 2 still has to prove itself in the field. It has been criticized because of its complexity. Where the authentication and privacy functions of version 2 are used, the protocol will use far greater system resources than version 1. But version 2 is not a frivolous elaboration of version 1. It was designed to solve hard problems. In today's network environment, there may not be any usable solutions that are less complex.

## 2.17    RECOMMENDED READING

RFC documents describing network management standards are available at many online sites within the Internet. Appendix B of this book lists the source RFC documents for Simple Network Management Protocol standards.

There are a number of books about the Internet that make interesting reading. The *Whole Internet Users Guide and Catalog* by Ed Krol (O'Reilly and Associates) is an entertaining introduction. RFC 1462, *What Is the Internet?*, is a publicly available expansion of chapter 2 of Krol's book. Daniel Dern's *Internet Guide for New Users* contains many helpful end-user tips on "where to find it and how to use it."

*The Internet for Everyone: A Guide for Users and Providers,* by Richard Wiggins (McGraw-Hill) is a very comprehensive tour of the Internet from someone who understands just what end users need and even shows how to provide those services.

Brendon Kehoe's *Zen and the Art of the Internet: A Beginner's Guide to the Internet,* is a very clearly written introduction to the golden treasures of information that pave the Internet highways. It is available in electronic form at various Internet archives, or in a nicely presented book from Prentice-Hall.

RFC 1463 contains a short bibliography of Internet readings.

# 3

# Overview of Simple Network Management

## 3.1 INTRODUCTION

Network devices contain information about themselves. For example, every device has been configured with some selection of parameters. A device has a current status that indicates whether it is in healthy running condition. Devices often keep internal statistics that count incoming and outgoing traffic and various observed errors.

Some devices contain a wealth of very interesting knowledge about their neighbors. A *network monitor* is designed to eavesdrop on a LAN or wide-area link and find out which stations are active, gather traffic statistics, check for conditions that signal a possible problem, or even capture a copy of a selected stream of traffic.

All of this information is at the heart of Simple Network Management. The key elements are:

- *What information is interesting?* Working groups of technology experts have hammered out a consensus of what information is interesting. As a side effect, this has led to the standardization of the form and meaning of information stored across products from many different vendors.

- *How do we name it?* Naming is important, because you can't ask for an item of information unless it has a name. The management framework includes a well-defined way to assign names.

- *How do we get it or change it?* Although "SNMP" has become a popular nickname for the entire Simple Network Management framework, SNMP actually refers to one part of the framework. The

Simple Network Management Protocol is the component that gets information from devices and changes the values of configuration parameters.

## 3.2  THE NATURE OF MANAGEMENT INFORMATION

The designers of the Simple Network Management framework put management data in the center of the picture. What kinds of configuration, status, and statistical information are associated with a device?

- Any network node has one or more interfaces to media.
- A network interface has a defined configuration type, such as Ethernet, Token-Ring, X.25, or Serial Line.
- An interface will have an operational status of up, down, or testing.
- A system normally counts interface statistics such as the number of frames sent and received, and number of frames discarded due to errors.

SNMP initially was targeted at managing TCP/IP networks. Hence, information relating to IP and TCP—IP address to physical address translation, incoming and outgoing IP datagram counts, a tabulation of TCP connections—received early notice.

Later, it was very natural to turn to information that described the activities of other protocols, such as DECnet, AppleTalk, and NetWare IPX/SPX. After all, every function of the multiprotocol routers that are the linchpins of today's enterprise networks needs to be managed.

Finally, work is proceeding on host management. Memory, CPU, and disk management are natural extensions of the framework. Currently, management of application services is being added.

## 3.3  MIBS

It is convenient to think of the configuration, status, and statistical information in a device as forming a "database." In reality, information may be stored at a device as a combination of switch settings, hardware counters, in-memory variables, in-memory tables, or files.

In the SNMP standards, this logical database of network management information is called a *Management Information Base* (MIB). We don't really care about the internal, physical form of this data. But we are very interested in being able to access this data.

## 3.4   THE INTERNET-STANDARD
## MANAGEMENT MODEL

The Internet-Standard Management Model is designed to enable network managers to examine device data and update appropriate configuration and status information.

*Agent* software is installed in each device. An agent receives incoming messages from a *manager*. These messages request reads or writes of the device's data. The agent carries out the requests and sends back responses. An agent does not always have to wait to be asked for information. When a serious problem arises or a significant event occurs, the agent sends a notification message called a *trap* to one or more managers.

Manager software at a *management station* sends request messages to agents and receives responses and spontaneous trap messages from agents. What protocol carries these messages? UDP is the preferred choice, but any transport protocol is acceptable.

To complete a network management system, we need one or more *applications* that enable an end user to control the manager software and view network information. The elements of this model are shown in Figure 3.1.

## 3.5   NETWORK MANAGEMENT
## APPLICATIONS

Network management applications are not standardized. Management station vendors compete vigorously in providing the best graphical user interface, the most intuitive information displays, and the best applications. They also provide customers with toolkits for adding new, specialized applications. We'll examine some examples of vendor applications later on. For now, let's look at a few examples in order to get a more solid idea of what they do.

Figure 3.2 shows two windows from a NetView/6000 display. The top window displays a map of the test LAN. This map was generated automatically. The "IPMap" application at the management station (*bluebell*) discovered the presence of the other stations, and sent each a query asking what type of system it was. The icon figures that were displayed were based on their answers. *Bluebell, sunflower,* and *tulip* are all workstations, while *crocus* is a PC.

Let's examine the lower window in Figure 3.2. *Bluebell* has been configured with a background application that periodically gets an interface traffic report from sunflower. The end user has started another application that graphs this data and displays it in the window.

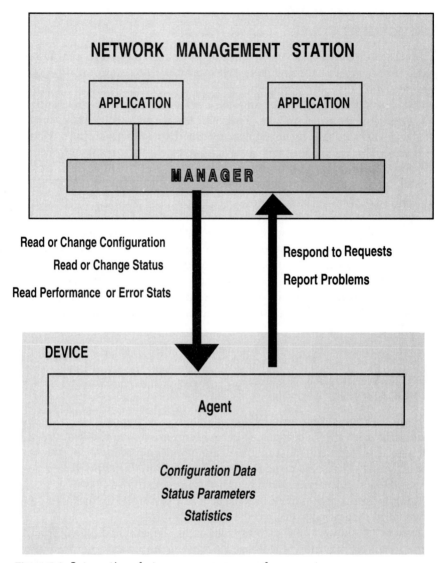

**Figure 3.1**  Interactions between a manager and an agent.

Finally, Figure 3.3 shows output from the NetView/6000 Events application. This application displays:

- Selected significant events learned by polling
- Spontaneous problem reports
- Warnings that user-specified thresholds have been exceeded
- Messages originating from other management applications

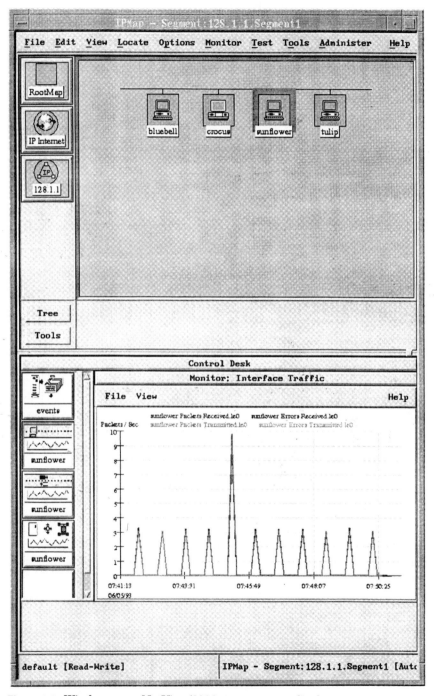

**Figure 3.2** Windows on a NetView/6000 management display.

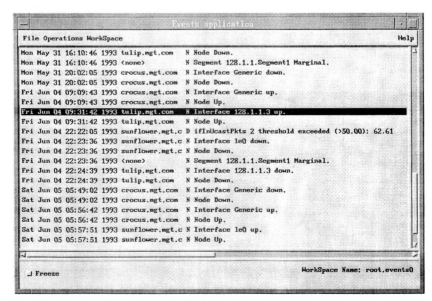

**Figure 3.3**  NetView/6000 Events application.

Network management station products such as NetView/6000, HP OpenView, and SunNet Manager draw network maps, allow different operators to work with customized submaps, and can talk to any SNMP agent. They provide built-in applications for retrieving, examining, and storing network information, and provide tools for building customized applications.

## 3.6  BRINGING IN THE LAN MONITORS

Information extracted from individual network nodes is extremely useful. However, LAN monitors add some special capabilities to network management.

A LAN monitor has the capability to examine all of the traffic on a LAN, providing a bird's-eye view of what is going on. A monitor can capture traffic based on many criteria, such as:

- All traffic for a given protocol
- Traffic between a selected pair of stations
- Traffic containing a selected byte pattern

Figure 3.4 was generated by a Network General *Sniffer* LAN monitor attached to an Ethernet LAN. The upper skyline graph displays the

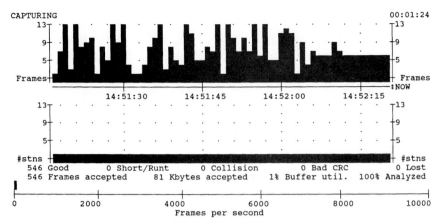

**Figure 3.4** LAN status reported by a Network General *Sniffer*.

number of frames per second on an Ethernet. The total time period shown is one minute, and 60 counts are graphed.

The lower skyline graph shows that only two stations are currently active. As a result, the graph is a flat bar.

The brief report at the bottom of the figure indicates that there were no problems—no frames that were too short (runts), no collisions, no bad CRC calculations, and no lost frames. The *Sniffer* has captured all of the traffic, and has used up only 1 percent of its buffer space in doing so. If there were a network problem, this traffic could be "replayed" or examined frame by frame. This capability makes a monitor a powerful diagnostic tool.

The gauge line at the bottom ranges from 0 to 10,000 frames per second. As can be seen, only a small part of the available bandwidth is in use.

A monitor can be configured to recognize and log errors and to display warnings—or make a loud beeping noise—whenever various types of errors begin to occur at dangerously high frequencies.

Clearly, monitors are powerful tools. RFC 1271, published in 1991, described how a management station could configure a network monitor and poll the monitor for many kinds of information. In 1993, LAN monitor implementations that supported this RFC were made available on the market.

## 3.7  MIB VARIABLES

What information should be kept in a device's MIB? The trick is to standardize without stifling useful additions and extensions. How do you do this? The SNMP community has used an evolutionary approach:

- Define groups of clearly useful parameters.
- After several months of field experience, fine-tune these groups. Throw away parameters that are not useful. Add new ones that are needed.
- Set up committees of industry experts to define MIB variables for special technologies, such as bridges or Token-Ring interfaces.
- Add vendor-specific extensions that cover special features of a vendor's products.

To get this level of flexibility, management information is structured as a *tree,* so that new branches can sprout wherever they are needed. Figure 3.5 shows a rough sketch of the tree of management information.

## 3.8   THE FIRST MIB—MIB-I

SNMP was originally developed to satisfy an immediate requirement to manage TCP/IP communications on the Internet. The first MIB, now called MIB-I, concentrated on information specific to TCP/IP. Sample variables from the original MIB included:

- A system description
- The number of networking interfaces (e.g., Ethernet adapters, Token-Ring adapters, or serial ports) that a system has
- The IP address associated with each network interface
- Counts of the numbers of incoming and outgoing datagrams
- A table of information about active TCP connections

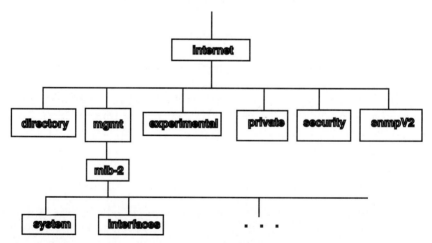

**Figure 3.5**  Part of the network management tree.

## 3.9    TUNING THE MIB TO GET MIB-II

After deployment in the field, the basic definitions were clarified and many new definitions were added. The results were published in RFC 1213: *Management Information Base for Network Management of TCP/IP-based Internets: MIB-II.* MIB-II has proved to be a robust basis for TCP/IP management.

At the time of writing, there were still network devices deployed that had not been upgraded from MIB-I to MIB-II. Life being what it is, this probably will persist for some time. However, the good news is that, since MIB-II is compatible with MIB-I, management stations can work with agents that support either MIB.

## 3.10    TECHNOLOGY EXTENSIONS

The management framework provided for experimentation and expansion. The IAB encouraged groups of vendors to form task forces and define the MIBs needed to manage their products. A spirit of cooperation and common sense has guided these efforts. RFC 1286, which describes a MIB for bridges, expresses the prevailing philosophy of MIB construction:

> To be consistent with IAB directives and good engineering practice, an explicit attempt was made to keep this MIB as simple as possible. This was accomplished by applying the following criteria to objects proposed for inclusion:
>
> (1) Start with a small set of essential objects and add only as further objects are needed.
>
> (2) Require objects be essential for either fault or configuration management.
>
> (3) Consider evidence of current use and/or utility.
>
> (4) Limit the total number of objects.
>
> (5) Exclude objects which are simply derived from others in this or other MIBs.
>
> (6) Avoid causing critical sections to be heavily instrumented. The guideline that was followed is one counter per critical section per layer.

The last point is important. "Instrumentation" means that while a device is doing its normal tasks, it also must count messages, events, and errors. But we do not want a device to become so involved in taking its own pulse by gathering statistics for network management that it cannot carry out its real duties efficiently!

The fifth point actually is a very terse expansion of this concept. Many managed devices are simple and dumb. A modem or an Ethernet repeater cannot devote internal resources to computing, comparing, and analyzing management data. Intelligent analysis is the job of a management station or a network monitor.

## 3.11   PRIVATE ENTERPRISE EXTENSIONS

We mentioned earlier that management information is structured into a tree. We'll look at that tree very carefully in Chapter 4.

Any vendor can contact the Internet Assigned Numbers Authority and request a *branch* or *subtree* in the tree of management information. The vendor can define any variables that are necessary for managing its products within its subtree. At a minimum, vendors are encouraged to define variables that provide standardized identifiers for their products. These variables can be very helpful in setting up an automated inventory of network equipment.

In addition, a vendor's products may have specific design elements or offer some control features that are not generic. Vendor-specific MIB variables may be needed to manage these features. The SNMP framework provides a way to define these special MIB variables and make them publicly available.

For example, Cisco Systems, Inc. has defined MIB variables relating to initialization of their routers by means of a download of software across a network, as well as variables that relate to managing the usage of memory within their routers.

MIB definitions are written in a standard language. Many management station products are capable of loading vendor definitions into their stations and managing the vendor's products.

Possession of a subtree is not limited to vendors. Any enterprise can register, be assigned a subtree, and start defining its own management parameters. The version of the *Assigned Numbers* document published as RFC 1340 included 461 registered vendors and enterprises. At the time of writing, there were over 800 registrants listed in file *snmp-vendors-contacts* in the *mib* directory at *venera.isi.edu*. The sampling that follows gives a flavor of the scope of participation.

| | |
|---|---|
| 1 | Proteon |
| 2 | IBM |
| 9 | cisco |
| 18 | Wellfleet |
| 36 | DEC |
| 45 | SynOptics |
| 63 | Apple Computer Inc |
| 75 | Ungermann-Bass |

| | |
|---|---|
| 100 | Ohio State University |
| 119 | NEC Corporation |
| 120 | Fibermux |
| 121 | FTP Software Inc. |
| 122 | Sony |
| 146 | American Airlines |
| 147 | Sequent Computer Systems |
| 148 | Bellcore |
| 156 | ENE (European Network Engineering) |
| 157 | Dansk Data Elektronik A/S |
| 180 | Hill Air Force Base |
| 182 | Japan Radio Co. |
| 221 | Microwave Bypass Systems, Inc. |
| 222 | Pyramid Technology Corp. |
| 223 | Unisys_Corp |
| 224 | LANOPTICS LTD. Israel |
| 231 | Siemens Nixdorf Informations Syteme AG |
| 232 | Compaq |
| 263 | Seiko Instruments, Inc. (SII) |
| 271 | TELECOM FINLAND |
| 311 | Microsoft |
| 312 | US West Advance Technologies |
| 313 | University College London |
| 314 | Eastman Kodak Company |
| 341 | Martin Marietta Energy Systems |
| 353 | ATM Forum |
| 360 | Morgan Stanley & Co. Inc. |
| 376 | Dassault Electronique |
| 447 | WilTel |
| 460 | Beame & Whiteside |

## 3.12  SIMPLE NETWORK MANAGEMENT PROTOCOL

So far we have focused on the information that is stored in a MIB. Now we will find out how to get at it. The Simple Network Management Protocol identifies:

- The types of messages that can be sent between a manager and an agent
- The formats of these messages
- The communications protocols to be used

Figure 3.6 illustrates the types of messages that are included in version 1 of SNMP:

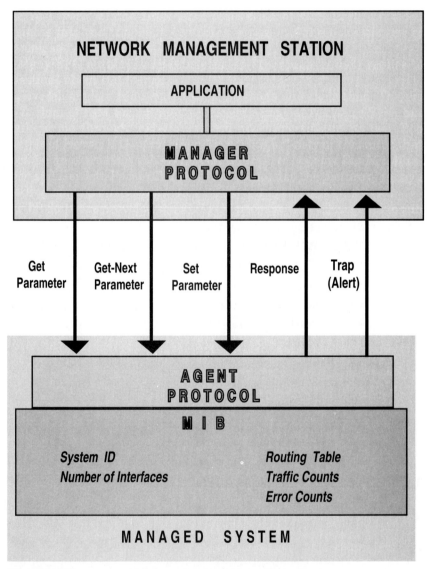

**Figure 3.6** Messages sent between a manager and an agent.

| | |
|---|---|
| *get-request* | Used to request the values of one or more MIB variables. |
| *get-next-request* | Used to read values sequentially. Often used to read through a table of values. After getting the first row with a get-request message, get-next-requests are used to read through the remaining rows. |
| *set-request* | Used to update one or more MIB values. |
| *get-response* | Returned to answer a get-request, get-next-request, or set-request message. |
| *trap* | Used to support significant events, such as a cold or warm restart or a link that has gone down. |

It is easy to see why SNMP was called "simple." We can read a single MIB variable or a list of MIB variables with a *get* message. We can read through the rows of a table—or from the beginning of a MIB to its end—with repeated *get-nexts*. We can write a parameter value with a *set* message. *Response* messages send back the results. A node can report problem events by sending *trap* messages to a manager.

However, these messages provide more power than might appear at first glance. Some writes to the MIB database are intended to trigger actions. For example, changing the status of an interface from enabled to disabled can trigger an action that turns off the interface. Setting a trigger variable to 1 can initiate a loopback test.

## 3.13   STRUCTURE AND IDENTIFICATION OF MANAGEMENT INFORMATION

Now we understand MIBs and the messages that are used to read and write a MIB, namely,

- Each device contains a database of information that it would be useful to know about. This database is called a MIB.

- SNMP defines a simple set of messages that let us read and write database variables, and receive trap reports of problem events.

There are still some important pieces missing.

1. How do we define and describe MIB variables?
2. How are different variables related to one another?
3. How do we identify a variable that we want to read or write?
4. How should these variables be represented (formatted)?

The answers to these questions were provided in RFC 1155, *Structure and Identification of Management Information for TCP/IP-based Internets*. This RFC follows the ISO/CCITT lead in dealing with these issues:

1. MIB variables are defined and described using a datatype definition language called Abstract Syntax Notation 1 (ASN.1). Like PL/I, Pascal, or C, ASN.1 allows you to define the data structures that you need to get your work done. ASN.1 has some additional capabilities that go beyond those found in ordinary programming languages.

2. Network management information has been incorporated into a large tree administered by ISO and CCITT. The tree structure helps us to visualize the relationships between variables.

3. Identifiers for network management parameters are derived from this tree. Each node in the tree is assigned a number. The name of a parameter is the sequence of numbers along the path from the root of the tree to the parameter. This will be described in detail in Chapter 4.

4. There are Basic Encoding Rules for translating values of ASN.1 variables into a fixed transmission format. When data values are transmitted between agents and managers, they always will be formatted in the same way. Agents and managers translate between this standard format and the local formats native to their systems.

## 3.14   ADVANTAGES OF A MODULAR APPROACH

The Simple Network Management framework has a very flexible, modular structure. This may have been a lucky choice, based on the desire to ease a later migration to ISO management standards. Or it is possible that some very bright people just had some very good ideas. Here is what modularity does for you:

- Adding new branches to the management information tree does not require any change to the protocol.

- The protocol is based on reads (*gets*), writes (*sets*), and event (*trap*) messages. If we want to be able to perform an action, such as "reboot the system," we just define a variable that causes a reboot when it is *set* to 1. To define a new action, such as "send test data," we just add another variable to a MIB. No change to the protocol is required.

What this means is that tremendous expansion in functionality is possible without *any* changes to agent protocol software.

The modularity of the structure was reflected in the use of separate RFC standards documents to define each component. To review briefly:

- RFC 1155, for the overall structure of network management information, the description of the naming tree, and the explanation of the method of assigning numerical and text identifiers to MIB parameters

- RFC 1212, to provide guidance to MIB writers who wish to create correct and useful MIB variable definitions

- RFC 1157, to define the SNMP messages (*get, get-next, set, get-response,* and *trap*) and describe how each should be handled

- RFC 1213 for the definition of MIB-II.

## 3.15  WHERE WE GO FROM HERE

Chapters 4 to 17 will tackle the components of the Simple Network Management framework. Chapter 4 discusses the tree structure of network management information, and explains exactly how identifiers are assigned to management parameters.

Chapter 5 introduces the Simple Network Management Protocol and Chapter 6 probes some of more technical aspects of the protocol.

Chapter 7 explains how MIBs are defined, and introduces MIB-II. Chapter 8 discusses traps.

Chapters 9 to 17 explore each group of MIB-II variables in detail, and explain the relevant protocols and technologies that are being managed.

Chapters 18 to 26 describe the management of a variety of interface technologies. Chapter 27 discusses bridge management, and Chapter 28 introduces the use of monitors. We'll visit AppleTalk in Chapter 29, and Novell's protocols in Chapter 30.

Chapters 31 to 34 explain SNMP version 2. Chapter 35 takes a close look at Abstract Syntax Notation 1.

## 3.16  RECOMMENDED READING

Appendix C contains the list of Private Enterprise Codes at the time of writing. Appendix D provides a concise summary of MIB-II. Appendix D also contains a table that lists the additional sets of Management Information Base definitions presented in the text, and indicates the chapter in which each can be found.

# Introduction to the Structure and Identification of Management Information

## 4.1 INTRODUCTION

Networks are complicated. There are many different devices—repeaters, modems, bridges, routers, computers. Within each device, there are numerous hardware and software components, each playing a specialized role in communications.

The designers of SNMP had to find a way to organize:

- *An administrative structure.* The only way to tackle a task of describing how each network component will be managed is to *delegate* the work within each particular specialty to experts in the field. The administrative structure is needed to describe and track the partitioning of the work and delegation of authority.

- *An information structure.* A massive amount of information is needed to manage today's complex multivendor networks. We need a network management information structure that we can extend as new requirements are discovered.

- *A naming structure.* There will be hundreds of variables that will be defined for network management. We need a consistent method of defining, describing, and naming these variables.

In this chapter, we will introduce the simple template that is used to define network management variables. We also will get acquainted with the tree-structured framework that is used to:

- Define administrative relationships
- Organize network management data
- Assign an identifier to every network management variable

This framework is called the *Structure of Management Information,* or SMI.

## 4.2   MANAGED OBJECTS

The network management community talks about network management *objects* rather than network management *variables*. What is an object? It is not complicated. An object has:

- A name
- Attributes
- A set of operations that can be performed on the object

SNMP standards describe *managed objects* that hold network information. A Management Information Base (MIB) consists of a set of *managed objects.*

Examples of managed objects include a system description, the number of incoming bytes received at an interface, and the IP address assigned to an interface. Aren't these just variables? It is very convenient to view them as objects instead, assigning to each:

- A unique name, called an OBJECT IDENTIFIER
- Attributes:
  —A datatype
  —A description that includes any details required to build a correct implementation
  —Status information, that is, whether this object definition is current or obsolete
- The valid operations, such as read and write, that can be performed on the object

### 4.2.1   Variables

A variable stored at a device is an individual *instance* of a managed object. A variable must be implemented so that it conforms to its MIB object definition—has the right datatype, behaves as described, and allows valid operations.

A standard formal template is used to define MIB objects. For example, let's take a look at the formal definition of *sysDescr,* as it appeared in RFC 1213.

```
sysDescr OBJECT-TYPE
     SYNTAX DisplayString (SIZE (0.255))
     ACCESS read-only
     STATUS mandatory
     DESCRIPTION
             "A textual description of the entity. This value
             should include the full name and version
             identification of the system's hardware type,
             software operating-system, and networking
             software. It is mandatory that this only contain
             printable ASCII characters."
     ::= { system 1 }
```

This definition tells us everything that we need to know to implement a system description variable. The datatype is a string of printable ASCII characters, at most 255 characters in length, that describes the system. Its value can be read by a management station. As we shall see a little later, the last line assigns a unique object identifier to *sysDescr.*

### 4.2.2   Datatypes for MIB Variables

What datatypes can be stored in a MIB? When they created their architecture, the designers of SNMP really stuck to their "keep it simple!" rule. MIB variables have elementary datatypes such as integer or octet strings.

### 4.2.3   Other Objects

One of the convenient things about an object-oriented point of view is that just about anything can be an object. For example, an organization or a document can be assigned an identifier and suitable attributes. As we shall see, the object-oriented approach has turned out to be very handy for recording administrative relationships, tracking documents, and building up an inventory of *Modules,* which are related sets of managed objects.

### 4.3   ISO AND CCITT STRUCTURE OF INFORMATION

The International Organization for Standardization (ISO) and the International Telegraph and Telephone Consultative Committee

(CCITT) promoted the idea of structuring information into a *global naming tree* and assigning an identifier to any object that needs a name. This tree (shown in Figure 4.1) is used to label just about anything of interest to a standards organization.

The administrative structure, information structure, and object name structure all are integrated into the global naming tree. The

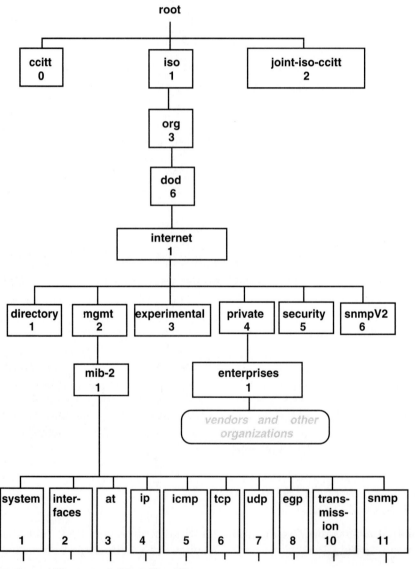

**Figure 4.1** The tree of object identifiers.

assignment of unique identifiers to standards documents even has its place in this tree.

### 4.3.1 Administrative Nodes in the ISO/CCITT Tree

Let's take a closer look at the tree in Figure 4.1. One of the convenient features of this tree is that a node can be used as a placeholder that indicates who is in charge of the objects under it.

This allows an organization to identify how it has delegated the work of defining objects; the organization defines a node in the tree for each administrative entity.

There are three nodes at the top of the global tree. Naturally, ISO administers the subtree that sprouts from its node. ISO has defined the *org* node in order to delegate authority to other organizations. One of these organizations is the United States Department of Defense (*dod*). The Department of Defense historically provided administration, operations, and information services to the Internet. The *internet* subtree under the *dod* node is owned by the Internet Architecture Board (IAB) and administered by the Internet Assigned Numbers Authority (IANA).

### 4.3.2 The Subtree Under Internet Control

Currently there are six nodes defined under *internet: directory, mgmt, experimental, private, security,* and *snmpV2.*

In our discussions of SNMP version 1, we will be concerned with three nodes—*mgmt, experimental,* and *private.* These nodes are administered by the Internet Assigned Numbers Authority. The *mgmt* (management) subtree holds all of the accepted, standard network management variables.

The scope of SNMP network management is enlarged through experimentation. New and unproved objects are placed under the *experimental* node. After a period of trial and revision, useful objects are moved from the *experimental* subtree to the *mgmt* subtree. For example, in June of 1991, objects for Token-Ring (as standardized in IEEE 802.5) and DS1 (T1 line) interfaces were moved from the *experimental* subtree to the *mgmt* subtree. The Token-Ring node is called *dot5,* referring to 802.5. Figure 4.2 shows the tree before and after June 1, 1991.

### 4.4 MIB MODULES

As described in Chapter 3, management information is treated as a virtual database called a *Management Information Base* or MIB. When

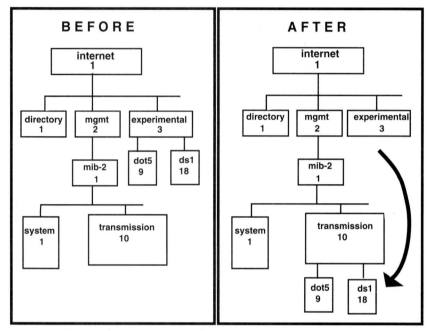

**Figure 4.2** Moving from *experimental* to *transmission* subtree.

a group of experts defines MIB objects for a particular area of technology, these are published as a *module.* RFC 1213, *Management Information Base for Network Management of TCP/IP-based Internets: MIB-II,* contains a module defining the basic objects needed to manage a TCP/IP network. Separate RFC documents contain modules defining objects for specific technologies such as Token-Ring interfaces, Open Shortest Path First (OSPF) routing, and Appletalk networking.

### 4.4.1  Groups

Within a large module, objects are organized into smaller units called *groups.* A vendor can implement the groups that are useful for a product and leave out those that are not.

For example, the *ethernet* module contains definitions of objects for any classic DIX,* 802.3, or starLan Ethernet interface. The module contains two groups. The *Ethernet-like Statistics* group contains required variables such as counts of Frame Check Sequence errors or numbers of collisions. On the other hand, the *Ethernet-like Collision Statistics* group is optional, and is used only for interfaces that have the capability to record very detailed collision information.

---

* "DIX" stands for Digital, Intel, and Xerox, three companies that cooperated on the original definition and implementation of Ethernet.

## 4.5  VENDOR MIB DEFINITIONS

The *private/enterprises* subtree enables equipment vendors, software developers, commercial enterprises, or universities to enhance the usefulness of SNMP. Each vendor or organization is assigned its own subtree under *private/enterprises*. Figure 4.3 shows some vendor subtrees attached to the enterprises node.

Into its subtree a vendor places product identifiers and MIB definitions that are needed to manage the vendor's products.

The product identifiers are very helpful in automating network inventory checks. Combined with the standard MIB-II system description variable, this information allows a device to identify itself very precisely. For example, the following display shows the messages printed when the FTP Software PC/TCP SNMP agent program is started using the *snmpd* command:

```
C:\>snmpd

FTP Software PC/TCP SNMPD Version 2.2 02/25/93 18:05

Copyright (c) 1986-1993 by FTP Software, Inc.   All rights
reserved.    Copyright 1990 by SNMP Research, Inc.

System Description = SNMPD v2.1 (9.3.1) IBM-PC MS-DOS FTP
Software

System Object Identifier = 1.3.6.1.4.1.121.1.1

Communities: 1 authentication, 1 trap
agent occupies 37792 bytes
```

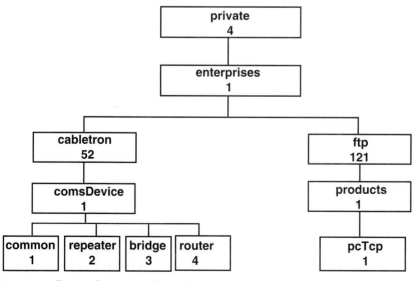

**Figure 4.3**  Parts of some vendor subtrees.

FTP Software has subtree 121 under private enterprises. The object identifier for this product is displayed, and is available to be retrieved by a remote management station.

A vendor can extend SNMP management to product features that are not covered by standard, generic MIB definitions. Appendix C contains a table of vendors and organizations and their enterprise subtree identifiers. This table is updated periodically and included in the *Assigned Numbers* RFC document maintained by the Internet Assigned Numbers Authority.

## 4.6    USING THE GLOBAL TREE TO ASSIGN IDENTIFIERS

The objects that we want to manage are represented by leaf nodes in the global ISO/CCITT tree. Every node in the tree is assigned a label consisting of an integer and a brief text description. The identifier of an object is the series of integers that mark the path from the root of the tree to the object. In the language of the standards makers, this formal name is called an OBJECT IDENTIFIER.

When written for human consumption, an OBJECT IDENTIFIER usually appears as a string of integers separated by dots, although occasionally spaces are used as separators. For example, following the path to *sysDescr* (system description) in Figure 4.1, we see that 1.3.6.1.2.1.1.1 is its formal OBJECT IDENTIFIER. The path to *ifOper-Status* (interface operational status), 1.3.6.1.2.1.2.2.1.8, is its formal OBJECT IDENTIFIER.

### 4.6.1    Text Descriptions

The text part of each node's label is intended to help people who may have trouble remembering and recognizing long strings of numbers. The user-friendly form of an identifier is often written as a series of text labels separated by underscores. The string:

```
iso_org_dod_internet_mgmt_mib-2_interfaces_
ifTable_ifEntry_ifOperStatus
```

identifies the operational status of an interface. It is easier to understand than 1.3.6.1.2.1.2.2.1.8, although it is not easier to write!

### 4.6.2    Picking Out What You Want with an Index

There is one more detail that we need to know in order to name a variable uniquely. A network node, such as a bridge or router, will be sure to have more than one interface. We need to be able to ask for information about a *specific* interface. For example, if a router has five interfaces, we might want to check up on the status of the third one. How is this done?

### 4.6.3 Variable Names

An OBJECT IDENTIFIER indicates the kind of object that we want to know about—in this case, the status of an interface. An *instance identifier* or *variable name* is used to indicate the precise value that we want to see—the status of the third interface. A variable name has the form:

```
OBJECT IDENTIFIER . which_one
```

In this case, to pick the specific interface, we add one last digit to the identifier. The path to *ifOperStatus* is:

```
1 . 3 . 6 . 1 . 2 . 1 . 2 . 2 . 1 . 8
```

If we want to get the operational status of the third interface on my router, we ask for:

```
1 . 3 . 6 . 1 . 2 . 1 . 2 . 2 . 1 . 8 . 3
```

The general principle is that:

> *To form a variable name from an OBJECT IDENTIFIER, add an index at the end that shows which item you want to access.*

Standards documents sometimes use the more formal term, *instance identifier,* instead of the less formal term, *variable name.*

### 4.6.4 One of a Kind

Sometimes an object is defined to be a one-and-only type of thing. For example, the description of a system or its location both are one-and-onlies. We want to be consistent with the rule that says: *to name a variable, always add an index at the end of an identifier.* Therefore, we add a 0 when accessing a one-and-only type. For example, the path to a *sysDescr* object is:

```
1 . 3 . 6 . 1 . 2 . 1 . 1 . 1
```

To get the system description, we will ask for:

```
1 . 3 . 6 . 1 . 2 . 1 . 1 . 1 . 0
```

The path to *sysLocation* is:

```
1 . 3 . 6 . 1 . 2 . 1 . 1 . 6
```

To find out the system location, we will ask for:

```
1 . 3 . 6 . 1 . 2 . 1 . 1 . 6 . 0
```

## 4.7   RETRIEVING VALUES USING SNMP

Let's use SNMP to interact with a real router to see how some of this works. The dialogue below uses a program tool named *snmplookup*. This program is part of a highly functional and flexible toolkit available from PSI (Performance Systems International, Inc.)

The *snmplookup* program lets you talk to devices using SNMP.* Although there are many products (including some built on top of *snmplookup*) that offer more sophisticated user interfaces, *snmplookup* is an ideal tool for letting you see exactly what the protocol does.

```
snmplookup
snmplookup Version 3.2
Copyright (C) PSI, Inc. 1990

default community name is public
default timeout is 10 seconds
default number of recv retries is 1
default prefix is _iso_org_dod_internet
```

In order to save some typing, a default prefix of _iso_org_dod_internet, i.e., 1.3.6.1, has been set up. Let's do it the hard way to start with, so that we can look at a few full-length identifiers. We'll set the prefix to null.

```
snmp> prefix
```

Next we have to pick an agent to talk to. We'll talk to a router. The true identity of the router has been changed to protect its privacy.

```
snmp> agent 128.1.1.1
```

---

\* Some of the *snmplookup* outputs have been edited slightly to improve readability.

The *query* command is used to get information from the router's MIB. The response to a *query* starts with the "user-friendly" version of an object identifier, followed by its values.

Below, we get the router's system description. Note that the response includes the string:

```
_iso_org_dod_internet_mgmt_mib_system_sysDescr_0
```

This is the text label for the object that we asked for. The rest of the response tells us that the system is a Cisco router and that its software was compiled in December of 1993 by jjones.

```
snmp> query 1.3.6.1.2.1.1.1.0
_iso_org_dod_internet_mgmt_mib_system_sysDescr_0 GS Software
(GS3-K), Version 9.1(2), SOFTWARE [fc1]
Copyright (c) 1986-1993 by cisco Systems, Inc.
Compiled Thu 10-Dec-93 12:15 by jjones
```

How many interfaces are on this router?

```
snmp> query 1.3.6.1.2.1.2.1.0
_iso_org_dod_internet_mgmt_mib_interfaces_ifNumber_0 0x5 5
```

There are five interfaces (0x5 5). Note that numeric values are written on the far right in both hexadecimal and decimal notation. Next we look at a description (*ifDescr*) of the router's third network interface. The interface is described as "Ethernet2."

```
snmp> query 1.3.6.1.2.1.2.2.1.2.3
_iso_org_dod_internet_mgmt_mib_interfaces_ifTable_ifEntry_if
Descr_3 Ethernet2
```

We don't really have to work this hard. First let's set a useful prefix that takes us to the interesting part of the naming tree:

```
snmp> prefix 1.3.6.1.2.1
```

Next, we can dump out all of the information under any node in the tree using the *mquery* command. For example, to get all system information:

```
snmp> mquery 1
d_internet_mgmt_mib_system_sysDescr_0GS Software (GS3-K),
Version 9.1(2), SOFTWARE [fc1]
```

```
Copyright (c) 1986-1993 by cisco Systems, Inc.
Compiled Thu 10-Dec-93 12:15 by jjones

d_internet_mgmt_mib_system_sysObjectID_0 1 3 6 1 4 1 9 1 1

d_internet_mgmt_mib_system_sysUpTime_0 0x09680628 157812264

d_internet_mgmt_mib_system_sysContact_0 jjones

d_internet_mgmt_mib_system_sysName_0 Main-Gateway.ABC.NET

d_internet_mgmt_mib_system_sysLocation_0 Room B14

d_internet_mgmt_mib_system_sysServices_0 0x6 6
```

After the prefix was set, the responses came back with labels that were truncated a bit on the left.

## 4.8   UNDERSTANDING MIB VARIABLES

Most MIB values are easy to understand. The *sysDescr* describes the node as a Cisco product. The person to contact if there are problems with the node is *jjones*. The node is named "Main-Gateway.ABC.NET" and it is located in room B14.

The value of the *sysObjectID* is a string of integers that looks suspiciously like an OBJECT IDENTIFIER. If we follow the tree path in Figure 4.1, we see that this takes us into node 9 under *private enterprises*. Cisco has been assigned node 9, and its own tree sprouts from this node.

This tree includes identifiers for each of Cisco's products, as well as vendor-specific MIB variables that Cisco feels are important for managing its routers and terminal servers. The value 1.3.6.1.4.1.9.1.1 is the OBJECT IDENTIFIER for this router product.

In order to make sense of some of the other responses, we have to look up their definitions in a MIB RFC document. Let's examine the definition of *sysUpTime*.

> sysUpTime OBJECT-TYPE
>     SYNTAX     TimeTicks
>     ACCESS     read-only
>     STATUS     mandatory
>     DESCRIPTION
>             "The time (in hundredths of a second) since the
>             network management portion of the system was last
>             re-initialized."
>     ::= { system 3 }

The last line of the definition assigns an OBJECT IDENTIFIER to *sysUpTime,* using the computer scientist's *assignment symbol, "::=".* Here, *"::= {system 3}"* means that *sysUpTime* is right below the *system* node in the tree, and its node number is 3. Thus, the complete *sysUp-Time* OBJECT IDENTIFIER is 1.3.6.1.2.1.1.3. .

Since *sysUpTime* is a one-and-only kind of variable, its full identifier is 1.3.6.1.2.1.1.3.0. The value that we read in the dialogue was hex 09680628, which translates to 157,812,264 hundredths of a second or a little more than 18 days.

What about the *sysServices* variable? Its definition begins:

```
sysServices OBJECT-TYPE
      SYNTAX    INTEGER (0.127)
      ACCESS    read-only
      STATUS    mandatory
      DESCRIPTION
                "A value which indicates the set of services that
                this entity primarily offers.
                The value is a sum."
```

The definition goes on to describe how the sum reveals the main functions that this system performs. The system that we have queried routes and bridges. The display below shows how the sum, 6, is calculated.

| Layer | Add to sum | Functionality |
|-------|-----------|---------------|
| 1 | 1 | Physical (e.g., repeaters) |
| 2 | 2 | Datalink/subnetwork (e.g., bridges) |
| 3 | 4 | Internet (e.g., IP routers) |
| 4 | 8 | End-to-end (i.e., TCP or UDP) |
| 7 | 64 | Applications (e.g., mail relays) |

As you can see, when you are viewing the results of SNMP queries, it is handy to have a glossary of MIB definitions on your desk. Many MIB objects are described in detail through this book. For easy reference, App. D of this volume lists MIB objects and points to the chapters in which their definitions can be found.

### 4.8.1 MIB Definitions at a Network Management Station

Well-designed network management stations provide online MIB definitions that can be accessed by pushing a help key or performing a point-and-click operation.

For example, Figure 4.4 shows the definition of *ifDescr* obtained by clicking on the object name.

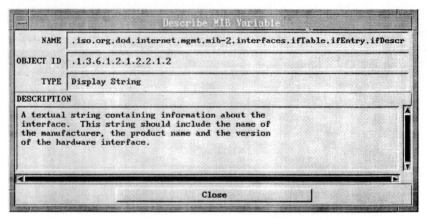

**Figure 4.4** Online description of a MIB variable.

## 4.9  RETRIEVING A LIST OF VARIABLES

Let's do another simple example. This time we'll get the full list of interface descriptions for this router. The object identifier for *ifDescr* is:

```
1 . 3 . 6 . 1 . 2 . 1 . 2 . 2 . 1 . 2
```

The variable names of the *ifDescr* values for the five interfaces are:

```
1.3.6.1.2.1.2.2.1.2.1
1.3.6.1.2.1.2.2.1.2.2
1.3.6.1.2.1.2.2.1.2.3
1.3.6.1.2.1.2.2.1.2.4
1.3.6.1.2.1.2.2.1.2.5
```

Our current prefix is 1.3.6.1.2.1, so we get a description of all of the interfaces by asking for everything under (1.3.6.1.2.1.)2.2.1.2.

```
snmp> mquery 2.2.1.2
d_internet_mgmt_mib_interfaces_ifTable_ifEntry_ifDescr_1 Ethernet0*
d_internet_mgmt_mib_interfaces_ifTable_ifEntry_ifDescr_2 Ethernet1
d_internet_mgmt_mib_interfaces_ifTable_ifEntry_ifDescr_3 Ethernet2
d_internet_mgmt_mib_interfaces_ifTable_ifEntry_ifDescr_4 Serial0
d_internet_mgmt_mib_interfaces_ifTable_ifEntry_ifDescr_5 Serial1
```

---

\* Note that this string does not include the manufacturer, full product name, and version of the hardware interface, as called for in the definition. In this case, the brief text probably was manually entered by an administrator, rather than provided by an interface board vendor.

We see that there are three Ethernet connections and two serial ports. Note how each text label ends with the index that tells you which interface it is describing. For example:

```
d_internet_mgmt_mib_interfaces_ifTable_ifEntry_ifDescr_3
```

## 4.10   TABLES

Often network information has a natural structure as a series of rows and columns organized into a table. Each row in a table is called an *entry*. For example, the following variables make up an IP address table entry:

1. IP address
2. The interface number associated with this IP address
3. The subnet mask
4. Whether to use 1s (the Internet standard) or 0s in broadcast addresses
5. The size of the biggest datagram that can be reassembled from IP fragments at this interface

Table 4.1 displays the IP address table for the router that we have queried in the previous sections. The router has five interfaces, so its IP address table has five rows.

### 4.10.1   Table Indices

A table is not much use without an index that lets you pick a specific row out of the table. The natural index to use here is the IP address.

Let's use PSI's *snmplookup* to retrieve all of the *subnet masks* for our sample router.* Each variable name ends with an index, which in this case is the IP address for the table entry. Instead of typing the long variable names, including the IP address indices, we use *mquery* to display the entire third column of the table. To simplify the appearance of the output, the first part of the label (*d_internet_mgmt_mib_ip_*) has been erased from each response.

```
>snmp mquery 4.20.1.3

ipAddrTable_ipAddrEntry_ipAdEntNetMask_128.1.1.1    255.255.255.0
ipAddrTable_ipAddrEntry_ipAdEntNetMask_130.92.5.26  255.255.255.248
```

---

\* A subnet mask looks like an IP address, but it has 1s in the network and subnet parts and 0s in the host part. A full discussion of subnet masks can be found in Chapter 12.

TABLE 4.1   An IP Address Table

| IP address | Interface number | Subnet mask | Broadcasts | Max reassembled datagram size |
|---|---|---|---|---|
| 128.1.1.1 | 1 | 255.255.255.0 | All 1s | 18024 |
| 130.92.5.26 | 2 | 255.255.255.248 | All 1s | 18024 |
| 130.92.27.129 | 5 | 255.255.255.248 | All 1s | 18024 |
| 130.92.54.207 | 4 | 255.255.255.248 | All 1s | 18024 |
| 192.122.21.45 | 3 | 255.255.255.0 | All 1s | 18024 |

```
ipAddrTable_ipAddrEntry_ipAdEntNetMask_130.92.27.129 255.255.255.248
ipAddrTable_ipAddrEntry_ipAdEntNetMask_130.92.54.207 255.255.255.248
ipAddrTable_ipAddrEntry_ipAdEntNetMask_192.12.211.66 255.255.255.0
```

Just to show that it can be done, we'll look up the subnet mask for IP address 130.92.54.207 (fourth in the list above) by adding the index (the IP address) to the end of the variable name. Remember that the prefix 1.3.6.1.2.1 will automatically be placed in front:

```
snmp> query 4.20.1.3.130.92.54.207
ipAddrTable_ipAddrEntry_ipAdEntNetMask_130.92.54.207 255.255.255.248
```

## 4.11   AN EXTREME CASE OF INDEXING

The purpose of an index is to identify a particular entry in a table. People who are familiar with tabular databases know that sometimes an index must be made up of more than one column. In other words, you can't pick out a *unique* row unless you specify the values of several columns.

The table of active TCP connections provides an extreme example of indexing. For each TCP connection, this table lists the local IP address and port, remote IP address and port, and the state of the connection. Table 4.2 shows part of a sample TCP connection table. The local system is at IP address 128.1.1.3. We can see that:

- The first two connections are logins from remote users at host 128.118.56.14 and remote ports 1611 and 1759 to the local telnet service port, 23.*

- An application at remote IP address 192.133.129.1 and remote port 2424 is just closing down its connection to the local electronic mail port, 25.

---

* Port numbers are described in Chapter 14.

**TABLE 4.2    Active Internet TCP Connections**

| Local IP address | Local port | Remote IP address | Remote port | Status |
|---|---|---|---|---|
| 128.1.1.3 | 23 | 128.118.56.14 | 1611 | ESTABLISHED |
| 128.1.1.3 | 23 | 128.118.56.14 | 1759 | ESTABLISHED |
| 128.1.1.3 | 25 | 192.133.129.1 | 2424 | TIME_WAIT |
| 128.1.1.3 | 119 | 192.67.256.24 | 60332 | ESTABLISHED |
| 128.1.1.3 | 3551 | 134.114.64.4 | 23 | ESTABLISHED |

- An application at remote IP address 192.67.256.24 and remote port 60332 is getting the network news from the local system at the standard news port, 119.

- The last entry shows that a local user at port 3551 has a telnet login to the system whose IP address is 134.114.64.4.

How many variables do we need to specify to be sure of identifying a row uniquely? Four—the local IP address, local port, remote IP address, and remote port! Therefore, to ask for the state of a connection corresponding to the first row in the table, we would start with object identifier:

```
iso org dod internet mgmt mib tcp tcpConnTable tcpConnEntry tcpConnState
1.  3.  6.   1.      2.   1.  6.      13.          1.            1.
```

and append the index:

```
Local       Local     Remote          Remote
IP Address  Port      IP Address      Port
128.1.1.3.  23.       128.118.56.14.  1611
```

The total variable name is:

```
1.3.6.1.2.1.6.13.1.1.128.1.1.3.23.128.118.56.14.1611
```

## 4.12    BETTER OUTPUT WITH A MANAGEMENT STATION

A basic tool like *snmplookup* can help us to understand what makes SNMP tick. However, we look to the vendors of network management stations to make life a little easier and free us from the need to work with long strings of digits, or even long strings of labels. A well-designed management station should provide an easy-to-use, intuitive user interface that takes the drudgery out of retrieving and displaying management information.

## 4.13   RECOMMENDED READING

The information structures used with SNMP are defined in RFC 1155, *Structure and Identification of Management Information for TCP/IP-based Internets*. RFC 1212, *Concise MIB Definitions,* provides an improved format for producing MIB documents. Marshall Rose's *Simple Book* offers quite a bit of insight into how SNMP and the Structure of Management Information evolved.

# Introduction to the Simple Network Management Protocol

## 5.1 INTRODUCTION

It is time for us to get acquainted with the protocol that carries information between managers and agents. We will take an informal approach, leaving the discussion of the formal aspects of the protocol to Chapter 6.

The designers of the Simple Network Management Protocol were very serious about the "simple" in the title. They wanted to stimulate quick and easy implementation and foolproof execution. The question was how to do this. Their solution was to adhere to some strict guidelines:

- Make it work over very uncomplicated transport protocols.

- Keep the number of protocol message types small.

- Stick to a unit of information that is a single value—such as an integer or text string.

## 5.2 UDP: THE PREFERRED PROTOCOL

UDP was picked as the preferred and recommended SNMP transport protocol.

This made sense because SNMP initially was targeted at managing Internet nodes and the predominant Internet protocol suite is TCP/IP. The choice of the TCP/IP suite continues to make sense because IP has become the protocol of choice for commercial backbone networks. Furthermore, users can count on a TCP/IP implementation to be available for any type of host or router.

Both TCP and UDP provide transport services. Why use UDP rather than TCP? TCP is a complicated protocol that consumes sizable chunks of memory and CPU resources. In contrast, UDP is easy to build and run. Vendors have built very simple versions of IP and UDP into devices like repeaters and modems. The total amount of transport software needed is small, and is easily packaged in read-only memory (ROM). UDP also is well suited to the brief request/response message exchanges characteristic of network management communications.

However, it is OK to exchange SNMP messages across any protocol. For example, RFC 1298 describes how SNMP messages can be carried over IPX, and there are some products designed for the NetWare environment that run SNMP on top of NetWare's IPX protocol.

## 5.3  SNMP PROTOCOL DATA UNITS

Recall that there are five message types in SNMP version 1:

- *get-request.*  Retrieves one or more values from a managed node's MIB.

- *get-next-request.*  Enables the manager to retrieve values sequentially. One popular use of the *get-next-request* is to read through the rows of a table.

- *set-request.*  Enables the manager to update appropriate variables.

- *get-response.*\*  Returns the results of a *get-request, get-next-request,* or *set-request* operation.

- *trap.*  Enables an agent to spontaneously report important events or problems.

### 5.3.1  Use of UDP Port Numbers

UDP application port numbers are used to identify the origination and destination endpoints for a message. Port numbers come in two flavors. Many standard services operate out of *well-known ports*†—their port numbers are predefined so that their partners know where to find them. Client applications borrow a port number out of a pool of available port numbers, and return it when they are done with it.

SNMP's use of UDP ports is illustrated in Figure 5.1. When a management application needs to communicate, it gets a port number from the pool and uses this port number as the source of its *get-request, get-next-request,* and *set-request* messages. The management application

---

\* Simply called a *response* in SNMP version 2.

† Well-known port numbers are listed in the *Assigned Numbers* RFC document.

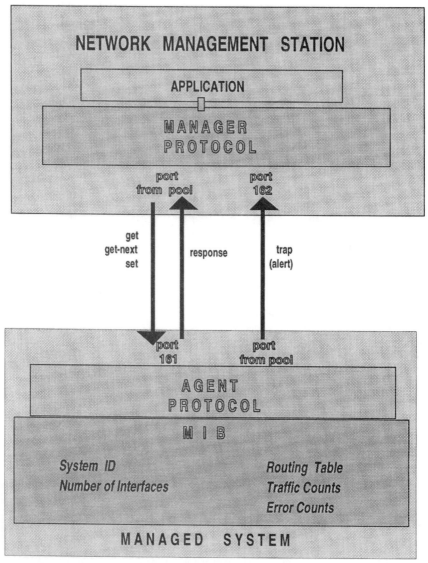

**Figure 5.1**  SNMP use of UDP port numbers.

sends the messages to the SNMP agent's *well-known* UDP port 161. The agent sends responses from port 161 back to the originating port at the manager. A manager receives *traps* at *well-known* UDP port 162.

## 5.4  THE UNIT OF INFORMATION

A *get-request* or *set-request* can read or write a single item or several items. Each item is a simple variable—for example, the system name, the number of bytes received at an interface, or the default value for the Time-to-Live field in IP headers. Another way of stating this is that SNMP recognizes variables that are *leaves* at the bottom of the big naming *tree*.

There was a good reason for this restriction during the early period of SNMP evolution. Groups of variables were being enlarged. Columns were added to tables. Occasionally, variables were dropped.

What happens when we replace an old implementation at an agent with a new one that has added several columns to a table? If a manager could simply ask for an entire table to be returned, the manager might be unable to handle mysterious columns that suddenly appeared in the new implementation. Since *gets* ask for a list of individual variables, this problem does not arise.

The *get-next-request* is a great helper in maintaining backward compatibility. A manager can walk through a MIB using *get-next-requests,* as shown in Figure 5.2, and the device will faithfully return all of the variables that it supports. Each variable will be accompanied by its OBJECT IDENTIFIER. The manager will then know the exact information available at the device.

Although new MIB variables may be added, the meanings of old MIB variables do not change, which also helps old and new implementations to work together.

## 5.5  SNMP MESSAGE FORMATS

The quickest way to get acquainted with the format of SNMP messages is to look at some examples.

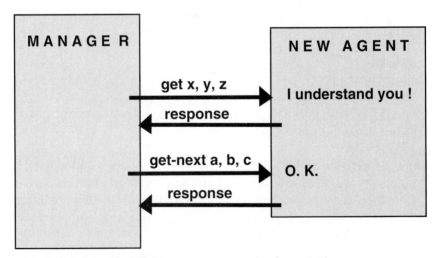

**Figure 5.2**  A manager talking to a new agent implementation.

### 5.5.1 A Sample Get-Request and Get-Response

The Network General *Sniffer* trace below shows an SNMP *get-request* message and its *get-response.*

The request asks for the value of the *icmpInEchos* variable. This value is a counter that records the number of ICMP Echo request messages that have been received at the node. The full identifier for this variable is 1.3.6.1.2.1.5.8.0.

```
SNMP: ----- Simple Network Management Protocol -----
SNMP:
SNMP: Version = 0
SNMP: Community = interop
SNMP: Command = Get request
SNMP: Request ID = 1426
SNMP: Error status = 0 (No error)
SNMP: Error index = 0
SNMP:
SNMP: Object = {1.3.6.1.2.1.5.8.0} (icmpInEchos.0)
SNMP: Value  = NULL
SNMP:


SNMP: ----- Simple Network Management Protocol -----
SNMP:
SNMP: Version = 0
SNMP: Community = interop
SNMP: Command = Get response
SNMP: Request ID = 1426
SNMP: Error status = 0 (No error)
SNMP: Error index = 0
SNMP:
SNMP: Object = {1.3.6.1.2.1.5.8.0} (icmpInEchos.0)
SNMP: Value  = 8 messages
SNMP:
```

Chapter 35 describes the way that these messages are formatted. For now, it is interesting to know that several fields have *variable length.* For example, "Object =" and "Value =" fields have whatever length is needed to hold their contents.

### 5.5.2 Request and Response Message Formats

SNMP request and response messages contain the fields:

■ Version: the version of SNMP.

- Community name: a password used to control access to node information.

- Command*: one of the five types of commands listed above.

- Request ID: used to correlate a request and its answer.

- Error status: in responses, used to indicate whether the request executed successfully.

- Error index: in responses, used to indicate which variable in the request caused a problem (if there was one).

- A list of (OBJECT IDENTIFIER, variable value) pairings. The formal name for this list is "*variable-bindings list*" or *VarBindList*. In the example, there is only a single identifier and value in the list.

The version number, 0, indicates that this is an SNMP version 1 message.[†] The *community* name, "interop" in this case, is a kind of password that tells the agent "It is OK to answer me—I am an authorized management station."

As you can see, a community name does not provide a lot of protection if anyone is eavesdropping on the LAN (e.g., with a monitor!). On the other hand, the information that is carried—the number of echo requests (pings) received—is not particularly sensitive.

A management station can shoot off dozens or hundreds of requests at a time. The request ID (1426 in this case) is used to match the response with its request.

Now let's look at the messages as a whole. Notice how the *get-request* and the *get-response* contain exactly the same fields. This makes it easy for an agent to construct an answer directly from a request by just filling in the blanks, minimizes the amount of software at the agent, and speeds execution.

To keep the formats identical, the *get-request* includes several place-holding fields that contain 0 or NULL values. For example, the error status and error index fields in a *get-request* are placeholders. They always are set to 0 in a request.

Finally, the *get-request* contains the identifier for *icmpInEchos*[‡] and a NULL placeholder for its value. When the response comes back, the value field has been filled in with the information that eight echo messages have been received by the node.

---

* See Chapter 35 for full formatting details.

[†] The fact that version 1 is denoted by zero probably indicates that the standards writers also are C programmers.

[‡] The variable is identified as *icmpInEchos.0*. Recall that a one-of-a-kind variable name always ends with an index value of 0.

## 5.6   GET-REQUESTS FOR MULTIPLE VARIABLES

A *get-request* can contain a list of several variables to be retrieved. In this case, the *get-response* fills in the value for each variable on the list.

There is one unfortunate feature of SNMP *get-requests*. If there is a problem that prevents the agent from getting a value of even a *single* variable on the list, then the whole *get-request* fails and no useful information can be returned! Version 2 removes this unnecessarily severe restriction.

The *Sniffer* trace below shows a request that asks for two values and its corresponding response. The variable *ifInErrors* counts the number of inbound packets that were discarded because they contained errors. Similarly, *ifOutErrors* counts packets that could not be transmitted because of errors. The indexed identifiers, *ifInErrors.1* and *ifOutErrors.1,* indicate that the counts apply to the first interface for the device.

In this example, two values are retrieved. The number of variables that can be processed successfully in a single request is limited only by the maximum size of the messages that can be handled by the manager and agent.

What is this maximum size? It is not reasonable to expect simple devices to handle messages of arbitrary length. The SNMP standard sets a baseline expectation that any node must be able to handle lengths up to 484 bytes. Of course, where possible, an implementation should support even larger messages.

```
SNMP: ----- Simple Network Management Protocol -----
SNMP:
SNMP: Version = 0
SNMP: Community = interop
SNMP: Command = Get request
SNMP: Request ID = 591479902
SNMP: Error status = 0 (No error)
SNMP: Error index = 0
SNMP:
SNMP: Object = {1.3.6.1.2.1.2.2.1.14.1} (ifInErrors.1)
SNMP: Value  = NULL
SNMP:
SNMP: Object = {1.3.6.1.2.1.2.2.1.20.1} (ifOutErrors.1)
SNMP: Value  = NULL
SNMP:

SNMP: ----- Simple Network Management Protocol -----
SNMP:
SNMP: Version = 0
```

```
SNMP: Community = interop
SNMP: Command = Get response
SNMP: Request ID = 591479902
SNMP: Error status = 0 (No error)
SNMP: Error index = 0
SNMP:
SNMP: Object = {1.3.6.1.2.1.2.2.1.14.1} (ifInErrors.1)
SNMP: Value  = 3 packets
SNMP:
SNMP: Object = {1.3.6.1.2.1.2.2.1.20.1} (ifOutErrors.1)
SNMP: Value  = 0 packets
SNMP:
```

## 5.7   THE GET-NEXT-REQUEST

In his books on SNMP, Marshall Rose refers to the *get-next-request* as the "powerful get-next operator."* This title is well deserved, as the *get-next-request* contributes greatly to the strength and generality of SNMP.

The simplest use of the *get-next-request* is to walk through a table one row at a time. The example that follows shows how this is done.

### 5.7.1   A Trace of a Simple Get-Next Message

In the SNMP trace below, a request is made for the variable that follows 1.3.6.1.2.1.2.2.1.8.1 in the agent's database. 1.3.6.1.2.1.2.2.1.8.1 is the identifier for the operational status of the first network interface on the device. The response indicates that the next variable is 1.3.6.1.2.1.2.2.1.8.2, the operational status of the second interface. The current value of the status is 1, which means that the interface is up.

```
SNMP: ----- Simple Network Management Protocol -----
SNMP:
SNMP: Version = 0
SNMP: Community = interop
SNMP: Command = Get next request
SNMP: Request ID = 3
SNMP: Error status = 0 (No error)
SNMP: Error index = 0
SNMP:
SNMP: Object = {1.3.6.1.2.1.2.2.1.8.1} (ifOperStatus.1)
SNMP: Value = NULL
SNMP:
```

---

* In the context of Rose's writing it comes across as "**The POWERFUL get-next operator!!!**"

```
SNMP: ----- Simple Network Management Protocol -----
SNMP:
SNMP: Version = 0
SNMP: Community = interop
SNMP: Command = Get response
SNMP: Request ID = 3
SNMP: Error status = 0 (No error)
SNMP: Error index = 0
SNMP:
SNMP: Object = {1.3.6.1.2.1.2.2.1.8.2} (ifOperStatus.2)
SNMP: Value = 1 (up)
SNMP:
```

Note how the same overall format that we saw for *get-request* and *get-response* messages is again used for the *get-next-request*. The Command type identifies which is which.

### 5.7.2  Using Get-Next to Walk Through a MIB

How do we know what variables are stored at a node? Different sets of variables are appropriate for bridges, routers, and hosts. The variables at a pair of routers may be different because one interfaces to Ethernet and FDDI LANs, while the other interfaces to Token-Rings and T1 lines.

One approach to managing nodes is to manually create a master configuration database at a management station. In this database, we could record:

- The type of node (bridge, router, etc.)
- The categories of MIB variables supported at the node

We would have to maintain this database by hand, adding and deleting entries as the configuration changed at various nodes.

Another approach is to implement a management application that dynamically discovers nodes on the network, and then asks the nodes what they are and what variables they support. This is the way that a well-designed management station operates. The station is able to operate this way because of the *get-next-request* operator.

Here's how it works. The management station can send a message to an agent asking for the entry after:

```
iso.org.dod.internet.mgmt.mib-2
```

That is,

```
1.3.6.1.2.1
```

The identifier in the reply is used to form another *get-next-request*. This is repeated until an error message is returned at the end of the agent's database.

We will show how a management station walks through an agent's MIB database by looking at the results of a *LANWatch* trace that captured this process. *LANWatch* is an FTP Software product that runs on a PC and enables the PC to capture and analyze LAN traffic.

The *LANWatch* has captured a *get-next* dialogue between a NetView/6000 manager and a Sun workstation's agent. The complete *LANWatch* SNMP trace information for the first *get-next-request* is

```
SNMP:  len: 36 version: int(1) 0x00 comm: string(6) "public"
type: GET-NEXT
  req-id: int(2) 0x5ade error: int(1) 0x00 error-index:int(1) 0x00
  var: obj(5) 1 3 6 1 2 1  val: empty(0)
```

The *LANWatch* provides a very detailed analysis of the message structure. The actual message is a long string of hexadecimal codes.

The *LANWatch* tells us that this SNMP message is 36 bytes long and consists of a sequence of fields. Each field is made up of a header and a value. The header indicates the type and length of the value—for example, int(1) means a 1-byte integer and string(6) indicates a 6-byte character string. The values occupy a total of 16 bytes, which means that the field headers account for 20 bytes! The trace indicates that the values are:

| Field | Length of value | Value |
|---|---|---|
| version: | 1-byte integer | 0 |
| community: | 6-byte string | "public" |
| GET-NEXT PDU | Rest of message | Rest of fields |
| request-id: | 2-byte integer | 0x5ade (23,262) |
| error: | 1-byte integer | 0 |
| error-index: | 1-byte integer | 0 |
| variable identifier | 5 bytes* | 1.3.6.1.2.1 |
| variable value | 0 | empty (NULL) |

\* How does 1 3 6 1 2 1 fit into 5 bytes? ISO defines a formula that codes the first two digits in one byte. Each of the remaining digits of the identifier occupies a byte. Chapter 35 contains the details.

Figure 5.3 shows how the dialogue proceeds. Since we are primarily interested in the flow of messages, the information in the *LANWatch* trace has been simplified in the figure. In addition, annotations have been added to explain what is going on.

```
GET-NEXT                              What is the first variable in your
  var: obj(5) 1 3 6 1 2 1            MIB?
  val: empty(0)

RESPONSE
  var: obj 1 3 6 1 2 1 1 1 0         sysDescr
  val:  string  "Sun  SNMP  Agent,   This is a Sun SPARCStation
SPARCStation  1+,  Company  Property
Number 123456"

GET-NEXT                              What is after sysDescr?
  var: obj 1 3 6 1 2 1 1 1 0
  val: empty

RESPONSE
  var: obj 1 3 6 1 2 1 1 2 0         sysObjectID
  val: obj 1 3 6 1 4 1 42 2 1 1      The identifier assigned by the
                                     vendor.

GET-NEXT
  var: obj(8) 1 3 6 1 2 1 1 2 0      What is after sysObjectID?
  val: empty(0)

RESPONSE
  var: obj(8) 1 3 6 1 2 1 1 3 0      sysUpTime
  val: time(3) 0x0da372              893,810 hundredths of a second (about
                                     2.5 minutes) since initialization.

GET-NEXT
  var: obj(8) 1 3 6 1 2 1 1 3 0      What's after sysUpTime?
  val: empty(0)


  . . .                              Continue through sysContact, sysName,
                                     and sysLocation.

GET-NEXT
  var: obj 1 3 6 1 2 1 1 6 0         What's after sysLocation?
  val: empty

RESPONSE
  var: obj 1 3 6 1 2 1 1 7 0         sysServices
  val: int 0x48                      Hex code x' 48 means that this is a
                                     host that runs service applications.

GET-NEXT
  var: obj 1 3 6 1 2 1 1 7 0         What's after sysServices?
  val: empty

RESPONSE                             ifNumber
  var: obj 1 3 6 1 2 1 2 1 0         There are 2 interfaces for this
  val: int 0x02                      system.
```

**Figure 5.3** Using *get-next*.

We start off asking for the next (leaf) variable after 1.3.6.1.2.1. The response indicates that this is *sysDescr,* whose identifier is 1.3.6.1.2.1.1.1.0. The system is identified as a Sun SPARCStation.

### 5.7.3  Lexicographic Order

*Get-next-request* messages move you through a MIB in lexicographic order. This means that you start at the smallest leaf object identifier in the MIB tree (at the far bottom left) and march toward the largest leaf object identifier (at the far bottom right). How do you determine that one object identifier is larger than another? You compare the digits, *going from left to right.* Let's look at an example:

```
A   1.3.6.1.2.1.1.6.0          (sysLocation)
B   1.3.6.1.2.1.1.7.0          (sysServices)
```

B has a bigger digit in the first position at which they differ, so B is bigger than A. Here's another example:

```
A   1.3.6.1.2.1.2.2.1.5.3      (ifSpeed for 3rd interface)
B   1.3.6.1.2.1.4.2.0          (ipDefaultTTL)
```

Again, B is bigger than A.

### 5.7.4   Using Get-Next to Read a Table

One of the results of the fact that *get-next-requests* retrieve items in lexicographic order is that *get-next* reads tables by marching down the first column, then the second, then the third, etc.

For example, the SPARCStation that we queried in Figure 5.3 has information about two interfaces in its MIB. These are:

- lo0: The loopback interface. A logical interface used when TCP/IP is used to pass traffic between two processes residing on the station.
- le0: An Ethernet interface that connects the workstation to an Ethernet network.

The standard MIB-II interfaces table consists of 20 columns. For this example, there are two rows, corresponding to the number of interfaces. The first five columns are shown in Table 5.1. Every variable in the table has a name with structure:

```
1.3.6.1.2.1.2.2.1.(column number).index
```

For example, the complete variable name for the speed of interface number 2 is 1.3.6.1.2.1.2.2.1.5.2.

**TABLE 5.1   Columns from the Interfaces Table**

| Interfaces Table 1.3.6.1.2.1.2.2.1. | | | | |
|---|---|---|---|---|
| ifIndex<br>1 | ifDescr<br>2 | ifType<br>3 | ifMTU<br>4 | ifSpeed<br>5 |
| 1 | lo0 | 24 (0x18) software<br>LoopBack | 1536 octets (0x0600) | 10 Megabits/sec<br>(0x989680) |
| 2 | le0 | 6 (0x06) ethernet<br>-csmacd | 1500 octets (0x05dc) | 10 Megabits/sec<br>(0x989680) |

Below we see the responses (as reported by LANWatch) when *get-next* messages are used to read this table. The first value, just prior to the table, is the value of *ifNumber,* which indicates the number of rows in the table. Then, *get-next* reads each column from top to bottom, which in this case means that it reads a value for interface 1, and then one for interface 2.

```
var: obj(8)  1 3 6 1 2 1 2 1 0     val: int(1) 0x02         (ifNumber)
var: obj(10) 1 3 6 1 2 1 2 2 1 1 1 val: int(1) 0x01         (ifIndex1)
var: obj(10) 1 3 6 1 2 1 2 2 1 1 2 val: int(1) 0x02         (ifIndex2)
var: obj(10) 1 3 6 1 2 1 2 2 1 2 1 val: string(3) "lo0"     (ifDescr1)
var: obj(10) 1 3 6 1 2 1 2 2 1 2 2 val: string(3) "le0"     (ifDescr2)
var: obj(10) 1 3 6 1 2 1 2 2 1 3 1 val: int(1) 0x18         (ifType 1)
var: obj(10) 1 3 6 1 2 1 2 2 1 3 2 val: int(1) 0x06         (ifType 2)
var: obj(10) 1 3 6 1 2 1 2 2 1 4 1 val: int(2) 0x0600       (ifMTU 1)
var: obj(10) 1 3 6 1 2 1 2 2 1 4 2 val: int(2) 0x05dc       (ifMTU 2)
var: obj(10) 1 3 6 1 2 1 2 2 1 5 1 val: gauge(4) 0x00989680 (ifSpeed1)
var: obj(10) 1 3 6 1 2 1 2 2 1 5 2 val: gauge(4) 0x00989680 (ifSpeed2)
```

## 5.8   TRAP MESSAGES

*Trap* messages enable an agent to report a serious condition to a management station. The SNMP philosophy affirms that *traps* should be used carefully and sparingly. When a network gets in trouble, the last thing that we want to do is to set off a chorus of complaining voices that tell us something we already have figured out.

### 5.8.1   Trace of a *trap* Message

A Network General Sniffer trace of a *trap* message is shown below. As in the previous message types, the first field identifies the version (0 for SNMP version 1), and the next field contains the community password ("public"). After it is established that the type is *trap,* the format diverges, and there are five new fields. Some *traps* (but not this one) contain additional information in the form of a variable list at the end of the message—using the same format for the variable list as *gets* and *sets* do.

The *Enterprise* field contains an OBJECT IDENTIFIER which usually names the vendor product that sent the trap.* In this case, 1.3.6.1.4.1.121.1.1 tells us that FTP Software is the product vendor, and the agent is part of the PC/TCP product. The next field contains the IP address of the PC that sent the *trap*.

```
SNMP: ----- Simple Network Management Protocol -----
SNMP:
SNMP: Version = 0
SNMP: Community = public
SNMP: Command = Trap
SNMP: Enterprise = {1.3.6.1.4.1.121.1.1}
SNMP: Network address = [128.1.1.10]
SNMP: Generic trap = 0 (Cold start)
SNMP: Specific trap = 0
SNMP: Time ticks = 0
SNMP:
```

The "Generic trap = 0" statement indicates that it is a standard trap reporting that a cold start occurred at the sending system.

### 5.8.2   Codes in the *generic-trap* Field

The codes used in the *generic-trap* field include:

- *coldStart(0):* The sender is reinitializing, and its configuration may change.
- *warmStart(1):* The sender is reinitializing, but its configuration will not change.
- *linkDown(2):* There is a failure in one of the agent's links.
- *linkUp(3).*   One of the agent's links has come up.
- *authenticationFailure(4).*   The agent reports that it has received a protocol message that was not properly authenticated—i.e., the message had an inappropriate community name. It *should* be possible to configure an agent to suppress this trap.
- *egpNeighborLoss(5).*   An Exterior Gateway Protocol neighbor is down. The Exterior Gateway Protocol will be described in Chapter 16.
- *enterpriseSpecific(6).*   The *trap* is identified as *not* being one of the five basic ones.

Codes 0–5 in the *generic-trap* field identify standard traps. Code number 6 is special.

---

* It alternatively can contain the identifier for the MIB subtree of a technology for which the trap is defined, or can contain the identifier of the administrative body that defined the trap.

*et-next-requests*

ning read/write)
*t* messages from
will be honored.
:h explains why
.

sed by MIB authors or vendors
ieir MIBs or for their products.
*riseSpecific* traps.
MIB defined two X.25-specific
ontains:

```
ansmission.x25
```

dentify which of the two *traps*
ie first *trap* and a value of 2 is

ic trap fields seems a little con-
ually simplifies traps.

ipsed time between the initial-
)f the *trap*—in other words, the
is 0, since the system made a
).

can be explicitly

:s that shed additional light on
e, when a *linkDown* or *linkUp*
affected link. An *egpNeighbor-*
e neighbor that has stopped
i *trap* looks just like a variable-
list of pairs, consisting of an

he display below
PC/TCP agent,
*raps* will be sent
.1.1.2. The com-
." For this agent
ient stations. If
ach destination.

ts:

ommunity name. Every agent
nore community names, and to
to managers according to the
ieir messages.
shows a community name con-
t is:
ct. A request from *anywhere*
imunity name "public" will be

given READ access. This means that *get-requests* and
will be honored.

The system is pickier about who has WRITE (me:
privileges. *Get-request, get-next-request,* and *set-reque*
128.1.1.2 containing the community name "xy12%$3v
This is not exactly an iron-clad security system, wh
many organizations do not permit WRITE access at a

```
# This is the communityconfigurationfile
# that determines who may access the system.
# Each line consists of three items:
#
# First, the communityname.
# Second, the IP address of the remote site.
# If the address is 0.0.0.0, then any address
# may communicateusing that communityname.
#
# Third, the privilegesgiven that communitynam
# These currentlyconsist of READ for read only
# WRITE for read/write, or NONE to lock out
# a communityname.
# Permissionsmust be in UPPER CASE.
#
public      0.0.0.0       READ
xy12%$3v    128.1.1.2     WRITE
```

Note that a specific community name (such as public)
locked out of a device by defining an access of NONE.

## 5.10  COMMUNITIES FOR TRAPS

An agent also needs to know where to send its *traps*. T
shows a *trap* destination configuration file for the
which is implemented by a program called SNMPD. T
to port number 162 at the system with IP address 12
munity name in the *trap* message will be set to "publi
product, *traps* could be sent to up to five manager
desired, a different community name can be used for

```
# SNMPD presently sends two kinds of Trap pack
# ColdStart and AuthenticationFailure.
# Each kind will be sent to all destinations
# listed in this file (maximum of 5). The form
#
# community IP address  UDP port
#
public 128.1.1.2 162
```

## 5.11    PROXY AGENTS

Sometimes management needs to be done by proxy. What does this mean? Figure 5.4 shows the relationship between an SNMP manager, a proxy agent, and the information to be accessed.

Formally, a proxy agent is *any* agent that does not reside in the same system that holds the MIB data. Thus, a proxy is used in any situation where we want to get indirect access to management information.

For example, we might have a network management station attached to a LAN that uses frequent SNMP polls to gather information about LAN devices. All polling can be done locally at high speeds. The LAN-attached management station can act as a proxy, sending *traps* to a principal management station at the Network Operations Center, and responding to occasional, selective polls from the Network Operations Center. If the proxy polls its devices frequently, it could respond to requests from the Network Operations Center by using cached data, rather than by generating fresh local polls.

A proxy also is useful for managing a subnetwork that must be kept very secure. An external Network Operations Center can watch over

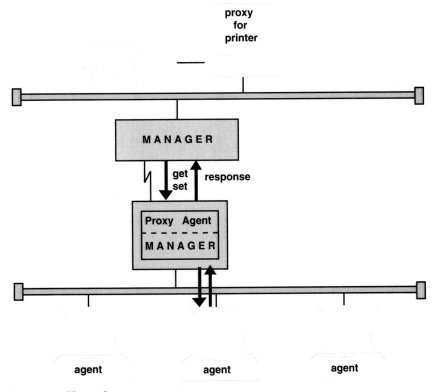

**Figure 5.4**  Uses of a proxy agent.

the subnetwork by communicating with an internal management station. No traffic to or from the outside world need appear within the subnetwork.

Another scenario for proxy use is that there may be older devices in the network that cannot be managed via SNMP, but *can* be managed by means of some proprietary protocol operating in a custom-designed management system. In some cases, it has been easy to add an SNMP *proxy agent* to the custom-designed management system. The proxy agent translates SNMP requests into proprietary requests, and reformats the device's data into MIB values.

SNMP version 2 provides an additional tool for partitioning the work of managing a network by defining a solid manager-to-manager protocol. A manager can be configured to send messages to a higher-level manager when a local problem-detecting statistic crosses a threshold.

## 5.12    GETTING TO KNOW SNMP

As protocols go, SNMP is indeed a simple one. We have seen that it has minimal transport needs. There are four straightforward messages that read and write MIB values, and a fifth that reports important events.

The request message formats were designed so that an agent just "fills in the blanks" and sends the answer back. The weakest point in the protocol is in the use of community names for authentication. However, agents can be configured to talk only to managers at prespecified IP addresses.

We shall see that "simple" does not mean "weak." The messages allow us to read *any* database of MIB variables. The scope of MIB definitions has grown explosively without requiring any changes to SNMP. The values of MIB variables can be tied to actions—for example, setting a value to 1 can start a loopback test or cause a reboot. Thus, an SNMP *set* can be used to test or cure a sick system.

This chapter has concentrated on SNMP's major structure and features. Chapter 6 will explore the details of how SNMP controls access to management data, and how various kinds of errors are handled. Chapter 6 also will explain how new *traps* are added to SNMP.

## 5.13    RECOMMENDED READING

SNMP version 1 is defined in RFC 1157.

# 6

# A Closer Look at SNMP

## 6.1 INTRODUCTION

Chapter 5 introduced SNMP and described its design concepts and capabilities. In this chapter we will go behind the scenes and consider some of the more technical details.

We will look at how a *community* defines the relationship between manager and agent. We'll see how an agent figures out what information a manager is entitled to access. There are times when an agent will turn down a request. We'll find out when this happens and what error messages will be sent back.

Another issue that needs to be resolved is that the original SNMP specification was not at all clear on how a manager could add a row to a table or delete a row from a table. We'll explain how table additions and deletions eventually were handled.

Finally, we will describe how vendors and organizations can meet their problem-reporting needs by defining new *traps*.

## 6.2 COMMUNITIES

Many of the pieces that are needed to make network management work have been assembled. But there are still some questions that need to be answered:

- Can I control which nodes are managed by a particular management station?
- Can several managers watch over a pool of nodes?
- Can I prevent a management station from writing configuration data into a MIB?
- Can I restrict the information that a management station can see?

These questions all relate to the administrative framework in which network management operates. Although the answer to all of the questions is "yes,"* the administrative mechanisms provided in version 1 of SNMP are quite primitive.

Sticking to basic mechanisms was necessary in order to get an easily implemented version out the door and into products. When we examine version 2 of SNMP, we shall see that one of its chief benefits is the introduction of a much more competent administrative framework.

## 6.3  CONFIGURING COMMUNITIES

SNMP administrative control is based on the use of *community* names. Each SNMP message includes a community name that functions like a password. The community name can be any string of octets.

The formal definition of a community is "a pairing of an agent with a set of application entities." The community relationship is implemented by configuring who will talk to whom, what community name will be included in the messages sent between them, and what data can be accessed for each community.

Many organizations allow *any* station that can run management software to view simple statistics. They do this by providing read access to statistical data for a community name such as "public." However, they restrict update privileges to a user at a specific IP address who knows a secret community password.

Figure 6.1 shows a *get* message with community name "public" that asks to read a statistic—the total number of incoming IP messages; the figure also shows a *set* message with a secret community name, "xy12%$3v" that changes the default Time-to-Live to 40.

In Chapter 5, we looked at configuration files that are used for a basic PC *agent*. The first file identified the acceptable IP addresses and community names for incoming *get* message (that read information) and *set* messages (that write updates). The second file defined the IP addresses and community names that the agent should use for sending *trap* messages. These files are displayed again below.

```
# This is the community configuration file
# that determines who may access the system.
# Each line consists of three items:
#
# First, the community name.
# Second, the IP address of the remote site.
# If the address is 0.0.0.0, then any address
# may communicate using that community name.
```

---

* "Yes, sort of" might be a more accurate answer for version 1 of SNMP.

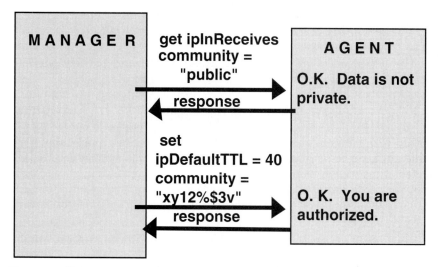

**Figure 6.1** Using a community name as a password.

```
#
# Third, the privileges given that community name.
# These currently consist of READ for read only,
# WRITE for read/write, or NONE to lock out
# a community name.
# Permissions must be in UPPER CASE.
#
public        0.0.0.0        READ
xy12%$3v      128.1.1.2      WRITE

# SNMPD presently sends two kinds of Trap packets:
# ColdStart and AuthenticationFailure.
# Each kind will be sent to all the destinations
# listed in this file (maximum of 5). The format is:
# community IP address    UDP port
public 128.1.1.2 162
```

These are very minimal configuration files. As we shall see, the vendor could have chosen to impose a more detailed level of access control. Since none of the MIB data in the PC is particularly secret or sensitive, the mechanisms were kept very simple.

## 6.4   COMMUNITY AUTHENTICATION SCHEME

How do we know that an SNMP message comes from a valid source? The SNMP version 1 specification pointed out the need for authentication, but did not mandate any specific solution. As a result, version 1 implementations rely on IP addresses and community names to check up on the validity of incoming messages. The community configuration files displayed above are typical.

The provision of more robust authentication and privacy services was at the top of the agenda for SNMP version 2.

## 6.5   RULES FOR READING AND WRITING

When can a management application read or write a particular variable in a device's MIB? There are several rules whose interaction determines who can do what:

- The *collection of variables* that are accessible by a given community can be restricted.

- The *type of access* to these variables might be limited—for example, to only reading values.

- Each individual *MIB definition* imposes its own limit on the access that is allowed.

We will work our way through all of these rules in the next few sections.

### 6.5.1   MIB View

A *MIB view* is a selected subset of the variables in a device's MIB. According to the SNMP access rules, a community can be restricted so that *only variables within a specific MIB view* can be accessed via messages carrying that community name.

Of course, this works only when the device's vendor provides customers a way to configure MIB views and assign them to communities. Many vendors have felt that this level of detailed control was not worth the extra development effort—or the extra processing overhead imposed by having to validate every variable in every message.

For example, for the configuration files shown in Section 6.3, there is only one MIB view, namely the PC's entire MIB.

### 6.5.2   Access Mode, Community Profile, and Access Policy

A level of access, READ-ONLY, READ-WRITE, or NONE, is called the *access mode*. The combination of a MIB view and an access mode which is applied to the *whole view* is called a *community profile*. Tie a *community profile* to a community and you have an *SNMP access policy*.

The formality of these definitions may seem like overkill, but the intention is simple. For example, suppose that we have a management station that is a multiuser system running many different management applications.

One of these applications may provide a user interface for a help-desk support person. Another may provide management functions to a network management staff person in charge of all of the network's routers. Each user's messages are sent out with a different community name. When we configure devices with community access policies:

- We can control which devices can be accessed by each operator.
- We can restrict which variables are accessed by each operator.
- We can prevent the help-desk operator from writing any values.

Of course, these restrictions work only if each operator's application plays by the rules and sends messages containing the appropriate community name.

### 6.5.3   Access Restrictions Within MIB Definitions

Every variable in a MIB has a built-in access restriction that is part of its MIB definition. We looked at some sample MIB definitions in Chapter 4. For example,

```
sysUpTime OBJECT-TYPE
    SYNTAX    TimeTicks
    ACCESS    read-only
    STATUS    mandatory
    DESCRIPTION
        "The time (in hundredths of a second) since the
        network management portion of the system was last
        re-initialized."
    ::= { system 3 }
```

Naturally, the ACCESS clause determines the level of access. The *sysUpTime* variable has been assigned read-only access. Read-only access means that a variable's value cannot be updated with a *set*. In version 1, a variable's ACCESS is assigned one of the values:

- *read-only.*   You can include this variable in a *get-request, get-next-request, get-response,* or *trap* message variable list.
- *read-write.*   You can include this variable in a *get-request, get-next-request, set-request, get-response,* or *trap* message variable list.
- *write-only.*   This variable can appear in a *set-request* and the answering *get-response.* Write-only access turned out to be useless, and was dropped in SNMP version 2.
- *not-accessible.*   This is used in the MIB definitions of compound objects: tables and table entries. A request message cannot simply

ask for ("access") a whole table. The message must ask for the individual variables that make up a table.

Defining an ACCESS of not-accessible may seem silly, but in fact it has a real meaning. We define a table as the *logical* organization of variables into columns and rows, even though the SNMP protocol *only can retrieve or update a list of individual variables.* The restriction to operating on *individual variables* has been absolutely critical to keeping SNMP flexible and extensible. Useless variables can be dropped from tables and new variables can be added without changing the SNMP software. A typical MIB variable that is not-accessible is:

```
ifTable OBJECT-TYPE
     SYNTAX   SEQUENCE OF IfEntry
     ACCESS   not-accessible
     STATUS   mandatory
     DESCRIPTION
        "A list of interface entries. The number of
        entries is given by the value of ifNumber."
        ::= { interfaces 2 }
```

Saying that the table is not-accessible means that we cannot retrieve a whole table by sending a *get* that contains only the OBJECT IDENTIFIER for the table, namely 1.3.6.1.2.1.2.2. We *will* be able to retrieve the table by sending the complete list of OBJECT IDENTIFIERs for the variables in the table, or by walking through the table with a series of *get-next-requests.*

### 6.5.4   Minimum or Maximum ACCESS?

In SNMP version 1, the ACCESS in a MIB definition was described as a *minimum* level. That meant that a particular vendor could implement a higher level of access. For example, a vendor might decide to implement its *sysUpTime* variable so that a management station could *set* it.

This turned out to be a bad idea. Variables that are read-only or not-accessible really are defined that way for very good reasons. Fortunately, few if any vendors took advantage of their freedom to provide inappropriate access to MIB variables.

SNMP version 2 correctly specifies that a variable's ACCESS, as defined in a MIB standard, is the *maximum* level that is acceptable.

### 6.6   CONTROLLING WHAT
### A MANAGER CAN READ

For every response to a *get,* and for each *trap* message, an agent has to answer the question: "What variable values am I *allowed* to send to this manager?" To find the answer, the agent has to answer three other questions:

1. Is this variable in the MIB view for the community that I am sending it to?
2. Does the community profile for this community have an access mode of either READ-ONLY or READ-WRITE (rather than NONE)?
3. Does the MIB definition for the variable give it an ACCESS of either read-only or read-write?

## 6.7 CONTROLLING WHAT A MANAGER CAN WRITE

For every *set-request* message that it receives, an agent has to answer the question: "What variable values is this manager *allowed* to write?" To get the answer, the agent has to answer three other questions:

1. Is this variable in the MIB view for the community that sent it?
2. Does the profile for this community give this MIB view an access mode of READ-WRITE?
3. Does the MIB definition for this variable give it an ACCESS of read-write?

## 6.8 TABULATING THE RULES FOR READING AND WRITING

The SNMP standard specifies what to do for each combination of MIB view access mode and MIB definition ACCESS clause. Table 6.1 shows exactly when it is valid to include a variable in a message under every possible combination of restrictions.

The rules in Table 6.1 boil down to common sense. If the overall MIB view access mode for your community is NONE, you can't read or write *any* of the variables in the MIB view. If the overall access mode is READ-ONLY, then you cannot *set* any values. If the overall access mode is READ-WRITE, then you can do anything that the MIB definition of each variable allows.

The usefulness of variables whose MIB definitions have an ACCESS clause of write-only is shrouded in some mystery. For example, the value for a write-only variable that is included in a *get-response* or a *trap* is "implementation-specific." Returning a random value to a manager that tries to read a write-only variable probably was introduced to avoid an error response. Since write-only variables are a disappearing (maybe nonexistent) breed, it does not pay to brood over this.

TABLE 6.1    Controlling Access to Variables

| MIB ACCESS clause for variable | MIB View Access Mode (Community Profile) | |
| --- | --- | --- |
| | READ-ONLY | READ-WRITE |
| | Valid In | |
| read-only | get-request<br>get-next-request<br>get-response<br>trap | get-request<br>get-next-request<br>get-response<br>trap |
| read-write | get-request<br>get-next-request<br>get-response<br>trap | get-request<br>get-next-request<br>get-response<br>trap<br>set-request |
| write-only | get-request<br>get-next-request<br>get-response*<br>trap* | get-request<br>get-next-request<br>get-response*<br>trap*<br>set-request |
| not-accessible | none | none |

* The value will be implementation-specific.

## 6.9   WHAT HAPPENS WHEN A REQUEST FAILS

In SNMP version 1, a request either succeeds completely or fails completely. If it succeeds, then the Error status and Error index in the *get-response* are set to 0. If it fails, the Error status and Error index provide clues to what went wrong.

Let's be specific. Suppose a *get-request* contains a list of six variables and the first three could be processed correctly but there is a problem with the fourth. What happens? The request will fail. You will get back a response that looks a lot like your original request, except for the fact that error information has been filled in.

In general (for version 1), if a request cannot be satisfied completely for any reason, the *whole request* will fail. SNMP version 1 is an all-or-nothing-at-all protocol. The agent will not *get* or *set any* values, and the response will not fill *any* data values into the variable list!

The agent will send back a response that looks just like the request, except that the message type will have changed and the *error status* field will indicate what went wrong. If the problem relates to a variable, the *error index* field will point to the variable that caused the problem.

Fortunately, SNMP version 2 has a more reasonable approach. A *get* is allowed to succeed even if some values are not available. However, a *set* still remains an all-or-nothing operation.

## 6.10   ERROR STATUS AND ERROR INDEX

What can go wrong? The integer codes that may appear in the error status field are:

- *noError(0).*   Well, this time nothing went wrong.

- *tooBig(1).*   The *get-response* message containing the results of an operation would be bigger than the local implementation can handle. (The error index will be 0.)

- *noSuchName(2).*   One of the requested variables does not match anything in the relevant MIB view that can be returned. The error index indicates which variable caused trouble. For example, "3" means the third variable in the list.

- *badValue(3).*   A *set-request* asked the agent to write an inappropriate value—for example, to write an integer where a text string was required. The error index indicates which variable caused the trouble.

- *readOnly(4).*   A *set-request* tried to write a variable that the operator is not allowed to write. Either the access mode is READ-ONLY or the variable's MIB definition does not permit write access. The error index indicates which variable caused the trouble.

- *genErr(5).*   A variable cannot be retrieved for some reason other than those listed above. The error index indicates which variable caused the trouble.

## 6.11   ELEMENTS OF TABLE MAINTENANCE

From the point of view of SNMP, a table is a *logical* structure, and SNMP worries only about reading or writing individual table values. Table maintenance was not given any attention—until real implementations hit the street and users could see that there were some holes in the specification. Many tables hold configuration information that will be updated by operators, and sometimes:

1. We need a way to delete a whole row.

2. We need a way to add a new row.

3. We need a way to manage contention when two different operators try to add a row with the same index at the same time!

Inventing a way to delete rows is easy. Any table that permits row deletions or additions just needs an extra column containing a entry status variable. We can *set* the value of this entry status variable to *invalid* in a row that we want to delete.

To create a new row, we have to establish values for every variable in the row. Some table definitions make this a bit easier by providing *default* values for some of the row variables.

The simplest way to add a row is to request a *set* that writes a new row of variables into a table, making sure that an unused index is selected and that the entry status variable gets *set* to *valid*. It is OK to omit values for variables whose definitions include *default* values.

If two or more operators try to create a row with the same index, the first *set* request will succeed, and the second operator's request will get an error response.

Sometimes creation of a new table entry will require more than one *set* by an operator—there may be just too many values to fit into a single message. We need a more finely tuned choice of values for the entry status variable when row creation takes a while and requires more than one operation. RFC 1271 defines values for an *entryStatus* variable that track the life of a table entry:

- *createRequest.*   Used in a *set* that requests creation of a new row.

- *underCreation.*   The operator is filling in the values for the row.

- *valid.*   The entry is complete and available.

- *invalid.*   The operator wants to delete the entry.

SNMP version 2 improves table management. First of all, version 2 makes a clear distinction between tables that an operator should be able to add to, such as configuration tables, and tables whose entries just report what is going on at a node—for example, a TCP connection table lists the currently active connections.

How do we indicate that it is OK to add new rows to a table? In SNMP version 2, row variables can be given ACCESS clause value "read-create" which actually means "read-write-create."* This makes it crystal clear that an operator is allowed to create a new row of variables in a table.

Version 2 also replaces *entryStatus* with a new row status (*rowStatus*) variable that does an even better job of controlling row creation and deletion. The details are in Chapter 31.

---

* What was gained by leaving out the word "write"? Confusion for the users!

## 6.12  RECOMMENDED READING

Some of the issues that we discussed are introduced in RFC 1157, *A Simple Network Management Protocol (SNMP)*. The easiest way to understand the use of communities to delineate the relationship between agents and management applications is to look at the configuration files in your own agent and management systems.

RFC 1212 described some rough guidelines for row creation. The *entryStatus* variable in RFC 1271 put row creation and deletion on a far more solid foundation. The enhanced *rowStatus* variable is described in RFC 1443.

# An Introduction to Management Information Bases

## 7.1 INTRODUCTION

It is time to focus our attention on the mixture of configuration, status, and statistical information that is stored at a device. Recall that the information may take many forms—a dip-switch setting, a hardware counter, a variable in PROM or RAM memory, or a table stored in memory or on disk.

A management station relies on the agent at a device to retrieve or update the information at the device. The information is viewed as a logical database, called a *Management Information Base,* or MIB. *MIB modules* describe MIB variables for a growing variety of device types and computer hardware and software components.

The original MIB for managing a TCP/IP internet (now called MIB-I) was defined in RFC 1066 in August of 1988. It was updated in RFC 1156 in May of 1990. The MIB-II version, published in RFC 1213 in May of 1991, contained some improvements, and has proved that it can do a good job of meeting basic TCP/IP management needs. MIB-II added a number of useful variables missing from MIB-I.

In this chapter, we will take a sightseeing trip through MIB-II, briefly visiting each of its groups. We will discover what guidelines MIB designers follow so that their MIBs will work well within the SNMP management framework, and find out just what goes into a MIB definition. We'll also take a look at how a management station's graphical user interface puts MIB information stored at many different devices within easy reach.

Chapters 8 to 16 will describe the components of MIB-II in greater detail. Later chapters will describe some of the MIBs defined by industry task forces for a variety of technologies, and also will look into some proprietary MIBs.

## 7.2   GUIDELINES FOR DEFINING MIBS

The first guideline for MIBs designed to fit into the Internet Management framework is to keep it simple. MIB variables are *elementary stand-alone quantities,* integers, octet strings, or object identifiers. Sometimes a bunch of MIB variables is *logically* organized into a table.

Measured by their computer resources, network management stations usually are big and strong. Network devices often are small and weak. It is important to keep the number of baseline MIB variables to an essential minimum. If a device is spending more time counting and recording what it is doing than it spends getting some useful work accomplished, something is definitely wrong!

MIBs should be defined so that the burden of computational work is shifted to the management applications. For example, if there is a variable that can be calculated from other MIB variables, let the management application do the calculation, and leave the computed variable *out* of the MIB.

## 7.3   EXTENSIBILITY

The tree of MIB variables can grow . . . and grow . . . and grow. It is very easy to graft new MIB modules onto the tree, and there currently are task forces working on MIBs for Asynchronous Transfer Mode, Host Management, Directory Services Management—and many other technologies.

Considering the scope of these efforts, it is not surprising that definitions need to be improved occasionally. If the improvement involves a major change, an updated version of the MIB will simply define a completely new variable and mark the old one as *deprecated* (on the way out) or outright *obsolete.*

For a while, it was the practice to place all new MIB definitions under the *experimental* node in the naming tree. After implementation, field experience and revision took place, the definitions were reviewed and moved to the appropriate place somewhere below the *mib-II* node.

The trouble with this was that products would have to be changed because all of the objects had been given new names. More recent MIB documents name objects to match their appropriate place in the naming tree as early as possible.

## 7.4   GROUPS AND HOW THEY ARE USED

MIB variables are defined in *groups*. This is a convenient arrangement. Each group usually has an identifier that appears in the naming tree, and objects are attached under that identifier. Thus all of the related variables within a group will have names that start with the same prefix.

The group concept is helpful in other ways. There are many, many groups of variables defined. Some groups are not at all relevant to a particular device. For example, a bridge probably would not support TCP.* If a group does not make sense for a device, the device simply does not support it. The *capabilities* of a device are easily summarized by listing the groups that the device supports.

In SNMP version 1, support for a group was an all-or-nothing-at-all decision. If a device provided a group, it was supposed to be able to handle requests that involved any variable in the group. This caused some problems, since some objects did not make sense for a vendor's product, or else the vendor just did not want to support some objects. This led to either a response of a 0 or NULL, or else an error response. SNMP version 2 handles conformance far more gracefully, allowing a vendor to list exactly what objects are supported, and to what degree.

## 7.5   A TOUR OF MIB-II

There are eleven groups referenced in the original MIB-II document. One of these, *cmot,* was intended to hold objects needed to run the ISO Common Management Information Services/Common Management Information Protocol on top of TCP/IP. When the effort to run ISO management on top of TCP/IP was abandoned, *cmot* was demoted to historical status, and dropped out of sight. The 10 remaining groups, along with one more group added slightly later, describe the most basic information needed to manage a TCP/IP internet. Many other useful MIBs have been written, but this chapter and the ones immediately following it concentrate on the MIB-II heartland.

Figure 7.1 displays the MIB-II groups and the OBJECT IDENTIFIERS that have been assigned to each group. The figure includes the *ifExtensions* group which was added after the publication of MIB-II and contains some very important definitions needed to manage interfaces.

---

* TCP certainly is not needed for a bridge's service function. However, a vendor might actually provide TCP to allow an administrator to log in to the bridge and configure it across a network. In any case, a simple version of IP and UDP would be implemented at a bridge to support SNMP.

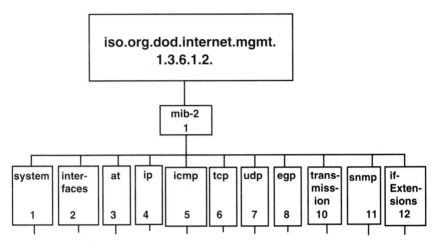

Figure 7.1   MIB-II.

Let's visit each of these groups briefly. Detailed descriptions of each group will be presented in the chapters that follow.

### 7.5.1   The *system* Group

The system group is so important that it is required for every device. The group includes configuration information that pinpoints what the device is, where it is, and who to call when something goes wrong. The *system* group will be described in Chapter 9.

### 7.5.2   The *interfaces* Group

A device connects to the world through interface hardware and software. A large amount of very important management information is included in the *interfaces* group.

MIB-II identifies 32 interface types—and more are being invented all the time! The display that follows lists some examples of interface types:

| LANs | Packet nets | Point-to-point |
|---|---|---|
| DIX Ethernet | X.25 | LAPB |
| 802.3 Ethernet | Frame Relay | ISDN |
| 802.5 Token-Ring | SMDS | DS1,E1 |
| FDDI | ATM | DS3 |

Variables in the interfaces group disclose:

- Configuration information, such as the interface type and speed
- The status of the interface (up or down)
- Incoming and outgoing traffic statistics
- Counts of various kinds of errors

The *interfaces* group, which is mandatory for all SNMP systems, will be described in Chapter 10.

### 7.5.3 The *ifExtensions* Group

Although the *ifExtensions* group is positioned several nodes away, it is closely tied to the *interfaces* group, and in fact contains some valuable extensions to the *interfaces* group. Among the information that has been added is:

- Separate counts of broadcast and multicast traffic
- Variables that fire off a test and record the test results
- The complete set of physical addresses (including broadcast and multicast addresses) for which an interface will absorb traffic

The *ifExtensions* group will be described in Chapter 10.

### 7.5.4 The *at* Group

For datagram-based protocols like IP, traffic is routed by choosing the next-hop system that is along the best path to the destination. Before a datagram can be transmitted, it must be wrapped in a frame. The frame header includes address information needed to deliver the frame. For example, as shown in Figure 7.2, to reach a system across an Ethernet LAN, the 6-octet Media Access Control (MAC) address of the Network Interface Card installed in the next-hop system must be included in the frame header.

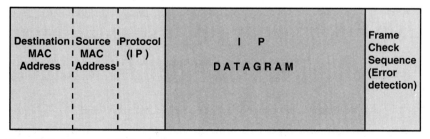

**Figure 7.2** Ethernet-II frame header.

The process of mapping the IP address of the next-hop system to the lower-layer frame address is called *address translation.* A list of network layer addresses and corresponding LAN or packet net addresses is stored in a translation table at a system. The address translation (*at*) group gives a management application access to this table information.

The *at* table was defined as part of MIB-I. In its original design, it had entries intended to translate any type of network layer address—IP, IPX, or whatever—to a corresponding lower-layer address. By the time the authors got around to writing MIB-II, they decided that they had made a mistake. The translation needs of protocols such as TCP/IP, NetWare IPX, DECnet, and AppleTalk differ in many details. The one-size-fits-all-protocols *at* table was not going to do the trick.

MIB-II defines the *at* table as *deprecated,* which means that it is on the way out. Instead, a separate IP address translation table is defined within the *ip* group. Other tables are defined as needed within other protocols.

There are still quite a few live systems in the field that support the original *at* table, so it is worth knowing that each table entry identifies an interface, a lower-layer address, and a network address. The *at* group will be discussed in Chapter 11.

### 7.5.5  The *ip* Group

The *ip* group covers the configuration and management needs of hosts and routers. The MIB includes:

- Configuration variables such as a default Time-to-Live and a reassembly timeout
- Incoming and outgoing traffic statistics
- Counts of various kinds of errors
- A table configuring each interface with an IP address, subnet mask, and other IP-related parameters
- A new IP-specific address translation table
- An IP routing table, used to select the next-hop destination when routing a datagram

The *ip* group, which is mandatory for all TCP/IP systems, will be covered in Chapter 12.

### 7.5.6  The *icmp* Group

Internet Control Message Protocol (ICMP) error messages are sent back to an IP datagram source to report problems encountered while trying to move a datagram to its destination. ICMP also supports some useful query messages. The *icmp* group is very straightforward. It consists of counts of every type of incoming and outgoing ICMP message. The *icmp* group, which is mandatory for all TCP/IP systems, will be described in Chapter 13.

### 7.5.7   The *tcp* Group

The *tcp* group lets a management application check up on some TCP configuration values, such as the top limit on the number of concurrent *tcp* connections that a system can handle. The MIB also records incoming and outgoing traffic and error statistics.

But perhaps the most useful diagnostic tool is the connection table, which allows a manager to view a list of active TCP sessions and get a pretty good idea of which applications are being accessed.

The *tcp* group, which is mandatory for all SNMP systems supporting TCP, will be described in Chapter 14.

### 7.5.8   The *udp* Group

The *udp* group also tracks traffic and errors, but since UDP is a very simple protocol, there are not a lot of variables needed to do this.

Since UDP applications just send stand-alone messages to each other, no record is kept of communicating partners. However, a management application can discover which UDP services are actively listening for partners to talk to.

The *udp* group, which is mandatory for all SNMP systems implementing UDP, will discussed in Chapter 15.

### 7.5.9   The *egp* Group

The Exterior Gateway Protocol (EGP) enables a router to talk to another router that is outside its own organization or administration. The two routers exchange some basic information needed to direct traffic from one network to the other.

Someone who has to support EGP is interested in the amounts of incoming and outgoing traffic, as well as how well the two routers are doing at keeping in touch with one another. The *egp* group meets these needs. The *egp* group, which is mandatory for all SNMP systems implementing EGP, will be discussed in Chapter 16.

### 7.5.10   The *transmission* Group

The *transmission* group opens the door to a whole world of new management functions. However, *transmission* never should have been called a group—it is just a node position in the naming tree. Many

MIBs, each containing groups that apply to different transmission technologies, are attached below this node.

Figure 7.3 shows some of the *transmission* subtrees. Chapters later in this book will describe the MIBs for specific transmission technologies. In the figure, *dot3, dot4,* and *dot5* refer to the standard LANs described in IEEE 802.3 (Ethernet), 802.4 (factory broadband) and 802.5 (Token-Ring) standards, and *sip* stands for SMDS Interface Protocol.

### 7.5.11  The *snmp* Group

With all of this wonderful information available out in the network, we can expect management stations to poll systems and ask for this data. We also can expect that *trap* traffic will appear on the network from time to time. If SNMP wants to track *everything,* maybe it should count its own traffic and errors. This is what the *snmp* group does. Specifically, the *snmp* group keeps track of the numbers of incoming and outgoing *gets, sets, responses,* and *traps,* and counts various errors, such as attempts to read nonexistent variables.

This is a mandatory group, required for every SNMP implementation, and will be described in Chapter 17.

### 7.6   CONTENTS OF A TYPICAL TRANSMISSION MIB

A number of transmission MIBs have reached draft or proposed standard level, and others are almost complete. Every popular technology

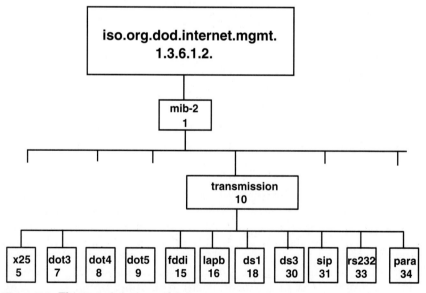

**Figure 7.3**  The transmission subtree.

is being addressed—for example, Ethernet, Token-Ring, FDDI, ISDN, DS1/E1 serial interfaces, higher-speed DS3/E3 serial interfaces, X.25, Frame Relay, SMDS, and Asynchronous Transfer Mode.

The *interfaces* and *ifExtensions* groups already provide variables that deal with interface configuration, traffic, status, and common errors. Why are separate MIBs needed?

They are needed primarily because there are configuration variables, status conditions, and errors that are specific to a technology, and there also are tests that make sense only for a distinctive technology. For example, the MIB for Ethernet-like interface types includes:

- A table that counts occurrences of several kinds of transmission problems and maintains overall collision counts
- A table that records a frequency histogram that shows how often 1 or 2 or 3 or _ collisions occurred when trying to transmit a frame
- The definition of a test (the Time-Domain Reflectometry test) used to locate an Ethernet cable fault

In contrast, a Token-Ring interface, which must execute a very complex LAN protocol, has a MIB that contains many more status variables and configuration variables—including 10 timer settings. Collisions are not a problem on a Token-Ring, but lost data frames and lost tokens are. The tests defined for a Token-Ring interface include a loopback that checks the path through the Token-Ring chipset, and a validation that the system is able to insert itself into the ring.

## 7.7 MANAGEMENT STATIONS

One of the great advantages of a network management standard is that it fosters inventiveness and competition in the design of network management stations.

Management station applications have the job of making the SNMP protocol tools easy to understand, easy to use, and as productive of results as is possible.

### 7.7.1 Browsing a MIB
### with a Management Station

Most network management stations provide a management application that can be used to peek at MIB values anywhere, anytime.

Figure 7.4 shows a NetView/6000 *Browse MIB* display. This screen was reached by clicking on a node to select it, and then clicking the *Browse MIB* menu choice.

In the top left window, we see the name of the selected node, *crocus.mgt.com.* Next to it is the community that will be used for the poll,

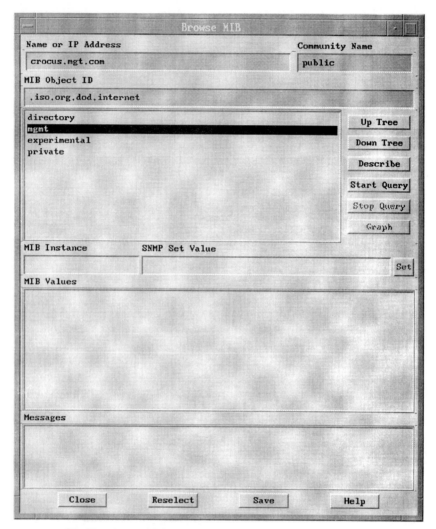

**Figure 7.4**  NetView/6000 MIB Browser.

*public.* The MIB Object ID window shows the tree labels leading to the current level of tree nodes, which are in the window below. To the right are our navigation buttons. We can go up or down the tree, ask for a description, start or stop a MIB query, or graph numeric results.

Figure 7.5 shows the result of clicking on *mgmt.* All of the standard MIB groups are listed. We could retrieve all of the values in a group from crocus, or click on a group and select one or more specific values. The results of a query would be shown in the scrollable window of Figure 7.5.

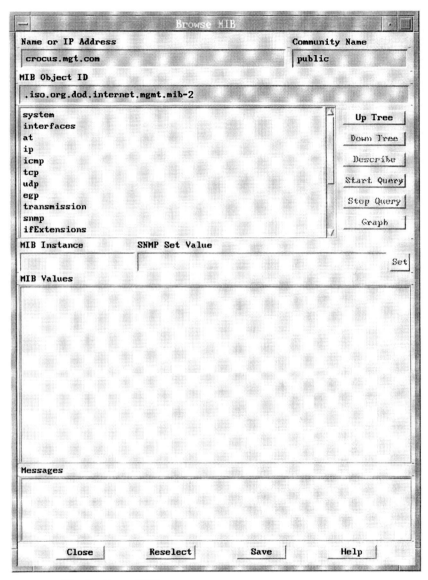

**Figure 7.5**  Navigating a MIB.

Note the slot about halfway down the screen labeled "MIB Instance." We can, if we like, provide an index value for a specific MIB variable. For example, we might want information about one particular network interface. Then to the right is a slot labeled "SNMP set value," which naturally is used to *set* a value. However, an attempt to *set* using community name *public* would (certainly should) be refused.

The *Describe* button presents a description of any object in the tree. In Chapter 4, Figure 4.4 showed the result of selecting an item further down the tree within the interfaces group and pushing *Describe*.

### 7.7.2   Setting Up Polls and Thresholds

Ad hoc polls are helpful for spot troubleshooting, but organized, scheduled data collection is how we get to understand a network's normal behavior and can spot trouble building up. Management stations can poll systems for selected statistics at regular intervals.

Figure 7.6 shows a NetView/6000 screen that configures some variables for regular collection. The buttons at the right of the top window allow us to add or delete variables, start or stop collection, and view collected data.

In the window of Figure 7.6, we can pick out the systems to be polled for this particular set of values, choose a polling interval, and indicate if we want the results stored in a file.

When a count for a variable goes above or below its configured upper or lower threshold, an event will be triggered. Event details are defined elsewhere, but typically an entry will be written in a log, and, in some cases, the management station operator will be notified immediately. Why do we need two thresholds? Usually one threshold means "We are in trouble!" while the other means "Back to normal." See Chapter 28 for a discussion of thresholds.

## 7.8   INTRODUCTION TO PROPRIETARY MIBS

### 7.8.1   Vendor and Enterprise MIBs

Any vendor can obtain a node under *private.enterprises,* and build whatever subtrees are needed in order to manage its products. Standards task forces and vendors do not have an exclusive lock on MIB definition. Any end-user enterprise also can register, obtain a subtree, and start writing MIB definitions that meet its specific needs.

### 7.8.2   Loading Proprietary MIBs

MIB variables are defined using a standard, high-level language. Many management stations include a *MIB compiler* that can integrate new sets of definitions into the family of objects managed by the station.

A good management station makes it easy for an operator to load and use proprietary MIBs. For example, Figure 7.7 shows a display of MIBs that already have been included in a NetView/6000 station.

When we push the *Load* button, we will get a display of MIB definition files, and can select more of them for inclusion. All management

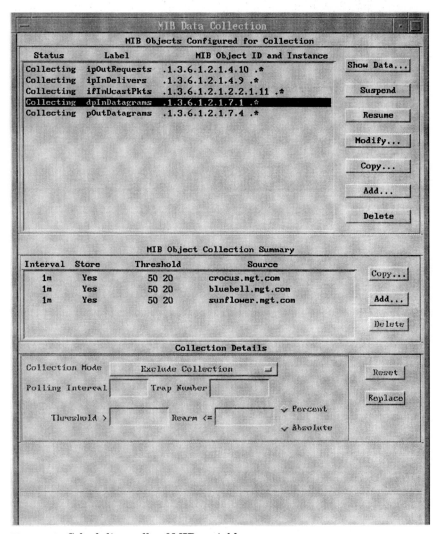

**Figure 7.6**  Scheduling polls of MIB variables.

station applications and tools can be used on the new variables in exactly the same way that the tools apply to the old variables.

## 7.9   DEFINING MIB DATATYPES WITH ASN.1

In earlier chapters, we looked at formal MIB definitions for *sysUpTime* and *sysServices*. These definitions are written in a special datatype definition language called *Abstract Syntax Notation 1* (ASN.1).

ASN.1 was one of the successful ideas introduced during the CCITT work that resulted in the X.400 electronic messaging recommendations.

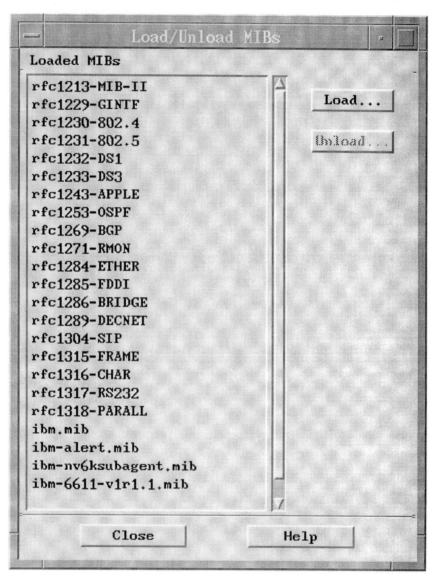

**Figure 7.7** Loading vendor MIBSs.

Historically, data communications specifications defined message formats bit by bit and byte by byte. The X.409 committee had a better idea. Why not use a high-level-language tool when defining the formats used in data communications protocols? Then let a compiler take care of all of the grubby work of converting ideas into a byte stream that a computer can understand. ASN.1 is the high-level language that has evolved and is now used whenever a complex communications standard must be designed.

How do we convert our high-level definitions into bytes that can be sent in messages? There are standard *Basic Encoding Rules* that convert the value of an ASN.1 variable into formatted bytes that can be sent across a network. These Basic Encoding Rules have been used to build compilers for MIB definitions.

In the next few sections, we will describe what you need to know about ASN.1 in order to read a MIB easily. A fuller description of ASN.1 is presented in Chapter 35.

## 7.10   DATATYPES THAT CAN BE USED IN MIBS

In its full strength, ASN.1 is a very powerful language, capable of describing extremely complicated data structures. The designers of SNMP were determined to *keep things simple*. They put on the brakes, restricting ASN.1 definitions of MIB variables to a few indispensable datatypes.

### 7.10.1   Introduction to Basic SNMP Datatypes

The fundamental ASN.1 datatypes used with SNMP version 1 are:

- OBJECT IDENTIFIER
- INTEGER
- OCTET STRING
- NULL

Version 2 adds the BIT STRING type. The full ASN.1 language has many more basic types. *However, every datatype comes with an encoding rule, and all of these rules have to be turned into software.* The designers of SNMP look at every new datatype definition with one thought in mind: "How many lines of code will it add to the implementation?" As a result, they have been very stingy about adding new datatypes, and practice recycling zealously.

### 7.10.2   Textual Conventions

One of the tricks used to keep the number of datatypes down is to suppress the instinct to create a new type, but instead define a *textual convention* that assigns a nickname for an existing datatype. The purpose is to make MIB definitions easier to read. For example,

- *PhysAddress.*   Another name for an OCTET STRING that represents a media or physical level address.

Sometimes there also is some restriction on possible values implied when the alternative name is used. For example,

- *DisplayString.* Another name for an OCTET STRING that is restricted to the Network Virtual Terminal (NVT) ASCII character set. The NVT ASCII printable character set was defined in the TCP/IP Telnet standard.

What is the practical meaning of using a nickname? Suppose that the value of a *DisplayString* variable has to be transmitted in a message. The Basic Encoding Rules require a *DisplayString* value to be encoded the same way that an octet string is encoded, namely,

'04'H    length-of-string    string-of-octets

The '04'H identifier means "I am an OCTET STRING." It is up to a programmer writing agent or manager software to make sure that only NVT ASCII characters appear in the octets on the right.

By the way, some programmers were unaware that an NVT ASCII line ends with carriage-return/line-feed. The result is that text sent back from their agents sometimes looks a bit strange when displayed on a manager's screen.

### 7.10.3  SNMP Application Datatypes

Austerity has been relaxed far enough to allow a *few* special datatypes to be defined for SNMP, even though they actually are special cases of INTEGERs and OCTET STRINGs. These new types were defined because of the frequency of their use, their importance, and the preciseness of their definitions. Each has its own encoding identifier. An example of one of these types is:

- *Counter:* An integer that grows to a maximum level and then wraps around.

According to the encoding rules, a plain integer is introduced by '02'H. In contrast, a *Counter* is assigned its own introducer of '41'H.

We will not worry any further about encoding rules until Chapter 35, where they are explained in full.

### 7.10.4  Table Entries and Tables

ASN.1 allows us to define new datatypes by combining variables into more complicated structures. However, the SNMP designers prevent us from getting too fancy. They have laid down the law: we can define a list of simple variables that make up a logical row, organize the rows into a logical table, and that's that!

## 7.11    BASIC SNMP DATATYPES

We'll discuss all of the valid data types more fully in the following sections.

### 7.11.1    OBJECT IDENTIFIERs

As we have seen earlier, an OBJECT IDENTIFIER is a series of digits used to name an object. We need to send OBJECT IDENTIFIERs in *get* and *set* messages in order to name the variables that we want to read and write.

There even are some MIB variables whose *values* are OBJECT IDENTIFIERs. For example, the value of the *sysObjectID* variable is an OBJECT IDENTIFIER assigned to a product by its vendor. In the *snmplookup* dialogue of Chapter 4, Section 4.7, we interacted with a Cisco router product that has been given the product identifier 1.3.6.1.4.1.9.1.1.

### 7.11.2    INTEGERs

Many variables have INTEGER datatype. For example, *ifNumber* is an INTEGER that reports the number of network interfaces on a system. Its formal definition* is as follows:

```
if Number OBJECT-TYPE
    SYNTAX INTEGER
    ACCESS read-only
    STATUS mandatory
    DESCRIPTION
        "The number of network interfaces (regardless of
        their current state) present on this system."
    ::= { interfaces 1 }
```

Recall that the last item, "::= { interfaces 1 }", indicates that the *ifNumber* node is right under the *interfaces* node in the tree, and its label is 1. Therefore, the OBJECT IDENTIFIER for its node is 1.3.6.1.2.1.2.1.

### 7.11.3    Refining the Range of an INTEGER

Some variables with INTEGER datatype have values that lie in a specific range. For example, an IP datagram never can be larger than 64 kilobytes, so the size of the largest reassembled datagram is limited:

---

* The sample definitions used in this section are taken from RFC 1213.

```
ipAdEntReasmMaxSize OBJECT-TYPE
SYNTAX INTEGER (0..65535)
ACCESS read-only
STATUS mandatory
DESCRIPTION
"The size of the largest IP datagram which this
entity can re-assemble from incoming IP fragmented
datagrams received on this interface."
::= { ipAddrEntry 5 }
```

Note the use of two dots "(0..65535)" to show a range of values. A restriction placed on the set of values that a datatype can assume is called a *SYNTAX refinement.*

### 7.11.4   Using INTEGERs for Enumerations

Sometimes an INTEGER datatype is used to identify a selection from a collection of possible answers. This is called an *enumerated* INTEGER type. For example, to see if a particular network interface is up, down, or in a testing mode:

```
ifOperStatus OBJECT-TYPE
SYNTAX INTEGER {
    up(1),          — ready to pass packets
    down(2),
    testing(3)      — in some test mode
                }
ACCESS read-only
STATUS mandatory
DESCRIPTION
    "The current operational state of the interface.
    The testing(3) state indicates that no operational
    packets can be passed."
::= { ifEntry 8 }
```

Some other uses for INTEGERs are considered special enough to be given their own datatypes—namely, counters, gauges, and timeticks.

### 7.11.5   Counters

There are many characteristics that we wish to count, such as the number of bytes (octets) of traffic received at an interface or the number of inbound packets that have contained errors. The Structure of Management Information (SMI) version 1 framework limits a counter to a 4-byte quantity,* so there is a top limit on how large it can get. What should a device do when the top limit is reached? Wrap around and start counting again! Formally,

---

* Version 2 also has 8-octet counters.

- *Counter:* A nonnegative integer that increases to a maximum of $2^{32} - 1$ (4,294,967,295) and then wraps around.

For example,

```
ifInOctets   OBJECT-TYPE
   SYNTAX    Counter
   ACCESS    read-only
   STATUS    mandatory
   DESCRIPTION
      "The total number of octets received on the
      interface, including framing characters."
   ::= { ifEntry 10 }
```

The current value of a counter is not good for anything. What a manager is interested in is how much the counter has *changed* over a period of time. Typically, a network management station will poll a device fairly often, and compute the difference between the current and prior counter value. Thus, to find out how many bytes of traffic were sent in an interval (such as 20 minutes), the management station would poll every 20 minutes and calculate the difference.

### 7.11.6   Gauges

A *Gauge* is an integer quantity that behaves differently from a Counter. A Counter keeps increasing until it wraps around, while the value of a Gauge goes up and down. A Gauge is used to measure variables such as queue lengths or number of current TCP connections. Formally,

- *Gauge:* A nonnegative integer ranging from 1 to $2^{32} - 1$ (4,294,967,295) which may increase or decrease, but which latches at a maximum value.

For example,

```
ifOutQLen   OBJECT-TYPE
   SYNTAX    Gauge
   ACCESS    read-only
   STATUS    mandatory
   DESCRIPTION
   "The length of the output packet queue (in
      packets)."
   ::= { ifEntry 21 }
```

There was a lot of confusion among implementors about what was meant by "latches at a maximum value." The intention was that if a measurement hit the ceiling, it would stay fixed at the maximum value until the quantity being measured decreased below the maximum. Fig-

MAXIMUM VALUE FOR GAUGE

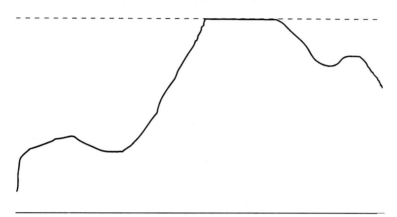

**Figure 7.8** Behavior of a gauge for large measurements.

ure 7.8 shows what ought to happen to a gauge when a measured value is very large.

### 7.11.7   TimeTicks

Integers used to measure time intervals are called *TimeTicks*. Formally,

- *TimeTicks:* A nonnegative integer ranging from 1 to $2^{32} - 1$ (4,294,967,295) measuring the number of hundredths of a second since some specified starting point.

For example, *sysUpTime* measures the number of hundredths of a second since the network part of a system has been initialized. Although 8,640,000 *TimeTicks* are added to *sysUpTime* for each day that passes, it would take more than 497 days to exhaust a 32-bit counter. We would expect network software to be restarted far more often than once per year.

```
sysUpTime OBJECT-TYPE
    SYNTAX TimeTicks
    ACCESS read-only
    STATUS mandatory
    DESCRIPTION
        "The time (in hundredths of a second) since the
    network management portion of the system was last
    re-initialized."
    ::= { system 3 }
```

The *sysUpTime* variable is very important. For example, it is a good idea to include it in every *get* that asks for counter values. That way, you can track the time differences between counter readings, and also can check whether a device has restarted during an interval.

### 7.11.8 OCTET STRINGs

What is an OCTET STRING? It is simply a series of bytes. Other conventional datatypes are defined by putting restrictions on the contents of an OCTET STRING. OCTET STRINGs are used for text strings, physical addresses, and anything else that needs to be represented by a series of bytes. The SYNTAX clause in an OCTET STRING definition often includes a SIZE refinement that limits the maximum number of bytes in the string. For example,

```
x25ClearedCircuitClearFacilities OBJECT-TYPE
   SYNTAX OCTET STRING (SIZE (0..109))
   ACCESS read-only
   . . .
```

### 7.11.9 DisplayString Textual Convention

One of the common uses of an OCTET STRING is to carry text information. A *DisplayString* is just an OCTET STRING that contains text characters and has been renamed according to a textual convention.

In the following definition, *sysDescr* values contain a string of characters from the printable NVT ASCII character set and the string is limited to at most 255 characters:

```
sysDescr OBJECT-TYPE
   SYNTAX DisplayString (SIZE (0..255))
   ACCESS read-only
   STATUS mandatory
   DESCRIPTION
      "A textual description of the entity. This value
      should include the full name and version
      identification of the system's hardware type,
      software operating-system, and networking
      software. It is mandatory that this only contain
      printable ASCII characters."
   ::= { system 1 }
```

### 7.11.10 Physical Address Textual Convention

A *PhysAddress* is an OCTET STRING whose length and format conform to the rules for the particular type of physical address. For example, 6-octet physical addresses are assigned to Ethernet interface boards. A PhysAddress is just an OCTET STRING that has been renamed by a textual convention.

```
ifPhysAddress OBJECT-TYPE
    SYNTAX PhysAddress
    ACCESS read-only
    STATUS mandatory
    DESCRIPTION
        "The interface's address at the protocol layer
        immediately 'below' the network layer in the
        protocol stack. For interfaces which do not have
        such an address (e.g., a serial line), this object
        should contain an octet string of zero length."
    ::= { ifEntry 6 }
```

Some uses for OCTET STRINGs are considered special enough to be given their own datatypes—namely, *IpAddresses* and *Opaque* data.

### 7.11.11   IpAddress Datatype

An *IpAddress* is a datatype with the structure of an OCTET STRING of length 4. A related type, *NetworkAddress,* refers to an network layer address for any type of protocol.

*IpAddresses* show up in many MIB definitions. For example, a routing table entry contains a destination to be reached and the IP address of the next router to be visited on the way to the destination:

```
ipRouteNextHop OBJECT-TYPE
    SYNTAX IpAddress
    ACCESS read-write
    STATUS mandatory
    DESCRIPTION
        "The IP address of the next hop of this route."
    ::= { ipRouteEntry 7 }
```

### 7.11.12   Opaque Data

An OCTET STRING may be used to carry *Opaque* data, which can be anything at all. *Opaque* data was defined as a kind of escape mechanism in case a management station needed to exchange information with an agent using a nonstandard format. You can take *Opaque* to mean "none of the above." For example, *Opaque* data could be used to send encrypted values between two stations.

*Opaque* data is not popular. It has been hard enough to win the war against network chaos and get all of the multivendor equipment to talk to each other. There has been no enthusiasm for adding strange, unspecified *Opaque* data to the list of problems to be debugged.

The burden of communicating in a secure environment has been left to SNMP version 2. SNMP version 2 does *not* use *Opaque* data.

### 7.11.13  NULL Values

NULL values are used as placeholders in the value fields in *get-request* and *get-next-request* messages. They also are used as placeholders in responses when a request has failed and no values can be returned.

## 7.12  HOW TO DEFINE A MIB OBJECT

Like the other parts of the Internet management scheme, the art of defining MIB datatypes has evolved and improved. The definitions described below follow the guidelines set out in RFC 1212, which paved the way for more elegant and concise definitions.

ASN.1 can be used much like an ordinary programming language to define datatypes. But ASN.1 also is a very powerful superlanguage that allows standards writers to set up templates ("macros") for datatype definitions.

### 7.12.1  Working with the OBJECT-TYPE Template

We already are somewhat familiar with the template used to define MIB variables because we have looked at quite a few examples. Let's now take a closer look at the template. We'll start with an easy definition.

```
sysLocation OBJECT-TYPE
    SYNTAX DisplayString (SIZE (0..255))
    ACCESS read-write
    STATUS mandatory
    DESCRIPTION
        "The physical location of this node (e.g.,
        'telephone closet, 3rd floor')."
    ::= { system 6 }
```

Each definition starts with a name. This definition describes an object named *sysLocation*. The last line of the definition assigns an OBJECT IDENTIFIER to *sysLocation*. Specifically,

```
    ::= { system 6 }
```

means that this object is attached under the *system* node, and its node number is 6. This is a one-and-only kind of object, so we must append a 0 when getting or setting a value for this variable. Thus the full OBJECT IDENTIFIER for a *sysLocation* variable that appears in a message will be

```
1 . 3 . 6 . 1 . 2 . 1 . 1 . 6 . 0
```

The SYNTAX clause defines the datatype for a *sysLocation* value. Here, the type is a *DisplayString,* i.e., an OCTET STRING of printable ASCII characters.

The ACCESS clause defines the level of access that a management station will need for this type. The kinds of access for SNMP version 1 (SNMPv1) are as follows:

- Read-only

- Read-write

- Write-only

- Not-accessible

As we would expect, *sysLocation* is a read-write variable.

The STATUS clause tells implementors whether they have to support this object type. The kinds of status for SNMPv1 are as follows:

- Mandatory

- Optional

- Obsolete

- Deprecated

We see that currently implementors must provide the *sysLocation* variable. The meaning of the mandatory, optional, and obsolete categories is clear. Of course, a deprecated variable is one that is on the road to becoming obsolete.

The use of optional variables is on the way out. After lots of MIBs had been produced, it became clear that either you need a variable or else you should leave it out of the MIB completely. In SNMP version 2 (SNMPv2), the status clause simply tells you whether an object is current, deprecated, or obsolete.

The DESCRIPTION clause is optional—a MIB author does not *have* to include a DESCRIPTION clause in each definition, but should! A DESCRIPTION clause can provide significant guidance on how to implement a variable. Fortunately, most MIB authors include DESCRIPTION clauses.

### 7.12.2 The REFERENCE Clause

Occasionally, a REFERENCE clause will appear in a definition. The REFERENCE does just what it sounds like. It provides some kind of cross reference. In the definition that follows, an IEEE document called *IEEE 802.3 Layer Management* is referenced for information about counting deferred frames.

```
dot3StatsDeferredTransmissions   OBJECT-TYPE
   SYNTAX   Counter
   ACCESS   read-only
   STATUS   mandatory
   DESCRIPTION
      "A count of frames for which the first
      transmission attempt on a particular interface
      is delayed because the medium is busy.
      The count represented by an instance of this
      object does not include frames involved in
      collisions."
   REFERENCE
      "IEEE 802.3 Layer Management"
   ::= { dot3StatsEntry 7 }
```

### 7.12.3   The DEFVAL Clause

The DEFVAL clause can be used to assign a default value to a variable that belongs to a logical table row. Default values fill in the blanks when you add a new row to a table but do not specify values for every variable in the row.

The example below defines a variable from an entry in a frame relay circuit table. The variable defines the amount of data that the network has promised to transfer across this circuit per time interval. If there is no firm, committed data rate, the value can be defaulted to a 0 setting.

```
frCircuitCommittedBurst OBJECT-TYPE
   SYNTAX   INTEGER
   ACCESS   read-write
   STATUS   mandatory
   DESCRIPTION
      "This variable indicates the maximum amount of
      data, in bits, that the network agrees to
      transfer under normal conditions, during the
      measurement interval."
   REFERENCE
      "Draft American National Standard T1.617-1991,
      Section 6.5.19"
   DEFVAL   { 0 } — the default indicates no commitment
   ::= { frCircuitEntry 12 }
```

## 7.13   DEFINING TABLES

Much network information has a natural structure as a table. Let's take a look at the features of a MIB table definition:

```
ipAddrTable   OBJECT-TYPE
  SYNTAX   SEQUENCE OF IpAddrEntry
  ACCESS   not-accessible
  STATUS   mandatory
  DESCRIPTION
    "The table of addressing information relevant to
    this entity's IP addresses."
  ::= { ip 20 }
```

This definition names an object called *ipAddrTable*. The OBJECT
IDENTIFIER for *ipAddrTable* is

1 . 3 . 6 . 1 . 2 . 1 . 4 . 20

The ACCESS clause says that the table is *not-accessible*. Does this
mean that we cannot read it? Of course we can read the *values* in the
table. But we can't use an SNMP message to say "get me that table";
we have to say "get me this bunch of variables" and "get me the next
bunch." Of course, a management station can provide a *user interface*
that lets an operator request a table, and then converts this request to
the messages that are needed in order to retrieve the table.

Like all tables, *ipAddrTable* is a SEQUENCE OF entries (rows). The
definition of an entry in this table is

```
ipAddrEntry   OBJECT-TYPE
  SYNTAX   IpAddrEntry
  ACCESS   not-accessible
  STATUS   mandatory
  DESCRIPTION
    "The addressing information for one of this
    entity's IP addresses."
  INDEX   { ipAdEntAddr }
  ::= { ipAddrTable 1 }
```

The object identifier for *ipAddrEntry* is

1 . 3 . 6 . 1 . 2 . 1 . 4 . 20 .1

Beyond that, the definition does not tell us much. But the definition
allows the MIB designer to explain the overall purpose of a row in the
table, and to identify the *index* that will be used to access a row. Since
an entry is made up of several fields, the entry also has an ACCESS
clause of not-accessible.

This *ipAddrEntry* definition points us at the *IpAddrEntry* definition
(note the switch to a capital *I*) to see the list of variables in the row:

```
IpAddrEntry ::=
  SEQUENCE {
  ipAdEntAddr            IpAddress,
  ipAdEntIfIndex         INTEGER,
  ipAdEntNetMask         IpAddress,
  ipAdEntBcastAddr       INTEGER,
  ipAdEntReasmMaxSize    INTEGER (0..65535)
  }
```

The datatype of each variable is indicated. However, full object definitions for each of the five variables still are needed. For example,

```
ipAdEntAddr   OBJECT-TYPE
  SYNTAX   IpAddress
  ACCESS   read-only
  STATUS   mandatory
  DESCRIPTION
    "The IP address to which this entry's addressing
    information pertains."
    ::= { ipAddrEntry 1 }
```

## 7.14   RECOMMENDED READING

MIB-II is defined in RFC 1213. In this chapter, we revisited RFC 1155: *Structure and Identification of Management Information for TCP/IP-based Internets,* for some key ideas. RFC 1212 describes the template for writing concise MIB definitions. RFC 1442 presents improvements that introduced for SNMP version 2.

# 8

# Traps

## 8.1 INTRODUCTION

In Chapter 5, we introduced the SNMP version 1 *trap* message, used to report important events or problems. It is part of the SNMP philosophy to use *traps* sparingly. When a network is in serious trouble, the last thing that you want to do is cause the network to be flooded with *trap* messages!

Recall that six basic *trap* types (numbered 0 to 5) were defined. An additional type (numbered 6) is used by MIB authors and product vendors to add their own *Enterprise Specific* traps. The trap types are:

- *coldStart(0).* The sender is reinitializing, and its configuration may change.
- *warmStart(1).* The sender is reinitializing, but its configuration will not change.
- *linkDown(2).* There is a failure in one of the agent's links.
- *linkUp(3).* One of the agent's links has come up.
- *authenticationFailure(4).* The agent has received a protocol message that was not properly authenticated.
- *egpNeighborLoss(5).* An Exterior Gateway Protocol neighbor is down.
- *enterpriseSpecific(6).* A form to be used as needed to define additional *trap* messages.

## 8.2 TRACE OF A SAMPLE TRAP MESSAGE

The SNMP version 1 *trap* message that follows was described in Chapter 5. It is a generic cold-start trap.

```
SNMP: ----- Simple Network Management Protocol -----
SNMP:
SNMP: Version = 0
SNMP: Community = public
SNMP: Command = Trap
SNMP: Enterprise = {1.3.6.1.4.1.121.1.1}
SNMP: Network address = [128.1.1.10]
SNMP: Generic trap = 0 (Cold start)
SNMP: Specific trap = 0
SNMP: Time ticks = 0
SNMP:
```

This is a particularly simple trap. The *generic-trap* field value of 0 tells us that this *trap* reports a cold start. The *specific-trap* code field is set to 0, as it must be unless the *generic-trap* field is 6.

The content of the *Enterprise* field is an OBJECT IDENTIFIER, 1.3.6.1.4.1.121.1.1 in this case. This tells us that FTP Software is the product vendor, and the agent is part of their PC/TCP product.

The *network-address* field contains the IP address of a PC that sent the trap.

Some traps will have a variable list at the end. For example, when a *linkDown* or *linkUp* trap is sent, the *trap* will carry a variable that identifies the interface that connects to the link.

## 8.3   ENTERPRISE-SPECIFIC TRAPS

Generic traps 0–5 are simple and unchanging. But trap type 6 can be used to define dozens, hundreds, or thousands of Enterprise-specific trap types. Enterprise-specific traps are defined as they are needed.

The "Enterprises" that define new traps are MIB standards groups, vendors, and corporate network management organizations. MIB standards groups add technology-specific traps, vendors add product-specific traps, and corporate groups add traps that meet their special management needs.

Figure 8.1 summarizes what a management station needs to find out when it receives a trap. The manager wants to know who defined the trap, which of their traps this is, and what useful variables the trap contains.

### 8.3.1   Defining a New *trap*

How does a standards committee or Enterprise define a new trap? They need to specify:

- The OBJECT IDENTIFIER that goes into the *Enterprise* field
- The *specific-trap* number

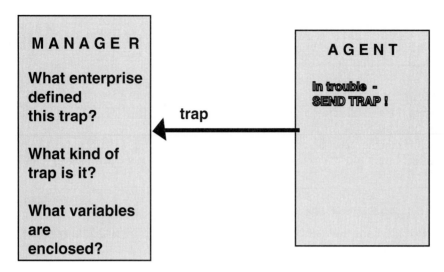

**Figure 8.1**  A manager receiving a trap.

- The *variable-list* to be included
- A description of the event that is reported by the trap

### 8.3.2   The Role of the *Specific-trap* Number

Defining a new version 1 *trap* is different from defining a new MIB object. Each *trap* is uniquely identified by the combination of two things:

- The *Enterprise* OBJECT IDENTIFIER that reveals the type of device that is the source of the trap
- The *specific-trap* number that tells which (of possibly many) traps this one is

### 8.3.3   An Example of a Standard MIB *trap*

The authors of the Frame Relay MIB have defined a *trap* that reports that a Frame Relay circuit has changed state.

- The Enterprise field contains the OBJECT IDENTIFIER for the *frame-relay* subtree (located under *transmission*), 1.3.6.1.2.1.10.32.
- The specific trap number is 1.
- The trap message will include variables that identify the Frame Relay interface, the circuit, and the current state.

- The description of the trap says: "This trap indicates that the indicated Virtual Circuit has changed state. It has either been created or invalidated, or has toggled between the active and inactive states."

When translated into a *trap* message, the *Enterprise* field will contain 1.3.6.1.2.1.10.32, the *generic-trap* field will be 6, the *specific-trap* field will be 1, and the *variable-list* will include (OBJECT IDENTIFIER, value) pairings for the *trap* variable list.

Of course, the description will not be included within a *trap* message, but it can be displayed to an operator at a network management station.

### 8.3.4   An Example of a Vendor *trap*

Novell's Ethernet LANtern is a LAN monitor product. The product's OBJECT IDENTIFIER is:

```
iso.org.dod.internet.private.enterprises.
novell.productType.networkMonitor
```

That is,

```
1 . 3 . 6 . 1 . 4 . 1 . 23 . 1 . 1 . 1
```

The Novell LANtern MIB defines twelve different traps. Trap number 3 reports that a duplicate IP address has been discovered by the monitor.

- The trap's Enterprise field will contain the *ethernetLANtern* product identifier, 1.3.6.1.4.1.23.1.1.1.
- The specific trap number is 3.
- Variables that provide a unique trap "handle" (identifier), the date, time, IP address, and physical MAC addresses are included.
- The description states: "A *duplicateIPAddr*(3) trap is generated whenever the LANtern network monitor first detects more than one host using the same IP address."

### 8.4   A TRAP DEFINITION MACRO

The examples above make it clear that new *traps* have a set of common elements. RFC 1215 defined a useful TRAP-TYPE macro template that helps MIB designers or vendors to define SNMP version 1 *traps*. The macro lets us identify:

- The *Enterprise* field for the *trap* definition. This will either point to a MIB subtree, or identify a product for which the trap has been defined.

- The value to be placed in the *specific-trap* field. This will number the traps as they are defined.
- A list of MIB variables to be carried in the trap message. These variables can assist in diagnostics.
- A description of the *trap.*
- Optionally, a reference clause that relates the *trap* to another *trap,* an alarm, an event, or whatever else may be relevant in some MIB module.

Using the macro, the Frame Relay *trap* described earlier is written as follows:

```
frDLCIStatusChange TRAP-TYPE
     ENTERPRISE frame-relay
     VARIABLES { frCircuitIfIndex, frCircuitDlci, frCircuitState }
     DESCRIPTION
          "This trap indicates that the indicated Virtual
          Circuit has changed state. It has either been
          created or invalidated, or has toggled between
          the active and inactive states."
     ::= 1
```

It is easy to see how the macro defines the Enterprise, variable-list, and description for the trap. The *specific-trap* number is assigned in the last line of the macro, "::= 1."

The macro definition of the *trap* that will be sent by a Novell LANtern monitor product when it discovers that there is more than one system using the same IP address is

```
duplicateIPAddr TRAP-TYPE
     ENTERPRISE ethernetLANtern
     VARIABLES { adminTrapHandle, adminDateAndTime,
                 ipDupeIPAddr, ipDupeGoodMACAddr,
                 ipDupeBadMACAddr }
     DESCRIPTION
               "A duplicateIPAddr(3) trap is generated whenever
               the LANtern network monitor first detects more than
               one host using the same IP address."
     ::= 3
```

Again, the macro displays the Enterprise, variable-list, and description for the trap. The specific-trap number is assigned in the last line of the macro, "::= 3."

In the remainder of this book, we will display trap definitions in the tabular format shown in Table 8.1.

## 8.5   FLEXIBILITY OF TRAP DEFINITIONS

The trap definition template is very flexible. A vendor chooses the variables that need to be included in a product-specific message. If real-world use shows that more data is needed, the vendor just adds some more variables to the list.

Working on a real implementation can change your point of view. A product developer might realize that the MIB definers had forgotten to include an important variable in the list when they wrote a *trap* definition.

The developer does not have to wait for a revision of the official specification before fixing the oversight. RFC 1215 states that an agent implementation legally can append extra variables at the end of the official variable-list. Since each variable value is accompanied by its OBJECT IDENTIFIER, a management application will be able to understand the additional information that has been bundled into the package.

SNMP version 2 improves trap definitions. The format of the trap message is simplified—in fact, version 2 *traps* have the same format as *gets* and *sets*. The basic idea is to move the timestamp and trap-type identifier into the variable-bindings list. Chapter 32 will present the details.

## 8.6   HANDLING INCOMING TRAPS

A good management station should be able to handle *traps* from any enterprise. What does a management application do with an incoming *trap?* Pass it an application that will log it, add a count to any relevant thresholds that have been set for the *trap,* and check a configuration file to see if some event needs to be triggered—such as setting off a buzzer to get the attention of an operator.

**TABLE 8.1   An Enterprise-Specific *trap***

| Enterprise iso.org.dod.internet.private.enterprises. novell.productType.networkMonitor.ethernetLANtern 1.3.6.1.4.1.23.1.1.1 | | | |
| --- | --- | --- | --- |
| Name | Specific-trap | Variables | Description |
| duplicate IPAddr | 3 | adminTrapHandle, adminDateAndTime, ipDupeIPAddr, ipDupeGoodMACAddr, ipDupeBadMACAddr | Generated when the LANtern network monitor first detects more than one host using the same IP address. |

## 8.7    TRAP-DIRECTED POLLING

Some organizations like to put *traps* into the spotlight and build a network management strategy around *trap* messages. The argument goes like this: If a network has a very large number of devices, then polling all agents for all of their data will use up huge amounts of bandwidth and device resources. Why not poll infrequently—say, once or twice a day—unless a *trap* is received? If the *trap* does not contain all of the information that is needed to troubleshoot a problem, then the management station can be configured so that the *trap* triggers a poll.

Is this a good strategy? For some devices and some problems, yes. For others, it is useless. There are many different ways to get and use management information. We shall discuss quite a few in later chapters. Network managers need to use a mixture of tools and tactics.

## 8.8    RECOMMENDED READING

The SNMP *trap* message is defined in RFC 1157, *A Simple Network Management Protocol (SNMP)*. RFC 1215, *A Convention for Defining Traps for Use with the SNMP,* has complete details on the TRAP-TYPE macro. RFC 1448, *Protocol Operations for Version 2 of the Simple Network Management Protocol (SNMPv2)* describes version 2 traps.

# 9

# The MIB-II System Group

## 9.1 INTRODUCTION

Every managed node must be capable of returning basic system information. This information is valuable because it allows nodes to identify and describe themselves. A management station can poll a device for its *system* information and automatically generate a configuration database for the network. This frees an operator from the laborious job of manually entering configuration information into a database (and possibly making a lot of errors along the way).

Some management station products use information returned in the *system* values to generate a map of the network. In the map, each node is represented by an icon that shows what it is—e.g., a bridge, router, PC, workstation, or computer. Figure 9.1 shows a map of a simple LAN that was automatically generated by a NetView/6000 management station.

## 9.2 THE *SYSTEM* SUBTREE

The system subtree contains the variables shown in Figure 9.2. The *system* objects are described in Table 9.1. Note that the name of a contact person (*sysContact*), the administrative name of the system (*sysName*), and a description of the location (*sysLocation*) all are read-write variables, which means that they can be updated from a central management station. The remaining variables are read-only.

### 9.2.1 The *sysObjectID* Object

One of the uses of the *private.enterprises* part of the global tree is to define and name vendor products. Each product is assigned an

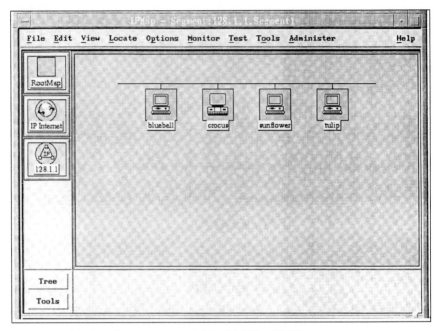

**Figure 9.1** A network map generated by NetView/6000.

OBJECT IDENTIFIER. A node's *sysObjectID* is this OBJECT IDEN-
TIFIER.

For example, the product identifier for a Vitalink bridge is
1.3.6.14.1.29.1.1. The number 29 under the enterprises tree has been
assigned to Vitalink, and the Vitalink subtree contains a product identifier as well as definitions of product specific variables.

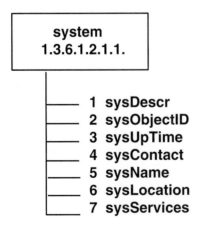

**Figure 9.2** The *system* subtree.

**TABLE 9.1    The System Group of Variables**

| iso.org.dod.internet.mgmt.mib-2.system. 1.3.6.1.2.1.1. | | | |
|---|---|---|---|
| OBJECT IDENTIFIER | Syntax | Access | Definition |
| sysDescr 1.3.6.1.2.1.1.1 | DisplayString (SIZE (0..255)) | read-only | A text description, which should include information about the type of hardware, operating system, and networking software. |
| sysObjectID 1.3.6.1.2.1.1.2 | OBJECT IDENTIFIER | read-only | An authoritative identifier assigned to this product by its vendor. |
| sysUpTime 1.3.6.1.2.1.1.3 | TimeTicks | read-only | The time (in hundredths of a second) since the network management portion of the system was last reinitialized. |
| sysContact 1.3.6.1.2.1.1.4 | DisplayString (SIZE (0..255)) | read-write | A person responsible for the node, along with information such as a phone number. |
| sysName 1.3.6.1.2.1.1.5 | DisplayString (SIZE (0..255)) | read-write | An administratively assigned name (usually the TCP/IP domain name). |
| sysLocation 1.3.6.1.2.1.1.6 | DisplayString (SIZE (0..255)) | read-write | The physical location of the device. |
| sysServices 1.3.6.1.2.1.1.7 | INTEGER (0..127) | read-only | A coded number that indicates the layer(s) for which this node performs services. |

### 9.2.2    The *sysUpTime* Object

*SysUpTime* measures the time since a system's network management was last initialized. This is a convenient variable to include in most polls. Make sure that your management system also adds its own local timestamp to your polling data before storing it.

When you read statistical counters, if you also read *sysUpTime,* you will be able to see how much the counters have changed during a time interval. Checking consecutive reads of *sysUpTime* against the management station's own timestamps will uncover a reboot that may have set counters (and elapsed time) back to 0.

### 9.2.3  The *sysServices* Object

The *sysServices* object provides a succinct way to indicate the kind of node this is. This integral value is calculated by summing $2^{(layer-1)}$ for each ISO layer for which the node provides service. Another way of saying this is as follows:

| Service | Layer | Add |
|---|---|---|
| Application | 7 | 64 |
| Transport | 4 | 8 |
| Network | 3 | 4 |
| Data link | 2 | 2 |
| Physical | 1 | 1 |

If a node is a repeater, its score would be 1 (physical layer service). If the node is a bridge router, its score would be $2 + 4 = 6$ (data link + network layers). A host running TCP or UDP and applications would rate an $8 + 64 = 72$ (transport + application).

Yet another way of viewing this is by treating the bits in an octet as flags. Each bit corresponds to an OSI layer, and the flag bit for layer 1 is at the far right. A flag value is set equal to 1 if the node provides service at the corresponding layer. Then we translate the octet's binary value into a decimal number.

There is no layer 8 in the OSI model, and TCP/IP does not use layers 5, 6, or 7, so some flag bits are always 0. Let's look at some examples. A repeater would have flags set to

```
0 0 0 0 0 0 0 1 = Decimal 1
```

A router would have flags set to

```
0 0 0 0 0 1 0 0 = Decimal 4
```

A bridge/router would have flags set to

```
0 0 0 0 0 1 1 0 = Decimal 6
```

For a host supporting layer 4 TCP/UDP and layer 7 applications,

```
0 1 0 0 1 0 0 0 = Decimal 72
```

## 9.3  A *SYSTEM* GROUP EXAMPLE

The example that follows displays output obtained using PSI's useful *snmplookup* program. First we set an OBJECT IDENTIFIER *prefix* to take us down the tree to the *mib* level. Then we provide the IP address of a router to be queried. The *mquery* command launches *get-next-requests* until the entire system group has been read.

```
snmp>
snmp> prefix 1.3.6.1.2.1
snmp> agent 128.193.70.01
snmp> mquery 1
d_internet_mgmt_mib_system_sysDescr_0 GS Software (GS3-K),
Version 9.1 (4.3), MAINTENANCEINTERIMTEST SOFTWARE
Copyright (c) 1986-1993 by cisco Systems, Inc.
CompiledMon 19-Apr-9311:59 by hlong


d_internet_mgmt_mib_system_sysObjectID_01 3 6 1 4 1 9 1 1
d_internet_mgmt_mib_system_sysUpTime_0 0x9454137 155533623
d_internet_mgmt_mib_system_sysContact_0 H. Long, 218-5532
d_internet_mgmt_mib_system_sysName_0 Main-Gateway.ABC.COM
d_internet_mgmt_mib_system_sysLocation_0Building 3, Room 402
d_internet_mgmt_mib_system_sysServices_00x6 6
snmp>
```

The *sysDescr* contains detailed product information. The *sysObjectID* is the definitive product identifier. Note that Cisco Systems owns node number 9 under enterprises.

The display of *sysUpTime* could be friendlier. The number of hundredths of a second since last initialization is shown in hex and decimal. It works out to about 18 days.

The *sysContact, sysName,* and *sysLocation* complete the configuration information for this system. Any management station authorized to access this node will be assured of obtaining identical, accurate information.

The *sysServices* variable indicates that the device is a combined bridge/router.

## 9.4  NETWORK MANAGEMENT CONSIDERATIONS

Periodic polls of system information are used to update a network inventory database and construct a map of active devices. The poll frequency depends on what you need to accomplish. For example, you might store a baseline map showing all bridges, routers, and host servers, and poll once each hour to check that all are present. The absence of a device could trigger a warning, and also could be used to trigger a procedure that polls the device every few minutes until it comes back up.

Alternatively, you might broadcast more frequent polls designed to discover active workstations on the network. This kind of job is carried out more effectively by network monitors, which can sense station activity without polling. Also, monitors can do their job even when the network management software at the workstations has not been initialized.

The values of the system contact and device location should be kept up-to-date by the network manager. These values enable problem reports to be routed to the personnel who can handle them, and immediately pinpoint the location of the device that is in trouble.

# 10

# Managing Interfaces

## 10.1  INTRODUCTION

An *interface* is software and hardware that is sandwiched between a Network Layer protocol and a physical network medium. MIB-II contains a group of variables that describe generic configuration, status, and performance information for any type of interface—whether to a serial line, a packet net, or a LAN.

Unlike most of the other objects in MIB-II, interface objects are protocol-neutral—an interface may be used to transmit and receive data for any protocol: for example, IP, NetWare IPX, or AppleTalk. In fact, an interface may transmit and receive traffic for several protocols at the same time.

MIB-II defines the most-wanted interface variables. However, these tell far less than the whole story. Additional interface variables were defined in the document, *Extensions to the Generic-Interface MIB,* published as RFC 1229. In turn, this document was updated in RFC 1573, *Evolution of the Interfaces Group of MIB-II.*

There are many other variables that only make sense for a particular type of interface. For example, you count the number of collisions for an Ethernet, and you count the number of times the token was lost on a Token-Ring. A set of MIB groups, each defining variables for a specific type of interface, is located under the *transmission* subtree.

This chapter refers to a number of technologies that will be described in detail in later chapters: e.g., Ethernet, Token-Ring, X.25, and frame relay. The MIB-II *interfaces* group deals with features that are common across technologies, such as the operational status of an interface or a count of the number of received octets.

### 10.1.1   Frame versus Packet Terminology

What's in a name? Plenty of confusion, if you are in the field of data communications. At the physical layer, signals representing 0s and 1s are impressed on a medium. Good. When these signals are organized into recognizable MAC layer or link layer data units, what do you call them? In his classic book, *Computer Networks,* Andrew Tannenbaum tried to establish the use of the term *frames.* We have used this term fairly consistently in this book.

However, many standards documents, user manuals, and screen displays employ the term *packet* instead. We will use *packet* in cases where the defining standards document does so, since one of the goals of this book is to enable the reader to consult these documents quickly and easily. The data communications vocabulary being what it is, the reader should not be surprised when *packet* reappears at layer 3, layer 4, and sometimes even at the application layer.

## 10.2   LAN INTERFACE ADDRESSES

Every LAN interface is assigned a physical address. The interface absorbs traffic sent to that address. Six-octet hexadecimal numbers are used for Ethernet or Token-Ring physical addresses. These addresses are administered by the IEEE, which assigns blocks of numbers to Network Interface Card (NIC) vendors.

There are many LAN protocols based on broadcasting. In addition to receiving traffic addressed to its unique physical address, an interface usually is configured to accept frames that have been sent to the *broadcast* address. An all-ones address (hex FF-FF-FF-FF-FF-FF) is the most common form for the broadcast address.

An interface also may be configured to receive frames sent to a *multicast* address. As the name implies, *multicasting* means sending to multiple systems on a LAN. A multicast address is associated with membership in some group or with a role performed by a system. For example:

- Frames sent to bridges participating in the "spanning tree" bridge protocol are addressed to 01-80-C2-00-00-00.

- Frames multicast to a group of Hewlett-Packard systems for the purpose of locating one of them are sent to 09-00-09-00-00-01.

In order to distinguish an interface's own physical address from broadcast or multicast addresses, the term *unicast address* was invented. It is no surprise that a frame sent to a unicast address is called a *unicast frame.* Just to complicate life a little bit more, occasionally there are situations where it is convenient to assign *several* unicast addresses to the *same* interface!

## 10.3   WAN INTERFACE ADDRESSES

What kinds of wide area networking options do we have? There are

- Point-to-point telephone, ISDN, or satellite circuits
- Packet Data Network circuits via X.25, frame relay, SMDS, or ATM

### 10.3.1   Circuits: A Short Digression

When you make a phone call from New York City to Los Angeles, you will spend a few seconds listening to some clicks and beeps while the telephone system sets up a circuit path for your call. The same circuit path will be used throughout your call—but the next time you call the same number, a completely different circuit path might be used, passing through telephone switches that are hundreds of miles away from the original path's switches.

Traditionally, packet switched data services have been engineered differently from telephone services. When you make a data call on a packet switched data network, the circuit path is allowed to change during the call. For this reason, data network people use the term *virtual circuit* instead of plain *circuit*.

### 10.3.2   Permanent Circuits

An organization may contract for a *permanent* telephone or ISDN circuit. We usually call this a *leased* line. When we contract for a permanent Packet Data Network circuit, we call it a *permanent virtual circuit* or PVC. Physical addresses are not needed for permanent circuits.*

### 10.3.3   Switched Circuits

*Switched* circuits are set up dynamically, by requesting a call to an identified party. Dial-up telephone or ISDN destinations are identified by their telephone numbers.

For a Packet Data Network, the counterpart to placing a telephone call is to set up a *switched virtual circuit*. A numbering scheme similar to the international telephone numbering plan is used to identify X.25 destinations and SMDS destinations. At the time of writing, a global numbering plan also was being introduced for use with frame relay.

---

* The one exception is a two-wire telephone connection for which the echoes of frames that the system has sent can look like incoming frames. In this case, each end is assigned a different address.

## 10.4   THE MIB-II INTERFACES SUBTREE

The MIB-II *interfaces* subtree contains a table with an entry for each
system interface. There is exactly one stand-alone variable, *ifNumber*.
It declares the total number of network interfaces.* The version of the
*interfaces* tree defined in MIB-II is shown in Figure 10.1.

## 10.5   COUNTING THE TRAFFIC FLOW
## WITH CASE DIAGRAMS

The *Case diagram* tool was invented by Jeffrey Case as a way of making sure that MIB counters were tracking the fate of all datagrams.
Case diagrams provide a very intuitive way to look at traffic flows and
to see the relationship between the incoming and outgoing traffic
counts. Specifically, the Case diagram tool:

- Helps MIB authors to visualize traffic flows so that they account for
  all messages.
- Helps the users of management tools to understand traffic flows, and
  the relationships between MIB variables.

The *interfaces* table records fairly careful counts of incoming traffic,
outgoing traffic, and the errors that cause frames to be discarded. The
flow of traffic, as shown in the Case diagram in Figure 10.2, is quite
simple. Frames are counted as they arrive from the network. Some are
discarded during error screening, and the rest are delivered to an
appropriate protocol.

Incoming frames are delivered to a "higher" layer or sublayer. However, "higher" is interpreted fairly loosely; for example, frames may be
passed to bridge forwarding software that determines how they should
be handled. Frames are delivered to whatever software module needs
to process them next.

## 10.6   ABOUT INTERFACE TYPES

The *ifType* variable identifies the type of technology for an interface.
Table 10.1 lists the official type number assignments at the time of
writing, and briefly describes each technology. The Internet Assigned
Numbers Authority now has the job of maintaining an up-to-date list
of defined types in its Assigned Numbers document. New types that
are being assigned numbers include *localTalk, smds-dxi, frameRelay-*

---

* Some devices need to add and remove interfaces dynamically. If this is the case, the
*ifNumber* will indicate the current number of interfaces.

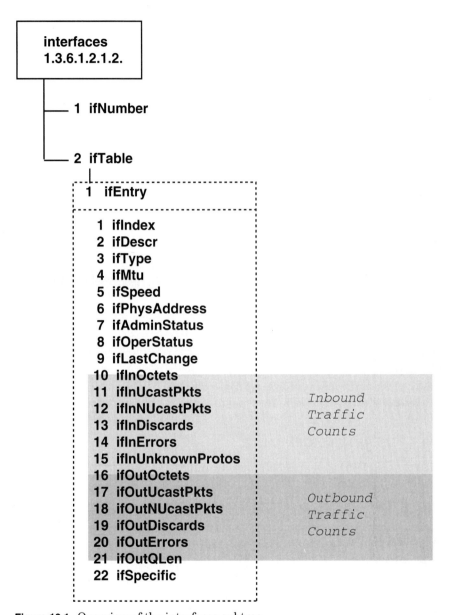

**Figure 10.1** Overview of the interfaces subtree.

*Service, v35, hssi, hippi,* and *modem.* Future implementations will refer to *IANAifType,* rather than *ifType.*

The first column in Table 10.1 contains the labels that have been assigned to each technology. Note the use of ISO standard numbers in the labels for the LAN technologies. The 802.3, 802.4, and 802.5 LAN

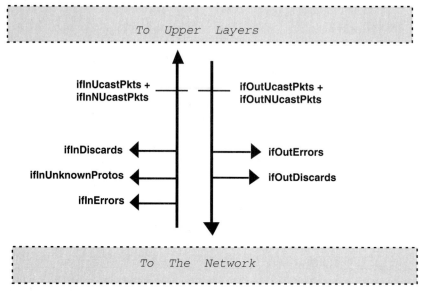

**Figure 10.2**  A Case diagram showing packet flows.

standards that were published by the IEEE have been adopted as ISO standards. ISO assigns its own numbers to standards; in this case, they picked numbers 88023, 88024, and 88025, which are pretty consistent with their IEEE counterparts.

## 10.7   THE *INTERFACES* TABLE

Table 10.2, the *interfaces* table, is an important part of MIB-II. Many other MIB tables refer back to it.

It also is the first MIB table that we have examined. Every MIB table has one or more indices. To make the table index or indices stand out, we will tag each one with the boldface symbol:

▶**Index**

### 10.7.1   Contents of the *interfaces* Table

The *interfaces* table contains several configuration variables: a description of the interface, its type (as selected from Table 10.1), the biggest Protocol Data Unit that can be carried, the interface speed, and the physical address.

A physical address (*physAddress*) is represented in Table 10.2 as an OCTET STRING. The recommended way to *display* a physical address is to separate the hex representations of each octet by "-" characters.

**TABLE 10.1   Types of Network Interfaces**

| Technology | Type | Description |
|---|---|---|
| other | 1 | None of those below. |
| regular1822 | 2 | Classic ARPANET asynchronous protocol (now obsolete) between a host and Interface Message Processor (IMP). |
| hdh1822 | 3 | Later version of the host-IMP protocol, using a synchronous link. |
| ddn-x25 | 4 | Version of X.25 required for connection to the Department of Defense packet network. For DDN-X.25, there is a formula that maps IP addresses to the interface's X.25 address. |
| rfc877-x25 | 5 | More flexible version of X.25, using a public packet switching network to carry IP datagrams, defined in 1983 and updated in 1992. |
| ethernet-csmacd | 6 | CSMA/CD Ethernet Media Access Control (MAC) protocol, as defined by Digital, Intel, and Xerox ("DIX"). |
| iso88023-csmacd | 7 | IEEE 802.3 version of the Ethernet protocol. Like all 802-standard interfaces, 802.3 requires that the information field of a MAC information frame must start with an 802.2 header. |
| iso88024-tokenBus | 8 | IEEE 802.4 Token Bus MAC protocol, intended for use on broadband cables installed in the factory environment. |
| iso88025-tokenRing | 9 | IEEE 802.5 Token-Ring protocol, as submitted by IBM for standardization. |
| iso88026-man | 10 | IEEE 802.6 protocol for attachment to Metropolitan Area Networks (adopted by Bellcore as SMDS interface). |
| starLan | 11 | A version of Ethernet marketed by AT&T, running on a twisted pair star. |
| proteon-10Mbit | 12 | Proprietary Proteon Token-Ring LAN. |
| proteon-80Mbit | 13 | Proprietary Proteon Token-Ring LAN. |
| hyperchannel | 14 | Network Systems Corporation interface to one of its high-speed proprietary coaxial cable or fiber-optic LANs. |
| fddi | 15 | Fiber Distributed Data Interface (FDDI), an interface to a fiber-optic LAN with a token passing protocol. |
| lapb | 16 | Link Access Procedures Balanced (LAPB), link protocol used with X.25. |
| sdlc | 17 | Synchronous Data Link Control (SDLC), link protocol used by IBM on point-to-point and multipoint lines. |
| ds1 | 18 | Interface to a T1 (1.544 megabits/sec) digital transmission line. |
| e1 | 19 | The European counterpart of T1, running at 2.048 megabits per second. |

TABLE 10.1    Types of Network Interfaces (*Continued*)

| Technology | Type | Description |
|---|---|---|
| basicISDN | 20 | Basic rate ISDN, supporting two 64 kilobits/sec B channels and a 16 kilobits/sec D signaling channel. |
| primaryISDN | 21 | Primary rate ISDN. In the U.S., supporting 23 B channels and a 64 kilobit/sec D channel (T1 bandwidth). In Europe, 30 B + D (E1 bandwidth). |
| propPointToPointSerial | 22 | Proprietary point-to-point serial interface that may offer special features such as data compression and multiple protocols. |
| ppp | 23 | Point-to-Point Protocol standard, supporting multiprotocol transmission. |
| softwareLoopback | 24 | Interface used for communication between processes in the same system. |
| eon | 25 | "Experimental OSI-based Network." OSI Connectionless Network Protocol can treat an IP internet as a logical interface type. |
| ethernet-3Mbit | 26 | 3 megabit/sec version of Ethernet. |
| nsip | 27 | XNS can treat an IP internet as a logical interface type. |
| slip | 28 | Serial Line Interface Protocol. A very simple protocol for framing IP datagrams sent across a serial line. |
| ultra | 29 | A proprietary high-speed fiber-optic interface technology from Ultra Network Technologies. |
| ds3 | 30 | U.S. Digital Signaling level 3 interface for T3 transmission at 44.736 megabits per second. |
| sip | 31 | Switched Multimegabit Data Services (SMDS) Bellcore interface, built on top of physical DS1 or DS3 interfaces using 802.6 Media Access Control. |
| frame-relay | 32 | A link layer interface to a packet switching network, typically supporting capacities ranging up to T1 (1.544 megabits/sec) or E1 (2.048 megabits/sec). |
| rs232 | 33 | RS-232. |
| para | 34 | Parallel port. |
| arcnet | 35 | ARCnet. |
| arcnetPlus | 36 | ARCnet Plus. |
| atm | 37 | Asynchronous Transfer Mode cells. |
| miox25 | 38 | Multiprotocol interconnect on X.25 and ISDN. |
| sonet | 39 | SONET or Synchronous Digital Hierarchy (SDH). |
| x25ple | 40 | X.25 Packet Layer Entity. |
| iso88022llc | 41 | ISO number for IEEE 802.2 Logical Link Control. |
| localTalk | 42 | Apple's older LocalTalk twisted pair interface. |
| smdsDxi | 43 | SMDS Data Exchange Interface. |

TABLE 10.1  Types of Network Interfaces (*Continued*)

| Technology | Type | Description |
|---|---|---|
| frameRelayService | 44 | Frame Relay Service-side interface. |
| v35 | 45 | V.35. |
| hssi | 46 | High Speed Serial Interface. |
| hippi | 47 | High Performance Parallel Interface. |
| modem | 48 | Generic Modem. |
| aal5 | 49 | ATM Adaptation Layer 5 (simple ATM format). |
| sonetPath | 50 | Sonet Path. |
| sonetVT | 51 | Sonet Virtual Tributary. |
| smdsIcip | 52 | SMDS InterCarrier Interface. |
| propVirtual | 53 | Proprietary virtual/internal. |
| propMultiplexor | 54 | Proprietary multiplexing. |

TABLE 10.2  The Interfaces Table

| iso.org.dod.internet.mgmt.mib-2.interfaces.ifTable.ifEntry 1.3.6.1.2.1.2.2.1 | | | |
|---|---|---|---|
| OBJECT IDENTIFIER | Syntax | Access | Description |
| ifIndex 1.3.6.1.2.1.2.2.1.1 ▶ **index** | INTEGER | read-only | Unique index for this entry. |
| ifDescr 1.3.6.1.2.1.2.2.1.2 | Display String | read-only | Text describing the interface: e.g., product name, manufacturer, hardware version. |
| ifType 1.3.6.1.2.1.2.2.1.3 | INTEGER | read-only | The type of interface. See Table 10.1. |
| ifMtu 1.3.6.1.2.1.2.2.1.4 | INTEGER | read-only | The size (in octets) of the largest protocol data unit that can be sent or received on the interface. |
| ifSpeed 1.3.6.1.2.1.2.2.1.5 | Gauge | read-only | Estimate of current bandwidth in bits per second. If value is constant or cannot be measured, nominal bandwidth is used. |
| ifPhysAddress 1.3.6.1.2.1.2.2.1.6 | PhysAddress | read-only | If applicable, a physical address such as an Ethernet MAC address, a phone number, or a Packet Data Net address. Where not relevant, a 0-length octet string. |

**TABLE 10.2   The Interfaces Table (*Continued*)**

iso.org.dod.internet.mgmt.mib-2.interfaces.ifTable.ifEntry
1.3.6.1.2.1.2.2.1

| OBJECT IDENTIFIER | Syntax | Access | Description |
|---|---|---|---|
| ifAdminStatus 1.3.6.1.2.1.2.2.1.7 | INTEGER up(1), down(2), testing(3) | read-write | *Desired* interface state. |
| ifOperStatus 1.3.6.1.2.1.2.2.1.8 | INTEGER up(1), down(2), testing(3) | read-only | The current actual operating state. |
| ifLastChange 1.3.6.1.2.1.2.2.1.9 | TimeTicks (hundredths of seconds) | read-only | The value of *sysUpTime* when the interface entered its current operational state (0 if the current state was entered before last initialization of management entity). |
| ifInOctets 1.3.6.1.2.1.2.2.1.10 | Counter | read-only | The total number of octets received on the interface, including framing octets. |
| ifInUcastPkts 1.3.6.1.2.1.2.2.1.11 | Counter | read-only | The number of unicast packets delivered to an appropriate protocol. |
| ifInNUcastPkts 1.3.6.1.2.1.2.2.1.12 | Counter | read-only | The number of non-unicast (i.e., broadcast or multicast) packets delivered to an appropriate protocol. |
| ifInDiscards 1.3.6.1.2.1.2.2.1.13 | Counter | read-only | The number of inbound packets discarded although no errors were found (e.g., because of lack of buffer memory). |
| ifInErrors 1.3.6.1.2.1.2.2.1.14 | Counter | read-only | The number of inbound packets discarded because they contained errors. |
| ifInUnknown Protos 1.3.6.1.2.1.2.2.1.15 | Counter | read-only | The number of inbound packets discarded because they were directed to an unknown or unsupported protocol. |

**TABLE 10.2    The Interfaces Table (*Continued*)**

| OBJECT IDENTIFIER | Syntax | Access | Description |
|---|---|---|---|
| iso.org.dod.internet.mgmt.mib-2.interfaces.ifTable.ifEntry 1.3.6.1.2.1.2.2.1 | | | |
| ifOutOctets 1.3.6.1.2.1.2.2.1.16 | Counter | read-only | The total number of transmitted octets, including framing octets. |
| ifOutUcastPkts 1.3.6.1.2.1.2.2.1.17 | Counter | read-only | The total number of unicast packets whose transmission to a single address was requested. |
| ifOut NUcastPkts 1.3.6.1.2.1.2.2.1.18 | Counter | read-only | The total number of packets whose transmission to a multicast or broadcast address was requested. |
| ifOutDiscards 1.3.6.1.2.1.2.2.1.19 | Counter | read-only | The number of outbound packets that were free of error, but were discarded (e.g., to free up memory). |
| ifOutErrors 1.3.6.1.2.1.2.2.1.20 | Counter | read-only | Number of outbound packets discarded because of errors. |
| ifOutQLen 1.3.6.1.2.1.2.2.1.21 | Gauge | read-only | Number of packets in the outbound queue. |
| ifSpecific 1.3.6.1.2.1.2.2.1.22 | OBJECT IDENTIFIER | read-only | The identifier for a MIB that contains additional definitions that relate to this interface type. |

For example, 00-00-C0-BF-45-5B is the physical address of the Ethernet interface in the PC being used to write this book.

The table also contains statistical variables that record incoming traffic, outgoing traffic, and error counts.

At this point, we will change gears and start to say "packet" instead of "frame" in order to be consistent with the wording in the MIB-II standard.

### 10.7.2    Controlling an Interface

Note that the current operational status (up, down, or testing) and the time of the last status change can be read from the *interfaces* table.

There also is an administrative status *control* variable in the table. If you want to change the operational status of an interface—for example, from down to up—you *set* the value of the administrative status to the state that you want.

Will the status change? That depends on whether the vendor has built in the software to make it happen. Unfortunately, lots of vendors don't.

### 10.7.3  The *ifSpecific* Variable

What is the purpose of the last variable, *ifSpecific*? Although an entry in the *interfaces* table contains many vital statistics, it might not tell the whole story of an interface's activities. The *ifSpecific* variable is supposed to point to a MIB subtree that defines additional variables for this type of interface. For example, if this entry describes an Ethernet interface, then the value of *ifSpecific* could identify a MIB subtree defining objects specific to Ethernet. (If there is no additional information for *ifSpecific* to point to, then its value should be {0 0}.)

The current wisdom is that this variable has caused a lot of confusion and is not really useful—after all, if the *ifType* is Ethernet, you probably could guess that the Ethernet subtree is the place to look for more detailed information. The *ifSpecific* object has been deprecated in the pending update of the *interfaces* MIB.

### 10.7.4  The *ifIndex*

Many MIB tables refer back to the *interfaces* table. For example, there is an Ethernet table that counts error and collision statistics. Each of this table's entries starts with the *ifIndex* value telling us which interface we are talking about. This enables us to look up the other generic information that we need to know about that interface.

### 10.8  POLLING FOR INTERFACE STATISTICS

The PSI *snmpLookup* dialogue that follows shows some sample responses from a router that was polled for its interface statistics. First, we get the system description, *sysDescr,* and the *sysUpTime.*

```
snmp> prefix 1.3.6.1.2.1
snmp> agent 128.1.20.1
snmp> query 1.1.0
d_internet_mgmt_mib_system_sysDescr_0 GS Software (GS3-K),
Version 9.1(4.3), MAINTENANCE INTERIM TEST SOFTWARE
Copyright (c) 1986-1993 by cisco Systems, Inc.
Compiled Mon 19-Apr-93 11:59 by jimkeith
snmp>
```

```
snmp> query 1.3.0
d_internet_mgmt_mib_system_sysUpTime_0 0xda67858 229013592
```

This system is a Cisco router and has been up for 229013592 hundredths of a second—roughly 26 days and 12 hours. Let's look at the configuration information obtained from an "mquery 2" command. Part of the long text prefix in the output has been omitted to improve readability. Some comments have been inserted to explain the output:

```
snmp> mquery 2
ifNumber_0    0x5   5
ifTable_ifEntry_ifIndex_1 0x1    1
ifTable_ifEntry_ifIndex_2 0x2    2
ifTable_ifEntry_ifIndex_3 0x3    3
ifTable_ifEntry_ifIndex_4 0x4    4
ifTable_ifEntry_ifIndex_5 0x5    5
```

There are five interfaces, naturally indexed 1–5. Note that the answers to the query are shown in both hexadecimal and decimal form. Much of the output of *snmplookup* appears this way.

```
ifTable_ifEntry_ifDescr_1 Ethernet0
ifTable_ifEntry_ifDescr_2 Serial0
ifTable_ifEntry_ifDescr_3 Serial1
ifTable_ifEntry_ifDescr_4 Ethernet1
ifTable_ifEntry_ifDescr_5 Serial2
```

The *ifDescr* is just an informal text comment.

```
ifTable_ifEntry_ifType_1  0x6     6
ifTable_ifEntry_ifType_2  0x16    22
ifTable_ifEntry_ifType_3  0x16    22
ifTable_ifEntry_ifType_4  0x6     6
ifTable_ifEntry_ifType_5  0x16    22
```

An integer is used for *formal* identification of the type. Checking back to Table 10.1, we see that interfaces 1 and 4 have DIX Ethernet type, while 2, 3, and 5 are proprietary serial interfaces.

```
ifTable_ifEntry_ifMtu_1   0x5dc 1500
ifTable_ifEntry_ifMtu_2   0x5dc 1500
ifTable_ifEntry_ifMtu_3   0x5dc 1500
ifTable_ifEntry_ifMtu_4   0x5dc 1500
ifTable_ifEntry_ifMtu_5   0x5dc 1500
```

The Maximum Transmission Unit for each of these interfaces is 1500 bytes.

```
ifTable_ifEntry_ifSpeed_1 0x989680        10000000
ifTable_ifEntry_ifSpeed_2 0x177000        1536000
ifTable_ifEntry_ifSpeed_3 0x178f40        1544000
ifTable_ifEntry_ifSpeed_4 0x989680        10000000
ifTable_ifEntry_ifSpeed_5 0x178f40        1544000
```

The speed for the Ethernet interfaces is 10 megabits per second. There are three T1 serial interfaces. The first reports a payload of only 1.536 megabits per second because some of the bandwidth is used for telephone company framing bits. The other two T1s appear to be configured for their full bandwidth, so no telco framing is in use.

```
ifTable_ifEntry_ifPhysAddress_1   0x00000c002a1b
ifTable_ifEntry_ifPhysAddress_2
ifTable_ifEntry_ifPhysAddress_3
ifTable_ifEntry_ifPhysAddress_4   0x00000c000c5d
ifTable_ifEntry_ifPhysAddress_5
```

Six-octet physical addresses are assigned to the two Ethernet interfaces.

```
ifTable_ifEntry_ifAdminStatus_1   0x1    1
ifTable_ifEntry_ifAdminStatus_2   0x1    1
ifTable_ifEntry_ifAdminStatus_3   0x2    2
ifTable_ifEntry_ifAdminStatus_4   0x2    2
ifTable_ifEntry_ifAdminStatus_5   0x2    2
ifTable_ifEntry_ifOperStatus_1    0x1    1
ifTable_ifEntry_ifOperStatus_2    0x1    1
ifTable_ifEntry_ifOperStatus_3    0x2    2
ifTable_ifEntry_ifOperStatus_4    0x2    2
ifTable_ifEntry_ifOperStatus_5    0x2    2
```

The desired administrative status matches the actual operational status. Currently, only interfaces 1 and 2 are up (1). The rest are down (2).

```
ifTable_ifEntry_ifLastChange_1   0xd768192    225870226
ifTable_ifEntry_ifLastChange_2   0xd767dab    225869227
ifTable_ifEntry_ifLastChange_3   0xd766c6c    225864812
ifTable_ifEntry_ifLastChange_4   0xd766c42    225864770
ifTable_ifEntry_ifLastChange_5   0xd766c6c    225864812
```

The status of all of the interfaces was last changed about 8 hours earlier.

### 10.8.1   Changes Over Time

Table 10.3 shows the remaining interface variable values, and compares them with values obtained 2 hours later. The hex version of the output is omitted.

**TABLE 10.3    Reviewing Two Sets of Interface Statistics**

| ifTable_ifEntry Object | Initial reading | 2 hours later | Difference |
|---|---|---|---|
| ifInOctets_1 | 3332972548 | 3450914300 | 117,941,752 |
| ifInOctets_2 | 2081061173 | 2565366471 | 484,305,278 |
| ifInOctets_3 | 0 | 0 | 0 |
| ifInOctets_4 | 0 | 0 | 0 |
| ifInOctets_5 | 0 | 0 | 0 |
| ifInUcastPkts_1 | 79593616 | 80241914 | 648,298 |
| ifInUcastPkts_2 | 136170982 | 138919610 | 2,748,628 |
| ifInUcastPkts_3 | 0 | 0 | 0 |
| ifInUcastPkts_4 | 0 | 0 | 0 |
| ifInUcastPkts_5 | 0 | 0 | 0 |
| ifInNUcastPkts_1 | 556899 | 571951 | 15,052 |
| ifInNUcastPkts_2 | 523610 | 532867 | 9,257 |
| ifInNUcastPkts_3 | 0 | 0 | 0 |
| ifInNUcastPkts_4 | 0 | 0 | 0 |
| ifInNUcastPkts_5 | 0 | 0 | 0 |
| ifInDiscards_1 | 0 | 0 | 0 |
| ifInDiscards_2 | 0 | 0 | 0 |
| ifInDiscards_3 | 0 | 0 | 0 |
| ifInDiscards_4 | 0 | 0 | 0 |
| ifInDiscards_5 | 0 | 0 | 0 |
| ifInErrors_1 | 143017 | 143018 | 1 |
| ifInErrors_2 | 833 | 833 | 0 |
| ifInErrors_3 | 0 | 0 | 0 |
| ifInErrors_4 | 0 | 0 | 0 |
| ifInErrors_5 | 0 | 0 | 0 |
| ifInUnknownProtos_1 | 0 | 0 | 0 |
| ifInUnknownProtos_2 | 0 | 0 | 0 |
| ifInUnknownProtos_3 | 0 | 0 | 0 |
| ifInUnknownProtos_4 | 0 | 0 | 0 |
| ifInUnknownProtos_5 | 0 | 0 | 0 |
| ifOutOctets_1 | 1688233427 | 2167580045 | 479,346,618 |
| ifOutOctets_2 | 2617713061 | 2731485448 | 113,772,387 |
| ifOutOctets_3 | 0 | 0 | 0 |
| ifOutOctets_4 | 1899 | 1899 | 0 |
| ifOutOctets_5 | 0 | 0 | 0 |
| ifOutUcastPkts_1 | 136415494 | 139171510 | 2,756,016 |
| ifOutUcastPkts_2 | 78258595 | 78904717 | 646,122 |
| ifOutUcastPkts_3 | 0 | 0 | 0 |
| ifOutUcastPkts_4 | 2 | 2 | 0 |
| ifOutUcastPkts_5 | 0 | 0 | 0 |
| ifOutNUcastPkts_1 | 412412 | 418379 | 5,967 |
| ifOutNUcastPkts_2 | 0 | 0 | 0 |
| ifOutNUcastPkts_3 | 0 | 0 | 0 |
| ifOutNUcastPkts_4 | 13 | 13 | 0 |
| ifOutNUcastPkts_5 | 0 | 0 | 0 |
| ifOutDiscards_1 | 47048 | 47070 | 22 |
| ifOutDiscards_2 | 1314737 | 1314780 | 43 |
| ifOutDiscards_3 | 0 | 0 | 0 |
| ifOutDiscards_4 | 0 | 0 | 0 |
| ifOutDiscards_5 | 0 | 0 | 0 |
| ifOutErrors_1 | 4934 | 4935 | 1 |
| ifOutErrors_2 | 0 | 0 | 0 |

TABLE 10.3    Reviewing Two Sets of Interface Statistics (*Continued*)

| ifTable_ifEntry Object | Initial reading | 2 hours later | Difference |
|---|---|---|---|
| ifOutErrors_3 | 0 | 0 | 0 |
| ifOutErrors_4 | 0 | 0 | 0 |
| ifOutErrors_5 | 0 | 0 | 0 |
| ifOutQLen_1 | 0 | 0 | 0 |
| ifOutQLen_2 | 0 | 0 | 0 |
| ifOutQLen_3 | 0 | 0 | 0 |
| ifOutQLen_4 | 0 | 0 | 0 |
| ifOutQLen_5 | 0 | 0 | 0 |

When polling, don't forget that counters will wrap around to zero after they reach 4,294,967,295. Be sure that you poll for rapidly changing counters (such as the number of bytes received at an interface) often enough so that the counter has not wrapped a couple of times during the interval. SNMP version 2 introduces 64-bit counters that take a very long time to wrap.

The values in Table 10.3 clearly reflect the fact that only interfaces 1 and 2 are active. A large amount of traffic has come into the router across the serial line—roughly 2.7 million frames or 484 million bytes. Traffic flow into the router's Ethernet interface is actually substantially less—roughly .6 million frames or 118 million bytes. The reason for this was that users on the Ethernet copy a lot of files from remote locations to their local systems.

Since there are only two active interfaces, shouldn't the traffic coming in from the T1 line be exactly equal to the traffic sent out through the Ethernet interface? The answer is no. Not all traffic goes *through* a router—a router is the originator or recipient of a fairly robust amount of traffic. Routing table updates are exchanged with other routers. The router receives SNMP polls and sends out responses. Most routers support Telnet logins for administrative purposes, creating other traffic for which the router is an endpoint.

Note that in the 2-hour period, a few frames queued for output on the Ethernet and serial interfaces were discarded, probably because of a brief memory shortage. One incoming Ethernet frame and one outgoing Ethernet frame were discarded because of errors.

Let's examine the last interface variable separately:

```
ifTable_ifEntry_ifSpecific_1    0 0
ifTable_ifEntry_ifSpecific_2    0 0
ifTable_ifEntry_ifSpecific_3    0 0
ifTable_ifEntry_ifSpecific_4    0 0
ifTable_ifEntry_ifSpecific_5    0 0
```

Recall that this variable is supposed to hold an OBJECT IDENTIFIER pointing to further MIB variables for this type of interface. Like most implementations, this one returns the conventional *null* OBJECT IDEN-TIFIER, 0 0, meaning "I really don't understand what to fill in here!"

## 10.9   EXTENDING THE INTERFACES MIB

The MIB-II designers did not want to burden implementations with so many management tasks that the performance of devices would be degraded. Hence, MIB-II included only basic variables that were clearly needed for management of interfaces.

However, hands-on use of the *interfaces* MIB revealed that some important things had been left out. As a result, extensions to the generic interface MIB subtree were proposed in RFC 1229. These included:

- *The Generic Interface Extension Table.*   Additional general interface variables.

- *The Generic Interface Test Table.*   Variables that can launch a test, and variables that contain the results of the most recent test.

- *The Generic Receive Address Table.*   For each interface, a list of *all* of the addresses for which the interface will accept traffic.

The last item needs some explanation. Every LAN interface has its own distinctive physical address. In addition, it is commonplace to con-figure most LAN interfaces to accept frames sent to the broadcast address. Occasionally, an interface also will need to recognize one or more multicast addresses. And in some rare cases, extra unicast addresses are assigned to the interface.

There was no convenient way to include all of these physical addresses in the original interfaces table. The Generic Receive Address Table was designed as a place to park this extra information.

By the way, although we are more accustomed to seeing multiple addresses for LAN interfaces, there also are some packet network tech-nologies with interfaces that can receive multicasts or broadcasts. The Generic Receive Address Table incorporates this information too.

The interface extension objects were placed under node:

```
iso.org.dod.internet.mgmt.mib-2.ifExtensions
```

or

```
1 . 3 . 6 . 1 . 2 . 1 . 12
```

The Generic Extensions tables are described in Sections 10.10, 10.11, and 10.12. Implementations of these tables may persist in products for some time to come. However, substantial clarifications and improvements of *interfaces* objects have been proposed in RFC 1573. These will be adopted as part of the migration to SNMP version 2, and are discussed at the end of this chapter.

## 10.10   THE GENERIC INTERFACE EXTENSION TABLE

Table 10.4, the Generic Interface Extension Table, counts multicast and broadcast traffic. A useful configuration variable has been added. Bridges and monitoring devices need to examine *every* frame on a medium. To do this, they set network interfaces into *promiscuous* mode. The *ifExtnsPromiscuous* variable indicates whether an interface is operating in this mode. This variable is listed as read-only, but ven-

**TABLE 10.4   The Generic Interface Extension Table**

iso.org.dod.internet.mgmt.mib-2.ifExtensions.ifExtnsTable.ifExtnsEntry
1.3.6.1.2.1.12.1.1

| OBJECT IDENTIFIER | Syntax | Access | Description |
|---|---|---|---|
| ifExtnsIfIndex 1.3.6.1.2.1.12.1.1.1 ▶ **Index** | INTEGER | read-only | The index (ifIndex) for this interface. |
| ifExtnsChipSet 1.3.6.1.2.1.12.1.1.2 | OBJECT IDENTIFIER | read-only | The OBJECT IDENTIFIER registered for the chipset used in this product. If not assigned or unknown, coded as {0 0}. |
| ifExtnsRevWare 1.3.6.1.2.1.12.1.1.3 | DisplayString (SIZE (0..255)) | read-only | ASCII text describing the firmware version for the main interface software. |
| ifExtnsMulticasts TransmittedOks 1.3.6.1.2.1.12.1.1.4 | Counter | read-only | Number of frames successfully transmitted to a subnetwork or link-layer multicast (group or functional) address. Broadcasts are not included. |
| ifExtnsBroadcasts TransmittedOks 1.3.6.1.2.1.12.1.1.5 | Counter | read-only | Number of frames successfully transmitted to a subnetwork or link-layer broadcast address. |
| ifExtnsMulticasts ReceivedOks 1.3.6.1.2.1.12.1.1.6 | Counter | read-only | Number of successfully received multicast frames. |
| ifExtnsBroadcasts ReceivedOks 1.3.6.1.2.1.12.1.1.7 | Counter | read-only | Number of successfully received broadcast frames. |
| ifExtns Promiscuous 1.3.6.1.2.1.12.1.1.8 | INTEGER true(1), false(2) | read-only | If true, the interface will accept all frames transmitted on the medium. |

dors are permitted to implement it as read-write. Products such as network monitors or bridges may need the ability to turn the promiscuous mode on and off for selected interfaces.

The table also contains configuration information identifying the hardware chipset and software firmware version for each interface. The chipset and software variables will be dropped in SNMP version 2 *interfaces* MIB update—equipment often contains a mixture of chipsets and software modules, and it has been difficult for vendors to come up with clear-cut values for these variables.

## 10.11  THE GENERIC INTERFACE TEST TABLE

The ability to test whether interface equipment is functioning properly is a fundamental network management requirement. How can we use SNMP to manage testing when SNMP does not include command messages, such as "start test" or "report test results"?

In SNMP you get something done by *setting* a variable that triggers a command within a device. The variables that start tests and record test results are gathered together in Table 10.7, the Generic Interface Test Table. Before studying the formal table, let's look at Table 10.5, which shows some sample test entries.

There is one entry per interface. A full-duplex loopback test has been performed on the first interface. The test failed, and the expected loopback data did not come back. Let's walk through the first test.

- A manager sent a *set* request with community name "Manager-1" and request identifier 2111067.

- The request said "set the value of the test-type variable for interface 1 equal to *full-duplex loopback test*." Since there was no test in progress for interface 1 and the Manager-1 community name was authorized to start tests, the request succeeded.

**TABLE 10.5  Sample Test Table Entries**

| Interface index | Community | Request-ID | Test type | Test result | Code |
|---|---|---|---|---|---|
| 1 | Manager-1 | 2111067 | Run full-duplex loop-back test | failed | Expected data was not received. |
| 2 | Manager-2 | 100035 | Test the Interface Token-Ring Insertion Logic | inProgress | None. |

- When the test completed, the result "failed" was recorded. The fact that the expected loopback data was not received was indicated in the code variable.

- The management station that started the test sent a *get-request* for the community name, request-ID, result and code variables, in order to find out what happened.

The second interface in the example is connected to a Token-Ring, and the ring insertion logic currently is being tested.

### 10.11.1   When Tests Collide

Why do we bother to put the community name and request identifier into the test table? Suppose the following series of events occurs:

- Manager-1 requests test-A for interface 1.
- Test-A completes.
- Manager-2 requests test-B for interface 1.
- Test-B completes.
- Manager-1 reads the result and code expecting to find out what happened for test-A, but actually gets back the result and code for test-B.

The results of test-A are lost forever, but at least Manager-1 can figure out what happened if the community name and request-ID are read along with the result and the code.

### 10.11.2   Identifying Tests

Standards writers and vendors want to define tests. Each type of test needs to be assigned a name. How is this done?

Each test type is assigned an OBJECT IDENTIFIER (of course!). At first glance this might seem cumbersome. But the reward for using these long test IDs is convenience and flexibility. A task force defining MIB variables for a new technology can create a branch in its own MIB subtree that can hold any new test-type IDs that are needed.

### 10.11.3   Some Sample Test IDs

Let's look at Table 10.6 to see some sample test identifiers that are located in different MIB subtrees.

Under *ifExtensions,* the *wellKnownTests* subtree has been set aside for standard tests. The first entry above shows that a full-duplex loopback test has been given an identifier in this subtree. To request a full-duplex loopback, a manager would *set* the test-type variable to 1.3.6.1.2.1.12.4.1.

**TABLE 10.6    Same Test Type Identifiers**

| Test label | Test identifier | Description |
|---|---|---|
| iso.org.dod.internet.mgmt.mib-2. ifExtensions.wellKnownTests. testFullDuplexLoopBack | 1.3.6.1.2.1.12.4.1 | Perform a full-duplex loop-back test. |
| iso.org.dod.internet.mgmt.mib-2. transmission.dot5. dot5Tests.testInsertFunc | 1.3.6.1.2.1.10.9.3.1 | Test the ring insertion logic for a Token-Ring interface. |
| iso.org.dod.internet.mgmt.mib-2. transmission.dot3. dot3Tests.dot3TestTdr | 1.3.6.1.2.1.10.7.6.1 | Test an Ethernet coax cable with a Time-domain Reflectometry test. |

The agent at the device would then be responsible for executing the test and storing the result and code (if any) in the test table.

Tests relating specifically to Token-Ring interfaces are defined under the Token-Ring *dot5* tree, in subtree *dot5Tests*. The second entry in Table 10.6 shows the identifier for a test that is used to check that a Token-Ring interface can insert a station into a ring correctly.

Tests relating specifically to Ethernet interfaces are defined under the Ethernet *dot3* tree, in subtree *dot3Tests*. The third entry in Table 10.6 shows the identifier for a test that is used to find the approximate distance to a coaxial cable fault.

### 10.11.4    Test Results

Values of the test result variable include:

1. none
2. success
3. inProgress
4. notSupported
5. unAbleToRun
6. aborted
7. failed

Only one test at a time can be in progress at a given interface, so if a test is running and another test request arrives, an agent should reject the new request.

### 10.11.5    Test Codes

Sometimes it is not enough to know only whether a test has succeeded or failed. We may want to know *why* a test failed. Or we may want to read a *measurement* that has been returned by a successful test. The test code variable has been designed to do *either* job. What kind of value is flexible enough to provide simple codes *or* point to a measurement value? An OBJECT IDENTIFIER.* To see how it works, let's look at two examples:

- If a loopback test of an Ethernet interface fails, then a test code value of 1.3.6.1.2.1.10.7.7.1 means that the MAC chip could not be initialized for the test.

- A Time-domain Reflectometry test is used to locate an Ethernet coaxial cable fault. The test result is a time measurement that is used in a formula calculating the distance to a fault. In this case, the test code value contains an OBJECT IDENTIFIER that *names* a separate variable that holds the time measurement.

### 10.11.6   Definitions for the Test Table

Now we are ready to look at Table 10.7. The variable definitions are quite straightforward.

## 10.12   THE GENERIC RECEIVE ADDRESS TABLE

It is commonplace for LAN interfaces to receive traffic addressed to one specific physical address and to the LAN broadcast address. Sometimes a LAN interface also must accept multicasts. And occasionally, an interface will be assigned more than one unicast physical address. Table 10.8, the Generic Receive Address Table, identifies all of the configured physical addresses for which the interface will absorb frames. There is a separate entry for each address.

Even an interface that is capable of operating promiscuously needs an address that identifies the traffic that specifically is sent to this device. For example, a bridge must be able to examine all traffic, but the bridge also needs to recognize an SNMP *get-request* that is addressed to the bridge, and respond to it.

## 10.13   AUGMENTING A TABLE

The intention of the Generic Interface Extension Table is to add a new set of variables that will be maintained for each interface. The new table should be a logical extension of the original interfaces table, equivalent to adding more columns.

---

* As usual in SNMP, we make the tradeoff of using up some extra bytes in messages in return for a lot of flexibility.

**TABLE 10.7 The Generic Interface Test Table**

iso.org.dod.internet.mgmt.mib-2.
ifExtensions.ifExtnsTestTable.ifExtnsTestEntry
1.3.6.1.2.12.2.1

| OBJECT IDENTIFIER | Syntax | Access | Description |
|---|---|---|---|
| ifExtnsTest IfIndex 1.3.6.1.2.1.12.2.1.1 ▶ **Index** | INTEGER | read-only | The interface *index* (ifIndex) for this entry. |
| ifExtnsTest Community 1.3.6.1.2.1.12.2.1.2 | OCTET STRING | read-only | The community name for the current or most recently launched test request for this interface. |
| ifExtnsTest RequestId 1.3.6.1.2.1.12.2.1.3 | INTEGER | read-only | The request-id of the SNMP PDU that invoked the current or most recent test of this interface. |
| ifExtnsTest Type 1.3.6.1.2.1.12.2.1.4 | OBJECT IDENTIFIER | read-write | Starts a named test. If set to noTest, {0 0}, aborts a test. When read, it returns the last value that it was set to. |
| ifExtnsTest Result 1.3.6.1.2.1.12.2.1.5 | INTEGER | read-only | The result of the most recently requested test, or none(1) if no test has been requested. See Sec. 10.11.2. |
| ifExtnsTest Code 1.3.6.1.2.1.12.2.1.6 | OBJECT IDENTIFIER | read-only | A value that adds specific information about how a test turned out. |

**TABLE 10.8 The Generic Receive Address Table**

iso.org.dod.internet.mgmt.mib-2.
ifExtensions.ifExtnsRcvAddrTable.ifExtnsRcvAddrEntry
1.3.6.1.2.1.12.3.1

| OBJECT IDENTIFIER | Syntax | Access | Description |
|---|---|---|---|
| ifExtnsRcv AddrIfIndex 1.3.6.1.2.1.12.3.1.1 ▶ **Index** | INTEGER | read-only | The *ifIndex* for this interface. |
| ifExtnsRcv Address 1.3.6.1.2.1.12.3.1.2 ▶ **Index** | PhysAddress | read-only | An address at which this interface will receive frames. |
| ifExtnsRcv AddrStatus 1.3.6.1.2.1.12.3.1.3 | INTEGER other(1), invalid(2), volatile(3), nonVolatile(4) | read-write | *Volatile* addresses are deleted when the system restarts. For *other* addresses, it is not known what their status will be after restart. |

In other words, if a new interface is added to one of the tables, it must be added to the other table too. If an interface is deleted from either table, it should be deleted from both.

Unfortunately, version 1 of SNMP provided no way to describe this relationship. Version 2 repairs this omission by defining the notion of *augmenting* a previously defined table with additional columns. For example, if the columns of the Generic Interface Extension Table have been implemented, then these are viewed as additional columns in the interfaces table. Rows added to the interfaces table will have values in the new columns, and row deletions also will run across all columns.

## 10.14   SOME VERSION 2 IMPROVEMENTS

The MIB-II *interfaces* group is extremely useful—but there always is room for improvement. Life at the lower layers of networking is complicated. To cite some examples:

- An interface often is made up of several sublayers—for example, the X.25 packet layer on top of the X.25 data link layer on top of an RS-232 physical interface.
- Traffic from several serial interfaces may be directly multiplexed onto a T1 line.
- The popularity of *Multi-Link-Procedure* (MLP), which makes several serial lines look like a single logical link, is increasing. MLP provides robustness and flexibility.

We want our management stations to get the information that they need in order to manage all of the pieces of an interface implementation. The solution is:

- If necessary in order to manage an interface effectively, put an entry into the *interfaces* table for every sublayer of an interface. An entry's traffic counts should reflect data sent and received by whatever sublayer or layer is directly above this one. For example, an entry for an RS-232 interface should record the traffic sent and received by the Data Link layer above it.
- Create a new "stack" table that identifies how the layers and sublayers that make up an interface are related to one another.

Another problem has been posed by access to ever-greater bandwidths, resulting in the current 32-bit counters wrapping around far too quickly. The solution is simple—introduce some 64-bit counters. These enhancements are among the many introduced in RFC 1573.

## 10.15    INTERFACES GROUP EVOLUTION

In this section, we will outline the improvements introduced in RFC 1573. The updated MIB is made up of five tables:

- The original MIB-II interface table, with a few definitions switched to *deprecated* status
- An improved version of the *interfaces* extensions table
- A stack table that describes the relationships between interface sublayers
- The generic interfaces test table, improved and updated with SNMP version 2 features
- A slightly modified receive address table, listing the media addresses for an interface

### 10.15.1    Changes to the *interfaces* Table

The updated *interfaces* table contains the same objects, but several have been *deprecated*. This means that they may be implemented during a transitional period, but they are on the way out. The deprecated variables are:

ifInNUcastPkts

ifOutNUcastPkts

ifOutQLen

ifSpecific

Counts of nonunicast (broadcast and multicast) frames have been placed in the new Interfaces Extension Table, and the last two variables have not been useful.

### 10.15.2    The New Interfaces Extensions Table

The remaining updates are sufficiently different to require a new subtree, namely,

```
iso.org.dod.internet.mgmt.mib-2.ifMIB
```

or

```
1 . 3 . 6 . 1 . 2 . 1 . 31
```

The new extensions table takes care of a number of problems. Broadcasts and multicasts are counted here. New, higher-speed interfaces have traffic counts that can run through the old 32-bit counters quickly—High-Capacity (HC) 64-bit counters are introduced, to be used where needed.

Since so many interfaces seem to be made up of two or more sublayers, it is handy to attach a name to the interface as a whole; hence, the new *ifName* variable has been introduced. Another problem is the fact that when something goes wrong with a layered interface, *all* of the sublayers might generate traps for the same problem. The *ifLinkUp-DownTrapEnable* object lets a manager choose which trap(s) should be sent.

Table 10.9 presents a summary overview of the new extensions, which should be viewed as additional columns that optionally can *augment* the interfaces table. This is an SNMP version 2 table, and so includes some new datatypes in the SYNTAX column. Their names are self-explanatory. Full definitions of SNMP version 2 datatypes can be found in Chapter 35.

**TABLE 10.9    Interface Extensions**

| iso.org.dod.internet.mgmt.mib-2.ifMIB. ifMIBObjects.ifXTable.ifXEntry 1.3.6.1.2.1.31.1.1.1 | | |
|---|---|---|
| OBJECT IDENTIFIER | Syntax | Description |
| ifName | Display String | A text name for the interface, suitable for use at a management console. |
| ifInMulticastPkts | Counter32 | Incoming multicast packets. |
| ifInBroadcastPkts | Counter32 | Incoming broadcasts. |
| ifOutMulticastPkts | Counter32 | Outgoing multicasts. |
| ifOutBroadcastPkts | Counter32 | Outgoing broadcasts. |
| ifHCInOctets ifHCInUcastPkts ifHCInMulticastPkts ifHCInBroadcastPkts ifHCOutOctets ifHCOutUcastPkts ifHCOutMulticastPkts ifHCOutBroadcastPkts | Counter64 | Counters for High Capacity interfaces. |
| ifLinkUpDown TrapEnable | INTEGER | Whether this sublayer should send Up/Down traps. |
| ifHighSpeed | Gauge32 | Bandwidth in 1,000,000 of bits per second. |
| ifPromiscuousMode | Truth Value | Indicates if all packets are absorbed. |
| ifConnectorPresent | Truth Value | Indicates if this sublayer has a physical connector. |

### 10.15.3    The Interface Stack Table

Table 10.10, the interface stack table, simply relates pairs of interface sublayers, indicating which is "higher" and which is "lower."

### 10.15.4    The Interface Test Table

Table 10.11, the Interface Test Table, replaces the *ifExtnsTestTable*. This table consists of columns which optionally augment the *interfaces* table.

**TABLE 10.10    The Stack Table**

| OBJECT IDENTIFIER | iso.org.dod.internet.mgmt.mib-2.ifMIB. ifMIBObjects.ifStackTable.ifStackEntry 1.3.6.1.2.1.31.1.2.1 | |
| --- | --- | --- |
| | Syntax | Description |
| ifStackHigher Layer ▶ **Index** | Integer32 | The ifIndex for the "top" of this pair. |
| ifStackLower Layer ▶ **Index** | Integer32 | The ifIndex for the "bottom" of this pair. |
| ifStackStatus | RowStatus | Status of this entry (e.g., active or destroy). |

**TABLE 10.11    The Interface Test Table**

| OBJECT IDENTIFIER | iso.org.dod.internet.mgmt.mib-2.ifMIB. ifMIBObjects.ifTestTable.ifTestEntry 1.3.6.1.2.1.31.1.3.1 | |
| --- | --- | --- |
| | Syntax | Description |
| ifTestId | TestAndIncr | An integer that identifies the current test invocation. |
| ifTestStatus | INTEGER notInUse(1), inUse(2) | A new test request cannot be started unless the value currently is notInUse. |
| ifTestType | Autonomous Type | An OBJECT IDENTIFIER that names a test. |
| ifTestResult | INTEGER | Success or failure of the test (see list in Section 10.16.4). |
| ifTestCode | OBJECT IDENTIFIER | A value that adds specific information about how a test turned out. |
| ifTestOwner | OwnerString | The entity that started the current or most recent test. |

The *ifTestId* variable prevents a new test request from interrupting a test that is in progress. The *ifTestResult* variable indicates how the test turned out:

1     none (no test yet requested)

2     success

3     inProgress

4     notSupported

5     unAbleToRun (due to the state of the system)

6     aborted

7     failed

### 10.15.5   The Generic Receive Address Table

Table 10.12, the Generic Receive Address Table, is very similar to the table that it replaces, the *ifExtnsRcvAddr* table. The table is indexed by both *ifIndex* and *ifRcvAddressAddress*. However, only *ifRcvAddressAddress* appears in Table 10.12. Instead of repeating a variable like *ifIndex* over and over again in many tables, a variable can be used as an index without occupying a visible column in the table.

## 10.16   NETWORK MANAGEMENT CONSIDERATIONS

The type and speed of every interface on a network can be discovered by polling the *interfaces* MIB. This information should be stored in a configuration database.

**TABLE 10.12   The Generic Receive Address Table**

| iso.org.dod.internet.mgmt.mib-2.ifMIB. ifMIBObjects.ifRcvAddressTable.ifRcvAddressEntry 1.3.6.1.2.1.31.1.4.1 | | |
|---|---|---|
| OBJECT IDENTIFIER | Syntax | Description |
| ifRcvAddress Address ▶ **Index** | PhysAddress | An address for which this interface will accept packets/frames. |
| ifRcvAddress Status | RowStatus | Status variable used to create and delete table entries. |
| ifRcvAddress Type | INTEGER other(1), volatile(2), nonVolatile(3) | Indicates whether this entry will still exist after the next restart. |

The operational status of bridge, router, and service host interfaces that ought to be "up" should be checked periodically (e.g., every 10 minutes) in case an administrator turned an interface off for some reason, but then forgot to set its status back to "up." A system that loses a link because of a network problem will send a trap message. If this message is lost, the operational status poll will pick up the fact that there is a problem.

### 10.16.1    Bringing in the Version 2
*inform-request*

Systems should be checked for problems that are signaled by unusual levels of traffic, discards, errors, and for congested output queues. Is polling the best way to find out about these problems? For "dumb" systems, yes. But what about smart, capable systems?

Much SNMP literature preaches that traps should be defined and used very sparingly. The original basis for this opinion was that "devices" are dumb and are too busy to check when some statistic has passed a critical threshold, while management stations are smart and are devoted to doing nothing else.

But lots of service hosts, routers, and bridges are quite smart and have the resources to carry out threshold checks for critical problems. It makes a lot more sense to have a *capable* device send a notification when it self-diagnoses a problem. Polling then can be carried out at more widely spaced intervals.

The *inform-request* defined in SNMP version 2 is ideal for this purpose. A system can be dynamically configured to send *inform-request* messages when thresholds are crossed. This is defined as a Manager-to-Manager message; however, any smart system can be built to include a small manager entity.

### 10.16.2    Self-Diagnosis and Cure

Perhaps at a future time, systems will be configured to carry this self-diagnosis one step further, and automatically apply a remedy to problems that have a purely local solution. Consider a simple example. Suppose that the administrative status of an interface has been set to UP, and the interface has failed. A vendor could construct its device to automatically recover that interface (for example, by triggering a reinitialization) as soon as it is able. This would not require any protocol change—it is a matter of interpreting the scope of an administrative setting.*

---

* This already is done, for example, by the proprietary network management software used by Prodigy. This enables a very large network to be kept at a high level of availability by a small staff.

Polling for error statistics still will be important, because some problems can only be diagnosed using data gathered from several devices. The trick is to strike a balance, avoiding a glut of too-frequent polls and long lists of warnings and errors appearing at the management station, and instead carefully selecting information to be polled each 10 or 15 minutes.

It is important to get a sense of normal traffic counts for each hour of the day, and to set thresholds that signal an unusual level of activity. Periodic polls (say, every 15 minutes) can check current levels of activity. If a network monitor is available, accurate traffic counts can be captured without the overhead introduced by polling. Monitors also are capable of checking counts against thresholds and sending traps to signal impending trouble.

## 10.17   RECOMMENDED READING

For a discussion of Case diagrams, see *Case Diagrams: A First Step to Diagrammed Management Information Bases,* Jeffrey D. Case and Craig Partridge, Computer Communication Review, May 1990.

RFC 1229 extended the interfaces MIB. RFC 1573, *Evolution of the Interfaces Group of MIB-II,* describes several improvements to the *interfaces* group, and supersedes RFC 1229.

An extensive set of RFCs defining technology-specific MIB variables has been published and more are in progress. To cite a few, RFC 1398 on Ethernet, RFC 1231 on Token-Ring, RFC 1317 on RS-232, RFC 1315 on frame relay, RFCs 1381 and 1382 on X.25, RFC 1512 on FDDI, and RFC 1304 on SMDS. Check a current version of *rfc-index.txt* in the *rfc* directory at *ds.internic.net* for the latest technologies and versions.

# 11

# Address Translation

## 11.1 INTRODUCTION

Datagram-based protocols like IP route traffic by examining the Network Layer destination address and choosing the next-hop system that is along the current best path to that destination. The next-hop system is adjacent to the local system; that is, both the local system and the next-hop system are connected to the same LAN, serial line, or packet network.

The next-hop system may be a router or it may be the final destination. In either case, for IP, the next-hop choice is expressed as:

- The IP address of the next-hop system
- The identity of the interface leading toward the next-hop system

A datagram is then wrapped in a *frame* for transmission to the next-hop system. Although frame formats vary, all frame headers include some type of destination address field that holds lower-layer address information. It is the job of address translation to provide this lower-layer information.

### 11.1.1 Address Translation for a LAN

Each LAN Network Interface Card (NIC) is identified by a 6-octet physical address. The physical address of the destination NIC card must be discovered before a datagram can be framed and transmitted. The process of mapping an IP address to a corresponding physical address is called *Address Translation.*

For example, to deliver an IP message to a system named *popeye* on an Ethernet LAN, we would need to identify our interface to the LAN, know *popeye*'s IP address, and be aware of the physical address on *popeye*'s Ethernet NIC card. A specific example would look like:

Our Interface Index = 1

Popeye's IP Address = 128.36.12.8

Popeye's Physical Address = 08-00-20-07-C7-B7

### 11.1.2   Address Translation for a Packet Network

Address translation also is needed when an interface connects to a packet network such as X.25, frame relay, or SMDS. In that case, the packet net address or circuit number for the next-hop system must be looked up. For a system attached to an X.25 network, its packet net address is called its X.121 address, because CCITT recommendation X.121 defines a worldwide packet numbering plan (analogous to the worldwide telephone numbering plan).

### 11.1.3   Address Translation for Serial Lines

If the interface is a permanent point-to-point telephone line or ISDN circuit, address translation is trivial; traffic is passed to the device driver for the appropriate serial interface. The driver builds a frame around the datagram and transmits it across the line. The address field in the frame header does not matter.

If several circuits are multiplexed across a leased line, then address field values need to be tabulated for each of the circuits.

Finally, if the interface is used to set up dial-up circuits on demand, then the telephone or ISDN number to be called in order to reach a given IP address must be tabulated.

### 11.1.4   The Address Translation MIB Subtree

The Address Translation group was defined in MIB-I and consists of a single table that maps a network layer address to a physical LAN address, packet net address, telephone number, or whatever—any address that is needed to build and send a frame. Figure 11.1 shows the *at* subtree, which consists of the Address Translation Table.

## 11.2   THE ADDRESS TRANSLATION TABLE

Table 11.1, the *Address Translation Table,* contains the address mappings. The two index variables in the table are marked with the ▶**Index** symbol.

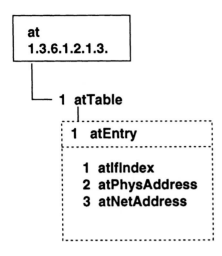

**Figure 11.1** The address translation subtree.

What addresses need to be listed in an Address Translation Table? We are only interested in mappings that we absolutely need to know in order to transmit traffic to a next-hop system. We want to know:

- Addresses that are on directly connected subnetworks
- Addresses that are needed in order to route datagrams *now* (as compared to yesterday!)

How are address translation entries generated?

- Some may be entered manually—e.g., telephone numbers or X.121 numbers.

**TABLE 11.1    Address Translation Table**

| OBJECT IDENTIFIER | Syntax | Access | Description |
|---|---|---|---|
| iso.org.dod.internet.mgmt.mib.at.atTable.atEntry 1.3.6.1.2.1.3.1.1 | | | |
| atIfIndex 1.3.6.1.2.1.3.1.1.1 ▶ **Index** | INTEGER | read-write | The index of this interface. |
| atPhysAddress 1.3.6.1.2.1.3.1.1.2 | Phys Address | read-write | The Physical address. If the value is null, then this entry is not in use. |
| atNetAddress 1.3.6.1.2.1.3.1.1.3 ▶ **Index** | Network Address | read-write | The Network Address (e.g., IP Address) corresponding to the physical address. |

- Some may be discovered automatically, e.g., by a special protocol such as the *Address Resolution Protocol,* used when running IP across a LAN.

- Some may be calculated automatically. Addresses for some protocols are assigned by using a standard mapping function that converts physical addresses to Network Layer addresses.

## 11.3   SAMPLE ADDRESS TRANSLATION PRINTOUT

Below we see a raw printout of the result of an SNMP address translation query sent by the PSI *snmplookup* program. The responses show that the node has two interfaces. There are entries for three systems that can be reached through the first interface and entries for two systems that can be reached through the second interface.

Each variable name ends with the *two* indices needed to select an instance: the interface number and the IP address. Thus, the first object identifier ends with *_atIfIndex_1.1.130.15.22.57,* meaning interface 1, IP address 130.15.22.57.

The values of *atIfIndex* and *atNetAddress* are the table indices, and just repeat the *ifIndex* numbers and IP addresses that are the index part of the variable's name. The *atIfIndex* value is printed twice—once in hex and once in decimal. The *atPhysAddress* variable provides the information that we are interested in—a 6-octet hex physical address.

```
snmp> mquery 3
atIfIndex_1.1.130.15.22.57          0x1                     1
atIfIndex_1.1.130.15.22.58          0x1                     1
atIfIndex_1.1.130.15.22.59          0x1                     1
atIfIndex_2.1.130.15.22.65          0x2                     2
atIfIndex_2.1.130.15.22.66          0x2                     2
atPhysAddress_1.1.130.15.22.57      0x00000c005880
atPhysAddress_1.1.130.15.22.58      0x00000c005884
atPhysAddress_1.1.130.15.22.59      0x020701029efa
atPhysAddress_2.1.130.15.22.65      0x00000c005881
atPhysAddress_2.1.130.15.22.66      0x00000c005885
atNetAddress_1.1.130.15.22.57       130.15.22.57
atNetAddress_1.1.130.15.22.58       130.15.22.58
atNetAddress_1.1.130.15.22.59       130.15.22.59
atNetAddress_2.1.130.15.22.65       130.15.22.65
atNetAddress_2.1.130.15.22.66       130.15.22.66
```

### 11.3.1   A Table of Results

The results are more attractive when rearranged into a tabular format, as shown in Table 11.2.

TABLE 11.2    Sample Address Translation Output

| Address Translation Table Example | | |
| --- | --- | --- |
| atIfIndex | atPhysAddress | atNetAddress |
| 1 | 0x00000c005880 | 130.15.22.57 |
| 1 | 0x00000c005884 | 130.15.22.58 |
| 1 | 0x020701029efa | 130.15.22.59 |
| 2 | 0x00000c005881 | 130.15.22.65 |
| 2 | 0x00000c005885 | 130.15.22.66 |

## 11.4   CREATING AN ADDRESS TRANSLATION TABLE

How do you create an Address Translation Table? For LAN physical address entries, most network administrators prefer to use a protocol that gets the answers automatically because it saves a lot of work and keeps up with network changes very efficiently.

### 11.4.1   The Address Resolution Protocol (ARP)

The *Address Resolution Protocol* (ARP) was designed to operate in a LAN environment. ARP's job is to discover the LAN *physical layer address* that corresponds to a given *network layer address*. LAN physical addresses are called *Media Access Control* (MAC) addresses.

Although ARP was constructed so that it could find out address translations for lots of network layer protocols, we will concentrate on the use of ARP with IP, since that is its current primary application.

ARP generates IP address to physical address mappings by broadcasting the question "Who has this IP address?" The broadcast message contains an IP network layer protocol address and asks the owner to send back the corresponding physical address. Initially, ARP was very widely used on Ethernet LANs. Later, its use was extended to Token-Rings and FDDI LANs—and beyond.

### 11.4.2   An ARP Example

The SNMP *at* table provides information similar to that displayed by the UNIX *arp -a* command. In the example below, the 6-octet physical address of each interface board is shown at the far right. In the display, the octets in the physical address are separated by ":" delimiters. The IP address is displayed in the middle column. To make the display more user-friendly, *arp* displays the system name at the left:

```
arp -a
casper.cs.yale.edu (128.36.12.1)  at 8:0:20:8:59:ec
cantor.cs.yale.edu (128.36.12.26) at 8:0:20:8:6e:a0
popeye.cs.yale.edu (128.36.12.8)  at 8:0:20:7:c7:b7
```

There is a timer associated with the ARP table. When the timer expires, the automatic entries are flushed and must be "relearned."

### 11.4.3   ARP with SMDS

Automatic translation is so attractive that ARP has been adapted for use in wide area *Switched Multimegabit Data Service* (SMDS), a service offered by Regional Bell Operating Companies.

Extension of ARP to SMDS is simple. One of the things that SMDS does is to support *Logical IP Subnets*. This means that when some routers and hosts belonging to an organization are connected to an SMDS service provider, the provider assigns them IP addresses belonging to a single IP network and subnet. The systems on the logical subnet SMDS will function very much like a backbone LAN (such as a high-speed Token-Ring or FDDI ring) within the organization's larger network. Since SMDS can operate at 45 megabits per second, this logical subnet could operate at very high speeds!

Each system on the logical subnet also would be assigned a unique SMDS lower-level address as well as an SMDS group address to be used for ARP broadcasts. A message sent to the group address would be delivered to every system on the logical subnet. Hence, ARP will work exactly as it does on a LAN.

### 11.4.4   ARP with Frame Relay

A single link between a customer premise and a frame relay service provider network can carry several virtual circuits, each leading to a different distant endpoint. An ARP request can be sent out on each virtual circuit, and the system with the requested IP address will respond, indicating which circuit to use to reach the desired IP address.

However, this is not a very efficient way to get address mappings. For example, if there were five interfaces and five remote IP addresses, we would send five ARP messages to map each IP address to a circuit, for a total of $5 \times 5 = 25$ messages.

The preferred implementation is to use *Inverse ARP*, which asks the reversed question "What is your IP address?" A single Inverse ARP message can be sent down each circuit asking for the remote IP address. This way, five messages provide all of the answers needed for the Address Translation Table.

### 11.4.5    Entries for X.25 Interfaces

If an interface connects to an X.25 public packet switching network, the usual procedure is to manually enter appropriate address mappings into an Address Translation Table. Nodes on X.25 networks are assigned numbers under the worldwide numbering plan defined in CCITT Recommendation X.121. Normally, a table entry is needed to indicate the X.121 address that corresponds to a given IP address. However, on a DDN-X.25 network, there is a formula that maps an IP address to its corresponding X.25 address.

## 11.5    DEPRECATED STATUS OF *at* IN MIB-II

When MIB-II was written, the old *at* group was *included without change, but was deprecated.* In general, an object is deprecated either because it hasn't proved to be particularly useful, or because a better, more useful definition has been found.

The original intent was that the *at* table would hold mappings for any datagram-style routing protocol. But in fact, the original MIB-II table currently is used only for IP address translation. The Address Translation variables shown in Table 11.1 do not meet the needs of protocols such as DECnet, AppleTalk, and NetWare IPX.

### 11.5.1    Separate Address Translation Tables
### for Each Protocol

It was decided that it was better to place separate, tailored address translation tables within the MIBs for each different Network Layer protocol. In fact, it turned out that the *at* variables even needed some enhancement for IP use. A modestly improved version, the *ipNetToMediaTable,* has been defined and placed within the MIB-II *ip* group. (See Chapter 12.)

Thus MIB-II contains two very similar address translation tables. The benefit of keeping the deprecated table is that it provides a transition period for updating products from MIB-I to MIB-II.

## 11.6    NETWORK MANAGEMENT
## CONSIDERATIONS

The *at* table is a useful troubleshooting tool. When a user cannot reach systems that are up and interacting with other users, it is possible that the problem stems from bad information in the local address translation table.

- Manually entered static information may have been entered incorrectly.

- A value that was discovered dynamically, e.g., via ARP, may have been kept for so long that it is stale.

A manager can poll the user's system and check whether the entries are valid. Since write access can be granted to the *at* variables, an authorized network manager would be able to fix incorrect information with a *set-request.*

If stale data caused the problem, it is possible that the timeout value configured for dynamic entries at the system is too large. Currently the timeout variable is not included in MIB-II, so if the timeout needs to be changed, the update would have to be made by an administrator for the system.

# 12

# Managing IP

## 12.1 INTRODUCTION

The IP protocol is responsible for directing datagrams from a source computer to a destination computer. How does IP work? If the source and destination are directly connected, datagrams flow across the single hop between them. Figure 12.1 shows traffic passing between two hosts on a LAN.

If a source and destination are attached to different parts of an internet, then traffic passes through one or more routers along the way. Figure 12.2 shows two paths between a source and destination.

## 12.2 THE ELEMENTS OF THE IP PROTOCOL

The next few sections will review the elements of the IP protocol, and sketch IP terminology and concepts. They are intended to be a reminder of how IP works—not a complete initiation into the world of IP. See the *Recommended Reading* section at the end of the chapter to find out where to get more information.

### 12.2.1 IP Addresses

An IP network can consist of a single LAN, as in Figure 12.1, or an *internet* made up of a number of subnetworks joined by routers. The internet in Figure 12.2 contains seven subnetworks: two Ethernets, a Token-Ring, a packet network, and three point-to-point links.

Every system in an internet needs to be assigned an IP address. IP addresses are 32 bits (4 bytes) long and, as shown in Figure 12.3, consist of a network part and a local part.

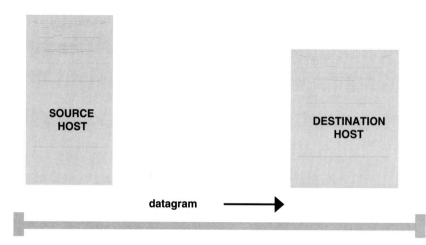

**datagram** ──────▶

**Figure 12.1**  IP traffic between two hosts on a LAN.

Addresses are written for human consumption in a user-friendly dot notation that converts each byte to a decimal number.

An organization usually enrolls its network with a *registration authority,** and is assigned the use of one or more unique network address prefixes. These address prefixes form the network part of their IP addresses. Although an organization can own and use several network address prefixes, it is assigned a single *Autonomous System* number that *uniquely* identifies its entire internet.

### 12.2.2  Address Classes

For many years, there were three classes of network address prefixes—A, B, and C—that were given to organizations. As shown in Table 12.1, a class A network address prefix allows for over 16 million local addresses. Extremely large and important organizations (such as the Navy and IBM) received class A addresses.

Large and medium-sized companies received class B addresses. Class C addresses were appropriate for small networks. The class was easily determined by the number in the first byte of the address, as shown in Table 12.1.

The assignment of large blocks of class A and class B addresses was extremely inefficient. The pool of popular class B addresses was

---

* Currently, primary registration services are provided by Network Solutions, Inc., in Herndon, Virginia. Other registration authorities are being set up around the world.

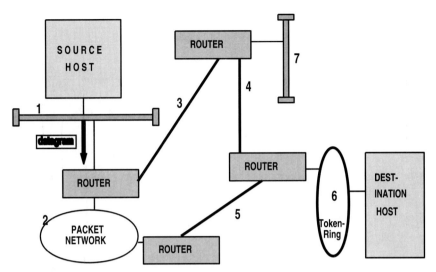

**Figure 12.2** IP traffic routed through an internet.

being depleted rapidly. This has led to a new *Classless* system, in which contiguous clumps of class C addresses are assigned to an organization.

### 12.2.3  Subnets

We've been using the informal term *subnetwork* for a LAN, point-to-point line, or packet network used to build up a network. The term *subnet* denotes a *logical* chunk of an internet. In real practice, this usually is a LAN, point-to-point line, or packet network. But it could be a logical subset of a LAN or packet network. For example, two work groups sharing the same LAN medium might be configured as separate *subnets*.

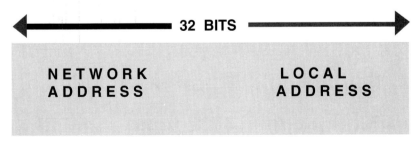

**Figure 12.3** IP address format.

TABLE 12.1   IP Addresses

| | IP Address Structures | | | |
|---|---|---|---|---|
| Class | Network address size | First byte of network address | Local address size | Number of local addresses* |
| A | 1 byte | 0-127 | 3 bytes | 16,777,216 |
| B | 2 bytes | 128-191 | 2 bytes | 65,536 |
| C | 3 bytes | 192-223 | 1 byte | 256 |
| Classless | 2 bytes plus as many bits as are needed for a total of $n$ bits. | 192-223 | 32-$n$ bits | $2^{32-n}$ |

* A few local addresses are reserved for special purposes.

### 12.2.4   Subnet Addressing

The purpose of defining *subnets* is to add some hierarchical structure to an IP address. The local field in an IP address can be divided into a subnet part and host part.

It is common practice to use the third byte in a class B address as the *subnet* part. For example, for the network address prefix 128.1, the *subnets* would be 128.1.1, 128.1.2, and so forth. The final byte identifies systems on a subnet. For example, host number 21 on subnet 4 and network 128.1 would be given IP address 128.1.4.21.

### 12.2.5   Subnet Mask

An organization has the freedom to choose *any* number of bits in its (local) part of the address to number its subnets—hence the need for a piece of configuration information known as the *subnet mask*. The purpose of the subnet mask is to show exactly how many bits are being used for the subnet part of addresses. The subnet mask is a 32-bit quantity with 1s in the network and subnet bits and 0s in the host address bits.

What can the subnet mask do for you? Suppose that:

- A source host on a LAN has IP address 128.1.4.21.
- The destination host has IP address 128.1.4.50.
- The subnet mask is 255.255.255.0.

Using the zero part of the mask to zero out the host addresses, we see that the network and subnet parts are the same—namely, 128.1.4. This tells you that both are on the same LAN, which is a useful fact to know.

### 12.2.6   Routing Masks

*Routing masks* are used to cut down on the size of routing tables. For example, a single routing table entry can suffice to direct all traffic to some external network—say, 190.77. Associating the mask 255.255.0.0 with an entry "190.77.0.0" indicates that this route is valid for *all* destination addresses starting with 190.77.

What if there is a better route to *some* of the systems in network 190.77? For example, suppose that a different next hop should be used to reach subnets 16 through 31 in network 190.77. Masks enable a routing table to express this finer granularity.

The address of *every* host on *any* of these subnets starts with the unique bit pattern:

```
10111110 01001101 0001xxxx xxxxxxxx
```

Filling the "don't care" x values with 0s, we get 190.77.16.0. Suppose that we put the following entries into the routing table:

| Destination | Routing mask | Next hop |
|---|---|---|
| 190.77.0.0 | 255.255.0.0 | 128.1.1.3 |
| 190.77.16.0 | 255.255.240.0 | 128.1.1.7 |

The mask 255.255.240.0 corresponds to:

```
11111111  11111111  11110000  00000000
  255.       255.      240.       0
```

When we apply the mask to an address like 190.77.21.75, the last 15 bits of the address are zeroed out and we get 190.77.16.0—a match!— so we will relay the datagram to 128.1.1.7. Of course, it is important to know that when IP searches a routing table, it looks for the entry providing the *longest match* of the destination address, so this entry would override the previous one.

### 12.2.7   Routing Masks and Classless IP Addressing

Finally, including masks in routing tables is essential in order to support classless IP addressing. Suppose that an organization has been assigned a clump of addresses ranging from 200.104.32.0 to 200.104.63.254. All of these addresses start with the unique bit pattern:

```
11001000 01101000 001xxxxx xxxxxxxx
```

Using a mask of:

```
11111111  11111111  11100000  00000000
  255.      255.      224.        0
```

enables the use of a single routing table entry to route to this clump of numbers.

## 12.3  PROCESSING DATAGRAMS

IP's job is to use the IP header and internal tabular information to route a datagram from its source to its destination. Let's follow a datagram from its source on one LAN to its destination on another. The source host:

- Uses the subnet mask to find out if the destination is on the local LAN.
- If yes, the source finds out the physical address of the destination and delivers the datagram.
- If no, the source looks up the destination in a routing table. If an appropriate router* can be selected, the source finds out the physical address of the router and forwards the datagram.

Routers use their local subnet masks and routing tables to forward the datagram until it reaches its destination.

At any point along the way, the datagram may prove to be too large to be carried in a legally sized frame for the next hop on its path. The datagram may need to be fragmented.

Sometimes datagrams run into trouble and cannot be delivered.

- The datagram may be lost during transmission across a link.
- The IP header may become corrupted.
- It may be impossible to route to the destination.
- The datagram may wander around in the internet for too long.

If a datagram does not run into any mishap and reaches a destination system, the destination IP also has a role to play. The destination IP needs to deliver each datagram to an appropriate upper-layer protocol, such as TCP or UDP. The destination IP checks the *protocol field* in the IP header to find out who gets the datagram.

---

* Recall that many of the older TCP/IP standards used the term *gateway* instead of *router*.

With this background, we are ready to look at the MIB variables in the *ip* group.

## 12.4   THE IP MIB SUBTREE

The *ip* subtree is made up of some individual configuration and statistics variables and three tables. Figure 12.4 shows an overview.

## 12.5   BASIC IP CONFIGURATION

Table 12.2 lists two IP configuration parameters that can be *set* by a management application. The sections that follow explain each variable.

### 12.5.1   Forwarding Role

Hosts are sources and destinations for application traffic. Routers act as intermediate switching nodes for datagrams. However, occasionally, a host system will be configured so that it also acts as a router. The *ipForwarding* variable indicates whether a system will forward (route) datagrams.

If the value of this variable is "not-forwarding" does it mean that it will *never* forward a datagram? Well, almost. An application that wants to make sure that its data follows a secure path to a destination can stick an IP source route into each IP header. An IP source route can include hosts. A host that is part of a source route will do as it's told and relay source-routed datagrams.

### 12.5.2   Default Time-To-Live

During a period of path adjustment, some IP datagrams may be misrouted and circle around for a while. The Time-To-Live hop counter in the datagram header gets decremented at each router, and datagrams that have outlived their usefulness are discarded.

A programmer can control the Time-To-Live value in datagrams sent by an application. If an application programmer does not call for a particular value, this default is used.

## 12.6   CONFIGURING THE IP
## ADDRESS TABLE

More configuration information is found in Table 12.3, the IP Address Table. Every network interface is assigned an IP address and some associated information. There is a table entry for each IP address, and so the IP address is used as the table's index.

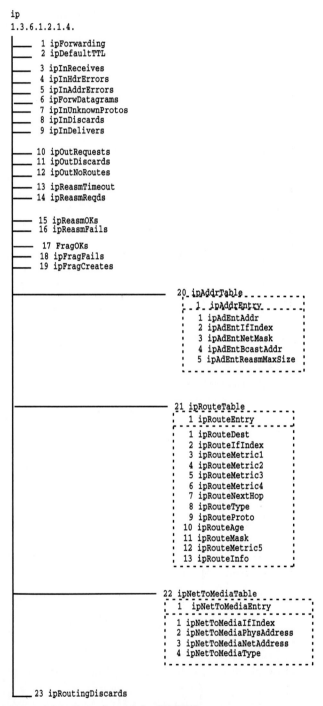

**Figure 12.4** Overview of the IP MIB.

**TABLE 12.2   Basic IP Configuration Parameters**

| | iso.org.dod.internet.mgmt.mib-2.ip. 1.3.6.1.2.1.4. | | |
|---|---|---|---|
| OBJECT IDENTIFIER | Syntax | Access | Description |
| ipForwarding 1.3.6.1.2.1.4.1 | INTEGER forwarding(1), not-forwarding(2) | read-write | Indicates whether the system will route datagrams. |
| ipDefaultTTL 1.3.6.1.2.1.4.2 | INTEGER | read-write | Default Time-To-Live value, used when an application does not specify a value. |

How many entries will appear in a system's IP Address Table? Most hosts communicate through a single interface, but a few have two or more. Routers, of course, always have two or more interfaces. Sometimes the number of IP addresses actually is *larger* than the number of interfaces. This is because a single interface *can* be assigned more than one IP address.*

All of the information in this table is read-only, and thus we should expect that it will be configured directly at the device.

Recall that in SNMP version 1, the access given in a MIB is stated to be the *minimum* level that a vendor should provide. However, most vendors have built their products using the defined MIB access as a maximum level. You will often discover that read-write variables have been implemented as read-only for a device. But you will rarely see a read-only variable implemented as read-write.

### 12.6.1   Selecting the Broadcast Format

Examples of standard forms of IP broadcast address are:

- 255.255.255.255: Broadcast on the LAN connected to this interface.

- 130.15.5.255: Broadcast on subnet 5 of network 130.15.

In general, a subnet broadcast address usually is formed by placing 1s in every host address position. However, there are some older implementations that used 0s instead of 1s for broadcasts, and this option still can be configured. The *ipAdEntBcastAddr* variable in Table 12.3 is set to 1 for the 1s form, and to 0 for the 0s form of broadcast.

---

* For example, sometimes nodes on a single physical LAN are organized as two or more logical subnets. A router attached to the LAN will be given a separate IP address for each logical subnet.

TABLE 12.3    IP Address Table

| iso.org.dod.mgt.mib-2.ip.ipAddrTable.ipAddrEntry 1.3.6.1.2.1.4.20.1 | | | |
|---|---|---|---|
| OBJECT IDENTIFIER | Syntax | Access | Description |
| ipAdEntAddr 1.3.6.1.2.1.4.20.1.1 ▶ **Index** | IpAddress | read-only | The 32-bit (4-byte) IP address for this entry. |
| ipAdEntIfIndex 1.3.6.1.2.1.4.20.1.2 | INTEGER | read-only | The corresponding network interface (*ifIndex*). |
| ipAdEntNet Mask 1.3.6.1.2.1.4.20.1.3 | IpAddress | read-only | The subnet mask for this IP address. |
| ipAdEnt BcastAddr 1.3.6.1.2.1.4.20.1.4 | INTEGER | read-only | Indication of the broadcast format for the interface. 1 for the all 1s standard, 0 for the all 0s format. |
| ipAdEntReasm MaxSize 1.3.6.1.2.1.4.20.1.5 | INTEGER (0.65535) | read-only | The biggest datagram that can be reassembled from fragments received at this interface. |

## 12.7  IP ROUTING TABLE

The IP Routing table contains information needed to route datagrams. IP looks up a destination in the table in order to choose the adjacent next-hop system to which a datagram should be sent. MIB documents refer to entries as providing *routes,* although an entry in fact only determines one hop along a route.

Where do routes come from? Routing information can be obtained:

- From stable, manually configured entries.

- Via an Internet Control Message Protocol (ICMP) *Redirect* message. When a system sends a datagram to the wrong local router, the router sends a Redirect message back. The Redirect message contains the correct next hop for this destination.

- From neighboring routers that provide information via an automatic routing protocol.

A host routing table usually is very simple—it often contains a single entry that identifies a local *default* router. For example, in most cases a LAN is connected to the rest of an enterprise network via single router, which is the default for all remote traffic.

### 12.7.1    Routing Protocols

An automatic routing protocol is a must for routers in a large, complex IP network. Routers use the automatic protocol to recalculate their routes after link failure, equipment failure, or when new a new router is added to the network. A routing protocol specifies:

- The rules whereby routers maintain awareness of each other and exchange current information with each other
- The algorithm used to calculate routes based on current information

Many routing protocols, both public and proprietary, are in use today. Modern routers even are capable of running several routing protocols at the same time. A router may speak to some of its neighbors using RIP and to others using IGRP, OSPF, or EGP.

Table 12.4, the IP Routing Table, has been designed to be flexible enough to encompass information used by many different routing protocols.

### 12.7.2    How Routes Are Learned

The *ipRouteProto* variable reveals how a route was learned. Its values include:

1. *other*          None of the following
2. *local*          Manually configured
3. *netmgt*         Entered via a network management *set*
4. *icmp*           Obtained via an ICMP redirect
5. *egp*            Exterior Gateway Protocol, a long-lived Internet standard, used between neighboring autonomous systems
6. *ggp*            Gateway-to-Gateway Protocol, a classic Internet backbone protocol
7. *hello*          Developed for "Fuzzball" gateways and used early in the history of the NSFnet research network
8. *rip*            Routing Information Protocol, a popular and widely available protocol
9. *is-is*          ISO Intermediate System (router) to Intermediate System protocol
10. *es-is*         ISO End System to Intermediate System protocol
11. *ciscoIgrp*     Cisco's proprietary Interior Gateway Routing Protocol

| 12. *bbnSpfIgp* | Bolt, Beranek and Newman's Shortest Path First gateway protocol |
| 13. *ospf* | Open Shortest Path First, a recent standard |
| 14. *bgp* | Border Gateway Protocol, a standard for routing between autonomous systems |

### 12.7.3   Facts About the Routing Table

The routing table is indexed by the destination IP address. All of the table's variables are read-write, except for *ipRouteProto* and *ipRoute-Info*. It is assumed that these values are configured at the device.

Every routing protocol uses some kind of *metric* or combination of *metrics* to decide which route is the best one. A metric may be as simple as a count of the number of hops needed to reach a destination. Or, combined metrics may take bandwidth, delay, and price factors into consideration. The meaning of the primary and alternate metrics in a table entry is determined by the routing protocol for that entry. The value for any metric that is not used will be set to –1, which is coded as 'FFFFFFFF'H.

The *ipRouteType* is an important variable that indicates the status and type of a routing table entry. Its values are:

| 1. *other* | None of the following |
| 2. *invalid* | No longer valid: logically, out of the table |
| 3. *direct* | Destination is on a directly connected subnet |
| 4. *indirect* | Destination is not on a directly connected subnet |

When an automatic routing protocol is used, routing table entries will be updated dynamically.* For most protocols, an entry will be thrown away if it is stale—meaning that no fresh information showing that this route is still valid has arrived for a long time. The *ipRouteAge* variable keeps track of how long it has been since an entry was refreshed.

Sometimes a router throws away perfectly valid entries because it needs to add some new entries to its table but has run out of space. There is a statistical counter that reports the number of valid routing table entries that have been discarded. We present the definition in Table 12.5 since it relates directly to the routing table.

The next two sections contain sample Route Table entries obtained from a Cisco router using the PSI *snmplookup* tool. Like several of the high-end router products that are available, the Cisco router can learn routes by using several different routing protocols at the same time.

---

\* However, an administrator has the option of entering some permanent entries manually.

**TABLE 12.4  The IP Routing Table**

| OBJECT IDENTIFIER | Syntax | Access | Description |
|---|---|---|---|
| iso.org.dod.mgt.mib-2.ip.ipRouteTable.ipRouteEntry<br>1.3.6.1.2.1.4.21.1 | | | |
| ipRouteDest<br>1.3.6.1.2.1.4.21.1.1<br>▶ **Index** | IpAddress | read-write | A destination IP address. 0.0.0.0 is used for a default entry. |
| ipRouteIfIndex<br>1.3.6.1.2.1.4.21.1.2 | INTEGER | read-write | The index of the interface (*ifIndex*) through which traffic to this destination should be transmitted. |
| ipRouteMetric1<br>1.3.6.1.2.1.4.21.1.3 | INTEGER | read-write | The primary routing metric for this route. Its meaning depends on the routing protocol (see the ipRouteProto variable). |
| ipRouteMetric2<br>1.3.6.1.2.1.4.21.1.4 | INTEGER | read-write | Another routing metric. |
| ipRouteMetric3<br>1.3.6.1.2.1.4.21.1.6 | INTEGER | read-write | Another routing metric. |
| ipRouteMetric4<br>1.3.6.1.2.1.4.21.1.6 | INTEGER | read-write | Another routing metric. |
| ipRouteNextHop<br>1.3.6.1.2.1.4.21.1.7 | IpAddress | read-write | The IP address of the next hop of this route. |
| ipRouteType<br>1.3.6.1.2.1.4.21.1.8 | INTEGER<br>other(1),<br>invalid(2),<br>direct(3),<br>indirect(4) | read-write | The status or type of the route. |
| ipRouteProto<br>1.3.6.1.2.1.4.21.1.9 | INTEGER | read-only | The protocol by which the route was learned (see Sec. 12.7.2). |
| ipRouteAge<br>1.3.6.1.2.1.4.21.1.10 | INTEGER | read-write | Number of seconds since last update or validation of this route. |
| ipRouteMask<br>1.3.6.1.2.1.4.21.1.11 | IpAddress | read-write | Routing mask for the entry. Some newer protocols carry this information. |
| ipRouteMetric5<br>1.3.6.1.2.1.4.21.1.12 | INTEGER | read-write | Yet another route metric. |
| ipRouteInfo<br>1.3.6.1.2.1.4.21.1.13 | OBJECT IDENTIFIER | read-only | A pointer to more MIB variables for the protocol. If not specified, the value should be {0 0}. |

**TABLE 12.5  Statistic for IP Routing Discards**

| Object | Syntax | Access | Description |
|---|---|---|---|
| iso.org.dod.internet.mgmt.mib-2.ip<br>1.3.6.1.2.1.4 | | | |
| ipRouting Discards<br>1.3.6.1.2.1.4.23 | Counter | read-only | The number of valid routing entries that were discarded—possibly to free up memory. |

### 12.7.4  A Sample RIP Entry

The example below shows a Cisco router's *ipRouteTable* entry for a route that has been learned using the RIP routing protocol.

```
ipRouteDest_128.1.2.0       128.1.2.0
ipRouteIfIndex_128.1.2.0    0x1            1
ipRouteMetric1_128.1.2.0    0x1            1
ipRouteMetric2_128.1.2.0    0xffffffff    -1 (not applicable)
ipRouteMetric3_128.1.2.0    0xffffffff    -1 (not applicable)
ipRouteMetric4_128.1.2.0    0xffffffff    -1 (not applicable)
ipRouteNextHop_128.1.2.0    128.1.5.55
ipRouteType_128.1.2.0       0x4            4
ipRouteProto_128.1.2.0      0x8            8
ipRouteAge_128.1.2.0        0x2            2
ipRouteMask_128.1.2.0       255.255.255.0
ipRouteMetric5.128.1.2.0    0xffffffff    -1 (not applicable)
ipRouteInfo.128.1.2.0       0 0
```

By looking at the destination, 128.1.2.0, and checking the route mask, *ipRouteMask,* which is 255.255.255.0, we can conclude that this is an entry for a subnet. The route type is indirect, meaning that the next hop is a router. The address of the next-hop router on the way to destination 128.1.2.0 is 128.1.5.55, and this router can be reached through interface 1. Protocol type 8 is RIP.

RIP uses only a single route metric. Metric 1 is set to 1 while the others are set to –1. It has been 2 seconds since this route last was determined to be correct.

### 12.7.5  A Sample IGRP Entry

The Internet Gateway Routing Protocol, IGRP, is Cisco's proprietary routing protocol. The route that follows has been learned using the IGRP protocol.

```
ipRouteDest_128.6.0.0       128.6.0.0
ipRouteIfIndex_128.6.0.0    0x2            2
ipRouteMetric1_128.6.0.0    0x31a6         12710
ipRouteMetric2_128.6.0.0    0x600          1536
ipRouteMetric3_128.6.0.0    0xf230         62000
ipRouteMetric4_128.6.0.0    0x3            3
ipRouteNextHop_128.6.0.0    130.9.1.49
ipRouteType_128.6.0.0       0x4            4
ipRouteProto_128.6.0.0      0xb            11
ipRouteAge_128.6.0.0        0x1            1
ipRouteMask_128.6.0.0       255.255.0.0
ipRouteMetric5.128.6.0.0    0xff           255
ipRouteInfo.128.6.0.0       0 0
```

The next-hop router on the way to destination 128.6.0.0 is 130.9.1.49. By checking the subnet mask, *ipRouteMask,* which is 255.255.0.0, we see that the destination is a network rather than subnet or an individual host. The route type is indirect, meaning that the next hop is a router. Protocol type 11 is IGRP. It has been 1 second since this route last was determined to be correct.

IGRP chooses routes based on bandwidth, delay, reliability, loading, and Maximum Transmission Unit size. All five of the routing metrics in the table are used.

## 12.8   A PROPOSED EXPANDED ROUTING TABLE

The *ipRouteTable* as defined above does not capture some of the strong capabilities in newer routing protocols. For example, the Open Shortest Path First routing protocol makes it possible to use several paths to a destination at the same time.

A second lack in the *ipRouteTable* is that it does not provide a way to define *routing policies.* For example, there is a Type-of-Service field in the IP header that indicates a datagram delivery characteristic such as desired priority, delay, or reliability. One route may be selected from several alternatives based on this field.

Another policy issue is whether you want the routers in *your* organization to carry traffic that originates and terminates in external organizations. (See Figure 12.5.)

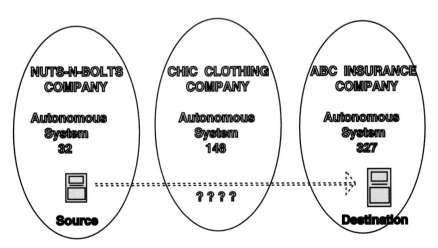

**Figure 12.5** A routing policy decision.

### 12.8.1   The *ipForwardTable*

The *ipForwardTable* below is the proposed alternative to the original *ipRouteTable*. In the future, the original *ipRouteTable* may be deprecated, with the *ipForwardTable* becoming the standard. However, at this writing, the new table still was undergoing testing and possible revision.

The original table was indexed only by the route destination. The new table is indexed by destination, protocol used, forwarding policy, and next hop. Indexing by the next hop as well as the destination supports multipathing. Indexing by protocol enables IP to search first for routes learned via a more advanced protocol, such as OSPF.

To accommodate the *ipForwardTable* and one additional variable, a new node is created under ip:

```
ipForward { ip 24 }
```

or

```
1 . 3 . 6 . 1 . 2 . 1 . 4 . 24
```

The first variable under this node is a Gauge variable that counts the number of valid entries in the *ipForwardTable*.

```
ipForwardNumber 1.3.6.1.2.1.4.24.1
```

The *ipForwardProto* variable in Table 12.6, the *ipForwardTable*, takes on the same values as the *ipRouteProto* variable in the older routing table. A new 15th value, *idpr* or Inter Domain Policy Routing, has been added to the list.

## 12.9   IP ADDRESS TRANSLATION TABLE

We have one more table in the *ip* group containing configuration information. Table 12.7, the IP Address Translation Table, maps IP addresses to technology-specific addresses. This table is intended to replace the now deprecated Address Translation table described in Chapter 10. The new table also improves on the old version by including the *ipNetToMediaType* variable. This variable indicates whether an entry is a static manually entered type, or was discovered by a dynamic protocol such as ARP. An entry can be deleted from the table by setting this variable to *invalid*.

The table is indexed by two variables: *ipNetToMediaIfIndex,* the *ifIndex* for the interface to be used, and *ipNetToMediaNetAddress,* the IP address of the system that we want to reach.

**TABLE 12.6    Proposed IP Forwarding Table**

iso.org.dod.internet.mgmt.mib-
2.ip.ipForward.ipForwardTable.ipForwardEntry
1.3.6.1.2.1.4.24.2.1

| OBJECT IDENTIFIER | Syntax | Access | Description |
|---|---|---|---|
| ipForwardDest<br>1.3.6.1.2.1.4.24.2.1<br>▶ **Index** | IpAddress | read-only | A destination IP address.* 0.0.0.0 is used for a default entry. |
| ipForwardMask<br>1.3.6.1.2.1.4.24.2.2 | IpAddress | read-write | Logical-AND this mask to a destination address before comparing it with the *ipForwardDest* of this row. |
| ipForwardPolicy<br>1.3.6.1.2.1.4.24.2.3<br>▶ **Index** | INTEGER | read-only | A value indicating the Type of Service on this route, or some other protocol-specific policy for route choice. |
| ipForwardNext Hop<br>1.3.6.1.2.1.4.24.2.4<br>▶ **Index** | IpAddress | read-only | For a remote route, the address of the next-hop system; otherwise, 0.0.0.0. |
| ipForwardIf Index<br>1.3.6.1.2.1.4.24.2.5 | INTEGER | read-write | The *ifIndex* of the interface used to reach the next hop. |
| ipForwardType<br>1.3.6.1.2.1.4.24.2.6 | INTEGER other(1), invalid(2), local(3), remote(4) | read-write | Type of route. |
| ipForwardProto<br>1.3.6.1.2.1.4.24.2.7<br>▶ **Index** | INTEGER | read-only | The method by which the route was learned (see Sec. 12.7.2). |
| ipForwardAge<br>1.3.6.1.2.1.4.24.2.8 | INTEGER | read-only | Number of seconds since the route was updated or otherwise found to be correct. |
| ipForwardInfo<br>1.3.6.1.2.1.4.24.2.9 | OBJECT IDENT-IFIER | read-write | An OBJECT IDENTIFIER referencing a MIB for this route's protocol. ({0 0} if unavailable.) |
| ipForwardNext HopAS<br>1.3.6.1.2.1.4.24.2.10 | INTEGER | read-write | If the next-hop router is in a different administration, the Autonomous System number for the next hop, otherwise 0. |

**TABLE 12.6     Proposed IP Forwarding Table (*Continued*)**

iso.org.dod.internet.mgmt.mib-
2.ip.ipForward.ipForwardTable.ipForwardEntry
1.3.6.1.2.1.4.24.2.1

| OBJECT IDENTIFIER | Syntax | Access | Description |
|---|---|---|---|
| ipForwardMetric1 1.3.6.1.2.1.4.24.2.11 | INTEGER | read-write | Primary routing metric for this route. Its meaning depends on the protocol. If not used, set to −1. |
| ipForwardMetric2 1.3.6.1.2.1.4.24.2.12 | INTEGER | read-write | An alternate routing metric. Its meaning depends on the protocol. If not used, set to −1. |
| ipForwardMetric3 1.3.6.1.2.1.4.24.2.13 | INTEGER | read-write | An alternate routing metric. Its use depends on the protocol. If not used, set to −1. |
| ipForwardMetric4 1.3.6.1.2.1.4.24.2.14 | INTEGER | read-write | An alternate routing metric. Its use depends on the protocol. If not used, set to −1. |
| ipForwardMetric5 1.3.6.1.2.1.4.24.2.15 | INTEGER | read-write | An alternate route metric. Its use depends on the protocol. If not used, set to −1. |

* There can be multiple entries with the same destination, since some protocols allow traffic to be split across several routes.

## 12.10   IP STATISTICS

The next sets of variables record counts of incoming and outgoing IP traffic and errors.

### 12.10.1   A *netstat* Example

Some readers may be familiar with the UNIX *netstat -s* command, used to display TCP/IP statistics.* The display below shows counts for incoming IP traffic:

```
netstat -s
ip:
   650331 total packets received
   0 bad header checksums
```

---

* The netstat command has been ported to many other systems.

**TABLE 12.7   IP Address Translation Table**

iso.org.dod.internet.mgmt.mib-
2.ip.ipNetToMediaTable.ipNetToMediaEntry
1.3.6.1.2.1.4.22.1

| OBJECT IDENTIFIER | Syntax | Access | Description |
|---|---|---|---|
| ipNetToMedia IfIndex 1.3.6.1.2.1.4.22.1.1 ▶ **Index** | INTEGER | read-write | The index of this interface. |
| ipNetToMedia PhysAddress 1.3.6.1.2.1.4.22.1.2 | Phys Address | read-write | A Physical address of the interface. |
| ipNetToMedia NetAddress 1.3.6.1.2.1.4.22.1.3 ▶ **Index** | IpAddress | read-write | The IP address. |
| ipNetToMedia Type 1.3.6.1.2.1.4.22.1.4 | INTEGER other(1), invalid(2), dynamic(3), static(4) | read-write | How the entry was learned. Also, use invalid to delete the entry. |

```
0 with size smaller than minimum
0 with data size < data length
0 with header length < data size
0 with data length < header length
1199 fragments received
0 fragments dropped (dup or out of space)
1 fragment dropped after timeout
0 packets forwarded
0 packets not forwardable
0 redirects sent
0 ip input queue drops
```

## 12.10.2   Definitions of Statistics

Table 12.8 defines a similar set of counters that record what happens to incoming datagrams. Some get discarded, some are delivered to protocols (such as TCP or UDP) at the system, and some are forwarded.

The table also defines counters that record outgoing datagram activity. Datagrams may be discarded for one reason or another. Among those successfully forwarded, some need to be fragmented first.

Who forwards datagrams? Routers do, because that is their main job. Some hosts may be configured so that they also are capable of rout-

**TABLE 12.8　IP Statistics**

| | iso.org.dod.internet.mgmt.mib-2.ip 1.3.6.1.2.1.4. | | |
|---|---|---|---|
| OBJECT IDENTIFIER | Syntax | Access | Description |
| ipInReceives 1.3.6.1.2.1.4.3 | Counter | read-only | Total number of incoming datagrams. |
| ipInHdr Errors 1.3.6.1.2.1.4.4 | Counter | read-only | Input datagrams discarded due to header errors (bad checksums, version number mismatch, format errors, time-to-live exceeded, bad IP options, etc.) |
| ipInAddr Errors 1.3.6.1.2.1.4.5 | Counter | read-only | Input datagrams discarded because the destination IP address was not valid here. |
| ipForw Datagrams 1.3.6.1.2.1.4.6 | Counter | read-only | Number of incoming datagrams for which forwarding was attempted. |
| ipIn Unknown Protos 1.3.6.1.2.1.4.7 | Counter | read-only | Datagrams addressed to this system whose protocol was unknown or unsupported. |
| ipInDiscards 1.3.6.1.2.1.4.8 | Counter | read-only | Correct datagrams that were discarded anyway, possibly because of lack of buffer memory. |
| ipInDelivers 1.3.6.1.2.1.4.9 | Counter | read-only | The number of IP datagrams delivered to local protocols. |
| ipOutRequests 1.3.6.1.2.1.4.10 | Counter | read-only | Total number of datagrams originating locally. |
| ipOutDiscards 1.3.6.1.2.1.4.11 | Counter | read-only | Output datagrams discarded although there was no error (but possibly a lack of buffer space). |
| ipOutNo Routes 1.3.6.1.2.1.4.12 | Counter | read-only | Output datagrams discarded because no route can be found. |
| ipReasm Timeout 1.3.6.1.2.1.4.13 | INTEGER | read-only | The maximum number of seconds that received fragments are held for reassembly. |
| ipReasm Reqds 1.3.6.1.2.1.4.14 | Counter | read-only | The number of IP fragments received which needed to be reassembled. |
| ipReasmOKs 1.3.6.1.2.1.4.15 | Counter | read-only | The number of IP datagrams successfully reassembled. |
| ipReasmFails 1.3.6.1.2.1.4.16 | Counter | read-only | The number of times that reassembly failed. |

**TABLE 12.8   IP Statistics (*Continued*)**

| OBJECT IDENTIFIER | iso.org.dod.internet.mgmt.mib-2.ip 1.3.6.1.2.1.4. | | |
| --- | --- | --- | --- |
| | Syntax | Access | Description |
| ipFragOKs 1.3.6.1.2.1.4.17 | Counter | read-only | Number of successfully fragmented datagrams. |
| ipFragFails 1.3.6.1.2.1.4.18 | Counter | read-only | Number of IP datagrams discarded because they needed to be fragmented but could not be. |
| ipFragCreates 1.3.6.1.2.1.4.19 | Counter | read-only | Number of IP datagram fragments created. |

ing. Even a host that is configured as *nonforwarding* has to forward datagrams if it is on a source route list in an IP header.

Occasionally, datagram fragments arrive and must be held until all of the pieces are put together.

Note that even at a router, some datagrams are delivered to a local protocol—routing information updates and network management messages are two examples.

All of the counters are read-only. The values cannot be reset. Meaningful numbers are obtained by calculating the *difference* between the counter's reading at the end and beginning of an interval. Each counter will increase to $2^{32} - 1$ and then wrap around to 0. Of course, if the network management process reinitializes (e.g., due to system restart) counters may be reset (e.g., to 0), so it is best to check *sysUpTime* when reading counters.

One of the variables listed is not a statistical counter. It is the timeout on holding fragments for reassembly into a complete datagram.

## 12.11   COUNTING DATAGRAM FLOW WITH CASE DIAGRAMS

Figure 12.6 shows a Case diagram of the flow of incoming datagrams arriving at the IP layer. Some datagrams are fragments that need to be reassembled. Some are discarded. Some are delivered to local protocols such as TCP, UDP, ICMP, RIP, or OSPF.

Some need to be forwarded. These join the flow of outgoing datagrams that originated at higher layers in the local system. Some of these are discarded, some are fragmented and rejoin the outbound flow as multiple smaller datagrams.

Figure 12.6 shows datagrams leaving or joining the flows into and out of the system.

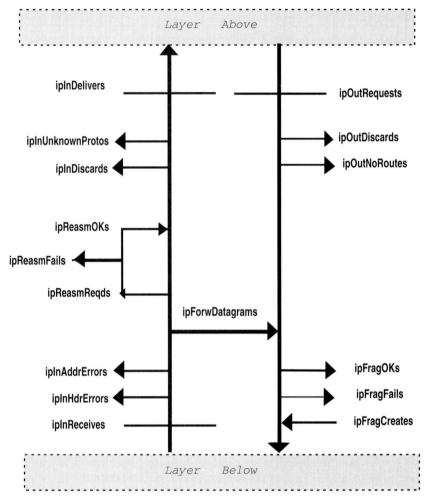

**Figure 12.6** Case diagram datagram flows.

## 12.12   PROPRIETARY VARIABLES OF INTEREST

Router vendors can define MIBs that contain variables that assist in controlling their products. Proprietary router MIBs tend to be quite large, because of the advanced multiprotocol routing, memory management, security, and priority functions performed by high-end routers.

Below we show the result of a poll of a Cisco router for a few of its memory management variables. The router has small, medium, and large memory buffers. Routing lookups are cached in buffers for fast reuse.

First, we list some brief definitions for the variables:

| | |
|---|---|
| *freeMem* | Amount of free memory in bytes |
| *bufferElFree* | Total number of free buffer elements |
| *bufferElMax* | Maximum number of buffer elements |
| *bufferElHits* | Number of buffer element hits |
| *bufferElMiss* | Number of buffer element misses |
| *bufferElCreate* | Number of buffer element creates |
| *bufferSmSize* | Size of small buffers |
| *bufferSmTotal* | Number of small buffers |
| *bufferSmFree* | Number of free small buffers |

The PSI *snmplookup* poll below shows that the router has more than 13.7 million bytes of free memory. There are 500 free buffer elements. There have been over 24 million buffer hits, no misses, and no creates. Small buffers consist of 104 bytes. There are 120 small buffers and 118 of them are free.

```
enterprises_cisco_local_1system_freeMem_0          0xd21590    13768080
enterprises_cisco_local_1system_bufferElFree_0     0x1f4       500
enterprises_cisco_local_1system_bufferElMax_0      0x1f4       500
enterprises_cisco_local_1system_bufferElHit_0      0x16ee668   24045160
enterprises_cisco_local_1system_bufferElMiss_0     0x0         0
enterprises_cisco_local_1system_bufferElCreate_0   0x0         0
enterprises_cisco_local_1system_bufferSmSize_0     0x68        104
enterprises_cisco_local_1system_bufferSmTotal_0    0x78        120
enterprises_cisco_local_1system_bufferSmFree_0     0x76        118
```

## 12.13   THE HELPFUL *GET-NEXT*

The easiest way to query a router to check up on some or all of its entries relating to a destination is to use *get-next* to locate the relevant entries. The *get-next-request* does not require that the OBJECT IDEN-TIFIER in the request exactly match an entry in the routing table. A management application should start a search with an entry that is lexicographically smaller than the destination and continue until it reaches an entry that is larger.

## 12.14   NETWORK MANAGEMENT CONSIDERATIONS

From the point of view of the overall health of an internet, the most important issue is whether the routers' tables are correct. Symptoms of a routing problem would include:

- High ICMP counts (see Chapter 13) for Destination Unreachable or Time-to-Live expired messages
- Complaints from end users who cannot set up connections
- Excessive *ipOutNoRoutes*

If you know that there is a problem reaching a particular destination, you can use the *traceroute* tool* to display the path that is followed toward that destination. Then you can poll routers that appear to be in trouble and check their current routing table entries. Check the *default* entries at routers very carefully—they can lead to routing loops or very strange routes.

It is important to avoid frequent congestion at a router. ICMP source quenches will signal this problem, but it is helpful to get a warning *before* the network starts to throw traffic away. Checking on memory utilization on a regular basis provides an early warning system for congestion conditions. It may be possible to rearrange the memory allocated to router queues, or just add more memory to the system, so that more is available for the most heavily used routes.

Another variable that can signal that there is a potential problem at a router is a high rate of discarding good routes (*ipRoutingDiscards*). The router may not have sufficient resources to record all of the routes that it needs to remember. Reconfiguration, additional memory, or a software upgrade may be needed.

Periodic counts of incoming and outgoing datagrams retrieved from major service hosts and routers on the network are useful in establishing baseline behavior at different times of day. It is a good idea to perform occasional spot checks of error and fragmentation counts, in order to pinpoint a misconfigured application.

## 12.15  RECOMMENDED READING

The author's earlier book, *TCP/IP: Architecture, Protocols, and Implementation,* contains detailed discussions of the TCP/IP protocol suite. Douglas Comer's books on *Internetworking with TCP/IP* are textbook standards. Volume II contains a complete sample TCP/IP implementation written in C code.

RFC 1354, *IP Forwarding Table MIB,* defines the proposed improved routing table. Reading the manuals for router products can provide good insights into router configuration and management.

---

* The *traceroute* tool will be described in Chapter 13.

# 13

# Managing with ICMP

## 13.1 INTRODUCTION

The Internet Control Message Protocol (ICMP) is an essential component of IP. When IP runs into a problem delivering a datagram, an ICMP message is sent back to the source. There also are some very useful ICMP service messages—most notably the echo message, which is the basis of the *ping* function used to check whether systems are active and to test response time.

## 13.2 THE ELEMENTS OF THE ICMP PROTOCOL

### 13.2.1 Error Reporting

IP is not responsible for reliable delivery but just makes a best effort at delivering datagrams to a destination.

The higher layers using IP need to know when there are problems in the network. Is it impossible to find a path to the destination? Is there congestion along the way? It is ICMP's job to send the word back.

Specifically, when a router or host runs into a problem in handling an incoming IP datagram, the problem is turned over to an ICMP procedure that generates a descriptive error message and sends it back to the source of the datagram. Error messages include:

- *Destination unreachable.* The datagram could not be delivered because a network, host, or service could not be reached, or fragmentation was required but was forbidden.

- *Time exceeded.* The datagram's Time-To-Live hop count expired, or else a destination host timed out while trying to reassemble a fragmented datagram.

- *Redirect.*   A local router informs a host that there is another router on the local network with a better route to the destination in the datagram.

- *Source quench.*   A router or host reports that it is congested, and requests a traffic slowdown.

- *Parameter problem.*   Some field (most frequently an option field) in the IP header is invalid.

When a system receives an ICMP error message, it is handled by a procedure that accepts and records incoming error messages and notifies the upper-layer protocols appropriately.

### 13.2.2   Service Messages

ICMP also provides a trio of service requests and responses. The *echo request* and *echo response* are the basis of the popular *ping* function. The *address mask request* and *address mask reply* enable systems on a LAN that have not been configured with a mask to find out what subnet address mask is in use. The timestamp request and reply can indicate a rough idea of the difference between the times at two systems.

### 13.3   REPORTING ICMP TRAFFIC

As noted in Chapter 12, many host TCP/IP products include a *netstat* command with a subcommand that displays statistics for local protocol traffic. The lines that follow are taken from a *netstat* report on ICMP activity counts, measured since the system was booted:

```
Input histogram:
    destination unreachable: 54
    source quench: 177
    echo: 1016
    time exceeded: 15

Output histogram:
    echo reply: 1016
    destination unreachable: 472
```

*Netstat* shows what is going on at the local host. Suppose that you want to get statistics for remote systems. A management station uses SNMP to gather similar counts from systems anywhere in the network.

## 13.4   THE *icmp* SUBTREE

The *icmp* MIB subtree is made up of a list of statistical counts and one configuration parameter. The subtree is displayed in Figure 13.1.

## 13.5   ICMP STATISTICS
## FOR INCOMING TRAFFIC

Table 13.1 lists the counts that are kept on incoming ICMP messages. As usual, keep in mind that counters will continually be incremented

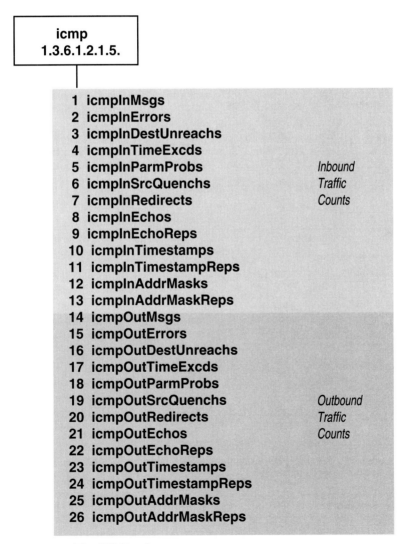

**Figure 13.1**  The ICMP subtree.

**TABLE 13.1     Statistics for Incoming ICMP Messages**

| OBJECT IDENTIFIER | Syntax | Access | Description |
|---|---|---|---|
| iso.org.dod.internet.mgmt.mib-2.icmp. 1.3.6.1.2.1.5. | | | |
| icmpInMsgs 1.3.6.1.2.1.5.1 | Counter | read-only | Total number of incoming ICMP messages. |
| icmpInErrors 1.3.6.1.2.1.5.2 | Counter | read-only | Number of incoming ICMP messages that contained errors (e.g., bad checksum, length, type). |
| icmpIn DestUnreachs 1.3.6.1.2.1.5.3 | Counter | read-only | Number of incoming ICMP Destination Unreachable messages. |
| icmpIn TimeExcds 1.3.6.1.2.1.5.4 | Counter | read-only | Number of incoming ICMP Time Exceeded messages. These signal expired Time-To-Lives and timeouts on reassembly of fragments. |
| icmpIn ParmProbs 1.3.6.1.2.1.5.5 | Counter | read-only | Number of incoming ICMP Parameter Problem messages (most often relate to problems in optional IP header fields). |
| icmpIn SrcQuenchs 1.3.6.1.2.1.5.6 | Counter | read-only | Number of incoming ICMP Source Quench messages. |
| icmpIn Redirects 1.3.6.1.2.1.5.7 | Counter | read-only | Number of incoming ICMP Redirect messages. A host should update its routing table based on the Redirect information. |
| icmpInEchos 1.3.6.1.2.1.5.8 | Counter | read-only | Number of incoming ICMP Echo request messages |
| icmpIn EchoReps 1.3.6.1.2.1.5.9 | Counter | read-only | Number of ICMP Echo Reply messages received. |
| icmpIn Timestamps 1.3.6.1.2.1.5.10 | Counter | read-only | Number of incoming ICMP Timestamp requests received. |
| icmpIn Timestamp Reps 1.3.6.1.2.1.5.11 | Counter | read-only | Number of incoming ICMP Timestamp Reply messages received. |
| icmpIn AddrMasks 1.3.6.1.2.1.5.12 | Counter | read-only | Number of incoming ICMP Address Mask Requests received. |
| icmpInAddr MaskReps 1.3.6.1.2.1.5.13 | Counter | read-only | Number of incoming ICMP Address Mask Reply messages received. |

until they wrap around. Hence, only differences in value across a sampling interval have significance.

## 13.6   ICMP STATISTICS
## FOR OUTGOING TRAFFIC

Table 13.2 lists the counts that are kept for outgoing ICMP messages. Here again, the most interesting numbers from the network management point of view are the counts of Source Quenches, Time-to-Live Expired, and Destination Unreachables. A large count during an interval can signal routing problems or congestion at the node being polled.

## 13.7   COUNTING MESSAGES
## WITH A CASE DIAGRAM

The Case diagram for ICMP is very simple. (See Figure 13.2.) The total number of incoming ICMP messages is counted by the *icmpInMsgs* variable. Some of the incoming messages are badly formed—e.g., have bad checksums or bad type fields. These are discarded. The rest of the incoming flow is split into the various message types, and these are handled by an ICMP procedure.

The total number of outgoing messages passed to the lower layers for transmission is counted in *icmpOutMsgs*. This flow is the sum of the different types of messages generated by the appropriate ICMP procedure, minus those that get discarded before a send can be attempted—typically because of a shortage of buffer memory.

## 13.8   SAMPLE OUTPUT
## OBTAINED WITH SNMP

The dialogue below shows part of an interaction between a management station and a router obtained using the PSI *snmplookup* tool. To simplify the display, some of the text label prefixes have been omitted.

```
snmp> agent 128.1.1.50
snmp> query 1.1.0
mib_system_sysDescr_0    GS   Software   (GS3-K),   Version
9.1(4.3), MAINTENANCE INTERIM TEST SOFTWARE
Copyright (c) 1986-1993 by cisco Systems, Inc.
Compiled Mon 19-Apr-93 11:59 by daveu
snmp>
snmp> query 1.3.0
mib_system_sysUpTime_0    0xda67858    229013592
```

**TABLE 13.2    Statistics for Outgoing ICMP Messages**

| | iso.org.dod.internet.mgmt.mib-2.icmp. 1.3.6.1.2.1.5. | | | |
|---|---|---|---|---|
| OBJECT IDENTIFIER | Syntax | Access | Description |
| icmpOutMsgs 1.3.6.1.2.1.5.14 | Counter | read-only | Total number of ICMP messages that the entity attempted to send. |
| icmpOut Errors 1.3.6.1.2.1.5.15 | Counter | read-only | Number of failed attempts to send ICMP messages due to problems such as lack of buffer space. |
| icmpOut DestUnreachs 1.3.6.1.2.1.5.16 | Counter | read-only | Number of ICMP messages sent to report unreachable destinations. |
| icmpOut TimeExcds 1.3.6.1.2.1.5.17 | Counter | read-only | Number of ICMP messages sent to report Time Exceeded. |
| icmpOut ParmProbs 1.3.6.1.2.1.5.18 | Counter | read-only | Number of ICMP messages sent to report a Parameter Problem. |
| icmpOut SrcQuenchs 1.3.6.1.2.1.5.19 | Counter | read-only | Number of ICMP Source Quench messages sent. |
| icmpOut Redirects 1.3.6.1.2.1.5.20 | Counter | read-only | For a router, the number of ICMP Redirect messages sent. (Hosts do not send Redirects.) |
| icmpOutEchos 1.3.6.1.2.1.5.21 | Counter | read-only | Number of ICMP Echo Request messages sent. |
| icmpOut EchoReps 1.3.6.1.2.1.5.22 | Counter | read-only | Number of ICMP Echo Reply messages sent. |
| icmpOut Timestamps 1.3.6.1.2.1.5.23 | Counter | read-only | Number of ICMP Timestamp Request messages sent. |
| icmpOut Timestamp Reps 1.3.6.1.2.1.5.24 | Counter | read-only | Number of ICMP Timestamp Reply messages sent. |
| icmpOut AddrMasks 1.3.6.1.2.1.5.25 | Counter | read-only | Number of ICMP Address Mask Request messages sent. |
| icmpOut AddrMask Reps 1.3.6.1.2.1.5.26 | Counter | read-only | Number of ICMP Address Mask Reply messages sent. |

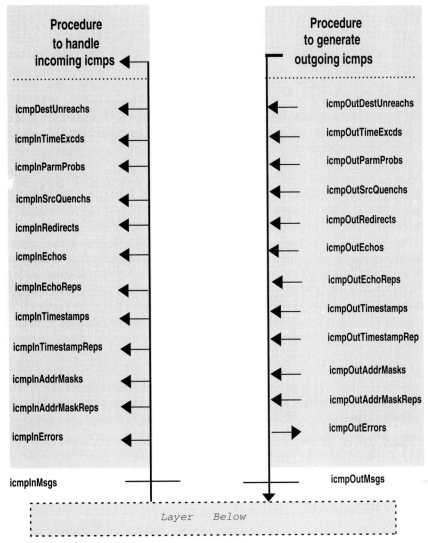

**Figure 13.2**  A Case diagram for ICMP data flow.

Recall that *sysUpTime* is measured in hundredths of a second. The system has been up for approximately 26 days and 12 hours.

```
snmp> mquery 5
mib_icmp_icmpInMsgs_0            0x2912b      168235
mib_icmp_icmpInErrors_0         0x0          0
mib_icmp_icmpInDestUnreachs_0   0xa3         163
mib_icmp_icmpInTimeExcds_0      0xf1         241
```

```
mib_icmp_icmpInParmProbs_0          0x0        0
mib_icmp_icmpInSrcQuenchs_0         0x0        0
mib_icmp_icmpInRedirects_0          0x2fa      762
```

## 13.9   CHECKING THE CHANGES BETWEEN TWO POLLS

The raw numbers are not particularly informative. Table 13.3 shows the results of two polls of ICMP statistics obtained using *snmplookup*.

The time between these two polls is about 12 hours; normally we would poll over shorter intervals, such as 15 minutes. There were 1441 incoming messages during that time period consisting of 1420 echo requests and 21 Time-to-Live expired messages. Other systems were probably using echo requests to check the router on a regular basis to make sure that it was running.

There were 3832 outgoing messages. These broke down into 2406 destination unreachables, 1420 replies to the echo requests, and 6 Time-to-Live exceeds.

*Snmplookup* is a basic tool. It is up to applications at a management station to display these values into a format that shows you what you need to know, highlight changes of interest in event logs, and perhaps even trigger an automatic procedure to explore for more data or initiate recovery from a problem.

## 13.10   WATCHING OUT FOR MISLEADING "ERRORS"

It is important to keep in mind that sometimes network tools can create misleading "error" counts.

### 13.10.1   TTL Exceededs Generated by the Traceroute Tool

For example, the very useful *traceroute* tool charts the path to a destination. Going from a location in Princeton, New Jersey, to a node in New Zealand whose nickname is *archie.nz* (and whose real name is *tahi.isor.vuw.ac.nz*), our path is:

```
traceroute archie.nz
traceroute to tahi.isor.vuw.ac.nz (130.195.9.4), 30 hops max, 40 byte packets
 1  net-gateway (128.127.15.3)  2 ms  2 ms  2 ms
 2  ford-gateway (130.94.0.49)  4 ms  3 ms  4 ms
 3  enss (192.12.211.3)  4 ms  3 ms  4 ms
 4  t3-1.New-York-cnss33.t3.ans.net  (140.222.33.2)  17 ms  6 ms  6 ms
 5  t3-3.New-York-cnss32.t3.ans.n  (140.222.32.4)  8 ms  6 ms  6 ms
```

**TABLE 13.3   Reviewing Two Sets of ICMP Statistics**

| icmp Object | Initial reading | 12 hours later | Difference |
|---|---|---|---|
| icmpInMsgs_0 | 168235 | 169676 | 1,441 |
| icmpInErrors_0 | 0 | 0 | 0 |
| icmpInDestUnreachs_0 | 163 | 163 | 0 |
| icmpInTimeExcds_0 | 241 | 262 | 21 |
| icmpInParmProbs_0 | 0 | 0 | 0 |
| icmpInSrcQuenchs_0 | 0 | 0 | 0 |
| icmpInRedirects_0 | 762 | 762 | 0 |
| icmpInEchos_0 | 75521 | 76941 | 1,420 |
| icmpInEchoReps_0 | 91516 | 91516 | 0 |
| icmpInTimestamps_0 | 0 | 0 | 0 |
| icmpInTimestampReps_0 | 0 | 0 | 0 |
| icmpInAddrMasks_0 | 16 | 16 | 0 |
| icmpInAddrMaskReps_0 | 16 | 16 | 0 |
| icmpOutMsgs_0 | 281520 | 285352 | 3,832 |
| icmpOutErrors_0 | 0 | 0 | 0 |
| icmpOutDestUnreachs_0 | 100893 | 103299 | 2,406 |
| icmpOutTimeExcds_0 | 1723 | 1729 | 6 |
| icmpOutParmProbs_0 | 0 | 0 | 0 |
| icmpOutSrcQuenchs_0 | 0 | 0 | 0 |
| icmpOutRedirects_0 | 11500 | 11500 | 0 |
| icmpOutEchos_0 | 91925 | 91925 | 0 |
| icmpOutEchoReps_0 | 75521 | 76941 | 1,420 |
| icmpOutTimestamps_0 | 0 | 0 | 0 |
| icmpOutTimestampReps_0 | 0 | 0 | 0 |
| icmpOutAddrMasks_0 | 0 | 0 | 0 |
| icmpOutAddrMaskReps_0 | 0 | 0 | 0 |

```
 6  t3-1.Cleveland-cnss40.t3.ans.net  (140.222.40.2)  18 ms   22 ms   18 ms
 7  t3-2.Chicago-cnss24.t3.ans.net  (140.222.24.3)  25 ms   25 ms   25 ms
 8  t3-1.San-Francisco-cnss8.t3.ans.net  (140.222.8.2)  65 ms   65 ms   65 ms
 9  t3-0.San-Francisco-cnss9.t3.ans.net  (140.222.9.1)  66 ms   68 ms   66 ms
10  t3-0.enss144.t3.ans.net  (140.222.144.1)  68 ms   67 ms   68 ms
11  ARC2.NSN.NASA.GOV  (192.52.195.11)  69 ms   70 ms   68 ms
12  132.160.254.2  (132.160.254.2)  674 ms   673 ms   673 ms
13  feba-aotearoa.waikato.tuia.net.nz(140.200.128.3)  676 ms   675 ms   676 ms
14  gw-fr.vuw.tuia.net.nz  (140.200.240.4)  708 ms   777 ms   708 ms
15  csc.net.vuw.ac.nz  (130.195.254.1)  710 ms   1649 ms   709 ms
16  tahi.isor.vuw.ac.nz  (130.195.9.4)  712 ms   709 ms   710 ms
```

*Traceroute* launches three UDP datagrams toward the destination with Time-to-Live (TTL) set to 1. At the first router, the TTL of each is decremented to 0. ICMP error messages reporting TTL expired are sent back to the source, which reports the round-trip times. The *traceroute* example above triggered a total of 48 TTL expired messages. An administrator who used *traceroute* to check up on several routes could trigger transmission of many TTL errors!

### 13.10.2   Destination Unreachables
### Generated by MTU Discovery

The *Maximum Transmission Unit* (MTU) *discovery* procedure can be the source of misleading Destination Unreachable messages. The purpose of MTU discovery is to find the size of the largest datagrams that can be sent to a destination without requiring fragmentation.

A source launches probing datagrams with the "Don't Fragment" flag set on. If a router cannot deliver the datagram without fragmentation, a Destination Unreachable ICMP message is sent back. This message contains the largest datagram size that *could* have been forwarded. MTU discovery would cause both hosts and routers to report a large number of Destination Unreachable messages that did not result from any routing problems.

## 13.11   CUSTOMIZED ICMP POLLING

NetView/6000 makes it very easy to build customized polling functions that can be launched by clicking on a menu line. Figure 13.3 shows the results of running a customized function *Check incoming ICMP errors,* that displays ICMP statistics.

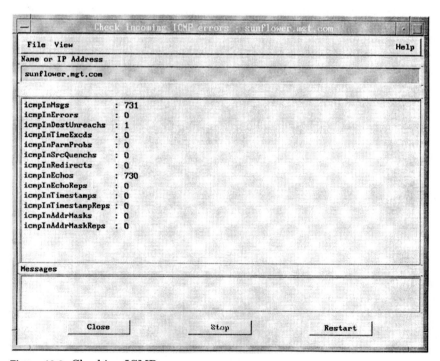

**Figure 13.3**  Checking ICMP errors.

The poll includes some variables that are not very interesting for network management—for example, counts of timestamp and address mask messages. Figure 13.4 (Modify MIB Application) illustrates how the function can be modified to add or delete poll variables.

## 13.12 NETWORK MANAGEMENT CONSIDERATIONS

The most interesting numbers from the network management point of view are the numbers of Source Quenches, Time-to-Live Expired, and Destination Unreachables.

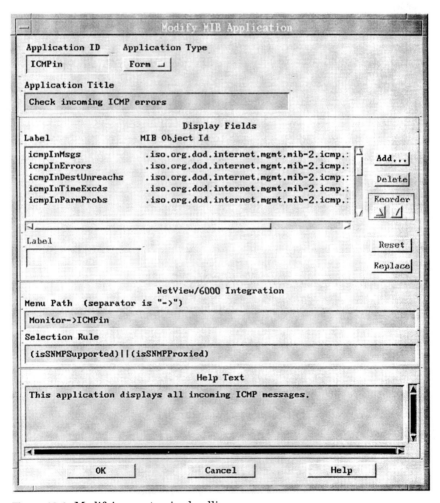

**Figure 13.4** Modifying customized polling.

A high count of *icmpInSrcQuenchs, icmpInTimeExcds,* or *icmpIn-DestUnreachs* messages is usually a symptom of trouble on the network. When this happens, it is a good idea to check that critical routers and links are operating. Fortunately, the ICMP *echo* message enables you to perform quick checks of connectivity.

A large number of parameter problems may signal a poorly implemented or misconfigured system.

A host that has access to more than one local router may receive some redirect messages. There are several problems that might cause a system to receive a large number of redirects:

- Significant transient changes to routing on the network.

- Incorrect manually entered static records in the system's routing table.

- A poorly implemented TCP/IP product that throws away redirect messages and stubbornly continues to misroute datagrams. Some PC products do this.

The most commonly seen incoming *service* messages are *echo* (ping) requests or responses. Occasionally, a few address mask requests or replies are logged. Routers usually are configured so that they can reply to address mask requests. However, not very many systems rely on the use of the address mask request to find out their subnet masks. Exchanges of timestamp requests and replies are even rarer.

# 14

# Managing TCP

## 14.1  INTRODUCTION

TCP is responsible for setting up connections, supporting reliable exchanges of data between the connection partners, and terminating connections. The TCP Protocol Data Unit is called a *segment.* Specifically, a segment is a TCP message which consists of a TCP header and (optionally*) some application data.

## 14.2  THE ELEMENTS OF THE TCP PROTOCOL

TCP is a layer 4 protocol. TCP segments are packaged in IP datagrams for transmission across a network. The protocol field in IP header is set to 6, signaling that a TCP segment is enclosed.

### 14.2.1  Socket Addresses

An endpoint of a TCP connection is identified by its *socket address,* which is the combination of its IP address and application *port number.* Permanent "well-known" port numbers ranging from 1 to 1023 are assigned to standard applications services. For example, a file transfer server operates at application port number 21. In contrast, client applications are assigned port numbers from a shared pool of numbers ranging from 1024 to 65535. A TCP connection is uniquely identified by the socket addresses at the two ends.

---

\* Sometimes no data is sent along with the TCP header. The header alone can be used to acknowledge received data, to report a change in receive buffer size, or to make sure that the partner at the other end is still awake.

### 14.2.2  Connection States

Typically, a server program initializes and passively starts to *listen* for clients. A client actively requests a connection with the server.

The connection is opened by means of *synchronize* (or *syn*) messages exchanged by the connection partners. After a successful opening, the connection is in an *established* state.

The connection is terminated with an exchange of *fin* messages. The connection advances through several intermediate states during termination, finally *closing*. However, old duplicate data could still be making its way toward either of the partners after the connection has been closed. For this reason, the connection sticks around in a *time wait* state so that data stragglers can be discarded gracefully.

### 14.2.3  A *netstat* Display

One of the many *netstat* command options reports on current active connections. It also lists server applications that are *listening* for clients. The display below shows part of a *netstat* report of the TCP connections for a system.

The *Local Address* and *Foreign Address* columns contain the socket addresses for the ends of each connection. The display replaces numeric IP addresses and ports with system and service names wherever it can.

```
netstat-a
Active Internet connections (including servers)
Proto Recv-Q Send-Q Local Address                Foreign
Address        (state)
tcp  0      0       tigger.telnet minnie.1052     ESTABLISHED
tcp  0      0       tigger.smtp   mickey.3543      TIME_WAIT
tcp  0      0       tigger.nntp   uranus.COM.1364  ESTABLISHED
tcp  0      523     tigger.telnet vanderbilt.23050 ESTABLISHED
tcp  0      0       tigger.pop-3  bambi.57841      ESTABLISHED
tcp  0      0       tigger.telnet chip.1012        ESTABLISHED
tcp  0      0       *.gopher      *.*              LISTEN
tcp  0      0       *.printer     *.*              LISTEN
tcp  0      0       *.pop-3       *.*              LISTEN
tcp  0      0       *.nntp        *.*              LISTEN
tcp  0      0       *.login       *.*              LISTEN
tcp  0      0       *.telnet      *.*              LISTEN
tcp  0      0       *.ftp         *.*              LISTEN
```

We see that an exchange of electronic mail with the Simple Mail Transfer Protocol (*smtp*) server at *tigger* has just completed. One client is picking up the Network News (*nntp*). There are several *telnet* terminal logins. A user at *bambi* is peeking at mail (*pop-3*) that is waiting at *tigger*.

The entries containing "*" characters, such as *\*.gopher,* represent server applications that are waiting (*listening*) for clients.

### 14.2.4 Flow Control

TCP manages flow control, making sure that a sender never transmits more data than the receiver's buffers can absorb. The current MIB-II *tcp* group does not address the issue of configuring buffer sizes or checking up on overall memory utilization.

### 14.2.5 Reliability

TCP provides session reliability by:

- Numbering data
- Setting a timer when data is transmitted
- Retransmitting when the timer expires before receipt of an acknowledgment

### 14.2.6 Retransmission Timeouts and Congestion Avoidance

How long should TCP wait before timing out and retransmitting an unacknowledged segment? This is a very important value, and has impact on the overall behavior of a network. If systems retransmit too quickly, the network can be loaded with unnecessary extra traffic. If the network gets congested and starts to discard datagrams, even more retransmissions will be produced.

The right thing for TCP to do is:

- Watch each individual connection.
- Base the retransmission timeout for a connection on the actual observed times that it takes to get back an acknowledgment.
- *Slow down* if the network is congested!

It is important for TCP/IP implementations to use appropriate algorithms for computing retransmission timeouts and avoiding congestion.

### 14.3 THE TCP MIB SUBTREE

The *tcp* subtree is made up of some individual configuration and statistics variables and a table that records TCP connection activity. Figure 14.1 shows an overview.

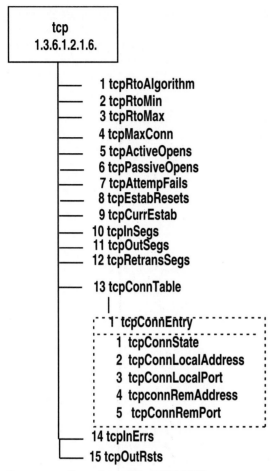

**Figure 14.1** Overview of the TCP MIB.


## 14.4 CONFIGURING TCP

The four defined TCP configuration parameters are described in Table 14.1. Note that these parameters are read-only, and cannot be configured from a management station.

The first parameter in Table 14.1 identifies the algorithm that will be used to compute the retransmission timeout. The choices are:

1. other      None of those below
2. constant    A fixed value
3. rsre       Defined in MIL-STD-1778, app. B
4. vanj      Van Jacobson's algorithm

RFC 1122, *Requirements for Internet Hosts—Communication Layers,* mandates use of Van Jacobson's algorithm. The Van Jacobson algorithm produces far better results than an earlier algorithm defined in the 1983 Military Standard version of TCP.

Use of a constant value is a poor choice. There is just too much variation between values that are needed for connections to a nearby lightly loaded LAN server, a busy local host, a system reached via a slow serial link, or hosts that are reached via a path through many routers. Further, a value that is good at one time of day may be terrible at other times.

The last parameter in Table 14.1 specifies an upper limit on the number of concurrent TCP connections that can be supported by a system.

## 14.5  TCP CONNECTION STATISTICS

An outgoing TCP connection is requested whenever a user asks for a connection-oriented service such as *telnet* terminal access or *ftp* file transfer. A user request results in a TCP *active open.*

Remote users may also access the local computer in order to log in, perform file transfer, pick up mail, or get the network news. A server runs as a background task, waiting for remote users to connect and request access. Incoming requests are counted as TCP *passive opens.*

**TABLE 14.1   TCP Configuration: Basic Parameters**

| iso.org.dod.internet.mgmt.mib-2.tcp. 1.3.6.1.2.1.6 | | | |
|---|---|---|---|
| OBJECT IDENTIFIER | Syntax | Access | Description |
| tcpRto Algorithm 1.3.6.1.2.1.6.1 | INTEGER other(1), constant(2), rsre(3), vanj(4) | read-only | The algorithm used to compute the retransmission timeout. |
| tcpRtoMin 1.3.6.1.2.1.6.2 | INTEGER | read-only | Minimum lower bound in milliseconds on the retransmission timeout. Its meaning depends on the algorithm. |
| tcpRtoMax 1.3.6.1.2.1.6.3 | INTEGER | read-only | Maximum upper bound in milliseconds allowed for a retransmission timeout (Rto). Its meaning depends on the algorithm. |
| tcpMax Conn 1.3.6.1.2.1.6.4 | INTEGER | read-only | A limit on the maximum number of concurrent TCP connections. −1 means that it is dynamically determined. |

The TCP Connection Statistics, shown in Table 14.2, count the outgoing and incoming connection attempts. More than a handful of abrupt closes indicates that some system may have been implemented incorrectly, and should be investigated. The number of current sessions gives a rough measure of the TCP network load at the computer.

## 14.6    TCP INCOMING AND OUTGOING TRAFFIC COUNTS

TCP traffic counts can provide a barometer of the network health of a host. Sometimes the TCP traffic counts from even a single (server) host can provide a useful indication of network conditions.

Table 14.3 counts incoming and outgoing segments. A large number of retransmissions is a sure sign of trouble. *Resets* are sent to refuse requests for connections, report a "strange" incoming segment, or abort a connection.

## 14.7    COUNTING SEGMENT FLOW WITH CASE DIAGRAMS

The flow of segments, as shown in the Case diagram in Figure 14.2, is quite simple. Segments are counted as they arrive from the network. Some are discarded during error screening, and the rest are delivered to their destination ports.

**TABLE 14.2    TCP Connection Statistics**

| OBJECT IDENTIFIER | Syntax | Access | Description |
|---|---|---|---|
| iso.org.dod.mgt.mib-2.tcp. 1.3.6.1.2.1.6. | | | |
| tcpActive Opens 1.3.6.1.2.1.6.5 | Counter | read-only | The number of outgoing connection requests from this system. |
| tcpPassive Opens 1.3.6.1.2.1.6.6 | Counter | read-only | The number of incoming connection requests to this system. |
| tcpAttempt Fails 1.3.6.1.2.1.6.7 | Counter | read-only | The number of failed connection requests— incoming and outgoing. |
| tcpEstab Resets 1.3.6.1.2.1.6.8 | Counter | read-only | The number of established or gracefully closing connections that have been terminated abruptly. |
| tcpCurrEstab 1.3.6.1.2.1.6.9 | Gauge | read-only | The number of TCP connections that are in either ESTABLISHED or CLOSE-WAIT state. |

**TABLE 14.3    Segment Counts**

| | iso.org.dod.mgt.mib-2.tcp. 1.3.6.1.2.1.6. | | |
|---|---|---|---|
| OBJECT IDENTIFIER | Syntax | Access | Description |
| tcpInSegs 1.3.6.1.2.1.6.10 | Counter | read-only | Total number of segments received, including those received in error. |
| tcpOutSegs 1.3.6.1.2.1.6.11 | Counter | read-only | Total number of segments sent, excluding those containing only retransmitted octets. |
| tcpRetrans Segs 1.3.6.1.2.1.6.12 | Counter | read-only | Total number of segments containing retransmitted data.* |
| tcpInErrs 1.3.6.1.2.1.6.14 | Counter | read-only | Total number of segments received with errors (e.g., bad TCP checksums). |
| tcpOutRsts 1.3.6.1.2.1.6.15 | Counter | read-only | Total number of TCP segments sent with the reset (RST) flag set to 1. |

\* When TCP retransmits data, it can repackage the segment so that some new bytes are included along with the retransmitted bytes.

TCP in the local system creates segments for three reasons:

- New application data has been submitted for transmission.
- A timeout has expired without reception of an expected acknowledgment, prompting a retransmission.
- An incoming segment that violates protocol rules prompts a reset. (For example, a very late duplicate segment arrives after a connection has been terminated.)

## 14.8    VIEWING ACTIVE TCP CONNECTIONS

In Sec. 14.2.3, we saw a display of current local TCP connections produced by the UNIX *netstat* command. Table 14.4, the TCP connection table, provides the same information to a remote network management station. Naturally enough, the table is indexed by the local and remote socket addresses. More precisely, a complete index has the form:

```
local-IP-address.local-TCP-port.remote-IP-address.remote-TCP-port
```

For example, the first line of the *netstat* display in Sec. 14.2.3 was:

```
tcp    0    0  tigger.telnet    minnie.1052    ESTABLISHED
```

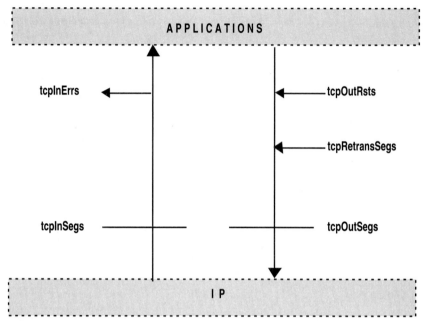

**Figure 14.2** A Case diagram showing segment flows.

The local host was tigger (128.121.50.145). The local port was 23, the well-known port for *telnet* logins. The remote host was minnie (128.121.50.141) and the remote port was 1052. Hence the complete index corresponding to this entry would be:

```
128.121.50.145.23.128.121.50.141.1052
```

Like the *netstat* display, the TCP connection table consists of the list of connection endpoints and the state of each connection.

### 14.8.1  Local Addresses

There is one technical point about the local address variable, *tcp-ConnLocalAddress*. For a host with only one IP address, its meaning is clear.

But suppose that the host is a server that happens to be connected to more than one subnet and has several IP addresses? If the server accepts clients from only one particular subnet, then the corresponding IP address is filled in. If the host is willing to accept clients through any of its interfaces, then address 0.0.0.0 is entered into the table.

If a local server is listening, waiting for a client to connect, a zero value is used as a placeholder for the remote address. In addition to

**TABLE 14.4    The TCP Connection Table**

| iso.org.dod.internet.mgmt.mib-2.tcp.tcpConnTable.tcpConnEntry 1.3.6.1.2.1.6.13.1 | | | |
|---|---|---|---|
| **OBJECT IDENTIFIER** | Syntax | Access | Description |
| tcpConnState 1.3.6.1.2.1.6.13.1.1 | INTEGER | read-write | The current state for the connection. |
| tcpConnLocal Address 1.3.6.1.2.1.6.13.1.2 ▶ **Index** | IpAddress | read-only | The local IP address for this TCP connection. |
| tcpConnLocal Port 1.3.6.1.2.1.6.13.1.3 ▶ **Index** | INTEGER (0.65535) | read-only | The local port number for this TCP connection. |
| tcpConnRem Address 1.3.6.1.2.1.6.13.1.4 ▶ **Index** | IpAddress | read-only | The remote IP address for this TCP connection. |
| tcpConnRem Port 1.3.6.1.2.1.6.13.1.5 ▶ **Index** | INTEGER (0.65535) | read-only | The remote port number for this TCP connection. |

established connections on which information is being transferred, the connection table also displays:

- Local services that are in a listen state, waiting for new clients to arrive (listen)
- Connections that are in the process of being set up (e.g., synSent or synReceived)
- Connections that are in the process of being terminated (finWait1, finWait2, closeWait, lastAck, closing, timeWait)

### 14.8.2    The Connection State

The *tcpConnState* variable reports on the current status of a connection. The values are:

1. closed
2. listen
3. synSent
4. synReceived
5. established

6. finWait1

7. finWait2

8. closeWait

9. lastAck

10. closing

11. timeWait

12. deleteTCB

A management station can *kill* a connection by *setting* the *tcp-ConnState* value to *deleteTCB,* meaning delete the *Transmission Control Block.* A connection's Transmission Control Block contains all of the information about the connection. This is the only state that can be written by a management station.

## 14.9   A MANAGEMENT STATION EXAMPLE

To get another view of a connection table, in Figure 14.3 we examine a NetView/6000 display that shows current activity at *sunflower.* There are *telnet* logins from users at *bluebell* and *crocus.* There also are five sessions with "loopback" address.

A "loopback" address means that both the client and the server are at sunflower. Pairs of applications were communicating within the

**TCP Connection Table : sunflower.mgt.com**

| File   View | | | Help |
|---|---|---|---|

**Name or IP Address**

sunflower.mgt.com

| Local Address | Remote Address | (state) |
|---|---|---|
| loopback.1080 | loopback.sunrpc | TIME-WAIT |
| loopback.1081 | loopback.sunrpc | TIME-WAIT |
| loopback.1082 | loopback.sunrpc | TIME-WAIT |
| loopback.1083 | loopback.sunrpc | TIME-WAIT |
| loopback.1084 | loopback.sunrpc | TIME-WAIT |
| sunflower.mgt.com.telnet | bluebell.mgt.com.1105 | ESTABLISHED |
| sunflower.mgt.com.telnet | crocus.mgt.com.4874 | ESTABLISHED |

**Messages**

| Close | Stop | Restart |
|---|---|---|

**Figure 14.3**   A NetView/6000 connection report.

same machine using TCP/IP, which is perfectly OK. Note that all of the loopback sessions are in TIME-WAIT state, which means that they have been terminated.

This management application offers a number of conveniences. We can push a button to save the results; we can change to a view that shows us numeric IP addresses and port numbers; or we can push a button that sends out a fresh poll.

## 14.10   NETWORK MANAGEMENT CONSIDERATIONS

Regular polls of important servers for connection statistics provide valuable usage information. Since the counters will advance relatively slowly, hourly polls suffice.

A high percentage of retransmissions is an indicator of network problems. A value of 2 percent or less is the normal retransmission rate. Therefore, frequent polls of the number of outgoing segments and number of retransmissions can be helpful. Alternatively, a monitor system can be configured to watch for excessive retransmissions, and to send a trap when a threshold (such as 5 percent) is exceeded.

If users complain of slow response or difficulty in connecting to a server, a check of the maximum permitted connections and of current connection activity can indicate whether the system is operating close to maximum network capacity. Work is under way on implementing a Host MIB. The Host MIB will provide information about overall system resource usage. Other MIBs currently being defined will provide statistics on usage for specific services, such as mail and file transfer.

# 15

# Managing UDP

## 15.1 INTRODUCTION

An application calls on the User Datagram Protocol (UDP) when it wants to send a stand-alone message to another application.

Many simple query/response applications are built on UDP. In fact, SNMP uses UDP to send *set-requests, get-requests, responses,* and *traps.*

## 15.2 THE ELEMENTS OF THE UDP PROTOCOL

UDP is a layer 4 protocol, and UDP messages are packaged in layer 3 IP datagrams for transmission across a network. UDP messages are called *UDP datagrams.* UDP datagrams are carried in IP datagrams with the protocol field in the IP header set to 17.

### 15.2.1 Socket Addresses

An endpoint of a UDP connection is identified by its socket address, which is the combination of its IP address and application port number. A pair of communicating UDP partners is uniquely identified by the socket addresses at the two ends.

### 15.2.2 Protocol Features

Unlike TCP, UDP does not guarantee delivery or provide flow control. It is up to the application that sends UDP datagrams to provide any extra support that may be needed. For example, an application that sends a query to a server asking for information can time out and retransmit if an answer does not come back in a reasonable amount of time.

Sometimes a client sends a query to a remote service that isn't there—no application is *listening* on the destination port. The remote system will throw the UDP datagram away.

## 15.3   THE UDP MIB SUBTREE

The UDP subtree is made up of some individual statistics variables and a table that records UDP services that are actively listening for clients. Figure 15.1 shows an overview.

## 15.4   UDP TRAFFIC STATISTICS

UDP is a very simple protocol, and its statistics, which are defined in Table 15.1, reflect that fact. There are counts of incoming and outgoing UDP datagrams. The number of incoming datagrams sent to a port without a listener is counted.

### 15.4.1   Viewing UDP Statistics

The PSI *snmplookup* dialog below queries a Cayman gatorbox for system information and UDP statistics. We see that Cayman has subtree 7 under *enterprises*. The system has been up for almost 20 hours. In that time, 2625 datagrams have arrived and 2502 datagrams have been sent. For 44 of the incoming datagrams, the appropriate destination application port had not been activated, and the datagrams had to be discarded. There were no other errors.

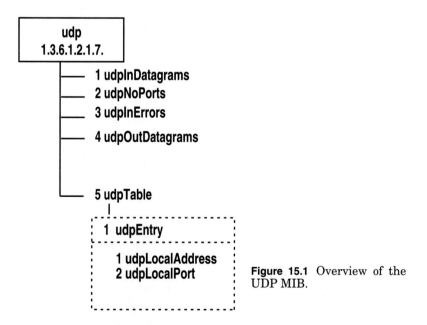

**Figure 15.1** Overview of the UDP MIB.

**TABLE 15.1    Incoming and Outgoing UDP Traffic**

| | | | |
|---|---|---|---|
| | iso.org.dod.internet.mgmt.mib-2.udp.<br>1.3.6.1.2.1.7. | | |
| OBJECT<br>IDENTIFIER | Syntax | Access | Description |
| udpIn<br>Datagrams<br>1.3.6.1.2.1.7.1 | Counter | read-<br>only | Total number of UDP<br>datagrams delivered to<br>UDP applications. |
| udpNoPorts<br>1.3.6.1.2.1.7.2 | Counter | read-<br>only | Total number of received<br>UDP datagrams for which<br>there was no application at<br>the destination port. |
| udpInErrors<br>1.3.6.1.2.1.7.3 | Counter | read-<br>only | Number of UDP datagrams<br>that could not be delivered<br>for some other reason—<br>e.g., a bad checksum or<br>insufficient memory<br>resources. |
| udpOut<br>Datagrams<br>1.3.6.1.2.1.7.4 | Counter | read-<br>only | Total number of outbound<br>UDP datagrams. |

```
snmp> mquery 1
d_internet_mgmt_mib_system_sysDescr_0      GatorShare version
                                           1.5.0 (build 1)
/  d_internet_mgmt_mib_system_sysObjectID_0   1 3 6 1 4 1 7 2 1
   d_internet_mgmt_mib_system_sysUpTime_0     0x6d0c86    7146630

snmp> mquery 7
d_internet_mgmt_mib_udp_udpInDatagrams_0  0xa41   2625
d_internet_mgmt_mib_udp_udpNoPorts_0      0x2c    44
d_internet_mgmt_mib_udp_udpInErrors_0     0x0     0
d_internet_mgmt_mib_udp_udpOutDatagrams_0 0x9c6   2502
```

## 15.5  COUNTING FLOW
## WITH A CASE DIAGRAM

The Case diagram in Figure 15.2 represents the flows of UDP data-grams entering and leaving a system.

## 15.6  A *netstat* DISPLAY

The *netstat* command that displayed TCP connection information in Chapter 14 also can be used to view UDP services. The UDP information in a *netstat* display usually follows the TCP entries:

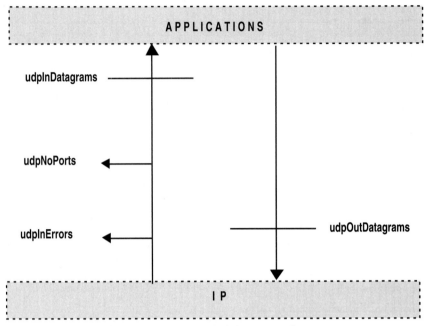

**Figure 15.2** A Case diagram showing UDP datagram flows.

```
netstat -a
Active Internet connections (including servers)
Proto Recv-Q Send-Q LocalAddressForeignAddress   (state)
tcp  0       0      tigger.telnetminnie.1052     ESTABLISHED
tcp  0       0      tigger.smtp  mickey.3543     TIME_WAIT
tcp  0       0      tigger.nntp  uranus.COM.1364 ESTABLISHED
. . .
udp  0       0      *.quotd      *.*
udp  0       0      *.chargen    *.*
udp  0       0      *.daytime    *.*
udp  0       0      *.discard    *.*
udp  0       0      *.echo       *.*
udp  0       0      *.time       *.*
udp  0       0      *.talk       *.*
udp  0       0      *.biff       *.*
udp  0       0      *.name       *.*
```

The first UDP service on the list is the quote of the day (*quotd*) or fortune cookie server, which answers every query with words of wisdom:

```
> fortune
Bradley's Bromide:
    If computers get too powerful, we can organize them into a
    committee -- that will do them in.
```

**TABLE 15.2    Information on Current UDP Listeners**

| iso.org.dod.internet.mgmt.mib-2.udp.udpTable.udpEntry 1.3.6.1.2.1.7.5.1 | | | |
|---|---|---|---|
| OBJECT IDENTIFIER | Syntax | Access | Description |
| udpLocal Address 1.3.6.1.2.1.7.5.1.1 ▶ **Index** | IpAddress | read-only | The local IP address for this UDP listener. |
| udpLocalPort 1.3.6.1.2.1.7.5.1.2 ▶ **Index** | INTEGER (0.65535) | read-only | The local port number for this UDP listener. |

```
>fortune
    If all else fails, immortality can always be assured by
    spectacular error.
        -- John Kenneth Galbraith
```

## 15.7    THE UDP LISTENER TABLE

Table 15.2, the UDP Table, records the socket addresses—that is, the IP addresses and UDP port numbers—in use by local applications that are waiting for UDP datagrams. These applications are called *listeners*. The table is indexed by IP address and UDP port number—and contains no other variables! Note that this table corresponds to the *netstat* display shown above.

# 16

# Managing the Exterior Gateway Protocol

## 16.1 INTRODUCTION

The set of routers administered by an organization is called an *Autonomous System*. When an organization receives its official domain name and network number(s) from a registration authority, it also receives a unique Autonomous System number.

One element of the TCP/IP protocol suite has been very flexible over the years. Within its own Autonomous System, an organization can choose how its routers will obtain routing information—by manual configuration, by automatic router-to-router updates using a standard *Interior Gateway Protocol* such as RIP or OSPF, or by a proprietary protocol.

But suppose that two organizations want to connect their networks. Or suppose that an organization wants to establish connectivity between some of its networks and the global Internet. How can different Autonomous Systems exchange meaningful routing information when, internally, they might be using completely different routing protocols?

Even if they use a common protocol, an Autonomous System might not want to provide the full disclosure of its topology and complete integration of routers that would occur if the boundary between the Autonomous Systems was ignored.

## 16.2 ELEMENTS OF THE EXTERIOR GATEWAY PROTOCOL

The *Exterior Gateway Protocol* (EGP), defined in RFC 904, was designed to solve these problems. EGP enables *neighboring* routers in different Autonomous Systems* to exchange limited, but useful, information. What does it take to be a *neighbor?*

- The routers should be connected to a common network. (For example, this could be a point-to-point link or a packet network.)
- The routers need to be configured so they know that they are neighbors.

The *Exterior Gateway Protocol* (EGP) provides the simplest information needed in order to route data from one network to another. An EGP router uses the protocol to announce:

- The *IP addresses of routers* that are in its Autonomous System and are attached to the same common network as the neighbor
- The internal *networks* that can be reached through each of these routers
- The *distance* from a router to each network that it can reach

Of course, the EGP router is also concerned with:

- Setting up communication by *acquiring* neighbors
- Periodically *checking* that the neighbors are still there
- Obtaining currently valid information about the *reachability* of remote networks

An EGP router is configured with a list of its EGP *neighbors.* The EGP protocol enables EGP routers to exchange network reachability information with its EGP neighbors. EGP messages are carried in IP datagrams with the protocol field in the IP header set to 8.

## 16.3   EGP SCENARIO

The easiest way to understand the operation of EGP is to walk through a scenario. One of the neighbors in an EGP pairing plays an *active* role, while the other is *passive.*

1. As the result of a *start* command generated by an operator or an automatic system procedure, the active EGP sends a request to a passive neighbor. The neighbor sends back a confirm response. This exchange is called *neighbor acquisition.*

---

* Actually, there is no law that says that neighbors in the same Autonomous System can't exchange EGP messages, but the real utility of the protocol is its ability to pass information across a border.

2. Periodically, the *active* EGP sends *Hello* messages. The *passive* EGP answers with "I Hear You" (*I-H·U*) responses.

3. Periodically, each neighbor sends *Poll* messages to the other asking for routing information. The information is returned in *Update* messages.

4. *Error* messages are sent to report problems such as the inability to provide requested information, receipt of multiple messages within a polling interval, or the receipt of garbled data.

Actually, both EGP routers can play the active role and send Hellos. However, this just uses up bandwidth without adding any functional benefit.

EGP neighbors are configured with a *Hello* interval and poll interval. The active system will replace every fourth *Hello* with a poll; hence, the polling interval should be four times the *Hello* interval. The minimum Hello and poll intervals are 30 seconds and 2 minutes.

## 16.4   THE EGP MIB SUBTREE

The *egp* subtree is made up of some overall statistics, a table of neighbor information, and a variable that contains the local Autonomous System number. Figure 16.1 shows an overview.

## 16.5   MANAGING THE EXTERIOR GATEWAY PROTOCOL

The MIB variables in Table 16.1 were defined in RFC 1213 as part of MIB-II. The first set of *egp* variables contains overall counts of incoming and outgoing EGP messages, as well as counts of EGP messages that were defective.

## 16.6   THE EGP NEIGHBOR TABLE

Table 16.2, the EGP Neighbor Table, contains the information needed to communicate with neighbors and tracks statistics on message traffic exchanged with neighbors.

Each router that has been configured as an EGP neighbor is represented by an entry in the table. An entry contains configuration information such as the neighbor's IP address, Autonomous System number, and the role (active or passive) that the local EGP will play in the relationship with this neighbor.

There are two timer configuration variables, *t1* and *t3*. If this is an active EGP, it will send a *Hello* every *t*1/100 seconds. For either role, a

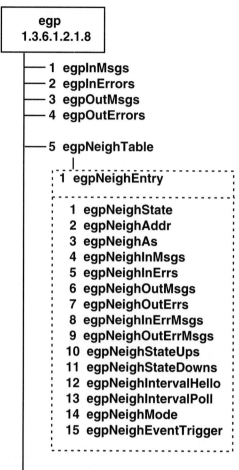

**Figure 16.1** The *egp* subtree.

*poll* will be sent every $t3/100$ seconds. There should be several *Hellos* between *polls*. If this is an active EGP, then a scheduled *poll* replaces one of the *Hellos*.

An entry also contains counts of the incoming and outgoing messages for the neighbor, and counts of significant state transition events.

There is one command element provided. An SNMP management station can ask the local EGP to start up (or reinitialize) acquisition of a particular neighbor, or to stop the exchange of information with a neighbor. The configuration variable, *egpNeighEventTrigger,* enables a manager to do this by setting the value of the variable to 1 (start) or 2 (stop).

TABLE 16.1    EGP Message Counts

| iso.org.dod.internet.mgmt.mib-2.egp 1.3.6.1.2.1.8 | | | |
|---|---|---|---|
| OBJECT IDENTIFIER | Syntax | Access | Description |
| egpInMsgs 1.3.6.1.2.1.8.1 | Counter | read-only | Number of EGP messages received without error. |
| egpInErrors 1.3.6.1.2.1.8.2 | Counter | read-only | Number of EGP messages received that proved to be in error. |
| egpOutMsgs 1.3.6.1.2.1.8.3 | Counter | read-only | Total number of EGP messages generated locally. |
| egpOutErrors 1.3.6.1.2.1.8.4 | Counter | read-only | Number of locally generated EGP messages not sent because of resource limitations. |

TABLE 16.2    The EGP Neighbor Table

| iso.org.dod.internet.mgmt.mib-2. egp.egpNeighTable.egpNeighEntry 1.3.6.1.2.1.8.5.1 | | | |
|---|---|---|---|
| OBJECT IDENTIFIER | Syntax | Access | Description |
| egpNeighState 1.3.6.1.2.1.8.5.1.1 | INTEGER idle(1), acquisition(2), down(3), up(4), cease(5) | read-only | The current EGP state of the local system with respect to this neighbor. |
| egpNeighAddr 1.3.6.1.2.1.8.5.1.2 ▶ Index | IpAddress | read-only | The IP address of this neighbor. |
| egpNeighAs 1.3.6.1.2.1.8.5.1.3 | INTEGER | read-only | The Autonomous System (AS) number of this neighbor. This is set to 0 if not yet known. |
| egpNeighInMsgs 1.3.6.1.2.1.8.5.1.4 | Counter | read-only | Number of incoming EGP messages from this neighbor without errors. |
| egpNeighInErrs 1.3.6.1.2.1.8.5.1.5 | Counter | read-only | Number of incoming EGP messages from this neighbor with errors (e.g., bad checksum field within the EGP message). |
| egpNeigh OutMsgs 1.3.6.1.2.1.8.5.1.6 | Counter | read-only | Number of locally generated EGP messages for this neighbor. |

TABLE 16.2 The EGP Neighbor Table (*Continued*)

iso.org.dod.internet.mgmt.mib-2.
egp.egpNeighTable.egpNeighEntry
1.3.6.1.2.1.8.5.1

| OBJECT IDENTIFIER | Syntax | Access | Description |
|---|---|---|---|
| egpNeigh OutErrs 1.3.6.1.2.1.8.5.1.7 | Counter | read-only | Number not sent because of lack of resources (e.g., buffer memory). |
| egpNeigh InErrMsgs 1.3.6.1.2.1.8.5.1.8 | Counter | read-only | Number of EGP-defined error messages from this neighbor. |
| egpNeigh OutErrMsgs 1.3.6.1.2.1.8.5.1.9 | Counter | read-only | Number of EGP-defined error messages sent to this neighbor. |
| egpNeigh StateUps 1.3.6.1.2.1.8.5.1.10 | Counter | read-only | Number of transitions to EGP UP state with this neighbor. |
| egpNeigh StateDowns 1.3.6.1.2.1.8.5.1.11 | Counter | read-only | Number of transitions from UP to any other state with this neighbor. |
| egpNeigh IntervalHello 1.3.6.1.2.1.8.5.1.12 | INTEGER | read-only | The timer t1 for EGP Hello command retransmissions (in hundredths of a second) for this neighbor. |
| egpNeigh IntervalPoll 1.3.6.1.2.1.8.5.1.13 | INTEGER | read-only | The timer t3 for EGP Poll command retransmissions (in hundredths of a second) for this neighbor. |
| egpNeighMode 1.3.6.1.2.1.8.5.1.14 | INTEGER active(1), passive(2) | read-only | The polling mode (active or passive) for this neighbor. |
| egpNeigh EventTrigger 1.3.6.1.2.1.8.5.1.15 | INTEGER start(1), stop(2) | read-write | A control variable used to trigger operator-initiated Start and Stop events. A Start causes the local EGP to try to acquire this neighbor. |

## 16.7 CONFIGURING THE AUTONOMOUS SYSTEM NUMBER

There is one stand-alone MIB variable in the *egp* subtree. As shown in Table 16.3, this variable contains the Autonomous System number for the EGP router. The Autonomous System Number of the sender is included in the header of each EGP message that it transmits.

TABLE 16.3    The Autonomous System Number

<table>
<tr><td colspan="4" align="center">iso.org.dod.internet.mgmt.mib-2.egp<br>1.3.6.1.2.1.8</td></tr>
<tr><td>OBJECT<br>IDENTIFIER</td><td>Syntax</td><td>Access</td><td>Description</td></tr>
<tr><td>egpAs<br>1.3.6.1.2.1.8.6</td><td>INTEGER</td><td>read-<br>only</td><td>The Autonomous System number<br>for this EGP entity.</td></tr>
</table>

## 16.8   POLLING AN EGP ROUTER FOR SYSTEM INFORMATION

The display that follows shows an SNMP dialog with a border router that has two EGP neighbors. The identities of all of the routers have been changed in order to preserve their privacy.

First, we establish the identity of the border router by getting system information:

```
snmplookup
        snmplookup Version 3.2
      Copyright (C) PSI, Inc. 1990
default community name is public
default timeout is 10 seconds
default number of recv retries is 1
default prefix is _iso_org_dod_internet

snmp> prefix 1.3.6.1.2.1
snmp> agent 135.11.51.12
snmp>
mquery 1
sysDescr_0        GS Software (GS3-K), ExperimentalVersion
                  9.1 (811)
Copyright (c) 1986-1993 by cisco Systems, Inc.
Compiled Tue 15-Jun-93 09:39
sysObjectID_0     1 3 6 1 4 1 9 1 1
sysUpTime_0       173290920
sysContact_0      Henry Hemmings
sysName_0         MAIN-GATE3.NET.CAMPUS.EDU
sysLocation_0     Room 17
sysServices_0     6
snmp>
```

Let's check the autonomous system number:

```
snmp> query 8.6.0
egpAs_0                 1310
```

## 16.9   EXAMPLES: POLLING
## FOR INFORMATION

Next we will display configuration information and statistics obtained by polling. Rather than show the *snmplookup* printout directly, we'll examine the output in a more compact tabular format.

The values in Tables 16.4 and 16.5 were obtained by actual polls taken 69.5 minutes apart. There are a few anomalies. The total number of reported incoming messages is less than the sum of the incoming messages from the two neighbors. The total number of reported outgoing messages is bigger than the sum for the two neighbors.

**TABLE 16.4   General EGP Statistics**

|  | First poll | 1 hour later | Difference |
|---|---|---|---|
| egpInMsgs_0 | 95250 | 95490 | 240 |
| egpInErrors_0 | 0 | 0 | 0 |
| egpOutMsgs_0 | 103394 | 103658 | 264 |
| egpOutErrors_0 | 0 | 0 | 0 |

**TABLE 16.5   EGP Neighbor Table**

|  | First poll | 1 hour later | Difference (or comments) |
|---|---|---|---|
| egpNeighState_ 130.91.20.1 | 4 | 4 | (State is up) |
| egpNeighState_ 192.43.12.4 | 4 | 4 | (State is up) |
| egpNeighAddr_ 130.91.20.1 | 130.91.20.1 | 130.91.20.1 | (Neighbor) |
| egpNeighAddr_ 192.43.12.4 | 192.43.12.4 | 192.43.12.4 | (Neighbor) |
| egpNeighAs_ 130.91.20.1 | 199 | 199 | (Autonomous System) |
| egpNeighAs_ 192.43.12.4 | 25 | 25 | (Autonomous System) |
| egpNeighInMsgs_ 130.91.20.1 | 47143 | 47265 | 122 |
| egpNeighInMsgs_ 192.43.12.4 | 48107 | 48230 | 123 |
| egpNeighInErrs_ 130.91.20.1 | 0 | 0 | 0 |
| egpNeighInErrs_ 192.43.12.4 | 0 | 0 | 0 |
| egpNeighOutMsgs_ 130.91.20.1 | 47261 | 47383 | 122 |

**TABLE 16.5  EGP Neighbor Table (*Continued*)**

|  | First poll | 1 hour later | Difference (or comments) |
|---|---|---|---|
| egpNeighOutMsgs_<br>192.43.12.4 | 48113 | 48236 | 123 |
| egpNeighOutErrs_<br>130.91.20.1 | 0 | 0 | 0 |
| egpNeighOutErrs_<br>192.43.12.4 | 0 | 0 | 0 |
| egpNeighInErrMsgs_<br>130.91.20.1 | 0 | 0 | 0 |
| egpNeighInErrMsgs_<br>192.43.12.4 | 0 | 0 | 0 |
| egpNeighOutErrMsgs_<br>130.91.20.1 | 0 | 0 | 0 |
| egpNeighOutErrMsgs_<br>192.43.12.4 | 0 | 0 | 0 |
| egpNeighStateUps_<br>130.91.20.1 | 1 | 1 | 0 |
| egpNeighStateUps_<br>192.43.12.4 | 1 | 1 | 0 |
| egpNeighStateDowns_<br>130.91.20.1 | 0 | 0 | 0 |
| egpNeighStateDowns_<br>192.43.12.4 | 0 | 0 | 0 |
| egpNeighIntervalHello_<br>130.91.20.1 | 6 | 6 | (Units?) |
| egpNeighIntervalHello_<br>192.43.12.4 | 6 | 6 | (Units?) |
| egpNeighIntervalPoll_<br>130.91.20.1 | 18 | 18 | (Units?) |
| egpNeighIntervalPoll_<br>192.43.12.4 | 18 | 18 | (Units?) |
| egpNeighMode_<br>130.91.20.1 | 2 | 2 | (Passive) |
| egpNeighMode_<br>192.43.12.4 | 2 | 2 | (Passive) |
| egpNeighEventTrigger_<br>130.91.20.1 | 0 | 0 | (No trigger used yet) |
| egpNeighEventTrigger_<br>192.43.12.4 | 0 | 0 | (No trigger used yet) |

The strangest entries are those shown for the timers *t1* and *t3,* the *Hello* and poll timers. Recall that the minimum interval for *Hellos* should be 30 seconds, and for polls, 2 minutes. In this case, 122 messages arrived from a neighbor over 69.5 minutes, which averages out to 34 seconds between messages—very much what should be expected. The table values are supposed to represent the interval in hundredths of a second, so we would expect a *t1* entry of 3000, rather than 6!

It is possible that the *t1* and *t3* values are just the result of an administrator typing in incorrect values which were overridden by the router software, which includes checks to ensure that parameters meet the protocol requirements.

## 16.10   NETWORK MANAGEMENT CONSIDERATIONS

A management station can perform a daily poll to validate the IP addresses and Autonomous System numbers of routers in adjacent networks, and map their points of connectivity to the local Autonomous System.

An initial set of polls can be used to establish baseline expectations for maintaining connectivity, and for message and error counts. Regular hourly polls can then detect trends that depart from the baseline.

Repeated loss and recovery of connectivity with a neighbor are signaled by the *egpNeighStatUps* and *egpNeighStatDowns* variable. For systems that have a record of instability, these variables should be polled more frequently. The ability to set a threshold and receive a trap signaling excessive interruptions in communications with a neighbor would be useful.

## 16.11   RECOMMENDED READING

The Exterior Gateway Protocol is defined in RFC 904.

# Reporting SNMP Traffic

## 17.1 INTRODUCTION

In earlier chapters, we have examined MIB variables that measure traffic for interfaces, IP, TCP, and UDP. MIB-II also includes variables that count incoming and outgoing SNMP traffic! In fact, support for the *snmp* group of objects is mandatory for all implementations that support the SNMP protocol.

## 17.2 THE *snmp* SUBTREE

The *snmp* MIB subtree is made up of a list of statistical counts and a single configuration variable. The subtree is displayed in Figure 17.1. There are 28 MIB definitions, with identifiers ranging from 1 to 30. Note that identifiers 7 and 23 are not used.

## 17.3 STATISTICS FOR INCOMING
## SNMP TRAFFIC

Table 17.1 describes the *snmp* variables that count *incoming* SNMP traffic. In addition to counting the overall total, each of the message types (*get-request, get-next-request, set-request, get-response,* and *trap*) are tracked for incoming SNMP messages.

All of the errors that can occur in processing an incoming SNMP message are tallied. For a security-conscious site, the counts of attempts to access the system with a bad community name, or to *set* variables using a community name that only supports *gets* may be of interest.

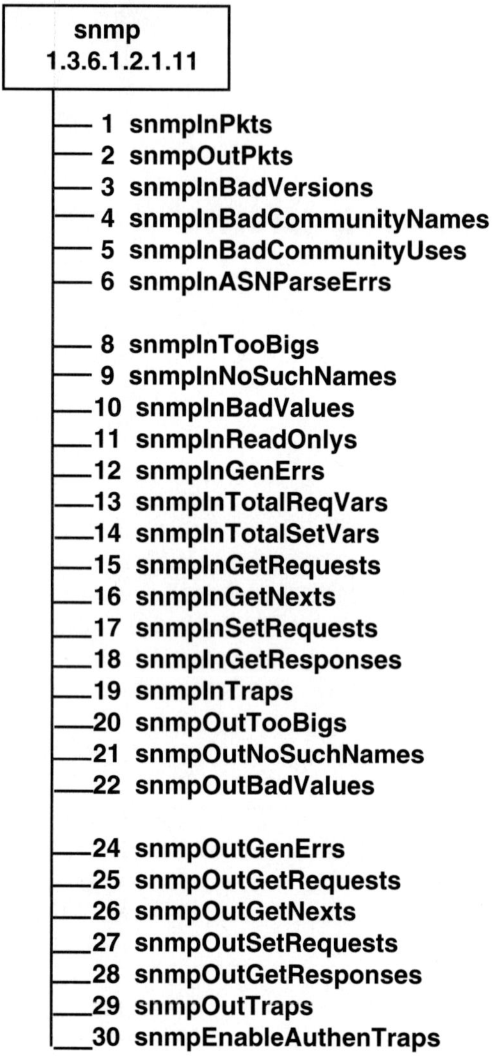

```
┌─────────────────────┐
│        snmp         │
│  1.3.6.1.2.1.11     │
└─────────────────────┘
        │── 1  snmpInPkts
        │── 2  snmpOutPkts
        │── 3  snmpInBadVersions
        │── 4  snmpInBadCommunityNames
        │── 5  snmpInBadCommunityUses
        │── 6  snmpInASNParseErrs

        │── 8  snmpInTooBigs
        │── 9  snmpInNoSuchNames
        │──10  snmpInBadValues
        │──11  snmpInReadOnlys
        │──12  snmpInGenErrs
        │──13  snmpInTotalReqVars
        │──14  snmpInTotalSetVars
        │──15  snmpInGetRequests
        │──16  snmpInGetNexts
        │──17  snmpInSetRequests
        │──18  snmpInGetResponses
        │──19  snmpInTraps
        │──20  snmpOutTooBigs
        │──21  snmpOutNoSuchNames
        │──22  snmpOutBadValues

        │──24  snmpOutGenErrs
        │──25  snmpOutGetRequests
        │──26  snmpOutGetNexts
        │──27  snmpOutSetRequests
        │──28  snmpOutGetResponses
        │──29  snmpOutTraps
        └──30  snmpEnableAuthenTraps
```

**Figure 17.1**  The *snmp* subtree.

## 17.4   STATISTICS FOR OUTGOING SNMP TRAFFIC

Table 17.2 describes the *snmp* variables that count *outgoing* SNMP traffic and errors.

## 17.5   CONFIGURING THE USE OF AUTHENTICATION TRAPS

There is one configuration parameter in the subtree. A station can be configured to send a *trap* whenever an improperly authenticated mes-

**TABLE 17.1 Incoming SNMP Traffic Counts**

| | iso.org.dod.internet.mgmt.mib-2.snmp 1.3.6.1.2.1.11 | | |
|---|---|---|---|
| OBJECT IDENTIFIER | Syntax | Access | Description |
| snmpInPkts 1.3.6.1.2.1.11.1 | Counter | read-only | Total number of incoming SNMP messages delivered by the transport service. |
| snmpInBad Versions 1.3.6.1.2.1.11.3 | Counter | read-only | Number of incoming messages with an unsupported version. |
| snmpInBad Community Names 1.3.6.1.2.1.11.4 | Counter | read-only | Number of incoming messages with an unknown community name. |
| snmpInBad Community Uses 1.3.6.1.2.1.11.5 | Counter | read-only | Number of incoming messages requesting an operation not supported for the community name. |
| snmpInASN ParseErrs 1.3.6.1.2.1.11.6 | Counter | read-only | Number of times message decoding failed. |
| snmpInToo Bigs 1.3.6.1.2.1.11.8 | Counter | read-only | Number of incoming messages with an error-status field of 'too big.' This means that the response would not fit into the largest permissible message allowed between this agent and manager. |
| snmpInNo SuchNames 1.3.6.1.2.1.11.9 | Counter | read-only | Number of incoming messages with an error-status field of 'noSuchName.' This means that a requested object is not supported by the agent. |
| snmpInBad Values 1.3.6.1.2.1.11.10 | Counter | read-only | Number of incoming messages with an error-status field of 'badValue.' This means that a value in a corresponding outgoing set-request had a bad data type, incorrect length, or inappropriate value. |
| snmpInRead Onlys 1.3.6.1.2.1.11.11 | Counter | read-only | Number of incoming messages with an error-status field of 'readOnly.' This signals that there is a local implementation error because an inappropriate set-request was sent. |
| snmpInGen Errs 1.3.6.1.2.1.11.12 | Counter | read-only | Number of incoming messages with an error-status field of 'genErr,' which means an error different from those listed above. |

**TABLE 17.1    Incoming SNMP Traffic Counts (*Continued*)**

| | iso.org.dod.internet.mgmt.mib-2.snmp 1.3.6.1.2.1.11 | | |
|---|---|---|---|
| OBJECT IDENTIFIER | Syntax | Access | Description |
| snmpInTotal ReqVars 1.3.6.1.2.1.11.13 | Counter | read-only | The total number of local MIB objects that have been retrieved successfully as a result of incoming get-requests and get-next-requests. |
| snmpInTotal SetVars 1.3.6.1.2.1.11.14 | Counter | read-only | The total number of local MIB objects that have been updated successfully as a result of incoming set-requests. |
| snmpInGet Requests 1.3.6.1.2.1.11.15 | Counter | read-only | Number of incoming get-requests accepted and processed. |
| snmpInGet Nexts 1.3.6.1.2.1.11.16 | Counter | read-only | Number of incoming get-next-requests accepted and processed. |
| snmpInSet Requests 1.3.6.1.2.1.11.17 | Counter | read-only | Number of incoming set-requests accepted and processed. |
| snmpInGet Responses 1.3.6.1.2.1.11.18 | Counter | read-only | Number of incoming get-responses accepted and processed. |
| snmpInTraps 1.3.6.1.2.1.11.19 | Counter | read-only | Number of incoming traps accepted and processed. |

**TABLE 17.2    Outgoing SNMP Traffic Counts**

| | iso.org.dod.internet.mgmt.mib-2.snmp 1.3.6.1.2.1.11 | | |
|---|---|---|---|
| OBJECT IDENTIFIER | Syntax | Access | Description |
| snmpOutPkts 1.3.6.1.2.1.11.2 | Counter | read-only | Total number of outgoing SNMP messages passed to the transport service. |
| snmpOutTooBigs 1.3.6.1.2.1.11.20 | Counter | read-only | Number of outgoing messages sent with the error-status field set to 'tooBig.' |
| snmpOutNoSuch Names 1.3.6.1.2.1.11.21 | Counter | read-only | Number of outgoing messages sent with the error-status field set to 'noSuchName.' |
| snmpOutBad Values 1.3.6.1.2.1.11.22 | Counter | read-only | Number of outgoing messages sent with the error-status field set to 'badValue.' |

**TABLE 17.2    Outgoing SNMP Traffic Counts (*Continued*)**

iso.org.dod.internet.mgmt.mib-2.snmp
1.3.6.1.2.1.11

| OBJECT IDENTIFIER | Syntax | Access | Description |
|---|---|---|---|
| snmpOutGenErrs 1.3.6.1.2.1.11.24 | Counter | read-only | Number of outgoing messages sent with error-status field set 'genErr.' |
| snmpOutGet Requests 1.3.6.1.2.1.11.25 | Counter | read-only | Number of outgoing get-requests generated. |
| snmpOutGetNexts 1.3.6.1.2.1.11.26 | Counter | read-only | Number of outgoing get-next-requests generated. |
| snmpOutSet Requests 1.3.6.1.2.1.11.27 | Counter | read-only | Number of outgoing set-requests generated. |
| snmpOutGet Responses 1.3.6.1.2.1.11.28 | Counter | read-only | Number of outgoing get-responses generated. |
| snmpOutTraps 1.3.6.1.2.1.11.29 | Counter | read-only | Number of outgoing traps generated. |

**TABLE 17.3    Enabling/Disabling Authentication Traps**

iso.org.dod.internet.mgmt.mib-2.snmp
1.3.6.1.2.1.11

| OBJECT IDENTIFIER | Syntax | Access | Description |
|---|---|---|---|
| snmpEnable AuthenTraps 1.3.6.1.2.1.11.30 | INTEGER enabled(1), disabled(2) | read-write | Indicates whether the agent is allowed to generate authentication-failure traps. |

sage arrives. However, there may be environments in which these messages are more of a nuisance than a help.

For example, a management station configured with an incorrect community name may be performing a large number of polls automatically. The *snmpEnableAuthenTraps* variable is used to turn authentication trapping on or off. Its value overrides any local configuration at a system.

## 17.6    POLLING FOR SNMP COUNTS

The dialogue on the next page shows part of an interaction between a management station and a router obtained using the PSI *snmplookup* tool. The counts are given in hexadecimal and in ordinary decimal.

A number of the counters are not perfectly consistent with one another. For example, there were 15,890 get-requests and 5,773 get-next-requests, for a total of 21,663. However, the total count of *snmp* messages received is listed as 21,649! The outgoing message count also is slightly low. Of course, we really would be examining differences in counts across a time interval, and the size of these discrepancies is not large.

This router sent out 198 traps, 2 of which were authentication failures. There were 60 requests for unknown variables.

In 59 cases, an error response had to be sent because too many variables were requested, and the answer would have been too big to process. A management station should be smart enough to take notice of this, and reduce the number of variables in its future request lists.

```
snmp>mquery 11
snmpInPkts_0                    0x5491    21649
snmpOutPkts_0                   0x5557    21847
snmpInBadVersions_0             0x0       0
snmpInBadCommunityNames_0       0x0       0
snmpInBadCommunityUses_0        0x0       0
snmpInASNParseErrs_0            0x0       0
snmpInTooBigs_0                 0x0       0
snmpInNoSuchNames_0             0x0       0
snmpInBadValues_0               0x0       0
snmpInReadOnlys_0               0x0       0
snmpInGenErrs_0                 0x0       0
snmpInTotalReqVars_0            0x385b9   230841
snmpInTotalSetVars_0            0x0       0
snmpInGetRequests_0             0x3e12    15890
snmpInGetNexts_0                0x168d    5773
snmpInSetRequests_0             0x0       0
snmpInGetResponses_0            0x0       0
snmpInTraps_0                   0x0       0
snmpOutTooBigs_0                0x3b      59
snmpOutNoSuchNames_0            0x3c      60
snmpOutBadValues_0              0x0       0
snmpOutGenErrs_0                0x0       0
snmpOutGetRequests_0            0x0       0
snmpOutGetNexts_0               0x0       0
snmpOutSetRequests_0            0x0       0
snmpOutGetResponses_0           0x54a9    21673
snmpOutTraps_0                  0xc6      198
snmpEnableAuthTraps_0           0x2       2
snmp>
```

# 18

# Managing an Ethernet Interface

## 18.1 INTRODUCTION

As one of the oldest, and currently still the most popular, LAN technologies, it is appropriate to start off the study of the groups under the transmission node with the Ethernet MIB. At the time of writing, the current Ethernet MIB document was RFC 1398, *Definitions of Managed Objects for the Ethernet-like Interface Types*.

Note the term *Ethernet-like* in the title. As might be expected for a technology that has been around as long as Ethernet, there are quite a few variations on the basic theme. The technology originally was defined by Digital, Intel, and Xerox ("DIX Ethernet") and later, the IEEE 802 committee described a slightly modified version in standard 802.3. AT&T marketed a version called *StarLAN*. Strictly speaking, the term "Ethernet" should be reserved for the DIX version, but hardly anyone makes this distinction.

The definitions in this MIB are quite solid. They were based on a very detailed IEEE specification on the management of 802.3 interfaces. Further, the initial version of the Ethernet MIB already has been revised based on field experience.

## 18.2 THE PHYSICAL STRUCTURE OF AN ETHERNET

A "thick" Ethernet LAN conforming to DIX version 2 or IEEE 802.3 is constructed using a thick, fairly rigid .4-inch diameter grade of coaxial cable. A branching bus is built out of segments up to 500 meters long, joined by repeaters.

As shown in Figure 18.1, a station is connected to an *Attachment Unit Interface* (AUI) 4-wire-pair drop cable. The AUI cable connects to

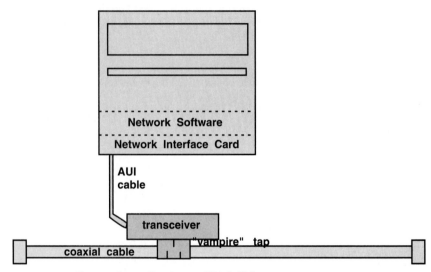

**Figure 18.1** Connecting a Station to Thick Ethernet.

a *transceiver* that clamps onto the cable. The transceiver contains a *vampire tap* that actually penetrates the coaxial cable.

The IEEE calls transceivers *Medium Attachment Units* or MAUs. This is somewhat unfortunate, because Token-Ring vendors use the term "MAU" for a hub product that concentrates the Token-Ring twisted pair wiring.

Ethernet has been around for a long time, and little by little, other media were introduced:

- A thinner, ¼-inch-thick coaxial cable
- Broadband coaxial cable
- Twisted pair of various grades
- Fiber-optic cable

Segment sizes and the method of attachment vary according to the medium. However, the most popular physical layout today is to use twisted pair cable to connect stations to a hub. Multiple hubs are connected by a high-quality grade of shielded twisted pair or by fiber-optic cable.

The common Ethernet transmission speed is 10 megabits per second (Mbps). The original AT&T StarLAN ran at 1 Mbps. There have been variants running at 3 and 5 Mbps. Standards committees currently are working on a 100-Mbps version.

## 18.3   HOW DOES AN ETHERNET WORK?

Ethernet is based on a very simple *Media Access Control* (MAC) rule called *Carrier Sense Multiple Access with Collision Detection* (CSMA/CD).

Figure 18.2 illustrates how the protocol works. A station wanting to send a frame listens to the medium. If the medium is not in use, the station transmits its frame. The frame header contains the physical address of the destination station. All of the stations on the LAN hear the frame, but only the destination station accepts it.

If two or more stations transmit at the same time, they can hear their data "collide," and they back off for a random amount of time and try again. The protocol requires a few more rules to operate correctly:

- There is a minimum time that stations must wait between transmissions in order to give a receiver time to finish processing one frame before having to receive another. This time is 9.6 microseconds.

- Frames must be large enough so that they stay on the medium long enough so that if there is a collision, all—not just some—of the stations will hear it. The minimum required length is 64 octets. Frames that are too short (usually as a result of hearing a collision) are called *runts*.

- There also is a maximum frame size of 1518 octets. Frames that are too long (sometimes resulting from a misbehaving transceiver) are called *jabbers*.

A transceiver uses one pair in an AUI drop cable to transmit a collision detection signal to the station. This signal is called *Signal Quality*

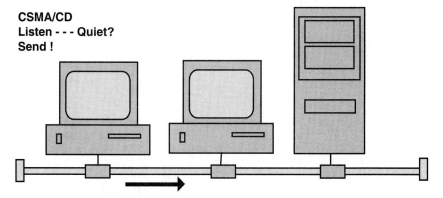

**CSMA/CD**
**Listen - - - Quiet?**
**Send !**

**Figure 18.2**  The CSMA/CD protocol.

*Error* or SQE. An SQE also is sent to report improper signals on the medium, or in response to an "output idle" signal from the station. The latter exchange is used to test the circuitry.

### 18.3.1   Ethernet Frame Format

Figure 18.3 shows the formats for the family of Ethernet frames. All frames in the family start with a *MAC header* that consists of a 6-octet physical destination address, 6-octet physical source address, and a third field that contains:

- For DIX Ethernet, a 2-octet identifier for the protocol type for the frame's information—for example, X'0800 for an IP datagram, or X'8137 for a NetWare datagram.
- For 802.3, a length field.

For 802.3 LANs, protocols are identified in the 802.2 Logical Link Control (LLC) header that immediately follows the MAC header. In fact, the same 802.2 header is used for all 802 LANs. No 802.2 header is present when using DIX Ethernet. The LLC header consists of:

- A 1-octet Destination Service Access Point (DSAP) identifier.
- A 1-octet Source Service Access Point (SSAP) identifier.

**DIX Ethernet**

| Destination Address | Source Address | Ether-type | INFORMATION | Frame Check Sequence |
|---|---|---|---|---|
| 6 | 6 | 2 | 48 to 1502 | 4 octets |

**IEEE 802.3 with 802.2 LLC Header**

| Destination Address | Source Address | Length | LLC | INFORMATION | Frame Check Sequence |
|---|---|---|---|---|---|
| 6 | 6 | 2 | 3 - 4 | 44 to 1499 | 4 octets |

**IEEE 802.3 with 802.2 LLC Header and SNAP**

| Destination Address | Source Address | Length | LLC | SNAP | INFORMATION | Frame Check Sequence |
|---|---|---|---|---|---|---|
| 6 | 6 | 2 | 3 - 4 | 5 | 39 to 1494 | 4 octets |

**Figure 18.3**  Format of an Ethernet MAC frame.

- A 1- or 2-octet control field. For TCP/IP—and many LAN protocols—this is set to '03'H, meaning "unnumbered information." For SNA, the control field is used to set up links, number and acknowledge data, and perform link flow control.

The purpose of DSAPs and SSAPs is to identify the protocol entities that are the frame's destination and source. This is exactly what the old DIX Ethertype field did. Within 802.2, classic Ethertype values are used to identify protocol destinations and sources by setting:

```
DSAP = 'AA'H    SSAP = 'AA'H
```

and adding yet another header, the Sub-Network Access Protocol (SNAP) header. This has a 3-octet introducer which is followed by the old 2-octet Ethertype code.

The physical addresses that appear in MAC headers are administered by the IEEE. The IEEE assigns sets of 3-octet codes to each manufacturer of Ethernet interfaces.* For example, boards with addresses that start with X'02608C or X'080002 are built by 3Com. The manufacturer then assigns the remaining 3 octets so that every interface board will have a unique identifier.

The Frame Check Sequence (FCS) field of a frame holds the result of a mathematical calculation performed on the message. The calculation is repeated at the receiving end, and if the answers do not agree, the frame is judged to have been corrupted and is discarded.

## 18.4   THE ETHERNET MIB

The *interfaces* group and its extensions include detailed counts of incoming and outgoing traffic. The Ethernet MIB adds:

- A statistics table that contains counts of Ethernet errors
- A statistics table used to build a histogram of collision frequencies
- Information needed to configure and trigger a *Time-domain Reflectometry* (TDR) test, used to check the distance to a cable fault
- OBJECT IDENTIFIERs for popular chipsets

Note that the numbering of objects in the MIB starts at 2, and that some numbers are skipped. This is because of the deletion of objects

---

* See the Assigned Numbers RFC for a list of vendor assignments.

from an earlier version of the MIB. Numbers for useful objects do not get changed when a MIB is revised. This enables management stations to get consistent data even when devices implement different MIB versions. It also makes it easier for a vendor to upgrade to a new MIB version.

Consistency does not cost anything—there are lots of free integers available!

## 18.5   THE ETHERNET-LIKE STATISTICS TABLE

Statistics for a variety of error conditions are shown in Table 18.1, the Ethernet-like Statistics Table. Sometimes a frame will exhibit several errors at once. In all but one case, only one of the errors is counted.

**TABLE 18.1   The Ethernet-like Statistics Table**

iso.org.dod.internet.mgmt.mib-2.transmission.
dot3.dot3StatsTable.dot3StatsEntry
1.3.6.1.2.1.10.7.2.1

| OBJECT IDENTIFIER | Syntax | Access | Description |
|---|---|---|---|
| dot3StatsIndex 1.3.6.1.2.1.10.7.2.1.1 ▶ **Index** | INTEGER | read-only | The index for the interface (*ifIndex*). |
| dot3Stats AlignmentErrors 1.3.6.1.2.1.10.7.2.1.2 | Counter | read-only | Number of frames with an alignment error—i.e., the length is not an integral number of octets and the frame cannot pass the FCS test. |
| dot3Stats FCSErrors 1.3.6.1.2.1.10.7.2.1.3 | Counter | read-only | Number of frames with frame-check errors—i.e., there is an integral number of octets, but an incorrect FCS. |
| dot3StatsSingle CollisionFrames 1.3.6.1.2.1.10.7.2.1.4 | Counter | read-only | Number of successfully transmitted frames for which there was exactly one collision. |
| dot3StatsMultiple CollisionFrames 1.3.6.1.2.1.10.7.2.1.5 | Counter | read-only | Number of successfully transmitted frames for which there were multiple collisions. |
| dot3StatsSQETest Errors 1.3.6.1.2.1.10.7.2.1.6 | Counter | read-only | Number of times that the Signal Quality Error TEST ERROR message was generated by the interface. |
| dot3StatsDeferred Transmissions 1.3.6.1.2.1.10.7.2.1.7 | Counter | read-only | Number of times the first transmission attempt was delayed because the medium was busy. |

TABLE 18.1    The Ethernet-like Statistics Table (*Continued*)

iso.org.dod.internet.mgmt.mib-2.transmission.
dot3.dot3StatsTable.dot3StatsEntry
1.3.6.1.2.1.10.7.2.1

| OBJECT IDENTIFIER | Syntax | Access | Description |
|---|---|---|---|
| dot3Stats LateCollisions 1.3.6.1.2.1.10.7.2.1.8 | Counter | read-only | Number of times that a collision was detected later than 64 octets into the transmission. (Also added into collision count.) |
| dot3StatsExcessive Collisions 1.3.6.1.2.1.10.7.2.1.9 | Counter | read-only | Number of frames for which transmission failed because of excessive collisions. |
| dot3StatsInternal MacTransmit Errors 1.3.6.1.2.1.10.7.2.1.10 | Counter | read-only | Number of frames for which transmission failed because of an internal MAC layer transmit error (i.e., transmit errors not picked up in any other count). |
| dot3StatsCarrier SenseErrors 1.3.6.1.2.1.10.7.2.1.11 | Counter | read-only | Number of transmission attempts that failed because the carrier sense condition was lost or never asserted. |
| dot3StatsFrame TooLongs 1.3.6.1.2.1.10.7.2.1.13 | Counter | read-only | Number of received frames that were bigger than the maximum permitted size. |
| dot3Stats Internal MacReceiveErrors 1.3.6.1.2.1.10.7.2.1.16 | Counter | read-only | Number of frames for which reception failed because of an internal MAC layer receive error (i.e., the receive errors not picked up in any other count). |

## 18.6    THE COLLISION HISTOGRAM TABLE

Table 18.2 contains the information needed to build a collision histogram. What happens when you try to transmit a frame? You might be successful on the first try, or there might be one or more collisions before you either succeed or give up.

An entry in the table counts the number of frames for which there were "*n*" collisions before the frame either was successfully transmitted or the attempt was abandoned. Each entry corresponds to a "cell" in a histogram.

When the histogram is plotted, each cell appears as one of the block rectangles in the picture, as shown in Figure 18.4. For example, the first block shows that within the measurement period, there were eight frames that collided on the first try, but were transmitted successfully on the second try. There were six frames that collided on both the first and second tries, but then were transmitted without a problem. No frame experienced more than five collisions during the attempt to send it.

TABLE 18.2    The Ethernet Collision Statistics Table

iso.org.dod.internet.mgmt.mib-2.transmission.
dot3.dot3CollTable.dot3CollEntry
1.3.6.1.2.1.10.7.5.1

| OBJECT IDENTIFIER | Syntax | Access | Description |
|---|---|---|---|
| dot3CollIndex<br>1.3.6.1.2.1.10.7.5.1.1<br>► **Index** | INTEGER | read-<br>only | The index (*ifIndex*) for the interface whose collisions are being counted. |
| dot3CollCount<br>1.3.6.1.2.1.10.7.5.1.2<br>► **Index** | INTEGER<br>(1.16) | read-<br>only | Number of collisions reported in this histogram cell. |
| dot3Coll<br>Frequencies<br>1.3.6.1.2.1.10.7.5.1.3 | Counter | read-<br>only | Number of frames for which this number of collisions occurred during the attempt to transmit. |

## 18.7  TESTING AN INTERFACE

Looking at statistics never tells the whole story. A network manager must be able to *test* an interface.

The extension to the interfaces MIB enables a management station to test interfaces. Specifically, there is a test table (*ifExtnsTestTable*) that works as follows:

- A variable (*ifExtnsTestType*) can be *set* to start or stop a test. The value is an OBJECT IDENTIFIER that names a specific test. For

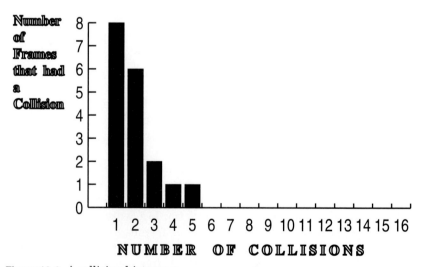

**Figure 18.4**  A collision histogram.

example, the OBJECT IDENTIFIER for a full-duplex loopback test is:

```
1 . 3 . 6 . 1 . 2 . 1 . 12 . 4 . 1
```

- A variable (*ifExtnsTestResult*) provides the status of the current or most recently completed test.

- A variable (*ifExtnsTestCode*) provides more specific information. The value is an OBJECT IDENTIFIER.

  For example, if the test result for a *loopback* test of an Ethernet-like interface is *failed(7),* then more specific information may be provided by the OBJECT IDENTIFIERS:

| | |
|---|---|
| 1.3.6.1.2.1.10.7.7.1 | Could not initialize MAC chip for test |
| 1.3.6.1.2.1.10.7.7.2 | Expected data not received, or not received correctly in loopback test |

### 18.7.1  TDR Test

The Ethernet MIB defines an additional test that can be applied to coaxial cable implementations. The Time-domain Reflectometry (TDR) test is used to check the approximate distance to an Ethernet coaxial cable fault. To start a TDR test, the test-type variable (*ifExtnsTestType*) must be *set* to hold OBJECT IDENTIFIER:

```
1 . 3 . 6 . 1 . 2 . 1 . 10 . 7 . 6 . 1
```

The test result is defined as the time interval between the start of the test transmission and subsequent detection of a collision or "deassertion" (absence) of carrier. The result is measured in 100-nanosecond units.

Where is the result? First you *get* the *ifExtnsTestResult* variable, which will tell you whether the test succeeded. If it did, the *ifExtnsTestCode* value will be an OBJECT IDENTIFIER of an object that contains the test result.*

### 18.8  HARDWARE CHIPSET IDENTIFICATION

The identity of the Ethernet chipset used in an Ethernet interface might be a useful piece of configuration information. The interface extensions MIB defined the *ifExtnsChipSet* variable to hold this information. The variable contains an OBJECT IDENTIFIER that names a chipset.

---

* There is an error in RFC 1398 on this point. The RFC states that *ifExtnsTestResult* contains the OBJECT IDENTIFIER pointing to the answer, but this is impossible. The next update of the MIB will correct this.

TABLE 18.3    OBJECT IDENTIFIERs for Chipsets

| iso.org.dod.internet.mgmt.mib-2.transmission. dot3.dot3ChipSets 1.3.6.1.2.1.10.7.8 | | |
|---|---|---|
| Vendor | Chipset name | Object identifier |
| dot3ChipSetAMD | | 1.3.6.1.2.1.10.7.8.1 |
| | dot3ChipSetAMD7990 | 1.3.6.1.2.1.10.7.8.1.1 |
| | dot3ChipSetAMD79900 | 1.3.6.1.2.1.10.7.8.1.2 |
| dot3ChipSetIntel | | 1.3.6.1.2.1.10.7.8.2 |
| | dot3ChipSetIntel82586 | 1.3.6.1.2.1.10.7.8.2.1 |
| | dot3ChipSetIntel82596 | 1.3.6.1.2.1.10.7.8.2.2 |
| dot3ChipSetSeeq | | 1.3.6.1.2.1.10.7.8.3 |
| | dot3ChipSetSeeq8003 | 1.3.6.1.2.1.10.7.8.3.1 |
| dot3ChipSetNational | | 1.3.6.1.2.1.10.7.8.4 |
| | dot3ChipSetNational8390 | 1.3.6.1.2.1.10.7.8.4.1 |
| | dot3ChipSetNationalSonic | 1.3.6.1.2.1.10.7.8.4.2 |
| dot3ChipSetFujitsu | | 1.3.6.1.2.1.10.7.8.5 |
| | dot3ChipSetFujitsu86950 | 1.3.6.1.2.1.10.7.8.5.1 |
| | dot3ChipSetFujitsu86960 | 1.3.6.1.2.1.10.7.8.5.2 |

The Ethernet MIB includes identifiers for some popular chipsets. These are displayed in Table 18.3. Note that each chipset is named by assigning it an OBJECT IDENTIFIER. It is possible that chipset identification will be dropped from the *interfaces* MIB, so don't be surprised if your products do not provide these values.

## 18.9   RECOMMENDED READING

The specification for 802.3 network management, *IEEE 802.3 Layer Management,* was published by the IEEE in November of 1988. This document includes meticulous detail on how parameters should be measured and even provides Pascal psuedocode.

This chapter is based on RFC 1398, *Definitions of Managed Objects for the Ethernet-like Interface Types.* RFC 1398 follows the lead of the *IEEE 802.3 Layer Management* document very closely.

The IEEE document describing the standardized form of Ethernet is *Carrier Sense Multiple Access with Collision Detection (CSMA/CD) Access Method and Physical Layer Specifications,* ANSI/IEEE Standard 802.3-1985. ISO adopted this standard as 8802/3.

Extensions to the generic interface MIB were defined in RFC 1229.

# Managing a Token-Ring Interface

## 19.1 INTRODUCTION

Just as was the case for an Ethernet interface, many of the variables needed to monitor a Token-Ring interface—incoming and outgoing traffic counts, interface speed, and operational status—were defined in MIB-II and the *interfaces* extensions.

However, there are many variables that relate to the specific Token-Ring interface technology that are not available in the basic MIB modules. These variables are described in this chapter. At the time of writing, RFC 1231 defined the Token-Ring MIB. The Token-Ring variables include:

- A table of Token-Ring specific configuration parameters
- A table of statistics and error counters
- An optional table of timer values
- Additional variables that cause interface tests to be initiated when their values are *set*

A *Token-Ring station* can be a PC, Macintosh, LAN server, minicomputer, router, mainframe, or specialized communications gear (such as an IBM 3174 communications controller). This use of the term *station* will be followed in the discussions in this chapter.

The sections that follow provide a brief introduction to Token-Ring terminology and concepts so that the reader will be able to understand the configuration and statistical variables that have been defined for the purpose of Token-Ring interface management.

Note that the MIB variables described in this chapter focus on managing a station's interface. These variables do not relate to information about IBM's *source routing protocol*. However, a discussion of source routing is included for completeness. This material will provide useful background for Chapter 27, which contains a description of the MIB variables used to manage source routing bridges.

## 19.2   THE PHYSICAL STRUCTURE OF A TOKEN-RING

A *ring topology* implies that stations are arranged in a ring, and data is passed from station to station around the ring, as illustrated in Figure 19.1.

Token-Ring LANs, as standardized in IEEE 802.5 and implemented by IBM, have a ring topology, but real implementations look like a sequence of stars cabled together, as shown in Figure 19.2.

A station's interface card connects to a very simple device called a *Trunk Coupling Unit* or TCU by means of two twisted pair wires, called a *lobe* of wire. The job of the TCU is to sense if the lobe is active. If not, the TCU causes signals to bypass the station.

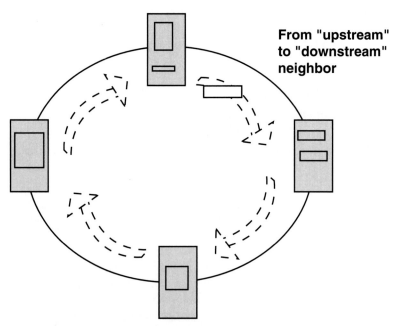

From "upstream" to "downstream" neighbor

**Figure 19.1**  A ring topology.

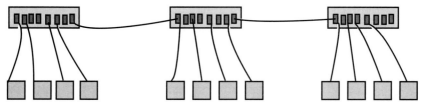

**Figure 19.2** A Token-Ring.

Typically, from 8 to 80 Trunk Coupling Units are packaged in a *Multiple Access Unit* (MAU)\* or *Communications Access Unit* (CAU). A lobe of wire connects a station at one end to a Multiple Access Unit at the other end. The MAU concentrator is stored in a convenient location, such as a wiring closet. Large rings are formed by cabling several Multiple Access Units together.

Token-Ring networks run at 4 or 16 megabits per second. Newer interface cards run at either speed, and the first station that comes up on a ring establishes the speed that will be used. However, if any other station comes up at a different speed, there will be transmission errors, stations will start to drop off the ring, and the telephone at the network control center will start to chime!

Each interface card has an associated 6-octet physical address. In SNMP messages, these are encoded as OCTET STRINGs. For convenience, the Textual Convention *MacAddress* is used when referring to these addresses.

### 19.3   HOW DOES A TOKEN-RING WORK?

The Token-Ring protocol defines the format of Media Access Control (MAC) frames and the rules for operating the ring. The basic idea behind the Token-Ring protocol is simple. A special MAC frame called a *token* circulates from station to station. When a station has information to transmit, it captures the token, creates a frame whose header contains the destination address, and sends its information. A destination address *usually* identifies a unique station, but alternatively it could identify a group of stations, or indicate that the frame should be broadcast.

Tokens and data are received from the *upstream* direction and are sent in the *downstream* direction.

---

\* Unfortunately, the IEEE's term for an Ethernet transceiver is "Medium Attachment Unit," which has the same acronym.

### 19.3.1    Role of the Token-Ring NIC

In the normal mode of operation, every information frame travels all the way around the ring. Therefore, one of the jobs of the Token-Ring Network Interface Card (NIC) in a station is to act as a repeater, transmitting the bits that it has received to the next station in the ring.

Of course, the original sender will not repeat its own frame. When the sender detects its own frame, it either will start transmitting a new frame or else will transmit a token, enabling another station to take control. The amount of time that a NIC can "hold" a token—that is, have the right to transmit frames—is limited, so that every station will get its turn within a predictable amount of time.

When a NIC detects an incoming frame, it must make a decision:

- Should I copy this frame into my memory?

If the destination address in the frame header is

- A unicast address assigned to the NIC
- A group (multicast) address assigned to the NIC
- A broadcast address

then the answer is yes.

### 19.3.2    Token-Ring Protocol Issues

There is quite a lot more to the Token-Ring protocol. Consider some of the main issues:

1. What happens if the token is corrupted and lost?
2. What happens if a sender crashes and fails to remove its frame from the ring?
3. How does a system that just powered up join the ring and get ready so that it is open for business?
4. How does a system close down and leave the ring?
5. What if there is a cabling problem, or one station's interface malfunctions, distorting messages or disobeying the rules?

There are many types of control frames used to deal with these issues. In addition, one of the stations plays a special role, detecting and curing ring problems.

## 19.4  ELEMENTS OF THE TOKEN-RING PROTOCOL

### 19.4.1  The Active Monitor

The use of one of the stations as an *Active Monitor* solves the problems posed by questions 1 and 2. An Active Monitor keeps a close watch on the ring. When the Active Monitor observes that a token is long overdue or that data is repeatedly circling around the ring, it sends a *purge* frame to reinitialize the ring, and then releases a new token.

### 19.4.2  Standby Monitors

The other stations have the job of acting as *Standby Monitors.* Periodically, all stations participate in a round-robin protocol that identifies each station's upstream neighbor. The stations identify themselves at regular intervals by sending *Standby Monitor Present* frames.

### 19.4.3  Procedures

A station that has just been activated or that has been reset will perform an initialization procedure. It will make sure that there is an Active Monitor. It must check that its address is not being used by another station by sending a *Duplicate Address Test* frame. When the station reaches the *opened* state, it is ready to send and receive information.

Similarly, a *closing* process enables the station's upstream and downstream neighbors to realize that they now are adjacent.

It is important for a station to know who its upstream neighbor is. Cabling problems and malfunctioning interfaces are detected by the station downstream from the problem and cause it to send a *Beacon* frame that indicates the location of the source of the trouble.

Does this solve all of our problems? Not quite. Suppose that the Active Monitor crashes? While it is alive, the Active Monitor periodically sends out *Active Monitor Present* frames to let the other stations know that it is there. If the other stations have not heard from the Active Monitor for a long time, they hold an election to pick another Active Monitor by sending out *Claim Token* frames. The election is won by the station whose address is the biggest number. The election protocol also is held when the ring is initialized.

### 19.4.4  Frame Formats

The Ethernet protocol has only one frame type—an information frame— with a very simple MAC header. As we have seen, quite a few control

| SD | AC | FC | Destination Address | Source Address | Routing Information Field (optional) | INFORMATION (optional) | FCS | ED | FS |
|----|----|----|---------------------|----------------|--------------------------------------|------------------------|-----|----|----|
|    |    |    |                     |                |                                      |                        |     |    |    |

SD = Starting Delimiter

AC = Access Control (Shows if this frame is a token)
FC = Frame Control (Type of frame)

Routing Information Field (Used to set up route,
                    then Contains route)

FCS = Frame Check Sequence

ED = Ending Delimiter
FS = Frame Status
     (Receiver indicates if
      frame was seen and
      copied)

**Figure 19.3** Token-Ring frame format.

frames are needed to make a Token-Ring work. Even more frame types are needed for the IBM (as opposed to IEEE) version of the protocol, which incorporates error reporting, route discovery, and source routing.

The format of Token-Ring frames is shown in Figure 19.3. The fields are as follows:

- Starting Delimiter: Identifies the start of a frame.

- Access Control: Indicates if the frame is a token. Used to implement frame priority. Inspected by the Active Monitor to detect whether this frame already has gone all the way around the ring.

- Frame Control: Defines the type of frame.

- Destination Address: 6-byte MAC address of the destination.

- Source Address: 6-byte MAC address of the source.

- Routing Information Field: Used by IBM's source routing protocol. Included if the frame is going to leave the source ring and pass through one or more source routing bridges.

- Information: Included in information (noncontrol) frames.

- Frame Check Sequence: Used to detect transmission errors.

- End Delimiter: Marks the end of the frame, can indicate whether this is an intermediate frame of a multiframe transmission, and can flag the fact that an error was detected in the frame.

An 802.2 Logical Link Control (LLC) header occupies the first few bytes of an information field.

## 19.5   SOURCE ROUTING

As shown in Figure 19.4, several rings can be bridged to form a single local area network. IBM has chosen to use *source routing* as the

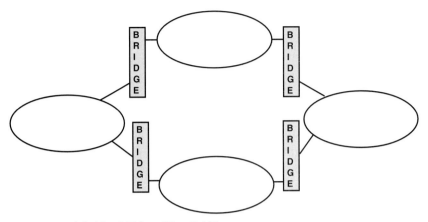

**Figure 19.4**  A bridged Token-Ring LAN.

method of establishing the paths that frames will follow across a bridged LAN.

A source station sends an *explorer* message that discovers a path to a destination, and records the path that is followed. The destination sends the message back to the source. Subsequent frames sent to the destination contain the path to be traversed. The Routing Information Field is the key to making this work.

### 19.5.1   Use of the Routing Information Field

To discover where a partner is located, we want to send a message that will provoke a response from the destination. Either of two messages defined as part of the IEEE 802.2 protocol will do the job:

XID           Exchange ID, which discloses attributes of the sender and
              elicits an XID response

TEST          Causes the partner to respond with a TEST message

The steps in the route discovery protocol are:

1. Check whether the destination is on the local ring. To do this, send an XID or TEST that does *not* include a routing information field. If there is no response, proceed with step 2.

2. Send an XID or TEST, but this time include a routing information field, and in that field, indicate that the frame should be broadcast across all rings.

There are two methods of broadcast. We'll describe the *all-routes* method in detail here. The frame that is broadcast is called an *explorer*.

3. The explorer frame is propagated to the destination across all possible paths. Hence, several copies may be produced. As each proceeds, its route is recorded in the routing information field. The destination returns all of the frames, and the source chooses the preferred route according to a specified criterion—e.g., the route contained in the first frame to complete the round trip.

4. Subsequent frames will be sent along the preferred route.

When the *single-route* method is used, exactly one copy of the frame will cross each LAN segment.

### 19.5.2  Format of the Routing Information Field

Figure 19.5 shows the format of the Routing Information Field (RIF), which consists of:

- Routing Control Field: Indicates if this is a routing broadcast. Provides the length of the Routing Information Field. Indicates whether the route should be followed from left-to-right or right-to-left.

- Route Designator Fields: Up to eight fields, each containing a ring-number/bridge-number combination.

## 19.6  THE INTERFACE TABLE

Table 19.1, the 802.5 Table, contains configuration and state information specific to a Token-Ring interface. There are variables that indicate whether the interface is joining or leaving the ring, report a variety of physical-level problems, and indicate the speed of the ring. The *dot5Commands* variable provides a mechanism that enables a management station to open, reset, or close down an 802.5 interface.

Three important table variables, *dot5RingState, dot5RingOpenStatus,* and *dot5RingStatus,* track exactly what is happening to the interface.

| Routing Control | Ring Number  Bridge Number | Ring Number  Bridge Number | . . . . . . |
|---|---|---|---|
| 2 octets | 2 octets | 2 octets | |

**Figure 19.5**  Format of the Routing Information Field.

**TABLE 19.1    The 802.5 Table**

iso.org.dod.internet.mgmt.mib-2.
transmission.dot5.dot5Table.dot5Entry
1.3.6.1.2.1.10.9.1.1

| OBJECT IDENTIFIER | Syntax | Access | Description |
|---|---|---|---|
| dot5IfIndex<br>1.3.6.1.2.1.10.9.1.1.1<br>► **Index** | INTEGER | read-<br>only | The index (*ifIndex*) for<br>this interface. |
| dot5Commands<br>1.3.6.1.2.1.10.9.1.1.2 | INTEGER<br>no-op(1),<br>open(2),<br>reset(3),<br>close(4) | read-<br>write | A command variable<br>used to request a state<br>change. Open means<br>join the ring, close<br>means leave. |
| dot5RingStatus<br>1.3.6.1.2.1.10.9.1.1.3 | INTEGER<br>See Sec. 19.6.3 | read-<br>only | A bit map showing<br>current errors. |
| dot5RingState<br>1.3.6.1.2.1.10.9.1.1.4 | INTEGER<br>See Sec. 19.6.1 | read-<br>only | State with respect to<br>entering/leaving ring. |
| dot5Ring<br>OpenStatus<br>1.3.6.1.2.1.10.9.1.1.5 | INTEGER<br>See Sec. 19.6.2 | read-<br>only | Did the last attempt<br>to enter the ring<br>succeed? If not, why? |
| dot5RingSpeed<br>1.3.6.1.2.1.10.9.1.1.6 | INTEGER<br>unknown(1),<br>1 Mbps(2),<br>4 Mbps(3),<br>16 Mbps(4) | read-<br>write | The bandwidth for the<br>ring. |
| dot5UpStream<br>1.3.6.1.2.1.10.9.1.1.7 | Mac<br>Address | read-<br>only | MAC address of the<br>upstream neighbor. |
| dot5ActMon<br>Participate<br>1.3.6.1.2.1.10.9.1.1.8 | INTEGER<br>true(1),<br>false(2) | read-<br>write | If true, then this<br>station will participate<br>in the Active Monitor<br>selection protocol. |
| dot5Functional<br>1.3.6.1.2.1.10.9.1.1.9 | Mac<br>Address | read-<br>write | A bit mask used to<br>identify all functional<br>addresses for this interface. |

### 19.6.1    The Ring State (Joining and Leaving)

The *dot5RingState* variable provides state information about opening (joining the ring) and closing (leaving the ring). The values are:

1. opened

2. closed

3. opening

4. closing

5. openFailure

6. ringFailure

### 19.6.2   The Ring Open Status

The *dot5RingOpenStatus* indicates whether the last attempt to enter the ring was successful, and if not, why not. The values are:

1. noOpen
2. badParam
3. lobeFailed
4. signalLoss
5. insertionTimeout
6. ringFailed
7. beaconing
8. duplicateMAC
9. requestFailed
10. removeReceived
11. open

### 19.6.3   The Ring Status

The *dot5RingStatus* is an error-reporting variable whose bits act as flags to signal one or more problems. Its integer value is computed as the sum of:

$$0 = \text{No Problems detected}$$

$$32 = \text{Ring Recovery}$$

$$64 = \text{Single Station}$$

$$256 = \text{Remove Received}$$

$$512 = \text{Reserved}$$

$$1024 = \text{Auto-Removal Error}$$

$$2048 = \text{Lobe Wire Fault}$$

$$4096 = \text{Transmit Beacon}$$

$$8192 = \text{Soft Error}$$

$$16384 = \text{Hard Error}$$

$$32768 = \text{Signal Loss}$$

$$131072 = \text{Open not completed}$$

The value is 131072 until an open is completed.

### 19.6.4   Functional Addresses

A Token-Ring interface can be assigned one or more *functional* addresses for which this interface will accept frames. A functional address is associated with a specific role in the network. Functional addresses have been defined for bridges, load servers, the Active Monitor, a LAN Manager station, and other roles.

## 19.7   THE STATISTICS TABLE

Table 19.2, the Statistics Table, counts traffic, physical problems, and protocol errors. A few technical facts are needed to understand some of the counters:

- A frame's End Delimiter byte contains two important flags. A pair of Address Recognized (A) bits are set to 1 by a destination station that recognizes its own address. A pair of Frame Copied (C) bits are set to 1 if the destination also has copied the frame into its receive buffer.

- There also is an error (E) bit at the end of a frame which is set to 1 by any station detecting an error.

- When the Active Monitor detects a serious error, it will transmit a Purge MAC frame which causes the ring to reinitialize itself.

The IBM version of the Token-Ring protocol includes error frames that can report a number of *soft errors.* These include conditions such as detection of an invalid character in a frame, a bad checksum, or a "lost" frame. A frame is lost if it was transmitted by the station, but never returned from its trip around the ring.

**TABLE 19.2   Token-Ring Statistics Table**

| iso.org.dod.internet.mgmt.mib-2. transmission.dot5.dot5StatsTable.dot5StatsEntry 1.3.6.1.2.1.10.9.2.1 | | | |
|---|---|---|---|
| OBJECT IDENTIFIER | Syntax | Access | Description |
| dot5StatsIfIndex 1.3.6.1.2.1.10.9.2.1.1 ▶ **Index** | INTEGER | read-only | The index (*ifIndex*) of this Token-Ring interface. |
| dot5Stats LineErrors 1.3.6.1.2.1.10.9.2.1.2 | Counter | read-only | Number of frames with E (error) bit 0 and: a nondata bit between the start and end delimiters or a bad Frame Check Sequence. |
| dot5Stats BurstErrors 1.3.6.1.2.1.10.9.2.1.3 | Counter | read-only | Number of times a station detected there were no signal transitions during five 1/2-bit timers. |

**TABLE 19.2    Token-Ring Statistics Table (*Continued*)**

iso.org.dod.internet.mgmt.mib-2.
transmission.dot5.dot5StatsTable.dot5StatsEntry
1.3.6.1.2.1.10.9.2.1

| OBJECT IDENTIFIER | Syntax | Access | Description |
|---|---|---|---|
| dot5Stats ACErrors 1.3.6.1.2.1.10.9.2.1.4 | Counter | read-only | For received Active Monitor Present and Standby Monitor Present frames: incremented when the A and C bits are wrong and indicate that some station is not setting these bits correctly. |
| dot5Stats AbortTransErrors 1.3.6.1.2.1.10.9.2.1.5 | Counter | read-only | Incremented when the station transmits an abort delimiter. |
| dot5Stats InternalErrors 1.3.6.1.2.1.10.9.2.1.6 | Counter | read-only | Incremented when a station diagnoses an internal error. |
| dot5Stats LostFrameErrors 1.3.6.1.2.1.10.9.2.1.7 | Counter | read-only | Incremented by a transmitting station when the trailer of a transmitted frame has not yet been received and the return-to-repeat timer (TRR) has expired. |
| dot5Stats ReceiveCongestions 1.3.6.1.2.1.10.9.2.1.8 | Counter | read-only | Incremented when there is not enough buffer space to receive an incoming frame. |
| dot5Stats FrameCopiedErrors 1.3.6.1.2.1.10.9.2.1.9 | Counter | read-only | Incremented when an incoming frame is addressed to this unique destination, but the A bits already have been set to 1. |
| dot5Stats TokenErrors 1.3.6.1.2.1.10.9.2.1.10 | Counter | read-only | Incremented by an Active Monitor that recognizes an error that means it needs to generate a new token. |
| dot5Stats SoftErrors 1.3.6.1.2.1.10.9.2.1.11 | Counter | read-only | Number of Soft Errors (errors recoverable by MAC protocol) that have been detected. |
| dot5Stats HardErrors 1.3.6.1.2.1.10.9.2.1.12 | Counter | read-only | Number of detected, immediately recoverable fatal errors—i.e., number of times the interface is transmitting or receiving beacon frames. |
| dot5Stats SignalLoss 1.3.6.1.2.1.10.9.2.1.13 | Counter | read-only | Number of times this interface detected loss of signal. |
| dot5Stats TransmitBeacons 1.3.6.1.2.1.10.9.2.1.14 | Counter | read-only | Number of times the interface has transmitted a beacon frame. |

TABLE 19.2    Token-Ring Statistics Table (*Continued*)

iso.org.dod.internet.mgmt.mib-2.
transmission.dot5.dot5StatsTable.dot5StatsEntry
1.3.6.1.2.1.10.9.2.1

| OBJECT IDENTIFIER | Syntax | Access | Description |
|---|---|---|---|
| dot5Stats Recoverys 1.3.6.1.2.1.10.9.2.1.15 | Counter | read-only | Number of Claim Token MAC frames received or transmitted after the interface has received a Ring Purge MAC frame. |
| dot5Stats LobeWires 1.3.6.1.2.1.10.9.2.1.16 | Counter | read-only | Number of times the interface has detected an open or short circuit in the lobe data path. |
| dot5Stats Removes 1.3.6.1.2.1.10.9.2.1.17 | Counter | read-only | Number of times the interface has received a Remove Ring Station request (which causes the interface to enter a close state.) |
| dot5Stats Singles 1.3.6.1.2.1.10.9.2.1.18 | Counter | read-only | Number of times this interface has sensed that it is the only station on the ring. |
| dot5Stats FreqErrors 1.3.6.1.2.1.10.9.2.1.19 | Counter | read-only | Number of times that the frequency of the incoming signal is not within expected bounds. |

## 19.8    THE TOKEN-RING TIMER TABLE

Table 19.3, the Token-Ring Timer Table, contains the values of the many timers required for Token-Ring operation. Note that *timer settings are measured in units of 100-microsecond intervals*. This table is an optional group.

This MIB was written following the convention that the ACCESS level is the *minimum* required. The timers in the table are assigned read-only access, but a vendor has the option of implementing them as read-write.

TABLE 19.3    The Token-Ring Timer Table

iso.org.dod.internet.mgmt.mib-2.
transmission.dot5.dot5TimerTable.dot5TimerEntry
1.3.6.1.2.1.10.9.5.1

| OBJECT IDENTIFIER | Syntax | Access | Description |
|---|---|---|---|
| dot5TimerIfIndex 1.3.6.1.2.1.10.9.5.1.1 ▶ **Index** | INTEGER | read-only | The index (*ifIndex*) for this 802.5 interface. |
| dot5Timer ReturnRepeat 1.3.6.1.2.1.10.9.5.1.2 | INTEGER | read-only | Time-out assuring that the interface will return to repeat state. |

**TABLE 19.3   The Token-Ring Timer Table (*Continued*)**

iso.org.dod.internet.mgmt.mib-2.
transmission.dot5.dot5TimerTable.dot5TimerEntry
1.3.6.1.2.1.10.9.5.1

| OBJECT IDENTIFIER | Syntax | Access | Description |
|---|---|---|---|
| dot5TimerHolding 1.3.6.1.2.1.10.9.5.1.3 | INTEGER | read-only | Token-holding time, during which a station can transmit frames. |
| dot5Timer QueuePDU 1.3.6.1.2.1.10.9.5.1.4 | INTEGER | read-only | Set after receiving an Active Monitor Present or Standby Monitor Present frame. When the timer expires, the station queues a Standby Monitor Present message for transmission. |
| dot5Timer ValidTransmit 1.3.6.1.2.1.10.9.5.1.5 | INTEGER | read-only | Timer used by the Active Monitor to detect the absence of valid transmissions. |
| dot5Timer NoToken 1.3.6.1.2.1.10.9.5.1.6 | INTEGER | read-only | Timer used to detect a lost token and other errors. |
| dot5Timer ActiveMon 1.3.6.1.2.1.10.9.5.1.7 | INTEGER | read-only | Timeout used by the Active Monitor for generating Active Monitor Present frames. |
| dot5Timer StandbyMon 1.3.6.1.2.1.10.9.5.1.8 | INTEGER | read-only | Timeout used by the Standby Monitors to detect that there is an Active Monitor Present and that tokens are being generated. |
| dot5Timer ErrorReport 1.3.6.1.2.1.10.9.5.1.9 | INTEGER | read-only | Timeout for sending a Report Error frame to report the values of error counters. |
| dot5Timer BeaconTransmit 1.3.6.1.2.1.10.9.5.1.10 | INTEGER | read-only | Timeout limit on sending beacon frames before a station enters the bypass state. |
| dot5Timer BeaconReceive 1.3.6.1.2.1.10.9.5.1.11 | INTEGER | read-only | Timeout limit on receiving beacon frames originating from the downstream neighbor before entering bypass. |

## 19.9   TESTS

Tests uniquely relating to a Token-Ring interface are identified under the Token-Ring subtree:

```
iso.org.dod.internet.mgmt.mib-2.transmission.dot5.dot5Tests
```

That is,

```
1 . 3 . 6 . 1 . 2 . 1 . 10 . 9 . 3
```

Tests that are relevant to a Token-Ring interface include the generic loopback test and a test of an interface's insert ring logic:

| OBJECT IDENTIFIER | Description |
|---|---|
| testFullDuplexLoopBack 1.3.6.1.2.1.12.4.1 dot5Tests 1.3.6.1.2.1.10.9.3.1 | Check the path from memory through the chipset's internal logic and back to memory. If the station is connected to an MAU, test the interface's insert ring logic. |

## 19.10   HARDWARE CHIPSET IDENTIFICATION

The identity of the chipset used in a Token-Ring interface is a useful piece of configuration information. The interface extensions MIB defined the *ifExtnsChipSet* variable to hold this information.

The variable *ifExtnsChipSet,* defined in RFC 1229, *Extensions to the Generic-Interface MIB,* holds the OBJECT IDENTIFIER of an interface's hardware chipset. The Token-Ring MIB includes identifiers for some popular chipsets. These are displayed in Table 19.4.

**TABLE 19.4   OBJECT IDENTIFIERs for Chipsets**

| iso.org.dod.internet.mgmt.mib-2.transmission. dot3.dot3ChipSets 1.3.6.1.2.1.10.7.8 | | |
|---|---|---|
| Vendor | Chipset name | Object identifier |
| IBM | chipSetIBM16 (4 or 16 Mbps) | 1.3.6.1.2.1.10.9.4.1 |
| TI | chipSetTItms380 (4Mbps) chipSetTItms380c16 (4 or 16 Mbs) | 1.3.6.1.2.1.10.9.4.2 1.3.6.1.2.1.10.9.4.3 |

## 19.11    RECOMMENDED READING

At the time of writing, the Token-Ring MIB was described in RFC 1231, *IEEE 802.5 Token Ring MIB.* The Token-Ring protocol is described in IEEE Standard 802.5, *Token Ring Access Method and Physical Layer Specifications.*

Use of the Token-Ring in IBM network environments is discussed in *IBM's Token-Ring Networking Handbook,* by George C. Sackett. IBM publication SC30-3374, *Token-Ring Network Architecture Reference,* contains a comprehensive description of the Token-Ring protocol.

# 20

# Managing an FDDI Interface

## 20.1 INTRODUCTION

The Fiber Distributed Data Interface (FDDI) technology defines a 100 megabit per second network primarily used as a backbone facility. With its diameter of 100 kilometers, an FDDI net can cover a significant area. However, sometimes FDDI is used for high-performance, high-bandwidth local area networks.

The FDDI technology is outside the scope of the IEEE 802 LAN committee. FDDI standards are under the control of the ANSI X3T9.5 Task Group. A Station Management subcommittee of the ANSI group devoted a great deal of effort to FDDI network management, and defined managed objects for the technology. The FDDI MIB defined in RFC 1512 is based directly on the ANSI work.

The FDDI specifications are particularly rich in acronyms. What is the probability that a random combination of any two or three characters is an FDDI acronym? Pretty high!

It is not possible to explain every FDDI timer and protocol element within the confines of this chapter. The current MIB is presented here, along with enough basic information so that the major protocol operations and most important error conditions can be understood.

## 20.2 FDDI LAN ARCHITECTURE

### 20.2.1 Topologies

FDDI is a very flexible technology. Data always follows a path that marches around a ring. However, like a Token-Ring, stations usually are attached to access units, forming a ring of stars. The access units are called *concentrators*. Moreover, concentrators can be attached below other concentrators, shaping the network into a ring of trees. The ring is allowed to shrink to a point, leaving only a tree that has a "null" concentrator as its root.

Different types of fiber-optic cable can be used within the same net. In fact, part of the net could be cabled with twisted pair.

### 20.2.2  Connectivity

All or part of an FDDI ring may be *dual-cabled* for fault tolerance. A dual-ring implementation has two rings: a primary and a secondary. A dual ring also is called a *trunk ring*. Concentrators can be used to build trees that extend out from the trunk. Figure 20.1 illustrates how complex a configuration can be.

Data normally travels around the primary ring, which may in fact be the only ring there is. A good use for a secondary ring is to connect a set of concentrators redundantly with dual attachments. If there is a break in a dual-cabled ring, the two nodes adjacent to the break can *wrap* the traffic onto the secondary connection. Figure 20.2 shows how traffic is wrapped and rerouted after a break.

An alternative recovery strategy called *Global Hold* switches all traffic from a broken ring to the other ring.

### 20.2.3  Stations and Concentrators

An *FDDI station* is an addressable node that can transmit, receive, and repeat information. Each station should contain exactly one Station

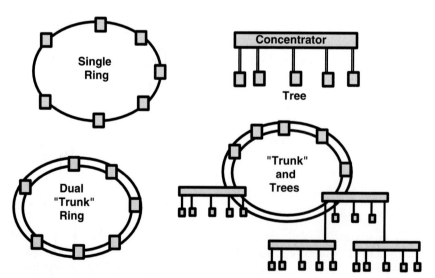

**Figure 20.1**  FDDI network topology.

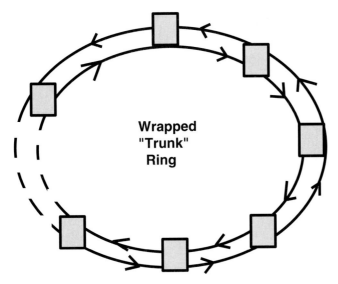

**Figure 20.2** "Wrapping" traffic to heal a broken ring.

Management (SMT) entity. However, the FDDI MIB provides for devices that support multiple SMTs. Each station also contains at least one Media Access Control (MAC) entity, and at least one physical *port*. A port provides connectivity to one fiber used to transmit data and a second fiber used to receive data.

There are two classes of station:

- *Class A or Dual-Attachment Station (DAS).* Has (at least) two ports, belongs to both the primary and secondary ring, and can *wrap* the ring to bypass a break.
- *Class B or Single-Attachment Station (SAS).* Has (at least) one port, belongs only to the primary ring, and cannot wrap the ring.

Stations can be attached to a *Ring Wiring Concentrator.* A concentrator can be a simple device dedicated to physical connectivity, or it may be a full-fledged class A station.

Some sites use the secondary ring as a second transmission path, bringing throughput up to 200 megabits per second. This is done by attaching Single-Attachment Stations (SAS) to the secondary ring. However, these stations will *not* be able to communicate with stations on the primary ring unless a bridge joins the two rings. The maximum number of stations attached to an individual ring is 500.

## 20.3    FDDI PROTOCOL ARCHITECTURE

### 20.3.1    Physical Protocol

It is unusual for a *physical* layer to be broken into sublayers, but this has been done for FDDI because it runs over so many different media.

The upper sublayer, called the Physical Layer Protocol (PHY), deals with all physical layer issues that are *independent* of the medium, such as clocking and buffering.

A different Physical Layer Medium-Dependent (PMD) protocol is defined for each media type. The PMD protocol must deal with issues such as cables, connectors, signals, acceptable bit error rates, and bypass management.

The first PMD specification was written for *multimode* fiber. Later, PMD specifications were written for *single mode* fiber,* SONET and copper twisted pair. Figure 20.3 shows the layering for different media.

An important fact to keep in mind is that data can be sent in only one direction on fiber. Hence a physical attachment consists of two fibers, one for each direction. A dual-attached station will require four fibers. A port, which controls a pair of fibers, is made up of a PHY/PMD combination. A port in a station connects to a port in a neighboring station or concentrator.

---

* This is not the place for a detailed description of types of optical fiber; the important fact is that *single mode* supports higher bandwidths and longer distances—and costs more.

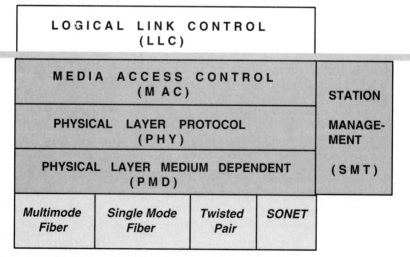

**Figure 20.3**  FDDI protocol layering.

### 20.3.2    MAC Layer

A token-passing protocol closely modeled on IEEE 802.5 is used for the FDDI Media Access Control (MAC) sublayer. Stations cooperate to monitor the ring and perform error detection and recovery. A logical FDDI ring is defined by the sequence of MAC entities through which data passes. There may be additional pieces of physical equipment (such as simple concentrators that do not contain any MACs) along the data path.

When a dual ring is configured, separate tokens rotate in opposite directions on the two rings.

The protocol supports *synchronous* or *asynchronous* transmission. Synchronous transmission means that stations get a certain amount of reserved bandwidth, and always will be allowed to send at least this much data. Asynchronous bandwidth is unreserved, and is used, within specified limits, on an as-needed basis. Normally FDDI networks operate asynchronously, but a mixture of asynchronous and synchronous traffic can be supported.

A Single-Attachment Station has a single MAC entity, but Dual-Attachment Stations may have one or two MACs. In other words, a single MAC could supervise two PHY/PMDs, or separate MACs could be used for each. A wiring concentrator can have many MAC entities.

### 20.3.3    MAC Timers

Each station knows how long it *should* take a token to circle the ring and how long it has been since a token last was seen. These values are kept in the timers.

- *Target Token Rotation Timer (TTRT).*   The target maximum elapsed time between token arrivals at each station. An operational value between 4 and 165 milliseconds is negotiated as follows. At initialization, each station requests a TTRT that meets its needs. Ring monitor negotiation assigns the minimum of these requests as the operational value.

- *Token Rotation Timer (TRT).*   Measures the time since this station last saw the token.

When a station receives a token, it has a quota of reserved time during which it can transfer data. It also can use any "leftover" period of time, TTRT-TRT, to transmit data. If there is no leftover, but in fact the TRT is much larger than the TTRT, the ring monitor function reports an error to the LAN manager. T_Max, a configured upper limit for TTRT, is used during initialization.

Each station checks for suspiciously long periods of inactivity using the *TVX* time:.

- *Valid-Transmission Timer (TVX).* Expires if no valid transmission has been seen by the station during the specified period.

If a TVX expires, the station will try to reinitialize the ring.

### 20.3.4   Station Management (SMT)

Station Management (SMT) is a term that covers all of the functions needed to make FDDI work. A Station Management entity must supervise activities at the Physical Layer Medium-Dependent (PMD) level, Physical Layer Protocol (PHY) level, and Media Access Control (MAC) level of an interface. What makes FDDI unusual is that SMT was built in as an integral part of the technology. Examples of SMT functions include:

- Controlling when a station joins or leaves the ring
- Monitoring and testing the physical layer
- Collecting statistics
- Communicating with external management stations

Station Management entities use SMT frames to exchange neighbor information, report status, and test the ring. There are several versions of the SMT protocol, and an individual station may be able to support a range of versions. A concentrator contains separate SMT entities for each of its interfaces.

The categories of station management functions include:

- *Connection Management (CMT).*   Establishes and maintains physical connections with neighboring stations and maintains the logical topology of the network.
- *Ring Management (RMT).*   Makes sure that ring activity is normal, and that there is a valid token.
- *Operational Management.*   Checks up on timers and other FDDI parameters. Communicates with an external management station.

Figure 20.3 showed the relationship between Station Management and the other components of an FDDI interface.

### 20.4   FDDI TEXTUAL CONVENTIONS

Two INTEGER and two OCTET STRING variables are given names specific to FDDI technology:

- *FddiTimeNano.*   An integer representing time measured in units of 1 nanosecond. The range is 0 to 2,147,483,647 (or 2.147 seconds). Note that ANSI uses a twos complement representation for time measurements, while the MIB represents time as ordinary integers.

- *FddiTimeMilli.*   An integer representing time measured in units of 1 millisecond. The range is 0 to 2,147,483,647 (or 2,147,483 seconds).

- *FddiResourceId.*   An INTEGER used to refer to an instance of a communications resource in an FDDI station. Resource types include Media Access Control (MAC), PORT (which implements the physical layer), or PATH (which identifies a path that data can take through a station). The range is (0..65535). Indexing begins at 1, and 0 indicates the absence of a resource.

- *FddiSMTStationIdType.*   An OCTET STRING identifying a station. It consists of 2 octets which are defined by an implementor, followed by the 6-octet IEEE MAC address.

- *FddiMACLongAddressType.*   An OCTET STRING containing an IEEE 6-octet MAC address.

## 20.5   THE FDDI MIB

As shown in Figure 20.4, there are five MIB groups, including:

- *fddimibSMT.*   FDDI node configuration and status information.

- *fddimibMAC.*   Configuration, status, and statistical information about the node's MAC entities and MAC protocol. The protocol resembles IBM's Token-Ring protocol.

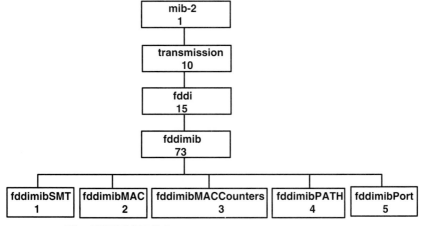

**Figure 20.4**  The FDDI MIB Subtree.

- *fddimibMACCounters.* An optional table of MAC error statistics.

- *fddimibPATH.* Two tables configuring PATHs through the node.

- *fddimibPORT.* A table that correlates a PORT with an exit MAC and valid PATHs. The table also sets thresholds for a variety of alarm conditions.

FDDI data rates are high, and the main job of an FDDI interface is to transmit and receive traffic. Maintaining perfect counts of the traffic has a secondary priority. Hence, the counters that appear in the MIB tables are expected to be close to the actual numbers, but might not be 100 percent accurate.

Before we look at the MIB variables, we need to understand the way that a port in one station is connected to a port in an adjacent station, and the types of paths that are followed by data as it enters and exits a station.

### 20.5.1 PORT Connector Types

A station is physically attached to a pair of fibers by a Media Interface Connector (MIC). A fiber can carry data in one direction only. Thus, every station needs at least one fiber to send data and another to receive data.

Saying that a station is *dual-attached* means that it connects to both the primary and secondary rings and therefore will have *two* ports, *two* Media Interface Connectors, and *four* fibers—a send and receive fiber that are part of the primary ring and a send and receive fiber that are part of the secondary ring.

Recall that a port is a PHY/PMD combination. There are four port *types* corresponding to the connectivity of its pair of cables, as shown in Figure 20.5. Each dual-attachment node contains a type A port and a type B port. A type A connects to a neighbor's type B. Concentrator nodes contain type M ports that connect to type S ports in single-attachment nodes. Specifically, the types are:

- Type A: One incoming primary, one outgoing secondary fiber.

- Type B: A partner for type A—one outgoing primary, one incoming secondary fiber.

- Type M: A Master in a concentrator, used to connect to a single-attachment station.

- Type S: In a single-attached station, used to connect to a concentrator.

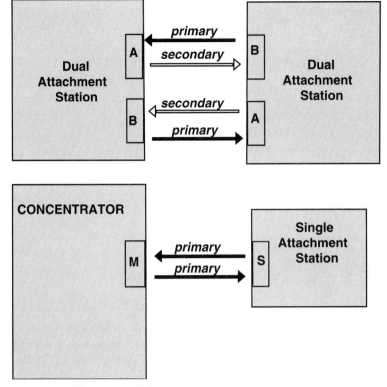

**Figure 20.5** Types of FDDI connectors.

A concentrator will have multiple type M ports. If the concentrator is attached to a dual trunk backbone, it will have a type A and type B port as well.

### 20.5.2 Connection Policy

What are the valid ways that a station can connect to a neighbor? All possible pairings of port types are listed as follows. Any combination except M-M is legal, but several are undesirable. Some combinations might be allowed because they are necessary to allow the ring to wrap and recover from a fault.

A station can be configured with a *connection policy* that indicates which combinations are unacceptable for the station. The policy is expressed by setting a flag bit for each combination that is rejected. The resulting binary number is then turned into an integer. The right-hand column shows the integer that is added into the sum when a flag bit is set to 1.

| Policy | Add |
|--------|------|
| A-A | 1 |
| A-B | 2 |
| A-S | 4 |
| A-M | 8 |
| B-A | 16 |
| B-B | 32 |
| B-S | 64 |
| B-M | 128 |
| S-A | 256 |
| S-B | 512 |
| S-S | 1024 |
| S-M | 2048 |
| M-A | 4096 |
| M-B | 8192 |
| M-S | 16384 |

### 20.5.3   Connection Management and PATHs

Let's examine the path followed by data entering the station from the primary ring and exiting the station onto the primary ring. As shown in Figure 20.6, a simple path is followed for a Single-Attachment Station, through PMD, PHY, MAC, PHY, and PMD.

For the Dual-Attachment Station, data normally enters via one PMD/PHY port and exits via the other. But if there is a break in the ring, the path can change so that data enters and leaves via the same PMD/PHY port—switching from the primary to the secondary ring in one station, and switching back again in another station.

Note that the simplest path of all is followed when a station is not actively participating in the ring. The station's bypass switch simply shunts incoming data to the appropriate output fiber.

In order to find out the state of the ring, management needs to know the path that currently is active. How can a path be described? Each port and MAC resource is assigned a *resource number*. A path is reported by indicating the order in which the resources are traversed. There also are some special types of paths:

- Optionally, a *Local* path may be defined that is not part of a primary or secondary path. It sometimes is used for diagnostics.

- An *isolated* path implements bypass. The MAC level of the station never sees the data.

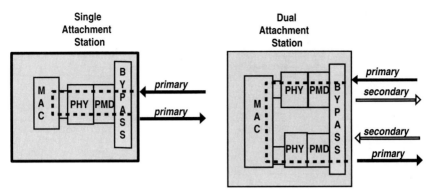

**Figure 20.6**  Paths through a station.

Connection management is responsible for inserting and removing ports from a ring, detecting faults, reconfiguring paths through a station using optical bypass,* and testing links.

## 20.6    THE STATION MANAGEMENT GROUP

The stand-alone variable, *fddimibSMTNumber,* indicates how many SMT implementations there are for a device. Its OBJECT IDENTIFIER is 1.3.6.1.2.1.10.15.73.1.1.

Table 20.1, the Station Management Table, contains configuration information about every facet of SMT. For example, it lists the number of MACs in the station or concentrator, counts ports of each type, configures and describes the type of PATHs through the system, indicates connection policies, and reports status. There also is an action variable that can be used to request that the station connect to the ring or disconnect from the ring. The number of entries cannot exceed *fddimibSMTNumber.*

## 20.7    MEDIA ACCESS CONTROL

The FDDI Media Access Control (MAC) protocol is similar to the 802.5 Token-Ring protocol.† IEEE 6-octet MAC addresses are used. A token, claim frames, purge frames, and beacon frames carry out protocol operations similar to Token-Ring operations. "A" bits at the end of a frame are set by a receiver to indicate "Address Recognized" and "C" bits are set to indicate "Frame Copied."

---

\* There are two types of bypass. A station may wrap the ring, or a station may isolate itself from the ring and just allow traffic to pass through.

† See Chapter 19.

**TABLE 20.1    The Station Management Table**

iso.org.dod.internet.mgmt.mib-2.transmission.
fddi.snmpFddiSMT.snmpFddiSMTTable.snmpFddiSMTEntry
1.3.6.1.2.1.10.15.73.1.2.1

| OBJECT IDENTIFIER | Syntax | Access | Description |
|---|---|---|---|
| fddimibSMT Index 1.3.6.1.2.1.10.15.73. 1.2.1.1 ▶ **Index** | INTEGER (1..65535) | read-only | A unique index for each SMT entity at this node. |
| fddimibSMT StationId 1.3.6.1.2.1.10.15.73. 1.2.1.2 | FddiSMT StationId Type | read-only | An 8-octet string uniquely identifying the FDDI station. |
| fddimibSMT OpVersionId 1.3.6.1.2.1.10.15.73. 1.2.1.3 | INTEGER (1..65535) | read-only | ANSI-defined version of SMT being used for operation. |
| fddimibSMT HiVersionId 1.3.6.1.2.1.10.15.73. 1.2.1.4 | INTEGER (1..65535) | read-only | Highest version of SMT that this station supports. |
| fddimibSMT LoVersionId 1.3.6.1.2.1.10.15.73. 1.2.1.5 | INTEGER (1..65535) | read-only | Lowest version of SMT that this station supports. |
| fddimibSMT UserData 1.3.6.1.2.1.10.15.73. 1.2.1.6 | OCTET STRING (SIZE (32)) | read-write | User information. An ASCII string. |
| fddimibSMT MIBVersionId 1.3.6.1.2.1.10.15.73. 1.2.1.7 | INTEGER (0..65535) | read-only | Version of the FDDI MIB of this station. |
| fddimibSMT MACCts 1.3.6.1.2.1.10.15.73. 1.2.1.8 | INTEGER (0..255) | read-only | Number of MACs in this station or concentrator. |
| fddimibSMT NonMasterCts 1.3.6.1.2.1.10.15.73. 1.2.1.9 | INTEGER (0..2) | read-only | Number of non-Master ports (A, B, or S ports) in the station or concentrator. |
| fddimibSMT MasterCts 1.3.6.1.2.1.10.15.73. 1.2.1.10 | INTEGER (0..255) | read-only | Number of Master (M) ports in the node. If node is not a concentrator, the value is zero. |
| fddimibSMT AvailablePaths 1.3.6.1.2.1.10.15.73. 1.2.1.11 | INTEGER (0..7) | read-only | Bit map indicating PATH types that are available (Primary(0), Secondary(1), Local(2)). |

**TABLE 20.1   The Station Management Table (*Continued*)**

iso.org.dod.internet.mgmt.mib-2.transmission.
fddi.snmpFddiSMT.snmpFddiSMTTable.snmpFddiSMTEntry
1.3.6.1.2.1.10.15.73.1.2.1

| OBJECT IDENTIFIER | Syntax | Access | Description |
|---|---|---|---|
| fddimibSMT Config Capabilities 1.3.6.1.2.1.10.15.73. 1.2.1.12 | INTEGER (0..3) | read-only | Bit map indicating capabilities. holdAvailable(0), CF-Wrap-AB(1) |
| fddimibSMT ConfigPolicy 1.3.6.1.2.1.10.15.73. 1.2.1.13 | INTEGER (0..1) | read-write | Bit map indicating the configuration policy (configurationHold(0)). |
| fddimibSMT Connection Policy 1.3.6.1.2.1.10.15.73. 1.2.1.14 | INTEGER (32768.. 65535) | read-write | Bit map indicating the connection types that will be rejected. See Sec. 20.5.4. |
| fddimibSMT TNotify 1.3.6.1.2.1.10.15.73. 1.2.1.15 | INTEGER (2..30) | read-write | Timer (in seconds) used in the Neighbor Notification protocol which is used to exchange address information and discover duplicate addresses. |
| fddimibSMT StatRptPolicy 1.3.6.1.2.1.10.15.73. 1.2.1.16 | INTEGER true(1), false(2) | read-write | Indicates whether the node implements the Status Reporting Protocol, which sends status messages to a ring manager station. |
| fddimibSMT TraceMaxExpiration FddiTimeMilli 1.3.6.1.2.1.10.15.73. 1.2.1.17 | FddiTime Milli | read-write | Estimates time for a Trace to propagate around the ring. Is a lower bound for detecting a nonrecovering ring. |
| fddimibSMT BypassPresent 1.3.6.1.2.1.10.15.73. 1.2.1.18 | INTEGER true(1), false(2) | read-only | Flag indicating if the station has a bypass on its AB port pair. |
| fddimibSMT ECMState 1.3.6.1.2.1.10.15.73. 1.2.1.19 | INTEGER ec0(1),... ec7(8) | read-only | Indicates current state of the Entity Coordination Management (ECM) state machine, such as Out, In, Path_Test, or Insert. |
| fddimibSMT CFState 1.3.6.1.2.1.10.15.73. 1.2.1.20 | INTEGER cf0(1),... cf12(13) | read-only | The attachment configuration for the station or concentrator, such as thru or wrap_ab. |

**TABLE 20.1   The Station Management Table (*Continued*)**

iso.org.dod.internet.mgmt.mib-2.transmission.
fddi.snmpFddiSMT.snmpFddiSMTTable.snmpFddiSMTEntry
1.3.6.1.2.1.10.15.73.1.2.1

| OBJECT IDENTIFIER | Syntax | Access | Description |
|---|---|---|---|
| fddimibSMT RemoteDisconnect Flag 1.3.6.1.2.1.10.15.73. 1.2.1.21 | INTEGER true(1), false(2) | read-only | A flag indicating that the station was remotely disconnected from the network as a result of a Parameter Management Frame command. |
| fddimibSMT StationStatus 1.3.6.1.2.1.10.15.73. 1.2.1.22 | INTEGER concat-enated(1), separated (2), thru(3) | read-only | Current status of the primary and secondary paths within this station. |
| fddimibSMT PeerWrapFlag 1.3.6.1.2.1.10.15.73. 1.2.1.23 | INTEGER true(1), false(2) | read-only | Value of the PeerWrapFlag. |
| fddimibSMT TimeStamp 1.3.6.1.2.1.10.15.73. 1.2.1.24 | FddiTime Milli | read-only | The value of the station TimeStamp, which is included in status report messages. |
| fddimibSMT TransitionTimeStamp 1.3.6.1.2.1.10.15.73. 1.2.1.25 | FddiTime Milli | read-only | The time of the most recent event or condition assertion at the station. |
| fddimibSMT StationAction 1.3.6.1.2.1.10.15.73. 1.2.1.26 | INTEGER | read-write | Triggers a connect, disconnect, test, or port Connector disable. |

A single-attachment station needs only a single MAC entity. A dual-attached station can be implemented with one* or two MAC entities. Two entities are used when both the primary and secondary ring are used to carry traffic concurrently. A concentrator will have many MAC entities.

In the MAC group, the stand-alone variable *fddimibMACNumber* reports the total number of MAC implementations at the entity, and hence the maximum number of entries in the Media Access Control Table. The OBJECT IDENTIFIER for *fddimibMACNumber* is:

```
1.3.6.1.2.1.10.15.73.2.1
```

---

* When used for backup only, the second set of connections in a dual configuration will have the same MAC address as the first.

### 20.7.1 The Media Access Control Table

A number of variables in Table 20.2, the Media Access Control Table, relate to timing on the ring.

One variable, *fddimibMACFrameErrorRatio,* is quite unusual because it is the result of a computation. The variable measures the proportion of error by calculating the quantity:

$$2^{16} \times \frac{(\text{delta fddimibMACLostCts} + \text{delta fddimibMACErrorCts})}{(\text{delta fddimibMACFrameCts} + \text{delta fddimibMACLostCts})}$$

This value will be compared to a threshold. SNMP usually leaves computational work and threshold checking to a management application. In this case, implementations already were providing the threshold check, so it was included in the MIB.

**TABLE 20.2  The MAC Table**

| iso.org.dod.internet.mgmt.mib-2.transmission. fddi.fddimibMAC.fddimibMACTable.fddimibMACEntry 1.3.6.1.2.1.10.15.73.2.2.1 | | | |
|---|---|---|---|
| OBJECT IDENTIFIER | Syntax | Access | Description |
| fddimibMAC SMTIndex 1.3.6.1.2.1.10.15.73. 2.2.1.1 ▶ **Index** | INTEGER (1..65535) | read-only | The value of the SMT index associated with this MAC. |
| fddimibMAC Index 1.3.6.1.2.1.10.15.73. 2.2.1.2 ▶ **Index** | INTEGER (1..65535) | read-only | Unique index for this MAC (which is its SMT resource index). |
| fddimibMAC IfIndex | INTEGER (1..65535) | read-only | The ifIndex for this MAC interface. |
| fddimibMAC FrameStatus Functions 1.3.6.1.2.1.10.15.73. 2.2.1.3 | INTEGER (0..7) | read-only | MAC's optional Frame Status processing functions (repeat, set, clear). |
| fddimibMAC TMaxCapability 1.3.6.1.2.1.10.15.73. 2.2.1.4 | FddiTime Nano | read-only | Maximum time value of fddiMACTMax that this MAC can support. |
| fddimibMAC TVXCapability 1.3.6.1.2.1.10.15.73. 2.2.1.5 | FddiTime Nano | read-only | Maximum time value of fddiMACTvxValue for this MAC. TVX is the Valid-Transmission Timer. |

**TABLE 20.2   The MAC Table (*Continued*)**

iso.org.dod.internet.mgmt.mib-2.transmission.
fddi.fddimibMAC.fddimibMACTable.fddimibMACEntry
1.3.6.1.2.1.10.15.73.2.2.1

| OBJECT IDENTIFIER | Syntax | Access | Description |
|---|---|---|---|
| fddimibMAC AvailablePaths 1.3.6.1.2.1.10.15.73. 2.2.1.6 | INTEGER (0..7) | read-only | Bit map of PATH types available for this MAC. Bits: Primary(0), Secondary(1), Local(2). |
| fddimibMAC CurrentPath 1.3.6.1.2.1.10.15.73. 2.2.1.7 | INTEGER | read-only | Path into which this MAC is currently inserted. isolated(1), local(2), secondary(3), primary(4), concatenated (5), thru(6). |
| fddimibMAC UpstreamNbr 1.3.6.1.2.1.10.15.73. 2.2.1.8 | FddiMAC LongAddress Type | read-only | Upstream neighbor's IEEE MAC address. |
| fddimibMAC DownstreamNbr 1.3.6.1.2.1.10.15.73. 2.2.1.8 | FddiMAC LongAddress Type | read-only | Downstream neighbor's IEEE MAC address. |
| fddimibMAC OldUpstreamNbr 1.3.6.1.2.1.10.15.73. 2.2.1.9 | FddiMAC LongAddress Type | read-only | Previous value of the upstream neighbor's MAC address. |
| fddimibMAC OldDownstreamNbr 1.3.6.1.2.1.10.15.73. 2.2.1.9 | FddiMAC LongAddress Type | read-only | Previous value of the downstream neighbor's MAC address. |
| fddimibMAC DupAddrTest 1.3.6.1.2.1.10.15.73. 2.2.1.10 | INTEGER none(1), pass(2), fail(3) | read-only | Value of duplicate address flag, indicates if the duplicate address test was passed. |
| fddimibMAC RequestedPaths 1.3.6.1.2.1.10.15.73. 2.2.1.11 | INTEGER (0..255) | read-write | Bit map showing permitted paths into which this MAC may be inserted. Bits: local(0), secondary-alternate(1), primary-alternate(2), concatenated-alternate(3), secondary-preferred(4) primary-preferred(5) concatenated-preferred(6) thru(7). |
| fddimibMAC DownstreamPORT Type 1.3.6.1.2.1.10.15.73. 2.2.1.12 | INTEGER a(1), b(2), s(3), m(4), none(5) | read-only | The Port Connector (PC) Type of the first port that is downstream of this MAC (the port that will exit the station). |

**TABLE 20.2    The MAC Table  (*Continued*)**

iso.org.dod.internet.mgmt.mib-2.transmission.
fddi.fddimibMAC.fddimibMACTable.fddimibMACEntry
1.3.6.1.2.1.10.15.73.2.2.1

| OBJECT IDENTIFIER | Syntax | Access | Description |
|---|---|---|---|
| fddimibMAC SMTAddress 1.3.6.1.2.1.10.15.73. 2.2.1.13 | FddiMAC LongAddress Type | read-only | 6-octet individual MAC address used for SMT frames. |
| fddimibMAC TReq 1.3.6.1.2.1.10.15.73. 2.2.1.14 | FddiTime Nano | read-only | The value of T_Req_value passed to the MAC; a timer that can trigger a recovery process. |
| fddimibMAC TNeg 1.3.6.1.2.1.10.15.73. 2.2.1.15 | FddiTime Nano | read-only | The value of the T-Neg timer. |
| fddimibMAC TMax 1.3.6.1.2.1.10.15.73. 2.2.1.16 | FddiTime Nano | read-only | The value of T_Max_value, the maximum Token Rotation Time passed to this MAC. |
| fddimibMAC TvxValue 1.3.6.1.2.1.10.15.73. 2.2.1.17 | FddiTime Nano | read-only | The value of the Valid-Transmission Timer, TVX, passed to this MAC. |
| fddimibMAC FrameCts 1.3.6.1.2.1.10.15.73. 2.2.1.20 | Counter | read-only | Count of number of frames received at this MAC. |
| fddimibMAC CopiedCts 1.3.6.1.2.1.10.15.73. 2.2.1. | Counter | read-only | Count of information frames addressed to and successfully copied to station's receive buffers by this MAC. |
| fddimibMAC TransmitCts 1.3.6.1.2.1.10.15.73. 2.2.1. | Counter | read-only | Number of information frames transmitted by this MAC. |
| fddimibMAC ErrorCts 1.3.6.1.2.1.10.15.73. 2.2.1.21 | Counter | read-only | Frames detected to be in error by this MAC (that had not been detected in error by another MAC). |
| fddimibMAC LostCts 1.3.6.1.2.1.10.15.73. 2.2.1.22 | Counter | read-only | Number of times this MAC detected a format error during frame reception. |
| fddimibMAC FrameError Threshold 1.3.6.1.2.1.10.15.73. 2.2.1.23 | INTEGER (0..65535) | read-write | A threshold used to determine when a MAC condition report shall be generated. |

**TABLE 20.2    The MAC Table  (*Continued*)**

iso.org.dod.internet.mgmt.mib-2.transmission.
fddi.fddimibMAC.fddimibMACTable.fddimibMACEntry
1.3.6.1.2.1.10.15.73.2.2.1

| OBJECT IDENTIFIER | Syntax | Access | Description |
|---|---|---|---|
| fddimibMAC FrameErrorRatio 1.3.6.1.2.1.10.15.73. 2.2.1.24 | INTEGER (0..65535) | read-only | Value of the ratio to be compared with the threshold (see formula in Sec. 20.7.1). |
| fddimibMAC RMTState 1.3.6.1.2.1.10.15.73. 2.2.1.25 | INTEGER | read-only | Current state of the Ring Management state machine (for example, isolated, Non_Op, or Ring_Op). |
| fddimibMAC DaFlag 1.3.6.1.2.1.10.15.73. 2.2.1.26 | INTEGER true(1), false(2) | read-only | Value of the Ring Management Duplicate Address Flag. |
| fddimibMAC UnaDaFlag 1.3.6.1.2.1.10.15.73. 2.2.1.27 | INTEGER true(1), false(2) | read-only | Flag set when the upstream neighbor reports a duplicate address condition. |
| fddimibMAC FrameErrorFlag 1.3.6.1.2.1.10.15.73. 2.2.1.28 | INTEGER true(1), false(2) | read-only | If true, the MAC Frame Error Condition is present. |
| fddimibMAC UnitdataAvailable 1.3.6.1.2.1.10.15.73. 2.2.1.29 | INTEGER true(1), false(2) | read-only | Has value of the Ring Management MAC_Avail flag. |
| fddimibMAC HardwarePresent 1.3.6.1.2.1.10.15.73. 2.2.1.30 | INTEGER true(1), false(2) | read-only | Indicates presence of hardware support for this MAC. |
| fddimibMAC UntdataEnable 1.3.6.1.2.1.10.15.73. 2.2.1.30 | INTEGER true(1), false(2) | read-write | Determines the value of the MA_UNITDATA_Enable flag in Ring Management. |

### 20.7.2   The Enhanced MAC Counters Group

Table 20.3, the Enhanced MAC Counters Table is optional. It includes a number of useful error counts. A station is expected to make the best effort that it can to keep fairly accurate counts. However, the station's functional responsibilities come first. The table is indexed by *fddimibMACSMTIndex* and *fddimibMACIndex*.

**TABLE 20.3    The Enhanced MAC Counters Table**

iso.org.dod.internet.mgmt.mib-2.transmission.
fddi.fddimib.fddimibMACCounters.
fddimibMACCountersTable.fddimibMACCountersEntry
1.3.6.1.2.1.10.15.73.3.1.1

| OBJECT IDENTIFIER | Syntax | Access | Description |
|---|---|---|---|
| fddimibMAC TokenCts 1.3.6.1.2.1.10.15.73. 3.1.1.1 | Counter | read-only | Number of times that the station has received a token at this MAC. |
| fddimibMAC TvxExpiredCts 1.3.6.1.2.1.10.15.73. 3.1.1.2 | Counter | read-only | Number of times that the Valid-Transmission Timer (TVX) has expired. |
| fddimibMAC NotCopiedCts 1.3.6.1.2.1.10.15.73. 3.1.1.3 | Counter | read-only | Number of frames that were addressed to this MAC but were not copied into its receive buffers. |
| fddimibMAC LateCts 1.3.6.1.2.1.10.15.73. 3.1.1.4 | Counter | read-only | Number of Token Rotation Time (TRT) expirations since this MAC was reset or a token was received. |
| fddimibMAC RingOpCts 1.3.6.1.2.1.10.15.73. 3.1.1.5 | Counter | read-only | Number of times the ring has entered the 'Ring_Operational' state from the 'Ring Not Operational' state. |
| fddimibMAC NotCopied Ratio 1.3.6.1.2.1.10.15.73. 3.1.1.6 | INTEGER (0..65535) | read-only | Value of the ratio defined in Sec. 20.7.2. |
| fddimibMAC NotCopiedFlag 1.3.6.1.2.1.10.15.73. 3.1.1.7 | INTEGER true(1), false(2) | read-only | True indicates that the Not Copied condition is present. |
| fddimibMAC NotCopied Threshold 1.3.6.1.2.1.10.15.73. 3.1.1.8 | INTEGER (0..65535) | read-write | Threshold for determining when a MAC condition report shall be generated. |

Like the MAC table, this table also contains a variable, *fddimib-MACNotCopiedRatio,* which is calculated. The ratio is:

$$2^{16} \times \frac{\text{delta fddiMACNotCopiedCts}}{(\text{delta fddiMACCopiedCts} + \text{delta fddiMACNotCopiedCts})}$$

## 20.8  THE PATH GROUP

The value of the stand-alone variable, *fddimibPATHNumber,* is the total number of PATHs possible through the entity. Its OBJECT IDENTIFIER is 1.3.6.1.2.1.10.15.73.4.1.

### 20.8.1  The PATH Table

Table 20.4, the PATH Table, sets some lower bounds on timers that can be used by a MAC entity that is on a given path. The data paths followed through port and MAC resources are described in Table 20.5, the PATH Configuration Table.

### 20.8.2  The PATH Configuration Table

See Table 20.5 for the PATH Configuration Table.

**TABLE 20.4    The PATH Table**

iso.org.dod.internet.mgmt.mib-2.transmission.
fddi.fddimib.fddimibPATH.
fddimibPATHTable.fddimibPATHEntry
1.3.6.1.2.1.10.15.73.4.2.1

| OBJECT IDENTIFIER | Syntax | Access | Description |
|---|---|---|---|
| fddimibPATH SMTIndex 1.3.6.1.2.1.10.15.73. 4.2.1.1 ▶ **Index** | INTEGER (1..65535) | read-only | The value of the SMT index associated with this PATH. |
| fddimibPATH Index 1.3.6.1.2.1.10.15.73. 4.2.1.2 ▶ **Index** | INTEGER (0..65535) | read-only | Index variable for uniquely identifying the primary, secondary, and local PATH object instances. Local PATH object instances are represented with integer values 3 to 255. |
| fddimibPATH TVXLowerBound 1.3.6.1.2.1.10.15.73. 4.2.1.3 | FddiTime Nano | read-write | Configurable minimum time value of *fddiMACTvxValue* that shall be used by any MAC that is configured in this path. Initial value is 2.5 ms. |
| fddimibPATH TMaxLowerBound 1.3.6.1.2.1.10.15.73. 4.2.1.4 | FddiTime Nano | read-write | Configurable minimum time value of *fddiMACTMax* that shall be used by any MAC that is configured in this path. |
| fddimibPATH MaxTReq 1.3.6.1.2.1.10.15.73. 4.2.1.5 | FddiTime Nano | read-write | Configurable maximum time value of *fddiMACT-Req* that shall be used by any MAC that is configured in this path. Default is 165 ms. |

**TABLE 20.5    The PATH Configuration Table**

iso.org.dod.internet.mgmt.mib-2.transmission.
fddi.fddimib.fddimibPATH.
fddimibPATHConfigTable.fddimibPATHConfigEntry
1.3.6.1.2.1.10.15.73.4.3.1

| OBJECT IDENTIFIER | Syntax | Access | Description |
|---|---|---|---|
| fddimibPATHConfig SMTIndex 1.3.6.1.2.1.10.15.73. 4.3.1.1 ▶ **Index** | INTEGER (1..65535) | read-only | Value of the SMT index for this entry. |
| fddimibPATHConfig PATHIndex 1.3.6.1.2.1.10.15.73. 4.3.1.2 ▶ **Index** | INTEGER (1..65535) | read-only | Value of the PATH resource index for this entry. |
| fddimibPATHConfig TokenOrder 1.3.6.1.2.1.10.15.73. 4.3.1.3 ▶ **Index** | INTEGER (1..65535) | read-only | The Token order position for this resource. That is, if the Token passes through this resource third, the value would be 3. |
| fddimibPATHConfig ResourceType 1.3.6.1.2.1.10.15.73. 4.3.1.4 | INTEGER mac(2), port(4) | read-only | Type of resource (MAC or port) for this entry. |
| fddimibPATHConfig ResourceIndex 1.3.6.1.2.1.10.15.73. 4.3.1.5 | INTEGER (1..65535) | read-only | Value of the SMT resource index used to refer to this MAC or Port resource. |
| fddimibPATHConfig CurrentPath 1.3.6.1.2.1.10.15.73. 4.3.1.6 | INTEGER isolated(1), local(2), secondary(3), primary(4), concatenated(5), thru(6) | read-only | Current insertion status for this resource on this Path. |

## 20.9    MANAGING PORTS

The first variable in the PORT group is a stand-alone variable that counts the total number of port implementations—across all SMTs—at the entity. This corresponds to the maximum number of entries in the Port table.

The OBJECT IDENTIFIER for this object is:

```
1.3.6.1.2.1.10.15.73.5.1
```

### 20.9.1    The PORT Table

Table 20.6, the PORT Table, describes the type of port, indicates how it is connected to a neighbor station port, describes timers, and counts errors. Note that "PC type" means Port Connector type. The types are A, B, S, or M, as defined in Sec. 20.5.3.

The stand-alone *fddimibPORTNumber* variable is a count of all PORT implementations across all SMTs for the node, and hence is a bound on the number of entries in the PORT table.

**TABLE 20.6    The PORT Table**

iso.org.dod.internet.mgmt.mib-2.transmission.
fddi.fddimibPORT.fddimibPORTTable.fddimibPORTEntry
1.3.6.1.2.1.10.15.73.5.2.1

| OBJECT IDENTIFIER | Syntax | Access | Description |
|---|---|---|---|
| fddimibPORT SMTIndex 1.3.6.1.2.1.10.15.73. 5.2.1.1 ► **Index** | INTEGER (1..65535) | read-only | Value of the SMT index associated with the port. |
| fddimibPORT Index 1.3.6.1.2.1.10.15.73. 5.2.1.2 ► **Index** | INTEGER (1..65535) | read-only | Unique value for each port within a given SMT, equal to the SMT resource index. |
| fddimibPORT MyType 1.3.6.1.2.1.10.15.73. 5.2.1.3 | INTEGER a(1), b(2), s(3), m(4), none(5) | read-only | Port Connector (PC) type. |
| fddimibPORT NeighborType 1.3.6.1.2.1.10.15.73. 5.2.1.4 | INTEGER a(1), b(2), s(3), m(4), none(5) | read-only | Type of the remote port, as determined in Physical Connection Management (PCM). |
| fddimibPORT ConnectionPolicies 1.3.6.1.2.1.10.15.73. 5.2.1.5 | INTEGER (0..3) | read-write | A bit map indicating the node's desired port policies. |
| fddimibPORT MACIndicated 1.3.6.1.2.1.10.15.73. 5.2.1.6 | INTEGER | read-only | The indication, in PC-Signaling of the intent to place a MAC in the output token PATH to a port. |
| fddimibPORT CurrentPath 1.3.6.1.2.1.10.15.73. 5.2.1.7 | INTEGER ce0(1) isolated ce1(2) local ce2(3) secondary ce3(4) primary ce4(5) concat ce5(6) thru | read-only | Path(s) into which this port is currently inserted. |
| fddimibPORT RequestedPaths 1.3.6.1.2.1.10.15.73. 5.2.1.8 | OCTET STRING (SIZE (3)) | read-write | List of permitted Paths. First octet: none; second: tree; third: peer. |

**TABLE 20.6   The PORT Table (*Continued*)**

iso.org.dod.internet.mgmt.mib-2.transmission.
fddi.fddimibPORT.fddimibPORTTable.fddimibPORTEntry
1.3.6.1.2.1.10.15.73.5.2.1

| OBJECT IDENTIFIER | Syntax | Access | Description |
|---|---|---|---|
| fddimibPORT MACPlacement 1.3.6.1.2.1.10.15.73. 5.2.1.9 | Fddi ResourceId (0..65535) | read-only | MAC, if any, whose transmit path exits the station via this port. |
| fddimibPORT AvailablePaths 1.3.6.1.2.1.10.15.73. 5.2.1.10 | INTEGER (0..7) | read-only | A bit map that indicates the path types (Primary, Secondary, Local) available to this port. |
| fddimibPORT PMDClass 1.3.6.1.2.1.10.15.73. 5.2.1.11 | INTEGER multimode(1), single-mode1(2), single-mode2(3), sonet(4), low-cost-fiber(5), twisted-pair(6), unknown(7), unspecified(8) | read-only | Type of physical medium for this port. |
| fddimibPORT Connection Capabilities 1.3.6.1.2.1.10.15.73. 5.2.1.12 | INTEGER (0..3) | read-only | Connection capabilities of the port. |
| fddimibPORT BSFlag 1.3.6.1.2.1.10.15.73. 5.2.1.13 | INTEGER true(1), false(2) | read-only | Flag indicating the Break State. |
| fddimibPORT LCTFailCts 1.3.6.1.2.1.10.15.73. 5.2.1.14 | Counter | read-only | Number of consecutive times the link confidence test (LCT) has failed during connection management. |
| fddimibPORT LerEstimate 1.3.6.1.2.1.10.15.73. 5.2.1.15 | INTEGER (4..15) | read-only | A long-term average Link Error Rate. Ranges from $10^{-4}$ to $10^{-15}$ and is reported as the absolute value of the base 10 logarithm. |
| fddimibPORT LemRejectCts 1.3.6.1.2.1.10.15.73. 5.2.1.16 | Counter | read-only | Link Error Monitoring count of the times that a link has been rejected. |
| fddimibPORT LemCts 1.3.6.1.2.1.10.15.73. 5.2.1.17 | Counter | read-only | Aggregate Link Error Monitor Error count. (0 on station initialization.) |

TABLE 20.6    The PORT Table (*Continued*)

iso.org.dod.internet.mgmt.mib-2.transmission.
fddi.fddimibPORT.fddimibPORTTable.fddimibPORTEntry
1.3.6.1.2.1.10.15.73.5.2.1

| OBJECT IDENTIFIER | Syntax | Access | Description |
|---|---|---|---|
| fddimibPORT LerCutoff 1.3.6.1.2.1.10.15.73. 5.2.1.18 | INTEGER (4..15) | read-write | Link Error Rate at which a link will be broken. Reported as absolute value of the base 10 logarithm. |
| fddimibPORT LerAlarm 1.3.6.1.2.1.10.15.73. 5.2.1.19 | INTEGER (4..15) | read-write | Link Error Rate threshold at which an alarm will be generated. |
| fddimibPORT ConnectState 1.3.6.1.2.1.10.15.73. 5.2.1.20 | INTEGER disabled(1), connecting(2), standby(3), active(4) | read-only | Connect state of this port. |
| fddimibPORT PCMState 1.3.6.1.2.1.10.15.73. 5.2.1.21 | INTEGER | read-only | Detailed state of Port Connect state machine. |
| fddimibPORT PCWithhold 1.3.6.1.2.1.10.15.73. 5.2.1.22 | INTEGER none(1), m-m(2), otherincompatible(3), pathnotavailable(4) | read-only | The value of PC_Withhold. |
| fddimibPORT LerFlag 1.3.6.1.2.1.10.15.73. 5.2.1.23 | INTEGER true(1), false(2) | read-only | Condition active when Link Error Rate estimate is less than or equal to Alarm level. |
| fddimibPORT HardwarePresent 1.3.6.1.2.1.10.15.73. 5.2.1.24 | INTEGER true(1), false(2) | read-only | Indicates presence of hardware support for this port. |
| fddimibPORT Action 1.3.6.1.2.1.10.15.73. 5.2.1.25 | INTEGER other(1), maintPORT(2), enablePORT(3), disablePORT(4), startPORT(5), stopPORT(6) | read-write | Requests an action. |

## 20.10    RECOMMENDED READING

*Metropolitan Area Networks,* by Gary C. Kessler and Davis A. Train, contains a detailed discussion of FDDI technology. The FDDI MIB is defined in RFC 1512. The MIB definitions are based on the ANSI document, *FDDI Station Management (SMT),* produced by the X3T9.5 committee.

# Managing an RS-232-like Hardware Interface

## 21.1 INTRODUCTION

Most of us have had the experience of connecting one end of an RS-232 cable to a serial interface on a personal computer, connecting the other end to an interface on a modem, plugging a telephone line into the modem and into a wall receptor, and making a data call across a telephone line.

The venerable design of RS-232 interfaces was standardized by the Electronic Industries Association (EIA). There have been several variants of RS-232 over the years. The most widely available form of RS-232 is RS-232-C, although the most current version is EIA/TIA-232-E. The CCITT equivalent is defined in V.24 (which defines functional behavior) and V.28 (which specifies the electrical characteristics).*

## 21.2 RS-232 TECHNOLOGY

Just about every computer has one or more RS-232 hardware interfaces, which also are called *RS-232 ports*. An RS-232 cable connects the computer, or DTE, to a communications box (DCE), such as a modem. The acronyms stand for:

DTE    Data Terminal Equipment

DCE    Data Circuit-terminating Equipment

Figure 21.1 shows two computers communicating across a wide area network. An RS-232 cable connects each computer to its modem. The modems interface to the switched telephone network.

---

* Modems support both EIA and CCITT standards.

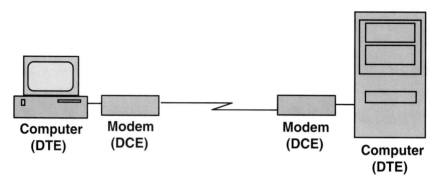

**Figure 21.1** RS-232 connections between computers and modems.

### 21.2.1   RS-232 Hardware

The most common DTE hardware connector has 25 "male" pins arranged in two rows. The DCE usually has 25 "female" sockets. The RS-232 cable terminates in a socket connector at one end and a pin connector at the other so that it can be connected to its DTE and DCE mates.

The connectors at the ends of the RS-232 cable are joined by a bundle of wires. Ordinarily, several (but not all) of the pins and wires are used actively. At least two of the wires carry data and others carry control signals. Each wire that is used for communications or control carries a signal in one direction—either from the DTE or to the DTE.

Data is transmitted from DTE pin 2 and received at pin 3. Data and control signals are represented by raising and lowering the voltage levels on a wire. For example, the DTE raises the voltage on wire 4 in order to signal "request to send." One wire is used to define a "ground-level" voltage against which other voltage levels are measured. Figure 21.2 illustrates features of the usual configuration.

Sometimes two computers need to be directly connected to one another without intervening DCEs. In this case, a *null modem* cable is used. Inside a null modem cable, several pairs of wires cross, so that inputs at one end become outputs at the other end. For example, a system transmits data through pin 2. This wire has to connect to pin 3 at the other end, because that's where data is received.

Occasionally there is a direct connection for which both communicating ends play DCE roles. In either case, DTE-to-DTE or DCE-to-DCE, special care is needed in configuring the interfaces.

### 21.2.2   RS-232-like Interfaces

The purpose of the RS-232-like Hardware Device MIB is to define a set of MIB variables that apply to a *range* of serial interfaces. What these interfaces have in common is that they use a similar set of control signals.

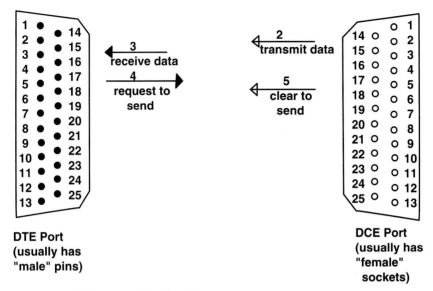

Figure 21.2  RS-232 interface hardware.

In addition to RS-232, other standards specifically referenced in the RS-232-like MIB include RS-422, RS-423, and V.35.

RS-232 is a Physical Layer interface. Recall that sometimes interface sublayers need to be stacked on top of one another.* For example, Figure 21.3 shows the relationship between the standard interfaces MIB variables, the MIB for the Point-to-Point protocol that controls and configures serial communications,† and the RS-232 hardware interface MIB.

---

\* See Chapter 10, Sec. 10.14.

† See Chapter 22.

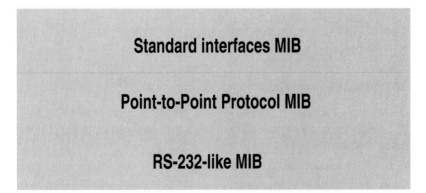

Figure 21.3  Use of several layers of interface MIBs.

### 21.2.3   RS-232 Signals

A DTE and DCE coordinate their exchange of data by means of a set of signals *asserted* on the various connecting wires. Signal assertions consist simply of setting a high voltage on a wire. Voltage is measured *relative* to the voltage level on a "ground" wire.

Separate wires are used to transmit data, receive data, and signal control information that indicates:

- The status of a device
- Its desire to transmit data
- An event

### 21.2.4   Control Signals

Control signals perform many important functions. For example:

- A modem signals that it is ready.
- A modem signals that it detects a carrier frequency on the telephone line.
- A DTE signals that it is ready.
- A modem signals that there is ringing on the line.
- A DTE signals that it wants to send some data.

Each signal is sent out via a pin connected to a separate wire. RS-232-like interfaces have up to 25 pins. The set of pins that is actively used—and the way that they are used—depends on how the systems are communicating. For example:

- Half-duplex or full-duplex
- Asynchronous or synchronous
- DTE-to-DCE, DTE-to-DTE, or DCE-to-DCE

### 21.3   THE RS-232 MIB

The RS-232-like Hardware Device MIB consists of:

- *The RS-232-like Port Table.*   For each RS-232-like port (interface) for a device, this table records the number of input and output signals, and the input and output speeds.
- *The RS-232-like Asynchronous Port Table.*   For each asynchronous RS-232-like port, this table records configuration information such as number of data bits, number of stop bits and parity, and also tracks some error counters.

- *The RS-232-like Synchronous Port Table.*  For each synchronous port, this table records the clock source and tracks error counters.

- *The RS-232-like Input Signal Table.*  For each RS-232-like port, this table lists the supported input signals, their current state, and how often that state has changed.

- *The RS-232-like Output Signal Table.*  For each RS-232-like port, this table lists the supported output signals, their current state, and how often that state has changed.

Note that these MIB tables record how a device has been configured and make this information accessible to a management station. This could speed problem resolution significantly.

## 21.4    THE RS-232 PORT TABLE

The generic *rs232* group of variables includes a table that provides general configuration information about an RS-232-like port, such as its hardware type and speed. This information is described in Table 21.1.

**TABLE 21.1    The RS-232 Port Table**

| OBJECT IDENTIFIER | Syntax | Access | Description |
|---|---|---|---|
| iso.org.dod.internet.mgmt.mib-2.transmission. rs232.rs232PortTable.rs232PortEntry 1.3.6.1.2.1.10.33.2.1 | | | |
| rs232PortIndex 1.3.6.1.2.1.10.33.2.1.1 ▶ **Index** | INTEGER | read-only | A unique value for each port, ranging from 1 to *rs232Number.* If possible, index values should map directly to external connectors. |
| rs232PortType 1.3.6.1.2.1.10.33.2.1.2 | INTEGER other(1), rs232(2), rs422(3), rs423(4), v35(5) | read-only | The hardware type. |
| rs232Port InSigNumber 1.3.6.1.2.1.10.33.2.1.3 | INTEGER | read-only | Number of detectable input signals for the port. The signals will be listed in the *rs232PortInSigTable.* |
| rs232Port OutSigNumber 1.3.6.1.2.1.10.33.2.1.4 | INTEGER | read-only | Number of output signals that the port can assert. The signals will be listed in *rs232PortOutSigTable.* |
| rs232PortInSpeed 1.3.6.1.2.1.10.33.2.1.5 | INTEGER | read-write | The port's input speed in bits per second. |
| rs232PortOutSpeed 1.3.6.1.2.1.10.33.2.1.6 | INTEGER | read-write | The port's output speed in bits per second. |

The first variable in the *rs232* group is a stand-alone read-only integer variable that records the total number of entries in the RS-232 port table. The stand-alone variable is:

```
iso.org.dod.internet.mgmt.mib-2.transmission.rs232.rs232Number
 1.  3.  6.   1.   2.  1.      10.        33.     1
```

## 21.5  ASYNCHRONOUS PORT CHARACTERISTICS

If a device is communicating through asynchronous interfaces, then the Asynchronous Port Table should be implemented.

Data that is transmitted asynchronously is sent one character at a time. Each character is delimited by a start bit. After the character bits, a parity bit and one or more stop bits are sent. Today, most transmission is based on 8-bit characters. However the number of bits is configurable.

A parity bit is appended to each character to provide basic error checking.* How is the parity bit set? This is configurable. The parity bit settings are:

*ODD*    The bit is set so that there is an odd number of 1s in the combined character-plus-parity field.

*EVEN*   Set so that there is an even number of 1s.

*NONE*   Ignore the parity bit.

*MARK*   Set the bit to 1 always.

*SPACE*  Set the bit to 0 always.

The trouble with having a lot of choices is that unless both ends use the same parity setting, they won't understand each other! The *rs232AsyncPortParityErrs* variable below is a good indicator of whether the two ends agree in their parity settings.

The *rs232AsyncPortFramingErrs* variable could be used as a quick indicator of whether both ends agree on their character format and stop bits. Of course, both parity errors and framing errors also can be the result of poor line quality.

### 21.5.1   The RS-232-like Asynchronous Port Group

Table 21.2, the Asynchronous Port Table, records configuration information for an asynchronous interface—namely, the number of bits per

---

* Note that although just about all asynchronous communication of ASCII characters carries a parity bit, the bit actually is rarely used.

**TABLE 21.2    The Asynchronous Port Table**

iso.org.dod.internet.mgmt.mib-2.transmission.rs232.
rs232AsyncPortTable.rs232AsyncPortEntry
1.3.6.1.2.1.10.33.3.1

| OBJECT IDENTIFIER | Syntax | Access | Description |
|---|---|---|---|
| rs232AsyncPortIndex<br>1.3.6.1.2.1.10.33.3.1.1<br>▶ **Index** | INTEGER | read-<br>only | The *rs232PortIndex* for the<br>port. (See the generic RS-<br>232 port table, Table 21.1) |
| rs232AsyncPortBits<br>1.3.6.1.2.1.10.33.3.1.2 | INTEGER<br>(5.8) | read-<br>write | Number of bits in a<br>character. |
| rs232AsyncPort<br>StopBits<br>1.3.6.1.2.1.10.33.3.1.3 | INTEGER<br>one(1),<br>two(2),<br>one-and-half(3),<br>dynamic(4) | read-<br>write | The number of stop bits. |
| rs232AsyncPort<br>Parity<br>1.3.6.1.2.1.10.33.3.1.4 | INTEGER<br>none(1),<br>odd(2),<br>even(3),<br>mark(4),<br>space(5) | read-<br>write | The type of parity bit for<br>each character. |
| rs232AsyncPort<br>Autobaud<br>1.3.6.1.2.1.10.33.3.1.5 | INTEGER<br>enabled(1),<br>disabled(2) | read-<br>write | Choose whether the port will<br>sense input speed, parity,<br>and character size<br>automatically (if it can). |
| rs232AsyncPort<br>ParityErrs<br>1.3.6.1.2.1.10.33.3.1.6 | Counter | read-<br>only | Total number of characters<br>input from the port with a<br>parity error. |
| rs232AsyncPort<br>FramingErrs<br>1.3.6.1.2.1.10.33.3.1.7 | Counter | read-<br>only | Total number of characters<br>input from the port with a<br>framing error. |
| rs232AsyncPort<br>OverrunErrs<br>1.3.6.1.2.1.10.33.3.1.8 | Counter | read-<br>only | Total number of characters<br>input from the port with an<br>overrun error. |

character, number of stop bits, parity type, and whether the interface can sense the speed, parity, and character size of incoming data.

In addition, the table provides counts of parity errors, character framing errors, and overrun errors. All of the error counters are measured from the time of the last system reinitialization and while the port state was 'up' or 'test'.

## 21.6    SYNCHRONOUS PORT CHARACTERISTICS

Synchronous transmission offers higher speeds and far better error control than asynchronous transmission—at a higher price. The mechanisms used include:

- Use of transmit and receive clock signals to synchronize the two ends. There are designated pins for clock signals.
- Use of flag patterns, "01111110," to delimit messages.
- Zero bit insertion and removal within the data portion of a frame to prevent a "01111110" pattern in the data to be mistaken for a flag.
- Use of a long string of 1s to signal that a frame is being aborted.

Clocking for the synchronous signal can be provided by a DCE or a DTE. Most often it is provided by the DCE. When both parties play a DTE role, or both act as DCEs, it is important to get the clocking sorted out in a consistent way.

There are lots of clocking configurations—including split timing, which uses an internal clock for transmitting and an external clock for receiving.

### 21.6.1   The RS-232-like
Synchronous Port Group

The synchronous port group consists of a table of variables listed in Table 21.3. The table indicates the source for synchronously clocking, and reports various types of errors. Port underrun and overrun errors are caused by the inability of interface hardware or software to keep up with the rate of the outgoing or incoming bit stream.

All counters are measured from the time of the last system reinitialization for the period that the port state was 'up' or 'test'.

### 21.7   SIGNALS

The pins in the various RS-232-like modems (and corresponding cable wires) can express a variety of signals.

Generally, only a very few of these signals are used. Characteristics of the available hardware determine which signals are available. Even when available, the operating environment may require that some signals be configured as disabled.

Some vendors provide *full-duplex* capability by splitting up the analog telephone bandwidth between the main data channel and a *secondary channel*. The extra secondary channel is used for signaling or error reporting. Some of the following definitions relate to signaling for a secondary channel.

The common use of the signals is summarized as follows. (Keep in mind that a DTE/DCE pair might be the originator of a call or the recipient of a call.)

*rts*     *to Send:* Used by DTE to inform a half-duplex DCE of desire to send.

*cts*     *Clear to Send:* Used by a half-duplex DCE to notify the DTE that it is safe to send.

*dsr*     *Data Set Ready:* The modem has either initiated or received a call and has heard or sent an answer tone. However, for microcomputers, it just means that the modem is powered up and ready.

*dtr*     *Data Terminal Ready:* Used by the DTE to signal that it is ready to open a communication. The signal is maintained throughout the session.

*ri*      *Ring Indicator:* The DCE signals the DTE that there is ringing on the line.

**TABLE 21.3    The Synchronous Port Table**

iso.org.dod.internet.mgmt.mib-2.transmission.rs232.
rs232SyncPortTABle.rs232SyncPortEntry
1.3.6.1.2.1.10.33.4.1

| OBJECT IDENTIFIER | Syntax | Access | Description |
| --- | --- | --- | --- |
| rs232SyncPort Index 1.3.6.1.2.1.10.33.4.1.1 ▶ **Index** | INTEGER | read-only | The *rs232PortIndex* for the port. |
| rs232SyncPort ClockSource 1.3.6.1.2.1.10.33.4.1.2 | INTEGER internal(1), external(2), split(3) | read-write | Source of the port's bit rate clock. 'Split' means that the transmit clock is internal and the receive clock is external. |
| rs232SyncPort FrameCheckErrs 1.3.6.1.2.1.10.33.4.1.3 | Counter | read-only | Number of incoming frames with an invalid Frame Check Sequence. |
| rs232SyncPort TransmitUnderrun Errs 1.3.6.1.2.1.10.33.4.1.4 | Counter | read-only | Number of frames that failed to be transmitted because data was not presented to the transmitter in time. |
| rs232SyncPort ReceiveOverrun Errs 1.3.6.1.2.1.10.33.4.1.5 | Counter | read-only | Number of frames that failed to be received because the receiver could not accept the data in time. |
| rs232SyncPort InterruptedFrames 1.3.6.1.2.1.10.33.4.1.6 | Counter | read-only | Number of frames that failed to be received or transmitted on the port due to loss of modem signals. |
| rs232SyncPort AbortedFrames 1.3.6.1.2.1.10.33.4.1.7 | Counter | read-only | Number of frames aborted on the port due to receiving an abort sequence. |

| | |
|---|---|
| *dcd* | *Received Line Signal Detector (Data Carrier Detect):* The DCE signals the DTE that remote carrier has been received. This signal is maintained throughout the session. |
| *sq* | *Signal Quality Detector:* DCE indicates that the received signal is of adequate quality to transmit correct data. |
| *srs* | *Data Signaling Rate Selector:* If two data rates are supported, *srs* is used to signal use of the higher rate. |
| *srts* | *Secondary Request to Send:* DTE requests to send on the secondary channel. |
| *scts* | *Secondary Clear to Send:* DCE notifies the DTE that it is safe to send on the secondary channel. |
| *sdcd* | *Secondary Received Line Signal Detector:* DCE signals the DTE of Data Carrier Detect for the secondary channel. |

### 21.7.1    The Input Signal Table

There are separate entries in Table 21.4, the Input Signal Table, for each supported port/signal combination. The table indicates which signal inputs are available, the current state of each, and a count of the number of signal transitions between *on* and *off*.

The *rs232InSigName* variable identifies the signal for the entry using the integer code:

1. rts      Request to Send
2. cts      Clear to Send
3. dsr      Data Set Ready
4. dtr      Data Terminal Ready
5. ri       Ring Indicator
6. dcd      Received Line Signal Detector
7. sq       Signal Quality Detector
8. srs      Data Signaling Rate Selector
9. srts     Secondary Request to Send
10. scts    Secondary Clear to Send
11. sdcd    Secondary Received Line Signal Detector

### 21.7.2    The Output Signal Table

Like the input signal table, Table 21.5, the Output Signal Table, is indexed by port and signal. The table indicates which signal outputs are available, the current state of each, and a count of the number of transitions between *on* and *off*.

The same integer codes used to identify input signals are used for *rs232OutSigName* as were used for *rs232InSigName*.

**TABLE 21.4    The RS-232 Input Signal Table**

iso.org.dod.internet.mgmt.mib-2.transmission.rs232
rs232InSigTable.rs232InSigEntry
1.3.6.1.2.1.10.33.5.1

| OBJECT IDENTIFIER | Syntax | Access | Description |
|---|---|---|---|
| rs232InSigPort Index 1.3.6.1.2.1.10.33.5.1.1 ▶ **Index** | INTEGER | read-only | The *rs232PortIndex* for this port. |
| rs232InSigName 1.3.6.1.2.1.10.33.5.1.2 ▶ **Index** | INTEGER | read-only | Integer code identifying the hardware signal. |
| rs232InSigState 1.3.6.1.2.1.10.33.5.1.3 | INTEGER none(1), on(2), off(3) | read-only | The current signal state. |
| rs232InSigChanges 1.3.6.1.2.1.10.33.5.1.4 | Counter | read-only | The number of times the signal has changed from 'on' to 'off' or from 'off' to 'on'. |

**TABLE 21.5    The RS-232 Output Signal Table**

iso.org.dod.internet.mgmt.mib-2.transmission.rs232.
rs232OutSigTable.rs232OutSigEntry
f1.3.6.1.2.1.10.33.6.1

| OBJECT IDENTIFIER | Syntax | Access | Description |
|---|---|---|---|
| rs232OutSigPortIndex 1.3.6.1.2.1.10.33.6.1.1 ▶ **Index** | INTEGER | read-only | The *rs232PortIndex* for this port. |
| rs232OutSigName 1.3.6.1.2.1.10.33.6.1.2 ▶ **Index** | INTEGER | read-only | Integer code identifying the hardware signal. |
| rs232OutSigState 1.3.6.1.2.1.10.33.6.1.3 | INTEGER none(1), on(2), off(3) | read-only | The current signal state. |
| rs232OutSigChanges 1.3.6.1.2.1.10.33.6.1.4 | Counter | read-only | The number of times the signal has changed from 'on' to 'off' or from 'off' to 'on'. |

## 21.8   NETWORK MANAGEMENT CONSIDERATIONS

Considering the number of things that can be misconfigured, it is no surprise that problems sometimes arise when setting up RS-232-like serial communications. An *accurate* implementation of the RS-232-like MIB would be very helpful, replacing a painstaking testing process. Some of the things that may be set up incorrectly are:

- *Both* ends of the ground wire are grounded. This induces a current (*ground loop*) across the wire that is used as a common measure of "zero-level" voltage.

- A normal cable is used where a null modem cable is needed. This would cause transmitted data to arrive at the remote transmitted data pin instead of the received data pin.

- Use of signals at the ends of an RS-232 cable is configured in an incompatible manner. For example, a DTE may expect the DCE to hold CTS and DTR on permanently where the DCE has not been configured to do this.

- For asynchronous communication, the configuration of the number of data bits, stop bits, or parity for the two end-to-end DTEs does not match.

## 21.9   RECOMMENDED READING

At the time of writing, RFC 1317 contained the RS-232-like device MIB definitions. A detailed discussion of RS-232 and related interfaces can be found in *Data Communications, Networks, and Distributed Processing,* by Uyless D. Black. Good expositions can be found in *RS-232 Made Easy,* by Martin Seyer, and *Technical Aspects of Data Communication,* by John McNamara.

# 22

# Managing a PPP Interface

## 22.1 INTRODUCTION

One of the certainties of a network manager's life is that the bill for wide area communications will arrive every month. Another certainty is that more users and applications will join the network, and that the hunger for bandwidth will grow.

The hunger for bandwidth expands dramatically when an organization decides to tie its LANs together into an enterprise network. Often, these LANs are of many different types, such as TCP/IP, NetWare, DECnet, AppleTalk, Vines, LAN Manager, or LAN Server. The first five protocols listed use different routing procedures, while the last two are based on NetBeui, which cannot be routed at all, and must be bridged.

One of the impressive achievements of the router industry has been the development of multiprotocol bridge-routers that can handle all of these protocols—and more—concurrently. If all of the protocol traffic between two locations can be multiplexed onto a single long-distance line, an organization can buy bandwidth in bulk (e.g., a T1 line), saving money and getting a bandwidth bonus in the bargain.

But to make this happen, the bridge-router vendors had a problem on their hands. There was no single standard format or protocol for point-to-point communications, and certainly no standard way to carry multiple protocols—as well as bridged traffic! The old HDLC link specification was really a set of options for a *family* of link disciplines, and, in addition, did nothing to address the multiprotocol problem.

An IETF task force that included a mixture of academic members and personnel from router, bridge, and modem companies has been working on a comprehensive Point-to-Point Protocol (PPP).

### 22.1.1    Requirements for PPP

There are many different link protocols in use today. The reason is that users have many different requirements; vendors and standards bodies have responded with protocols that meet particular sets of requirements. The result is a glut of incompatible methods for crossing a point-to-point line.

RFC 1547, *Point-to-Point Protocol Requirements,* surveys user requirements and strategies for meeting them. Among the points cited are that PPP must:

- Make efficient use of bandwidth.
- Be simple enough to enable fast processing of frames.
- Carry multiple types of Protocol Data Units (e.g., IP, DECnet, IPX).
- Run over a selection of physical interfaces, such as EIA RS-232-C, EIA RS-422, EIA RS-423, and CCITT V.35.
- Run over any type of link: synchronous or asynchronous, switched or permanent.
- Work symmetrically, without requiring preassigned master/slave roles.
- Be able to detect when a link is failing, failed, or in a loopback state.
- Support dynamic network address identification. During setup of a dial-up link, the systems can identify themselves. Or, when a PC calls a network server, the server can identify itself and dynamically assign an address to the PC.
- Support the use of data compression. Traffic streams for different protocols are allowed to use different compression algorithms.

Suppose that you do not need link-failure detection, or identification, or data compression. PPP has a basic, predefined default configuration. If additional features are needed, they are negotiated at link setup, enabling an implementation to be as functional—or as simple—as the situation requires.

## 22.2    ENVIRONMENTS FOR PPP

PPP was designed to work over any full-duplex synchronous *or* asynchronous link. Traffic for many routed protocols, as well as bridged traffic, can share a single link. PPP can be carried in an HDLC-compatible frame format, so it works with commonly used hardware, and takes advantage of a hardware-calculated Frame Check Sequence when it is available.

IETF groups are working on specifications that will define how PPP will be used over a switched ISDN line or a SONET circuit.

## 22.3   PPP FEATURES AND BENEFITS

The primary benefit of PPP is its ability to multiplex many protocols across a single point-to-point link. It was designed to be flexible enough so that a wide variety of equipment built by different vendors could interwork. Since wide area bandwidth is costly, PPP also was designed with low overhead in mind.

A PPP link is set up with a link control negotiation. One of things that can be negotiated is the maximum size of the information that can be carried. For a poor-quality link, throughput can be improved by using shorter frames. Another negotiable feature is the use of a compressed frame format. When sending across a wide-area serial link, every byte counts! Both ends also can agree to compress selected protocol data. For example, Van Jacobson compression of IP and TCP headers can reduce the combined headers from 40 octets to 3–5 octets.

PPP can be used for heavy-duty long-haul connections in a corporate network. It also has features needed by dial-up telecommuters who want to set up a link to the corporate network in order to reach their LAN server and log in to network hosts. To provide security where it is needed—for example, for dial-up links—the use of an authentication protocol can be negotiated.

PPP can carry control information such as XON/XOFF across an asynchronous link, or remove extraneous control characters, such as those injected by a PBX.

Automatic link monitoring is another useful option. If desired, the quality of the link can be watched on a regular basis. A link also can be checked to make sure that it is not in a looped-back condition.

## 22.4   THE PROTOCOLS

PPP actually is a *family* of special-purpose protocols. There is a PPP *Link Control Protocol* (LCP) that is used to negotiate link options and open a link. LCP negotiation can compress the frame format, adjust limits on frame sizes, choose an Authentication protocol, and initiate link monitoring.

One of the optional *Authentication Protocols* can be used to validate the identity of the partners when the link is set up. Authentication is important when a switched virtual circuit or dial-up line is used for PPP access.

There are separate *Network Control Protocols* (NCPs) used to negotiate options for the different types of traffic that PPP will carry, such as IP, IPX, or DECnet. So-called *Network Protocols* define the rules for encapsulating each type of traffic that is transmitted across the PPP link.

Finally, an optional *Link Quality Monitoring Protocol* enables each partner to find out what percentage of its data is being successfully transmitted.

## 22.5  LAYERING INTERFACES

Is PPP an interface? The answer is yes, PPP is considered an interface, and PPP entities will be listed in the *interfaces* table. However, PPP will usually be layered on top of another, lower-level interface, such as an RS-232, as shown in Figure 22.1.

This lower-level interface also will have an entry in the *interfaces* table! It seems like a good idea to show the relationship between these two interfaces. There is a variable in the PPP MIB that contains the value of the *ifIndex* for the lower-level interface.*

## 22.6  THE PPP MIB

The PPP MIB is made up of several groups, defined in a series of RFC documents—and the MIB is still growing! In this chapter we will introduce the following groups:

- *PPP Link Group.*  The Link Group is made up of a Link Status Table and a Link Configuration Table.

---

\* The *pppLinkStatusPhysicalIndex* variable in the PPP Link Status Table holds the lower-level *ifIndex*.

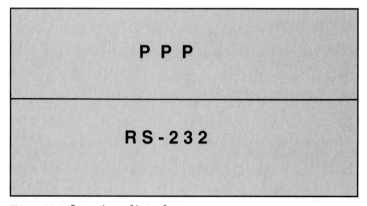

**Figure 22.1**  Layering of interfaces.

- *PPP LQR Group.* The Link Quality Group configures and tracks the use of the Link Quality Report protocol. The Link Quality Report Group is made up of a table of parameters and statistics and a configuration table.

- *PPP LQR Extensions Group.* The Link Quality Report Extensions Group holds the most recently received LQR packet, as well some locally tabulated values that help to determine link status.

- *PPP IP Group.* The IP Group is made up of configuration, status, and control variables that relate to running IP over PPP.

- *PPP Bridge Group.* The Bridge Group is made up of configuration, status, and control variables that relate to Bridging over PPP.

- *PPP Security Group.* The Security Group is made up of configuration and control variables that relate to PPP security. Currently, this is restricted to authentication of the communication partners.

## 22.7   THE PPP ENCAPSULATION

An important goal is to make PPP adaptable to use over any type of link—asynchronous, bit-oriented synchronous HDLC or X.25 LAPB, byte-oriented synchronous BISYNC or DDCMP—or whatever.

Figure 22.2 displays PPP encapsulation within an HDLC link frame. As will be the case with many link protocols, the address and control fields remain constant for PPP traffic. The HDLC address field is set to 'FF'H, the All-Stations address. The HDLC control field is set to '03'H, the code for unnumbered information.

### PPP  in  an  HDLC  Frame

| Flag | Address | Control | Prot-ocol 16 bits | INFORMATION | pad-ding | FCS | Flag |
|------|---------|---------|-------------------|-------------|----------|-----|------|
| 01111110 | 11111111 | 00000011 | | | | | 01111110 |

*PPP  Encpsulation*

### Address, Control, and Protocol field Compression

| Flag | Prot-ocol 8 bits | INFORMATION | pad-ding | FCS | Flag |
|------|------------------|-------------|----------|-----|------|
| 01111110 | | | | | 01111110 |

*PPP  Encpsulation*

**Figure 22.2**  The PPP frame format.

The PPP encapsulation starts with a 2-octet protocol field indicating whether a frame carries a Link Control message, a Network Control Protocol negotiation message, or information belonging to a particular protocol—e.g., an IP datagram.

The Information field carries network layer PDUs or bridged data. Occasionally it is convenient to include *padding*. For example, suppose that Ethernet bridging is supported across the link. Ethernet frames must be padded if their transmitted frame size is less than 64 octets. The maximum size for the Information field (including padding) is called the *Maximum Receive Unit* or MRU. The default MRU is 1500 octets.

As shown in Figure 22.2, the number of overhead octets can be reduced by negotiating "compression" (i.e., noninclusion) of the frame Address and Control fields. During information transmission, the Protocol field can be reduced to 1 octet.

## 22.8  PPP OVER ASYNC

The same frame format, including flags, is used across an asynchronous link. Octets are sent with 1 start bit, 8 data bits, and 1 stop bit. There are a number of special problems that need to be dealt with:

1. What if the flag octet appears in data?

2. Communications equipment (e.g., a modem) may mistake a data octet with value less than '20'H (i.e., decimal 0 to 31) as a control command. How do we transmit these values?

3. Communications equipment may inject extra control characters into the data stream!

These problems are solved with "byte stuffing." A flag or a low-value octet that we need to protect is *mapped* to a 2-octet sequence: the Control Escape character, '7D'H, followed by the original character with bit 6 complemented.*

By default, all characters less than '20'H will be mapped. A '7D'H in the data also needs to be mapped so that it will be understood correctly when it appears as normal information.

Of course, the link partner will unmap these patterns as they are received. If a low-value octet that normally would be mapped arrives in an incoming message, then I can assume that it has been injected by intervening equipment and remove it.

Let's look at some examples of mapping and unmapping:

---

* Note that complementing bit 6 either adds or subtracts 2 from the first hex digit representing an octet.

| Source | | Network | | Destination |
|--------|------|---------|------|-------------|
| 7E | → | 7D 5E | → | 7E |
| 7D | → | 7D 5D | → | 7D |
| 11 | → | 7D 31 | → | 11 |
| 18 | → | 7D 38 | → | 18 |

Mapping and unmapping burns up CPU resources and adds extra overhead bytes to the data stream. Suppose that I want to inform my partner exactly which characters (in the decimal range 0–31) need to be mapped and which do not in order to get through my communications equipment? I send the partner a 4-octet bit map called the *Remote Async-Control-Character Map* or Remote ACC Map. Any position set to 1 means "map the corresponding value." For example, the map 00 00 00 03 says "map '00'H or '01'H, but don't bother to map the rest."

Mapping occurs *after* the Frame Check Sequence has been computed, and unmapping at the receiving end occurs *before* the Frame Check sequence is computed.

## 22.9  STARTING UP A PPP LINK

The default format for a PPP frame is used during initial link setup and negotiation. However, every byte counts on a long distance link, and configuration messages can reshape the format that will be used for *information* transfer.

Each side negotiates what it wants to receive by sending Configure-Request messages. The negotiation is completed by an exchange of Configure-ACK messages. The two ends do not have to agree to one common format—I agree to send you what you want, and you agree to send me what I want!

Features that can be negotiated include:

- The Maximum Receive Unit, i.e., the biggest size for the information field in incoming frames.

- Compression of the Protocol field from 2 octets to 1. All of the codes (e.g., '0021'H for IP) currently defined can be reduced to 1 octet.

- Compression of the Address and Control fields. Since these fields always hold the same values they are "compressed" by leaving them out completely.

- For an asynchronous link, an Async-Control-Character-Map (ACC Map) flagging characters that I want my partner to map when transmitting to me. This is optional, as the default is to map *all* low-octet characters. Using this map assures that I can receive any character sent to me through my modem, and also can detect any low-byte characters injected by my modem.

There are some other optional features that can be negotiated, including a choice of Authentication protocol and Link Quality Monitoring protocol to be used. These will be discussed in later sections.

## 22.10   LINK PROTOCOL ELEMENTS

A value of *'C021'H* in a PPP frame's protocol field indicates that the information field contains a Link Control Protocol Packet. The first byte of this packet is a *code* that identifies the packet type. For example, a code of 9 identifies an Echo-Request packet.

The packet types used by the Link Control Protocol to set up a link include:

- *Configure-Request(1).*   Contains the sender's choices for link options.
- *Configure-Ack(2).*   Accepts a set of options.
- *Configure-Nak(3).*   Returns a list of acceptable values for options whose proposed values were not acceptable.
- *Configure-Reject(4).*   Returns a list of those options that were not recognizable, or not acceptable for negotiation.

Packets used to terminate a link include:

- *Terminate-Request(5).*   Sent by a PPP that wishes to close a connection.
- *Terminate-Ack(6).*   Sent to acknowledge closure.

Packets used to manage a link include:

- *Code-Reject(7).*   Reports reception of a packet with an unrecognized code.
- *Protocol-Reject(8).*   Reports reception of a packet with an unrecognized protocol identifier in the frame's protocol field.
- *Echo-Request(9).*   Asks the receiver to loop this message back.
- *Echo-Reply(10).*   Responds to an Echo-Request.
- *Discard-Request(11).*   A simple one-way test of a link. The receiver should discard the packet.

Some or all of these packet types are reused in other protocols in the PPP family.

For example, the IP Network Control Protocol, used to initialize and terminate the use of IP across the PPP link, uses code types 1 to 7. The protocol field in the frame header will be set to *'8021'H,* indicating that the IP NCP protocol is in effect.

## 22.11    USE OF THE PROTOCOL FIELD

The protocol field in the PPP header identifies the various types of PPP packets. Link Control packets have a protocol field of 'C021'H. Sample values for the protocol field during Network Control negotiations follow (see the *Assigned Numbers* RFC for a complete list):

| | |
|------|------|
| 8021 | Internet Protocol Control Protocol |
| 8023 | OSI Network Layer Control Protocol |
| 8025 | Xerox NS IDP Control Protocol |
| 8027 | DECnet Phase IV Control Protocol |
| 8029 | Appletalk Control Protocol |
| 802b | Novell IPX Control Protocol |
| 8031 | Bridging NCP |
| 8035 | Banyan Vines Control Protocol |

Sample values for the protocol field during information transfer include:

| | |
|------|------|
| 0021 | Internet Protocol |
| 0023 | OSI Network Layer |
| 0025 | Xerox NS IDP |
| 0027 | DECnet Phase IV |
| 0029 | Appletalk |
| 002b | Novell IPX |
| 002d | Van Jacobson Compressed TCP/IP |
| 0031 | Bridging PDU |
| 0035 | Banyan Vines |
| 0201 | 802.1d Hello Packets |

## 22.12    THE LINK CONTROL PROTOCOL MIB

RFC 1471 defines MIB variables for the PPP Link Control Protocol. The RFC defines objects for three groups:

- The PPP Link Group
- The PPP Link Quality Report Group
- The PPP Tests Group

## 22.13    THE PPP LINK GROUP

The PPP Link Group includes the Link Status Table and the Link Configuration Table.

### 22.13.1   The PPP Link Status Table

Table 22.1, the PPP Link Status Table, records configuration choices that have been established for open links and also includes some error counts. Note that some configuration settings on an open link depend on the results of the Link Control Protocol negotiation. If a parameter has not been included in a PPP Configure-Request, then the parameter's default value is used.

**TABLE 22.1   The PPP Link Status Table**

iso.org.dod.internet.mgmt.mib-2.
transmission.ppp.pppLep.pppLink.
pppLinkStatusTable.pppLinkStatusEntry
1.3.6.1.2.1.10.23.1.1.1.1

| OBJECT IDENTIFIER | Syntax | Access | Description |
|---|---|---|---|
| pppLinkStatus PhysicalIndex 1.3.6.1.2.1.10.23.1.1.1.1.1 | INTEGER (0.. 2147483647) | read-only | Value of *ifIndex* for the lower-level interface (e.g., HDLC or RS-232) over which the PPP link operates. |
| pppLinkStatus BadAddresses 1.3.6.1.2.1.10.23.1.1.1.1.2 | Counter | read-only | Number of received packets with an incorrect Address Field. |
| pppLinkStatus BadControls 1.3.6.1.2.1.10.23.1.1.1.1.3 | Counter | read-only | Number of received packets with an incorrect Control Field. |
| pppLinkStatus PacketTooLongs 1.3.6.1.2.1.10.23.1.1.1.1.4 | Counter | read-only | Number of received packets discarded because their length exceeded the Maximum Receive Unit (MRU). |
| pppLinkStatus BadFCSs 1.3.6.1.2.1.10.23.1.1.1.1.5 | Counter | read-only | Number of received packets discarded due to having an incorrect FCS. |
| pppLinkStatus LocalMRU 1.3.6.1.2.1.10.23.1.1.1.1.6 | INTEGER (1.. 2147483648) | read-only | Current value of the Maximum Receive Unit (MRU) for the local PPP Entity. |
| pppLinkStatus RemoteMRU 1.3.6.1.2.1.10.23.1.1.1.1.7 | INTEGER (1.. 2147483648) | read-only | Current value of the MRU for the remote PPP Entity. |
| pppLinkStatus Local ToPeerACCMap 1.3.6.1.2.1.10.23.1.1.1.1.8 | OCTET STRING (SIZE (4)) | read-only | Current value of the Async-Control-Character (ACC) Map used when sending packets from the local PPP entity to the remote PPP entity. |

**TABLE 22.1    The PPP Link Status Table (*Continued*)**

iso.org.dod.internet.mgmt.mib-2.
transmission.ppp.pppLep.pppLink.
pppLinkStatusTable.pppLinkStatusEntry
1.3.6.1.2.1.10.23.1.1.1.1

| OBJECT IDENTIFIER | Syntax | Access | Description |
|---|---|---|---|
| pppLinkStatus PeerToLocalACCMap 1.3.6.1.2.1.10.23.1.1.1.1.9 | OCTET STRING (SIZE (4)) | read-only | ACC Map used by the remote PPP entity when sending packets to the local PPP entity. |
| pppLinkStatus LocalToRemote ProtocolCompression 1.3.6.1.2.1.10.23.1.1.1.1.10 | INTEGER enabled(1), disabled(2) | read-only | Indicates whether the local PPP will compress the Protocol field in frames sent to the remote PPP. |
| pppLinkStatus RemoteToLocal ProtocolCompression 1.3.6.1.2.1.10.23.1.1.1.1.11 | INTEGER enabled(1), disabled(2) | read-only | Indicates whether the remote PPP will compress the Protocol field in frames sent to the local PPP. |
| pppLinkStatus LocalToRemote ACCompression 1.3.6.1.2.1.10.23.1.1.1.1.12 | INTEGER enabled(1), disabled(2) | read-only | Indicates whether the local PPP will compress (omit) the Address and Control fields for frames sent to the remote PPP. |
| pppLinkStatus RemoteToLocal ACCompression 1.3.6.1.2.1.10.23.1.1.1.1.13 | INTEGER enabled(1), disabled(2) | read-only | Indicates whether the remote PPP will compress (omit) the Address and Control fields for frames sent to the local PPP. |
| pppLinkStatus TransmitFcsSize 1.3.6.1.2.1.10.23.1.1.1.1.14 | INTEGER (0..128) | read-only | Size in bits of the Frame Check Sequence (FCS) in packets that the local PPP will send to the remote PPP. |
| pppLinkStatus ReceiveFcsSize 1.3.6.1.2.1.10.23.1.1.1.1.15 | INTEGER (0..128) | read-only | Size in bits of the Frame Check Sequence (FCS) in packets that the remote PPP will send to the local PPP. |

The tables in the PPP MIB follow a practice of using *ifIndex* as an index, rather than using a variable that is defined within the table.

## 22.13.2    The PPP Link Configuration Table

The PPP link status table reported the configurations in use on live links. Table 22.2, the PPP Link Configuration Table, contains precon-figured parameter choices desired by the local end.

TABLE 22.2   The PPP Link Configuration Table

iso.org.dod.internet.mgmt.mib-2.
transmission.ppp.pppLcp.pppLink.
pppLinkConfigTable.pppLinkConfigEntry
1.3.6.1.2.1.10.23.1.1.2.1

| OBJECT IDENTIFIER | Syntax | Access | Description |
|---|---|---|---|
| pppLinkConfig InitialMRU 1.3.6.1.2.1.10.23.1.1.2.1.1 | INTEGER (0.. 2147483647) | read- write | Maximum Receive Unit (MRU) that the local PPP will request. If 0, then the default of 1500 is OK. |
| pppLinkConfig ReceiveACCMap 1.3.6.1.2.1.10.23.1.1.2.1.2 | OCTET STRING (SIZE (4)) | read- write | The Asynchronous Control Character (ACC) Map that the local PPP will request the remote PPP to use to assure that the local modem will successfully receive all characters. |
| pppLinkConfig TransmitACCMap 1.3.6.1.2.1.10.23.1.1.2.1.3 | OCTET STRING (SIZE (4)) | read- write | The ACC Map that defines characters that must be mapped in order to be transmitted correctly through the local modem. |
| pppLinkConfig MagicNumber 1.3.6.1.2.1.10.23.1.1.2.1.4 | INTEGER false (1), true (2) | read- write | If true(2) then the local node will attempt to perform Magic Number negotiation with the remote node. |
| pppLinkConfig FcsSize 1.3.6.1.2.1.10.23.1.1.2.1.5 | INTEGER (0..128) | read- write* | Size in bits of the Frame Check Sequence that will be used for outgoing frames (not negotiable). |

* In RFC 1471, this variable is listed as a read-write configuration variable. This is an error, and the variable actually should not have been defined in this table.

Parameters taken from the table can be proposed during the link configuration dialogue. The other end can selectively reject any parameter that it cannot support. The local end will have to modify its request until it is acceptable to the other side (or else abort the link). For example, a Maximum Receive Unit can be proposed in a Configure-request.

Configuration values for Authentication and Link Quality Monitoring are defined in separate parts of the MIB that deal with these functions.

### 22.13.3   Configuring Async-Control-Character Maps

Recall that some data communications equipment interprets various low-value octets as control commands. One approach (the simplest) is to map all low-value octets to escaped 2-octet codes before sending, and to unmap them on receiving.

If you want to save the CPU and bandwidth overhead imposed by mapping everything, you can be selective, but it is a bit complicated:

1. I know which characters need to be mapped in order to be received through my modem safely. I send you my map.

2. You know which characters *you* need to map to be sure that when you transmit, characters will be sent through *your* modem safely. You combine my map with yours.*

3. When you send characters to me, you use the combined map to decide which ones to map.

4. If I receive a low-octet value that was flagged in the map that I sent you, I know that it has been injected by communications equipment and discard it.

### 22.13.4   Magic Numbers

The optional *Magic-Number* parameter is used to check whether a link is in a looped-back state.

The easiest way to use Magic-Numbers is to preassign a unique number to each PPP entity. For example, a system's serial number might be used. If a PPP sends a request with a unique Magic-Number in it and gets a request back with the same Magic-Number, then the link is looped back.

As an alternative to using preassigned unique numbers, a local PPP can pick a random number. Now if a request comes back with the same Magic-Number, it is only *likely* that the link is looped back—the other end conceivably could have picked the same number and might be sending its own requests! The local PPP should pick another random number and try again. If the same result is repeated a few times, then it is reasonable to believe that the link is looped back.

Suppose that the link is not looped back at start-up time, but falls into that state later? After a unique Magic-Number has been discovered it continues to be useful, since it will be included as a parameter in other messages, and a ping-pong message can be detected immediately.

### 22.14   Monitoring Link Quality

It often is difficult to find out how well a link is performing—or whether it may even be broken! PPP partners can agree to monitor their link. Following the modular architectural approach used

---

* The two maps can simply be ORed—that is, create a map that has a 1 in any position holding a 1 in either map.

throughout the design of PPP, the partners can choose a monitoring protocol from several that may be available.

There is only one PPP monitoring protocol defined at the time of writing, the Link-Quality-Report (LQR) protocol. Neither, one, or both ends of a PPP link can ask a partner to transmit quality reports at regular intervals.

How do I determine if a link is healthy? First of all, is my traffic reaching the other end? I know how many octets and frames I have sent. The peer PPP knows how many good octets and frames have arrived, and how many errors it has received.

Similarly, I know what I have received and the peer knows what it has sent. By periodically exchanging Link Quality Reports, we pool our knowledge, find out how much good traffic is getting through, and how much is being lost.

When do we say that a link is "good"? This evaluation is left up to each implementation to decide, but it is assumed that some kind of criterion can be established outside of the protocol.

### 22.14.1   The PPP Link Quality Report Table

Table 22.3, the PPP Link Quality Report (LQR) Table, contains information about the present status of Link Quality Reporting. It indicates whether the link is currently good and records the local and remote timers that determine how often reports are sent.

**TABLE 22.3   PPP LQR Table**

| iso.org.dod.internet.mgmt.mib-2. transmission.ppp.pppLcp.pppLqr. pppLqrTable.pppLqrEntry 1.3.6.1.2.1.10.23.1.2.1.1 | | | |
|---|---|---|---|
| OBJECT IDENTIFIER | Syntax | Access | Description |
| pppLqrQuality 1.3.6.1.2.1.10.23.1.2.1.1.1 | INTEGER good(1), bad(2), not-determined(3) | read-only read- | Current quality of the link according to local Link-Quality Management The local LQR reporting |
| 1.3.6.1.2.1.10.23.1.2.1.1.3 | (1.. 2147483648) | only | period, in hundredths of a second. |
| pppLqrRemotePeriod 1.3.6.1.2.1.10.23.1.2.1.1.4 | INTEGER (1.. 2147483648) | read-only | The remote LQR reporting period, in hundredths of a second. |
| pppLqrOutLQRs 1.3.6.1.2.1.10.23.1.2.1.1.5 | Counter | read-only | Value of the *OutLQRs* counter for this link on the local node. |
| pppLqrInLQRs 1.3.6.1.2.1.10.23.1.2.1.1.6 | Counter | read-only | Value of the *InLQRs* counter for this link on the local node. |

A Link Quality Report contains cumulative counts of:

- Number of packets and octets that have been sent
- Number of received packets
- Number of incoming error packets, and packets discarded for some reason such as lack of memory
- Number of good octets that have been received

All of the values except for the last are obtained from variables already defined in the interfaces MIB. For this reason, the number of good octets and the total number of Link Quality Reports that have been sent and received (*pppLqrOutLQRs* and *pppLqrInLQRs*) are the only counters needed in this table.

### 22.14.2   The PPP LQR Configuration Table

To indicate that monitoring should be configured for a link, an entry is created in Table 22.4, the PPP Link Quality Report (LQR) Configuration Table. The entry is indexed by its *ifIndex* value. The maximum desired time interval between reports from the partner is defined, and the value of *pppLqrConfigStatus* is set to "enabled."

### 22.14.3   The Link Quality Report
### Extensions Table

What should we look at to decide whether a link is "good" or "bad"? It seems reasonable to examine the last-received Link Quality Request (LQR) packet.

**TABLE 22.4    The PPP LQR Configuration Table**

| iso.org.dod.internet.mgmt.mib-2. transmission.ppp.pppLcp.pppLqr. pppLqrConfigTable.pppLqrConfigEntry 1.3.6.1.2.1.10.23.1.2.2.1 | | | |
|---|---|---|---|
| OBJECT IDENTIFIER | Syntax | Access | Description |
| pppLqrConfigPeriod 1.3.6.1.2.1.10.23.1.2.2.1.1 | INTEGER (0.. 2147483647) | read-write | The LQR Reporting Period that the local PPP will attempt to negotiate with the remote PPP, in units of hundredths of a second. |
| pppLqrConfigStatus 1.3.6.1.2.1.10.23.1.2.2.1.2 | INTEGER disabled(1), enabled(2) | read-write | If enabled(2), then the local node will attempt to perform LQR negotiation with the remote node. If disabled(1), the entry may choose to remove the entry from the table. |

TABLE 22.5   The Link Quality Report Extensions Table

iso.org.dod.internet.mgmt.mib-2.
transmission.ppp.pppLcp.pppLqr.
pppLqrExtnsTable.pppLqrExtnsEntry
1.3.6.1.2.1.10.23.1.2.3.1

| OBJECT IDENTIFIER | Syntax | Access | Description |
|---|---|---|---|
| pppLqrExtnsLast ReceivedLqrPacket 1.3.6.1.2.1.10.23.1.2.3.1.1 | OCTET STRING (SIZE(68)) | read-only | The most recently received LQR packet. |

The (optional) extensions table, shown in Table 22.5, was introduced to hold data that can be used to evaluate the condition of the link. The table holds only one variable for each PPP interface, namely, the last Link Quality Request packet.

This packet actually is logically extended with the values of several purely local counters: the total number of received LQR packets, the total number of incoming packets, the total number of errored incoming packets, and the total number of good incoming octets.

## 22.15   PPP TESTS

Recall that the framework for testing an interface was defined in RFC 1229, *Extensions to the Generic-Interface MIB*. Tests are launched, and results are viewed, by means of entries in the *ifExtnsTestTable*.

The test to be run is named in the *ifExtnsTestTable* by means of an OBJECT IDENTIFIER. OBJECT IDENTIFIERS for tests uniquely relating to a PPP link are defined in the subtree:

```
iso.org.dod.internet.mgmt.mib-2.transmission.ppp.pppLcp.pppTests
```

```
( 1 . 3 . 6 . 1 . 2 . 1 . 10 . 23 . 1 . 3 )
```

There are two tests. Recall that Echo-Request and Discard-Request packets are defined within the PPP protocol. As their names suggest, the partner should send back an echo and throw away a discard. The tests consist of sending an echo or a discard.

| OBJECT IDENTIFIER | Description |
|---|---|
| pppEchoTest 1.3.6.1.2.1.10.23.1.3.1 | Send a PPP Echo Packet on the line. Success(2) means that the packet came back properly. |
| pppDiscardTest 1.3.6.1.2.1.10.23.1.3.2 | Send a PPP Discard Packet on the line. Success(2) means that the packet was successfully transmitted. |

## 22.16   PPP AUTHENTICATION PROTOCOLS

One of PPP's strong features is that it can be used on a switched or dial-up link. However, before allowing a dial-up system to join a network, it makes sense to find out its identity! Two protocols have been defined for PPP Authentication.

The Password Authentication Protocol (PAP) depends on a simple two-way handshake. After the link has been established, an identifier and password are repeatedly sent to the other end. The partner will either acknowledge the authentication or close down the link. PAP packets are sent in frames whose protocol field is set to 'C023'H.

The stronger Challenge-Handshake Authentication Protocol (CHAP) avoids the transmission of passwords:

- The challenger sends down a *Value* (e.g., a random number).

- The receiver concatenates a secret key, computes a "hash" or "digest" function on the *key + Value* octets, and sends the answer back. The answer also contains the receiver's identifier.

- The challenger looks up the name in a table, retrieves the secret key for that identity, computes the hash function against the original number, and compares answers.

For the price of a bit more software and a quick computation, this protocol offers far safer and more robust authentication. The challenge values are automatically changed all the time. No passwords are sent on the link.

The challenge can be repeated periodically throughout the connection, if desired. This can be useful for dial-ups; occasionally a user's modem will drop a connection which accidentally gets picked up by the next dial-in user. The challenge would uncover this event.

CHAP packets are sent in frames whose protocol field is set to 'C223'H.

### 22.16.1   Identifying the Security Protocols

One of the items negotiated during link setup is the security protocol (if any) to be used. A protocol is identified by an OBJECT IDENTIFIER in the subtree:

```
iso.org.dod.internet.mgmt.mib-2.transmission.
ppp.pppSecurity.pppSecurityProtocols

( 1 . 3 . 6 . 1 . 2 . 1 . 10 . 23 . 2 . 1 )
```

The protocols are:

| OBJECT IDENTIFIER | Description |
|---|---|
| pppSecurityPapProtocol 1.3.6.1.2.1.10.23.2.1.1 | The Password Authentication Protocol. |
| pppSecurityChapMD5Protocol 1.3.6.1.2.1.10.23.2.1.2 | The Challenge-Handshake Authentication Protocol, using the MD5* hash function. |

* See Chapter 33 for more information about MD5.

### 22.16.2   The PPP Security Configuration Table

Table 22.6, the PPP Security Configuration Table, configures the protocols that will be proposed during link negotiation and the order of preference in which they will be proposed.

### 22.16.3   The PPP Security Secrets Table

How many systems will I contact using PPP? It may be one, or it may be many. I will need a separate identity and secret for each of these systems. I may also need to challenge remote systems for their identities. All of this information is stored in Table 22.7, the PPP Security Secrets Table.

TABLE 22.6   PPP Security Configuration Table

| iso.org.dod.internet.mgmt.mib-2. transmission.ppp.pppSecurity. pppSecurityConfigTable.pppSecurityConfigEntry 1.3.6.1.2.1.10.23.2.2.1 | | | |
|---|---|---|---|
| OBJECT IDENTIFIER | Syntax | Access | Description |
| pppSecurityConfig Link 1.3.6.1.2.1.10.23.2.2.1.1 ▶ Index | INTEGER (0.. 2147483647) | read-write | The *ifIndex* for the corresponding interface. If 0, then this is a default value for all interfaces. |
| pppSecurityConfig Preference 1.3.6.1.2.1.10.23.2.2.1.2 ▶ Index | INTEGER (0.. 2147483647) | read-write | The relative preference of this security protocol. More than one protocol can be supported. Lower numbers mean more preferred. |
| pppSecurityConfig Protocol 1.3.6.1.2.1.10.23.2.2.1.3 | OBJECT IDENTIFIER | read-write | Identifies the security protocol to be attempted on the link for this preference level. |
| pppSecurityConfig Status 1.3.6.1.2.1.10.23.2.2.1.4 | INTEGER invalid(1), valid(2) | read-write | The invalid setting is used to request deletion of this entry. |

**TABLE 22.7    The PPP Security Secrets Table**

iso.org.dod.internet.mgmt.mib-2.
transmission.ppp.pppSecurity.
pppSecuritySecretsTable.pppSecuritySecretsEntry
1.3.6.1.2.1.10.23.2.3.1

| OBJECT IDENTIFIER | Syntax | Access | Description |
|---|---|---|---|
| pppSecuritySecrets Link 1.3.6.1.2.1.10.23.2.3.1.1 ▶ **Index** | INTEGER (0..2147483647) | read-only | The link to which this ID/Secret pair applies. If 0, the data applies to all links. |
| pppSecuritySecrets IdIndex 1.3.6.1.2.1.10.23.2.3.1.2 ▶ **Index** | INTEGER (0..2147483647) | read-only | A unique index for each ID/Secret pair defined for this link. |
| pppSecuritySecrets Direction 1.3.6.1.2.1.10.23.2.3.1.3 | INTEGER local-to-remote(1), remote-to-local(2) | read-write | The direction for this ID/Secret pair. |
| pppSecuritySecrets Protocol 1.3.6.1.2.1.10.23.2.3.1.4 | OBJECT ID | read-write | The security protocol (e.g., CHAP or PAP) to which this ID/Secret pair applies. |
| pppSecuritySecrets Identity 1.3.6.1.2.1.10.23.2.3.1.5 | OCTET STRING (SIZE (0..255)) | read-write | The Identity parameter for the ID/Secret pair. Exact meaning (e.g., userid) depends on the protocol. |
| pppSecuritySecrets Secret 1.3.6.1.2.1.10.23.2.3.1.6 | OCTET STRING (SIZE(0..255)) | read-write | The secret (or key) used for this ID/Secret pair. |
| pppSecuritySecrets Status 1.3.6.1.2.1.10.23.2.3.1.7 | INTEGER invalid(1), valid(2) | read-write | Setting to invalid is used to request deletion of this entry. |

## 22.17    A NETWORK CONTROL PROTOCOL FOR IP

Once the link has been established and any necessary authentication is complete, PPP will start negotiating the Network Control Protocols for the layer 3 traffic that will be carried on the link.

Recall that the IP Network Control Protocol, used to initialize and terminate the use of IP across the PPP link, uses a subset of the same kinds of packets used by the Link Control Protocol. However, the protocol field in the frame header will be set to '8021'H (rather than 'C021'H) indicating that the IP NCP protocol is in effect.

### 22.17.1    TCP/IP Header Compression

Compression of TCP/IP headers can save significant amounts of overhead on a serial link. Many sites have implemented the Van Jacobson header compression algorithm for this purpose.

Van Jacobson header compression is based on the fact that very few fields in the TCP and IP headers change value during a TCP connection. If I store the header for each of my TCP connections in an array, then I can just send and receive header changes across the link.

The use of header compression in one or both directions is one of the items that can be requested during IP NCP negotiation. Although it may seem strange to compress traffic in one direction but not in the return direction, the PPP philosophy allows this to be done!

Negotiation can also be used to report the local IP address to the peer, or else to ask the peer to assign an IP address.*

Once negotiation is complete and the use of IP reaches open state, IP datagrams will be transmitted in the information field of frames whose protocol field is '0021'H—or, if protocol field compression is used, just '21'H.

### 22.17.2    The PPP IP Table

Table 22.8, the PPP IP Table, reports IP NCP status information for a device's PPP links. It indicates whether the IP NCP has reached an opened state, and reports the use of compression in either direction.

---

* PPP is being extended to include compression of the *contents* of messages too.

**TABLE 22.8    The PPP IP Table**

| iso.org.dod.internet.mgmt.mib-2. transmission.ppp.pppIp.pppIpTable.pppIpEntry 1.3.6.1.2.1.10.23.3.1.1 | | | |
|---|---|---|---|
| OBJECT IDENTIFIER | Syntax | Access | Description |
| pppIpOperStatus 1.3.6.1.2.1.10.23.3.1.1.1 | INTEGER opened(1), not-opened(2) | read-only | Set to opened when PPP option negotiation has completed and the IP network protocol has reached opened state. |
| pppIpLocalToRemote CompressionProtocol 1.3.6.1.2.1.10.23.3.1.1.2 | INTEGER none(1), vj-tcp(2) | read-only | The TCP/IP compression protocol used when sending to the remote end. |
| pppIpRemoteToLocal CompressionProtocol 1.3.6.1.2.1.10.23.3.1.1.3 | INTEGER none(1), vj-tcp(2) | read-only | The TCP/IP compression protocol used by the remote end when sending to the local end. |
| pppIpRemoteMax SlotId 1.3.6.1.2.1.10.23.3.1.1.4 | INTEGER (0..255) | read-only | The remote end's Max-Slot-Id parameter, used with Van Jacobson TCP/IP compression. |
| pppIpLocalMaxSlotId 1.3.6.1.2.1.10.23.3.1.1.5 | INTEGER | read-only | The local end's Max-Slot-Id parameter, used with Van Jacobson TCP/IP compression. |

If compression is used, then TCP/IP headers will be stored in an array. The size of the array, described as the number of *slots* available, limits the number of TCP/IP connections that can be compressed. The sizes for the local and remote ends are recorded.

The PPP IP table is indexed by the *ifIndex* of the PPP link. The IP address in use is not included in this table, but is available elsewhere in the MIB.*

### 22.17.3   The PPP IP Configuration Table

The PPP IP table reported the status for links on which the IP NCP was being negotiated or had been established. Table 22.9, the PPP IP Configuration Table, indicates whether TCP/IP compression should be negotiated. The table is indexed by *ifindex*. This table provides a variable that an operator can set to request that use of IP on a PPP link be opened or closed.

## 22.18   A NETWORK CONTROL PROTOCOL FOR IPX

The IPX Control Protocol configures, initializes, and terminates the exchange of Novell IPX datagrams across a PPP link.

The IPX Control Protocol uses a subset of the same kinds of packets used by the Link Control Protocol. However, the protocol field in the frame header will be set to '802B'H. After initialization is complete, IPX datagrams are sent with PPP protocol field equal to '002B'H.

Codes 1 through 7 (Configure-Request, Configure-Ack, Configure-Nak, Configure-Reject, Terminate-Request, Terminate-Ack, and Code-Reject) are used.

---

* It is not a good idea to try to record the same information in two different places.

TABLE 22.9   The PPP IP Configuration Table

| OBJECT IDENTIFIER | Syntax | Access | Description |
|---|---|---|---|
| iso.org.dod.internet.mgmt.mib-2. transmission.ppp.pppIp.pppIpConfigTable.pppIpConfigEntry 1.3.6.1.2.1.10.23.3.2.1 | | | |
| pppIpConfig AdminStatus 1.3.6.1.2.1.10.23.3.2.1.1 | INTEGER open(1), close(2) | read-write | The desired status of the IP Network Protocol. |
| pppIpConfig Compression 1.3.6.1.2.1.10.23.3.2.1.2 | INTEGER none(1), vj-tcp(2) | read-write | If > 1, the local node will try to negotiate the indicated header compression algorithm |

### 22.18.1   IPX Configuration Options

IPX configuration options include:

- *IPX-Network-Number.*   The IPX network number to be used for the link. Both ends of the link must use the same network number. Sometimes a pair of routers ("half routers") are configured so that the link between them is invisible. In this case no number is assigned to the link, which in fact is the default.

- *IPX-Node-Number.*   Allows the local node to inform its peer of its node number, or to be assigned a node number by the peer. (Default value is no node number.)

- *IPX-Compression-Protocol.*   Used to negotiate the use of a specific compression protocol. Current values include:

  0002    Telebit Compressed IPX

  0235    Shiva Compressed NCP/IPX

  The default value is no compression.

- *IPX-Routing-Protocol.*   Requests use of one or more routing protocols. Current values include:

  0    No routing protocol required

  1    RESERVED

  2    Novell RIP/SAP required

  4    Novell NLSP required

  The default is to use Novell's Routing Information Protocol (RIP) and Server Advertising Protocol (SAP).

- *IPX-Router-Name.*   Provides an ASCII string naming a NetWare server.

- *IPX-Configuration-Complete.*   Indicates that all needed parameters have been provided.

### 22.19   A NETWORK CONTROL PROTOCOL FOR BRIDGING

PPP can carry layer 2 bridged traffic as well as an assortment of layer 3 protocols. The Bridge Network Control Protocol, used to initialize and terminate the use of bridging across the PPP link, uses a subset of the same kinds of packets used by the Link Control Protocol. However, the protocol field in the frame header will be set to '8031'H, indicating that the Bridge NCP protocol is in effect. Packets with code values 1–7 are used.

Parameters that can be negotiated are:

- *Tinygram Compression support.* DIX Ethernet and 802.3 MAC frames have a required minimum size. Tiny frames are padded with 0s to reach this minimum size. Tinygram compression removes the padding before transmitting across the PPP link, and restores the padding at the destination.

- *LAN Identification support.* An identifier can be used to tag LANs that belong to a user community. Traffic will only be moved between LANs that belong to a common community.

- *Remote Ring and Bridge Identification.* In order to carry out remote bridging of 802.5 Token-Ring LANs, each bridge needs to know its partner's ring and bridge numbers.

- *802.5 Line Identification.* An option that allows the PPP link to be treated like a logical Token-Ring by assigning the line a Ring Number.

- *MAC Types supported.* Note that the size of the Maximum Receive Unit may limit which MAC types can be carried.

### 22.19.1   The PPP Bridge Table

Table 22.10, the PPP Bridge Table, reports Bridge NCP status information for a device's PPP links. The table is indexed by *ifIndex*. It indicates whether the Bridge NCP has reached an opened state, reports on whether tinygram compression is in use, and indicates whether a LAN identification field will be included in packets.

**TABLE 22.10    The PPP Bridge Table**

iso.org.dod.internet.mgmt.mib-2.
transmission.ppp.pppBridge.pppBridgeTable.pppBridgeEntry
1.3.6.1.2.1.10.23.4.1.1

| OBJECT IDENTIFIER | Syntax | Access | Description |
|---|---|---|---|
| pppBridgeOperStatus 1.3.6.1.2.1.10.23.4.1.1.1 | INTEGER opened(1), not-opened(2) | read-only | Set to opened when the Bridge Network Control Protocol has reached opened state. |
| pppBridgeLocalTo RemoteTinygram Compression 1.3.6.1.2.1.10.23.4.1.1.2 | INTEGER false(1), true(2) | read-only | If true, the local node will perform tinygram compression. |
| pppBridgeRemoteTo LocalTinygram Compression 1.3.6.1.2.1.10.23.4.1.1.3 | INTEGER | read-only | If true, the remote node will perform tinygram compression. |
| pppBridgeLocalTo RemoteLanId 1.3.6.1.2.1.10.23.4.1.1.4 | INTEGER | read-only | If true, the local node will include the LAN Identification field. |
| pppBridgeRemoteTo LocalLanId 1.3.6.1.2.1.10.23.4.1.1.5 | INTEGER | read-only | If true, the remote node will include the LAN Identification field. |

### 22.19.2  The PPP Bridge Configuration Table

Table 22.11, the PPP Bridge Configuration Table, contains configuration information for PPP bridging. The table (which is indexed by *ifIndex*) also provides a control variable that an operator can set to request that use of Bridging on a PPP link be opened or closed.

### 22.19.3  The PPP Bridge Media Table

We need to figure out which MAC types will be sent and received on each interface. Table 22.12, the PPP Bridge Media Table, records which types of MAC frames can be sent and received across each of the system's interfaces. Naturally, the table is indexed by *ifIndex* and *pppBridgeMediaMacType*. MAC-type identifiers are assigned by the Internet Assigned Numbers Authority. Current types include:

**TABLE 22.11   The PPP Bridge Configuration Table**

iso.org.dod.internet.mgmt.mib-2.transmission.ppp.
pppBridge.pppBridgeConfigTable.pppBridgeConfigEntry
1.3.6.1.2.1.10.23.4.2.1

| OBJECT IDENTIFIER | Syntax | Access | Description |
|---|---|---|---|
| pppBridgeConfig AdminStatus 1.3.6.1.2.1.10.23.4.2.1.1 | INTEGER open(1), close(2) | read-write | The desired status of the Bridging Network Protocol. |
| pppBridgeConfig Tinygram 1.3.6.1.2.1.10.23.4.2.1.2 | INTEGER false(1), true(2) | read-write | If true, the local Bridge NCP will negotiate the option of sending compressed tinygrams. |
| pppBridgeConfig RingId 1.3.6.1.2.1.10.23.4.2.1.3 | INTEGER false(1), true(2) | read-write | If true, the local Bridge NCP will send its ring number and bridge number. |
| pppBridgeConfig LineId 1.3.6.1.2.1.10.23.4.2.1.4 | INTEGER false(1), true(2) | read-write | For 802.5 bridging, if true, then the PPP line will be treated like a logical Token-Ring. The local Bridge NCP will send the line's ring number, and its own bridge number. |
| pppBridgeConfig LanId 1.3.6.1.2.1.10.23.4.2.1.5 | INTEGER false(1), true(2) | read-write | If true, the local Bridge NCP will negotiate the option of including LAN Identification. |

**TABLE 22.12    The PPP Bridge Media Table**

| iso.org.dod.internet.mgmt.mib-2.transmission.ppp. pppBridge.pppBridgeMediaTable.pppBridgeMediaEntry 1.3.6.1.2.1.10.23.4.3.1 | | | |
|---|---|---|---|
| OBJECT IDENTIFIER | Syntax | Access | Description |
| pppBridgeMedia MacType 1.3.6.1.2.1.10.23.4.3.1.1 | INTEGER (0.. 2147483647) | read-only | The MAC type for which this entry provides status information. |
| pppBridgeMedia LocalStatus 1.3.6.1.2.1.10.23.4.3.1.2 | INTEGER accept(1), dont-accept(2) | read-only | Indicates if the local PPP is willing to accept the above MAC type in this interface. |
| pppBridgeMedia RemoteStatus 1.3.6.1.2.1.10.23.4.3.1.3 | INTEGER accept(1), dont-accept(2) | read-only | Indicates whether the local PPP believes that the remote PPP reached across this interface will accept the above MAC type. |

| | |
|---|---|
| 0 | Reserved |
| 1 | IEEE 802.3 or Ethernet |
| 2 | IEEE 802.4 |
| 3 | IEEE 802.5 |
| 4 | FDDI |

## 22.19.4    The PPP Bridge Media Configuration Table

Finally, in Table 22.13, we look at the configuration information that will be used to negotiate the MAC types to be sent and received across each interface. Again, this table is indexed by the *ifIndex* and *pppBridgeMediaConfigMacType*.

**TABLE 22.13    The PPP Bridge Media Configuration Table**

| iso.org.dod.internet.mgmt.mib-2.transmission.ppp. pppBridge.pppBridgeMediaTable.pppBridgeMediaEntry 1.3.6.1.2.1.10.23.4.4.1 | | | |
|---|---|---|---|
| OBJECT IDENTIFIER | Syntax | Access | Description |
| pppBridgeMedia ConfigMacType 1.3.6.1.2.1.10.23.4.4.1.1 | INTEGER (0.. 2147483647) | read-write | The MAC type for this entry. |
| pppBridgeMedia ConfigLocalStatus 1.3.6.1.2.1.10.23.4.4.1.2 | INTEGER accept(1), dont-accept(2) | read-write | If the value is accept, then the local PPP will accept MAC frames of the above type. |

## 22.20   RECOMMENDED READING

PPP is a useful protocol family, and it is growing. At the time of writing, the defining RFCs for the protocols were:

- RFC 1548, *The Point-to-Point Protocol (PPP)*
- RFC 1549, *PPP in HDLC Framing*
- RFC 1332, *The PPP Internet Control Protocol (IPCP)*
- RFC 1552, *The PPP Internetwork Packet Exchange Control Protocol (IPXCP)*
- RFC 1333, *PPP Link Quality Monitoring*
- RFC 1334, *PPP Authentication Protocols*
- RFC 1220, *Point-to-Point Extensions for Bridging*
- RFC 1471, *The Definitions of Managed Objects for the Link Control Protocol of the Point-to-Point Protocol*
- RFC 1472, *The Definitions of Managed Objects for the Security Protocols of the Point-to-Point Protocol*
- RFC 1473, *The Definitions of Managed Objects for the IP Network Control Protocol of the Point-to-Point Protocol*
- RFC 1474, *The Definitions of Managed Objects for the Bridge Network Control Protocol of the Point-to-Point Protocol*

RFC 1547, *Requirements for an Internet Standard Point-to-Point Protocol,* contains a lucid and comprehensive discussion of point-to-point protocol requirements, and evaluates existing vendor and standards body link protocols.

# 23

# Managing a DS1/ES1 (T1 or E1) Interface

## 23.1  INTRODUCTION

Most people are familiar with the use of plain old telephone service for data communications. After installing some simple software and attaching a modem to a serial interface on a PC or workstation, we can call computers and access remote applications. The modem (*modula-tor/dem*odulator) converts between digital computer signals and analog phone-line signals.

The use of the analog phone system for data communications has a long history. However, the phone system itself is built upon a *digital* backbone, and starting in the 1970s, businesses began to make use of faster, more reliable digital services.

In this chapter, we will need to introduce a fairly substantial amount of telecommunications language and lore in order to understand the MIBs that enable us to manage these digital interfaces.

## 23.2  THE TRADITIONAL U.S. DIGITAL HIERARCHY

Within the digital phone system, a voice channel is transformed into 64,000 bits of digital data per second. United States phone systems use *T1 carriers* to combine 24 channels for high-speed transmission. The T1 transmission rate is 1.544 megabits per second (Mbps). For telephony use, this is made up of:

- $24 \times 64{,}000 = 1.536$ Mbps of payload
- 8000 extra bits used to align the channels and carry signaling and related network information

The United States phone system performs higher levels of multiplexing. T1s are multiplexed together to form *T2 carriers,* and T1s or T2s are multiplexed into *T3 carriers.*

These *Digital Signaling levels* of multiplexing make up the *U.S. Digital Hierarchy.* For example, Digital Signaling level 0 (DS0) is a single 64,000 bit per second (bps) channel, while Digital Signaling level 1 (DS1) multiplexes 24 DS0 channels.

A *T1 carrier* implements DS1. A *T2 carrier* implements Digital Signaling level 2 (DS2), and a *T3 carrier* implements Digital Signaling level 3 (DS3).

These carriers are full-duplex; an equal number of channels is carried in each direction. However, in talking about the carriers, we usually focus on the flow in one direction. This flow has a *source* and a *sink.* The source is said to be *upstream* while the sink is *downstream.*

## 23.3   DS1 FRAMES

When the bits for many separate channels are sent down a wire together, we need a way to sort out where the bits for each channel are located. The bits are sent in a pattern called a *frame.* These frames are very different from the frames that we are used to dealing with in data communications!

A DS1 frame consists of 24 eight-bit *samples* (one sample byte for each channel), arranged in order and preceded by an extra bit, called the *framing bit.* Figure 23.1 shows the format of a DS1 frame.

The framing bits are important. They repeat a pattern that is used to find out where frames begin and end, so that the right sample gets delivered to the right channel.

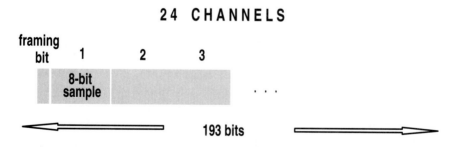

### 24 CHANNELS

8000 x 193 = 1.544 million bits/second

**Figure 23.1**   DS1 framing format.

In all, DS1 interfaces insert 8000 framing bits per second into the data stream, making the total T1 carrier bit rate 1,544,000 bits per second.* Thus framing adds about .5 percent overhead to the bit stream.

What happens if you lose frame alignment? Until you lock back onto the framing pattern, you have to throw away all of the bits that are flowing into the interface!

## 23.4   EVOLVING USE OF THE FRAMING BITS

The meaning of the extra framing bits injected into the data stream has evolved over time. For many years, *D4 framing* was the standard for DS1 interfaces. For D4 framing, a set of *12 frames* was considered a framing unit called a *Superframe. All* of the extra bits were used to locate the start of each Superframe unit and the start of each frame within the Superframe—i.e., alignment was the only purpose of the extra bits. The extra bits were set in a special pattern (100011011100), that was repeated every 12 frames.

Later, *Extended Superframes* (ESF) were introduced. With extended framing, a set of *24 frames* is considered a Superframe unit.

ESF was an important breakthrough. It turned out that alignment would work perfectly well if only 6 of the 24 extra frame bits were used for alignment. This left 18 bits that could be exploited to do a lot of useful things. Some provided an error-checking Cyclic Redundancy Code (CRC)[†] and some made up a *Facility Data Link (FDL)*, used to notify the remote end of local error conditions.

It may seem strange to think of the spare bits that are used to send facilities information as a data link, but a second look shows that it is perfectly natural. We have some bits that occur periodically in a regular position. This is exactly what any telecommunications channel is! The Facility Data Link runs at 4 kilobits per second.

Dedicating some of the extra bits to forming a Facility Data Link has proved to be an extremely valuable idea. An interface can always track its *near-end* (local) error statistics, but with a Facility Data Link, the interface also can receive reports of *far-end* (remote) statistics. If the T1 line runs end-to-end between customer locations, then the statistics are sent from the far-end Customer Premise Equipment. If channels in the T1 are switched by a telco service provider, then the statistics are sent from intermediate telco equipment.

---

* If an organization has its own transmission lines and is not interfacing with a telecommunications service provider, it could decide to use this full bandwidth for data, dispensing with all framing bits.

[†] The CRC is computed against the bits in the *previous* Extended Superframe.

A Facility Data Link also can be used to signal alarms, carry control information, or to initiate a loopback test.

There are two different industry standards specifying uses of the Facility Data Link: AT&T 54016 and ANSI T1.403.

### 23.4.1 Alarms and the Facility Data Link

In the telecommunications world, an interface raises an alarm only when an error has persisted for a significant amount of time. For example, if your interface loses alignment for a few milliseconds but then fixes itself, it does not raise an alarm. But if an outage lasts a significant amount of time, you do raise an alarm.

Just how long is "a significant amount of time"? It is up to telecommunications standards to decide this. For example, if the local end fails to find the far end's framing alignment pattern in an incoming stream for more than 2.5 (plus or minus .5) seconds, the local end enters a *red alarm* condition. To notify the other end of the problem, the pattern

```
1 1 1 1 1 1 1 1 0 0 0 0 0 0 0 0
```

is signaled on the Facility Data Link.\* This pattern is called a *yellow alarm.*

Naturally, the DS1 MIB is largely concerned with reporting problems and alarm conditions. Basically, the kinds of errors and problems that are of concern are:

- Bad signals on the line—that is, the incoming signal contains something other than properly encoded 0s and 1s.

- The signal has been lost completely—no signal pulses are seen.

- Loss of frame alignment.

- Receipt of Cyclic Redundancy Check (CRC) codes that indicate that a Superframe contained bit errors.

- Detection of repeated or deleted payload bits, usually caused by timing differences at the source and destination.

There are many technical definitions in this MIB. They associate time periods with each problem in order to nail down when alarms should be raised. They describe when and how errors should be counted. Not all details are included within this chapter. In particular, many timing constraints must be looked up in the MIB or in the source telecommunications standards.

---

\* Keep in mind that a facilities data link is not available for the old Superframe format. In this case, a yellow alarm is sent using bits out of the payload.

### 23.4.2   Framing and Transmission Rates

Recall that T1 carriers can be multiplexed into higher-rate T2 or T3 carriers. Each of the U.S. carrier types has a specific framing format. Extra bits are inserted into the data flow to align the channels, to provide CRC or parity error checks, and to send signals on a Facility Data Link. For example, we have seen that because of the extra framing bits, the T1 transmission rate requires 1,544,000 bits per second to carry a framed payload of 1,536,000 bits per second.

The following display shows the numbers of channels, payload, and total transmission rates for the U.S. transmission Digital Signaling (DS) level hierarchy for telecommunications interfaces.

| Level | Channels | Payload (bits/sec) | Rate (bits/sec) | Carrier |
|-------|----------|--------------------|-----------------|---------|
| DS0 | 1 | 64,000 | 64,000 | |
| DS1 | 24 | 1,536,000 | 1,544,000 | T1 |
| DS2 | 96 | 6,144,000 | 6,312,000 | T2 |
| DS3 | 672 | 43,008,000 | 44,736,000 | T3 |

## 23.5   E1 TRANSMISSION

Outside of North America and Japan, phone systems use *E1 carriers* to combine 32 channels. The E1 transmission rate is 2.048 Mbps.

Two of the channels are reserved for signaling and related network functions. Hence, for telephony use, an E1 carrier is made up of:

- $30 \times 64,000 = 1.920$ Mbps of payload
- 128,000 extra bits used to align the channels and carry signaling and related network information

E1 originally was defined by the *Conference of European Postal and Telecommunications Associations* (CEPT).

Instead of using the term *SuperFrames,* E1 frames are grouped into units called *Multiframes.*

Channel 0 is used for individual frame alignment, alarms, and network synchronization information. During proper alignment, channel 0 contains 0011011 in bits 2–8 of alternate frames.

Channel 16 (also called Time Slot 16 or TS16) is used for signaling information. Channel 16 of frame number 0 in each multiframe also helps out with multiframe alignment, and contains 0000 in bits 1–4.

There are several choices for European E1 framing formats. For example, some lines will provide a CRC while others will not.

## 23.6   DS1 LINE TYPES

Throughout the rest of this chapter, a DS1 interface will mean an interface to a T1 or E1 line. As noted earlier, there are a number of flavors of T1 and E1 line types. The following list shows the T1/E1 line types that are referenced in the DS1 MIB:

1. other             Not listed below
2. dsx1ESF           Extended SuperFrame DS1
3. dsx1D4            AT&T D4 format DS1
4. dsx1E1            Based on CCITT G.704 without CRC
5. dsx1E1-CRC        Based on CCITT G.704 with CRC
6. dsx1E1-MF         Based on CCITT G.704 with Time Slot 16 multi-framing, without CRC
7. dsx1E1-CRC-MF     Based on CCITT G.704 with Time Slot 16 multi-framing, with CRC

## 23.7   THE EVOLUTION OF SIGNALING

Originally, T1 was introduced purely to serve voice needs in the United States. Older D4 equipment "robbed" bits from fixed places in the T1 Superframe in order to convey signaling information. This does not hurt voice particularly, but does not serve data well.

If the European E1 model was followed, the signaling bits were sent in a reserved channel. This was called Associated Signaling, because specific bits in the reserved channel were associated with each service channel.

Modern systems use a reserved channel but send signaling information across the extra channel in formatted messages. For T1, channel 24 is used. For E1, channel 16 is used. A field in each message identifies the corresponding service channel.

## 23.8   T1 CSUS AND DSUS

In place of the modem used to interface to an *analog* line, the equipment used to interface to *digital* service consists of two components—a Channel Service Unit (CSU) and a Data Service Unit (DSU). Often these are packaged together.

As shown in Figure 23.2, the CSU faces out toward the service network. It is the job of a CSU to physically terminate the network's digital line. The CSU also performs signal regeneration, alarms, and loopback testing.

The DSU connects the CSU to your premise equipment. A DSU matches local clocking to network clocking, and provides a physical interface—such as RS-232, RS-449, or V.35—to local equipment.

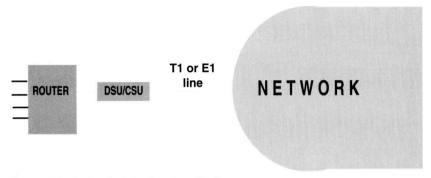

**Figure 23.2**  A simple interface to a T1 line.

## 23.9  PHYSICAL CONFIGURATION FOR MANAGED CSU/DSUS

In some cases, we wish to use an SNMP agent to manage a single DS1 interface. Or, we may have a whole shelf of CSU/DSU units that provide multiple DS1 interfaces.

In today's routed networks, the configuration may be more complicated. A router may connect directly to a shelf of CSU/DSUs. An SNMP agent in the router may be acting as agent for the router and proxy agent for the CSU/DSUs. The router agent now has to watch *both* the interfaces between the router and CSU/DSUs, *and* the interface between the network and the DS1 interfaces. Figure 23.3 illustrates this type of configuration.

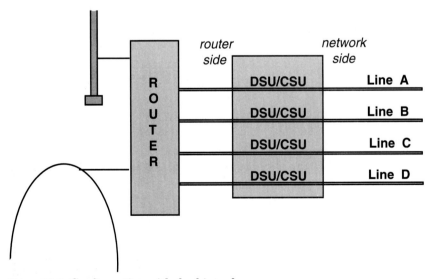

**Figure 23.3**  Configuration with dual interfaces.

Each line to the outside world actually represents a pair of lines. The DS1 MIB introduces a convention for numbering lines in this kind of situation.

- Choose a starting number bigger than the total number of interfaces. For example, the router in Figure 23.3 has five interfaces, so we could start with the number 6.
- Number lines on the equipment side with even numbers.
- Assign an adjacent odd number to the corresponding line on the network side. For example, the first line on the equipment side of the router in Figure 23.3 is assigned number 6, and its corresponding network line is numbered 7.

We treat each pair of lines like a *single* interface. After all, traffic just passes through the pair of lines. Identical interface traffic counts should not have to be recorded twice.

To sort out the relationship between lines and interfaces, a line identification variable, *dsx1LineIndex,* is introduced. Values of *dsx1Line-Index* based on Figure 23.3 are tabulated as follows:

| Line | dsx1LineIndex | ifindex |
| --- | --- | --- |
| A, Router Side | 6 | 2 |
| A, Network Side | 7 | 2 |
| B, Router Side | 8 | 3 |
| B, Network Side | 9 | 3 |
| C, Router Side | 10 | 4 |
| C, Network Side | 11 | 4 |
| D, Router Side | 12 | 5 |
| D, Network Side | 13 | 5 |

Suppose that we have a shelf of CSU/DSU units with its own internal agent. Then, as far as a line is concerned, it has only one side—a network side.* We still assign a value to the *dsx1LineIndex* variable, but that value is simply the *ifIndex* value for the line.

## 23.10  GATHERING STATISTICS

The statistics that appear in the DS1 MIB are derived from long custom in the phone system.

In the phone system, the standard measurement period is a 15-minute interval. Statistics are collected 24 hours per day. Hence, a total of 96 sets of statistics are gathered each day.

---

* The device will have some local interfaces as well, which will be handled directly as separate interfaces.

The T1/E1 MIB tracks statistics for the current 15-minute period, and also stores the values for the previous 96 periods. In addition, totals across the previous 24 hours are maintained. Of course, if the interface has been initialized some time in the last 24 hours, then less than the full 96 sets of statistics will be available.

## 23.11   LINE CODING
## AND THE ZEROS PROBLEM

It would be nice if we did not have to worry about how telephone service providers represent 0s and 1s on a line. Unfortunately, there are a number of alternatives, and it is important to be aware of which one is in use.

For a long time, a scheme called *Alternate Mark Inversion* (AMI) was very popular with AT&T and other carriers. AMI represents a "0" as a zero voltage and "1s" as alternatively positive (+) and negative (−) voltage pulses. That is, if the last 1 was positive, the next 1 will be negative, and vice versa. For example, the following is valid:

```
1   1   0   1   0   0   1
+   −   0   +   0   0   −
```

There is one unfortunate problem with Alternate Mark Inversion—if there are too many zeros in a row, bit timing can be completely lost!

There are a number of solutions to this problem. Some of them are crude and clumsy. One of them turns a violation into a benefit.

Failure to *change* from high-positive to low-negative polarity, or from low-negative to high-positive polarity is called a *bipolar violation*. A handy solution to too many zeros in the data is to replace a string of zeros with a special bipolar violation pattern.

The method that has been chosen to handle repeated zeros for a line is indicated by storing one of the following numeric codes in MIB variable *dsx1LineCoding*.

1. *dsx1JBZS*    Jammed Bit Zero Suppression: Solves the problem by setting 1 selected bit out of each 8 bits to 1. Thus only 7 bits per channel can be used for data, cutting a DS0 channel to 56,000 bits per second, and cutting the T1 payload to 1,344,000 bits per second!

2. *dsx1B8ZS*    Bipolar with 8-Zero Substitution: Replaces a sequence of 8 zeros with an 8-bit pattern that cannot be confused with normal data, because it contains bipolar violations.

3. *dsx1HDB3*    High Density Bipolar 3-Zero Maximum Coding: A different substitution pattern, used on European E1 links. Replaces 4 zeros with a 4-bit pattern containing a bipolar violation. Adjacent blocks of zeros have different patterns, with alternate polarity, to avoid introducing a direct-current component into the signal.

4. *dsx1ZBTSI*    Zero-Byte Time Slot Interchange, an ANSI standard coding that also provides full use of a channel. A scrambling/unscrambling algorithm is used to transform long strings of 0s to an acceptable signal. Some of the framing bits are reserved for use with this algorithm.

5. *dsx1AMI*    Alternate Mark Inversion, as used on European links. It is left to higher layers to assure that the data contains no long strings of zeros.

6. *other*    None of the above.

## 23.12  LINE CODING
## AND THE ONES PROBLEM

The reason that some implementations change the polarity for successive 1s is that the line behaves best when there is a balance between positive and negative pulses. When positives and negatives are not balanced, a Direct-Current component is introduced onto the line, and this component causes distortion of the signal.

We shall see in later sections that codings often are designed keeping in mind the goal to balance out the number of positive and negative pulses.

## 23.13  ERROR EVENTS

Inevitably, things sometimes will go wrong. Why? The clocks at the two ends may not be synchronized correctly. There may be bit errors on the line. Some piece of equipment may be malfunctioning.

Problems surface through a number of error events, defined as:

- *Bipolar Violation (BPV).*  For AMI, a bipolar violation—that is, a high when the last nonzero signal was high, or a low when the last nonzero signal was low. Of course, when zero substitution is in use (B8ZS or HDB3), a bipolar violation is not an error unless it is clearly not part of a zero substitution.

- *Excessive Zeroes (EXZ).*  For Alternate Mark Inversion, more than 15 contiguous zeros. For B8ZS, more than 7 contiguous zeros.

- *Line Coding Violation (LCV).*  Either a Bipolar Violation (BPV) or Excessive Zeroes (EXZ) Error Event.

- *Path Coding Violation (PCV).*  For D4 or E1 without CRC, a frame synchronization bit error. For Extended SuperFrame (ESF) or E1 with CRC, a CRC error.

- *Controlled Slip (CS).*  A repetition or deletion of an incoming frame by the receiving equipment. Controlled Slip might result from a timing problem.

## 23.14   PERSISTENT PROBLEMS
## AND LINE FAILURES

More serious conditions are defined as follows. These conditions are cleared when the symptom has not appeared for a prespecified time period. For details on how long each time period lasts, see the MIB document or appropriate telephony standards.

- *Out of Frame Defect (OOF).*   The receiver does not see the expected framing pattern.

  —More precisely, for T1, two or more framing errors have been detected within a 3-millisecond period for ESF signals and within 0.75 milliseconds for D4 signals—or two or more errors out of five or less consecutive framing-bits.

  —For E1, three consecutive frame alignment signals have been received with an error.

  —An Out of Frame defect ends when the signal is back in frame.

- *Loss of Signal Failure (LOS).*   The receiver sees no positive or negative pulses.

  —More precisely, for T1, the Loss of Signal failure is declared after $175 \pm 75$ contiguous pulse positions with no pulses of either positive or negative polarity.

  —For E1, the Loss of Signal failure is declared when more than 10 consecutive zeros are detected.

- *Loss of Frame Failure (LOF).*   Nothing useful is coming in.

  —More precisely, for T1, failure is declared when an Out of Frame (OOF) or Loss of Signal (LOS) has persisted for a specified number of seconds.

  —For E1, Loss of Frame Failure is declared when an OOF defect is detected.

- *Alarm Indication Signal (AIS).*   The source has a problem that prevents it from sending its normal, framed payload. Instead, it sends an unframed stream of 1s.

  —More precisely, for D4 and ESF links, the sink detects this as an unframed signal with a 1s density of at least 99.9 percent present for a specified time.

  —For E1 links, "all 1s" is a string of 512 bits containing fewer than 3 zero bits.

- *TS16 Alarm Indication Signal Failure (T16AIS):* For E1 only. Recall that normally, *Time Slot 16* (TS16) of frame 0 should have 0000 in bits 1–4. The TS16 Alarm Indication Signal failure is declared when time slot 16 is received as all 1s for all frames of two consecutive multiframes.

- *Loss of MultiFrame Failure (LOMF).* Only for E1 operating in "Channel Associated Signaling" mode. Declared when two consecutive multiframe alignment signals (bits 4 through 7 of Time Slot 16 of frame 0) have been received with an error.

- *Far-End Loss of Multiframe Failure (FarEndLOMF).* Only for E1 operating in "Channel Associated Signaling" mode. Declared when bit 2 of time slot 16 of frame 0 is received set to one on two consecutive occasions.

## 23.15   LINE ALARM CONDITIONS

The status of a line can be fairly complex. A loopback may be in progress, and there also may be several line failure alarm conditions that have not yet cleared.

The line status is represented by the *dsx1LineStatus* variable, which is an integer that represents a bit map. Each bit indicates whether a particular condition is present. Note that the conditions were defined in the previous section. In the following list, the bit assignments are translated to decimal numbers—e.g., 100 becomes 4:

| | |
|---|---|
| 1 dsx1NoAlarm | No Alarm Present. |
| 2 dsx1RcvFarEndLOF | Far-End Loss of Frame (signaled by a received Yellow Alarm). |
| 4 dsx1XmtFarEndLOF | Near end is sending Loss of Frame Indication (i.e., sending Yellow Alarm). |
| 8 dsx1RcvAIS | Far end is sending Alarm Indication Signal. |
| 16 dsx1XmtAIS | Near end is sending Alarm Indication Signal. |
| 32 dsx1LossOfFrame | Near end is experiencing Loss of Frame (in a Red Alarm condition). |
| 64 dsx1LossOfSignal | Near end is experiencing Loss of Signal (i.e., not detecting 1s). |
| 128 dsx1LoopbackState | Near end is looped. |
| 256 dsx1T16AIS | Have received an Alarm Indication Signal on an E1 link (signaled by a 1s pattern in time slot 16). |
| 512 dsx1RcvFarEndLOMF | For E1, a Loss of Multiframe Failure, diagnosed from bad multiframe alignment signals in time slot 16. |
| 1024 dsx1XmtFarEndLOMF | Near End is sending a time slot 16 Loss of Multiframe Failure. |

| 2048 | dsx1RcvTestCode | Near End detects a test code. |
| 4096 | dsxOtherFailure | None of the above. |

## 23.16  TESTING A LINE

Most of the time, we expect that the information being sent across a DS1 interface will be normal data. However, when problems arise, there are various tests that are used to help with diagnosis.

For example, there are two types of loopback tests. A *payload loopback* is received by a device, reframed by the device, and then sent back. A *line loopback* is simply turned around and sent back without going through the device and being reframed.

Other tests involve sending fixed or random patterns to an interface. Status information about an interface includes the type of data currently being received. The type of data is indicated by a code number in variable *dsx1SendCode*. The choice of codes includes:

| Value | Sending |
| --- | --- |
| 1. dsx1SendNoCode | Looped or normal data |
| 2. dsx1SendLineCode | Request for a line loopback |
| 3. dsx1SendPayloadCode | Request for a payload loopback |
| 4. dsx1SendResetCode | Request for loopback termination |
| 5. dsx1SendQRS | A Quasi-Random Signal test pattern |
| 6. dsx1Send511Pattern | A 511-bit fixed test pattern |
| 7. dsx1Send3in24Pattern | A fixed test pattern of 3 bits set within 24 |
| 8. dsx1SendOtherTestPattern | Some other test pattern |

## 23.17  TIMING

Timing is of critical importance for the accurate transmission of data. Bits must arrive at a DS1 interface within close tolerances of when the local hardware expects them to arrive. Bits must be transmitted so that their arrival will synchronize with the equipment at the far end. There are three ways that an interface can establish its transmit clock:

1. *loopTiming*    Synchronize with the network by recovering the receive clock.

2. *localTiming*    Use a local, internal clock source.

3. *throughTiming*    If there are several DS1 interfaces, the receive clock from another interface can be used as this interface's transmit clock.

We finally are ready to look at the DS1 MIB!

## 23.18   LOOPBACK STATES

Data reception can be suspended in order to participate in a loopback test across a line. The loopback state is stored in configuration variable *dsx1LoopbackConfig*. The state is coded by the integer values:

1. *dsx1NoLoop*          Not in Loopback state.
2. *dsx1PayloadLoop*     The received signal is looped through the local device.
3. *dsx1LineLoop*        The received signal does not go through the device, but is looped back.
4. *dsx1OtherLoop*       Another type of loopback is configured.

## 23.19   THE DS1 NEAR-END GROUP TABLES

Our first concern is to find out how our end of a line is behaving. The DS1 Near-End Group consists of four tables:

- The DS1 Configuration Table contains line configuration and status information.
- The DS1 Current Table records error statistics for the current 15-minute interval.
- The DS1 Interval Table records error statistics for earlier, completed 15-minute intervals.
- The DS1 Total Table contains sums of error statistics over the past 24-hour period.

Note that the OBJECT IDENTIFIER numbering of tables in this MIB does not start at 1. This is because there was an earlier MIB version from which some definitions were dropped.

### 23.19.1   The DS1 Configuration Table

Table 23.1, the DS1 Configuration Table, contains general configuration information about a DS1 interface such as the type of line (e.g., DS4 Superframe or Extended SuperFrame) and kind of coding used to deal with blocks of zeros. It also includes status information indicating:

- The number of seconds since the current measurement period started
- The number of previous intervals for which data has been stored
- The current type of code being sent across the interface (e.g., normal data or some kind of test pattern)
- The current status of the line, especially with regard to alarms that may be in effect

**TABLE 23.1    The DS1 Configuration Table**

iso.org.dod.internet.mgmt.mib-2.
transmission.ds1.dsx1ConfigTable.dsx1ConfigEntry
1.3.6.1.2.1.10.18.6.1

| OBJECT IDENTIFIER | Syntax | Access | Description |
|---|---|---|---|
| dsx1LineIndex<br>1.3.6.1.2.1.10.18.6.1.1<br>► **Index** | INTEGER<br>(1..'7fffffff'h) | read-only | Line index. |
| dsx1IfIndex<br>1.3.6.1.2.1.10.18.6.1.2 | INTEGER<br>(1..'7fffffff'h) | read-only | This is the *ifIndex* for the corresponding interface. |
| dsx1TimeElapsed<br>1.3.6.1.2.1.10.18.6.1.3 | INTEGER<br>(0..899)<br>i.e., up to<br>15 minutes. | read-only | Number of seconds that have elapsed since the beginning of the current error-measurement period. |
| dsx1ValidIntervals<br>1.3.6.1.2.1.10.18.6.1.4 | INTEGER<br>(0..96) | read-only | Number of previous intervals (up to 96) for which valid data was collected. |
| dsx1LineType<br>1.3.6.1.2.1.10.18.6.1.5 | INTEGER<br>other(1),<br>dsx1ESF(2),<br>dsx1D4(3),<br>dsx1E1(4),<br>dsx1E1-CRC(5),<br>dsx1E1-MF(6),<br>dsx1E1-CRC-MF(7) | read-write | Type of line.<br>See Sec. 23.6. |
| dsx1LineCoding<br>1.3.6.1.2.1.10.18.6.1.6 | INTEGER<br>dsx1JBZS(1),<br>dsx1B8ZS(2),<br>dsx1HDB3(3),<br>dsx1ZBTSI(4),<br>dsx1AMI(5),<br>other(6) | read-write | The kind of Zero Code Suppression used on the link. See Sec. 23.11. |
| dsx1SendCode<br>1.3.6.1.2.1.10.18.6.1.7 | INTEGER<br>(1–8) | read-write | Type of data being sent across the DS1 interface, e.g., normal or looped data, or some type of test pattern. See Sec. 23.16. |
| dsx1Circuit<br>Identifier<br>1.3.6.1.2.1.10.18.6.1.8 | DisplayString<br>(SIZE (0..255)) | read-write | The transmission vendor's circuit identifier, used to facilitate troubleshooting. |
| dsx1LoopbackConfig<br>1.3.6.1.2.1.10.18.6.1.9 | INTEGER<br>(1–4) | read-write | Whether the interface is looped back, and if so, which type. |

TABLE 23.1     The DS1 Configuration Table (*Continued*)

iso.org.dod.internet.mgmt.mib-2.
transmission.ds1.dsx1ConfigTable.dsx1ConfigEntry
1.3.6.1.2.1.10.18.6.1

| OBJECT IDENTIFIER | Syntax | Access | Description |
|---|---|---|---|
| dsx1LineStatus<br>1.3.6.1.2.1.10.18.6.1.10 | INTEGER<br>(1..8191) | read-<br>only | An integer representing a bit map. It can report loopback, failure, received alarm, and transmitted alarm information. See Sec. 23.15. |
| dsx1SignalMode<br>1.3.6.1.2.1.10.18.6.1.11 | INTEGER<br>none(1),<br>robbedBit(2),<br>bitOriented(3),<br>message<br>Oriented(4) | read-<br>write | The method (if any) used for signaling on this channel. |
| dsx1Transmit<br>ClockSource<br>1.3.6.1.2.1.10.18.6.1.12 | INTEGER<br>loopTiming(1),<br>localTiming(2),<br>throughTiming(3) | read-<br>write | Source of transmit clocking. |
| dsx1Fdl<br>1.3.6.1.2.1.10.18.6.1.13 | INTEGER<br>other(1),<br>ANSI-T1-403(2),<br>AT&T-54016(4),<br>none(8) | read-<br>write | The Facility Data Link protocol that is supported. |

The first variable in Table 23.1 is the line index. Recall that depending on the type of equipment, there may be a 1-1 or a 2-1 relationship between lines and interfaces. In brief, if a line has a 1-1 relationship with an interface, then *dsx1LineIndex* has the same value as the corresponding *ifIndex*. Otherwise, the value exceeds the total number of interfaces (as recorded in the *ifNumber* variable). Inside interfaces are given an even number and outside interfaces are given an odd number.

There are different ways to use the Facility Data Link. ANSI T1.403 sends priority bit-oriented signals on the link as needed, and sends out message-oriented performance reports once per second. AT&T's 54016 standard uses a command-response protocol across the link. The *dsx1Fdl* variable found in Table 23.1 indicates which protocol is used on the link.

### 23.19.2     Error Statistics Tables

Although we may not care much about infrequent and transient errors, errors that recur frequently are a cause for concern. In order to track these errors, the MIB keeps counts of the number of seconds in which various kinds of errors occur.

The MIB also contains counts of the total numbers of Line Coding Violations and Path Coding Violations. Recall that Line Coding Violations are the result of Bipolar Violations or excessive zeros, while Path Coding Violations are the result of bad framing bits or incorrect CRC codes.

Table 23.2, the DS1 Current Table, contains statistics that are being collected for the current 15-minute interval. The same statistics are gathered for each completed measurement interval in the previous 24-hour period, and are recorded in the DS1 Interval Table. Finally, totals of the same variables are recorded in the DS1 Total Table.

Note that a *gauge* datatype is used to count numbers of errors rather than a *counter* datatype. This is because we want to keep a record of the total number of errors *for a specific period.* If the number reaches the maximum that can be held in 32 bits, we do not want it to wrap around to 0, as it would for a counter. A gauge value will stick at the maximum value, and even without knowing how many more errors have occurred, we will have a pretty clear idea that something went wrong in that interval!

A few more definitions are needed in order to understand the counts in these tables:

- *Errored Seconds (ES).*  For ESF and E1-CRC links, a second with one or more Path Code Violations *or* one or more Out of Frame defects *or* one or more Controlled Slip events *or* a detected AIS defect.

    For D4 and E1 non-CRC links, a second in which Bipolar Violations occurred.

- *Severely Errored Seconds (SES).*  For ESF, a second with 320 or more Path Code Violation Error Events *or* one or more Out of Frame defects *or* a detected AIS defect.

    For E1-CRC signals, a second with 832 or more Path Code Violation error events *or* one or more Out of Frame defects.

    For E1 non-CRC signals, a second with 2048 or more Line Coding Violations.

    For D4 signals, Severely Errored Seconds counts 1-second intervals with Framing Error events, *or* an OOF defect, *or* 1544 or more Line Coding Violations.

- *Severely Errored Framing Second (SEFS).*  A second with one or more Out of Frame defects *or* a detected AIS defect.

- *Unavailable Seconds (UAS).*  Number of seconds that the interface is unavailable. A DS1 interface is unavailable from the onset of 10 contiguous Severely Errored Seconds, or the onset of the condition leading to a failure (see Failure States).

**TABLE 23.2    The DS1 Current Table**

iso.org.dod.internet.mgmt.mib-2.
transmission.ds1.dsx1CurrentTable.dsx1CurrentEntry
1.3.6.1.2.1.10.18.7.1

| OBJECT IDENTIFIER | Syntax | Access | Description |
|---|---|---|---|
| dsx1CurrentIndex<br>1.3.6.1.2.1.10.18.7.1.1<br>► **Index** | INTEGER<br>(1..'7ffffffff'h) | read-only | The line index (same as *dsx1LineIndex*) for this interface. |
| dsx1CurrentESs<br>1.3.6.1.2.1.10.18.7.1.2 | Gauge | read-only | Number of errored seconds in the current 15-minute interval. |
| dsx1CurrentSESs<br>1.3.6.1.2.1.10.18.7.1.3 | Gauge | read-only | Number of Severely Errored Seconds in the current 15-minute interval. |
| dsx1CurrentSEFSs<br>1.3.6.1.2.1.10.18.7.1.4 | Gauge | read-only | Number of Severely Errored Framing Seconds in the current 15-minute interval. |
| dsx1CurrentUASs<br>1.3.6.1.2.1.10.18.7.1.5 | Gauge | read-only | Number of Unavailable Seconds in the current 15-minute interval. |
| dsx1CurrentCSSs<br>1.3.6.1.2.1.10.18.7.1.6 | Gauge | read-only | Number of Controlled Slip Seconds in the current 15-minute interval. |
| dsx1CurrentPCVs<br>1.3.6.1.2.1.10.18.7.1.7 | Gauge | read-only | Total number of Path Coding Violations in the current 15-minute interval. |
| dsx1CurrentLESs<br>1.3.6.1.2.1.10.18.7.1.8 | Gauge | read-only | Number of Line Errored Seconds in the current 15-minute interval. |
| dsx1CurrentBESs<br>1.3.6.1.2.1.10.18.7.1.9 | Gauge | read-only | Number of Bursty Errored Seconds in the current 15-minute interval. |
| dsx1CurrentDMs<br>1.3.6.1.2.1.10.18.7.1.10 | Gauge | read-only | Number of Degraded Minutes in the current 15-minute interval. |
| dsx1CurrentLCVs<br>1.3.6.1.2.1.10.18.7.1.11 | Gauge | read-only | Total number of Line Code Violations in the current 15-minute interval. |

- *Controlled Slip Seconds (CSS).* A second in which one or more controlled slips is detected. Recall that a controlled slip is a replication or deletion of information payload bits in a DS1 frame.
- *Line Errored Seconds (LES).* A second in which one or more Line Coding Violation error events were detected. Recall that a Line Coding Violation is either a Bipolar Violation or Excessive Zeros Error Event.
- *Bursty Errored Seconds (BES).* A second with 1–319 Path Coding Violation error events, no Severely Errored Frame defects and no detected incoming AIS defects.
- *Degraded Minutes.* A minute in which the estimated error rate exceeds 1 in 1,000,000 but does not exceed 1 in 1000. (Remove severely errored seconds before counting errors.)

### 23.19.3   The DS1 Current Table

Table 23.2, the DS1 Current Table, contains statistics that are being collected for the current 15-minute interval.

### 23.19.4   The DS1 Interval Table

The DS1 Interval Table contains error statistics for up to 96 intervals prior to the current one. If the interface has been up for less than 24 hours, then less than 96 intervals will be recorded. The error statistics that are tracked are identical to those in Table 23.2, the DS1 Current Table. The OBJECT IDENTIFIER for the table is:

```
iso.org.dod.internet.mgmt.mib-2.transmission.ds1.dsx1IntervalTable
```

or

```
1 . 3 . 6 . 1 . 2 . 1 . 10 . 18 . 8
```

### 23.19.5   The DS1 Total Table

The DS1 Total Table contains cumulative sums of error statistics for the 24-hour period preceding the current interval. The error statistics that are tracked are identical to those in Table 23.2, the DS1 Current Table. The OBJECT IDENTIFIER for the table is:

```
iso.org.dod.internet.mgmt.mib-2.transmission.ds1.dsx1TotalTable
```

or

```
1 . 3 . 6 . 1 . 2 . 1 . 10 . 18 . 9
```

## 23.20   INTRODUCTION TO THE DS1 FAR-END GROUP

When troubleshooting a DS1 interface, you need all of the information that you can get. Knowledge of status and statistics for the far-end partner would be very helpful. Some DS1 products can make use of a Facility Data Link, or of some proprietary channel arrangement, to get information about the far end.

The DS1 far-end group is made up of three tables containing information about the far end. As in the previous group, the first table provides values for the current 15-minute interval, the second records error activity for intervals during the previous 24 hours, and the last contains totals over the entire 24-hour period.

### 23.20.1   The DS1 Far-End Current Table

Far-end statistics for the current interval are recorded in Table 23.3. All of the statistics counted for the local end that also make sense for the far end appear in the table. The order of the PCVs and LESs variables is switched in this table. This was done accidentally when the MIB was written. The OBJECT IDENTIFIER definitions must be used as they appear in the MIB.

### 23.20.2   The DS1 Far-End Interval Table

Far-end statistics for all of the completed intervals in the last 24 hours are recorded in the DS1 Far-End Interval Table. The error statistics that are tracked are identical to those in the DS1 Far-End Current Table. The OBJECT IDENTIFIER for the table is:

```
iso.org.dod.internet.mgmt.mib-2.transmission.ds1.dsx1FarEndIntervalTable
```

or

```
1 . 3 . 6 . 1 . 2 . 1 . 10 . 18 . 11
```

### 23.20.3   The DS1 Far-End Total Table

The DS1 Far-End Total Table contains cumulative sums of statistics for the 24-hour period preceding the current interval. The error statistics that are tracked are identical to those in the DS1 Far-End Current Table. The OBJECT IDENTIFIER for the table is:

```
iso.org.dod.internet.mgmt.mib-2.transmission.ds1.dsx1FarEndTotalTable
```

or

```
1 . 3 . 6 . 1 . 2 . 1 . 10 . 18 . 12
```

**TABLE 23.3     The DS1 Far-End Current Table**

iso.org.dod.internet.mgmt.mib-2.transmission.
ds1.dsx1FarEndCurrentTable.dsx1FarEndCurrentEntry
1.3.6.1.2.1.10.18.10.1

| OBJECT IDENTIFIER | Syntax | Access | Description |
|---|---|---|---|
| dsx1FarEnd CurrentIndex 1.3.6.1.2.1.10.18.10.1.1 ▶ **Index** | INTEGER (1..'7fffffff'h) | read-only | Index uniquely identifying the DS1 line interface (*dsx1LineIndex*). |
| dsx1FarEnd TimeElapsed 1.3.6.1.2.1.10.18.10.1.2 | INTEGER (0..899) | read-only | Number of seconds that have elapsed since the beginning of the far-end current error measurement period. |
| dsx1FarEnd ValidIntervals 1.3.6.1.2.1.10.18.10.1.3 | INTEGER (0..96) | read-only | Number of previous far-end intervals for which valid data was collected. |
| dsx1FarEnd CurrentESs 1.3.6.1.2.1.10.18.10.1.4 | Gauge | read-only | Number of Far-End Errored Seconds in the current 15-minute interval. |
| dsx1FarEnd CurrentSESs 1.3.6.1.2.1.10.18.10.1.5 | Gauge | read-only | Number of Far-End Severely Errored Seconds in the current 15-minute interval. |
| dsx1FarEnd CurrentSEFSs 1.3.6.1.2.1.10.18.10.1.6 | Gauge | read-only | Number of Far-End Severely Errored Framing Seconds in the current 15-minute interval. |
| dsx1FarEnd CurrentUASs 1.3.6.1.2.1.10.18.10.1.7 | Gauge | read-only | Number of Far-End Unavailable Seconds in the current 15-minute interval. |
| dsx1FarEnd CurrentCSSs 1.3.6.1.2.1.10.18.10.1.8 | Gauge | read-only | Number of Far-End Controlled Slip Seconds in the current 15-minute interval. |

TABLE 23.3    The DS1 Far-End Current Table (*Continued*)

iso.org.dod.internet.mgmt.mib-2.transmission.
ds1.dsx1FarEndCurrentTable.dsx1FarEndCurrentEntry
1.3.6.1.2.1.10.18.10.1

| OBJECT IDENTIFIER | Syntax | Access | Description |
| --- | --- | --- | --- |
| dsx1FarEnd CurrentLESs 1.3.6.1.2.1.10.18.10.1.9 | Gauge | read-only | Number of Far-End Line Errored Seconds in the current 15-minute interval. |
| dsx1FarEnd CurrentPCVs 1.3.6.1.2.1.10.18.10.1.10 | Gauge | read-only | Number of Far-End Path Coding Violations in the current 15-minute interval. |
| dsx1FarEnd CurrentBESs 1.3.6.1.2.1.10.18.10.1.11 | Gauge | read-only | Number of Far-End Bursty Errored Seconds in the current 15-minute interval. |
| dsx1FarEnd CurrentDMs 1.3.6.1.2.1.10.18.10.1.12 | Gauge | read-only | Number of Far-End Degraded Minutes in the current 15-minute interval. |

## 23.21    THE DS1 FRACTIONAL GROUP

There are times when a DS1 interface is not used as a single data pipe, but instead is broken into several conveniently sized logical *fractional* interfaces. The whole physical DS1 interface will be treated as an interface and will have an assigned *ifIndex*. But, in addition, each logical interface also is assigned its own *ifIndex*.

To configure logical interfaces, we need to know:

- The *ifIndex* for the DS1 interface as a whole
- Which of the channels (of the 24 for T1 or 32 for E1) belong to each logical interface
- The *ifIndex* assigned to each logical interface

For example, suppose that a DSU/CSU unit has two DS1 interfaces. Suppose that the first interface is used as a big data pipe, but for the second, channels 1–6 form one logical interface, channels 7–12 form another, while channels 13–24 make up 12 separate 64,000 bit/sec logical interfaces.

**TABLE 23.4    Assignment of Logical Interface Numbers**

| Real DS1 interface dsx1FracIndex | Channel number dsx1FracNumber | Fractional interface dsx1FracIfIndex |
|:---:|:---:|:---:|
| 2 | 1 | 3 |
| 2 | 2 | 3 |
| 2 | 3 | 3 |
| 2 | 4 | 3 |
| 2 | 5 | 3 |
| 2 | 6 | 3 |
| 2 | 7 | 4 |
| 2 | 8 | 4 |
| 2 | 9 | 4 |
| 2 | 10 | 4 |
| 2 | 11 | 4 |
| 2 | 12 | 4 |
| 2 | 13 | 5 |
| 2 | 14 | 6 |
| 2 | 15 | 7 |
| 2 | 16 | 8 |
| 2 | 17 | 9 |
| 2 | 18 | 10 |
| 2 | 19 | 11 |
| 2 | 20 | 12 |
| 2 | 21 | 13 |
| 2 | 22 | 14 |
| 2 | 23 | 15 |
| 2 | 24 | 16 |

Table 23.4 shows an assignment of values that describes the fractional logical channels created over interface number 2.

Fractional interfaces are sometimes used so that a customer can subscribe to (and pay for!) a fractional part of the DS1 bandwidth. In this case, some DS0 channels are simply turned off and unused. For example, a customer might contract for half of the normal DS1 bandwidth. In this case, unused channels are assigned a fractional interface index of 0.

Note that logical channel structure is a DSU function. CSUs manage physical layer characteristics and don't care about fractional content. Therefore a shelf of CSU units will not support these MIB variables.

Table 23.5 contains the formal definitions of these variables.

## 23.22    RECOMMENDED READING

At the time of writing, RFC 1406 defined the MIB for DS1 and E1 interfaces. ANSI standard T1.403 describes the DS1 interface. ANSI Standards T1.107 and T1.107a define DS1, DS2, and DS3 frame formats.

TABLE 23.5    The DS1 Fractional Table

| iso.org.dod.internet.mgmt.mib-2.transmission.<br>ds1.dsx1FracTable.dsx1FracEntry<br>1.3.6.1.2.1.10.18.13.1 | | | |
|---|---|---|---|
| OBJECT IDENTIFIER | Syntax | Access | Description |
| dsx1FracIndex<br>1.3.6.1.2.1.10.18.13.1.1<br>► **Index** | INTEGER<br>(1..'7fffffff'H) | read-<br>only | Index uniquely identifying the<br>DS1 line interface (same as<br>*dsx1LineIndex* value). |
| dsx1FracNumber<br>1.3.6.1.2.1.10.18.13.1.2<br>► **Index** | INTEGER<br>(1..31) | read-<br>only | The channel number for this<br>entry. |
| dsx1FracIfIndex<br>1.3.6.1.2.1.10.18.13.1.3 | INTEGER<br>(1..'7fffffff'H) | read-<br>write | An index that uniquely<br>defines this interface. If the<br>channel is being used, the<br>index matches a value of<br>*ifIndex*. Otherwise, the value<br>should be 0. If the interface<br>occupies multiple time slots,<br>the same *ifIndex* value will be<br>found in multiple time slots. |

CCITT Recommendations G.703, G.704, G.706, and G.732 describe physical characteristics, framing, and signaling.

Performance measurements are discussed in ANSI T1M1.3/92-005R1, CCITT .162, and CCITT G.821.

There are many relevant AT&T technical specifications, such as Publication 62411—*High Capacity Digital Service Channel Interface Specifications;* Compatibility Bulletin 142—*The Extended Framing Format Interface Specification.*

# Managing a DS3/ES3 (T3 or E3) Interface

## 24.1 INTRODUCTION

Originally intended for internal telephone company use, a DS3 interface can multiplex 28 DS-1 Extended SuperFrame inputs (the equivalent of 672 DS0 channels) into a 44.736 megabit per second T3 stream. Note that:

$$28 \times 1,544,000 = 43,232,000$$

which is 1,504,000 megabits less than the T3 rate. The extra bits are used for framing, alarms, CRC checks, and parity checks.

In Europe, E3 service multiplexes 16 E1 inputs (the equivalent of 480 DS0 channels) and combines them into a 34,368,000 bits per second stream.

## 24.2 DS3 FRAME FORMAT

DS3 frames have a three-tiered structure:

- 84 bits of payload data plus 1 framing bit form an 85-bit *block.*
- 8 blocks form a 680-bit *M-subframe.*
- 7 M-subframes form a 4760-bit *M-frame.*

Figure 24.1 shows the structure of a DS3 frame. In all, there are 56 framing bits spread through an M-frame. Groups of these framing bits have different roles:

**FIRST M-SUBFRAME**
680 bits

| X1 | 84 info | F1 | 84 info | C1 | 84 info | F2 | 84 info | C2 | 84 info | F3 | 84 info | C3 | 84 info | F4 |
|----|---------|----|---------|----|---------|----|---------|----|---------|----|---------|----|---------|----|

**M-FRAME**
4760 bits

| X1 | 679 bits | X2 | 679 bits | P1 | 679 bits | P2 | 679 bits | M1 | 679 bits | M2 | 679 bits | M3 |
|----|----------|----|----------|----|----------|----|----------|----|----------|----|----------|----|

**Figure 24.1**  DS3 Frame Format.

- M1, M2, and M3 repeat a fixed pattern that enables the interface to align the M-frame and locate the M-subframes.

- F1, F2, F3, and F4 repeat a fixed pattern that enables the interface to align the M-subframes and locate the blocks.

- P1 and P2 report the result of a parity sum calculation on the *previous frame*.* If the sum is odd, P1=P2=1.

- X1 and X2 are normally set to 1. If the interface loses frame alignment on received frames, or is receiving a special payload pattern called an Alarm Indication Signal, it sets the outgoing X-bits to 0 to signal Yellow Alarm.

- The C-bits, C1, C2, and C3, take a little more explaining. We will tackle them in the next section.

## 24.3  LOADING PAYLOAD INTO A DS3 FRAME

Knowing the way that standards work, it may not surprise the reader to learn that there are three different ways to assemble payload into a DS3 M-Frame!

All three methods *interleave* data from several converging bit streams—that is, a bit from the first stream is inserted, then a bit from the second stream, then a bit from the third, etc. Figure 24.2 shows two methods for interleaving DS1 data streams. The third method is a variation on the first one shown in the figure that involves special use of the C-bits.

---

* The values in P-bit parity bits may be recalculated and replaced at intermediate switching equipment, and will not in general be valid for end-to-end error measurement.

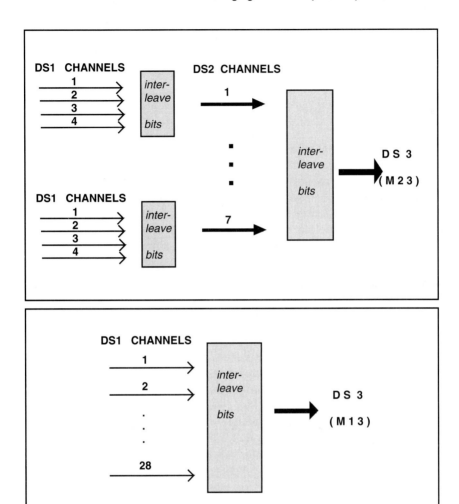

**Figure 24.2**  Interleaving payload bits into a frame.

In telecom language, an interleaving method, along with a characteristic way to handle configuration, diagnostics, and testing, is called an *application*.

### 24.3.1  M23 Multiplex Application

The first DS3 application fills bits into an M-frame in a two-step procedure. First of all, a DS2 (T2) signal is formed by interleaving four T1 channels and adding appropriate framing. Then seven T2s are interleaved to form a DS3 (T3) signal. This gives us a total of 28 DS1 channels.

Sometimes it is necessary to *stuff* in extra bits (S-bits) to allow for timing differences between the channels as they are multiplexed. M23 uses the C-bits to indicate whether stuff bits have been inserted at various positions in the M-frame.

### 24.3.2   The M13 or SYNTRAN
### Multiplex Application

The M13 application, often called the SYNTRAN application, skips the intermediate formation of a DS2 signal, and simply interleaves 28 DS1 channels. SYNTRAN stands for Synchronous Transmission, meaning that stuff bits are *not* used. This frees up the $7 \times 3 = 21$ C-bits in every T3 M-frame so that they can be used to form network operations and maintenance channels.

Less formally stated, using C-bits, an interface can talk to *the far end of the line* about configuration, can report problems that it is experiencing, or can ask for a loopback line test. Specifically, SYNTRAN C-bits are allocated to functions such as:

- Remote configuration via a Facility Data Link made up by bits C11 through C18
- Reporting received CRC errors to the far end (via a *Far-End Block Error* or "FEBE" bit)
- Reporting loss of synchronization of the received signal, or an idle condition
- Activating and deactivating a line loopback function

### 24.3.3   The C-Bit Parity Application

The C-bit Parity application* multiplexes 28 DS1 signals in a two-step procedure, just as M23 does. However, every possible stuff bit is included automatically, so that the C-bits are not needed to flag stuff bits. The C-bits are put to work as spare end-to-end channels. For the C-bit Parity application, maintenance functions include:

- *Far-End Alarm and Control* (FEAC) signaling that sends alarm or status information to the remote end, or else initiates or terminates loopback tests. Many different conditions can be reported, such as equipment failure, loss of framing, AIS or idles received, or loss of signal.
- Performing *end-to-end* parity checks. The C-bits used to do this are called *CP bits.*
- Reporting received CRC errors to the far end (via a *Far-End Block Error* or FEBE bit).

---

\* Also called the asynchronous DS3 C-bit Parity application.

Some of the C-bits are used for a LAPD* link that can carry a variety of configuration and maintenance messages.

### 24.3.4   DS3/E3 Interface Line Types

The M23, SYNTRAN, and C-bit Parity are the most important applications defined for the United States. The list below shows the complete set of T3/E3 application types that are referenced in the DS3 MIB:

1. dsx3other          Not one of those below (proprietary)
2. dsx3M23           M23, described in ANSI T1.107-1988
3. dsx3SYNTRAN      SYNTRAN, described in ANSI T1.107-1988; synchronous, easily demultiplexed transmission
4. dsx3CbitParity    C-bit Parity, based on ANSI T1.107a-1989
5. dsx3ClearChannel  A simplified use of C-bits, which are employed only for sending or receiving an Alarm Indication Signal (AIS), based on ANSI T1.102-1987
6. e3other           Other than the E3 types listed (proprietary)
7. e3Framed          Based on CCITT G.751
8. e3Plcp            Based on ETSI T/NA(91)18

## 24.4   T3 CSUS AND DSUS

Just as is the case for T1 service, the equipment used to interface to *digital* service consists of two components—a Channel Service Unit (CSU) and a Data Service Unit (DSU). Often these are packaged together.

The CSU faces out toward the service network. It is the job of a CSU to physically terminate the network's digital line. The CSU also performs signal regeneration, alarms, and loopback testing.

The DSU connects the CSU to your premise equipment. A DSU matches local clocking to network clocking, and provides a physical interface to local equipment.

Within a service provider's network, a T3 "line" supplied by a telecommunications company actually is a series of links. T3 networks are made up of *facility sections* that cover the lines between two sets of line-terminating equipment. Telephone companies monitor errors *within each facility section.*

## 24.5   PHYSICAL CONFIGURATION
## FOR CSU/DSUS

In some cases, we wish to use an SNMP agent to manage a single DS3 interface. Or, we may have a whole shelf of CSU/DSU units that provide multiple DS3 interfaces.

---

* The LAPD link protocol originally was introduced to carry ISDN signaling information.

In today's routed networks, the configuration may be more compli-cated. A router may connect directly to a shelf of CSU/DSUs. An SNMP agent in the router may be acting as agent for the router and proxy agent for the CSU/DSUs. The router agent now has to watch *both* the interfaces between the router and CSU/DSUs, *and* network and the DS3 interfaces.

This is exactly the same set of configurations described in Chapter 23, Sec. 23.9, and it is handled within the MIB in the same way. In addition to maintaining a variable that points to the *ifIndex* for each interface, there is a second variable, *dsx3LineIndex*. The *dsx3Line-Index* variable can differentiate between external, network side lines and internal, router side lines.

## 24.6    GATHERING STATISTICS

Just as for DS1 and E1 interfaces, DS3 and E3 statistics are collected in 15-minute intervals, 24 hours a day, for a total of 96 sets of statistics per day.

The DS3/E3 MIB tracks statistics for the current 15-minute period, and also stores the values for active periods over the prior 24 hours. In addition, totals for the previous 24 hours are maintained. Of course, if the interface has been initialized some time in the last 24 hours, then less than the full 96 sets of statistics will be available.

## 24.7    LINE CODING
## AND THE ZEROS PROBLEM

T3 and E3 lines are subject to the same consecutive zeros problem as T1 and E1 lines. In fact, the problem is even more severe because the high line speeds require very accurate timing, and strings of zeros cause loss of timing.

T3 lines use Binary 3 Zero Substitution (B3ZS) coding, which substi-tutes a violation of the form "1 0 1" or "–1 0 –1" for three zeros, "0 0 0." The polarity is determined by preceding pulses—recall that a balance in the number of positive and negative pulses always is desirable.

E3 lines use the High-Density Bipolar 3-Zero (HDB3) substitution described in Chapter 23. That is, a string of four zeros is replaced with a pattern containing a bipolar violation.

## 24.8    ERROR EVENTS

Many of the DS3/E3 error events are very similar to those defined for DS1/E1 in Chapter 23. Events include:

- *Bipolar Violation (BPV).*  A bipolar violation that is not part of a B3ZS or HDB3 zero substitution code.

- *Excessive Zeros (EXZ).*  An occurrence of more than three zeros for T3 (with B3ZS) and more than four zeros for E3 (with HDB3).

- *Line Coding Violation (LCV).*  The occurrence of either a bipolar violation (BPV) or of excessive zeros (EXZ).

- *P-bit Coding Violation (PCV).*  (Applies to DS3.) Detection of a parity error by means of a received P-bit.

- *C-bit Coding Violation (CCV).*  For SYNTRAN, a CRC error. For C-bit Parity, an end-to-end parity error detected by the CP bits.

## 24.9  PERSISTENT PROBLEMS AND LINE FAILURES

Serious conditions are defined below. These conditions are cleared when the symptom has not appeared for a specified time period. For detailed time periods, see the MIB document or appropriate telephony standards.

- *Out of Frame (OOF).*  For DS3, detected when any three or more errors in 16 or fewer consecutive F-bits occur within a DS3 M-frame. An OOF defect may also be called a Severely Errored Frame (SEF) defect.

  For E3, detected when four consecutive frame alignment signals have been incorrectly received in their allotted positions in an E3 signal.

- *Loss of Frame (LOF).*  For DS3, declared when the DS3 OOF defect persists for 2 to 10 seconds.

- *Loss of Signal (LOS).*  Declared upon observing 175 ($\pm$75) contiguous pulse positions with no pulses of either positive or negative polarity.

- *Alarm Indication Signal (AIS).*  Declared when a special AIS payload pattern is received persistently for a period of .2 to 100 milliseconds. For DS3, the AIS payload pattern is 1010..., and specific values also are assigned to several framing bits. For example, X bits are 1 and C bits are 0.

  For E3, the payload pattern is a stream of 1s.

- *The Remote Alarm Indication (RAI).*  For SYNTRAN, declared after detecting the Yellow Alarm Signal on the alarm channel.

  For C-bit Parity DS3, declared after detecting one of several far-end alarm signals, including Yellow Alarm.

  Also declared when Loss of Signal (LOS), Out of Frame (OOF), or incoming Alarm Indication Signal (AIS) persists for at least 2 to 10 seconds or Severely Errored Framing Seconds (SEFS).

- *Far-End Severely Errored Framing Seconds / Alarm Indication Signal.*  Detected when the two X-bits in an incoming M-frame are set to zero.

### 24.9.1   Line Alarm Conditions
### (The *dsx3LineStatus* Variable)

The status of a line can be fairly complex. A loopback may be in progress, and there may be several line failure alarm conditions that have not yet cleared. The line status is represented by the *dsx3LineStatus* variable, which is an integer that represents a bit map. Each bit indicates whether a particular condition is present. Note that the conditions were defined in the previous section. The bit assignments are:

| | | |
|---|---|---|
| 1 | dsx3NoAlarm | No alarm present |
| 2 | dsx3RcvRAIFailure | Receiving Yellow/Remote Alarm Indication |
| 4 | dsx3XmitRAIAlarm | Transmitting Yellow/Remote Alarm Indication |
| 8 | dsx3RcvAIS | Receiving AIS failure state |
| 16 | dsx3XmitAIS | Transmitting AIS |
| 32 | dsx3LOF | Receiving LOF failure state |
| 64 | dsx3LOS | Receiving LOS failure state |
| 128 | dsx3LoopbackState | Looping the received signal |
| 256 | dsx3RcvTestCode | Receiving a Test Pattern |
| 512 | dsx3OtherFailure | Any line status not defined above |

### 24.9.2   Testing a Line

When problems arise, there are various tests that are used to help with the diagnosis of line problems.

For example, there are two types of loopback test. A *payload loopback* is received by a device, reframed by the device, and then sent back. Note that for a payload loopback, reframing is performed on *each* DS1 or E1 within a DS3 or E3 frame.

In contrast, a *line loopback* is simply turned around by a device and sent back without going through the device and being reframed.

Other tests involve sending fixed or random patterns to an interface. Status information about an interface includes the type of data currently being received. The status is indicated by a code number. The choice of codes (used for the *dsx3SendCode* variable) includes:

| | | |
|---|---|---|
| 1. | dsx3SendNoCode | Sending looped or normal data |
| 2. | dsx3SendLineCode | Requesting a line loopback |
| 3. | dsx3SendPayloadCode | Requesting a payload loopback |
| 4. | dsx3SendResetCode | Requesting a loopback deactivation |
| 5. | dsx3SendDS1LoopCode | Requesting a loopback of a *particular* DS1/E1 within a DS3/E3 frame |
| 6. | dsx3SendTestPattern | Sending a test pattern |

Use of these values is optional for E3 interfaces.

## 24.10   TIMING

DS3/E3 interfaces operate at high bit speeds. If the timing at the receiving end is not closely synchronized with the timing at the sending end, the line will not be able to operate. The three methods that an interface uses to derive its timing are:

1. loopTiming      Synchronize with the network by recovering the receive clock.

2. localTiming     Use a local, internal clock source.

3. throughTiming   Use the receive clock from another interface.

## 24.11   INTRODUCTION TO THE DS3/E3 NEAR-END GROUP

The DS3 Near-End Group is made up of four tables containing information about the near-end—that is, local—interface. The first table contains configuration information. The next three tables report error statistics. The tables provide statistics for the current 15-minute interval, for intervals during the previous 24 hours, and finally, totals over the entire 24-hour period.

### 24.11.1   The DS3/E3 Configuration Table

Table 24.1, the DS3/E3 configuration table, records the same type of information as the DS1 configuration table.* It includes information about a DS3/E3 interface such as the type of application (e.g., M23, SYNTRAN, or C-bit Parity) and the kind of coding used to deal with blocks of zeros. It also includes status information indicating:

- The number of seconds since the current measurement period started

- The number of previous intervals for which data has been stored

- The current type of payload being sent across the interface (e.g., normal data or some kind of test pattern)

- The current status of the line, especially with regard to alarms that may be in effect

### 24.11.2   Error Statistics Tables

Although we may not care much about infrequent and transient errors, errors that recur frequently are a cause for concern. In order to track

---

* There is one more variable in the DS1 table. It describes the use of the DS1 facilities data link.

**TABLE 24.1    The DS3/E3 Configuration Table**

iso.org.dod.internet.mgmt.mib-2.
transmission.ds3.dsx3ConfigTable.dsx3ConfigEntry
1.3.6.1.2.1.10.30.5.1

| OBJECT IDENTIFIER | Syntax | Access | Description |
|---|---|---|---|
| dsx3LineIndex 1.3.6.1.2.1.10.30.5.1.1 ▶ **Index** | INTEGER (1..65535) | read-only | The line number. |
| dsx3IfIndex 1.3.6.1.2.1.10.30.5.1.2 | INTEGER (1..65535) | read-only | The *ifIndex* for the corresponding interface. |
| dsx3TimeElapsed 1.3.6.1.2.1.10.30.5.1.3 | INTEGER (0..899) i.e., up to 15 minutes. | read-only | Number of seconds that have elapsed since the beginning of the near-end current error-measurement period. |
| dsx3ValidIntervals 1.3.6.1.2.1.10.30.5.1.4 | INTEGER (0..96) | read-only | Number of previous intervals (up to 96) for which valid data was collected. |
| dsx3LineType 1.3.6.1.2.1.10.30.5.1.5 | INTEGER dsx3other(1), dsx3M13(2), dsx3SYNTRAN(3), dsx3CbitParity(4), dsx3ClearChannel(5), e3other(6), e3Framed(7), e3Plcp(8) | read-write | Type of DS3/E3 application. |
| dsx3LineCoding 1.3.6.1.2.1.10.30.5.1.6 | INTEGER dsx3Other(1), dsx3B3ZS(2), e3HDB3(3) | read-write | The kind of Zero Code Suppression used on the interface. |
| dsx3SendCode 1.3.6.1.2.1.10.30.5.1.7 | INTEGER dsx3SendNoCode(1), dsx3SendLineCode(2), dsx3SendPayloadCode(3), dsx3SendResetCode(4), dsx3SendDs3LoopCode(5), dsx3SendTestPattern(6) | read-write | Type of payload code being sent across the DS3 interface. (Optional for E3 interfaces.) |
| dsx3Circuit Identifier 1.3.6.1.2.1.10.30.5.1.8 | DisplayString (SIZE (0..255)) | read-write | The transmission vendor's circuit identifier, used to facilitate troubleshooting. |

**TABLE 24.1    The DS3/E3 Configuration Table (*Continued*)**

iso.org.dod.internet.mgmt.mib-2.
transmission.ds3.dsx3ConfigTable.dsx3ConfigEntry
1.3.6.1.2.1.10.30.5.1

| OBJECT IDENTIFIER | Syntax | Access | Description |
|---|---|---|---|
| dsx3Loopback Config 1.3.6.1.2.1.10.30.5.1.9 | INTEGER dsx3NoLoop(1), dsx3PayloadLoop(2), dsx3LineLoop(3), dsx3OtherLoop(4) | read-write | Line status— normal data, reframed and looped, or just turned around. |
| dsx3LineStatus 1.3.6.1.2.1.10.30.5.1.10 | INTEGER (1..1023) See 23.9.1. | read-only | An integer representing a bit map that can report loopback and failure-state information. |
| dsx3Transmit ClockSource 1.3.6.1.2.1.10.30.5.1.11 | INTEGER loopTiming (1), localTiming (2), throughTiming (3) | read-write | Source of transmit clocking See Sec. 24.10. |

these errors, the MIB keeps track of the number of seconds in which various kinds of errors occur.

The MIB also counts the total number of errors of certain types, such as bad parity bits or incorrect CRC codes for the incoming payload.

Table 24.2, the DS3/E3 Current Table, contains statistics that are being collected for the current 15-minute interval. The same statistics are gathered for each completed measurement interval in the previous 24-hour period, and are recorded in the DS3/E3 Interval Table. Finally, totals of the same variables are recorded in the DS3/E3 Total Table.

Note that just as in Chapter 23, a *gauge* datatype rather than a *counter* datatype is used to record error counts. That is because we do not want to lose track of the total for an integer because a counter has wrapped around to 0!

A few more definitions are needed in order to understand the counts in these tables. For completeness and convenience, we'll repeat a few of the definitions given earlier:

- *Line Coding Violation (LCV).*   The occurrence of either a bipolar violation (BPV) or of excessive zeros (EXZ).

- *P-bit Coding Violation (PCV).*   (Applies to DS3.) A parity error detected via a received P-bit.

- *C-bit Coding Violation (CCV).*   For SYNTRAN, a CRC error. For C-Bit Parity, an end-to-end parity error detected by the CP bits.

MIB variables will count:

- *Line Errored Second (LES).* A second in which one or more Coding Violations *or* one or more Loss of Signal defects occurred.

- *P-bit Errored Second (PES).* A second with one or more Parity bit (P-bit) Coding Violations *or* one or more Out of Frame defects *or* a detected incoming Alarm Indication Signal.

- *P-bit Severely Errored Second (PSES).* A second with 44 or more P-bit Coding Violations (PCVs) *or* one or more Out of Frame defects *or* a detected incoming Alarm Indication Signal.

- *C-bit Errored Second (CES).* (For SYNTRAN and C-bit Parity applications.) A second with one or more C-bit Coding Violations (CCVs) *or* one or more Out of Frame defects *or* a detected incoming Alarm Indication Signal.

- *C-bit Severely Errored Second (CSES).* (For SYNTRAN and C-bit Parity applications.) A second with 44 or more C-bit Coding Violations (CCVs) *or* one or more Out of Frame defects *or* a detected incoming Alarm Indication Signal.

- *Severely Errored Framing Second (SEFS).* A second with one or more Out of Frame defects *or* a detected incoming Alarm Indication Signal.

- *Unavailable Seconds (UAS).* Number of seconds that the interface is unavailable.*

### 24.11.3 The DS3/E3 Current Table

Now we are ready to look at Table 24.2, DS3/E3 Current Table, which contains statistics that are being collected for the current 15-minute interval.

### 24.11.4 The DS3/E3 Interval Table

The DS3/E3 interval table contains error statistics for up to 96 intervals prior to the current one. If the interface has been operating for less than 24 hours, then less than 96 intervals will be recorded. The error statistics that are tracked are identical to those in the Current Table. The OBJECT IDENTIFIER for the DS3/E3 Interval Table is:

```
iso.org.dod.internet.mgmt.mib-2.transmission.ds3.dsx3IntervalTable

1 . 3 . 6 . 1 . 2 . 1 . 10 . 30 . 7
```

---

* See the MIB definition for a detailed discussion of unavailability.

**TABLE 24.2    The DS3/ES3 Current Table**

iso.org.dod.internet.mgmt.mib-2.
transmission.ds3.dsx3CurrentTable.dsx3CurrentEntry
1.3.6.1.2.1.10.30.6.1

| OBJECT IDENTIFIER | Syntax | Access | Description |
|---|---|---|---|
| dsx3CurrentIndex<br>1.3.6.1.2.1.10.30.6.1.1<br>▶ **Index** | INTEGER<br>(1..65535) | read-<br>only | Index uniquely identifying the<br>DS3/E3 line interface (same<br>value as *dsx3LineIndex*). |
| dsx3CurrentPESs<br>1.3.6.1.2.1.10.30.6.1.2 | Gauge | read-<br>only | Number of P-bit Errored<br>Seconds in the current 15<br>minute interval. |
| dsx3CurrentPSESs<br>1.3.6.1.2.1.10.30.6.1.3 | Gauge | read-<br>only | Number of P-bit Severely<br>Errored Seconds in the current<br>15 minute interval. |
| dsx3CurrentSEFSs<br>1.3.6.1.2.1.10.30.6.1.4 | Gauge | read-<br>only | Number of Severely Errored<br>Framing Seconds in the current<br>15 minute interval. |
| dsx3CurrentUASs<br>1.3.6.1.2.1.10.30.6.1.5 | Gauge | read-<br>only | Number of Unavailable Seconds<br>in the current 15 minute<br>interval. |
| dsx3CurrentLCVs<br>1.3.6.1.2.1.10.30.6.1.6 | Gauge | read-<br>only | Number of Line Coding<br>Violations in the current 15<br>minute interval. |
| dsx3CurrentPCVs<br>1.3.6.1.2.1.10.30.6.1.7 | Gauge | read-<br>only | Number of P-bit Coding<br>Violations in the current 15<br>minute interval. |
| dsx3CurrentLESs<br>1.3.6.1.2.1.10.30.6.1.8 | Gauge | read-<br>only | Number of Line Errored<br>Seconds in the current 15<br>minute interval. |
| dsx3CurrentCCVs<br>1.3.6.1.2.1.10.30.6.1.9 | Gauge | read-<br>only | Number of C-bit Coding<br>Violations in the current 15<br>minute interval. |
| dsx3CurrentCESs<br>1.3.6.1.2.1.10.30.6.1.10 | Gauge | read-<br>only | Number of C-bit Errored<br>Seconds in the current 15<br>minute interval. |
| dsx3CurrentCSESs<br>1.3.6.1.2.1.10.30.6.1.11 | Gauge | read-<br>only | Number of C-bit Severely<br>Errored Seconds in the current<br>15 minute interval. |

### 24.11.5    The DS3/E3 Total Table

The DS3/E3 Total Table contains cumulative sums of error statistics
for the 24-hour period preceding the current interval. The error statistics that are tracked are identical to those in the current table. The
OBJECT IDENTIFIER for the DS3/E3 Total Table is:

```
iso.org.dod.internet.mgmt.mib-2.transmission.ds3.dsx3TotalTable
1 . 3 . 6 . 1 . 2 . 1 . 10 . 30 . 8
```

## 24.12    INTRODUCTION TO THE DS3 FAR-END GROUP

Information about the far end of a line is essential for efficient troubleshooting. Recall that there are two implementations—SYNTRAN and C-bit Parity—that use channels made up of the 21 "C" framing bits to transmit far-end configuration and diagnostic information. The Far-End Group can be used with these implementations.

The DS3 Far-End Group is made up of four tables. The first table contains configuration information. The next three tables report error statistics. As in the Near-End Group, these tables provide error statistics for the current 15-minute interval, for intervals during the previous 24 hours, and finally, totals over the entire 24-hour period.

### 24.12.1    The DS3 Far-End Configuration Table

Table 24.3 contains far-end information that enables network personnel to identify the type of system at the far end and pinpoint its location. The configuration information is sent back within a *Path Identification Message.*

**TABLE 24.3    The Far-End Configuration Table**

| iso.org.dod.internet.mgmt.mib-2.transmission. ds3.dsx3FarEndConfigTable.dsx3FarEndConfigEntry 1.3.6.1.2.1.10.30.9.1 | | | |
|---|---|---|---|
| OBJECT IDENTIFIER | Syntax | Access | Description |
| dsx3FarEnd LineIndex 1.3.6.1.2.1.10.30.9.1.1 ▶ Index | INTEGER (1..65535) | read- only | Index uniquely identifying the DS3/E3 line interface (same as *dsx3LineIndex*). |
| dsx3FarEnd EquipCode 1.3.6.1.2.1.10.30.9.1.2 | Display String (SIZE (0..10)) | read- write | The Far-End Equipment Identification code. |
| dsx3FarEnd LocationIDCode 1.3.6.1.2.1.10.30.9.1.3 | Display String (SIZE (0..11)) | read- write | The Far-End Location Identification code describing the equipment's location. |
| dsx3FarEnd FrameIDCode 1.3.6.1.2.1.10.30.9.1.4 | Display String (SIZE (0..10)) | read- write | The Far-End Frame Identification code, identifying where the equipment is within a building at a given location. |
| dsx3FarEnd UnitCode 1.3.6.1.2.1.10.30.9.1.5 | Display String (SIZE (0..6)) | read- write | The Far-End code identifies the equipment location within a bay. |
| dsx3FarEnd FacilityIDCode 1.3.6.1.2.1.10.30.9.1.6 | Display String (SIZE (0..38)) | read- write | Identifies a specific Far-End DS3 path. |

### 24.12.2    The DS3 Far-End Current Table

Table 24.4 contains far-end statistics for the current interval. These statistics are based on information sent from the far end in a block error code within the C bits.

The error statistics in the far-end current table are a subset of those found in the near-end current table. Counts are provided for C-bit errors and unavailable seconds.

### 24.12.3    The DS3 Far-End Interval Table

The DS3 Far-End Interval Table contains cumulative sums of statistics for the 24-hour period preceding the current interval. The error statistics that are tracked are the same as those in the DS3 Far-End Current Table. The OBJECT IDENTIFIER for the DS3 Far-End Interval Table is:

```
iso.org.dod.internet.mgmt.mib-2.transmission.ds3.dsx3FarEndIntervalTable
```

```
1 . 3 . 6 . 1 . 2 . 1 . 10 . 30 . 11
```

**TABLE 24.4    The DS3 Far-End Current Table**

| | | | |
|---|---|---|---|
| iso.org.dod.internet.mgmt.mib-2.transmission. ds3.dsx3FarEndCurrentTable.dsx3FarEndCurrentEntry 1.3.6.1.2.1.10.30.10.1 | | | |
| OBJECT IDENTIFIER | Syntax | Access | Description |
| dsx3FarEnd CurrentIndex 1.3.6.1.2.1.10.30.10.1.1 ▶ **Index** | INTEGER (1..65535) | read-only | Index uniquely identifying the DS3 line interface (same as *dsx3LineIndex*). |
| dsx3FarEnd TimeElapsed 1.3.6.1.2.1.10.30.10.1.2 | INTEGER (0..899) | read-only | Number of seconds that have elapsed since the beginning of the far-end current error measurement period. |
| dsx3FarEnd ValidIntervals 1.3.6.1.2.1.10.30.10.1.3 | INTEGER (0..96) | read-only | Number of previous far-end intervals for which valid data was collected. |
| dsx3FarEnd CurrentCESs 1.3.6.1.2.1.10.30.10.1.4 | Gauge | read-only | Number of Far-End C-bit Errored Seconds in the current 15-minute interval. |
| dsx3FarEnd CurrentCSESs 1.3.6.1.2.1.10.30.10.1.5 | Gauge | read-only | Number of Far-End C-bit Severely Errored Seconds in the current 15-minute interval. |
| dsx3FarEnd CurrentCCVss 1.3.6.1.2.1.10.30.10.1.6 | Gauge | read-only | Number of Far-End C-bit Coding Violations in the current 15-minute interval. |
| dsx3FarEnd CurrentUASs 1.3.6.1.2.1.10.30.10.1.7 | Gauge | read-only | Number of Far-End Unavailable Seconds in the current 15-minute interval. |

### 24.12.4  The DS3 Far-End Total Table

The DS3 Far-End Total Table contains cumulative sums of error statistics for the 24-hour period preceding the current interval. The error statistics that are tracked are the same as those in the DS3 Far-End Current Table. The OBJECT IDENTIFIER for the DS3 Far-End Total Table is:

```
iso.org.dod.internet.mgmt.mib-2.transmission.ds3.dsx3FarEndTotalTable
```

```
1 . 3 . 6 . 1 . 2 . 1 . 10 . 30 . 12
```

## 24.13  INTRODUCTION TO THE DS3/E3 FRACTIONAL GROUP

DS1 or E1 channels within a DS3 or E3 can be grouped to form logical or fractional interfaces offering a variety of traffic capacities. Each fractional interface will appear in the *interfaces* table, just as if it were a real interface.

Fractional interfaces are sometimes used so that a customer can subscribe to (and pay for!) a fractional part of the DS3 bandwidth. In this case, some DS1 channels are simply turned off and unused.

### 24.13.1  The DS3/E3 Fractional Table

Table 24.5, the DS3/E3 Fractional Table, indicates which channels have been combined into a logical interface. First of all, the *dsx3FracIndex* identifies which DS3 interface is being chopped up into logical subinterfaces.

The channel numbers are in the variable *dsx3FracNumber,* and the variable *dsx3FracIfIndex* names a *logical* interface that the channel

**TABLE 24.5   The DS3/E3 Fractional Table**

| OBJECT IDENTIFIER | Syntax | Access | Description |
|---|---|---|---|
| iso.org.dod.internet.mgmt.mib-2.transmission. ds3.dsx3FracTable.dsx3FracEntry 1.3.6.1.2.1.10.30.13.1 | | | |
| dsx3FracIndex 1.3.6.1.2.1.10.30.13.1.1 ▶ **Index** | INTEGER (1..'7fffffff'H) | read-only | Index uniquely identifying the real DS3 or E3 line interface (same as *dsx3LineIndex* value). |
| dsx3FracNumber 1.3.6.1.2.1.10.30.13.1.2 ▶ **Index** | INTEGER (1..31) | read-only | The channel number for this entry. |
| dsx3FracIfIndex 1.3.6.1.2.1.10.30.13.1.3 | INTEGER (1..'7fffffff'H) | read-write | An index that uniquely defines this fractional interface. |

**TABLE 24.6    Dividing a DS3 into Fractional Interfaces**

| Real DS3 interface dsx3FracIndex | Channel Number dsx3FracNumber | Fractional interface dsx3FracIfIndex |
|---|---|---|
| 1 | 1 | 2 |
| 1 | 2 | 2 |
| 1 | 3 | 2 |
| 1 | 4 | 2 |
| 1 | 5 | 2 |
| 1 | 6 | 2 |
| 1 | 7 | 3 |
| 1 | 8 | 3 |
| 1 | 9 | 3 |
| 1 | 10 | 3 |
| 1 | 11 | 3 |
| 1 | 12 | 3 |
| 1 | 13 | 4 |
| 1 | 14 | 4 |
| 1 | 15 | 4 |
| 1 | 16 | 4 |
| 1 | 17 | 4 |
| 1 | 18 | 4 |
| 1 | 19 | 4 |
| 1 | 20 | 4 |
| 1 | 21 | 4 |
| 1 | 22 | 4 |
| 1 | 23 | 4 |
| 1 | 24 | 4 |
| 1 | 25 | 0 |
| 1 | 26 | 0 |
| 1 | 27 | 0 |
| 1 | 28 | 0 |

belongs to. For unused channels, the value of *dsx3FracIfIndex* simply is set to 0.

An example may be helpful. In Table 24.6, we show how a DS3 channel (which is the one and only interface for the device) has been divided into three fractional interfaces using 6, 6, and 12 channels respectively. The remaining four channels are unused. The real DS3 interface has *ifIndex* 1, so the logical channels are assigned new interface indices of 2, 3, and 4.

Note that there are 28 T1 channels for each DS3 interface and 16 E1 channels for each E3 interface.

## 24.14   RECOMMENDED READING

The DS3 MIB is defined in RFC 1407. The DS3 definitions used in the MIB are based on the DS3 specifications in ANSI T1.102-1987, ANSI T1.107-1988, ANSI T1.107a- 1990, and ANSI T1.404-1989. The E3 definitions are based on CCITT G.751.

# 25

# Managing an X.25 Interface

## 25.1 INTRODUCTION

Thanks to the worldwide telephone network, you can pick up a telephone in Dallas, Texas, and place a call to a friend in Bombay, India. The interworking of the global telephone net can be credited to cooperative *Recommendations* framed by the International Telegraph and Telephone Consultative Committee (CCITT).*

The CCITT tackled the job of building a worldwide *packet switching data network* in a series of Recommendations published in 1976, 1980, and 1984. These well-known X.25 Recommendations deal with the interface between a computer and a service network.

In CCITT language, this is called the interface between a *DTE* and a *DCE. Data Terminal Equipment,* or DTE, is a computer that is the source or destination for data. *Data Circuit-terminating Equipment,* or DCE, is equipment providing access to a network. A DCE is an integral part of the service network. Figure 25.1 shows the relationship between DTEs, DCEs, and a packet network.

The purpose of connecting all these systems to a network is, of course, so that they can communicate with one another. In the telephony world we talk to someone across a *telephone circuit.* A fixed bandwidth is reserved for our use until the telephone call is ended. In the packet data world, a pair of DTEs communicate across a virtual circuit. The term *virtual circuit* was adopted because a fixed amount of bandwidth is not reserved for the call—many data transmissions share a common set of lines that make up the service network.

---

* Now called the International Telecommunications Union–Telecommunications Standards Sector or ITU-T.

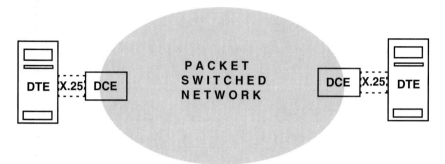

**Figure 25.1**  X.25 interface to a packet network.

### 25.1.1  Packet Switching Benefits

What are the benefits of packet switched wide area services? Data traffic tends to be bursty—briefly needing a lot of bandwidth, and, a few moments later, needing little or none. Leased lines are expensive. Significant savings are possible by building a mesh network that takes advantage of the on-again, off-again nature of data traffic and:

- Offers many entry points
- Enables its users to set up virtual circuits to lots of destinations
- Shares bandwidth in a fair manner
- Because of sharing, can offer cost savings

### 25.1.2  X.25 in Other Environments

In 1986, the International Organization for Standardization (ISO) published a standard that extended the use of a subset of X.25 technology to point-to-point lines and local area networks. Most of the discussion in this chapter will focus on the original purpose of X.25—to provide a standard way for a computer to attach to a service provider's data network.

## 25.2  X.25 TECHNOLOGY AND CONCEPTS

The X.25 Recommendations define a standard way to connect a DTE to a DCE that provides access to a service network. Many concurrent virtual circuits can be set up across the single DTE-to-DCE interface link. The standards allow for over 4000! Real interfaces are limited to a far smaller number of *logical channels* that can be used for calls, such as 32, 64, or 128 channels. Figure 25.2 shows an X.25 interface that has eight logical channels. There are active virtual circuits for channels 2, 5, 6, and 7.

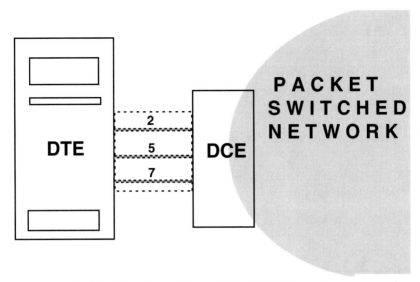

**Figure 25.2**  An X.25 interface with multiple logical channels.

### 25.2.1   Virtual Circuits

An X.25 interface can be preconfigured with a set of *Permanent Virtual Circuits* (PVCs) that are the packet switched equivalent of leased lines. A preselected logical channel is assigned to each PVC.

An interface also can support *Virtual Calls* (VCs) that are the equivalent of dial-up calls. Sometimes the term *Switched Virtual Circuit* or SVC is used instead of Virtual Call. During call setup (outgoing or incoming) an unused *logical channel* is assigned to a Virtual Call. When a Virtual Call is finished, the circuit will be closed down and the logical channel will be freed up for reuse.

### 25.2.2   Public Data Network
### Service Providers

There are many X.25 public data network service providers. In some countries, services are provided by official *Administrations* run by the government. The public X.25 data nets are chained together, offering access to DTEs all around the globe. There is a numbering plan for X.25 systems, analogous to the worldwide telephone numbering plan. The numbering plan is described in *Recommendation X.121*.

### 25.2.3   X.25 Facilities

Service providers offer many *facilities,* which are special options needed by their business customers. A few examples can give the flavor of the kinds of features offered:

- *Incoming Calls Barred.*    Only outgoing Virtual Calls are allowed at the interface.

- *One-way Logical Channel Incoming.*    Restricts a particular channel so that it can only be used to receive incoming Virtual Calls.

- *Closed User Group.*    If desired, DTEs that are members of a group will be allowed to communicate with each other, but not with other systems. The service provider sets up calls between nodes that belong to a customer's private network, while preventing contact with any external systems.

- *Reverse Charging.*    This is like 800-number calling. A DTE is billed for all of its incoming calls.

Endless variations on these themes are offered. A DTE may be permitted to belong to several Closed User Groups. Or a DTE may belong to Closed User Groups, but may also be allowed to place Virtual Calls to "open" DTEs that do not belong to any Closed User Group. Or a DTE may belong to Closed User Groups, but still receive calls from other DTEs.

### 25.2.4   Private X.25 Networks

Rather than sign on with a public service provider, some organizations build their own internal X.25 networks. This might be the most cost-effective approach if traffic levels to several locations were consistently high. The switches needed to build this type of network are marketed by several vendors.

### 25.2.5   Talking to the Network

Data network access with X.25 can be a little confusing to people used to working with end-to-end networking protocols. Although the purpose of connecting to a DCE is to get data delivered to a remote DTE, 99 percent of the protocol deals with interactions between a computer (DTE) and its network access point (DCE).

The DTE can negotiate with its DCE for features like message size, throughput, and window size. *The DTE at the other end of a call can negotiate a different set of parameters to be used with its own DCE!* That's OK. The *network** is allowed to repackage messages, adjust the flow of data, and do whatever it needs to do in order to make both DTEs as happy as possible.

---

* Keep in mind that the two ends of a circuit may even be attached to different, but interconnected, service providers.

### 25.2.6   How Reliable Is It?

X.25 is a three-layer communications protocol that allows a DTE to open concurrent virtual circuits to many different destinations. X.25 delivers data across each circuit reliably and in sequence.

Of course, there are occasional network problems. When reliable delivery fails, there are recovery procedures that *reinitialize* the circuit. In the process of reinitializing, the service network will throw away data that is in transit on the circuit.

### 25.2.7   X.25 Layering

The three layers for an X.25 DTE to DCE interface are *physical, data link,* and *packet.*

There are several physical layer standards for X.25. For example, the X.21 physical layer standard is based on the use of digital transmission between the DTE and DCE. An alternative standard uses an RS-232-like analog line.

A system connects to an X.25 service network using a *connection-oriented reliable* layer 2 link protocol called *Link Access Procedure Balanced* or LAPB. Then many separate connection-oriented layer 3 virtual circuits are multiplexed across the single LAPB link. The X.25 *Packet Layer Protocol* guides layer 3 activities. Figure 25.3 illustrates X.25 layering.

### 25.2.8   What is an Interface?

Interfaces were discussed back in Chapter 10. At that point, it all seemed quite straightforward. But let's take a closer look. We send traffic by means of a layer 3 *Packet Layer Entity* (PLE) that controls a bunch of virtual circuits. It seems reasonable to call that an interface.

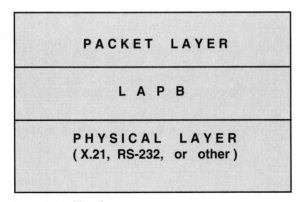

**Figure 25.3**  X.25 layers.

Then data for all of the virtual circuits is carried across a single layer 2 LAPB link. That is an interface too.

But the layer 2 LAPB link might be supported by an RS-232-like interface. Do we have three interfaces?

The MIB standards answer is yes! All three interfaces will appear as entries in the *interfaces* table.

### 25.2.9    Related Interfaces

How can we work out the relationship between the three entries in the *interfaces* table that make up a single X.25 entity? RFC 1381 outlines a pretty complicated scheme for doing this.

Here's the way it works. The configuration table for the layer 3 interface will include a variable whose value is the OBJECT IDENTIFIER for the supporting layer 2 interface index. This means that if we perform a *get* of that OBJECT IDENTIFIER, the response will contain the *ifIndex* for the layer 2 interface.

We track down the layer 1 interface in the same way. The following display shows exactly how this is done.

| Table | Variable | Description |
|-------|----------|-------------|
| x25OperTable | **x25OperIndex** | The *ifIndex* for the layer 3 Packet Layer Entity (PLE). |
| x25OperTable | x25OperDataLinkId | The OBJECT IDENTIFIER of the supporting layer 2 interface: in this case, the *lapbAdmnIndex*. |
| lapbAdmnTable | **lapbAdmnIndex** | The *ifIndex* for the LAPB interface. |
| lapbOperTable | lapbOperPortId | The OBJECT IDENTIFIER of the supporting physical interface: in this case, the *rs232PortIndex*. |
| rs232PortTable | **rs232PortIndex** | The *ifIndex* for the RS-232 interface. |

Not only is this complicated, but you have to search around in a lot of different tables to put the picture together. The proposed update of the *interfaces* MIB gathers all of the layer relationships into one simple stack table. As we saw in Chapter 10, the stack table simply relates pairs of interface sublayers, indicating which is "higher" and which is "lower."*

---

* See Chapter 10, Secs. 14 and 15 for a fuller description.

## 25.3   THE DATA LINK LAYER: LAPB

The X.25 data link layer protocol is called *Link Access Procedures Balanced* or LAPB. LAPB sets up a reliable, connection-oriented link between a DTE and DCE.* A layer 2 LAPB link can support many concurrent layer 3 (*packet layer*) virtual circuits.

For now, let's concentrate on the LAPB link. *Unnumbered* frames are used to set up a link, report serious errors, and terminate the link. *Supervisory* frames are used for flow control and to report a missing information frame.

Data is transmitted in numbered *Information* frames, and is retransmitted if an acknowledgment does not arrive within a timeout period. Acknowledgments are read from the headers of Information frames flowing in the reverse direction, and also are included in the headers of Supervisory frames.

Information frames usually are numbered modulo 8—that is 0, 1, 2, 3, 4, 5, 6, 7, 0, 1, . . . —but, in some cases, *extended* modulo 128 numbering is appropriate.

Figure 25.4 shows the format of an LAPB frame. The control field identifies the frame type, and also includes acknowledgment numbers and sequence numbers for relevant frame types. Supervisory frames include acknowledgments, while information frames include both sequence numbers and acknowledgments.

### 25.3.1   The Life and Death of an LAPB Link

After an LAPB link is opened, information frames are exchanged between the DTE and DCE. Special supervisory frames are used for flow control—one frame says "please be quiet" and later another is used to say "OK, you can talk again."

Note that when used to connect to a service provider's network, an LAPB link is *not* end-to-end.† An X.25 DCE has to take responsibility for reliable delivery of information frames to their remote destination.

The scenario that follows shows a typical DTE/DCE LAPB interaction and indicates how the various types of frames are used:

- The DTE or DCE initiates the link by sending a *Set Asynchronous Balanced Mode* (SABM) frame to its partner. (If modulo 128 num-

---

\* As mentioned previously, LAPB also has been adapted for DTE-to-DTE use. See ISO 7776 for details.

† There are exceptions. LAPB is sometimes used as a point-to-point protocol across a serial link. Sometimes it even is used for point-to-point access across a LAN, such as an Ethernet.

## LAPB FRAME FORMAT

| Flag | Address Field | Control Field | I N F O R M A T I O N | Frame Check Seq. | Flag |
|------|---------------|---------------|----------------------|------------------|------|

**Figure 25.4**   Format of a LAPB frame.

bering of information frames is desired, then a *Set Asynchronous Balanced Mode Extended* (SABME) frame is sent instead.)

- The partner responds with an *Unnumbered Acknowledgment* (UA) frame.

- The DCE and DTE start to send each other numbered *Information* frames. Numbering starts at 0. Several frames may be sent in quick sequence before receiving an acknowledgment. How many? That is determined by a *window* parameter (k) that must be less than the modulus that has been chosen (8 or 128).

- Suppose that some frame arrives whose sequence number is not the next one expected. The receiver sends a *Reject* (REJ) frame that asks for retransmission starting from the missing frame.

- Suppose neither an acknowledgment of the last transmitted information frame(s) nor a reject arrives within the timeout (T1) period. Then the frame(s) will be retransmitted.*

- Things are moving along pretty well now. Both sides are exchanging frames, and temporary glitches caused by loss of a frame now and then are handled easily. But suppose one end runs out of buffer space and wants the other end to be quiet for a while. It sends a *Receive Not Ready* (RNR) frame. The partner will stop sending until it gets a *Receive Ready* (RR) frame.

- Suppose one of the ends wants to close down the link. It sends a *Disconnect* (DISC) frame. The partner says OK by sending an *Unnumbered Acknowledgment* (UA).

There are many variations on the scenario:

- The SABM or SABME might be sent by the DCE, rather than the DTE.

- In fact, instead of starting with a SABM or SABME, a DISC or Disconnected Mode (DM) might be sent first, to make sure that both ends are starting from a disconnected state.

---

* Alternatively, a supervisory frame, such as Receive Ready or Receive Not Ready, can be sent with its poll bit set to 1.

- What happens if some error occurs that cannot be cured by simple retransmission, but we want to keep the link alive? The procedure is to *reset,* sending a fresh SABM or SABME, and resetting the numbering of information frames at 0 all over again.* One end can ask the other end to start off the reset by sending a *Frame Reject* (FRMR) frame.

There are several types of problems that could trigger a FRMR—for example, receipt of a frame with an information field that is too large or with an inappropriate acknowledgment value. The FRMR contains an information field that indicates what kind of problem turned up.

- One end might disconnect for some internal reason, and send a *Disconnected Mode* (DM) frame to report that it has disconnected.

- What else can go wrong? The other end may not be functioning at all. How can I tell? I can use an idle timer (T3) to sense an abnormal period without flags or frames.

- On the other hand, if the link is alive but neither end has had any frame traffic for a while (time T4), I might want to close down the link in order to conserve resources.

### 25.3.2  Borrowing X.25 Technology

Although designed to enable a DTE to talk to a DCE that provides access to a service network, the X.25 *link layer* has been reworked for use across a point-to-point line, or for point-to-point communications between two stations attached to a local area network. In these environments:

- A DTE talks directly to a DTE.

- An exchange ID (XID) protocol is used for mutual identification, and to negotiate some communication parameters.

A number of variables have been included in the LAPB MIB to cover the needs of these different environments.

ISO standard 7776 describes the use of LAPB DTE procedures. ISO 8885 describes the XID message, which is based on an earlier XID defined as an optional part of the HDLC protocol.

## 25.4  LAPB MIB LINK LAYER
## TEXTUAL CONVENTIONS

There are a number of X.25 MIB variables whose values are nonnegative integers—for example, the maximum size for a frame, and several

---

* Data may be lost!

timers that are measured in milliseconds. The MIB authors have defined the textual convention:

*PositiveInteger*    An INTEGER between 0 and 2147483647 (inclusively)

A second textual convention is defined for an INTEGER that is used as a table index:

*IfIndexType*    An INTEGER between 1 and 2147483647 (inclusively) whose value matches a corresponding value of *ifIndex* in the MIB-II *ifTable*

## 25.5 OVERVIEW OF THE LAPB MIB

There are four LAPB tables:

- *lapbAdmnTable.* A configuration table that sets link parameters such as frame size, window size, and timers.
- *lapbOperTable.* A table showing parameters (such as frame size, window size, and timers) *actually in use* on active links.
- *lapbFlowTable.* A table of statistical counts of significant link events such as timeouts, changes of state, busy endpoints, and serious problems.
- *lapbXidTable.* A table of configuration parameters to be used for interfaces that perform exchange ID (XID) negotiation. Identification and addressing information is included.

## 25.6 THE LAPB ADMINISTRATION TABLE

A device (for example, a router) might have more than one LAPB link. Table 25.1, the LAPB Administration Table, contains configuration parameters for each of a device's LAPB interfaces. The term "DXE" is used within the table. DXE denotes either a DTE or a DCE. If LAPB is being used as a point-to-point protocol or as a LAN protocol, then during negotiation, normally both ends will identify themselves as DTEs.

The transmit window size in the table is the maximum number (k) of sequentially numbered transmitted Information frames that may be outstanding—that is, no acknowledgment has been received for any of these frames. Similarly, the receive window size is the maximum number of outstanding unacknowledged frames that the partner can send.

## 25.7 THE LAPB OPERATIONAL TABLE

When a link is started up, values from an entry in the Administration Table are copied into an entry in the LAPB Operational Table. The last

**TABLE 25.1    The LAPB Administration Table**

iso.org.dod.internet.mgmt.mib-2.<br>
transmission.lapb.lapbAdmnTable.lapbAdmnEntry<br>
1.3.6.1.2.1.10.16.1.1

| OBJECT IDENTIFIER | Syntax | Access | Description |
|---|---|---|---|
| lapbAdmn Index 1.3.6.1.2.1.10.16.1.1.1 ▶ **Index** | IfIndex Type | read-only | The *ifIndex* for this LABP interface. |
| lapbAdmn StationType 1.3.6.1.2.1.10.16.1.1.2 | INTEGER dte(1), dce(2), dxe(3) | read-write | The desired station type DTE, DCE, or, if either is OK, DXE. |
| lapbAdmn ControlField 1.3.6.1.2.1.10.16.1.1.3 | INTEGER modulo8(1), modulo128(2) | read-write | Sequence numbering to be used. |
| lapbAdmn TransmitN1 FrameSize 1.3.6.1.2.1.10.16.1.1.4 | Positive Integer | read-write | Default desired maximum number (N1) of bits in a transmitted frame (excluding flags and inserted 0-bits). |
| lapbAdmn ReceiveN1 FrameSize 1.3.6.1.2.1.10.16.1.1.5 | Positive Integer | read-write | Default desired maximum number (N1) of bits in a received frame. |
| lapbAdmn TransmitK WindowSize 1.3.6.1.2.1.10.16.1.1.6 | INTEGER (1..127) | read-write | Transmit window size k. Default 7. |
| lapbAdmn ReceiveK WindowSize 1.3.6.1.2.1.10.16.1.1.7 | INTEGER (1..127) | read-write | Receive window size k (maximum number of unacked PDUs). Default 7. |
| lapbAdmn N2RxmitCount 1.3.6.1.2.1.10.16.1.1.8 | INTEGER (0..65535) | read-write | Maximum number (N2) of retransmissions that may be attempted before giving up. Default is 20. |
| lapbAdmn T1AckTimer 1.3.6.1.2.1.10.16.1.1.9 | Positive Integer | read-write | Default retransmission timeout (T1) in milliseconds. |
| lapbAdmn T2AckDelayTimer 1.3.6.1.2.1.10.16.1.1.10 | Positive Integer | read-write | The maximum delay time (T2) in milliseconds permitted before an acknowledgment of a received in-sequence frame must be sent. |
| lapbAdmn T3DisconnectTimer 1.3.6.1.2.1.10.16.1.1.11 | Positive Integer | read-write | Disconnect if link is idle (no flags or frames) for T3 milliseconds. 0 means only disconnect with the termination protocol. Default 60000. |

**TABLE 25.1    The LAPB Administration Table (*Continued*)**

iso.org.dod.internet.mgmt.mib-2.
transmission.lapb.lapbAdmnTable.lapbAdmnEntry
1.3.6.1.2.1.10.16.1.1

| OBJECT IDENTIFIER | Syntax | Access | Description |
|---|---|---|---|
| lapbAdmn<br>T4IdleTimer<br>1.3.6.1.2.1.10.16.1.1.12 | Positive<br>Integer | read-<br>write | Maximum time in ms<br>(T4) to retain an idle<br>link when no frames are<br>being sent. No timeout<br>if T4=2147483647. |
| lapbAdmn<br>ActionInitiate<br>1.3.6.1.2.1.10.16.1.1.13 | INTEGER<br>sendSABM(1),<br>sendDISC(2),<br>sendDM(3),<br>none(4),<br>other(5) | read-<br>write | Identifies the action the<br>local end will take to<br>initiate link setup.<br>Default sendSABM. |
| lapbAdmn<br>ActionRecvDM<br>1.3.6.1.2.1.10.16.1.1.14 | INTEGER<br>sendSABM(1),<br>sendDISC(2),<br>other(3) | read-<br>write | Identifies action local<br>end will take when it<br>receives a DM response.<br>Default sendSABM. |

two variables, which deal with initialization of the link, are not copied, but two more variables are included: the port for the physical interface supporting the link, and the LAPB protocol version identifier.

However, some of the values in an LAPB Operational Table entry might possibly differ from the values currently configured in the Administration Table. Why? There are two possibilities:

- If a manager changes some of a link's configuration parameters in the Administration Table *after* the link already is up, it may be impossible for the new values to take effect until the link is reinitialized.

- If the XID protocol is used for this link, then some of the parameters might be modified during XID negotiation.

Since the variables have identical definitions, the table is not included. The OBJECT IDENTIFIER for the LAPB Operational Table is:

```
iso.org.dod.internet.mgmt.mib-2.transmission.lapb.lapbOperTable
```

or

```
1 . 3 . 6 . 1 . 2 . 1 . 10 . 16 . 2
```

The *lapbProtocolVersion* subtree has been defined under *lapb* to hold OBJECT IDENTIFIERs that identify LAPB protocol versions. These include the following:

|                                        Protocol Versions<br>iso.org.dod.internet.mgmt.mib-2.<br>transmission.lapb.lapbProtocolVersion<br>1.3.6.1.2.1.10.16.5 | |
| --- | --- |
| OBJECT IDENTIFIER | Description |
| lapbProtocolIso7776v1986<br>1.3.6.1.2.1.10.16.5.1 | 1986 ISO version |
| lapbProtocolCcittV1980<br>1.3.6.1.2.1.10.16.5.2 | 1980 CCITT version |
| lapbProtocolCcittV1984<br>1.3.6.1.2.1.10.16.5.3 | 1984 CCITT version |

## 25.8   THE LAPB FLOW TABLE

Table 25.2 the LAPB Flow Table, counts significant events in the life of a link. For example, the table reports how often the remote end was busy, the number of reject (REJ) frames sent and received, and the number of retransmissions because of timeouts.

The Flow Table counts the number of *state changes* that have occurred on the link. For example, arrival of a SABM (or SABME) or a responding Unnumbered Acknowledgment (UA) frame causes the local end of the link to go from Not Started to Asynchronous Balanced Mode (Extended) state. State changes also are caused by arriving Disconnected Mode (DM) or Disconnect (DISC) frames. Other changes are caused by Frame Rejects and by having attempted the maximum-allowed number (N2) of retransmissions of a frame.

### 25.8.1   Reasons for State Change

A variable in the flow table (*lapbFlowChangeReason*) reports the reason for the *most recent* state change, which is one of the following:

| Reason for state change | Explanation |
| --- | --- |
| 1.  notStarted | Initial state |
| 2.  abmEntered | SABM or UA |
| 3.  abmeEntered | SABME or UA |
| 4.  abmReset | SABM in abm |
| 5.  abmeReset | SABME in abme |
| 6.  dmReceived | DM Response |
| 7.  dmSent | DM sent |
| 8.  discReceived | DISC Response |
| 9.  discSent | DISC Sent |
| 10. frmrReceived | FRMR Received |
| 11. frmrSent | FRMR Sent |
| 12. n2Timeout | N2 Timer Expired |
| 13. other | |

**TABLE 25.2    The LAPB Flow Table**

| iso.org.dod.internet.mgmt.mib-2.<br>transmission.lapb.lapbFlowTable.lapbFlowEntry<br>1.3.6.1.2.1.10.16.3.1 | | | |
|---|---|---|---|
| OBJECT IDENTIFIER | Syntax | Access | Description |
| lapbFlow<br>IfIndex<br>1.3.6.1.2.1.10.16.3.1.1<br>▶ **Index** | IfIndexType | read-only | The *ifIndex* for this LAPB interface. |
| lapbFlow<br>StateChanges<br>1.3.6.1.2.1.10.16.3.1.2 | Counter | read-only | The number of LAPB State Changes, including resets. |
| lapbFlow<br>ChangeReason<br>1.3.6.1.2.1.10.16.3.1.3 | INTEGER<br>See 24.7.1. | read-only | The reason for the most recent state change. |
| lapbFlow<br>CurrentMode<br>1.3.6.1.2.1.10.16.3.1.4 | INTEGER<br>See 24.7.2. | read-only | The current flow mode. |
| lapbFlow<br>BusyDefers<br>1.3.6.1.2.1.10.16.3.1.5 | Counter | read-only | The number of times this device could not transmit a frame because the remote end was busy—i.e., the remote end had sent RNR, or there was currently no send window space left. |
| lapbFlow<br>RejOutPkts<br>1.3.6.1.2.1.10.16.3.1.6 | Counter | read-only | The number of reject frames (REJ or SREJ) sent by this station. |
| lapbFlow<br>RejInPkts<br>1.3.6.1.2.1.10.16.3.1.7 | Counter | read-only | The number of reject frames received by this station. |
| lapbFlow<br>T1Timeouts<br>1.3.6.1.2.1.10.16.3.1.8 | Counter | read-only | The number of times that a T1 timer expired and caused a retransmission. |
| lapbFlow<br>FrmrSent<br>1.3.6.1.2.1.10.16.3.1.9 | OCTET<br>STRING<br>(SIZE (0..7)) | read-only | The information field from the most recently sent frame reject (FRMR). Recall that this field indicates what the problem was. |
| lapbFlow<br>FrmrReceived<br>1.3.6.1.2.1.10.16.3.1.10 | OCTET<br>STRING<br>(SIZE (0..7)) | read-only | The information field from the most recently received frame reject (FRMR). |
| lapbFlow<br>XidReceived<br>1.3.6.1.2.1.10.16.3.1.11 | OCTET<br>STRING<br>(SIZE (0..8206)) | read-only | The information field from the most recently received exchange ID (XID) frame. |

### 25.8.2 Current Flow Mode

Another Flow Table variable (*lapbFlowCurrentMode*) records the *current* flow mode. The possibilities are as follows:

| Current flow mode | Explanation |
|---|---|
| 1. disconnected | Initial state or DISC received. |
| 2. linkSetup | SABM sent. |
| 3. frameReject | Invalid frame received and FRMR sent. |
| 4. disconnectRequest | DISC sent. |
| 5. informationTransfer | Normal information transfer state. |
| 6. rejFrameSent | Invalid sequence number received, REJ sent. |
| 7. waitingAcknowledgement | T1 retransmission timer expired and RR sent. |
| 8. stationBusy | Receive Not Ready (RNR) sent. |
| 9. remoteStationBusy | Receive Not ready (RNR) received. |
| 10. bothStationsBusy | RNR received and RNR sent. |
| 11. waitingAckStationBusy | T1 expired, RNR sent. |
| 12. waitingAckRemoteBusy | T1 expired, RNR received. |
| 13. waitingAckBothBusy | T1 expired, RNR sent, RNR received. |
| 14. rejFrameSentRemoteBusy | REJ sent and RNR received. |
| 15. xidFrameSent | XID frame sent. |
| 16. error | Some other error state. |
| 17. other | None of the above. |

## 25.9 THE LAPB XID TABLE

Table 25.3, the LAPB Exchange ID Table, contains configuration information used in the XID protocol, but not already included in the LAPB Administration Table.

There are several variables in this table whose datatype (i.e., SYNTAX) is OCTET STRING. If no value has been assigned to a variable with OCTET STRING type, this will be indicated by returning a zero-length string.

## 25.10 THE X.25 PACKET LAYER

The discussion that follows describes the traditional DTE-to-DCE interactions used to send data across a data packet network.

### 25.10.1 Packet Layer Technology and Concepts

As we have seen, the LAPB protocol supports a reliable, connection-oriented link. Once the link has been started, it acts as a big pipeline between the DTE and the network. Many parallel virtual circuits can run through that pipeline at the same time. Data for each virtual cir-

**TABLE 25.3    The LAPB XID Table**

iso.org.dod.internet.mgmt.mib-2.
transmission.lapb.lapbXidTable.lapbXidEntry
1.3.6.1.2.1.10.16.4.1

| OBJECT IDENTIFIER | Syntax | Access | Description |
|---|---|---|---|
| lapbXid Index 1.3.6.1.2.1.10.16.4.1.1 ▶ **Index** | IfIndex Type | read-only | The *ifIndex* for this LAPB interface. |
| lapbXid AdRIdentifier 1.3.6.1.2.1.10.16.4.1.2 | OCTET STRING (SIZE (0..255)) | read-write | The value of the Address Resolution Identifier. Default "H. |
| lapbXid AdRAddress 1.3.6.1.2.1.10.16.4.1.3 | OCTET STRING (SIZE (0..255)) | read-write | The value of the Address Resolution Address. |
| lapbXid Parameter UniqueIdentifier 1.3.6.1.2.1.10.16.4.1.4 | OCTET STRING (SIZE (0..255)) | read-write | The value of the parameter unique Identifier. |
| lapbXid GroupAddress 1.3.6.1.2.1.10.16.4.1.5 | OCTET STRING (SIZE (0..255)) | read-write | The value of the parameter Group address. |
| lapbXid PortNumber 1.3.6.1.2.1.10.16.4.1.6 | OCTET STRING (SIZE (0..255)) | read-write | The port number assigned for this link. Default "H. |
| lapbXid UserDataSubfield 1.3.6.1.2.1.10.16.4.1.7 | OCTET STRING (SIZE (0..8206)) | read-write | A user data subfield, if any, to be transmitted in an XID frame. |

cuit is carried in layer 3 *packets* that are sent across the link inside of LAPB information frames.

There are many types of layer 3 packets. Some are used to set up or terminate Virtual Calls. Information packets contain data to be delivered to partners at the other end of permanent or switched virtual circuits. Some packet types are used to negotiate changes to call parameters, report errors, or signal a catastrophic loss of all circuits!

### 25.10.2    Numbering Logical Channels

Each virtual circuit is assigned to a *logical channel*. A logical channel is identified by a two-part number—a *logical channel group number* and a *logical channel number*. Some logical channels are preassigned to Permanent Virtual Circuits. On the other hand, Virtual Calls are set up on request from a DTE (like dialing a phone number). The assignment of an unused logical channel to a new circuit is part of the routine used to set up a Virtual Call.

### 25.10.3  The Packet Layer Entity (PLE) Interface

All virtual circuit activity is managed by a *Packet Layer Entity* (PLE) that acts as the layer 3 interface.

Calls are set up, maintained, and terminated by the Packet Layer Entity. The packet protocol used on each separate virtual circuit provides reliable, ordered delivery of data, flow control, and error diagnostics for *that* virtual circuit.

The PLE is in charge of sending and receiving the distinct packets used to set up a Virtual Call, exchange data, and clear a call. The PLE handles flow control by means of *packet layer* Receive Ready (RR) and Receive-Not-Ready (RNR) packets. Note that *this* flow control relates to just the one virtual circuit, not the whole link.

The PLE can send a special Interrupt packet that carries a small amount of out-of-band data to the partner. An Interrupt must be confirmed by the remote partner.

If problems arise on a virtual circuit, either end can ask for a Reset, which cleans data out of the circuit, and sets numbering back to 0.

To ensure reliable delivery, data packets are numbered and acknowledged. Suppose that a packet is missing from an incoming sequence of layer 3 packets—for example, 2, 3, 5, 6 arrive. We are very surprised, since the underlying LAPB link is supposed to guarantee that packets (wrapped in their frame headers and trailers) will arrive safely. Hence, a missing layer 3 packet is considered serious and leads to a circuit reset. Some networks support optional use of a REJ layer 3 packet that requests retransmission starting from a requested packet number.

### 25.10.4  Red Alert! Restart!

Without a doubt, the most dramatic event that can happen at the packet layer is a *Restart,* which can be requested by a DTE or a DCE (via a Restart packet). A Restart wipes away *all* Virtual Calls at the interface, and reinitializes every Permanent Virtual Circuit. A restart is a clean sweep.

### 25.10.5  More About Facilities

CCITT Recommendations do not have a reputation for simplicity, but no one can deny that they are flexible. A customer can sign on with a service provider for a set of facilities.

A customer who wants to keep their options open can ask for *online* facilities registration. Some facilities that will apply to *all* calls can be negotiated (using *Registration* packets) before any calls are set up. That seems reasonable. But even after some calls are in progress, you can change your mind, adding some general facilities and dropping others. Is that enough? No! There are facilities that you can ask for when setting up a call, to apply to that call only!

The network user may seem to be rather pampered, but in fact not all wishes have to be granted. The network has the right to give the user somewhat less than what is asked for.

## 25.11    INTRODUCTION TO THE X.25 PACKET LAYER MIB

As we have seen, the X.25 packet layer is quite complicated—mainly because different configuration choices and different facilities can be chosen for each call. Also remember that a single device might conceivably connect to more than one data network, and so might have multiple Packet Layer Entities to configure.

### 25.11.1    Tables in the Packet Layer MIB

There are seven MIB tables used for the packet layer. Three are used for configuration:

- *x25AdmnTable.* Each entry contains parameters that a network manager would set to configure a Packet Layer Entity. The variables include timer settings and limits on the number of retries for various actions.

- *x25ChannelTable.* A network manager uses this table to configure the way that channel numbers will be used. A set of channel numbers can be reserved for Permanent Virtual Circuits. Other sets can be dedicated to incoming Virtual Calls only or outgoing Virtual Calls only. A range of channel numbers also can be set up for use for either incoming or outgoing calls.

- *x25CallParmTable.* Each entry in the X.25 Call Parameter Table contains a set of Virtual Call parameters that describe features such as packet size, window size, and throughput, as well as facilities such as Closed User Group or Reverse Charging. Think of an entry as a template that can be picked if it has just what you need for a virtual circuit that you are setting up. A single entry can be selected for use by one circuit, or by many different circuits—perhaps even across many PLEs.

    How is this table used in a typical implementation? When setting up a call, software in the device could identify an entry that will be used for the parameters for this call. If an entry is not explicitly picked, then the *default* entry for the PLE would be used.

There are three tables used to record information about active inter-faces and their virtual circuits:

- *x25OperTable.* When a Packet Layer Entity is initialized, the parameters in the Administration Table are copied into an entry in the X.25 Operations Table. The Administration and Operation vari-ables are identical, except that the X.25 Operations Table includes an additional variable that points to the underlying layer 2 LAPB interface that supports the operating Packet Layer Entity.

  What happens if a network manager later makes a change to the Administrative Table? It will depend on the specific implementation. We should expect that often the changes will not take effect until the interface is reinitialized.

- *x25StatTable.* The X.25 Statistics Table contains counts of events for an operating Packet Layer Entity—such as number of incoming calls, outgoing calls, data packets sent and received, resets, restarts, and timeouts.

- *x25CircuitTable.* This table lists information about existing, live *circuits* for any of the Packet Layer Entities. It identifies the calling and called X.121 addresses. It tallies incoming and outgoing packet and octet counts. It counts retransmissions and resets.

  The *x25CircuitCallParamId* variable points to the entry in the X.25 Call Parameter Table that holds parameters for a given circuit.

Finally, there is one table used to record information about circuits that failed:

- *x25ClearedCircuitTable.* An entry is created in this table if a circuit terminates abnormally. This provides useful data for troubleshoot-ing. Variables record when the circuit was set up, when it was cleared, the amount of traffic, and diagnostic codes related to closing down the circuit. Optionally, an implementation can enter normal terminations into this table too.

### 25.11.2  Packet Layer Textual Convention

You can't make a Virtual Call unless you can identify the called DTE. Recommendation X.121 describes the plan used to number DTEs. The packet layer MIB expresses X.121 numbers as OCTET STRINGs:

- *X121Address.* An OCTET STRING 0 to 17 bytes in length consist-ing of a sequence of digits represented as ASCII characters.

### 25.11.3  Timeouts, Retries, and Recovery

Whatever you do in the course of a virtual call—send a call request, send data, ask for data retransmission, report an error, or try to clear (terminate) a call, you want some kind of indication that the partner heard you and will react appropriately. The Packet Layer Entity sets a timer for each of these actions.

On a timeout, what happens? The PLE tries again—within reason. There is a limit set on how often an action can be retried before giving up. What do you do then? In some cases, live with it. For example, if an attempt to register for new facilities fails, perhaps you can manage to communicate without those facilities. On the other hand, if resets or clears fail, you probably would declare the link to be broken and report this to network management. Or a failed restart might be reported to higher-layer software, which might have some built-in correction mechanism.

## 25.12  THE X.25 ADMINISTRATION TABLE

Table 25.4, the X.25 Administration Table, contains settings for the many timers that are used to determine that some action is taking too long. Times are measured in milliseconds. The table also sets limits on how often the PLE will retry an action that has timed out. The variables in an Administration Table entry are copied into the *x25OperTable* when the PLE interface starts up.

As part of initialization, the *default* parameters to be used for Virtual Calls also are established. The *x25AdmnDefCallParamId* variable points to an entry in the X.25 Call Parameter Table, *x25CallParmTable,* that contains these default settings.

## 25.13  THE X.25 OPERATIONAL TABLE

The X.25 Operational Table has variables identical to those in the operational table. However, these variables represent the values in actual use. The table is not reproduced here, since only the names have changed. For example, *x25AdmnIndex* appears instead of *x25AdmnIndex.*

The Administrative Table may have been reconfigured since the interface came up. In most implementations, the old operational values will persist until the interface is reinitialized.

## 25.14  THE X.25 STATISTICS TABLE

Table 24.5, the X.25 Statistics Table, contains counts of many packet layer events. It records the numbers of incoming and outgoing calls, resets, and many types of timeouts.

**TABLE 25.4   The X25 Administration Table**

iso.org.dod.internet.mgmt.mib-2.
transmission.x25.x25AdmnTable.x25AdmnEntry
1.3.6.1.2.1.10.5.1.1

| OBJECT IDENTIFIER | Syntax | Access | Description |
|---|---|---|---|
| x25Admn Index 1.3.6.1.2.1.10.5.1.1.1 ► **Index** | IfIndexType | read-only | The *ifIndex* for this X25 interface. |
| x25Admn InterfaceMode 1.3.6.1.2.1.10.5.1.1.2 | INTEGER dte (1), dce (2), dxe (3) | read-write | Identifies the mode for the interface—DTE or DCE. DXE means that the mode is determined by XID negotiation. |
| x25Admn MaxActiveCircuits 1.3.6.1.2.1.10.5.1.1.3 | INTEGER (0..4096) | read-write | Maximum number of concurrent circuits (including PVCs) that can be supported at this interface. |
| x25Admn PacketSequencing 1.3.6.1.2.1.10.5.1.1.4 | INTEGER modulo8(1), modulo128(2) | read-write | Sequence numbering to be used for packets. |
| x25Admn RestartTimer 1.3.6.1.2.1.10.5.1.1.5 | Positive Integer | read-write | T20, the timeout for receiving a restart confirmation. |
| x25Admn CallTimer 1.3.6.1.2.1.10.5.1.1.6 | Positive Integer | read-write | T21, the timeout for receiving a Call Accepted packet. |
| x25Admn ResetTimer 1.3.6.1.2.1.10.5.1.1.7 | Positive Integer | read-write | T22, the timout for receiving a Reset Confirmation. |
| x25Admn ClearTimer 1.3.6.1.2.1.10.5.1.1.8 | Positive Integer | read-write | T23, the timout for receiving a Clear Confirmation. |
| x25Admn WindowTimer 1.3.6.1.2.1.10.5.1.1.9 | Positive Integer | read-write | The T24 window status transmission timer in milliseconds. |
| x25Admn DataRxmtTimer 1.3.6.1.2.1.10.5.1.1.10 | Positive Integer | read-write | T25, the timout for receiving acknowledgment for data. 2147483647 means no timer. |
| x25Admn InterruptTimer 1.3.6.1.2.1.10.5.1.1.11 | Positive Integer | read-write | T26, the timout for receiving an interrupt confirmation. |
| x25Admn RejectTimer 1.3.6.1.2.1.10.5.1.1.12 | Positive Integer | read-write | T27, the timeout for receiving information after sending a Reject. |
| x25Admn Registration RequestTimer 1.3.6.1.2.1.10.5.1.1.13 | Positive Integer | read-write | The T28 registration timer in milliseconds. |

**TABLE 25.4    The X25 Administration Table (*Continued*)**

iso.org.dod.internet.mgmt.mib-2.
transmission.x25.x25AdmnTable.x25AdmnEntry
1.3.6.1.2.1.10.5.1.1

| OBJECT IDENTIFIER | Syntax | Access | Description |
|---|---|---|---|
| x25Admn MinimumRecall Timer 1.3.6.1.2.1.10.5.1.1.14 | Positive Integer | read-write | Minimum time interval between unsuccessful call attempts in milliseconds. |
| x25Admn RestartCount 1.3.6.1.2.1.10.5.1.1.15 | INTEGER (0..65535) | read-write | The R20 restart retransmission count. |
| x25Admn ResetCount 1.3.6.1.2.1.10.5.1.1.16 | INTEGER (0..65535) | read-write | The R22 Reset retransmission count. |
| x25Admn ClearCount 1.3.6.1.2.1.10.5.1.1.17 | INTEGER (0..65535) | read-write | The R23 Clear retransmission count. |
| x25Admn DataRxmtCount 1.3.6.1.2.1.10.5.1.1.18 | INTEGER (0..65535) | read-write | The R25 Data retransmission count. |
| x25Admn RejectCount 1.3.6.1.2.1.10.5.1.1.19 | INTEGER (0..65535) | read-write | The R27 reject retransmission count. |
| x25Admn Registration Request Count 1.3.6.1.2.1.10.5.1.1.20 | INTEGER (0..65535) | read-write | The R28 Registration retransmission count. |
| x25Admn NumberPVCs 1.3.6.1.2.1.10.5.1.1.21 | INTEGER (0..4096) | read-write | The number of Permanent Virtual Circuits (PVCs) configured for this interface. The PVCs use channel numbers from 1 to this number. |
| x25Admn DefCallParamId 1.3.6.1.2.1.10.5.1.1.22 | OBJECT IDENTIFIER | read-write | The index of the entry in the x25CallParmTable which contains the default call parameters for this PLE. |
| x25Admn LocalAddress 1.3.6.1.2.1.10.5.1.1.23 | X121Address | read-write | The local address for this PLE subnetwork. |
| x25Admn ProtocolVersion Supported 1.3.6.1.2.1.10.5.1.1.24 | OBJECT IDENTIFIER | read-write | Version of the X.25 protocol supported. See Sec. 25.19 for the appropriate OBJECT IDENTIFIERs. |

**TABLE 25.5 The X.25 Statistics Table**

iso.org.dod.internet.mgmt.mib-2.
transmission.x25.x25StatTable.x25StatEntry
1.3.6.1.2.1.10.5.3.1

| OBJECT IDENTIFIER | Syntax | Access | Description |
|---|---|---|---|
| x25Stat<br>Index<br>1.3.6.1.2.1.10.5.3.1.1<br>▶ **Index** | IfIndex<br>Type | read-<br>only | The *ifIndex* for this X.25 interface. |
| x25StatInCalls<br>1.3.6.1.2.1.10.5.3.1.2 | Counter | read-<br>only | Number of incoming calls received. |
| x25Stat<br>InCallRefusals<br>1.3.6.1.2.1.10.5.3.1.3 | Counter | read-<br>only | Number of incoming calls refused—<br>by the PLE and by higher layers. |
| x25Stat<br>InProvider<br>InitiatedClears<br>1.3.6.1.2.1.10.5.3.1.4 | Counter | read-<br>only | Number of clear requests with a<br>cause code other than DTE-initiated. |
| x25Stat<br>InRemotely<br>InitiatedResets<br>1.3.6.1.2.1.10.5.3.1.5 | Counter | read-<br>only | Number of reset requests received<br>with cause code DTE-initiated. |
| x25Stat<br>InProvider<br>InitiatedResets<br>1.3.6.1.2.1.10.5.3.1.6 | Counter | read-<br>only | Number of reset requests received<br>with cause code other than DTE-<br>initiated. |
| x25Stat<br>InRestarts<br>1.3.6.1.2.1.10.5.3.1.7 | Counter | read-<br>only | Number of remotely (including<br>provider) initiated restarts of an<br>already-established connection. |
| x25Stat<br>InDataPackets<br>1.3.6.1.2.1.10.5.3.1.8 | Counter | read-<br>only | Number of data packets received. |
| x25Stat<br>InAccusedOf<br>ProtocolErrors<br>1.3.6.1.2.1.10.5.3.1.9 | Counter | read-<br>only | Number of packets received<br>containing a procedure error cause<br>code. |
| x25Stat<br>InInterrupts<br>1.3.6.1.2.1.10.5.3.1.10 | Counter | read-<br>only | Number of interrupt packets<br>received. |
| x25Stat<br>OutCallAttempts<br>1.3.6.1.2.1.10.5.3.1.11 | Counter | read-<br>only | Number of outgoing calls<br>attempted. |
| x25Stat<br>OutCallFailures<br>1.3.6.1.2.1.10.5.3.1.12 | Counter | read-<br>only | Number of outgoing call attempts<br>which failed. |
| x25Stat<br>OutInterrupts<br>1.3.6.1.2.1.10.5.3.1.13 | Counter | read-<br>only | Number of interrupt packets sent by<br>the PLE. |

**TABLE 25.5    The X.25 Statistics Table (*Continued*)**

<table>
<tr><td colspan="4" align="center">iso.org.dod.internet.mgmt.mib-2.<br>transmission.x25.x25StatTable.x25StatEntry<br>1.3.6.1.2.1.10.5.3.1</td></tr>
<tr><th>OBJECT IDENTIFIER</th><th>Syntax</th><th>Access</th><th>Description</th></tr>
<tr><td>x25Stat<br>OutDataPackets<br>1.3.6.1.2.1.10.5.3.1.14</td><td>Counter</td><td>read-only</td><td>Number of data packets sent by the PLE.</td></tr>
<tr><td>x25Stat<br>OutgoingCircuits<br>1.3.6.1.2.1.10.5.3.1.15</td><td>Gauge</td><td>read-only</td><td>Number of active outgoing circuits, including call requests that have not yet been confirmed. (PVCs not included.)</td></tr>
<tr><td>x25Stat<br>IncomingCircuits<br>1.3.6.1.2.1.10.5.3.1.16</td><td>Gauge</td><td>read-only</td><td>Number of active incoming circuits including call indications that have not yet been acked. (PVCs not included.)</td></tr>
<tr><td>x25Stat<br>TwowayCircuits<br>1.3.6.1.2.1.10.5.3.1.17</td><td>Gauge</td><td>read-only</td><td>Number of active two-way circuits including those whose setup is not yet complete. (PVCs are not included.)</td></tr>
<tr><td>x25Stat<br>RestartTimeouts<br>1.3.6.1.2.1.10.5.3.1.18</td><td>Counter</td><td>read-only</td><td>Number of times the T20 restart timer has expired.</td></tr>
<tr><td>x25Stat<br>CallTimeouts<br>1.3.6.1.2.1.10.5.3.1.19</td><td>Counter</td><td>read-only</td><td>Number of times the T21 call timer has expired.</td></tr>
<tr><td>x25Stat<br>ResetTimeouts<br>1.3.6.1.2.1.10.5.3.1.20</td><td>Counter</td><td>read-only</td><td>Number of times the T22 reset timer has expired.</td></tr>
<tr><td>x25Stat<br>ClearTimeouts<br>1.3.6.1.2.1.10.5.3.1.21</td><td>Counter</td><td>read-only</td><td>Number of times the T23 clear timer has expired.</td></tr>
<tr><td>x25StatData<br>RxmtTimeouts<br>1.3.6.1.2.1.10.5.3.1.22</td><td>Counter</td><td>read-only</td><td>Number of times the T25 data timer has expired.</td></tr>
<tr><td>x25Stat<br>InterruptTimeouts<br>1.3.6.1.2.1.10.5.3.1.23</td><td>Counter</td><td>read-only</td><td>Number of times the T26 interrupt timer has expired.</td></tr>
<tr><td>x25StatRetry<br>CountExceededs<br>1.3.6.1.2.1.10.5.3.1.24</td><td>Counter</td><td>read-only</td><td>Number of times a retry counter was exhausted.</td></tr>
<tr><td>x25StatClear<br>CountExceededs<br>1.3.6.1.2.1.10.5.3.1.25</td><td>Counter</td><td>read-only</td><td>Number of times the R23 clear count was exceeded.</td></tr>
</table>

## 25.15    THE X.25 CHANNEL TABLE

Logical Channel Numbers are made up of a 4-bit Logical Channel Group Number (0–15) and 8-bit channel number (0–255), giving a total range of values from 0 to 4095. 0 is not used. The group number can be used, naturally, to group related channels together.

There are several categories of circuits, and each type is assigned a range of channel numbers:

- Permanent Virtual Circuits
- One-way incoming (only for incoming calls)
- Two-way (for incoming or outgoing calls)
- One-way outgoing (only for outgoing calls)

Figure 25.5 shows a typical layout for logical channel assignments. Suppose that some range is nonexistent; for example, suppose that no

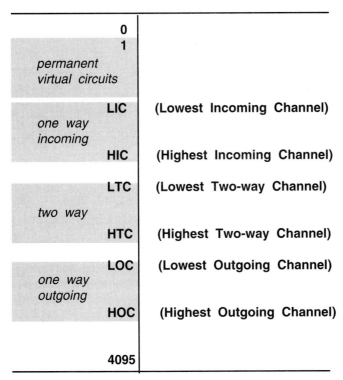

**LOGICAL CHANNEL NUMBERS**

**Figure 25.5**  X.25 logical channel assignments.

channels are dedicated to one-way incoming calls. Then LIC-HIC-0, and the range would be omitted from the figure.

The X.25 Channel Table provides configuration information about logical channel assignments. It assigns lower and upper bounds to incoming channels, two-way channels, and outgoing channels. The table's OBJECT IDENTIFIER is:

```
iso.org.dod.internet.mgmt.mib-2.transmission.x25.x25ChannelTable
```

or

```
1 . 3 . 6 . 1 . 2 . 1 . 10 . 5 . 4
```

## 25.16   THE X.25 CIRCUIT TABLE

Table 25.6, the X.25 Circuit Table, lists information about existing live circuits for any of the Packet Layer Entities. The table describes the current detailed status for each circuit. If the circuit belongs to a Virtual Call, the table records when the call was set up, and whether it was incoming or outgoing.

The table tallies incoming and outgoing packet and octet counts and also counts retransmissions and resets.

The table identifies the calling and called X.121 addresses. However, the called address may not be the same as the one originally asked for by the caller! Among the many facilities offered by service providers are hunt groups and call rerouting. What are these for? Think of the data equivalent of a business 800 number. Calls for information or service arrive, and are redirected to locations that have available resources to handle the call. To keep the record straight, there is a table variable that holds the address that originally was called.

### 25.16.1   Circuit Status

The important $x25CircuitStatus$ variable indicates the exact status of a circuit. Possible values are:

1. invalid
2. closed
3. calling
4. open
5. clearing
6. pvc
7. pvcResetting
8. startClear
9. startPvcResetting
10. other

**TABLE 25.6   The X.25 Circuit Table**

iso.org.dod.internet.mgmt.mib-2.
transmission.x25.x25CircuitTable.x25CircuitEntry
1.3.6.1.2.1.10.5.5.1

| OBJECT IDENTIFIER | Syntax | Access | Description |
|---|---|---|---|
| x25CircuitIndex<br>1.3.6.1.2.1.10.5.5.1.1<br>▶ **Index** | IfIndex<br>Type | read-<br>only | The *ifIndex* of the X.25<br>interface. |
| x25CircuitChannel<br>1.3.6.1.2.1.10.5.5.1.2<br>▶ **Index** | INTEGER<br>(0..4095) | read-<br>only | The channel number for this<br>circuit. |
| x25CircuitStatus<br>1.3.6.1.2.1.10.5.5.1.3 | INTEGER<br>See Section<br>24.15.1. | read-<br>write | The current status of this<br>circuit. |
| x25Circuit<br>EstablishTime<br>1.3.6.1.2.1.10.5.5.1.4 | TimeTicks | read-<br>only | The value of *sysUpTime*<br>when the channel was<br>associated with this circuit. |
| x25Circuit<br>Direction<br>1.3.6.1.2.1.10.5.5.1.5 | INTEGER<br>incoming(1),<br>outgoing(2),<br>pvc (3) | read-<br>write | The direction of the call<br>that established this circuit. |
| x25Circuit<br>InOctets<br>1.3.6.1.2.1.10.5.5.1.6 | Counter | read-<br>only | Number of octets of user data<br>delivered to upper layer. |
| x25Circuit<br>InPdus<br>1.3.6.1.2.1.10.5.5.1.7 | Counter | read-<br>only | Number of PDUs received. |
| x25Circuit<br>InRemotely<br>InitiatedResets<br>1.3.6.1.2.1.10.5.5.1.8 | Counter | read-<br>only | Number of Resets received<br>for this circuit with cause<br>code of DTE initiated. |
| x25Circuit<br>InProvider<br>InitiatedResets<br>1.3.6.1.2.1.10.5.5.1.9 | Counter | read-<br>only | Number of Resets received<br>for this circuit with cause<br>code other than DTE-<br>initiated. |
| x25Circuit<br>InInterrupts<br>1.3.6.1.2.1.10.5.5.1.10 | Counter | read-<br>only | Number of interrupt<br>packets received. |
| x25Circuit<br>OutOctets<br>1.3.6.1.2.1.10.5.5.1.11 | Counter | read-<br>only | Number of octets of user<br>data sent. |
| x25Circuit<br>OutPdus<br>1.3.6.1.2.1.10.5.5.1.12 | Counter | read-<br>only | Number of PDUs sent. |
| x25Circuit<br>OutInterrupts<br>1.3.6.1.2.1.10.5.5.1.13 | Counter | read-<br>only | Number of interrupt<br>packets sent. |

**TABLE 25.6    The X.25 Circuit Table (*Continued*)**

iso.org.dod.internet.mgmt.mib-2.
transmission.x25.x25CircuitTable.x25CircuitEntry
1.3.6.1.2.1.10.5.5.1

| OBJECT IDENTIFIER | Syntax | Access | Description |
|---|---|---|---|
| x25CircuitData Retransmission Timeouts 1.3.6.1.2.1.10.5.5.1.14 | Counter | read-only | Number of times the T25 data retransmission timer expired. |
| x25Circuit ResetTimeouts 1.3.6.1.2.1.10.5.5.1.15 | Counter | read-only | Number of times the T22 reset timer expired. |
| x25Circuit InterruptTimeouts 1.3.6.1.2.1.10.5.5.1.16 | Counter | read-only | Number of times the T26 Interrupt timer expired. |
| x25Circuit CallParamId 1.3.6.1.2.1.10.5.5.1.17 | OBJECT IDENTIFIER | read-write | The index for the entry in the *x25CallParmTable* which contains the call parameters in use with this circuit. |
| x25Circuit CalledDteAddress 1.3.6.1.2.1.10.5.5.1.18 | X121 Address | read-write | The called address. For incoming calls, it is taken from the call indication packet. For outgoing calls, it is taken from the call confirmation packet. |
| x25Circuit CallingDteAddress 1.3.6.1.2.1.10.5.5.1.19 | X121 Address | read-write | The calling address. For incoming calls, it is taken from the call indication packet. For outgoing calls, it is taken from the call confirmation packet. |
| x25Circuit OriginallyCalled Address 1.3.6.1.2.1.10.5.5.1.20 | X121 Address | read-write | The originally called address. If it has been changed for an incoming call, it will be the address in the call Redirection or Call Deflection Notification facility. |
| x25Circuit Descr 1.3.6.1.2.1.10.5.5.1.21 | Display String (SIZE (0..255)) | read-write | A descriptive string associated with this circuit. |

A network manager has limited power to *set* a few values of this variable in order to change the state of a circuit. By setting the variable to *startClear,* the network manager can clear a Virtual Call. The *startPvcResetting* value is used to reset a Permanent Virtual Circuit. The *invalid* setting is used to delete a circuit.

It is possible that some implementations might allow a network manager to create a Permanent Virtual Circuit. In this case, a new entry would be created with the value of *x25CircuitStatus* set to *pvc*.

## 25.17  THE X.25 CLEARED CIRCUIT TABLE

Table 25.7, the X.25 Cleared Circuit Table is used (primarily) to record information about circuits that were closed due to some error condition. The table may optionally also hold entries about circuits which have closed down normally.

The MIB defines two stand-alone variables that describe the requested and granted table size for the Cleared Circuit Table:

| | |
|---|---|
| *x25ClearedCircuit EntriesRequested* | A PositiveInteger showing the requested number of entries. The OBJECT IDENTIFIER is 1.3.6.1.2.1.10.5.6 |
| *x25ClearedCircuit EntriesGranted* | A PositiveInteger showing the granted number of entries. The OBJECT IDENTIFIER is 1.3.6.1.2.1.10.5.7 |

Note that the table index starts at 2147483647 and decreases to 1! This means that a *get-next* on index 0 will always get the most recent entry. If we have used up all of the entries down to 1, the next attempt to add an entry to the table will cause all of the entries to be erased, and numbering will start at 2147483647 again.

## 25.18  THE X.25 CALL PARAMETER TABLE

Table 25.8, the X.25 Call Parameter Table, contains call parameters that can be used for any of the device's X.25 interfaces. An entry from this table is selected when a call is set up.

### 25.18.1  References from Other Tables

Entries in other tables point to call configuration entries in this table:

- *X.25 Administration Table.*  The *x25AdmnDefCallParamId* variable points to an entry with the administratively set default settings for a Packet Layer Entity (PLE).

- *X.25 Operational Table.*  The *x25OperDefCallParamId* variable points to an entry with the operational default settings for a PLE.

- *X.25 Circuit Table.*  The *x25CircuitCallParamId* variable points to the entry that holds parameters for a circuit. If several circuits all use the same parameters, then they all will point to the same entry.

**TABLE 25.7    The X.25 Cleared Circuit Table**

iso.org.dod.internet.mgmt.mib-2.
transmission.x25.
x25ClearedCircuitTable.x25ClearedCircuitEntry
1.3.6.1.2.1.10.5.8.1

| OBJECT IDENTIFIER | Syntax | Access | Description |
| --- | --- | --- | --- |
| x25ClearedCircuit Index 1.3.6.1.2.1.10.5.8.1.1 ▶ **Index** | Positive Integer | read-only | A unique index for this entry. The index will start at 2147483647 and decrease by 1 for each new entry. |
| x25ClearedCircuit PleIndex 1.3.6.1.2.1.10.5.8.1.2 | IfIndex Type | read-only | The *ifIndex* for the PLE that cleared the circuit described in this entry. |
| x25ClearedCircuit TimeEstablished 1.3.6.1.2.1.10.5.8.1.3 | TimeTicks | read-only | The value of *sysUpTime* when the circuit was established. |
| x25ClearedCircuit TimeCleared 1.3.6.1.2.1.10.5.8.1.4 | TimeTicks | read-only | The value of *sysUpTime* when the circuit was cleared. |
| x25ClearedCircuit Channel 1.3.6.1.2.1.10.5.8.1.5 | INTEGER (0..4095) | read-only | Channel number used for this circuit. |
| x25ClearedCircuit ClearingCause 1.3.6.1.2.1.10.5.8.1.6 | INTEGER (0..255) | read-only | The Clearing Cause, taken from the clear request or clear indication packet. |
| x25ClearedCircuit DiagnosticCode 1.3.6.1.2.1.10.5.8.1.7 | INTEGER (0..255) | read-only | The Diagnostic Code, taken from the clear request or clear indication packet. |
| x25ClearedCircuit InPdus 1.3.6.1.2.1.10.5.8.1.8 | Counter | read-only | Number of PDUs received on the circuit. |
| x25ClearedCircuit OutPdus 1.3.6.1.2.1.10.5.8.1.9 | Counter | read-only | Number of PDUs transmitted on the circuit. |
| x25ClearedCircuit CalledAddress 1.3.6.1.2.1.10.5.8.1.10 | X121 Address | read-only | The called address. |
| x25ClearedCircuit CallingAddress 1.3.6.1.2.1.10.5.8.1.11 | X121 Address | read-only | The calling address. |
| x25ClearedCircuit ClearFacilities 1.3.6.1.2.1.10.5.8.1.12 | OCTET STRING (SIZE (0..109)) | read-only | The facilities field from the clear request or clear indication packet. |

**TABLE 25.8    The X.25 Call Parameter Table**

iso.org.dod.internet.mgmt.mib-2.
transmission.x25.
x25CallParmTable.x25CallParmEntry
1.3.6.1.2.1.10.5.9.1

| OBJECT IDENTIFIER | Syntax | Access | Description |
|---|---|---|---|
| x25CallParm Index 1.3.6.1.2.1.10.5.9.1.1 ▶ **Index** | Positive Integer | read-only | A unique index for this entry. |
| x25CallParm Status 1.3.6.1.2.1.10.5.9.1.2 | Entry Status | read-write | The status of this entry. If *invalid,* the entry slot can be reused. |
| x25CallParm RefCount 1.3.6.1.2.1.10.5.9.1.3 | Positive Integer | read-only | The reference counter for this entry. It should be incremented every time this entry is referenced in another table. |
| x25CallParm InPacketSize 1.3.6.1.2.1.10.5.9.1.4 | INTEGER (0..4096) | read-write | Maximum receive packet size (in octets) for a circuit. (DEFVAL 128.) |
| x25CallParm OutPacketSize 1.3.6.1.2.1.10.5.9.1.5 | INTEGER (0..4096) | read-write | Maximum transmit packet size (in octets) for a circuit. (DEFVAL 128.) |
| x25CallParm InWindowSize 1.3.6.1.2.1.10.5.9.1.6 | INTEGER (0..127) | read-write | Receive window size for a circuit. (DEFVAL 2.) |
| x25CallParm OutWindowSize 1.3.6.1.2.1.10.5.9.1.7 | INTEGER (0..127) | read-write | Transmit window size for a circuit. (DEFVAL 2.) |
| x25CallParm AcceptReverse Charging 1.3.6.1.2.1.10.5.9.1.8 | INTEGER default(1), accept(2), refuse(3), neverAccept(4) | read-write | Determines if the PLE will accept reverse charges. (DEFVAL is refuse.) |
| x25CallParm ProposeReverse Charging 1.3.6.1.2.1.10.5.9.1.9 | INTEGER default(1), reverse(2), local(3) | read-write | Determines if the PLE will propose reverse or local charging. (DEFVAL local.) |
| x25CallParm FastSelect 1.3.6.1.2.1.10.5.9.1.10 | INTEGER See Section 24.18.3. | read-write | Determines if Fast select will be used, and if so, whether it will be restricted. (DEFVAL is no.) |
| x25CallParm InThruPutClasSize 1.3.6.1.2.1.10.5.9.1.11 | INTEGER See Section 24.18.3. | read-write | The choice of incoming throughput class to be negotiated, if any. (DEFVAL is none.) |

**TABLE 25.8    The X.25 Call Parameter Table (*Continued*)**

iso.org.dod.internet.mgmt.mib-2.
transmission.x25.
x25CallParmTable.x25CallParmEntry
1.3.6.1.2.1.10.5.9.1

| OBJECT IDENTIFIER | Syntax | Access | Description |
|---|---|---|---|
| x25CallParm OutThruPutClasSize 1.3.6.1.2.1.10.5.9.1.12 | INTEGER See Section 24.18.3. | read-write | The choice for outgoing throughput class to negotiate, if any. (DEFVAL none.) |
| x25CallParm Cug 1.3.6.1.2.1.10.5.9.1.13 | DisplayString (SIZE(0..4)) | read-write | Choice (if any) for Closed User Group, identified by a string of two to four digits. DEFVAL is empty (none). |
| x25CallParm Cugoa 1.3.6.1.2.1.10.5.9.1.14 | DisplayString (SIZE(0..4)) | read-write | Choice (if any) for Closed User Group with Outgoing Access, identified by two to four digits. DEFVAL none. |
| x25CallParm Bcug 1.3.6.1.2.1.10.5.9.1.15 | DisplayString (SIZE(0..3)) | read-write | Choice (if any) of Bilateral Closed User Group, identified by two digits (or "DEF" for PLE default). |
| x25CallParm Nui 1.3.6.1.2.1.10.5.9.1.16 | OCTET STRING (SIZE(0..108)) | read-write | Network User Identification, if any. |
| x25CallParm ChargingInfo 1.3.6.1.2.1.10.5.9.1.17 | INTEGER default(1), noFacility(2), noCharging Info(3), charging Info(4) | read-write | If a DTE subscribes to this facility, the DTE can ask for charging information in a call request and network will provide charging information in the clear packet. |
| x25CallParm Rpoa 1.3.6.1.2.1.10.5.9.1.18 | DisplayString (SIZE(0..108)) | read-write | If the path request facility is supported, can contain identification of the sequence of transit networks to be used. |
| x25CallParm TrnstDly 1.3.6.1.2.1.10.5.9.1.19 | INTEGER (0..65537) | read-write | Transit delay requested for a call, in milliseconds. 65536 means none requested and 65537 means use PLE default. |
| x25CallParm CallingExt 1.3.6.1.2.1.10.5.9.1.20 | DisplayString (SIZE(0..40)) | read-write | Hex digits to be put into the Calling Extension facility |
| x25CallParm CalledExt 1.3.6.1.2.1.10.5.9.1.21 | DisplayString (SIZE(0..40)) | read-write | Hex digits to be put into the called extension facility. |
| x25CallParm InMinThuPutCls 1.3.6.1.2.1.10.5.9.1.22 | INTEGER (0..17) | read-write | The minimum input throughput class. |

**TABLE 25.8    The X.25 Call Parameter Table (*Continued*)**

iso.org.dod.internet.mgmt.mib-2.
transmission.x25.
x25CallParmTable.x25CallParmEntry
1.3.6.1.2.1.10.5.9.1

| OBJECT IDENTIFIER | Syntax | Access | Description |
|---|---|---|---|
| x25CallParm OutMinThuPutCls 1.3.6.1.2.1.10.5.9.1.23 | INTEGER (0..17) | read- write | The minimum output throughput class. |
| x25CallParm EndTrnsDly 1.3.6.1.2.1.10.5.9.1.24 | OCTET STRING (SIZE(0..6)) | read- write | End-to-end transit delay to be negotiated. |
| x25CallParm Priority 1.3.6.1.2.1.10.5.9.1.25 | OCTET STRING (SIZE(0..6)) | read- write | The priority facility to be negotiated. |
| x25CallParm Protection 1.3.6.1.2.1.10.5.9.1.26 | DisplayString (SIZE(0..108)) | read- write | The protection facility to be negotiated. |
| x25CallParm ExptData 1.3.6.1.2.1.10.5.9.1.27 | INTEGER default(1), noExpedited Data(2), expedited Data(3) | read- write | Whether to use expedited data. |
| x25CallParm UserData 1.3.6.1.2.1.10.5.9.1.28 | OCTET STRING SIZE (0..128)) | read- write | Call user data to be placed in a packet. (This value is used in preference to a default PLE value.) |
| x25CallParm CallingNetwork Facilities 1.3.6.1.2.1.10.5.9.1.29 | OCTET STRING (SIZE (0..108)) | read- write | Calling network facilities. |
| x25CallParm CalledNetwork Facilities 1.3.6.1.2.1.10.5.9.1.30 | OCTET STRING (SIZE (0..108)) | read- write | Called network facilities. |

In fact, there is a Call Parameter variable that counts the current number of references to its entry from other tables. Why? Well, it is not a good idea to delete a Call Parameter entry that is actively in use! An entry cannot be changed or deleted unless the reference count is 0.

## 25.18.2    Types of Call Parameter Entries

Each entry lists a set of parameters that can be used when placing a call or when answering a call. There are entries showing parameters in use on a live circuit, or parameters that have recently been used for a circuit. Different entries can be dedicated to specialized uses:

- An entry can provide *default* settings for outgoing Virtual Calls. These defaults might apply to one PLE or to more than one PLE.
- Another entry might be used to hold defaults for incoming Virtual Calls.
- Entries can be recorded that hold customized parameters, and selected for appropriate outgoing or incoming Virtual Calls.

### 25.18.3  Facilities

In the introduction to this chapter, we described some facilities such as Closed User Groups and Reverse Charging. There are lots of facilities in the Call Parameter Table. Some that have not yet been discussed include:

- *Bilateral Closed User Group.*  A Closed User Group made up of two DTEs.
- *Fast Select.*  Enables a small amount of data to be enclosed in call setup messages. A restricted Fast Select can support a brief ping-pong message exchange: a Connect Request containing a short message can be answered by a Clear (terminate) Request that contains a short message. The enumerated values in the table are:
  1. default (the PLE default)
  2. notSpecified
  3. fastSelect
  4. restrictedFastResponse
  5. noFastSelect
  6. noRestrictedFastResponse
- *Throughput Class.*  A service provider may allow a DTE to negotiate separate incoming and outgoing throughput classes with the remote DTE by means of fields in the call request packet. The call DTE picks the classes that will be used for the call and writes them into fields in the call accepted packet. The called DTE *must* choose values that are less than or equal to what the partner requested. Each value has a name consisting of "tc" for "throughput class" followed by bits per second. The enumerated values are:
  1. tcReserved1
  2. tcReserved2
  3. tc75
  4. tc150

5. tc300

6. tc600

7. tc1200

8. tc2400

9. tc4800

10. tc9600

11. tc19200

12. tc48000

13. tc64000

14. tcReserved14

15. tcReserved15

16. tcReserved0

17. tcNone

18. tcDefault

- *Network User Identification (NUI).* Used somewhat like a computer account identifier, the NUI identifies a DTE to the service provider.

- *RPOA Selection.* Long-distance data calls may pass through a chain of service providers in several countries. This facility allows a specific path to be selected through a list of administrations.

- *Expedited Data.* Ability to send an out-of-band message. An expedited data message must be confirmed by the remote partner before another can be sent.

### 25.18.4  Explaining Defaults

There are two different uses of the term *default* in this table. When an entry is created, if some of the variables in the entry have not been *set,* then their values will take on defaults that are defined in the OBJECT TYPE macro.

For example, the *x25CallParmAcceptReverseCharging* variable has an enumerated value. If no value has been *set,* then we use the DEFVAL for this OBJECT TYPE, which is "refuse the call!"

But if this value has been *set* to 1 (which is listed as "default"), it means "look up the value in the default entry for this PLE." OK?

### 25.19  THE X.25 PROTOCOL VERSION SUBTREE

The *x25ProtocolVersion* subtree (1.3.6.1.2.1.10.5.10) has been defined under *x25* to hold OBJECT IDENTIFIERs that identify different versions of the X.25 packet layer protocol. These include the following:

| | |
|---|---|
| Protocol Versions iso.org.dod.internet.mgmt.mib-2. transmission.x25.x25ProtocolVersion 1.3.6.1.2.1.10.5.10 | |
| OBJECT IDENTIFIER | Description |
| x25protocolCcittV1976 1.3.6.1.2.1.10.5.10.1 | CCITT 1976 version |
| x25protocolCcittV1980 1.3.6.1.2.1.10.5.10.2 | CCITT 1980 version |
| x25protocolCcittV1984 1.3.6.1.2.1.10.5.10.3 | CCITT 1984 version |
| x25protocolCcittV1988 1.3.6.1.2.1.10.5.10.4 | CCITT 1988 version |
| x25protocolIso8208V1987 1.3.6.1.2.1.10.5.10.5 | 1987 version of ISO 8208 |
| x25protocolIso8208V1989 1.3.6.1.2.1.10.5.10.6 | 1989 version of ISO 8208 |

## 25.20   X.25 TRAP TYPES

RFC 1382 defines two traps that are specific to X.25. The ENTER-PRISE field in the trap contains the OBJECT IDENTIFIER for the *x25* subtree, 1.3.6.1.2.1.10.5. The GENERIC TRAP field will contain 6. The SPECIFIC TRAP field will have the values 1 and 2, respectively. Variables will be included in the trap messages, as shown in Table 25.9 which describes the traps.

## 25.21   RECOMMENDED READING

At the time of writing, RFC 1381 defined the *SNMP MIB Extension for LAPB,* and RFC 1382 held the *SNMP MIB Extension for the X.25 Packet Layer.* CCITT Recommendations defining and refining X.25 were published in 1976, 1980, 1984, and 1988.

Standards providing the ISO view of X.25 include 8885 for the XID frame, 7776 for LAPB-compatible DTE data link procedures, and 8208 for the DTE packet layer protocol.

**TABLE 25.9    X.25 Traps**

| Name | Specific trap | Enclosed variables | Description |
|---|---|---|---|
| x25 Restart | 1 | x25OperIndex | The agent reports that an X.25 PLE has sent or received a restart packet. The agent that sends this trap should not send a linkdown or linkup trap. |
| x25 Reset | 2 | x25CircuitIndex x25CircuitChannel | The PLE has sent or received a reset. |

# 26

# Frame Relay and SMDS Interfaces

## 26.1 INTRODUCTION TO FRAME RELAY

For years, X.25 provided the standard interface joining a computer, router, or communications controller and a packet switching network. A new, simpler packet switching technology, *frame relay,* emerged in 1990. Like X.25, a single interface is used to access multiple destinations. Like X.25, frame relay sites exchange information across *virtual circuits,* as shown in Figure 26.1. Unlike X.25, frame relay operates at the physical and data link layers only, and offers a simple, best-effort frame delivery service.

The technology was originally targeted at access capacities ranging from 64,000 bits per second up to the T1 speed, 1.544 megabits per second (T1).* Some implementations now support up to T3 access speeds of roughly 45 megabits per second.

The frame relay technology was rushed into the marketplace at top speed, before stable standards were available. Vendors built switches, and service providers enrolled customers. This has resulted in the use of several different frame formats and in two different sets of standards that allow a user site to poll the service provider's network for performance and error statistics.

## 26.2 FRAME RELAY TECHNOLOGY AND CONCEPTS

Several service providers† offer frame relay connectivity. Alternatively, instead of using a service provider, an organization might buy its own frame relay switches and set up a private packet switching network.

---

* Frame relay equipment also can operate at the European E1 rate.

† For example, WilTel, AT&T, Sprint, CompuServe, and MCI.

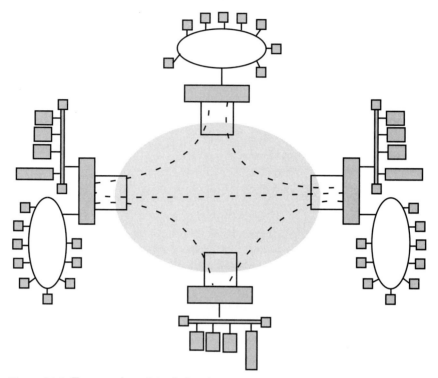

**Figure 26.1**   Frame relay virtual circuits.

### 26.2.1   Physical Interfaces

There are several different physical interfaces in use. Sites usually connect to a service provider via a CSU/DSU that provides T1 or fractional T1 access. Some services offer T3 or fractional T3 rates.

Routers and bridges usually are connected to private on-site frame relay switches via a standard V.35 interface.

### 26.2.2   Virtual Circuits

Typically, a set of *Permanent Virtual Circuits* (PVCs) are configured connecting a frame relay user's site to selected remote sites. What is *permanent* about a PVC is that it is contracted for and configured ahead of time. A particular PVC can crash and recover, or can be terminated and restored administratively. But when a PVC comes up, it always links the same pair of sites.

In Figure 26.2, site A is connected to sites B, C, and D by means of virtual circuits. Outgoing frames from site A to *anywhere* are multiplexed down a point-to-point link joining site A to the service provider's network. Similarly, incoming frames are passed to site A across the point-to-point link.

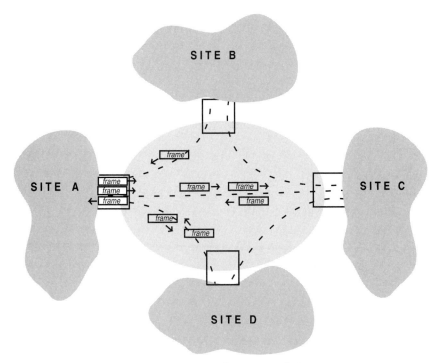

**Figure 26.2** Frames transmitted to and from several sites.

Some service providers are starting to offer *Switched Virtual Circuits* (SVCs) which allow calls to be set up on demand.

## 26.3   THE DATA LINK CONNECTION IDENTIFIER (DLCI)

Each outgoing and incoming frame contains a number that identifies its virtual circuit. This number is called the *Data Link Connection Identifier* (DLCI). The DLCI numbers have *local significance*—this means that the virtual circuit that is identified by number 37 at site A might appear as circuit number 17 at site C.* Once a frame is inside a provider's network, the network can use any method it likes to identify real message sources and destinations. But it is the network's job to fill in a DLCI that means something to site A before passing the frame down the link to site A. Figure 26.3 shows how local DLCIs might be assigned to the virtual circuits that join site A to sites B, C, and D.

---

* This is the normal case, but some implementations are configured so that the DLCIs at the two ends match.

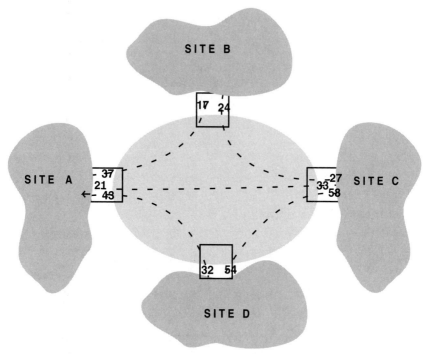

**Figure 26.3** Assignment of DLCIs.

## 26.4  FRAME FORMATS

There are several different formats for the frame relay header that have been in use, each with a different size for the DLCI: 11- and 13-bit sizes have been superseded; 10-, 16-, and 23-bit sizes are valid. The most popular format is the one shown in Figure 26.4 which has a 10-bit DLCI. This format provides a range of virtual circuit numbers from 0 to 1023. However, 0 is reserved for call control signaling, 1023 is reserved for management messages, and currently a few other numbers are reserved for future special assignments.*

There are several other bits in the frame header intended to serve a useful purpose:

- *Discard Eligibility (DE).*   When congested, the network will discard some frames. Frames with DE = 1 will be discarded in preference to those with DE = 0.

---

* Currently 1–15 and 1008–1022 are reserved.

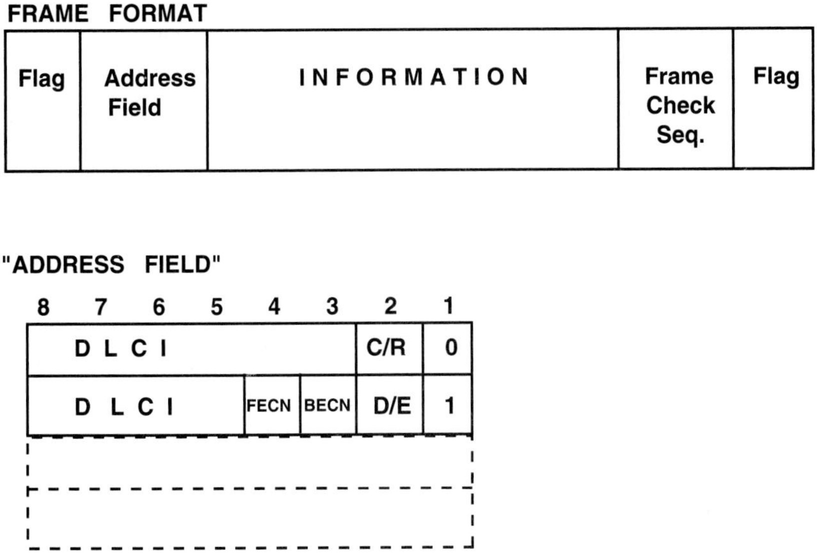

## FRAME  FORMAT

| Flag | Address Field | I N F O R M A T I O N | Frame Check Seq. | Flag |
|------|---------------|----------------------|------------------|------|

## "ADDRESS  FIELD"

| 8 | 7 | 6 | 5 | 4 | 3 | 2 | 1 |
|---|---|---|---|---|---|---|---|
| | D L C I | | | | | C/R | 0 |
| | D L C I | | | FECN | BECN | D/E | 1 |

**Figure 26.4**  Frame formats.

- *Forward Explicit Congestion Notification (FECN).*   When set to 1, it tells the receiver that there is congestion along the virtual circuit *to* the receiver.

- *Backward Explicit Congestion Notification (BECN).*   When set to 1, it tells the receiver that there is congestion along the virtual circuit *from* the receiver.

- *Extended Address (EA).*   A mechanism for extending the DLCI size. EA = 0 means "keep on going for another byte." Standards groups have, in fact, proposed 3- and 4-byte formats, but the 2-byte format is the one currently in most common use.

- *Command/Response (C/R).*   Has no function at present.

The Frame Check Sequence (FCS) at the end of the frame provides the usual error-detection function. If the recalculated value at the destination does not agree with the number in the FCS field, then the frame is discarded.

## 26.5   MEASURING INFORMATION RATES

Typically, a user will connect to a frame relay service provider's network by means of a leased line. Often a T1 line is used. However, the user may not want to pay for full T1 capacity, but may need some fraction of this bandwidth in order to support its virtual circuits.

What is a fair way to contract and pay for bandwidth? I might contract for, say, a 256 kilobit per second virtual circuit. The term *Committed Information Rate* (CIR) is used somewhat differently by the various service providers, but usually means an amount of bandwidth, such as 256 kilobits per second, that should be available to the user's virtual circuit.

Data traffic is bursty. As shown in Figure 26.5, the traffic rate will oscillate around an average *circuit throughput* rate.

The most sensible way to deal with this situation is to measure throughput by counting the total number of bits transmitted during a *measurement interval*. A frame relay interface allows a device to transmit at levels above and below an average rate, as long as the *total* for the interval stays within a bound called the *committed burst*. Some services even allow the transmission of a short *excess information burst* that exceeds the quota for the interval, as shown in Figure 26.5. However, the service does not guarantee to deliver all of it!

### 26.5.1   Frame Virtual Circuit Throughput Rate

The user and service provider agree to a set of specific information rates for the user's virtual circuits. The measurement that is used in the MIB circuit table is:

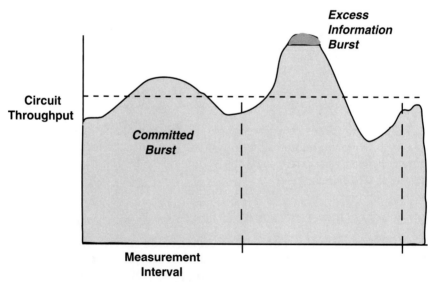

**Figure 26.5**  Traffic measurements for bursty data.

- *frCircuitThroughput.* The service provider guarantees that over a preset measurement interval, *on average,* this number of bits per second can be transmitted.

### 26.5.2  Circuit Committed Burst for an Interval

A related measurement, the *frCircuitCommittedBurst* is the maximum number of bits that the network agrees to transfer, under normal conditions, during an *entire* measurement interval. Simple arithmetic shows that:

Measurement interval = frCircuitCommittedBurst/frCircuitThroughput

### 26.5.3  Sending Excess Data

The user's pipeline to the network may have a greater capacity than the contracted rate. By agreement, the service provider might allow the user to send a burst of data and exceed the normal amount for an interval.

The *Excess Information Burst Size* is the maximum amount of excess data that the network will attempt to deliver over the measurement interval.* One way to handle excess data is to turn on the Discard Eligibility, giving this traffic a lower priority than normal traffic.

## 26.6  MANAGING THE LINK

A switch and a frame format are not all that it takes to bring packet switched virtual circuits into an enterprise network. Network managers need to control and monitor their circuits.

In 1990, since standards bodies had not yet addressed the management problem and vendors were eager to bring products to market, vendors took matters into their own hands. Digital Equipment Corporation, Northern Telecom, StrataCom, and Cisco together designed the *Local Management Interface* (LMI), which was accepted by an industry consortium called the Frame Relay Forum.

Eventually, ANSI came up with management specifications that carry out similar functions—but not in an interoperable way. The result is that most products support both and let the user choose which one to use. The management interface will be discussed further in Section 26.8.

---

* This sometimes is speed of the line that connects the user's premise equipment to the service network, e.g., T1 rate.

## 26.7  THE FRAME RELAY MIB

The sections that follow describe the frame relay MIB. At the time of writing, the MIB was defined in RFC 1315. There are three groups in the MIB:

- The Data Link Connection Management Table: information about the user-site-to-network-management interface.
- The Circuit Table: descriptions of the virtual circuits.
- The Error Table: information about the most recent error at each interface.

A couple of textual conventions are used to make the MIB more readable:

- *Index.*  An INTEGER that represents an interface number.
- *DLCI.*  An INTEGER that, of course, represents a Data Link Connection Identifier.

## 26.8  MANAGEMENT INTERFACES

A management interface provides a user's device with information about the virtual circuits at the user's frame relay interface.

The Local Management Interface (LMI) version from the Frame Relay Forum originally was designed to manage Permanent Virtual Circuits. (Its use was later extended to setting up Switched Virtual Calls.) The LMI uses the virtual circuit with DLCI 1023 to exchange management messages.

ANSI standards cover both permanent and switched virtual circuits, and management details differ depending on which type of circuits need to be managed. ANSI T1.617 Annex D discusses permanent virtual circuits, while ANSI T1.617 Annex B deals with switched virtual circuits.

Similar management mechanisms are used in all of the standards, and the MIB is able to accommodate all of them.

## 26.9  DATA LINK CONNECTION MANAGEMENT

What happens on a management circuit? At regular intervals the user device polls the network by sending a *keepalive status inquiry,* and the network responds. Periodically, instead of sending a keepalive, the user device requests a *full status report.* The status report lists all existing virtual circuits and indicates:

- Whether this is a new circuit that just was added
- Whether this circuit is currently active

The configuration parameters in Table 26.1 include the base polling interval and the number of intervals between status requests. If no answer is received to a specified number of polls during a configured time period, the interface is declared down.

Other table parameters indicate the maximum number of virtual circuits that can be opened and whether multicasting is supported. Multicasting can be quite useful. For example, a multicast to all circuit partners asking for their IP addresses can be used to build an address resolution table.

## 26.10   THE FRAME RELAY CIRCUIT TABLE

One frame relay interface can support multiple virtual circuits, each identified by a DLCI. A device might support several frame relay interfaces. Table 26.2, the Circuit Table, contains an entry for each interface/DLCI combination—that is, there is an entry for each circuit.

An entry records the Circuit Throughput, Committed Burst, and Excess Burst. It also contains counts of incoming and outgoing traffic, and indicates the frequency of incoming and outgoing congestion for each circuit. The entry keeps track of some circuit history, recording the creation time and the time since the last change of state. State changes include creation of a circuit and changes between active and inactive status.

The statistical counts for a virtual circuit are measured from the time that the virtual circuit was created.

## 26.11   THE FRAME RELAY ERROR TABLE

Table 26.3, the Frame Relay Error Table, only keeps track of the most recent error for each *interface* (not for each circuit). Each error is associated with receipt of a bad data frame or a bad management frame, and part of the improper frame is stored in a table variable, along with the value of *sysUpTime* at which the error was detected.

## 26.12   FRAME RELAY TRAP

A single enterprise-specific trap is defined for Frame Relay. The *status change trap* signals that a virtual circuit has been created or invalidated, or that a circuit's state has switched between active and inactive.

When a trap message is sent, it identifies the circuit by carrying variables *frCircuitIfIndex* and *frCircuitDlci*. The state is indicated by

**TABLE 26.1** **Data Link Connection Management Interface**

iso.org.dod.internet.mgmt.mib-2.
transmission.frame-relay.frDlcmiTable.frDlcmiEntry
1.3.6.1.2.1.10.32.1.1

| OBJECT IDENTIFIER | Syntax | Access | Description |
|---|---|---|---|
| frDlcmiIfIndex<br>1.3.6.1.2.1.10.32.1.1<br>▶ **Index** | Index | read-only | The *ifIndex* for this entry. |
| frDlcmiState<br>1.3.6.1.2.1.10.32.1.2 | INTEGER<br>noLmiConfigured(1)<br>lmiRev1(2),<br>ansiT1-617-D(3),<br>ansiT1-617-B(4) | read-write | The Data Link Connection Management scheme that is active at this interface (and, by implication, which circuit is used for management). |
| frDlcmiAddress<br>1.3.6.1.2.1.10.32.1.3 | INTEGER<br>q921(1),<br>q922March90(2),<br>q922November90(3),<br>q922(4) | read-write | Address format used.<br>(1) 13-bit DLCI<br>(2) 11-bit DLCI<br>(3) 10-bit DLCI<br>(4) Final Standard |
| frDlcmiAddress<br>Len<br>1.3.6.1.2.1.10.32.1.4 | INTEGER<br>two-octets (2),<br>three-octets (3),<br>four-octets (4) | read-write | Address length in octets. 2-octet form usually picked. For Q922 format, length includes both address and control portions. |
| frDlcmiPolling<br>Interval<br>1.3.6.1.2.1.10.32.1.5 | INTEGER<br>(5..30) | read-write | Number of seconds between status enquiry messages. (Typically 5–30 seconds.) |
| frDlcmiFull<br>EnquiryInterval<br>1.3.6.1.2.1.10.32.1.6 | INTEGER<br>(1..255) | read-write | Number of status enquiry intervals before issuance of a full status enquiry message. (Default 6.) |
| frDlcmiError<br>Threshold<br>1.3.6.1.2.1.10.32.1.7 | INTEGER<br>(1..10) | read-write | Maximum number of unanswered Status Enquiries allowed (during a time period specified in next variable) before declaring the interface down. |

TABLE 26.1    Data Link Connection Management Interface (*Continued*)

iso.org.dod.internet.mgmt.mib-2.
transmission.frame-relay.frDlcmiTable.frDlcmiEntry
1.3.6.1.2.1.10.32.1.1

| OBJECT IDENTIFIER | Syntax | Access | Description |
|---|---|---|---|
| frDlcmi MonitoredEvents 1.3.6.1.2.1.10.32.1.8 | INTEGER (1..10) | read-write | Number of intervals making up the period for counting the number of unanswered status messages. If the *frDlcmiError-Threshold* is exceeded, the interface is assumed to be down. |
| frDlcmiMax SupportedVCs 1.3.6.1.2.1.10.32.1.9 | INTEGER | read-write | Maximum number of virtual circuits allowed for this interface. |
| frDlcmiMulticast 1.3.6.1.2.1.10.32.1.10 | INTEGER nonBroadcast(1), broadcast(2) | read-write | Indicates whether the interface uses a multicast service. |

TABLE 26.2    The Frame Relay Circuit Table

iso.org.dod.internet.mgmt.mib-2.
transmission.frame-relay.frCircuitTable.frCircuitEntry
1.3.6.1.2.1.10.32.2.1

| OBJECT IDENTIFIER | Syntax | Access | Description |
|---|---|---|---|
| frCircuitIfIndex 1.3.6.1.2.1.10.32.2.1.1 ▶ **Index** | Index | read-only | The *ifIndex* for this interface. |
| frCircuitDlci 1.3.6.1.2.1.10.32.2.1.2 ▶ **Index** | DLCI | read-only | Data Link Connection Identifier (DLCI) for this virtual circuit. |
| frCircuitState 1.3.6.1.2.1.10.32.2.1.3 | INTEGER invalid(1), active(2),[default] inactive(3) | read-write | Desired operational state of this circuit. Setting an entry to invalid should cause the circuit to be deleted. |
| frCircuitReceived FECNs 1.3.6.1.2.1.10.32.2.1.4 | Counter | read-only | Number of received frames indicating forward congestion. |
| frCircuitReceived BECNs 1.3.6.1.2.1.10.32.2.1.5 | Counter | read-only | Number of received frames indicating backward congestion. |

**TABLE 26.2   The Frame Relay Circuit Table (*Continued*)**

iso.org.dod.internet.mgmt.mib-2.
transmission.frame-relay.frCircuitTable.frCircuitEntry
1.3.6.1.2.1.10.32.2.1

| OBJECT IDENTIFIER | Syntax | Access | Description |
|---|---|---|---|
| frCircuitSent Frames 1.3.6.1.2.1.10.32.2.1.6 | Counter | read-only | Number of frames sent on this virtual circuit. |
| frCircuitSent Octets 1.3.6.1.2.1.10.32.2.1.7 | Counter | read-only | Number of octets sent on this virtual circuit. |
| frCircuitReceived Frames 1.3.6.1.2.1.10.32.2.1.8 | Counter | read-only | Number of frames received on this virtual circuit. |
| frCircuitReceived Octets 1.3.6.1.2.1.10.32.2.1.9 | Counter | read-only | Number of octets received on this virtual circuit. |
| frCircuitCreation Time 1.3.6.1.2.1.10.32.2.1.10 | TimeTicks | read-only | Value of *sysUpTime* when the virtual circuit was created. |
| frCircuitLastTime Change 1.3.6.1.2.1.10.32.2.1.11 | TimeTicks | read-only | Value of *sysUpTime* when the state of the virtual circuit last changed. |
| frCircuitCommitted Burst 1.3.6.1.2.1.10.32.2.1.12 | INTEGER | read-write | Maximum bits of data that the network agrees to transfer under normal conditions, during the measurement interval. |
| frCircuitExcess Burst 1.3.6.1.2.1.10.32.2.1.13 | INTEGER | read-write | Maximum uncommitted bits of data that the network will attempt to transfer under normal conditions, during the measurement interval. |
| frCircuit Throughput 1.3.6.1.2.1.10.32.2.1.14 | INTEGER | read-write | Average number of Information Field bits transferred per second across a user/network interface in one direction, measured over the measurement interval. |

**TABLE 26.3    The Frame Relay Error Table**

iso.org.dod.internet.mgmt.mib-2.
transmission.frame-relay.frErrTable.frErrEntry
1.3.6.1.2.1.10.32.3.1

| OBJECT IDENTIFIER | Syntax | Access | Description |
|---|---|---|---|
| frErrIfIndex<br>1.3.6.1.2.1.10.32.3.1.1<br>► **Index** | Index | read-only | The *ifIndex* for this entry. |
| frErrType<br>1.3.6.1.2.1.10.32.3.1.2 | INTEGER<br>unknown Error(1),<br>receiveShort(2),<br>receiveLong(3),<br>illegalDLCI(4),<br>unknownDLCI(5),<br>dlcmiProtoErr(6),<br>dlcmiUnknownIE(7),<br>dlcmiSequenceErr(8),<br>dlcmiUnknownRpt(9),<br>noErrorSinceReset(10) | read-only | Type of error last seen on this interface. |
| frErrData<br>1.3.6.1.2.1.10.32.3.1.3 | OCTET STRING | read-only | Octet string containing as much of the error frame as possible. At a minimum, it must contain the address or as much of it as was delivered. |
| frErrTime<br>1.3.6.1.2.1.10.32.3.1.4 | TimeTicks | read-only | Value of *sysUpTime* when the error was detected. |

including variable *frCircuitState*. Table 26.4 shows the elements of the formal trap definition.

## 26.13    FRAME RELAY GLOBAL VARIABLES

Currently, there is only one global variable, as displayed in Table 26.5. By setting this variable, a manager can enable or disable sending the DLCI status change trap.

## 26.14    INTRODUCTION TO SMDS

Bellcore, the research facility that serves the United States Regional Bell Operating Companies, recently completed several years of design and planning for a new, high-speed packet switching service, Switched Multimegabit Data Service (SMDS). SMDS offers access at ranges from DS1 (1.544 megabits per second) to DS3 (44.736 megabits per second), and in the future will offer even higher capacities.

**TABLE 26.4    The Frame Relay DLCI Status Change Trap**

| | | Enterprise<br>iso.org.dod.internet.mgmt.mib-2.transmission.frame-relay<br>1.3.6.1.2.1.10.32 | |
|---|---|---|---|
| Name | Specific trap | Variables | Description |
| frDLCI<br>Status<br>Change | 1 | frCircuitIfIndex,<br>frCircuitDlci,<br>frCircuitState | Indicates that the virtual<br>circuit has changed state. It<br>has either been created or<br>invalidated, or has toggled<br>between the active and<br>inactive states. |

**TABLE 26.5    Enable or Disable Sending the Status Change Trap**

| | | iso.org.dod.internet.mgmt.mib-2.<br>transmission.frame-relay.frame-relay-globals<br>1.3.6.1.2.1.10.32.4 | |
|---|---|---|---|
| OBJECT IDENTIFIER | Syntax | Access | Description |
| frTrapState<br>1.3.6.1.2.1.10.32.4.1 | INTEGER<br>enabled(1),<br>disabled(2) | read-<br>write | Indicates whether the<br>system will produce the<br>*frDLCIStatusChange* trap. |

However, it should be noted that SMDS has a rather high level of overhead—more than 20 percent—so actual payloads are 1.2 and 34 megabits per second.

SMDS has been carefully planned as a wide area service offering, with attention to enabling regional services to interwork and offer nationwide access.

The *SMDS Interface Protocol* (SIP) is *not* based on virtual circuits. It can support sessions, deliver isolated datagrams, and support multicasting. A use that will be popular is to glue an enterprise IP network together with a virtual subnetwork, as shown in Figure 26.6.

Routers connect the network facilities at each site to an SMDS network. Each router is assigned an address on a single IP subnet. SMDS multicasting to group addresses is used to support ARP translation between IP addresses and SMDS addresses.

Note that SMDS is capable of running at LAN-level speeds, so that it has powerful potential as a network integrator.

Like the telephone system and X.25, SMDS has a global numbering scheme, which conforms to CCITT E.164 format. Thus, SMDS is adaptable to both private and public networking.

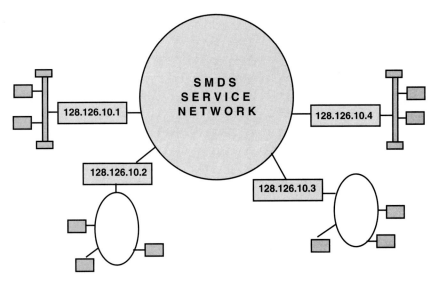

**Figure 26.6**  A virtual IP subnet.

## 26.15   THE SUBSCRIBER NETWORK INTERFACE (SNI)

There are several acceptable interfaces to an SMDS network. The simplest for a user is to simply connect a Point-to-Point (PPP) link to a router belonging to a service provider, and let the service provider perform the conversions necessary to conform to the *Subscriber Network Interface* (SNI) protocols. The official Subscriber Network Interface is made up of several components.

Before data is passed to an SMDS service provider it first is formatted into *frames,* and then these frames are repackaged as a sequence of 53 octet *cells.* Finally, the cells are sent across a T1 or T3 line. (A future interface to SONET is planned.)

Adapting cells to a T1 or T3 is called the *Physical Layer Convergence Procedure* (PLCP). Special DSUs must be used to transmit L2_PDU cells across T1 or T3 lines.

Figure 26.7 shows the many sublevels of the *SMDS Interface Protocol* (SIP). The frames are called Level 3 Protocol Data Units or L3_PDUs, and consist of a 36-octet header, up to 9188 octets of information, and 4 or more octets of trailer. An L3_PDU is *not* an OSI Layer 3 PDU. It is a Data Link layer frame.

The cells are called Level 2 Protocol Data Units or L2_PDUs, and consist of 7 octets of header, 44 octets of information, and a 2-octet trailer. Cell relay turns out to be very flexible and capable of high speeds. How-

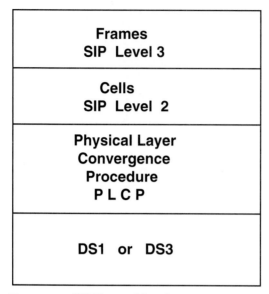

**Figure 26.7**  SIP Protocol Levels.

ever, it is the cell headers and trailers that impose most of the overhead burden. Figure 26.8 sketches the L3_PDU and L2_PDU formats.

The MAC protocol used at the SNI is based on the IEEE 802.6 Distributed Queue Dual Bus (DQDB) access protocol. This protocol would allow several routers at a customer site to share a single SNI interface. For some sites, this could provide a performance benefit.

## F R A M E

| . . . Destination  Source  . . . Address  Address | Information | Trailer |
|---|---|---|
| 36 octets | Up to 9188 octets | 4 octets |

| Cell | Cell | Cell | . . . |

## C E L L

| Header | Segmentation  Unit | Trailer |
|---|---|---|
| 7 octets | 44 octets | 2 octets |

**Figure 26.8**  Level 2 and Level 3 PDUs.

SMDS is the first *service* based on cell relay technology. The SMDS protocols operate at MAC and physical layers. SMDS defines a quite large MAC message—the largest information payload is 9188 bytes, large enough to encapsulate and bridge 802.3, 802.5, or FDDI frames.

Formally, a subscriber accesses an SMDS network across a *Subscriber Network Interface* (SNI). The various protocol levels define exactly how subscriber equipment must behave and how data must be formatted at the interface.

*SIP Level 3* defines the format and protocol actions for the large Level 3 messages. *SIP Level 2* relates to the 53 octet cells. The *Physical Layer Convergence Procedure* (PLCP) translates between *SIP Level 2* and the DS1 or DS3 bit stream.

## 26.16   SMDS ADDRESSES

SMDS MAC addresses are 8 octets long. The first 4 bits can have values:

| | |
|---|---|
| 1100 | An individual address |
| 1110 | A group address |

The next 4 bits are set to 0001. The next 40 bits contain the 10 binary-coded decimal digits that identify the interface. The last 16 bits are set to 1.

## 26.17   THE SIP LEVEL 3 TABLE

Table 26.6, the SIP Level 3 Table, contains traffic and error counts for each local interface. A SIP interface is called a *port*. Each SIP port corresponds to an entry in the *interfaces* table.

## 26.18   THE SIP LEVEL 2 GROUP

Table 26.7, the SIP Level 2 Table, contains Level 2 traffic and error counts. A Level 3 frame is segmented into a sequence of Level 2 cells. Cells are marked as Beginning of Message (BOM), MIDs, and End of Message (EOM).

## 26.19   THE SIP PLCP GROUP

SIP has DS1 and DS3 physical interfaces. The SIP Physical Layer Convergence Procedure performs the adaptation to T1 or T3 transmission.

Separate tables are defined for DS1 and DS3 interfaces. However, the variables in the DS3 PLCP Table have the same definitions as those in Table 26.8, the SIP DS1 PLCP Table. See Chapters 23 and 24 for definitions of DS1 and DS3 errors and alarms.

**TABLE 26.6　The SIP Level 3 Table**

iso.org.dod.internet.mgmt.mib-2.
transmission.sip.sipL3Table.sipL3Entry
1.3.6.1.2.1.10.31.1.1

| OBJECT IDENTIFIER | Syntax | Access | Description |
|---|---|---|---|
| sipL3Index<br>1.3.6.1.2.1.10.31.1.1.1<br>► **Index** | INTEGER<br>(1..65535) | read-only | The *ifIndex* of this SIP port. |
| sipL3Received<br>IndividualDAs<br>1.3.6.1.2.1.10.31.1.1.2 | Counter | read-only | Total number of individually addressed unerrored SIP Level 3 PDUs received from the remote system across the Subscriber Network Interface (SNI). |
| sipL3Received<br>GAs<br>1.3.6.1.2.1.10.31.1.1.3 | Counter | read-only | Total number of group addressed unerrored SIP Level 3 PDUs received from the remote system across the SNI. |
| sipL3Unrecognized<br>IndividualDAs<br>1.3.6.1.2.1.10.31.1.1.4 | Counter | read-only | Number of SIP Level 3 PDUs received from the remote system with invalid or unknown individual destination addresses. |
| sipL3Unrecognized<br>GAs<br>1.3.6.1.2.1.10.31.1.1.5 | Counter | read-only | Number of SIP Level 3 PDUs received from the remote system with invalid or unknown group addresses. |
| sipL3Sent<br>IndividualDAs<br>1.3.6.1.2.1.10.31.1.1.6 | Counter | read-only | Number of individually addressed SIP Level 3 PDUs transmitted by this system across the SNI. |
| sipL3SentGAs<br>1.3.6.1.2.1.10.31.1.1.7 | Counter | read-only | Number of group addressed SIP Level 3 PDUs transmitted by this system across the SNI. |
| sipL3Errors<br>1.3.6.1.2.1.10.31.1.1.8 | Counter | read-only | Total number of individual or group SIP Level 3 PDUs received from the remote system that were discarded because of errors (including protocol processing and bit errors but excluding addressing-related errors). |
| sipL3InvalidSMDS<br>AddressTypes<br>1.3.6.1.2.1.10.31.1.1.9 | Counter | read-only | Number of SIP Level 3 PDUs received from the remote system whose source or Destination addresses did not start with 1100 or 1110, or had a Source Address starting with 1110. |
| sipL3Version<br>Support<br>1.3.6.1.2.1.10.31.1.1.10 | INTEGER<br>(1..65535) | read-only | An integer computed from a bit map indicating the supported versions of SIP. Bit $n = 1$ means version $n$ is supported. |

**TABLE 26.7   The SIP Level 2 Table**

iso.org.dod.internet.mgmt.mib-2.
transmission.sip.sipL2Table.sipL2Entry
1.3.6.1.2.1.10.31.2.1

| OBJECT IDENTIFIER | Syntax | Access | Description |
|---|---|---|---|
| sipL2Index<br>1.3.6.1.2.1.10.31.2.1.1<br>▶ Index | INTEGER | read-only | The *ifIndex* of this SIP port. |
| sipL2Received<br>Counts<br>1.3.6.1.2.1.10.31.2.1.2 | Counter | read-only | Number of unerrored SIP Level 2 PDUs received from the remote system across the SNI. |
| sipL2SentCounts<br>1.3.6.1.2.1.10.31.2.1.3 | Counter | read-only | Number of SIP Level 2 PDUs that have been sent by this system across the SNI. |
| sipL2HcsOrCRC<br>Errors<br>1.3.6.1.2.1.10.31.2.1.4 | Counter | read-only | Number of received SIP Level 2 PDUs that were discovered to have either a Header Check Sequence error or a Payload CRC violation. |
| sipL2Payload<br>LengthErrors<br>1.3.6.1.2.1.10.31.2.1.5 | Counter | read-only | Number of received SIP Level 2 PDUs that had invalid Payload Lengths. |
| sipL2Sequence<br>NumberErrors<br>1.3.6.1.2.1.10.31.2.1.6 | Counter | read-only | Number of received SIP Level 2 PDUs that had a sequence number within the L2PDU not equal to the expected sequence number of the SMDS SS receive process. |
| sipL2MidCurrently<br>ActiveErrors<br>1.3.6.1.2.1.10.31.2.1.7 | Counter | read-only | Number of received SIP Level 2 PDUs that were Beginnings of Message when an active receive process had already started. |
| sipL2BomOrSSMs<br>MIDErrors<br>1.3.6.1.2.1.10.31.2.1.8 | Counter | read-only | Number of received SIP Level 2 PDUs that are SSMs with a MID not equal to zero or are BOMs with MIDs equal to zero. |
| sipL2Eoms<br>MIDErrors<br>1.3.6.1.2.1.10.31.2.1.9 | Counter | read-only | Number of received SIP Level 2 PDUs that are Ends of Message (EOMs) for which there is no active receive process for the MID. |

## 26.20   OTHER SIP GROUPS

To summarize the remaining SIP MIB data:

- The SIP Applications Group includes the IP over SMDS Table, which translates between SMDS and IP addresses, and indicates the SMDS address (individual or group) to which ARP requests are to be sent.

**TABLE 26.8    The SIP DS1 PLCP Table**

| | | | |
|---|---|---|---|
| iso.org.dod.internet.mgmt.mib-2. transmission.sip.sipPLCP.sipDS1PLCPTable.sipDS1PLCPEntry 1.3.6.1.2.1.10.31.3.1.1 | | | |
| OBJECT IDENTIFIER | Syntax | Access | Description |
| sipDS1PLCPIndex 1.3.6.1.2.1.10.31.3.1.1.1 ▶ **Index** | INTEGER (1..65535) | read-only | The *ifIndex* for the SIP port for this entry. |
| sipDS1PLCPSEFSs 1.3.6.1.2.1.10.31.3.1.1.2 | Counter | read-only | Count of Severely Errored Framing Seconds. |
| sipDS1PLCP AlarmState 1.3.6.1.2.1.10.31.3.1.1.3 | INTEGER | read-only | Indicates if there is an alarm: noAlarm (1), receivedFarEndAlarm (2), incomingLOF (3) |
| sipDS1PLCPUASs 1.3.6.1.2.1.10.31.3.1.1.4 | Counter | read-only | Number of Unavailable Seconds. |

■ The SIP Error Table stores the latest occurrence of various types of SIP L3_PDU errors.

## 26.21   RECOMMENDED READING

At the time of writing, RFC 1315 contained the most current version of the frame relay MIB.

Darren Spohn has a detailed description of Frame Relay technology, operation, and services in his book, *Data Network Design* (McGraw-Hill, 1993). Digital Equipment Corporation, Northern Telecom, Inc., and StrataCom, Inc. produced a brief but clear description of frame relay in their document, *Frame Relay Specification with Extensions.*

ANSI T1.606, *ISDN—Architectural Framework and Service Description for Frame Relaying Bearer Service,* provides a service overview. ANSI T1.617 Annex D, Additional Procedures for PVCs Using Unnumbered Information Frames, describes call control procedures and methods of recovering from loss of PVCs. ANSI T1.617 Annex B describes the use of ISDN mechanisms to set up frame relay calls on demand.

CCITT standard Q.922, ISDN Data Link Layer Specifications for Frame Mode Bearer Services, describes many elements of the frame relay protocol. Q.921 describes a header format that is now obsolete.

RFC 1304 defines MIB objects for the SMDS Interface Protocol. Gary Kessler and David Train's *Metropolitan Area Networks* contains a detailed description of SMDS protocols.

# 27

# Managing Bridges

## 27.1 INTRODUCTION

Local area networks tend to grow, and g r o w, and G R O W! Bridges help LANs to grow gracefully.

For example, an important characteristic of bridges, as shown in Figure 27.1, is that they keep purely local traffic local; only traffic whose source is in one segment and whose destination is in another will cross the bridge. Thus, a bridge can be used to separate a pair of work groups

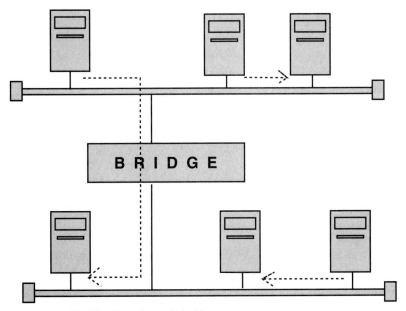

**Figure 27.1** Traffic flow through bridges.

that have an occasional need to exchange data. Installation of the bridge would improve performance for each work group.

Bridges also are used to glue together widely separated LANs. As shown in Figure 27.1, two LANs can be bridged together across a wide area link.

There are devices popularly call *brouters* which bridge some traffic, but route selected protocols (such as IP and DECnet). *The configuration information and statistics in the bridge MIB relate to only the bridged part of a brouter's traffic.* Traffic is sorted out according to protocol. For example, a brouter might route IP and DECnet traffic, and bridge NETBEUI LAN traffic and DEC LAT terminal access traffic.

## 27.2   USE OF FRAME FORMATS FOR BRIDGING

A bridge operates at a low protocol level. A bridge needs to worry about physical interfaces, Media Access Control (MAC) physical addresses, and MAC protocols. A MAC frame header contains the destination and source physical addresses. Recall that MAC physical addresses are administered by the IEEE.

Figure 27.2 shows a frame that is being transmitted between Network Interface Cards. The frame header contains source and destination addresses corresponding to the NIC addresses. A frame trailer contains a Frame Check Sequence (FCS) field, used to check whether a frame has been transmitted without error.

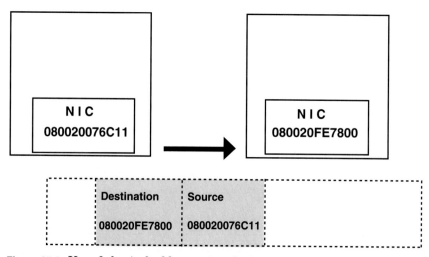

**Figure 27.2** Use of physical addresses in a frame.

Customers can override the manufacturer's addresses on their boards, assigning their own unique addresses. For example, fields in the user-assigned address might identify geographical location, or LAN number and host number. Customer-assigned addresses frequently are used on Token-Ring LANs.

## 27.3   BRIDGE PORTS AND SEGMENTS

The term *port,* rather than *interface,* is used in the bridging world. When connecting to an Ethernet or a Token-Ring, a port corresponds directly to an interface. A frame relay or X.25 interface, which can support several circuits, has a separate *port* for each circuit.

Bridges unite separate LANs into a single LAN. Bridge vendors prefer to say that a bridge joins two or more *segments* of a network together. The first bridges that were marketed joined Ethernets together, and so the terminology was very natural. Today, rings connected by a Token-Ring bridge also are called segments, which is not quite as natural.

By customer demand, bridging was extended across wide area links. A WAN point-to-point or virtual circuit link is called a segment too.

## 27.4   TRANSPARENT BRIDGES

The operation of the early bridges that connected Ethernet LANs together was completely transparent to the hosts on a network, and so they were called *transparent* bridges.

A transparent bridge looks at the destination MAC address in each frame. It checks its *Forwarding Database* to decide whether the frame's destination is local, or if the frame should be transmitted to another segment. A transparent bridge is easy to use, because it can build its Forwarding Table automatically by watching the traffic at each of its ports. Figure 27.3 illustrates a transparent bridge.

If a frame is sent to a destination that the transparent bridge has not yet recorded, the bridge will forward the frame onto all segments except for the one on which it arrived.*

### 27.4.1   Spanning Tree Protocol

As time went by, customers began to build very large bridged Ethernet networks. In some of these networks, failure of a bridge could not be tolerated, and automatic backup facilities were needed. Vendors began

---

* The segments to which the frame will be forwarded can be limited by configuring *filters.* This will be discussed later in the chapter.

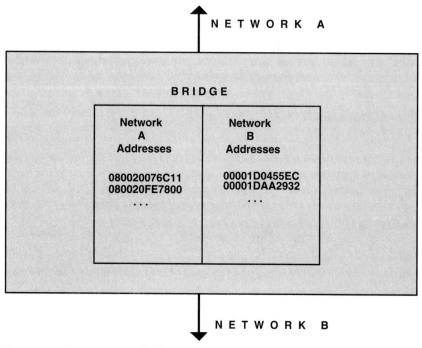

**Figure 27.3** A transparent bridge.

to ship Ethernet bridges that could communicate with one another. The bridges automatically calculated the best topology for the bridged LANs using the *Spanning Tree Protocol* (STP). If a port on some bridge failed, these Spanning Tree bridges could reconfigure the topology and switch traffic over to new paths. Figure 27.4 illustrates a network of bridges that use the Spanning Tree Protocol.

## 27.5   SOURCE ROUTING BRIDGES

IBM introduced a new kind of bridge for its Token-Ring protocol—the *source routing bridge*. Source routing does not just provide backup paths, it offers the luxury of multiple paths that can be used all of the time. The bridges do not have to be intelligent to make it happen. The cleverness is in the Token-Ring Network Interface Cards in each station.

A source station sends a message that finds its way to the destination, and records the path that it follows on the way. The destination sends the message back to the source along the same path. Once the source has discovered a path, each frame sent to the destination contains the path to be traversed. Note that the source plays the most active role. Token-Ring bridges just need to do as they are told! Section 27.15 contains a discussion of source routing.

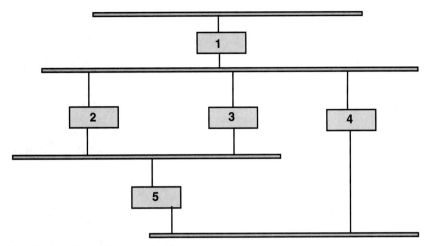

**Figure 27.4**  Spanning tree bridges.

Figure 27.5 illustrates bridges in a Token-Ring network. As originally conceived, a Token-Ring bridge has two ports—that is, it connects to exactly two rings. This makes life simple. Traffic entering one port always goes out the other.*

### 27.5.1  Source Route Transparent Bridge

Eventually, many customers ended up with some segments that were bridged transparently and others that were bridged via source routing. Bridge vendors wanted to provide devices that could do either or both. The ability to handle both kinds of traffic was especially attractive for the purpose of sharing wide area links. *Source route transparent* bridges were introduced to satisfy this desire. Source route transparent bridges can route traffic:

- From a transparent source to a transparent destination
- From a source routing originator to a source routing destination

These bridges connect like to like. Figure 27.6 illustrates source route transparent bridges.

### 27.5.2  Controlling the Flow

As bridges grew bigger and supported several ports, and as bridged networks grew larger and more complex, customers began to feel the

---

* Some products are more complicated, treating one box with a lot of ports as a set of *logical* Token-Ring bridges. Each logical bridge is assigned two ports.

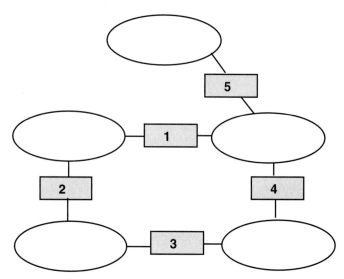

**Figure 27.5** Source routing bridges.

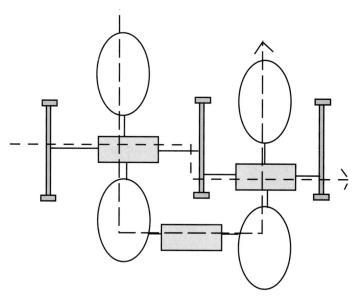

**Figure 27.6** Source route transparent bridges.

need to have greater control over bridged traffic. They wanted to apply *filtering,* turning a bridge into a traffic cop. Filtering allows a customer to say "If a frame has entered at port $A$ and has destination *nnnnnn,* then it may only be sent out through ports $X$ or $Y$." The ability to filter is used to:

- Improve performance by limiting the scope of broadcasts and multi-casts.

- Impose security, limiting which parts of a network users on a LAN segment will be able to reach.

Filtering information must be entered manually, so the price of this extra functionality is some extra up-front work.

## 27.6   THE BRIDGE MIB

Internet MIB documents define MIB variables for all of these bridge types. The Internet MIBs are closely based on the detailed definitions of managed objects specified by the IEEE in standards documents 802.1D and 802.5M.

Of course, a bridge need only support the groups of MIB variables that make sense for the type of bridging that it does. The MIB groups are:

- *The dot1dBase Group.*   Simple configuration and statistical information, required for any bridge.

- *The dot1dStp Group.*   Configuration, status, and statistical data relating to bridges supporting the Spanning Tree Protocol.

- *The dot1dSr Group.*   Configuration, status, and statistical data relating to Token-Ring bridges that rely on source route bridging.

- *The dot1dTp Group.*   Configuration, status, and statistical data relating to transparent bridging. Useful for transparent-only or Source Routing Transparent bridges.

- *The dot1dStatic Group.*   Static filtering information used to limit the forwarding of frames.

## 27.7   TEXTUAL CONVENTIONS
## FOR THE BRIDGE MIB

Recall that textual conventions do not introduce new datatypes, but simply allow meaningful names to be used for existing datatypes within a MIB module.

The bridging modules use the conventions:

- *MacAddress.*   A 6-byte OCTET STRING that holds the physical address of a LAN interface. Since bridges have two or more interfaces, there will be multiple MAC addresses associated with a bridge.

- *BridgeId.*   An 8-byte OCTET STRING, assigned as a bridge identifier for the Spanning Tree Protocol. It consists of:

—2-octet priority number

—6-octet MAC address (one of the MAC addresses assigned to the bridge—usually the one that is numerically the smallest)

- *Timeout.*   An INTEGER value for a Spanning Tree Protocol timer in units of 1/100 seconds.

Many MIB time parameters are represented in units of hundredths of a second. However, in the Spanning Tree Protocol standard (IEEE 802.1D), times are expressed in units of 1/256 seconds! The bridge MIB document contains a set of carefully stated algorithms for converting between 1/100 and 1/256 measurements.

While carefully converting between these different time measurements, keep in mind that the IEEE standard states that the settable granularity for a timer cannot be finer than 1 second.

## 27.8   BASIC BRIDGE INFORMATION

The *dot1dBase* group contains some basic configuration parameters and a table of generic port configuration information. The basic stand-alone configuration parameters in Table 27.1 include a MAC address selected to identify the bridge, the total number of ports, and the bridging protocol supported: transparent-only, source-routing-only, or source-route transparent.

## 27.9   THE GENERIC BRIDGE PORT TABLE

Table 27.2, the Generic Bridge Port Table, provides information relevant to transparent, source-route, *and* source-routing transparent

**TABLE 27.1    Basic Bridge Configuration Information**

| iso.org.dod.internet.mgmt.mib-2.dot1dBridge.dot1dBase 1.3.6.1.2.1.17.1 | | | |
| --- | --- | --- | --- |
| OBJECT IDENTIFIER | Syntax | Access | Description |
| dot1dBase BridgeAddress 1.3.6.1.2.1.17.1.1 | MacAddress | read-only | A MAC address used as an identifier for the bridge. (The numerically smallest MAC address is suggested.) |
| dot1dBase NumPorts 1.3.6.1.2.1.17.1.2 | INTEGER | read-only | Number of ports for this bridge. |
| dot1dBase Type 1.3.6.1.2.1.17.1.3 | INTEGER unknown(1), transparent-only(2), sourceroute-only(3), srt(4) | read-only | Type of bridging that this bridge can do. |

**TABLE 27.2  Generic Bridge Port Table**

| iso.org.dod.internet.mgmt.mib-2.dot1dBridge. dot1dBase.dot1dBasePortTable.dot1dBasePortEntry 1.3.6.1.2.1.17.1.4.1 | | | |
|---|---|---|---|
| OBJECT IDENTIFIER | Syntax | Access | Description |
| dot1dBasePort 1.3.6.1.2.1.17.1.4.1.1 ▶ Index | INTEGER (1..65535) | read-only | Port number for this entry. |
| dot1dBasePort IfIndex 1.3.6.1.2.1.17.1.4.1.2 | INTEGER | read-only | The *ifIndex* corresponding to this port. |
| dot1dBasePort Circuit 1.3.6.1.2.1.17.1.4.1.3 | OBJECT IDENTIFIER | read-only | Needed only when several ports share an interface index—for example, an X.25 interface with several circuits. |
| dot1dBasePort DelayExceeded Discards 1.3.6.1.2.1.17.1.4.1.4 | Counter | read-only | Number of frames discarded by this port due to excessive transit delay through the bridge. |
| dot1dBasePort MtuExceeded Discards 1.3.6.1.2.1.17.1.4.1.5 | Counter | read-only | The number of frames discarded by this port due to excessive size. |

ports. The table correlates ports with interfaces, and reports on the number of frames that were discarded because they have been delayed too long, or because their size is too big.

## 27.10  SPANNING TREE

A transparent bridge watches the traffic at each port. By recording the source addresses that the bridge sees, the bridge can build up a forwarding table of the form:

| MAC Address | port | Station Name |
|---|---|---|
| 02-00-08-A3-12-ED | 2 | MARS |
| 02-00-08-1B-44-31 | 3 | VENUS |
| . . . | . . . | |

Suppose that we want to bridge segment A to segment B, as shown in Figure 27.7, and that we don't want to lose connectivity if bridge 1 fails. What happens when we install bridge 2?

If both bridges are active and start to forward traffic, then bridge 1 and bridge 2 hear station MARS on segment A. They hear station

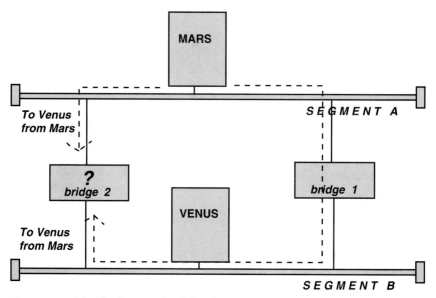

**Figure 27.7** A bridged network with a loop.

VENUS on segment B. OK. Now MARS sends a segment to station VENUS. Both bridges forward the frame. Now each bridge sees the *other* bridge's frame on segment B. It will look as if station MARS lives on segment B! Wow, are we confused!

The problem is that we have built a loop into our network and transparent bridges do not work properly where there are loops. We need the *Spanning Tree Protocol.*

The Spanning Tree Protocol makes it possible to build redundancy into a network connected by transparent bridges. In order to do this, the protocol removes loops from the network, configuring the network into a tree. The bridges exchange various protocol messages* to build the tree at start-up time, or to rebuild the tree after a bridge failure.

The protocol's first job is to select a *root* bridge. This is where we use the *bridge identifier,* which is made up of a priority number and the selected MAC address. The root bridge is the one with the smallest identifier number.

Next, each of the nonroot bridges must find its *root port.* Every bridge port is assigned a *path cost* that reflects the cost of transmitting a frame onto a LAN through that port. Slow LANs should be assigned higher costs than fast LANs. The best path is the one for which the sum of all of the costs along the way is least. The root port is the port that is on the lowest-cost path to the root.

---

* Formally, the bridges exchange Bridge Protocol Data Units (BPDUs).

Now, for each segment, we have to choose which bridge will be active for the segment. The next step in the protocol picks a single *Designated Bridge* for each segment. The Designated Bridge is the one for which the cost of the path to the root is the least. If there is a tie, the bridge identifier is used to break it. Any bridge that is not a Designated Bridge goes into a *standby mode* for the segment.

Figure 27.8 illustrates path costs. Bridge 1 is the root bridge. After exchanging information, adding up root path costs, and breaking the tie between bridges 2 and 3, bridges 3, 5, and 6 go into standby mode. Note that traffic from segment C to segment D must travel a path whose cost = 7. The path from the root is least cost—other paths are not optimal.

All bridges exchange protocol data units with their neighbors at regular intervals (typically 1–4 seconds) in order to check that none of the Designated Bridges has failed. When a failure is detected, the network reinitializes and regenerates its tree topology. One or more of the backup bridges will be called to active duty.

### 27.10.1 Spanning Tree Parameters

There is more than one version of the Spanning Tree Protocol. Digital Equipment Corporation (DEC) was an early implementer of Ethernet, and developed its own (LANbridge) version of the protocol. The IEEE published its version as standard IEEE 802.1D.

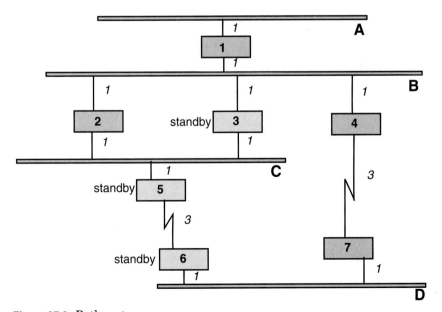

**Figure 27.8** Path costs.

The basic parameters shown in Table 27.3 apply to a bridge as a whole. The values include the version of the protocol, parameters used in determining the current tree topology, and settings for various timers. The MIB convention is to write time in hundredths of a second, but several timers actually require a setting with granularity in seconds. For these variables, a setting like 600 (6 seconds) is valid, while 650 is not.

The forward delay timer, *dot1dStpForwardDelay,* is used to help a Spanning Tree bridge make a graceful transition from *Blocking* (backup) to *Forwarding* (active) status. The bridge will first move to *Listening* state. When the timer *dot1dStpForwardDelay* expires, the bridge will move to *Learning* state. When the timer expires again, the bridge will move to *Forwarding* state.

### 27.10.2   The Spanning Tree Port Table

Table 27.4, the Spanning Tree Port Table, assigns a number, cost, and priority to each port. The priority is used to break ties if there are equally cost-effective paths from this bridge to the root.

The table also records status information: for example, the port's state and the current selection for the root bridge. Note that the table holds quite a bit of information about the current Designated Bridge for the segment attached to the port: its bridge identifier, its port on this segment, and the cost of its path to the root.

## 27.11   TRANSPARENT BRIDGING

The *dot1dTp* Group contains the remaining objects needed to manage transparent bridges. Of course, the group also applies to Source Route Transparent bridges. The group consists of two stand-alone variables: the bridge's Forwarding Database and a table that records port statistics.

### 27.11.1   Transparent Bridge Parameters

A transparent bridge depends on its Forwarding Database. A database entry records a destination MAC address and the port that should be used to reach that address.

No product has infinite memory. If there is a very large number of communicating systems on the network, a bridge could fill up its entire Forwarding Database, and might be unable to add new addresses that are discovered. One solution to this problem is to "age out" entries, throwing them away after a timeout.

The first two transparent bridge parameters in Table 27.5 configure the age timeout and count the number of entries that have to be thrown away because the Forwarding Database is full. A database that

**TABLE 27.3    Basic Spanning Tree Parameters**

iso.org.dod.internet.mgmt.mib-2.dot1dBridge.dot1dStp
1.3.6.1.2.1.17.2

| OBJECT IDENTIFIER | Syntax | Access | Description |
|---|---|---|---|
| dot1dStpProtocol Specification 1.3.6.1.2.1.17.2.1 | INTEGER unknown(1), decLb100(2), ieee8021d(3) | read-only | The version of the Spanning Tree Protocol that is being run. |
| dot1dStpPriority 1.3.6.1.2.1.17.2.2 | INTEGER (0..65535) | read-write | The first 2 octets of the bridge identifier. |
| dot1dStpTimeSince TopologyChange 1.3.6.1.2.1.17.2.3 | TimeTicks | read-only | Time (in hundredths of a second) since this bridge detected a topology change. |
| dot1dStpTopChanges 1.3.6.1.2.1.17.2.4 | Counter | read-only | Total number of topology changes detected by this bridge since last reset or initialization. |
| dot1dStpDesignated Root 1.3.6.1.2.1.17.2.5 | BridgeId | read-only | Bridge identifier of the node that this bridge believes is the current root of the spanning tree. |
| dot1dStpRootCost 1.3.6.1.2.1.17.2.6 | INTEGER | read-only | The total cost of the best path to the root. |
| dot1dStpRootPort 1.3.6.1.2.1.17.2.7 | INTEGER | read-only | The number of the port through which the lowest-cost path to the root is accessed. |
| dot1dStpMaxAge 1.3.6.1.2.1.17.2.8 | Timeout | read-only | Timeout on STP information learned from the network. Information that has not been refreshed will be discarded. |
| dot1dStpHelloTime 1.3.6.1.2.1.17.2.9 | Timeout | read-only | Interval for sending Configuration bridge PDUs if bridge is the root, or is trying to become the root. |

**TABLE 27.3   Basic Spanning Tree Parameters (*Continued*)**

iso.org.dod.internet.mgmt.mib-2.dot1dBridge.dot1dStp
1.3.6.1.2.1.17.2

| OBJECT IDENTIFIER | Syntax | Access | Description |
|---|---|---|---|
| dot1dStpHoldTime 1.3.6.1.2.1.17.2.10 | INTEGER | read-only | Length of interval for which, at most, two Configuration bridge PDUs should be transmitted by this node. |
| dot1dStpForwardDelay 1.3.6.1.2.1.17.2.11 | Timeout | read-only | Current value of the length of time spent in each of the Listening and Learning states while moving toward Forwarding state for this bridge. |
| dot1dStpBridge MaxAge 1.3.6.1.2.1.17.2.12 | Timeout (600..4000) | read-write | Value that all bridges use for MaxAge when this bridge is the root. (Granularity should be in seconds.) |
| dot1dStpBridge HelloTime 1.3.6.1.2.1.17.2.13 | Timeout (100..1000) | read-write | Value that all bridges use for HelloTime when this bridge is the root. (Granularity should be in seconds.) |
| dot1dStpBridge ForwardDelay 1.3.6.1.2.1.17.2.14 | Timeout (400..3000) | read-write | Value that all bridges use for ForwardDelay when this bridge is the root. (Granularity should be in seconds.) |

keeps overflowing means trouble. Aging entries out more quickly might help, but most likely more memory is needed—or else introducing some routers into the network.

### 27.11.2   The Forwarding Database Table

What goes into a Forwarding Database? First of all, it contains entries for individual (unicast) MAC addresses, not multicast or broadcast destinations.

**TABLE 27.4    The Spanning Tree Port Table**

| OBJECT IDENTIFIER | Syntax | Access | Description |
|---|---|---|---|
| iso.org.dod.internet.mgmt.mib-2.dot1dBridge.dot1dStp 1.3.6.1.2.1.17.2.15.1 | | | |
| dot1dStpPort 1.3.6.1.2.1.17.2.15.1.1 ▶ **Index** | INTEGER (1..65535) | read-only | Port number for this entry. |
| dot1dStpPort Priority 1.3.6.1.2.1.17.2.15.1.2 | INTEGER (0..255) | read-write | The port priority. |
| dot1dStpPortState 1.3.6.1.2.1.17.2.15.1.3 | INTEGER disabled(1), blocking(2), listening(3), learning(4), forwarding(5), broken(6) | read-only | Current state of the port. |
| dot1dStpPort Enable 1.3.6.1.2.1.17.2.15.1.4 | INTEGER enabled(1), disabled(2) | read-write | Administrative status of the port. |
| dot1dStpPort PathCost 1.3.6.1.2.1.17.2.15.1.5 | INTEGER (1..65535) | read-write | Contribution to the cost of paths through this port leading to the root. |
| dot1dStpPort DesignatedRoot 1.3.6.1.2.1.17.2.15.1.6 | BridgeId | read-only | Bridge Identifier of the current root, as identified in Bridge PDUs transmitted by the current Designated Bridge for the segment. |
| dot1dStpPort DesignatedCost 1.3.6.1.2.1.17.2.15.1.7 | INTEGER | read-only | Path cost for the Designated Port of the segment connected to this port. |
| dot1dStpPort DesignatedBridge 1.3.6.1.2.1.17.2.15.1.8 | BridgeId | read-only | The Bridge Identifier of the bridge which this port considers to be the Designated Bridge for this port's segment. |
| dot1dStpPort DesignatedPort 1.3.6.1.2.1.17.2.15.1.9 | OCTET STRING (SIZE (2)) | read-only | Port Identifier of the port on the Designated Bridge for this port's segment. |
| dot1dStpPort ForwardTransitions 1.3.6.1.2.1.17.2.15.1.10 | Counter | read-only | The number of times this port has transitioned from the Learning state to the Forwarding state. |

**TABLE 27.5** **Transparent Bridge Parameters**

| iso.org.dod.internet.mgmt.mib-2.dot1dBridge.dot1dTp 1.3.6.1.2.1.17.4 | | | |
|---|---|---|---|
| OBJECT IDENTIFIER | Syntax | Access | Description |
| dot1dTpLearned EntryDiscards 1.3.6.1.2.1.17.4.1 | Counter | read-only | Number of Forwarding Database entries which have been or would have been learned, but were discarded due to a lack of space. |
| dot1dTpAging Time 1.3.6.1.2.1.17.4.2 | INTEGER (10.. 1000000) | read-write | Timeout in seconds for aging out dynamically learned forwarding information. (Recommended default is 300 seconds.) |

There are entries for the MAC addresses for each of the bridge's own ports. There are entries that have been learned by watching the source addresses that show up on each of the connected segments.

Not all forwarding information must be learned dynamically. An administrator can manually enter forwarding information in a Static Table, which will be described in Sec. 27.12. There may possibly be other parts of the MIB that contain information that can be used to decide how to forward a frame to a particular MAC address.

Table 27.6 contains destination MAC addresses and the ports through which they should be forwarded. A port value of 0 means that the port number has not been learned, but the bridge has another source of information, such as the Static Table, that indicates how frames sent to this address should be handled.

### 27.11.3 The Transparent Bridge Port Table

Table 27.7 records the biggest information field that can be handled at each port, along with traffic statistics for each port. If the device is a brouter, traffic counts apply to bridged traffic only.

## 27.12 STATIC ADDRESS FILTERING

Many organizations have built complex bridged networks in which multiport bridges connect several bridged segments. Imposed on top of the physical structure, there also is an administrative structure, reflecting the organization's departments and functions.

Network management personnel need a way to control the traffic flows in the network, both to improve physical performance and to safeguard the security of critical systems.

**TABLE 27.6   Forwarding Database Table**

iso.org.dod.internet.mgmt.mib-2.
dot1dBridge.dot1dTp.dot1dTpFdbTable.dot1dTpFdbEntry
1.3.6.1.2.1.17.4.3.1

| OBJECT IDENTIFIER | Syntax | Access | Description |
|---|---|---|---|
| dot1dTpFdb Address 1.3.6.1.2.1.17.4.3.1.1 ▶ **Index** | MacAddress | read-only | A unicast MAC address. |
| dot1dTpFdb Port 1.3.6.1.2.1.17.4.3.1.2 | INTEGER | read-only | The number of the port at which the address was seen. |
| dot1dTpFdb Status 1.3.6.1.2.1.17.4.3.1.3 | INTEGER other(1), invalid(2), learned(3), self(4), mgmt(5) | read-only | Self(4) means this is the MAC address of a port on this bridge. Mgmt(5) means that this address is in the Static Table. |

**TABLE 27.7   The Transparent Bridge Port Table**

iso.org.dod.internet.mgmt.mib-2.
dot1dBridge.dot1dTp.dot1dTpPortTable.dot1dTpPortEntry
1.3.6.1.2.1.17.4.4.1

| OBJECT IDENTIFIER | Syntax | Access | Description |
|---|---|---|---|
| dot1dTpPort 1.3.6.1.2.1.17.4.4.1.1 ▶ **Index** | INTEGER (1..65535) | read-only | Port number. |
| dot1dTpPort MaxInfo 1.3.6.1.2.1.17.4.4.1.2 | INTEGER | read-only | Maximum size of the information field that this port will transmit or receive. |
| dot1dTpPortIn Frames 1.3.6.1.2.1.17.4.4.1.3 | Counter | read-only | Number of (bridge) frames received by this port from its segment. |
| dot1dTpPortOut Frames 1.3.6.1.2.1.17.4.4.1.4 | Counter | read-only | Number of (bridge) frames transmitted by this port to its segment. |
| dot1dTpPortIn Discards 1.3.6.1.2.1.17.4.4.1.5 | Counter | read-only | Number of valid incoming frames received that were discarded (filtered) by the Forwarding Process. |

Many bridge products enable network management personnel to control the actions of a bridge by manually entering static configuration information. This information filters, i.e., restricts the traffic flows through a multiport bridge.

Restrictions can be placed on unicast, multicast, and broadcast frames. A very useful application of this static configuration data is to limit the scope of broadcasts. Filtering also is used to control which parts of the network stations on any given segment can reach.

### 27.12.1   The Static Destination-Address Filtering Database

Filtering is configured by defining a limited set of permitted exit ports for traffic with a given port of entry and a specified destination.

The list of allowed exit ports is expressed as an OCTET STRING that is treated as a bit map. That is, if there are 16 ports or less in all and frames are allowed to exit ports 1, 2, 3, 9, and 10, the OCTET STRING would have the form:

```
PORT 1 2 3 4 5 6 7 8  9 10 11 12 13 14 15 16
     1 1 1 0 0 0 0 0  1  1  0  0  0  0  0  0
```

An entry in Table 27.8 might reflect a desired permanent network configuration, or it might be created to solve a temporary problem. The status parameter indicates whether and when deletion of an entry should occur. Specifically, setting the status parameter to:

- *permanent.*   Indicates that this entry should persist through resets.

- *invalid.*   The entry can be removed.

- *deleteOnReset.*   The entry should be removed after a bridge reset.

- *deleteOnTimeout.*   The entry should be removed on timeout.

## 27.13   TRAPS FOR BRIDGES

RFC 1493 defines two bridge traps, and both relate to the Spanning Tree Protocol. A bridge sends a trap when it begins an active role, transitions to a passive role, or becomes the root.

The ENTERPRISE field in each trap contains the OBJECT IDENTIFIER for the *dot1dBridge* subtree, 1.3.6.1.2.1.17. The SPECIFIC TRAP field will have the values 1 and 2, respectively. Variables will be included in the trap messages, as shown in Table 27.9, which describes the traps.

**TABLE 27.8    The Static Filtering Database Table**

iso.org.dod.internet.mgmt.mib-2.
dot1dBridge.dot1dStatic.dot1dStaticTable.dot1dStaticEntry
1.3.6.1.2.1.17.5.1.1

| OBJECT IDENTIFIER | Syntax | Access | Description |
|---|---|---|---|
| dot1dStatic Address 1.3.6.1.2.1.17.5.1.1.1 ▶ **Index** | MacAddress | read-write | The destination MAC address—unicast, group, or broadcast—for this entry. |
| dot1dStatic ReceivePort 1.3.6.1.2.1.17.5.1.1.2 ▶ **Index** | INTEGER | read-write | Entry applies to frames received on this port. If port is 0, applies to all ports for which there is no other entry. |
| dot1dStatic AllowedToGoTo 1.3.6.1.2.1.17.5.1.1.3 | OCTET STRING | read-write | The set of ports through which forwarding is allowed. (Expressed as a bit map.) |
| dot1dStaticStatus 1.3.6.1.2.1.17.5.1.1.4 | INTEGER other(1), invalid(2), permanent(3), deleteOnReset(4), deleteOnTimeout(5) | read-write | Indicates either that the entry is permanent, or else indicates conditions that cause automatic deletion. |

## 27.14   SOURCE ROUTING

Source routing for Token-Ring LANs was defined by IBM, and has been widely adopted in the marketplace. IEEE and ANSI have published source routing specifications. Some extra configuration is required to make source route bridging work. Every segment (ring) is assigned a ring number. Every bridge is assigned a bridge number.

**TABLE 27.9    Spanning Tree Traps**

| Name | Enterprise | Specific trap value | Enclosed variables | Description |
|---|---|---|---|---|
| newRoot | dotidBridge 1.3.6.1.2.1.17 | 1 | None | Indicates that the sender has become the new root of the Spanning Tree. |
| topology Change | dotidBridge 1.3.6.1.2.1.17 | 2 | None | Indicates a port transition from Learning to Forwarding, or from Forwarding to Blocking. |

As mentioned earlier, it is up to a frame's sender to discover the best way to get to a destination on a bridged Token-Ring LAN. Here's how this is done:

- Check to see if the destination is on the local segment. To do this, send a TEST or XID frame to the destination. If a response comes back, the destination is local, and no route is needed.

If a response does not came back, there is some work to be done! There are two different methods that can be used to find a route.

1. The *All Routes Explorer* method broadcasts a TEST or XID message on every possible route. As the message proceeds, the ring number and bridge number are recorded in the message by each bridge along the way. The destination turns around every message it receives, sending it back on the same route. The source station usually chooses to use the route in the message that wins the round-trip race.

2. The *Spanning Tree Explorer* method is similar, but makes sure that frames do not traverse a segment more than once, cutting down on unnecessary traffic.

Once a route to the destination has been set, the sequence of ring-numbers/bridge-numbers to be traversed is placed in a Routing Information Field in the Token-Ring frame header.

## 27.15   THE SOURCE ROUTE BRIDGE MIB

The Source Route Bridge MIB consists of the Source Routing group and the Port Pair group.

The Source Routing group is implemented within Source Routing and Source Routing Transparent bridges. The group includes the Source Routing Port Table, which contains port configuration and statistical variables. There also is one stand-alone variable—it identifies the version of the Routing Information Field format that the bridge uses.

The source routing MIB variables are in the subtrees:

```
iso.org.dod.internet.mgmt.mib-2.dot1dBridge.dot1dSr
1 . 3 . 6 . 1 . 2 . 1 . 17 . 3
```

and

```
iso.org.dod.internet.mgmt.mib-2.dot1dBridge.dot1dSr.dot1dPortPair
1 . 3 . 6 . 1 . 2 . 1 . 17 . 10
```

You may want to revisit the background material in Chapter 19, "Managing a Token-Ring Interface," before studying the source routing variables.

### 27.15.1   The Source Routing Group

Table 27.10, the Source Routing Port Table, contains an entry for each port on a Source Routing bridge. As was the case with transparent bridges, there often is a one-to-one correspondence between interfaces and ports. However, for interfaces such as frame relay and X.25 that provide multiple circuits, there will be a separate port for each circuit, and therefore several ports per X.25 or frame relay interface.

The table includes configuration parameters such as the bridge number and segment number. The table also includes statistical counts of source routed frames, Explorer frames, and errors.

**TABLE 27.10   The Source Routing Port Table**

iso.org.dod.internet.mgmt.mib-2.
dot1dBridge.dot1dSrPortTable.dot1dSrPortEntry
1.3.6.1.2.1.17.3.1.1

| OBJECT IDENTIFIER | Syntax | Access | Description |
|---|---|---|---|
| dot1dSrPort 1.3.6.1.2.1.17.3.1.1.1 ► **Index** | INTEGER (1..65535) | read-only | Port number. |
| dot1dSrPort HopCount 1.3.6.1.2.1.17.3.1.1.2 | INTEGER | read-write | Maximum number of routing descriptors allowed in All Paths or Spanning Tree Explorer frames. |
| dot1dSrPort LocalSegment 1.3.6.1.2.1.17.3.1.1.3 | INTEGER | read-write | Segment number for this port (0–4095). 65535 means none assigned. |
| dot1dSrPort BridgeNum 1.3.6.1.2.1.17.3.1.1.4 | INTEGER | read-write | Bridge number (0–15). 65535 means none assigned. |
| dot1dSrPort TargetSegment 1.3.6.1.2.1.17.3.1.1.5 | INTEGER | read-write | Target segment (0–4095). 65535 means none assigned. |
| dot1dSrPort LargestFrame 1.3.6.1.2.1.17.3.1.1.6 | INTEGER | read-write | Maximum size of the information field in frames that can be sent/received through this port. |
| dot1dSrPort STESpanMode 1.3.6.1.2.1.17.3.1.1.7 | INTEGER auto-span(1), disabled(2), forced(3) | read-write | How port handles Spanning Tree Explorer frames. *Forced* means accept and propagate. |

TABLE 27.10    The Source Routing Port Table (*Continued*)

iso.org.dod.internet.mgmt.mib-2.
dot1dBridge.dot1dSrPortTable.dot1dSrPortEntry
1.3.6.1.2.1.17.3.1.1

| OBJECT IDENTIFIER | Syntax | Access | Description |
|---|---|---|---|
| dot1dSrPort SpecInFrames 1.3.6.1.2.1.17.3.1.1.8 | Counter | read-only | Number of Source Routed frames received at this port. |
| dot1dSrPort SpecOutFrames 1.3.6.1.2.1.17.3.1.1.9 | Counter | read-only | Number of Source Routed frames transmitted by this port. |
| dot1dSrPort ApeInFrames 1.3.6.1.2.1.17.3.1.1.10 | Counter | read-only | Number of All Paths Explorer frames received at this port. |
| dot1dSrPort ApeOutFrames 1.3.6.1.2.1.17.3.1.1.11 | Counter | read-only | Number of All Paths Explorer frames transmitted by this port. |
| dot1dSrPort SteInFrames 1.3.6.1.2.1.17.3.1.1.12 | Counter | read-only | Number of Spanning Tree Explorer frames received at this port. |
| dot1dSrPort SteOutFrames 1.3.6.1.2.1.17.3.1.1.13 | Counter | read-only | Number of Spanning Tree Explorer frames transmitted by this port. |
| dot1dSrPort SegmentMismatch Discards 1.3.6.1.2.1.17.3.1.1.14 | Counter | read-only | Number of explorer frames discarded because of an invalid adjacent segment number in the routing descriptor field. |
| dot1dSrPort DuplicateSegment Discards 1.3.6.1.2.1.17.3.1.1.15 | Counter | read-only | Number of frames discarded because of a duplicate segment identifier in the routing descriptor field. |
| dot1dHopCount ExceededDiscards 1.3.6.1.2.1.17.3.1.1.16 | Counter | read-only | Number of explorer frames discarded because the maximum limit on the Routing Information Field size would be exceeded by adding another hop. |
| dot1dSrPort DupLanIdOrTree Errors 1.3.6.1.2.1.17.3.1.1.17 | Counter | read-only | Number of duplicate LAN IDs or Tree errors. Helps in detection of problems in networks containing older IBM Source Routing Bridges. |
| dot1dSrPort LanIdMismatches 1.3.6.1.2.1.17.3.1.1.18 | Counter | read-only | Number of explorer frames discarded because the last LAN ID in the Routing Information Field is not the LAN ID for this port's partner. |

The scalar in this group is:

| iso.org.dod.internet.mgmt.mib-2. dot1dBridge.dot1dSr 1.3.6.1.2.1.17.3 | | | |
|---|---|---|---|
| OBJECT IDENTIFIER | Syntax | Access | Description |
| dot1dSrBridge LfMode 1.3.6.1.2.1.17.3.2 | INTEGER mode3(1), mode6(2) | read-write | Indicates whether the bridge operates using older 3-bit length negotiation fields or the newer 6-bit length field in its Routing Information Field. |

## 27.15.2  The Port-Pair Group

Token-Ring bridging is quite straightforward when every bridge has two ports. Multiport bridges can be configured with port pairings, each corresponding to a unique source to target bridge path. The IEEE 802.5 SRT Addendum defines how this *direct multiport model* works.

An entry in Table 27.11, the Port-Pair Table, contains:

- The port numbers for a pair of ports
- A bridge number for the pair of ports
- A state variable indicating whether the bridge number is currently enabled or disabled

The port-pair group starts with a stand-alone variable that indicates the number of entries in the table:

| iso.org.dod.internet.mgmt.mib-2. dot1dBridge.dot1dPortPair. 1.3.6.1.2.1.17.10 | | | |
|---|---|---|---|
| OBJECT IDENTIFIER | Syntax | Access | Description |
| dot1dPortPair TableSize 1.3.6.1.2.1.17.10.1 | Gauge | read-only | Total number of entries in the Bridge Port-Pair Database. |

**TABLE 27.11   The Port-Pair Table**

iso.org.dod.internet.mgmt.mib-2.dot1dBridge.
dot1dPortPair.dot1dPortPairTable.dot1dPortPairEntry
1.3.6.1.2.1.17.10.2.1

| OBJECT IDENTIFIER | Syntax | Access | Description |
|---|---|---|---|
| dot1dPortPair LowPort 1.3.6.1.2.1.17.10.2.1.1 ► **Index** | INTEGER (1..65535) | read-write | Lower-numbered port for this pair. |
| dot1dPortPair HighPort 1.3.6.1.2.1.17.10.2.1.2 ► **Index** | INTEGER (1..65535) | read-write | Higher-numbered port for this pair. |
| dot1dPortPair BridgeNum 1.3.6.1.2.1.17.10.2.1.3 | INTEGER | read-write | Bridge number assigned so that the path between these low- and high-numbered ports is uniquely identified. |
| dot1dPortPair BridgeState 1.3.6.1.2.1.17.10.2.1.4 | INTEGER enabled(1), disabled(2), invalid(3) | read-write | Current state for this bridge number. *Invalid* means remove the entry. |

## 27.16   RECOMMENDED READING

At the time of writing, general parameters and transparent bridging objects were defined in RFC 1493, *Definitions of Managed Objects for Bridges.* Source Routing Bridge objects were defined in RFC 1525.

Both MIB documents were based on ANSI/IEEE specifications. The ANSI/IEEE 802.1D *Standard for MAC Bridges* describes the various bridging protocols. ANSI/IEEE P802.5M, *Source Routing Transparent Bridge Operation,* is still undergoing revision. Both of these documents define management objects. ANSI/IEEE 802.1y, *Source Routing Tutorial for End System Operation,* provides a good introduction to source routing.

# 28

# Monitors

## 28.1 INTRODUCTION

In order to keep SNMP simple so that any kind of device can partici-pate, the intelligence needed to analyze data usually is concentrated in the management station, and a low level of brainpower is assumed for the agent. But a network monitor does not need this kind of protection. A monitor is a smart, streetwise partner that is ready to jump into the middle of the fray.

A monitor can watch a LAN as a whole. It gathers information *with-out* polling and adding to traffic. A monitor can track the traffic flows that contribute the most to network activity. A monitor also can detect failures that are hard to find by polling. For example, a monitor can find duplicate IP address assignments.

Although we most often see monitors attached to LANs, a monitor also can watch wide area network interfaces, tracking traffic and checking whether errors stay within acceptable bounds.

Because a monitor is an intelligent host with CPU, memory, and disk resources, it can be configured to watch out for signs of trouble. For example, a monitor can be instructed to write a log entry or send a trap message when an error count passes a danger threshold.

Many organizations buy a monitor because it is invaluable for prob-lem diagnosis. For example, a monitor can lock onto any octet pattern and capture all frames containing that pattern for later study.

Monitors perform an important function for centrally managed net-works. A network problem may cause the Network Control Center to lose its link to a LAN. During this time, LAN devices cannot be polled, and important troubleshooting information might be lost. However, if a monitor is attached to the LAN, it will continue with its data-gathering duties. The information will be there for later study—or, if immediate analysis is needed, the monitor can be accessed via a dial-up link separate from the network.

## 28.2  OPERATING ENVIRONMENT

Most often, a monitor is attached to a *single* Ethernet, Token-Ring, or FDDI LAN. Because of its ability to see every packet on a LAN, it is kept in a secure location! An authorized local operator uses the monitor's keyboard and screen locally. The operator configures the jobs that the monitor should do, and checks the displays and reports produced by the monitor. The operator also listens for the beeping sounds produced when a network gets in trouble.

Monitors sometimes are shipped with multiple network interface cards. In some organizations, the unit is moved from Ethernet to Token-Ring to FDDI to WAN link, as a need for analysis arises. Given sufficient CPU, memory, disk (and a physical network configuration that allows it), monitors could be constructed to connect to and watch several interfaces at the same time.

Some hub vendors currently offer a product option that bundles a monitor with the hub chassis. A monitor also could be packaged with a router or a bridge.

## 28.3  THE RMON MIB

In 1991, the *Remote Network Monitoring Management Information Base* was published as RFC 1271, and immediately dubbed the "RMON MIB." The RMON MIB contains the tools that a network management station needs to configure and control a monitor, read out data and reports, and receive alarms.

## 28.4  ADMINISTRATIVE MODEL
## FOR SHARING A MONITOR

Controlling a monitor from remote management stations introduces some contention problems. For example, we might have a local operator and two remote management station operators all trying to configure the monitor at once. How should you handle this? You might want to do any of the following:

- Set up the monitor so that it can be configured only by a single local or remote operator, but allows others to read the results.

- Set up the monitor so that control authority is divided. For example, allow one operator to control Ethernet, while another controls Token-Ring.

- Give the monitor lots of extra CPU, memory, and disk, and give local and remote operators equal status.

The list of administration models could go on and on. Rather than decide which model is the *right* one, the RMON MIB simply provides control mechanisms that *could* be used to support any of these models. It is up to individual vendors to decide on the options that they want to give their users, and it is up to users to select their own administrative model.

## 28.5 RMON MIB MECHANISM FOR SHARING

The RMON MIB mechanism for sharing is straightforward. A local or remote operator enters configuration data by adding a new *entry* to a *control table*. One of the variables in the entry identifies the operator. This variable—along with SNMP authentication information—is used to implement the desired administrative model.

Once the control table entry is complete, has been assigned an index, and has a valid status, the monitor starts to do the job requested by the entry. For example, a Host Control Table entry might say that:

- This request comes from operator Joe Jones at station sunflower with IP address 128.1.1.2. His phone number is 203-888-9999.

- Joe Jones wants to monitor the Ethernet LAN connected to interface number 1.

- Joe Jones wants the monitor to collect host traffic statistics for the 100 most recently active hosts.

When the status of this entry becomes *valid,* the monitor begins to collect host table records that satisfy Joe Jones' request. Each resulting record includes a request index that shows that the record is part of Joe Jones' data.

## 28.6 FOCUS OF RFC 1271

RFC 1271 provides the general framework for statistics collection, alarms, and data capture. Some statistical variables are technology-specific. For example, we are interested in collisions on an Ethernet, and need to know about beaconing or ring purges on a Token-Ring.

RFC 1271 provides a large number of general variables, along with the specific variables needed to monitor an Ethernet. RFC 1513 adds Token-Ring data to the RMON. Work on RMON MIB variables for FDDI is in progress at the time of writing.

## 28.7 RMON MIB TERMINOLOGY

The term *packet* is used in the MIB to mean a Media Access Control (MAC) frame. Although the term *frame* is used through most of this book, we will follow the RMON convention in this chapter, and use the term *packet*.

Each technology has its own method for delimiting the beginning and end of a packet (frame). Delimiter bits are not included in traffic count statistics.

Frame headers and error-checking fields *are* included in octet counts. For example, an Ethernet packet is defined to begin with its 6-octet destination physical address and end with its Frame Check Sequence, inclusively. Octet counts will include these fields.

A LAN is monitored through a monitor network interface card that physically connects the monitor to the LAN. The RMON MIB often refers to the network *segment* attached via the interface, rather than the *LAN*.

## 28.8   MORE ABOUT CONFIGURING A MONITOR

Monitors can gather and tabulate many useful statistics. A monitor operator can configure a station to present these statistics in the way that is most helpful to the user.

For example, what time interval should be used for periodic statistics? 30 minutes? 15 minutes? How many periods should the monitor hang onto? Enough for a day? A week? A month? The operator creates a control table entry that outlines exactly how information should be gathered. Within the control table structure, it is possible that one management station might request statistics to be recorded for each 15-minute period in the last day, while another operator requests the *same* statistics to be recorded for each 30-minute period over the last week. If the monitor can handle it, each operator's request is granted and their results are distinguished by the index of their control table request.

## 28.9   ACCESS CONTROL VARIABLES

There are two control table variables that are used to sort out requests entered by different managers. The first variable identifies who wrote the request into the control table entry, and the other variable indicates the current status of the control table entry. These variables appear repeatedly, and are assigned labels following the textual conventions:

- *OwnerString.*  An NVT ASCII DisplayString containing an administratively assigned name for the owner of an entry. The definition suggests including information such as the IP address, management station name, operator's name, location, or phone number. The size of the string may range from 0 to 127 octets. If a request entry was configured right at the monitor, the owner's name should start with "monitor."

- *EntryStatus.* The normal life cycle of an entry starts with a *set* operation that launches the creation of a request in the control table. The monitor performs some initialization to prepare to produce results, and then the entry becomes *valid.* The monitor will begin to gather information. After a period of time, the operator sets the entry to *invalid* to end this particular task and to signal that all related information can be deleted. Formally, the EntryStatus is an INTEGER, with values:

—valid(1)

—createRequest(2)

—underCreation(3)

—invalid(4)

The entry's status variable is used to maintain the consistency of the table while an entry is being added, and to mark entries for deletion.

## 28.10   RMON MIB GROUPS

The RMON MIB contains a large number of groups. Listed in their order of presentation in the MIB, they are: *statistics, history, alarm, host, hostTopN, matrix, filter, packet capture,* and *event.* This ordering is used in assigning OBJECT IDENTIFIERs.

Unfortunately, this ordering hides the close relationship between some of the groups. In this chapter, we will present the groups in an order that emphasizes their natural structure.

### 28.10.1   Traffic and Error Statistics Groups

First of all, there are four groups that provide traffic and error statistics. Each group offers a different and useful view of traffic measurements:

- *statistics.*   Simple counts of traffic (in both packets and octets) and errors, accumulated since the start of the monitoring session.
- *history.*   Sets of statistics for a selected time interval—for example, counts for each 30-minute interval for the last month.
- *host.*   A monitor will discover hosts that are active on the network. Traffic and error statistics are recorded for each host.
- *hostTopN.*   The hosts that had the largest traffic or error counts over an interval are ordered and presented in a table.

### 28.10.2    Matrix of Flows Between Systems

We may have counted every byte that was sent on the LAN, but we don't know who is talking to whom. The matrix group takes care of this.

- *matrix.*    Simple counts of traffic (in both packets and octets) and errors between sources and destinations.

### 28.10.3    Filtering and Capturing Traffic

While gathering statistics is useful, the real diagnostic horsepower of a monitor is in its ability to capture traffic. A monitor can be configured to capture on the basis of just about anything—various errors, the presence of a specific octet pattern in some packet location, the absence of a pattern from some location. Note that the choice of octet patterns allows you to pick out packets belonging to a specific protocol, and/or packets sent to a given location, and/or packets that belong to a selected application, such as a TCP file transfer.

Monitors make it easy for you to choose what you want by providing a series of menus that contain popular selection criteria. Management stations will need to provide a similar helping hand.

The RMON MIB filter group is used to set up the criteria for a packet capture, or to detect packets that trigger events. Variables in the packet-capture group configure buffer memory that then is used to hold captured data.

- *filter.*    Parameters that can be used to select traffic that will be examined.

- *packet capture.*    Configuration and storage of captured packet data.

### 28.10.4    Alarms and Events

A monitor can watch what is going on and it is an intelligent device. This combination gives a monitor the power to execute its most valuable function. A monitor can watch various variables, detect that a threshold into a danger zone has been crossed, and trigger an event as a result. An early warning system helps a network manager to take action before little problems become big ones!

Alarms and events go hand in hand. You define an alarm by picking a variable, such as the number of Ethernet collisions, a time interval, such as 1 second, and a threshold, such as 60. Put it together, and we have said that if we exceed 60 collisions per second, we are in trouble. What do we do about it?

Each alarm is linked to an event in the event group. An event defines an action that will be triggered when the alarm condition holds. For example, when the number of collisions in the interval exceeds the threshold, the corresponding event could cause a trap message to be sent to a management station. An event can also trigger the start of packet capture.

To summarize:

- *alarm.*  A list of variables to be watched and pointers to events that are triggered when values cross given thresholds. Alarms are used to detect that things have gone wrong—and also are used to detect that normalcy has been restored!

- *event.*  An event may involve notification, such as writing a log entry or sending an SNMP trap. Or, an alarm may generate an event that starts or stops packet capture.

## 28.11   RELATIONSHIP TO MONITOR PRODUCTS

While all of the groups are optional, these groups do reflect the normal capabilities of monitors that are available in the marketplace. In this chapter, the information that these groups make available is illustrated by screens and reports generated by a Network General *Sniffer* attached to the test network.

## 28.12   CONFIGURATION, CONTROL, AND DATA TABLES

A monitor does a lot, but you have to know how to ask it to do something. Configuration is very important for this type of device, and this MIB contains a large number of configuration parameters.

Several of the groups in the MIB consist of pairs of tables. A *control table* configures what information is to be monitored, often sets a time interval, and puts a limit on the amount of data that needs to be recorded. A separate *data or results table* holds the information that is gathered. Each control entry is linked to the data that is gathered on its behalf.

Obviously, it would be disruptive to try to change a configuration parameter in the middle of a data-gathering operation. The usual procedure to be followed is to *set* the corresponding control table entry to *invalid.* This terminates the previous data-gathering activity and causes both the control entry and the gathered information to be discarded. Then a fresh activity is started by writing a new control entry into the control table.

We now should have enough of an idea of how all this works to take a close look at the RMON MIB.

## 28.13   GLOBAL STATISTICS

The *statistics* group defines global statistics measured for a whole LAN (or a WAN circuit). An entry in Table 28.1, the Ethernet Statistics Table, reports detailed statistics for one interface connected to one Ethernet LAN. The table can report statistics for multiple interfaces just by adding more entries.

Before taking a close look at the table, let's examine some displays of Ethernet statistics from the Network General *Sniffer* attached to the test network.

Figure 28.1 shows global statistics for a small Ethernet. Much of the information translates directly into MIB variables. However, the *Sniffer* uses the term *frames* where the MIB refers to *packets,* and the *Sniffer* uses the term *Cyclic Redundancy Check* (CRC) where the MIB refers to the equivalent term, *Frame Check Sequence* (FCS).

Within the upper-left-hand section of Figure 28.1, we see Total Frames and Total Bytes. These are counted (starting from 0) from the time that the *monitor* was started. Counts in the MIB statistics table will start from 0 when a *valid entry* is created.

The upper-right section of the display contains current counts, recording activity for a period of 1 second. The box at the lower left displays important error statistics: the number of runts, CRC/Align Errors, and Collisions. The monitor did not miss any frames due to lack of buffer space.

Figure 28.2 shows an alternative display that includes a graphic representation of network utilization over the current minute.

Figure 28.3 shows a monitor screen that displays the frame sizes for the LAN traffic. Frame size counts also appear in the MIB statistics

```
┌GLOBAL STATISTICS───────────────────────────────────Aug 06 09:01:24┐
                            Traffic Counts

     Total Stations        3            Active Stations       2
     Average Usage         0.85 %       Current Usage         0.13 %
     Total Frames       125,467         Current Frames        3
     Total Bytes     76,012,639         Current Bytes     1,634
     Avg Frame Size        605          Avg Frame Size      544

   ┌─────────────────────────────┬─────────────────────────────────┐
            Error Counts                     Timestamps

       Runt Frames        0         Monitor Started    Aug 06 06:58:01
       CRC/Align Errors   0         Monitor Active   0 day(s) 02:03:23
       Total Frame Errors 0
                                    First Activity     Aug 06 06:58:01
       Collisions        22         Last Activity      Aug 06 09:01:23
                                    Network Active   0 day(s) 02:03:22
       Missed/Lost Frames 0
```

**Figure 28.1**   Global monitor statistics for an Ethernet.

**TABLE 28.1    Ethernet Statistics Table**

iso.org.dod.internet.mgmt.mib-2.
rmon.statistics.etherStatsTable.etherStatsEntry
1.3.6.1.2.1.16.1.1.1

| OBJECT IDENTIFIER | Syntax | Access | Description |
|---|---|---|---|
| etherStatsIndex 1.3.6.1.2.1.16.1.1.1.1 ▶ **Index** | INTEGER (1..65535) | read-only | A unique index assigned to the entry. |
| etherStats DataSource 1.3.6.1.2.1.16.1.1.1.2 | OBJECT IDENTIFIER | read-write | The *ifIndex*. |
| etherStats DropEvents 1.3.6.1.2.1.16.1.1.1.3 | Counter | read-only | Number of times that the monitor detected that it had dropped packets because of lack of resources. |
| etherStatsOctets 1.3.6.1.2.1.16.1.1.1.4 | Counter | read-only | Total number of octets of data (including bad packets) received on the network. |
| etherStatsPkts 1.3.6.1.2.1.16.1.1.1.5 | Counter | read-only | Total number of packets (including error packets) received. |
| etherStats BroadcastPkts 1.3.6.1.2.1.16.1.1.1.6 | Counter | read-only | Total number of good broadcast packets received. |
| etherStats MulticastPkts 1.3.6.1.2.1.16.1.1.1.7 | Counter | read-only | Total number of good multicast (nonbroadcast) packets received. |
| etherStats CRCAlignErrors 1.3.6.1.2.1.16.1.1.1.8 | Counter | read-only | Total number with a length between 64 and 1518 octets, inclusive, that had a bad FCS or were not an integral number of octets in length. |
| etherStats UndersizePkts 1.3.6.1.2.1.16.1.1.1.9 | Counter | read-only | Number of otherwise well-formed packets received with length less than 64 octets. |
| etherStats OversizePkts 1.3.6.1.2.1.16.1.1.1.10 | Counter | read-only | Number of otherwise well-formed packets received with length greater than 1518 octets. |
| etherStats Fragments 1.3.6.1.2.1.16.1.1.1.11 | Counter | read-only | Total number not an integral number of octets or with a bad FCS, *and* less than 64 octets long. |
| etherStatsJabbers 1.3.6.1.2.1.16.1.1.1.12 | Counter | read-only | Total number longer than 1518 octets, and were not an integral number of octets or had a bad FCS. |
| etherStats Collisions 1.3.6.1.2.1.16.1.1.1.13 | Counter | read-only | Best estimate of the total number of collisions on this segment. |

**TABLE 28.1    Ethernet Statistics Table (*Continued*)**

iso.org.dod.internet.mgmt.mib-2.
rmon.statistics.etherStatsTable.etherStatsEntry
1.3.6.1.2.1.16.1.1.1

| OBJECT IDENTIFIER | Syntax | Access | Description |
|---|---|---|---|
| etherStats Pkts64Octets 1.3.6.1.2.1.16.1.1.1.14 | Counter | read-only | Total number received (including error packets) that were 64 octets in length. |
| etherStats Pkts65to127Octets 1.3.6.1.2.1.16.1.1.1.15 | Counter | read-only | Total number received (including error packets) that were 65–172 octets in length. |
| etherStats Pkts182to255Octets 1.3.6.1.2.1.16.1.1.1.16 | Counter | read-only | Total number received (including error packets) that were 128–255 octets in length. |
| etherStats Pkts256to511Octets 1.3.6.1.2.1.16.1.1.1.17 | Counter | read-only | Total number received (including error packets) that were 256–511 octets in length. |
| etherStats Pkts512to 1023Octets 1.3.6.1.2.1.16.1.1.1.18 | Counter | read-only | Total number received (including error packets) that were 512–1023 octets in length. |
| etherStats Pkts1024to 1518Octets 1.3.6.1.2.1.16.1.1.1.19 | Counter | read-only | Total number received (including error packets) that were 1024–1518 octets in length. |
| etherStatsOwner 1.3.6.1.2.1.16.1.1.1.20 | Owner String | read-write | The entity that configured this entry and is using the entry resources. |
| etherStatsStatus 1.3.6.1.2.1.16.1.1.1.21 | EntryStatus | read-write | The status of this *etherStats* entry. |

table, although the size ranges differ slightly (e.g., 128–255 rather than 129–256).

Table 28.1 contains 17 statistical counts. Their definitions are straightforward, and many correspond to the items in the *Sniffer* displays. Keep in mind that octet counts will include frame headers and Frame Check Sequences.

## 28.14   HISTORY STATISTICS

A monitor doesn't just report what is going on right now—it can record statistics for past time intervals. This is useful for many reasons. Normal daily traffic patterns can be studied. We have to know what is usual before we can recognize what is unusual behavior. For example, a suggested level for setting alarm thresholds is to take what is "nor-

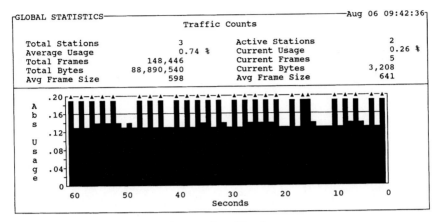

**Figure 28.2** Graphic display of network utilization.

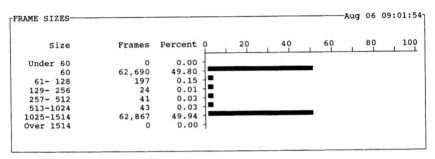

**Figure 28.3** Monitor display of frame sizes.

mal" and add 50 percent. History reports provide valuable input for topology design and capacity planning. And history reports can help with diagnostics.

Statistics are counted for a preset time interval. A monitor can save the statistical counts for a large number of intervals—for example, the monitor used for the illustrations in this book has been set up to save statistics for up to 1750 intervals.

Figure 28.4 shows part of a *Sniffer* monitor history table. The collection interval was set to 5 minutes; note that the station automatically adjusted the time boundary so that it would be aligned with the hours—for example, there are samples at 8:00, 8:05, 8:10. Only the results of completed intervals are shown.

### 28.14.1 The History Control Table

Table 28.2, the History Control Table, is used to set configuration parameters for history collection. The operator sets a *desired* number

```
┌GLOBAL HISTORY STATISTICS─────────────────────────────────┬Aug 06 09:02:45┐
│              Time      Frames   Errs           Bytes  Size  %Usage │
│  25  Aug 06 09:00:00    3,619     0         2,055,528   567   0.57  │
│  24         08:55:00    3,644     0         2,063,053   566   0.57  │
│  23         08:50:00    3,263     0         1,821,646   558   0.50  │
│  22         08:45:00    3,872     0         2,217,369   572   0.61  │
│  21         08:40:00    5,322     0         3,060,900   575   0.85  │
│  20         08:35:00    4,745     0         2,726,594   574   0.75  │
│  19         08:30:00    5,389     0         3,109,712   577   0.86  │
│  18         08:25:00    4,611     0         2,636,338   571   0.73  │
│  17         08:20:00    3,623     0         2,045,417   564   0.56  │
│  16         08:15:00    3,052     0         1,672,339   547   0.46  │
│  15         08:10:00    3,639     0         2,058,430   565   0.57  │
│  14         08:05:00    3,999     0         2,286,564   571   0.63  │
│  13         08:00:00    4,654     0         2,677,380   575   0.74  │
│  12         07:55:00    4,548     0         2,610,868   574   0.72 M│
│  11         07:50:00    3,933     0         2,238,105   569   0.62 o│
│  10         07:45:00    5,071     0         2,931,333   578   0.81 r│
│   9         07:40:00    5,191     0         2,998,669   577   0.83 e│
│   8         07:35:00    4,443     0         2,533,177   570   0.70 ↓│
└────────────────────────────────────────────────────────────────────┘
```

**Figure 28.4**  Monitor history display.

of intervals, and the monitor records the number closest to the requested value that it actually can (and will) provide. Time marches on, and when the limit on the number of records is reached, the history table will wrap around, replacing the oldest entries with new ones.

The operator sets the sampling interval, which can range from 1 second to 1 hour. As before, graceful management of table additions and deletions is provided by owner and status variables.

The table will have separate entries for different interfaces, and even can have multiple entries for an individual interface. Each entry stores a different configuration choice for gathering history records.

RFC 1271 suggests creating two separate reports for each interface—one short term (30 seconds) and the other long term (30 minutes). Of course, some monitor products may not be able to work with more than a single configuration.

### 28.14.2  Gathering History Samples

History data collection begins after an operator has completed a valid entry in the control table. The Ethernet History Table describes the database that contains the results of the actual history samples.

This database will contain a separate set of history records for each History Control Table entry that points to an Ethernet interface. Separate history data tables (e.g., a Token-Ring History Table) will be used for other media. This has to be the case, since the variables for each medium will be different.

The first table index identifies which History Control Table entry configured the collection of these statistics. The second index is used to identify the sample interval. The interval start time for each sample is recorded.

**TABLE 28.2    The History Control Table**

iso.org.dod.internet.mgmt.mib-2.
rmon.history.historyControlTable.historyControlEntry
1.3.6.1.2.1.16.2.1.1

| OBJECT IDENTIFIER | Syntax | Access | Description |
|---|---|---|---|
| historyControl Index 1.3.6.1.2.1.16.2.1.1.1 ► **Index** | INTEGER (1..65535) | read-only | An index for the entry. |
| historyControl DataSource 1.3.6.1.2.1.16.2.1.1.2 | OBJECT IDENTIFIER | read-write | The OBJECT IDENTIFIER of the ifIndex for the interface connecting to the LAN segment for which statistics are collected. |
| historyControl BucketsRequested 1.3.6.1.2.1.16.2.1.1.3 | INTEGER (1..65535) | read-write | Requested number of time intervals over which data should be saved. |
| historyControl BucketsGranted 1.3.6.1.2.1.16.2.1.1.4 | INTEGER (1..65535) | read-only | The number of intervals that the monitor actually will provide. |
| historyControl Interval 1.3.6.1.2.1.16.2.1.1.5 | INTEGER (1..3600) | read-write | The sampling interval, in seconds. |
| historyControl Owner 1.3.6.1.2.1.16.2.1.1.6 | Owner String | read-write | The owner of the entry. |
| historyControl Status 1.3.6.1.2.1.16.2.1.1.7 | Entry Status | read-write | The status of the entry. |

The *Sniffer* history display shown in Figure 28.4 would correspond to a control table entry that set the time interval to 5 minutes. Note how the *interval start time,* displayed as the time of day, has been aligned with 5-minute periods starting on the hour.

The statistics gathered in the Ethernet History Table are similar to those in the Global Statistics table, and so the definitions will not be reproduced here. However, the packet length counts have been dropped, and an estimate of the percent of bandwidth utilized has been added. The Ethernet History Table has OBJECT IDENTIFIER:

```
iso.org.dod.internet.mgmt.mib-2.rmon.history.etherHistoryTable
```

or

```
1 . 3 . 6 . 1 . 2 . 1 . 16 . 2 . 2
```

## 28.15   HOSTS

A monitor attached to a LAN can detect all of the active hosts on a LAN by watching the source and destination addresses of good MAC frames. In addition to finding who is on the LAN, we'd also like to get an idea of how much traffic each host generates.

The *Sniffer* display in Figure 28.5 lists active hosts and the total amount of incoming and outgoing traffic for each since monitoring began. It is the purpose of the hosts group to provide similar information. The hosts group consists of:

- A control table that sets the ground rules for host data collection
- A host table containing traffic statistics for each discovered host, and indexed by the host's physical address
- The host table reindexed by order of discovery

### 28.15.1   The Host Control Table

Table 28.3, the Host Control Table, is used to configure which of its attached LAN and WAN interfaces the monitor should watch. If all of the host table space gets filled, the monitor will start to delete entries. A recommended strategy is to dump the least recently used entries.

The control table includes the usual ownership and status information. Note that if the status of a control table entry is set to invalid, the host table is deleted—as is the hostTopN table, defined in the next group.

### 28.15.2   The Host Table

After an operator has completed a valid entry in the Host Control Table, the monitor begins the process of discovering hosts, adding them to the host table (Table 28.4), and tracking their traffic.

The table records the traffic into and out of each host in packets and in octets. All counts are computed from the time that the host was added to the table.

```
┌ABSOLUTE TRAFFIC STATISTICS TO AND FROM STATIONS──────────Aug 06 09:01:47┐
      Station              Frames   Errs        Bytes  Size  %Usage
  1   Sunflower           125,715      0   76,155,923   605    0.85
  2   Tulip                93,862      0   58,810,533   626    0.65
  3   Crocus               31,861      0   17,345,870   544    0.19
  4   Broadcast                 8      0          480    60    0.01



└                                                                         ┘
```

**Figure 28.5**  Active hosts and their traffic.

**TABLE 28.3    The Host Control Table**

| | iso.org.dod.internet.mgmt.mib-2. rmon.hosts.hostControlTable.hostControlEntry 1.3.6.1.2.1.16.4.1.1 | | |
|---|---|---|---|
| OBJECT IDENTIFIER | Syntax | Access | Description |
| hostControlIndex 1.3.6.1.2.1.16.4.1.1.1 ▶ **Index** | INTEGER (1..65535) | read-only | A unique index for this entry. |
| hostControl DataSource 1.3.6.1.2.1.16.4.1.1.2 | OBJECT IDENTIFIER | read-write | The *ifIndex* for the segment for which host information is being collected. |
| hostControl TableSize 1.3.6.1.2.1.16.4.1.1.3 | INTEGER | read-only | The number of *hostEntries* in the *hostTable* and the *hostTimeTable* associated with this *hostControlEntry*. |
| hostControl LastDelete 1.3.6.1.2.1.16.4.1.1.4 | TimeTicks | read-only | Value of *sysUptime* the last time an entry was deleted from the portion of the host table associated with this entry. |
| hostControl Owner 1.3.6.1.2.1.16.4.1.1.5 | Owner String | read-write | The owner of this entry. |
| hostControl Status 1.3.6.1.2.1.16.4.1.1.6 | Entry Status | read-write | The status of this entry. |

The table is indexed by the host's physical address and the corresponding control table entry (which selects the LAN to be monitored).

The host creation order index runs from 1 to N, where 1 corresponds to the host that has been in the table longest, and N is the size of the host table. The host with creation order index 1 was the first to be put into the table. If the oldest host entry is deleted, all of the other host creation-order indices will be renumbered.

### 28.15.3    The Host Time Table

The Host Time Table contains exactly the same information as the Host Table. The only difference is that instead of being indexed by a host's physical address, it is indexed by the *hostTimeCreationOrder*. This has some advantages. The table can be retrieved efficiently by a series of SNMP *gets* that will cause table entries to be packed into the smallest possible number of responses. The table information also is retrieved in a very natural display order.

TABLE 28.4   The Host Table

| | iso.org.dod.internet.mgmt.mib-2. rmon.hosts.hostTable.hostEntry 1.3.6.1.2.1.16.4.2.1 | | |
|---|---|---|---|
| OBJECT IDENTIFIER | Syntax | Access | Description |
| hostAddress 1.3.6.1.2.1.16.4.2.1 ▶ **Index** | OCTET STRING | read-only | The physical address of this host. |
| hostCreationOrder 1.3.6.1.2.1.16.4.2.1.2 | INTEGER (1..65535) | read-only | An index indicating when this host was added to the table. 1 means that the host was the first entry. |
| hostIndex 1.3.6.1.2.1.16.4.2.1.3 ▶ **Index** | INTEGER (1..65535) | read-only | The hostControlIndex. |
| hostInPkts 1.3.6.1.2.1.16.4.2.1.4 | Counter | read-only | Number of packets without errors transmitted to this physical address. |
| hostOutPkts 1.3.6.1.2.1.16.4.2.1.5 | Counter | read-only | Number of packets (including errors) transmitted by this address. |
| hostInOctets 1.3.6.1.2.1.16.4.2.1.6 | Counter | read-only | Number of octets in messages without errors transmitted to this address. |
| hostOutOctets 1.3.6.1.2.1.16.4.2.1.7 | Counter | read-only | Number of octets in messages (including those with errors) transmitted by this address. |
| hostOutErrors 1.3.6.1.2.1.16.4.2.1.8 | Counter | read-only | Number of error packets transmitted by this address. |
| hostOut BroadcastPkts 1.3.6.1.2.1.16.4.2.1.9 | Counter | read-only | Number of good broadcast packets transmitted by this address. |
| hostOut MulticastPkts 1.3.6.1.2.1.16.4.2.1.10 | Counter | read-only | Number of good multicast (non broadcast) packets transmitted by this address. |

Since the only difference is the index, this table will undoubtedly be implemented by means of an second index for the Host Table. The OBJECT IDENTIFIER for the Host Time Table is:

```
iso.org.dod.internet.mgmt.mib-2.rmon.hosts.hostTimeTable
```

or

```
1 . 3 . 6 . 1 . 2 . 1 . 16 . 4 . 3
```

## 28.16   HOST TOP N

Who really is busy on the network? Figure 28.6 shows a *Sniffer* report that reveals which stations are transmitting the most traffic. Let's take a closer look at the report. How has it been designed?

- Statistics for up to 10 stations transmitting the most octets will be shown.
- Hosts are ordered by the most octets transmitted.
- The start time and the monitoring period are shown.

It is possible to configure a *Sniffer* to produce similar reports that track the hosts that received the most frames or generated the most bad packets.

The *hostTopN* group provides the framework for configuring what we want a report to tell us, and gathering the data needed to generate the report. That is, the group includes a control table (*hostTopNControlTable,* Table 28.5) and a results table (*hostTopNTable,* Table 28.6). This group enables an operator to configure a monitor to choose the hosts that were most active according to *one* of the criteria:

1. Incoming packets (*hostTopNInPkts*)
2. Outgoing packets (*hostTopNOutPkts*)
3. Incoming octets (*hostTopNInOctets*)
4. Outgoing octets (*hostTopNOutOctets*)
5. Outgoing errors (*hostTopNOutErrors*)
6. Outgoing broadcast packets (*hostTopNOutBroadcastPkts*)
7. Outgoing multicast packets (*hostTopNOutMulticastPkts*)

A "Top N" report is designed by writing configuration information in Table 28.5, the *hostTopNControlTable,* including:

```
                       Top 10 Talkers

This report provides statistics for the 10 stations which have
transmitted the most traffic.  The stations are sorted by bytes
transmitted.

Monitoring Started:    Aug 06 06:58:01       Total Stations:      3
Monitoring Stopped:    Aug 06 10:29:52
Elapsed Time:          0 day(s) 03:31:51

Report Generated:      Aug 06 10:29:52


        Name                    Bytes    Errors    Size    % Rel

    1   Sunflower            76,740,387       0     1073    69.80
    2   Tulip                29,308,714       0      427    27.54
    3   Crocus                2,132,636       0       60     2.65
```

**Figure 28.6**  Top N hosts.

**TABLE 28.5    The Host Top N Control Table**

iso.org.dod.internet.mgmt.mib-2.
rmon.hostTopN.hostTopNControlTable.hostTopNControlEntry
1.3.6.1.2.1.16.5.1.1

| OBJECT IDENTIFIER | Syntax | Access | Description |
|---|---|---|---|
| hostTopN ControlIndex 1.3.6.1.2.1.16.5.1.1.1 ▶ **Index** | INTEGER (1..65535) | read-only | A unique index corresponding to one Top N report prepared for one interface. |
| hostTopNHostIndex 1.3.6.1.2.1.16.5.1.1.2 | INTEGER (1..65535) | read-write | The corresponding host table for this report, as identified by hostIndex. |
| hostTopNRateBase 1.3.6.1.2.1.16.5.1.1.3 | INTEGER 1-7 | read-write | The variable that top host selection is based on (e.g., most incoming octets). |
| hostTopN TimeRemaining 1.3.6.1.2.1.16.5.1.1.4 | INTEGER | read-write | Number of seconds left in the current interval. Setting this variable triggers a new report. |
| hostTopNDuration 1.3.6.1.2.1.16.5.1.1.5 | INTEGER | read-only | Total number of seconds in the collection interval. |
| hostTopN RequestedSize 1.3.6.1.2.1.16.5.1.1.6 | INTEGER | read-write | Maximum number of hosts *requested* for the Top N table. |
| hostTopN GrantedSize 1.3.6.1.2.1.16.5.1.1.7 | INTEGER | read-only | Actual maximum number of hosts that can appear in the Top N table. |
| hostTopN StartTime 1.3.6.1.2.1.16.5.1.1.8 | Time Ticks | read-only | Value of *sysUptime* when this report was last started. |
| hostTopNOwner 1.3.6.1.2.1.16.5.1.1.9 | Owner String | read-write | Owner of this entry. |
| hostTopNStatus 1.3.6.1.2.1.16.5.1.1.10 | Entry Status | read-write | Entry status. |

- The maximum number of hosts to be tracked
- One of the seven statistics above, used to select the most active hosts
- The time that monitoring started
- The duration of the reporting interval

Two copies of the time interval are created—one copy is counted down until the end of the interval. To be specific, the operator writes the desired reporting interval into the *hostTopNTimeRemaining* variable. The monitor then automatically copies the interval setting into the *hostTopNDuration* variable.

The duration variable is static and will not change. However, the *hostTopNTimeRemaining* variable will count down, second by second. When it reaches zero, the sampling results will be written into the *hostTopNTable*. To get a new report, the *hostTopNTimeRemaining* variable must be reset to a nonzero value.

The monitor may be short of memory resources and may not be able to create a data table that holds the requested number of hosts. In this case, the monitor will do the best that it can, and will report the actual size limit in the *hostTopNGrantedSize* variable.

The host group is a prerequisite for the host Top N group. Each host Top N report is linked back to a corresponding Host Table.

### 28.16.1  The Host Top N Table

The results of the counts configured in the control table are placed in the Host Top N Table after the selected interval has elapsed.

Hosts with the largest change in the selected variable are listed first. Hosts with the smallest change in the selected variable are listed last. That is, within each report, hosts are indexed by their Top N order.

## 28.17  MATRIX

So far, we have defined global LAN statistics, checked traffic flows in and out of hosts, and recorded which hosts produce the most traffic— or errors. Now we want to know who is talking to whom, and how much. That is the function of the matrix group.

Specifically, the flows of traffic and errors from each source to each destination will be counted. RFC 1271 refers to these flows as "conver-

**TABLE 28.6    The Host Top N Table**

| iso.org.dod.internet.mgmt.mib-2.<br>rmon.hostTopN.hostTopNTable.hostTopNEntry<br>1.3.6.1.2.1.16.5.2.1 | | | |
|---|---|---|---|
| OBJECT IDENTIFIER | Syntax | Access | Description |
| hostTopNReport<br>1.3.6.1.2.1.16.5.2.1.1<br>▶ **Index** | INTEGER<br>(1..65535) | read-<br>only | Identifies the control table entry for this report, i.e., *hostTopNControlIndex.* |
| hostTopNIndex<br>1.3.6.1.2.1.16.5.2.1.2<br>▶ **Index** | INTEGER<br>(1..65535) | read-<br>only | A unique index for this entry, giving its Top N position. |
| hostTopNAddress<br>1.3.6.1.2.1.16.5.2.1.3 | OCTET<br>STRING | read-<br>only | Physical address of this host. |
| hostTopNRate<br>1.3.6.1.2.1.16.5.2.1.4 | INTEGER | read-<br>only | Amount of change in the selected variable during this sampling interval. |

```
┌ABSOLUTE TRAFFIC STATISTICS─SINGLE STATION──────────────Aug 06 09:01:39┐
                                   Traffic TO and FROM Station
           Station: Sunflower     Current Usage               0.51 %
                                   Average Usage               0.85 %
                                   Total Frames            125,575
     Last sent to: Tulip          Total Errors                  0
     Last rcv from: Tulip         Total Bytes          76,075,103
                                   Avg Frame Size              605
 ├─────────────────────────────────┬─────────────────────────────────┤
          Traffic FROM Station     │       Traffic TO Station

     Current Usage          0.48 % │  Current Usage          0.03 %
     Average Usage          0.65 % │  Average Usage          0.20 %
     Total Frames          54,582  │  Total Frames          70,993
     Total Errors               0  │  Total Errors               0
     Total Bytes       59,222,757  │  Total Bytes       16,852,346
     Avg Frame Size         1085   │  Avg Frame Size          237
     Start Time   Aug 06 06:58:01  │  Start Time   Aug 06 06:58:01
     End Time     Aug 06 09:01:38  │  End Time     Aug 06 09:01:38
     Elapsed      0 day(s) 02:03:37│  Elapsed      0 day(s) 02:03:37
 └─────────────────────────────────┴─────────────────────────────────┘
```

**Figure 28.7** Data flows.

sations." Figure 28.7 shows a Sniffer display that describes the traffic flow between stations named Sunflower and Tulip.

The matrix group consists of a control table (*matrixControl Table*) and a data table (*matrixSDTable*) that measures the flow of packets between sources and destinations. A second data table, *matrix-DSTable,* also is defined. The *matrixDSTable* data is identical to the *matrixSDTable* data—and even has the same indices. The only difference between the two tables is the order of the indices. Clearly, the *matrixDSTable* would be implemented by means of software that changes the order of retrieval for the entries in the *matrixSDTable.*

### 28.17.1   The Matrix Control Table

As usual, we assume that a monitor might have several active interfaces. An entry in Table 28.7, the Matrix Control Table identifies an interface to be observed, and identifies the upper limit on the number of source-destination pairs that can be tracked.

There are, potentially, a very large number of pairings. When the table space fills up, old entries must be discarded to make way for new ones. It is suggested that the least recently used entries should be the candidates for deletion. The time of the last table deletion is recorded in the control table. This gives an idea of how likely it is that some active entries may have been lost because of insufficient table size. As usual, owner and status control information are included.

### 28.17.2   The Matrix
### Source-to-Destination Table

Table 28.8, the Matrix Source-to-Destination Table (*matrixSDTable*) contains sets of statistics that track the amount of traffic between two systems.

TABLE 28.7   The Matrix Control Table

iso.org.dod.internet.mgmt.mib-2.
rmon.matrix.matrixControlTable.matrixControlEntry
1.3.6.1.2.1.16.6.1.1

| OBJECT IDENTIFIER | Syntax | Access | Description |
|---|---|---|---|
| matrixControl Index 1.3.6.1.2.1.16.6.1.1.1 ▶ **Index** | INTEGER (1..65535) | read-only | A unique index for this entry. |
| matrixControl DataSource 1.3.6.1.2.1.16.6.1.1.2 | OBJECT IDENTIFIER | read-write | Interface that is the source for this data, expressed as the object identifier for the interface. |
| matrixControl TableSize 1.3.6.1.2.1.16.6.1.1.3 | INTEGER | read-only | The number of matrix table entries for this interface. |
| matrixControl LastDeleteTime 1.3.6.1.2.1.16.6.1.1.4 | TimeTicks | read-only | The value of *sysUpTime* the last time that an entry associated with this control information was deleted from one of the matrix statistics tables. |
| matrixControl Owner 1.3.6.1.2.1.16.6.1.1.5 | Owner String | read-write | The owner of this entry. |
| matrixControl Status 1.3.6.1.2.1.16.6.1.1.6 | INTEGER | read-write | The status of this entry. |

The table records simple counts of packets, bytes, and errors. The packet and byte counts include error packets in their tallies. The *matrixSDTable* counts traffic transmitted from a source to a destination.

In addition to keeping counts for traffic directed from one system to another, counts of packets and octets sent to multicast and broadcast addresses also are recorded.

The term "conversation" is used for a data flow. The table lists flows from one computer to another. The table also shows flows from a system to a multicast or broadcast address. The matrix table is indexed by the:

- Interface being monitored
- Source physical address
- Destination physical address

A monitor will create a new entry in the table when it detects a new flow. If a monitor runs out of table space, it will start to delete entries. The selection of entries to be deleted is, of course, up to the monitor. A sensible guideline would be to get rid of the least recently used entries.

**TABLE 28.8**    **The Matrix Source-to-Destination Table**

iso.org.dod.internet.mgmt.mib-2.
rmon.matrix.matrixSDTable.matrixSDEntry
1.3.6.1.2.1.16.6.2.1

| OBJECT IDENTIFIER | Syntax | Access | Description |
|---|---|---|---|
| matrixSD SourceAddress 1.3.6.1.2.1.16.6.2.1.1 ▶ **Index** | OCTET STRING | read-only | The source physical address. |
| matrixSD DestAddress 1.3.6.1.2.1.16.6.2.1.2 ▶ **Index** | OCTET STRING | read-only | The destination physical address. |
| matrixSDIndex 1.3.6.1.2.1.16.6.2.1.3 ▶ **Index** | INTEGER (1..65535) | read-only | The control table entry for this part of the table (corresponding to the *matrixControlIndex*). |
| matrixSDPkts 1.3.6.1.2.1.16.6.2.1.4 | Counter | read-only | Number of packets transmitted from the source address to the destination address. |
| matrixSDOctets 1.3.6.1.2.1.16.6.2.1.5 | Counter | read-only | Number of octets in all packets transmitted from the source address to the destination address. |
| matrixSDErrors 1.3.6.1.2.1.16.6.2.1.6 | Counter | read-only | Number of error packets transmitted from the source address to the destination address. |

### 28.17.3   The Matrix Destination-to-Source Table

The matrix Destination-to-Source Table (*matrixDSTable*) is identical to the matrix Source-to-Destination Table, except that the order of its indices is:

- Interface being monitored
- Destination physical address
- Source physical address

The only difference that this makes would be in the order in which *get-nexts* would retrieve table entries. For the *matrixSDTable,* the logical order of the table lists all flows for the first *source,* then all flows for the second *source,* etc. For *matrixDSTable,* the logical order of the table lists all flows for the first *destination,* then all flows for the second *destination,* etc. The OBJECT IDENTIFIER for the *matrixDSTable* is:

```
iso.org.dod.internet.mgmt.mib-2.rmon.matrix.matrixDSTable
```

or

$$1 . 3 . 6 . 1 . 2 . 1 . 16 . 6 . 3$$

## 28.18   Detailed Diagnostics

We now come to a set of groups that work together as a diagnostic team. When there is a network problem, we often need to focus attention on one particular kind of traffic. Maybe we want to watch for error packets. Perhaps we need to track TCP-based terminal logins to a specific host in order to watch for an attempt to breach security. Or, some users may be having trouble using a particular NetWare print server.

The filter group, packet group, and event group cooperate to give us a very finely tuned set of diagnostic tools. In order to get a preview of the RMON MIB toolkit, let's take a look at some *Sniffer* screens.

Figure 28.8 shows a screen that helps us to design a set of filtering criteria for capturing packets (frames). Let's focus on the bottom of the center panel. The check marks show that we want to capture three types of Ethernet error frames: bad CRCs, short frames, and collision frames.

We also want to capture specific good frames. The protocol submenu to the right allows us to check off which protocols we want to capture. The protocol field in each Ethernet frame will be examined, and any frame that matches one of the checkoffs will be captured.

Figure 28.9 shows that we also can use the **Destination Class** menu to specify whether we want broadcast, unicast, or both. The next menu pick, **Station Address,** would let use focus on a specific set of stations.

The most general filtering can be set up using the **Pattern Match** selection, as shown in Figure 28.10. We see that we can use the right panel to set up several patterns, and apply the patterns with **AND** or

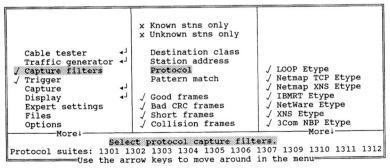

**Figure 28.8**  Packet filtering criteria.

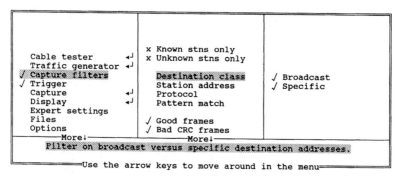

**Figure 28.9**  Filtering by destination class.

**OR** logic. In Figure 28.10, we can indicate that we want to check a pattern at a given offset—a successful check can be defined by either a **Match** or a **Don't Match** result.

Finally, Figure 28.11 shows how one or more patterns can be entered with "don't care" bytes between them.

Wow! How can the RMON MIB capture all of this complexity and choice? Well, it isn't easy, but let's tackle it.

## 28.19   THE FILTER GROUP

Monitors let us pick out the traffic that we want to watch closely. All of the traffic is subjected to a set of *filter* tests in order to separate out a particular logical stream of data called a *channel*. Each filter tests two things:

- Presence or absence of data patterns
- Presence or absence of particular errors

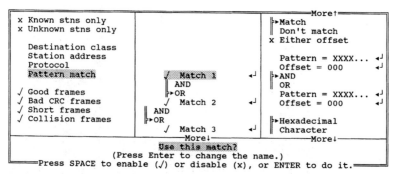

**Figure 28.10**  Filtering by pattern match.

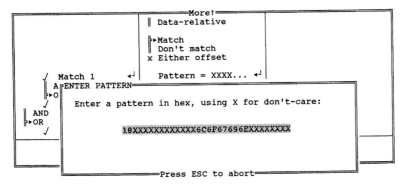

**Figure 28.11**  Entering a pattern.

To be accepted, traffic must pass the filter's data pattern-matching test *and* the filter's error-status check.

A channel is created by defining one or *more* filters. The channel consists of all traffic that is accepted by:

filter 1 **OR** filter 2 **OR** . . .

Let's take a close look at pattern matching first.

### 28.19.1   Pattern Matching in a Filter

How do we define pattern matching in a filter? First we set:

- An offset from the beginning of a packet (*filterPktDataOffset*). Pattern checking will start here.

Next, let's provide a pattern:

- A string of octets (*filterPktData*) forms a data pattern to be matched.

Now things start to get a bit more complicated. We might have two or more clumps of octets that we want to match, separated by "don't care" bytes. We use a mask to show which parts of a packet we pull out and compare with the pattern.

- A mask (*filterPktDataMask*) shows which bits in the packet should be compared with the data pattern.

The mask will be applied starting at the offset. The bits in the packet that correspond to 1s in the mask are selected for comparison. One technicality: suppose that there are more bits in the data pattern than there are 1s in the mask? Then the mask is automatically extended with 1s until it is long enough.

What comes next? The straightforward procedure is to compare the packet bits that we have pulled out (using the mask) with the data pattern and declare a match if they are the same. But we actually allow more elaborate comparisons to be made.

We define another mask (*filterPktDataNotMask*) that is applied to the packet bits that we have pulled out. If a bit in the *NotMask* is 0, then the corresponding packet bit *must* match the pattern. Now we look at all of the packet bits for which the *NotMask* is 1. *At least one* of these must be *different* from the corresponding pattern bit! In other words, the NotMask defines part of the pattern as **Match** data and part of the pattern as **Doesn't Match** data.

Another technicality: if the *NotMask* is shorter than the data pattern, it is extended with 0s until it is long enough.

If the *NotMask* consists entirely of 0s, then we do a simple pattern comparison. The use of 1s in the *NotMask* picks a set of bits that must differ *somewhere*. Putting it all together, here's what we do:

1. Is the packet so short that we can't pull out enough bits to compare with the pattern? If so, it is not a match.

2. Among the selected packet bits, is there a packet bit position with *NotMask=0* and bit value that does *not* match the corresponding data pattern bit? If so, it is not a match.

3. Among the selected bits, looking at those for which the *NotMask=1*, do they *all* match the data pattern? If so, it is not a match.

Any packets that *have* passed all three tests get thrown into the channel!

### 28.19.2    Error-Checking Filter

That takes care of pattern matching. Now let's look at screening for errors. The next criteria let us choose traffic with—or without—selected errors. The *filterPktStatus* variable selects errors of interest. Ethernet errors are defined as:

0. Packet is longer than 1518 octets.

1. Packet is shorter than 64 octets.

2. Packet experienced a CRC or Alignment error.

We pick out errors that may be of interest by setting flags in a bit map. For example, to request errors 0 and 2, we set bits 0 and 2:

|     | 0 | 0 | 0 | 0 | 0 | 1 | 0 | 1 |
| --- | - | - | - | - | - | - | - | - |
| *bit* | 7 | 6 | 5 | 4 | 3 | 2 | 1 | 0 |

The result is turned into an integer that is stored in the packet status variable, *filterPktStatus*.

The monitor will check each packet for errors and compute its packet status. Do we then compare the packet's status with the defined *filterPktStatus?* No! We define a mask (*filterPktStatusMask*). The comparison is made *only* for the packet status bits that correspond to mask bits with value 1.

It that all? No! Another mask (*filterPktStatusNotMask*) tells which are the bits we want to **Match.** Specifically, if a bit in the NotMask is 0, then the corresponding packet status bit must match the bit in the *filterPktStatus.* Now we look at all of the packet status bits for which the NotMask is 1. At least *one* of these must be *different* from the corresponding *filterPktStatus* bit! Putting this together, here's what we do:

1. Use the *filterPktStatusMask* to pull out the packet status bits that will be compared.

2. Among these packet status bits, is there a packet bit position with *NotMask=0* and bit value that does not match the corresponding *filterPktStatus* bit? If so, it is not a match.

3. Among these packet status bits, looking at those for which the *NotMask=1,* do they *all* match the corresponding *filterPktStatus* bits? If so, it is not a match.

Remember that a channel will be defined by one—or more—filters, so the conditions that choose packets for a channel can be as complicated as you like.

### 28.19.3   The Filter Table

Each entry in Table 28.9, the Filter Table, defines a filter. Each filter provides a set of criteria for screening every packet and deciding whether to it belongs to a logical channel. Several filter entries can be associated with the same channel. Remember that multiple filters are ORed to choose traffic for the channel.

A separate Channel Table, defined in the next section, contains control information that turns filtering on and off. The packet capture group configures the capture of a channel's packets.

### 28.19.4   The Channel Table

Recall that packets that are selected by a set of filter expressions form a logical data stream called a *channel.* What is a channel used for? Sometimes we use a channel to define a stream of packets that will be captured. Sometimes we will be searching for rare but important patterns, and want to generate an event whenever a packet is selected for the channel.

Table 28.10, the Channel Table, contains the control parameters needed to complete the description of a channel.

**TABLE 28.9    The Filter Table**

| | iso.org.dod.internet.mgmt.mib-2.<br>rmon.filter.filterTable.filterEntry<br>1.3.6.1.2.1.16.7.1.1 | | |
|---|---|---|---|
| OBJECT IDENTIFIER | Syntax | Access | Description |
| filterIndex<br>1.3.6.1.2.1.16.7.1.1.1<br>▶ **Index** | INTEGER<br>(1..65535) | read-<br>only | A unique index that identifies<br>each entry. |
| filterChannel<br>Index<br>1.3.6.1.2.1.16.7.1.1.2 | INTEGER<br>(1..65535) | read-<br>write | Identifier for the channel for<br>which this filter selects data, i.e.,<br>the corresponding channelIndex. |
| filterPkt<br>DataOffset<br>1.3.6.1.2.1.16.7.1.1.3 | INTEGER | read-<br>write | The offset from the beginning of<br>each packet where a match of<br>data will be attempted. |
| filterPktData<br>1.3.6.1.2.1.16.7.1.1.4 | OCTET<br>STRING | read-<br>write | The data that is to be matched<br>with the input packet. |
| filterPktDataMask<br>1.3.6.1.2.1.16.7.1.1.5 | OCTET<br>STRING | read-<br>write | The mask used to select data<br>from a packet before applying<br>the match process. |
| filterPkt<br>DataNotMask<br>1.3.6.1.2.1.16.7.1.1.6 | OCTET<br>STRING | read-<br>write | The mask that picks which data<br>needs to be matched, and which<br>should not match perfectly. |
| filterPktStatus<br>1.3.6.1.2.1.16.7.1.1.7 | INTEGER | read-<br>write | Status bits selecting error<br>conditions of interest. |
| filterPkt<br>StatusMask<br>1.3.6.1.2.1.16.7.1.1.8 | INTEGER | read-<br>write | The mask to be applied to a<br>packet's status bits to select which<br>ones will be used in the match<br>process. |
| filterPkt<br>StatusNotMask<br>1.3.6.1.2.1.16.7.1.1.9 | INTEGER | read-<br>write | The mask that picks which error<br>status bits need to be matched,<br>and which status bits should not<br>match perfectly. |
| filterOwner<br>1.3.6.1.2.1.16.7.1.1.10 | Owner<br>String | read-<br>write | The owner of this entry. |
| filterStatus<br>1.3.6.1.2.1.16.7.1.1.11 | Entry<br>Status | read-<br>write | The status of this entry. |

First of all, we need to identify the interface that will be watched. Next, this is our last chance to change our minds about what we want to filter; we can set a variable so that data will be accepted only if it *fails* either the packet data match or the packet error status match!

A control variable, *channelDataControl,* is used to turn a channel on or off—that is, to start or stop the filtering process. We also can specify an *event* that will set *channelDataControl* on and kick off filtering and another *event* that will set *channelDataControl* off and turn off filtering.

**TABLE 28.10    The Channel Table**

iso.org.dod.internet.mgmt.mib-2.
rmon.filter.channelTable.channelEntry
1.3.6.1.2.1.16.7.2.1

| OBJECT IDENTIFIER | Syntax | Access | Description |
|---|---|---|---|
| channelIndex<br>1.3.6.1.2.1.16.7.2.1.1<br>▶ **Index** | INTEGER<br>(1..65535) | read-<br>only | A unique identifier for the<br>entry. |
| channelIfIndex<br>1.3.6.1.2.1.16.7.2.1.2 | INTEGER<br>(1..65535) | read-<br>write | The *ifIndex* of the interface<br>to which to apply filters. |
| channelAccept<br>Type<br>1.3.6.1.2.1.16.7.2.1.3 | INTEGER<br>accept<br>Matched(1),<br>accept<br>Failed(2) | read-<br>write | 1 means accept packets that<br>satisfy the filter and 2<br>means accept only if either<br>the packet data match or<br>the packet status match<br>fails. |
| channelData<br>Control<br>1.3.6.1.2.1.16.7.2.1.4 | INTEGER | read-<br>write | Controls the flow of data,<br>status, and events through<br>this channel. |
| channelTurn<br>OnEventIndex<br>1.3.6.1.2.1.16.7.2.1.5 | INTEGER<br>(0..65535) | read-<br>write | The index of an event that<br>will turn *channelData<br>Control* from off to on<br>when the event is generated. |
| channelTurn<br>OffEventIndex<br>1.3.6.1.2.1.16.7.2.1.6 | INTEGER<br>(0..65535) | read-<br>write | The index of an event that<br>will turn *channelData<br>Control* from on to off<br>when the event is generated. |
| channelEvent<br>Index<br>1.3.6.1.2.1.16.7.2.1.7 | INTEGER<br>(0..65535) | read-<br>write | The *eventIndex* of an event<br>to be generated if a packet<br>is matched. |
| channelEvent<br>Status<br>1.3.6.1.2.1.16.7.2.1.8 | INTEGER<br>event<br>Ready(1),<br>event<br>Fired(2),<br>event<br>AlwaysReady(3) | read-<br>write | A control that can be used<br>to prevent a flood of events. |
| channelMatches<br>1.3.6.1.2.1.16.7.2.1.9 | Counter | read-<br>only | Number of times this<br>channel has matched a<br>packet. |
| channel<br>Description<br>1.3.6.1.2.1.16.7.2.1.10 | DisplayString<br>(SIZE(0..127)) | read-<br>write | A comment describing this<br>channel. |
| channelOwner<br>1.3.6.1.2.1.16.7.2.1.11 | OwnerString | read-<br>write | The owner of this entry. |
| channelStatus<br>1.3.6.1.2.1.16.7.2.1.12 | Entry<br>Status | read-<br>write | The status of this entry. |

If the channel is being used to find a packet and fire off an event, we set the *channelEventIndex* variable to point to the event. This event might cause a trap to be sent, or might trigger packet capture. Another variable is used to prevent too many events from being generated by repeated matches.

## 28.20 CAPTURING PACKETS

Finally, we come to the definition of parameters that control the capture of packets that match a given filter.

### 28.20.1 The Buffer Control Table

Table 28.11, the Buffer Control Table, configures the management of the buffer memory used for packet capture. Each entry identifies resources for capture for one selected channel. An operator can decide how much memory to allocate for capture, and whether to stop capturing or wrap around when that memory is exhausted.

For many diagnostics, it is not necessary to store entire packets. A table variable can be set to choose the number of bytes to save. Furthermore, to save bandwidth, an even smaller chunk of the packet may be selected for SNMP retrieval. Since SNMP implementations are not *required* to be able to accept messages larger than 484 bytes, it is important to have the ability to look at a piece of a packet.

### 28.20.2 The Capture Buffer Table

Table 28.12, the Capture Buffer Table, contains data from captured packets that is available for SNMP retrieval. There is an entry for each captured packet. Each is tied back to the Buffer Control Table entry that configured storage for the capture.

The length of the original packet, time of capture, and error status all are recorded. An additional flag has been added to the error status. The full list of error flags is:

| Bit | Error |
|-----|-------|
| 0 | Packet is longer than 1518 octets. |
| 1 | Packet is shorter than 65 octets. |
| 2 | Packet experienced a CRC or Alignment error. |
| 3 | This is the first packet in this capture buffer after it was detected that some packets were not processed correctly. |

## 28.21 ALARMS

When conditions on the network are deteriorating, you want to know. You do not want to wait until the network is in a state of collapse before getting some kind of notification.

**TABLE 28.11    The Buffer Control Table**

iso.org.dod.internet.mgmt.mib-2.
rmon.capture.bufferControlTable.bufferControlEntry
1.3.6.1.2.1.16.8.1.1

| OBJECT IDENTIFIER | Syntax | Access | Description |
|---|---|---|---|
| bufferControlIndex<br>1.3.6.1.2.1.16.8.1.1.1<br>▶ **Index** | INTEGER<br>(1..65535) | read-<br>only | A unique index for this<br>entry. |
| bufferControl<br>ChannelIndex<br>1.3.6.1.2.1.16.8.1.1.2 | INTEGER<br>(1..65535) | read-<br>write | The *channelIndex* of the<br>channel that is the source<br>of packets to be captured<br>into the buffer space. |
| bufferControl<br>FullStatus<br>1.3.6.1.2.1.16.8.1.1.3 | INTEGER<br>space<br>Available(1),<br>full(2) | read-<br>only | States whether the buffer<br>currently has room for<br>more packets or is full. |
| bufferControl<br>FullAction<br>1.3.6.1.2.1.16.8.1.1.4 | INTEGER<br>lockWhenFull(1),<br>wrapWhen<br>Full(2) | read-<br>write | What to do when the<br>buffer is full. If wrap is<br>chosen, the first packet<br>captured will be the first<br>to be overwritten. |
| bufferControl<br>CaptureSliceSize<br>1.3.6.1.2.1.16.8.1.1.5 | INTEGER | read-<br>write | Maximum number of<br>octets of each packet to be<br>saved in this capture<br>buffer. Default 100. |
| bufferControl<br>DownloadSliceSize<br>1.3.6.1.2.1.16.8.1.1.6 | INTEGER | read-<br>write | The maximum number of<br>octets that will be<br>returned in an SNMP<br>retrieval of that packet. |
| bufferControl<br>DownloadOffset<br>1.3.6.1.2.1.16.8.1.1.7 | INTEGER | read-<br>write | The offset of the first<br>octet of each packet that<br>will be returned in an<br>SNMP retrieval. |
| bufferControl<br>MaxOctets<br>Requested<br>1.3.6.1.2.1.16.8.1.1.8 | INTEGER | read-<br>write | The requested maximum<br>number of octets to be<br>saved in this buffer. |
| bufferControl<br>MaxOctetsGranted<br>1.3.6.1.2.1.16.8.1.1.9 | INTEGER | read-<br>only | The maximum number of<br>octets that the monitor is<br>able to save in this<br>buffer, including overhead. |
| bufferControl<br>CapturedPackets<br>1.3.6.1.2.1.16.8.1.1.10 | INTEGER | read-<br>only | The number of packets<br>currently in this buffer. |
| bufferControl<br>TurnOnTime<br>1.3.6.1.2.1.16.8.1.1.11 | TimeTicks | read-<br>only | Value of *sysUpTime* when<br>this capture buffer was<br>turned on. |
| bufferControl<br>Owner<br>1.3.6.1.2.1.16.8.1.1.12 | OwnerString | read-<br>write | The owner of this entry. |
| bufferControl<br>Status<br>1.3.6.1.2.1.16.8.1.1.13 | Entry<br>Status | read-<br>write | The status of this entry. |

**TABLE 28.12    The Capture Buffer Table**

iso.org.dod.internet.mgmt.mib-2.
rmon.capture.captureBufferTable.captureBufferEntry
1.3.6.1.2.1.16.8.2.1

| OBJECT IDENTIFIER | Syntax | Access | Description |
|---|---|---|---|
| captureBuffer ControlIndex 1.3.6.1.2.1.16.8.2.1.1 ▶ **Index** | INTEGER (1..65535) | read-only | The index of the buffer ControlEntry with which this packet is associated. |
| captureBuffer Index 1.3.6.1.2.1.16.8.2.1.2 ▶ **Index** | INTEGER | read-only | An index that uniquely identifies this packet within those captured in the buffer defined by the corresponding Buffer Control Table entry. |
| captureBuffer PacketID 1.3.6.1.2.1.16.8.2.1.3 | INTEGER | read-only | An index that describes the order of capture. The index will roll over at $2^{31}$. |
| captureBuffer PacketData 1.3.6.1.2.1.16.8.2.1.4 | OCTET STRING | read-only | Captured packet data, which starts from the offset specified by the associated *bufferControlDownload Offset* and is limited by the configured slice size. |
| captureBuffer PacketLength 1.3.6.1.2.1.16.8.2.1.5 | INTEGER | read-only | The original length of this packet, including FCS octets. |
| captureBuffer PacketTime 1.3.6.1.2.1.16.8.2.1.6 | INTEGER | read-only | Number of milliseconds after this capture buffer was turned on that this packet was captured. |
| captureBuffer PacketStatus 1.3.6.1.2.1.16.8.2.1.7 | INTEGER | read-only | The error status of this packet. |

The alarm group is tasked with the job of listing the set of symptoms that spell trouble. There is an art to configuring alarms. You have to pick the threshold for a danger zone. Some problems are signaled by too much activity—for example, too many collisions—while other problems are signaled by too little activity—for example, no traffic originating at a server host!

For example, in Figure 28.12, we see that a critical alarm will be written to a log when the collision rate exceeds 1 percent. This actually is much too low a setting, but the test network was so well behaved on the day on which these samples were recorded that an abnormally small rate had to be set in order to cause an alarm condition!

Figure 28.13 shows the Sniffer alarm log that reports an occurrence of a collision rate of more than 1 percent for an interval. The second critical event in Figure 28.13 was not caused by too much of anything, but by too little.

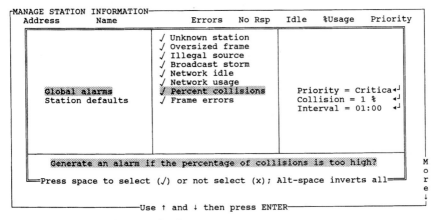

**Figure 28.12** Critical alarm display.

```
┌ALARM LOG──────────────────────────────────────────Aug 06 11:37:36┐
    Priority          Time  Source          Type/Description        Ack
  1 Critical  Aug 06 07:08:31  Global Network  Collisions exceeded 1.00%  √
  2 Critical  Aug 06 10:55:15  Global Network  Idle 15 minutes            √
│                                                                        │
│                                                                        │
│                                                                        │
│                                                                        │
│                                                                        │
└────────────────────────────────────────────────────────────────────┘
```

**Figure 28.13** Alarm log.

The log reports that the network was idle for a full monitoring period of 15 minutes. In this case, a low activity threshold was used to detect that the network was idle.

### 28.21.1 Rising and Falling Thresholds

Let's take a closer look at how alarms are set up. Suppose that we want to be warned when collisions on an Ethernet reach as high as 60 per second. Then we set up a *Rising Threshold* of 60 collisions within the last second. We configure an event number to be looked up in the event table when the threshold is exceeded. That entry in the event table says "Write this into the alarm log, and also send a trap message to Joe Jones."

Anyone who has worked with network management is familiar with the fact that when things go bad, they stay bad for a while. This situation could cause one identical alarm after another, and these extra alarms add nothing to our knowledge.

We really do not want to receive these repeated alarms. Once excessive collisions are detected, what we actually want to know is when things are back within a normal behavior range. Newer alarming systems do not keep repeating an alarm. Instead, they watch for a *Falling*

*Threshold.* For example, we might set a Falling Threshold of 30 collisions per second to indicate a return to acceptable behavior.

What happens after we cross a falling threshold that takes us back to normalcy? If we like, we can configure the Falling Threshold so that it also causes a log entry and trap message. In any case, the monitor now will be reset, and will react with a fresh event if the Rising Threshold is crossed again.

Figure 28.14 shows collision behavior increasing above a Rising Threshold. The first crossing causes an event. The next two crossings are ignored. Then the collision rate subsides to a normal level. A later crossing of the Rising Threshold causes an event.

Sometimes things are just the other way around! A Falling Threshold may be used to detect trouble, and a Rising Threshold to signal normalcy. For example, a suspiciously low (or zero!) level of network traffic might indicate that an important server is down. Rebooting the server would return the network to normal traffic levels which would be detected by the Rising Threshold. Figure 28.15 illustrates this situation.

### 28.21.2  Configuring Alarms

In order to describe an alarm condition, we need to nail down several values:

- The monitoring interval over which data is sampled
- A variable to be sampled
- *Rising* and *Falling* Thresholds used to detect when trouble starts and when it ends
- The event (if any) that takes place when a Rising Threshold is crossed
- The event (if any) that takes place when a Falling Threshold is crossed

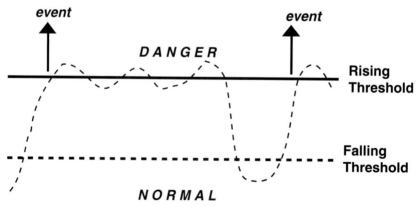

**Figure 28.14** Behavior crossing a Rising Threshold.

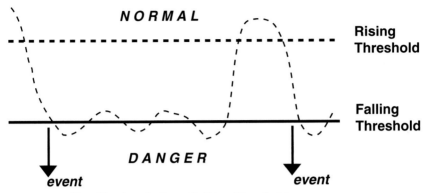

**Figure 28.15**  Trouble signaled by a Falling Threshold.

Thresholds can be set only for numeric variables. Hence, Table 28.13 configures alarms for INTEGER, Counter, Gauge, or TimeTick variables.

How do we use the thresholds? The value of a gauge rises and falls, so it makes sense to compare a gauge value with a threshold. But if the variable being checked is a Counter, what we are really interested in is checking how much the value has *changed* during an interval. In this case, the *delta value,* or change, that occurred over the interval is compared with the thresholds.

### 28.21.3  The Alarm Table

Now we are ready to tackle Table 28.13, the Alarm Table, in which an operator configures the symptoms that spell trouble. An entry in the alarm table identifies a variable, a time interval, and the kind of count that should be tested. It chooses whether we want to check the value of the variable or the change in the variable.

An entry also includes the thresholds: a Rising Threshold with corresponding event, a Falling Threshold with corresponding event. A 0 event index indicates "do nothing," which is fine when the threshold just measures a return to normalcy.

Sometimes we want the very first measurement interval to be handled a bit differently from the others. For example, normally, when the number of collisions goes too high, we might send a trap and write a log message. Then, when things go back to normal, we might record another log message showing when a proper level was reached.

But what about the first interval? If there are too many collisions, we would want to know, but suppose the first reading takes us below the Falling Threshold? We do not need a log entry to remind us that everything was OK.

**TABLE 28.13    The Alarm Table**

iso.org.dod.internet.mgmt.mib-2.
rmon.alarm.alarmTable.alarmEntry
1.3.6.1.2.1.16.3.1.1

| OBJECT IDENTIFIER | Syntax | Access | Description |
|---|---|---|---|
| alarmIndex<br>1.3.6.1.2.1.16.3.1.1.1<br>▶ **Index** | INTEGER<br>(1..65535) | read-<br>only | A unique index for the<br>entry. |
| alarmInterval<br>1.3.6.1.2.1.16.3.1.1.2 | INTEGER | read-<br>write | The interval in seconds<br>over which the data is<br>sampled and compared with<br>the Rising and Falling<br>thresholds. |
| alarmVariable<br>1.3.6.1.2.1.16.3.1.1.3 | OBJECT<br>IDENTIFIER | read-<br>write | The object identifier of the<br>variable to be sampled. |
| alarmSampleType<br>1.3.6.1.2.1.16.3.1.1.4 | INTEGER<br>absolute<br>Value(1),<br>deltaValue(2) | read-<br>write | Choice of whether to<br>compare the actual value or<br>delta change with the<br>thresholds. |
| alarmValue<br>1.3.6.1.2.1.16.3.1.1.5 | INTEGER | read-<br>only | The value of the statistic<br>during the last sampling<br>period. |
| alarmStartup<br>Alarm<br>1.3.6.1.2.1.16.3.1.1.6 | INTEGER<br>risingAlarm(1),<br>fallingAlarm(2),<br>risingOrFalling<br>Alarm(3) | read-<br>write | The start-up alarm, i.e.,<br>conditions for an alarm to<br>be sent as a result of the<br>first sample. |
| alarmRising<br>Threshold<br>1.3.6.1.2.1.16.3.1.1.7 | INTEGER | read-<br>write | The Rising Threshold. |
| alarmFalling<br>Threshold<br>1.3.6.1.2.1.16.3.1.1.8 | INTEGER | read-<br>write | The Falling Threshold. |
| alarmRising<br>EventIndex<br>1.3.6.1.2.1.16.3.1.1.9 | INTEGER<br>(1..65535) | read-<br>write | The index (*eventIndex*) of<br>the *eventEntry* that is used<br>when a Rising Threshold is<br>crossed. If 0, no event will<br>be generated. |
| alarmFalling<br>EventIndex<br>1.3.6.1.2.1.16.3.1.1.10 | INTEGER<br>(1..65535) | read-<br>write | The index (*eventIndex*) of<br>the *eventEntry* that is used<br>when a Falling Threshold is<br>crossed. If 0, no event will<br>be generated. |
| alarmOwner<br>1.3.6.1.2.1.16.3.1.1.11 | OwnerString | read-<br>write | The entity that configured<br>this entry and is therefore<br>using the resources assigned<br>to it. |
| alarmStatus<br>1.3.6.1.2.1.16.3.1.1.12 | Entry<br>Status | read-<br>write | Status of this alarm entry. |

The *alarmStartupAlarm* variable gives us control over the first interval. We can choose to be warned only if the Rising Threshold is crossed; or we can choose to be warned only if the Falling Threshold is crossed; or else, if either threshold is crossed.

## 28.22   EVENTS

The event group includes the Event Table and the Log Table. We think of an event as being "triggered" by current network conditions. The Event Table defines the notification that takes place when an event is triggered. One form of notification is to write an entry in the Log Table.

### 28.22.1   Events, Alarms, and Packet Matching

The Alarm Table sets up problem detection. A detected alarm points to an event that defines a warning or diagnostic action. Specifically:

- When an alarm rising or falling threshold is crossed, a corresponding event is defined in the *alarmRisingEventIndex* or *alarmFallingEventIndex* variable. The entry with this index is looked up in the Event Table. The table indicates what to do—nothing, write an entry in the log table, send a trap, or log *and* trap.

Packet pattern matching also can be tied to an event. Specifically:

- A Channel Table entry optionally identifies the index of an event to be triggered when a packet match is found. The event indicates what to do—log or trap.

An alarm, a resulting event, and packet capture all can be tied together. When the alarm condition occurs, the corresponding event is generated. In turn, this event can be linked to starting or ending packet capture. The *channelTurnOnEventIndex* and *channelTurnOffEventIndex* variables in the Channel Table provide this linkage. Specifically:

- A Channel Table entry optionally identifies an event that will cause packet capture to be turned on, and another event that will cause packet capture to be turned off.

### 28.22.2   The Event Table

Events are configured in Table 28.14, the Event Table. Each entry identifies an event and indicates an action, such as logging or sending a trap. If a trap will be generated, the *eventCommunity* variable identifies where the trap needs to be sent. The *eventLastTimeSent* variable

**TABLE 28.14    The Event Table**

| | iso.org.dod.internet.mgmt.mib-2. rmon.event.eventTable.eventEntry 1.3.6.1.2.1.16.9.1.1 | | |
| --- | --- | --- | --- |
| OBJECT IDENTIFIER | Syntax | Access | Description |
| eventIndex 1.3.6.1.2.1.16.9.1.1.1 ▶ **Index** | INTEGER (1..65535) | read-write | A unique identifier for this entry. |
| eventDescription 1.3.6.1.2.1.16.9.1.1.2 | DisplayString (SIZE(0..127)) | read-write | A comment describing this event entry. |
| eventType 1.3.6.1.2.1.16.9.1.1.3 | INTEGER none(1), log(2), snmp-trap(3), log-and-trap(4) | read-write | The type of event notification that will be done when the event occurs. |
| eventCommunity 1.3.6.1.2.1.16.9.1.1.4 | OCTET (SIZE(0..127)) | read-write | For version 1, if an SNMP trap is generated, it will be sent to this community. |
| eventLastTime Sent 1.3.6.1.2.1.16.9.1.1.5 | TimeTicks | read-only | The value of *sysUpTime* the last time that this entry caused an event. |
| eventOwner 1.3.6.1.2.1.16.9.1.1.6 | Owner String | read-write | The owner of this entry. |
| eventStatus 1.3.6.1.2.1.16.9.1.1.7 | Entry Status | read-write | The status of this entry. |

indicates the last time that this event was triggered. The usual owner and status variables are included for table update control.

### 28.22.3    The Log Table

Table 28.15, the Log Table, is the simplest of the tables in this chapter. It records each event that needs to be logged. It provides the event number, an index that distinguishes occurrences of the same event, the occurrence time, and an implementation-specific event description.

## 28.23    DESIGNING REPORTS

Monitors provide a ton of information. To digest it, it is important to be able to design and print out reports that present selected information in an orderly fashion. Generally, monitors offer some type of report design tool that makes it easy to select variables and display them in any format that you like. An unlimited number of designs is possible.

**TABLE 28.15    The Log Table**

| | iso.org.dod.internet.mgmt.mib-2. rmon.event.logTable.logEntry 1.3.6.1.2.1.16.9.2.1 | | |
|---|---|---|---|
| OBJECT IDENTIFIER | Syntax | Access | Description |
| logEventIndex 1.3.6.1.2.1.16.9.2.1.1 ▶ Index | INTEGER (1..65535) | read-only- | The event entry that generated this log entry. |
| logIndex 1.3.6.1.2.1.16.9.2.1.2 ▶ Index | INTEGER | read-only- | An index that uniquely identifies this entry among those associated with the same event entry. |
| logTime 1.3.6.1.2.1.16.9.2.1.3 | TimeTicks | read-only- | The value of *sysUpTime* when this log entry was created. |
| logDescription 1.3.6.1.2.1.16.9.2.1.4 | Display String (SIZE(0..255)) | read-only- | An implementation-dependent description of the event that activated this log entry. |

A few simple but useful reports are shown in the figures that follow. Figure 28.16 displays a report of traffic history information for a set of 5-minute intervals. The percent utilization of the network in each period is tracked, and a graphic display makes the relative usage in each period quite plain. Most likely, you would want a report that showed daily usage for 30-minute intervals.

Figure 28.17 shows LAN physical addresses. Figure 28.18 shows actual traffic counts for all station addresses.

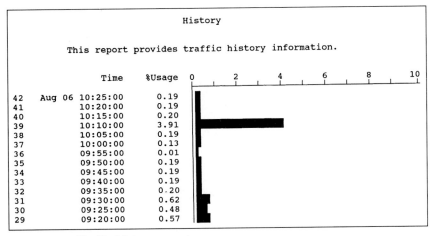

**Figure 28.16** Traffic history report.

```
                          Station List
This report lists the physical address and assigned name of each station.
The stations are sorted by address.


        00000F00A662   Tulip
        0000C0BF455B   Crocus
        000235031038   Sunflower
        030000000001   NetBIOS
```

**Figure 28.17**  LAN address report.

```
                          All Users
This report provides combined transmit and receive statistics for all
stations.  The stations are sorted by name.
                  Monitoring Started:   Aug 06 06:58:01
                  Monitoring Stopped:   Aug 06 10:31:34
                  Elapsed Time:         0 day(s) 03:33:33
```

| | Name | Frames | Errs | Bytes | Size | % Rel |
|---|---|---|---|---|---|---|
| 1 | Broadcast | 18 | 0 | 1,080 | 60 | 0.01 |
| 2 | Crocus | 53,671 | 0 | 29,028,427 | 540 | 26.99 |
| 3 | Sunflower | 175,752 | 0 | 108,493,949 | 617 | 99.95 |
| 4 | Tulip | 122,699 | 0 | 79,431,526 | 647 | 73.05 |

**Figure 28.18**  Traffic count report.

## 28.24  MONITORING A TOKEN-RING

RFC 1513, *Token-Ring Extensions to the Remote Network Monitoring MIB,* includes information that is needed to monitor the Token-Ring protocol elements.

In particular, the Token-Ring Media Access Control (MAC) protocol requires a number of packet (frame) types that are used purely to control access and handle errors. It is just as important to monitor these packets as it is to watch data packets.

The Token-Ring RMON MIB groups include:

- The Token Ring Mac-Layer Statistics Group: Includes overall counts of control traffic, plus counts of the many types of Token-Ring error conditions.

- The Token Ring Promiscuous Statistics Group: Includes overall counts of unicast, multicast, and broadcast data traffic, as well as a breakdown of the traffic by packet sizes.

- The Token Ring Mac-Layer History Group: Contains counts of control traffic and errors. The variables are similar to those in the Mac-Layer Statistics Group.

- The Token Ring Promiscuous History Group: Contains a sequence of counts of data traffic and errors. The variables are similar to those in the Promiscuous Statistics Group.

- The Token Ring Ring Station Group: Identifies and provides status and error statistics about every station on the local ring.

- The Token Ring Ring Station Order Group: Identifies the order of the stations as the ring is traversed.

- The Token Ring Ring Station Config Group: Provides detailed configuration information about stations, including such items as the assigned physical address, group addresses, functional addresses, and microcode version. Includes a control function that lets an operator remove a station from the ring.

- The Token Ring Source Routing Group: Statistics derived from source routing information in packets. Includes counts of traffic to and from other rings, and traffic breakdowns by the number of hops between the local and remote ring.

Figure 28.19 shows a *Sniffer* Token-Ring monitor screen. We can see that the reports listed on the screen relate to the information in the Token-Ring MIB groups. Figure 28.20 shows some preconfigured global alarms for a Token-Ring.

## 28.25 EXPERT CAPABILITIES

Monitors are getting smarter and smarter. The *Sniffer* used for the displays in this chapter can automatically diagnose network problems at every layer of network activity. A few examples are shown in Table 28.16 for each layer, in order to give a flavor of the kind of help that a monitor can offer. Default values are provided for the thresholds used to recognize problems. The operator can tune the thresholds to fit local conditions.

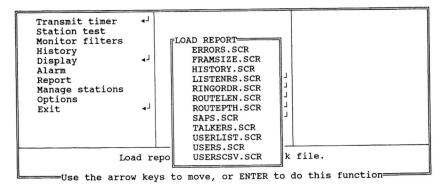

**Figure 28.19** Token-Ring monitor screen.

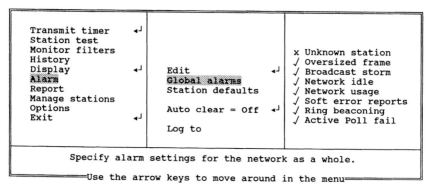

**Figure 28.20**  Configuring Token-Ring alarms.

## 28.26  MONITORS AND MANAGERS

Monitors offer a rich set of tools for finding out what is happening on your networks. Best of all, they get information without adding polling messages to the traffic.

We have seen that the designers of the RMON MIB tackled a difficult job and have done quite well at accomplishing what they set out to

**TABLE 28.16    Expert Diagnoses**

| Application Layer |
| --- |
| An excessive percentage of client requests are being refused. |
| Response time is too slow for a significant percentage of requests. |
| File transfers between two local stations are too slow. |
| File transfers between a local station and a remote station are too slow. |

| Connection Layer |
| --- |
| Station needs to retransmit data too frequently. |
| Excessive retransmissions—connection has been lost. |
| Receive window has been zero for a long time. |
| Connection has been idle for a suspiciously long period. |

| Network Layer |
| --- |
| There are stations with the same network layer address. |
| Too many routers are being used to route data to the same destination. |

| Data Link Control Station Layer |
| --- |
| There is a suspiciously large number of broadcasts. |
| The rate of physical errors is too high. |
| (For a WAN link.) The link is overloaded or underloaded. |

| MAC Layer |
| --- |
| (For a Token-Ring.) There are too many insertions—or deletions of stations. |
| (For a Token-Ring.) There are excessive ring purges. |

do. They have succeeded in giving an SNMP manager the ability to configure and control a monitor. The manager can extract useful information ranging from simple global statistics to detailed packet captures. Now it is up to the vendors of monitors and management stations to compete—or cooperate—to provide the most intuitive configuration screens, the best tables and graphs, and the most powerful report design tools.

## 28.27  RECOMMENDED READING

The RMON MIB was defined in RFC 1271, *Remote Network Monitoring Management Information Base*. Token-Ring extensions were defined in RFC 1513. Some of the best sources for understanding how to use this MIB are the manuals published by monitor vendors.

# 29

# Managing AppleTalk

## 29.1 INTRODUCTION

*AppleTalk* is a family of protocols originally developed for the purpose of networking Apple computers. The protocol has been ported to several other computer systems—primarily systems that wish to offer services to AppleTalk nodes.

Originally, AppleTalk ran only on Apple's proprietary *LocalTalk* LAN. LocalTalk was small-scale and slow, but very low in cost; in fact, it was virtually free, since Apple packaged all the necessary interface hardware and software in their Macintosh systems. LocalTalk enabled up to 32 devices to be joined on a twisted pair bus and communicate at speeds of up to 230.4 Kbits/second.

Later, AppleTalk graduated to a more sophisticated *Phase 2 architecture.* Phase 2 AppleTalk could run on popular LANs such as Ethernet or Token-Ring and even on internets consisting of multiple LANs, routers, serial lines, and backbone IP networks.

An outstanding characteristic of an AppleTalk network is that every resource has a user-friendly text name and end users ask for resources by name. Network addresses do not need to be preconfigured and, optionally, may change frequently. Several ingenious protocols are used to locate named resources (such as file servers or printers) dynamically, as the resources are needed.

## 29.2 THE APPLETALK MIB

Although it relates to a vendor protocol, the AppleTalk MIB is the work of an IETF task force and has been published in an RFC. As defined in RFC 1243, the AppleTalk MIB contains nine groups of variables*:

---

* At the time of writing, the AppleTalk MIB had Proposed Standard status.

- *LLAP.*  The LocalTalk Link Access Protocol was Apple's original simple LAN access protocol. This group includes traffic and error statistics for LLAP interfaces.

- *AARP.*  The AppleTalk Address Resolution Protocol, a protocol similar to ARP, is used to translate AppleTalk network layer addresses to physical addresses. This group tabulates physical addresses and their corresponding AppleTalk network layer addresses.

- *ATPort.*  This group tabulates configuration and status information associated with the *logical ports* for an AppleTalk router. A logical port identifies a network over which AppleTalk traffic can be transmitted. A port may map to a normal interface supported by AppleTalk, such as an LLAP, Ethernet, or Token-Ring interface.

  Alternatively, a port may correspond to a serial connection between AppleTalk nets, an interface to an IP network that will carry traffic between two AppleTalk nets (by *tunneling*), or an attachment to some other type of backbone network.

- *DDP.*  The Datagram Delivery Protocol, a protocol similar to IP, is responsible for end-to-end delivery of datagrams. This group tabulates traffic and error statistics for this AppleTalk routing protocol.

- *RTMP.*  The Routing Table Maintenance Protocol is a protocol similar to RIP that specifies router-to-router information exchanges and the contents of a router's routing table. This group tabulates RTMP routing table entries.

- *KIP.*  The Kinetics Internet Protocol is used to encapsulate and route AppleTalk datagrams across an IP internet. This group tabulates KIP routing table entries.

- *ZIP.*  A zone is a set of nodes in an AppleTalk internet that have some kind of logical association (e.g., a work group). Each zone has a name. The Zone Information Protocol (ZIP) enables routers to exchange zone information. ZIP also enables a user system to ask a local router to provide the list of valid zone names for its network. This group tabulates zone information.

- *NBP.*  The Name Binding Protocol is used to convert a user-friendly service name to the numeric addressing information needed to find the service. This group contains a configuration table that pairs each service with its zone.

- *ATEcho.*  The AppleTalk Echo Protocol is a protocol similar to the TCP/IP ICMP echo request and response. This group simply counts echo requests and responses.

There is ongoing work to enhance the AppleTalk MIB. Improvements include definitions of additional variables for the nine defined groups as well as the definition of new groups to cover management of the higher layers of the AppleTalk protocols, such as the AppleTalk Transaction Protocol, Printer Access Protocol, AppleTalk Session Protocol, and AppleTalk Data Stream Protocol. At the time of writing, these enhancements were still in the draft/experimental stage.

## 29.3 THE LOCALTALK LINK ACCESS PROTOCOL

The *LocalTalk Link Access Protocol* is the classic link protocol used on Apple's original simple twisted pair bus LAN. The LocalTalk Link Access Protocol is based on *Carrier Sense Multiple Access with Collision Avoidance*. When a node wishes to transmit a frame, it waits until the line has been idle for a preset time—and then waits for an additional short random period. If the line is still idle, the node sends a short request-to-send (RTS) frame to the destination. If a clear-to-send (CTS) is received, then the information frame is sent.

LocalTalk stations use a simple 1-byte address which they dynamically generate at start-up time:

- The station picks an address and asks if anybody else is using it.
- If the address is in use, another address is picked and the station asks again.
- The process is repeated until a free address is found.

Clients find services by broadcasting the service name to find out where the service resides.

Note that this network technology is proprietary, and the only frames that will be sent through a LocalTalk interface will be LocalTalk frames.

Table 29.1 lists the MIB variables for the LocalTalk Link Access Protocol. Note that in addition to the usual counts of good and bad incoming and outgoing frames, there are counts relating to request-to-sends that were not answered and clear-to-sends that did not match a request.

## 29.4 APPLETALK ADDRESS RESOLUTION PROTOCOL

In its Phase 2 version, AppleTalk was enhanced so that it could run on popular LAN technologies such as Ethernet and Token-Ring, and was extended to internets connected by routers. To support internet

**TABLE 29.1   Table of LLAP Statistics**

| iso.org.dod.internet.mgmt.mib-2.appleTalk.llapTable.llapEntry 1.3.6.1.2.1.13.1.1.1 | | | |
|---|---|---|---|
| OBJECT IDENTIFIER | Syntax | Access | Description |
| llapIfIndex ▶ **Index** 1.3.6.1.2.1.13.1.1.1.1 | INTEGER | read-only | The value of ifIndex for this interface. |
| llapInPkts* 1.3.6.1.2.1.13.1.1.1.2 | Counter | read-only | The total number of good frames received at this interface. |
| llapOutPkts* 1.3.6.1.2.1.13.1.1.1.3 | Counter | read-only | The total number of frames transmitted at this interface. |
| llapInNoHandlers* 1.3.6.1.2.1.13.1.1.1.4 | Counter | read-only | Number of good incoming frames whose destination protocol was not available. |
| llapInLengthErrors 1.3.6.1.2.1.13.1.1.1.5 | Counter | read-only | The number of incoming frames whose length did not match the length in the header. |
| llapInErrors* 1.3.6.1.2.1.13.1.1.1.6 | Counter | read-only | The total number of incoming frames containing errors. |
| llapCollisions 1.3.6.1.2.1.13.1.1.1.7 | Counter | read-only | Number of collisions diagnosed due to lack of a Clear-to-Send response. |
| llapDefers 1.3.6.1.2.1.13.1.1.1.8 | Counter | read-only | Total of number of times sending was deferred. |
| llapNoDataErrors 1.3.6.1.2.1.13.1.1.1.9 | Counter | read-only | Number of times a Request-to-Send was received, but no information frame arrived. |
| llapRandom CTSErrors 1.3.6.1.2.1.13.1.1.1.10 | Counter | read-only | Total of Clear-to-Send frames received when no request-to-send had been transmitted. |
| llapFCSErrors 1.3.6.1.2.1.13.1.1.1.11 | Counter | read-only | Total incoming frames with a Frame Check Sequence Error |

\* NOTE: These variables duplicate counts that are already available in the MIB-II *interfaces* group, and it is very likely that they will be deprecated in the next version of the AppleTalk MIB.

addressing, AppleTalk's Phase 2 datagram protocol uses 3-octet addresses of the form:

(2 octets)                          (1 octet)

net number                      node number

The AppleTalk MIB defines the textual convention *DdpAddress* to denote these OCTET STRINGS. Note that the net number can be set to 0 for a small stand-alone network.

In order to deliver data to Ethernet or Token-Ring destinations, the AppleTalk addresses must be translated to physical board addresses. This job is done by the *AppleTalk Address Resolution Protocol* (AARP), which is similar to the Address Resolution Protocol (ARP) used for IP address translation. The key information for the AppleTalk Address Resolution Protocol (AARP) is a table mapping AppleTalk Protocol Addresses to physical board addresses. Table 29.2 lists the variables in the address resolution table.

## 29.5  APPLETALK PORTS

Since node identifiers are only 1 octet long, the number of nodes in an AppleTalk network would appear to be quite restricted. However, this is not really a problem, since a physical LAN—such as an Ethernet or Token-Ring—can be assigned a *range* of network numbers.

An AppleTalk router needs to be aware of all of the network numbers that can be reached through each of its interfaces.

The concept of a logical port is used to sort out this information when configuring an AppleTalk router. A range of network numbers and a "zone" are associated with an AppleTalk port, as shown in Table 29.3, the AppleTalk Port Table. Zones will be explained later.

**TABLE 29.2    AppleTalk Address Resolution Protocol Table**

| OBJECT IDENTIFIER | Syntax | Access | Description |
|---|---|---|---|
| iso.org.dod.internet.mgmt.mib-2. appleTalk.aarp.aarpTable.aarpEntry 1.3.6.1.2.1.13.2.1.1. | | | |
| aarpIfIndex 1.3.6.1.2.1.13.2.1.1.1 ▶ **Index** | INTEGER | read-only | The value of *ifIndex* for this interface. |
| aarpPhysAddress 1.3.6.1.2.1.13.2.1.1.2 | OCTET STRING | read-only | The media-dependent Physical address. |
| aarpNetAddress 1.3.6.1.2.1.13.2.1.1.3 ▶ **Index** | DdpAddress | read-only | The AppleTalk Network Address |

**TABLE 29.3    Table of Logical Port Information**

| | | | |
|---|---|---|---|
| iso.org.dod.internet.mgmt.mib-2.appleTalk.atport.atport.Table.atport.Entry 1.3.6.1.2.1.13.3.1.1 | | | |
| OBJECT IDENTIFIER | Syntax | Access | Description |
| atportIndex 1.3.6.1.2.1.13.3.1.1.1 ▶ **Index** | INTEGER | read-only | A unique number assigned to the logical port. |
| atportDescr 1.3.6.1.2.1.13.3.1.1.2 | Display String | read-only | An ASCII text string describing the port. |
| atportType 1.3.6.1.2.1.13.3.1.1.3 | INTEGER other(1), localtalk(2), ethertalk1(3), ethertalk2(4), tokentalk(5), iptalk(6), serial-ppp(7), serial-nonstandard(8), virtual(9) | read-write | The type of supporting lower-layer protocol. |
| atportNetStart 1.3.6.1.2.1.13.3.1.1.4 | OCTET STRING (SIZE(2)) | read-write | The first network address in the range for this port. |
| atportNetEnd 1.3.6.1.2.1.13.3.1.1.5 | OCTET STRING (SIZE(2)) | read-write | The last network address in the range for this port. |
| atportNetAddress 1.3.6.1.2.1.13.3.1.1.6 | DdpAddress | read-write | The specific AppleTalk network address configured for this port. |
| atportStatus 1.3.6.1.2.1.13.3.1.1.7 | INTEGER operational(1), unconfigured(2), off(3), invalid(4) | read-write | The configuration status of the port. When set to invalid, the entry is logically deleted. |
| atportNetConfig 1.3.6.1.2.1.13.3.1.1.8 | INTEGER configured(1), garnered(2), guessed(3), unconfigured(4) | read-only | The source for network configuration info for this port. *Garnered* means obtained by observing the net. |
| atportZoneConfig 1.3.6.1.2.1.13.3.1.1.9 | INTEGER configured(1), garnered(2), guessed(3), unconfigured(4) | read-only | The source for zone configured info for this port. |
| atportZone 1.3.6.1.2.1.13.3.1.1.10 | OCTET STRING | read-write | Zone name configured for this AppleTalk port. |
| atportIfIndex 1.3.6.1.2.1.13.3.1.1.11 | INTEGER | read-write | The physical interface (*ifIndex*) for this port. |

## 29.6   THE DATAGRAM DELIVERY PROTOCOL

AppleTalk's *Datagram Delivery Protocol* (DDP) is similar in many ways to IP. DDP uses a RIP-like routing protocol. However, the hop counter in a DDP header initially is set to 0 and counts up to 15 instead of counting down to 0. The DDP group is made up of a set of datagram statistics, displayed in Table 29.4

## 29.7   THE ROUTING TABLE MAINTENANCE PROTOCOL

The *Routing Table Maintenance Protocol* (RTMP) enables AppleTalk routers to exchange routing information and dynamically update their routing tables. Its basic operation is similar to the Routing Information Protocol (RIP). Table 29.5, the AppleTalk Routing Table, contains routing information.

## 29.8   THE KINETICS INTERNET PROTOCOL

The *Kinetics Internet Protocol* (KIP) is used to encapsulate AppleTalk datagrams and route them across an IP internet. Table 29.6 displays KIP routing configuration information.

## 29.9   THE ZONE INFORMATION PROTOCOL

A *zone* is a set of nodes in an AppleTalk internet that have some kind of logical association (e.g., nodes in a work group or at some specific location). Each zone has a name.

Nodes on a single network may belong to different zones. The permissible zone names that can be *used* on any individual network are limited to a preconfigured list of up to 255 zones. A system must choose its zone name from this list.

The mapping of a range of network numbers to a list of permitted zone names is maintained at AppleTalk routers. Each router is configured with information for its connected networks.

When a router discovers one or more new networks on its internet, it uses the Zone Information Protocol (ZIP) to ask neighbor routers for the zone lists for the networks.

ZIP also enables ordinary systems to find out which zones are legitimate for the networks of the internet. Table 29.7 contains ZIP configuration information.

**TABLE 29.4  Datagram Delivery Protocol Statistics**

iso.org.dod.internet.mgmt.mib-2.appleTalk.ddp
1.3.6.1.2.1.13.4

| OBJECT IDENTIFIER | Syntax | Access | Description |
|---|---|---|---|
| ddpOutRequests 1.3.6.1.2.1.13.4.1 | Counter | read-only | Number of DDP datagrams submitted from local clients. |
| ddpOutShorts 1.3.6.1.2.1.13.4.2 | Counter | read-only | Number of transmitted short (1-byte) address DDP datagrams. |
| ddpOutLongs 1.3.6.1.2.1.13.4.3 | Counter | read-only | Number of transmitted long (3-byte) address DDP datagrams. |
| ddpInReceives 1.3.6.1.2.1.13.4.4 | Counter | read-only | Total number of incoming datagrams received by DDP, including errors. |
| ddpForw Requests 1.3.6.1.2.1.13.4.5 | Counter | read-only | Number of incoming datagrams for which forwarding was attempted. |
| ddpInLocal Datagrams 1.3.6.1.2.1.13.4.6 | Counter | read-only | Number of incoming datagrams for which this was the destination. |
| ddpNoProtocol Handlers 1.3.6.1.2.1.13.4.7 | Counter | read-only | Number of incoming datagrams for which destination protocol was not available. |
| ddpOutNo Routes 1.3.6.1.2.1.13.4.8 | Counter | read-only | Number of datagrams dropped because a route could not be found. |
| ddpTooShort Errors 1.3.6.1.2.1.13.4.9 | Counter | read-only | Number of incoming datagrams dropped because the received data length was less than indicated in the header, or the datagram was shorter than a header. |
| ddpTooLong Errors 1.3.6.1.2.1.13.4.10 | Counter | read-only | Number of incoming datagrams dropped because the received data length was greater than stated in the header or larger than the allowed maximum. |
| ddpBroadcast Errors 1.3.6.1.2.1.13.4.11 | Counter | read-only | Number of incoming datagrams, broadcast at the link level, dropped because this was not their DDP destination. |
| ddpShortDDP Errors 1.3.6.1.2.1.13.4.12 | Counter | read-only | Number of incoming datagrams dropped because this was not the destination and their type was short DDP. |
| ddpHopCount Errors 1.3.6.1.2.1.13.4.13 | Counter | read-only | Number of incoming datagrams dropped because this was not the final destination and the hop count would exceed 15. |
| ddpChecksum Errors 1.3.6.1.2.1.13.4.14 | Counter | read-only | Number of incoming datagrams dropped because of a header checksum error. |

**TABLE 29.5    AppleTalk Routing Table**

iso.org.dod.internet.mgmt.mib-2.
appleTalk.rtmp.rtmpTable.rtmpEntry
1.3.6.1.2.1.13.5.1.1

| OBJECT IDENTIFIER | Syntax | Access | Description |
|---|---|---|---|
| rtmpRangeStart 1.3.6.1.2.1.13.5.1.1.1 ▶ **Index** | OCTET STRING (SIZE(2)) | read-write* | The first network address in the range for this entry. |
| rtmpRangeEnd 1.3.6.1.2.1.13.5.1.1.2 | OCTET STRING (SIZE(2)) | read-write* | The last network address in the range for this entry. (This is 0 for a Phase 1 or nonextended network.) |
| rtmpNextHop 1.3.6.1.2.1.13.5.1.1.3 | OCTET STRING | read-write* | The next hop for this route— a DdpAddress if the route type is AppleTalk. |
| rtmpType 1.3.6.1.2.1.13.5.1.1.4 | INTEGER other(1), appletalk(2), serial-ppp(3), serial-nonstandard(4) | read-write* | The type of net for the next hop. DDP addresses are not assigned for serial links. |
| rtmpPort 1.3.6.1.2.1.13.5.1.1.5 | INTEGER | read-write* | The index of the AppleTalk port for this route. |
| rtmpHops 1.3.6.1.2.1.13.5.1.1.6 | INTEGER | read-write* | The number of hops to the destination network. |
| rtmpState 1.3.6.1.2.1.13.5.1.1.7 | INTEGER good(1), suspect(2), goingBad(3), bad(4) | read-write | The status of the information in this entry. A bad entry can be removed. |

* NOTE: These variables should not be settable by a management station. Their status will be changed to read-only in a future release.

## 29.10    THE NAME BINDING PROTOCOL

End users in an AppleTalk network identify resources using text names that are made up of three parts—object, type, and zone. For example, Helen:Mailbox@Chicago.

The AppleTalk *Name Binding Protocol* (NBP) dynamically maps the text name of a resource to its address. Each node stores names of resources that it offers in a local table. A remote client that wants to access a resource finds the resource by means of the Name Binding Protocol, which sends out a query using a zonewide multicast.

Table 29.8 lists the resources available at the local node.

**TABLE 29.6    Routing Table for KIP Encapsulation**

<table>
<tr><th colspan="4">iso.org.dod.internet.mgmt.mib-2.<br>appleTalk.kip.kipTable.kipEntry<br>1.3.6.1.2.1.13.6.1.1</th></tr>
<tr><th>OBJECT<br>IDENTIFIER</th><th>Syntax</th><th>Access</th><th>Description</th></tr>
<tr><td>kipNetStart<br>1.3.6.1.2.1.13.6.1.1.1<br>▶ **Index**</td><td>OCTET<br>STRING<br>(SIZE(2))</td><td>read-<br>write</td><td>The network number for<br>the first network in the<br>range.</td></tr>
<tr><td>kipNetEnd<br>1.3.6.1.2.1.13.6.1.1.2</td><td>OCTET<br>STRING<br>(SIZE(2))</td><td>read-<br>write</td><td>The network number for<br>the last number in the<br>range.</td></tr>
<tr><td>kipNextHop<br>1.3.6.1.2.1.13.6.1.1.3</td><td>IpAddress</td><td>read-<br>write</td><td>The IP address of the next<br>hop in the route to this<br>entry's destination network.</td></tr>
<tr><td>kipHopCount<br>1.3.6.1.2.1.13.6.1.1.4</td><td>INTEGER</td><td>read-<br>write</td><td>The number of hops to the<br>destination network.</td></tr>
<tr><td>kipBCastAddr<br>1.3.6.1.2.1.13.6.1.1.5</td><td>IpAddress</td><td>read-<br>write</td><td>The form of the IP address<br>used to broadcast on this<br>network.</td></tr>
<tr><td>kipCore<br>1.3.6.1.2.1.13.6.1.1.6</td><td>INTEGER<br>core(1),<br>notcore(2)</td><td>read-<br>write</td><td>Status: whether this is a<br>KIP core network.</td></tr>
<tr><td>kipType<br>1.3.6.1.2.1.13.6.1.1.7</td><td>INTEGER<br>kipRouter(1),<br>net(2),<br>host(3),<br>other(4)</td><td>read-<br>write</td><td>The type of destination<br>that this route points to.</td></tr>
<tr><td>kipState<br>1.3.6.1.2.1.13.6.1.1.8</td><td>INTEGER<br>configured(1),<br>learned(2),<br>invalid(3)</td><td>read-<br>write</td><td>The state of this network<br>entry.</td></tr>
<tr><td>kipShare<br>1.3.6.1.2.1.13.6.1.1.9</td><td>INTEGER<br>shared(1),<br>private(2)</td><td>read-<br>write</td><td>The value is "shared" if the<br>information in this entry is<br>propagated to other routers;<br>otherwise, private.</td></tr>
</table>

**TABLE 29.7    The Zone Information Protocol Table**

iso.org.dod.internet.mgmt.mib-2.
appleTalk.zip.zipTable.zipEntry
1.3.6.1.2.1.13.7.1.1

| OBJECT IDENTIFIER | Syntax | Access | Description |
|---|---|---|---|
| zipZoneName 1.3.6.1.2.1.13.7.1.1.1 | OCTET STRING | read-write* | The ASCII text name for the zone. |
| zipZoneIndex 1.3.6.1.2.1.13.7.1.1.2 ▶ Index | INTEGER | read-only | A unique integer is associated with each zone name in the table. |
| zipZoneNetStart 1.3.6.1.2.1.13.7.1.1.3 ▶ Index | OCTET STRING (SIZE(2)) | read-write* | The network number for the first network in the range. |
| zipZoneNetEnd 1.3.6.1.2.1.13.7.1.1.4 | OCTET STRING (SIZE(2)) | read-write* | The network number for the last number in the range. |
| zipZoneState 1.3.6.1.2.1.13.7.1.1.5 | INTEGER valid(1), invalid(2) | read-write | The state of the entry. If invalid, the entry should be considered deleted. |

* NOTE: These variables should not be settable by a management station. Their status will be changed to read-only in a future release.

**TABLE 29.8    Services at The Local Node**

iso.org.dod.internet.mgmt.mib-2.
appleTalk.nbp.nbpTable.nbpEntry
1.3.6.1.2.1.13.8.1.1

| OBJECT IDENTIFIER | Syntax | Access | Description |
|---|---|---|---|
| nbpIndex 1.3.6.1.2.1.13.8.1.1.1 ▶ Index | INTEGER | read-only | The index of the table entry. |
| nbpObject 1.3.6.1.2.1.13.8.1.1.2 | OCTET STRING | read-write | The first (object) part of the name. |
| nbpType 1.3.6.1.2.1.13.8.1.1.3 | OCTET STRING | read-write | The second (type) part of the name. |
| nbpZone 1.3.6.1.2.1.13.8.1.1.4 | OCTET STRING | read-write | The third (zone) part of the name. |
| nbpState 1.3.6.1.2.1.13.8.1.1.5 | INTEGER valid(1), invalid(2) | read-write | The state of the entry. |

**TABLE 29.9   Echo Protocol Statistics**

| iso.org.dod.internet.mgmt.mib-2. appleTalk.atecho 1.3.6.1.2.1.13.9 | | | |
|---|---|---|---|
| OBJECT IDENTIFIER | Syntax | Access | Description |
| atechoRequests 1.3.6.1.2.1.13.9.1. | Counter | read-only | The number of AppleTalk echo requests received. |
| atechoReplies 1.3.6.1.2.1.13.9.2 | Counter | read-only | The number of AppleTalk echo replies sent. |

## 29.11   THE APPLETALK ECHO PROTOCOL

The *AppleTalk Echo Protocol* functions very much like a TCP/IP ICMP echo request and reply, and is used to check whether a system is active. Echo statistics are defined in Table 29.9.

## 29.12   RECOMMENDED READING

*Inside AppleTalk* by G. Sidhu, R. Andrews, and A. Oppenheimer (Addison Wesley) contains succinct descriptions of all of the AppleTalk protocols. At the time of writing, RFC 1243 was the current version of the proposed MIB.

# 30

# Vendor MIBs: The Novell MIB

## 30.1 INTRODUCTION

Several standard MIBs have been presented in this book, and many more have been published. But in spite of the scope of standard MIBs, many vendors of communications products still feel that they need to define their own MIBs in order to configure and control special features of their products.

It is possible that as the number of standard MIBs grows and is refined, many of these proprietary equipment MIBs may shrink and even disappear. On the other hand, it is not such a bad situation for users if vendors continue to outpace standards writers in providing interesting new product capabilities!

One of the most important vendor MIBs is the one that is evolving to manage proprietary NetWare networks. With its huge installed base, NetWare clients and servers can be found within almost every large enterprise.

The Novell MIB is large enough to inspire a book on its own. Our goal in this chapter is to demonstrate that the proprietary Novell MIB is written in the same style as are standard MIBs, and show that there are no special problems in reading it. We will present a brief introduction to NetWare protocols, present a few MIB excerpts, and display a sample table.

## 30.2 FORMAT OF VENDOR MIBS

Vendors write their MIBs using ASN.1, and follow the macro conventions defined in the SNMP standards documents. Many vendor MIBs are publicly available.

An important issue for the use of vendor MIBs is the ease with which they can be integrated into your management environment. In Chapter 7, Figure 7.7 showed that MIBs can be loaded into NetView/6000 with a simple menu click. The ability to load vendor MIBs is an important management station feature.

## 30.3   A BRIEF INTRODUCTION
## TO NETWARE

NetWare communications form a family of protocols originally developed for the purpose of supporting Novell's file and print servers. The protocol has been ported to many computer systems that can act as servers for NetWare clients. NetWare runs over many types of LAN and wide area communications technologies, and is so widely implemented that it might be considered a de facto standard. NetWare communications are based on five protocols:

- *Internetwork Packet Exchange (IPX).*   A connectionless Network Layer protocol. IPX defines the network address, the datagram format, and routing procedures.

- *Routing Information Protocol (RIP).*   Defines messages passed between routers and the method of computing routing table entries. NetWare RIP also includes messages that enable hosts to discover routes.

- *Service Advertising Protocol (SAP).*   Enables servers to advertise their availability and the type of service that they offer. The information is propagated from the local router to all routers using SAP messages. Workstations use SAP messages to ask a local router for the name and address of the nearest server of a given type.

- *NetWare Core Protocol (NCP).*   Protocol controlling all aspects of file access, file maintenance, and print service.

- *Sequenced Packet Exchange (SPX).*   Provides reliable, connection-oriented communication.

The relationship between the protocols is shown in Figure 30.1. NetBIOS appears in the figure because NetBIOS messages can be tunneled across a NetWare network inside IPX datagrams.

A new protocol has been introduced into NetWare in addition to those listed above. NLSP is a routing protocol that offers improved routing functionality.

Like AppleTalk, parts of NetWare—IPX and RIP—were adapted from the Xerox Network System protocol family. However, several changes were introduced into both IPX and RIP.

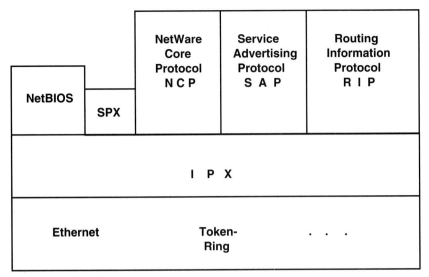

**Figure 30.1**  NetWare protocols.

## 30.4  IPX

Every network segment in an IPX internet is assigned a network number. Datagrams are routed based on their network numbers. A network destination of 0 usually means the local network. However, at initialization, a system will broadcast datagrams with both source and destination network numbers set to 0—e.g., to find the nearest server. The source system will receive responses that identify the source and destination network numbers.

Each communicating process has an IPX address consisting of:

- Network number for the system's network
- Node number for the system
- Socket number for the process

The system's node number is its physical (MAC) address. When a process at a system needs to communicate, it obtains a *socket number*. Socket numbers function like TCP or UDP port numbers to enable delivery of traffic to the correct destination process. Several socket numbers are reserved for well-known services, such as RIP or NetBIOS.

IPX headers are 30 octets long, and include destination and source addresses, along with some other fields. The address format is shown in Figure 30.2.

| NETWORK | NODE | SOCKET |
|---------|------|--------|
| 4  octets | 6  octets | 2  octets |

**Figure 30.2** IPX address format.

Historically, the maximum length of an IPX datagram was 576 octets. Newer implementations can support up to 65,536 octets. However, IPX does not support fragmentation, so that datagrams which are too large to be forwarded will be discarded.

Like AppleTalk, an increasing hop counter is used. A datagram is discarded when its count reaches 16.

### 30.5  RIP

A router exchanges routing information with its neighbor routers by means of periodic Routing Information Protocol (RIP) messages. RIP broadcasts also are triggered by network changes.

There also are RIP messages that are used by hosts. When a host needs to find out how to reach a destination at a remote network number, the host broadcasts a request. The router with the best path responds.

### 30.6  SAP

The Service Advertising Protocol (SAP) enables servers and routers to exchange information about the location of services. Routers propagate SAP information to other routers. Clients can then obtain information about a service anywhere on the network from their neighboring router. Like RIP, SAP messages are broadcast periodically, and also are triggered by changes in the location of network services.

### 30.7  THE NOVELL MIB

The Novell MIB is quite massive, containing many groups of variables. Not all parts have been published at the time of writing. The definitions for the *ipx* part of the Novell tree start off:

```
novell OBJECT IDENTIFIER::= { enterprises 23}
mibDoc OBJECT IDENTIFIER::= { novell 2}
ipx     OBJECT IDENTIFIER::= {mibDoc 5}

ipxSystem OBJECT IDENTIFIER::= {ipx 1}
ipxCircuit OBJECT IDENTIFIER::= {ipx 2}
ipxForwarding OBJECT IDENTIFIER::= {ipx 3}
ipxServices OBJECT IDENTIFIER::= {ipx 4}
ipxTraps OBJECT IDENTIFIER::= {ipx 5}
```

The textual convention *NetNumber* is a 4-byte OCTET STRING that represents an IPX network number. Definitions for the *ipx system group* start out with:

```
ipxBasicSysTableOBJECT-TYPE
   SYNTAX SEQUENCEOF IPXBasicSysEntry
   ACCESS not-accessible
   STATUS mandatory
   DESCRIPTION
      "The IPX System table - basic information."
   ::= {ipxSystem 1}

ipxBasicSysEntryOBJECT-TYPE
   SYNTAX IPXBasicSysEntry
   ACCESS not-accessible
   STATUS mandatory
   DESCRIPTION
      "Each entry corresponds to one instance of IPX running
      on the system."
   INDEX {ipxBasicSysInstance}
   ::= {ipxBasicSysTable1}
```

The initial individual definitions start with:

```
ipxBasicSysInstanceOBJECT-TYPE
   SYNTAX INTEGER
   ACCESS read-write
   STATUS mandatory
   DESCRIPTION
      "The unique identifier of the instance
      of IPX to which this row corresponds.
      This value may be written only when
      creating a new entry in the table."
   ::= {ipxBasicSysEntry1}
   ipxBasicSysExistStateOBJECT-TYPE
   SYNTAX INTEGER {
      off(1),
      on(2)
      }
   ACCESS read-write
   STATUS mandatory
   DESCRIPTION
      "The validity of this entry in the
      IPX system table. Setting this field
      to off indicates that this entry may be
      deleted from the system table at the IPX
      implementation's discretion."
   ::= {ipxBasicSysEntry2}
```

In fact, note that this MIB looks exactly like a standard MIB.

**TABLE 30.1  The Basic System Table**

iso.org.dod.internetprivate.enterprises.
novell.mibdoc.ipx.ipxSystem.ipxBasicSysTable.ipxBasicSysEntry
1.3.6.1.2.4.1.23.2.5.1.1.1

| OBJECT IDENTIFIER | Syntax | Access | Description |
|---|---|---|---|
| ipxBasicSys Instance 1.3.6.1.2.4.1.23.2. 5.1.1.1.1 ▶ **Index** | INTEGER | read-write | Unique index for this instance of IPX. |
| ipxBasicSys ExistState 1.3.6.1.2.4.1.23.2. 5.1.1.1.2 | INTEGER off(1), on(2) | read-write | Validity of entry. Off means that it can be deleted. |
| ipxBasicSys NetNumber 1.3.6.1.2.4.1.23.2. 5.1.1.1.3 | Net Number | read-write | Network number part of the IPX address of this entity. |
| ipxBasicSys Node 1.3.6.1.2.4.1.23.2. 5.1.1.1.4 | OCTET STRING (SIZE(6)) | read-write | The node number portion of the IPX address of this entity. |
| ipxBasicSys Name 1.3.6.1.2.4.1.23.2. 5.1.1.1.5 | OCTET STRING (SIZE(0..48)) | read-write | The readable name for this system. |
| ipxBasicSys InReceives 1.3.6.1.2.4.1.23.2. 5.1.1.1.6 | Counter | read-only | Total number of IPX packets received, including those received in error. |
| ipxBasicSys InHdrErrors 1.3.6.1.2.4.1.23.2. 5.1.1.1.7 | Counter | read-only | Number of IPX packets discarded due to errors in their headers, including any IPX packet with a size less than the minimum of 30 bytes. |
| ipxBasicSys InUnknown Sockets 1.3.6.1.2.4.1.23.2. 5.1.1.1.8 | Counter | read-only | Number of IPX packets discarded because the destination socket was not open. |
| ipxBasicSys InDiscards 1.3.6.1.2.4.1.23.2. 5.1.1.1.9 | Counter | read-only | Number of IPX packets received but discarded due to reasons other than header errors, unknown sockets, or decompression errors. |

**TABLE 30.1   The Basic System Table (*Continued*)**

iso.org.dod.internetprivate.enterprises.
novell.mibdoc.ipx.ipxSystem.ipxBasicSysTable.ipxBasicSysEntry
1.3.6.1.2.4.1.23.2.5.1.1.1

| OBJECT IDENTIFIER | Syntax | Access | Description |
|---|---|---|---|
| ipxBasicSys InBad Checksums 1.3.6.1.2.4.1.23.2.5.1.1.1.10 | Counter | read-only | Number of IPX packets received with incorrect checksums. |
| ipxBasicSys InDelivers 1.3.6.1.2.4.1.23.2.5.1.1.1.11 | Counter | read-only | Total number of IPX packets delivered locally, including packets from local applications. |
| ipxBasicSys NoRoutes 1.3.6.1.2.4.1.23.2.5.1.1.1.12 | Counter | read-only | Number of times no route to a destination could be found. |
| ipxBasicSys OutRequests 1.3.6.1.2.4.1.23.2.5.1.1.1.13 | Counter | read-only | Number of IPX packets originating locally. |
| ipxBasicSys OutMalformed Requests 1.3.6.1.2.4.1.23.2.5.1.1.1.14 | Counter | read-only | Number of IPX packets supplied locally that were malformed. |
| ipxBasicSys OutDiscards 1.3.6.1.2.4.1.23.2.5.1.1.1.15 | Counter | read-only | Number of outgoing IPX packets discarded due to reasons other than those that were malformed, were not filtered, or had a problem related to compression. |
| ipxBasicSys OutPackets 1.3.6.1.2.4.1.23.2.5.1.1.1.16 | Counter | read-only | Total number of IPX packets transmitted. |
| ipxBasicSys ConfigSockets 1.3.6.1.2.4.1.23.2.5.1.1.1.17 | Counter | read-only | Configured maximum number of IPX sockets that may be open at one time. |
| ipxBasicSys OpenSocket Fails 1.3.6.1.2.4.1.23.2.5.1.1.1.18 | Counter | read-only | Number of IPX socket open calls which failed. |

## 30.8   THE NOVELL BASIC SYSTEM TABLE

One sample table is included to convey the flavor of the definitions. Table 30.1, the Basic System Table, contains an entry for each instance of IPX running on the system. The table includes traffic and error counts. Note that the term *packet,* rather than *datagram,* is used for IPX Protocol Data Units.

The protocol supports a compression algorithm that can be used across dial-up or leased wide area lines. A NetWare router can be configured to apply filtering criteria to traffic, discarding selected packets. Both of these facts are referenced in the table.

## 30.9   RECOMMENDED READING

At the time of writing, Novell MIB modules were available in the */mib* directory at *venera.isi.edu.* Each file had a title starting with "novell-."

The *Programmer's Guide to NETWARE,* by Charles G. Rose, contains full details of the protocol and programming interface.

# 31

# Formal Changes
# in SNMP Version 2

## 31.1  INTRODUCTION

Live and learn. By the time that version 2 was created, MIB writers had discovered that more precision was needed in some datatype definitions to ensure interworking. They also were starting to wrestle with the problems of maintenance of revisions.

Some vendors needed to depart slightly from a few MIB definitions. For example, a device might have been engineered so that:

- Some specific enumerated values never occurred in their products.

- Some read-write variable might be impossible to *set*—for example, a change of value might require manually moving a switch on the device.

Vendors needed some kind of framework in which they could declare what MIB variables their products really were capable of supporting, as well as any deviations from the exact MIB definitions.

Solutions to these problems and other useful enhancements were proposed in SNMP version 2 and are described in the sections that follow. Figure 31.1 provides a snapshot overview of the improvements in SNMPv2 that are discussed in this chapter.

## 31.2  DATATYPE CHANGES

In order to improve the precision of definitions, the basic datatypes were expanded slightly. Counters and gauges will be defined with their proper implementation size: Counter32, Counter64, Gauge32. Other

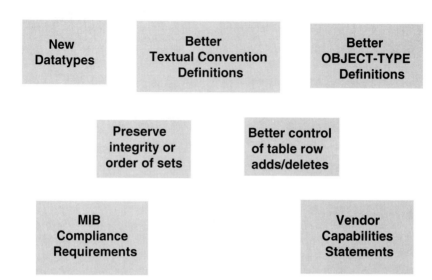

**Figure 31.1**  Some SNMPv2 improvements.

new types include UInteger32 (unsigned integer, 32 bits long) and NsapAddress (for OSI addresses).

An additional basic type, the BIT STRING datatype, was introduced. The version 1 MIB definitions that used INTEGERs to express a bunch of flag settings turned out to confuse vendors and users alike. A BIT STRING datatype is much more direct.

Only *enumerated* BIT STRINGs are allowed. This means that a meaning is assigned to each individual bit, not to clumps of bits.

## 31.3  TEXTUAL CONVENTIONS

SNMP version 2 takes many of the successful ideas in version 1 and solidifies and clarifies them. In version 1, textual conventions made MIBs easier to read, and avoided loading the protocol with lots of unnecessary new datatypes. However, textual conventions were defined quite casually. For example,

    MacAddress ::= OCTET STRING (SIZE (6))

Version 2 introduces a TEXTUAL-CONVENTION macro. The definitions created with this macro are much more informative. Let's look at the version 2 definition of MacAddress as presented in RFC 1443:

    MacAddress ::= TEXTUAL-CONVENTION
        DISPLAY-HINT "1x:"
        STATUS  current

DESCRIPTION
"Represents an 802 MAC address represented in the
'cannonical' order defined by IEEE 802.1a, i.e., as
if it were transmitted least significant bit
first, even though 802.5 (in contrast to other
802x protocols) requires MAC addresses to be
transmitted most significant bit first."
SYNTAX  OCTET STRING (SIZE (6))

This definition presents a clear description of *MacAddress,* and lets us
know that the status is current. It contains all but one of the TEXTUAL-
CONVENTION clauses; there also is an optional REFERENCE
clause.

The introduction of the DISPLAY-HINT clause is an interesting new
feature. The DISPLAY-HINT suggests how values should be presented
to a user. In this case, "1x:" means take each octet (1), display it as a hexadecimal number (x), and separate the octets by colons (:). For example,

```
08:00:20:3E:41:09
```

In addition to "x" for hexadecimal representation, hints specify "d" for
decimal, "o" for octal, "b" for binary, and "a" for ASCII.*

Let's look at two other examples of hints for presenting information
whose underlying type is OCTET STRING:

| Datatype | Display hint | Explanation |
|---|---|---|
| DisplayString | "255a" | Up to 255 ASCII characters. |
| DateAndTime | "2d-1d-1d,1d:1d:1d.1d, 1a1d:1d" | Year-month-day, hour:minutes:seconds.deci-seconds,+/–hours from UTC: minutes from UTC. |

For *DateAndTime,* the first field, "2d," indicates that the first 2 octets
should be combined and translated to a decimal number. This number
is the year. The eighth field, "1a1d," consists of the ASCII character "+"
or "−" followed by a decimal number.

## 31.4  SETTING VALUES

Because of the absence of authentication and security protection in version 1, most early implementation effort focused on reading data from a

---

* See RFC 1443 for details.

MIB. As we shall see in Chapter 33, a substantial portion of version 2 is devoted to wrapping SNMP in a security blanket. Hence, it now makes sense to get serious about performing *sets* on MIB variables.

But more than one management station may try to update a MIB at any time. Suddenly we are faced with some of the problems that real database applications must deal with.

The first problem is a classic. A husband and wife each are withdrawing money from a bank account at the same time, but from different branch locations. The balance is $500. The husband wants to withdraw $200 and the wife is withdrawing $100. The balance is read at each branch at the same time—$500. The new balances, $300 and $400, are calculated at each branch.

|  | Husband's branch | Wife's branch |
|---|---|---|
| Read balance | 500.00 | 500.00 |
| Withdraw | −200.00 | −100.00 |
| Update balance | 300.00 | 400.00 |

Depending on which update reaches the computer first, the account will have a balance of $300 or $400. In either case, the balance will be wrong.

Obviously, real banks don't operate this way. When a new value will be calculated from the current value, you need to make sure that the current value is *locked* in order to perform an *atomic* read and update. *Atomic* means that the *read and update* are grouped together as a single transaction, and nobody else can access the value until the transaction is complete.

Protection of some kind is needed for MIB updates when:

- The new value that is *set* depends on the current value.

or

- A management station wants to make sure that *set* operations are performed in a specific order.

The textual convention *TestAndIncr* facilitates atomic operations and ordered operations. Think of *TestAndIncr* as the brass ring on a merry-go-round. You reach out and try to grab the ring. If someone else grabs the ring ahead of you, you lose. Formally,

- *TestAndIncr.*   An integer ranging from 0 to 2,147,483,647. For a variable of this type, *the value in a set must be equal to the current value or else the set will fail.* But the result of a successful set is that the variable increases by 1.

What is this all about? First, let's look at what this says. Suppose that the *TestAndIncr* variable called *test* has a current value of 10. To succeed, the value in a *set-request* must be 10—but the result will be that *test* now holds the value 11.

Now suppose that management stations A and B are trying to read and then update some values, and that it is important for each to act in an atomic manner. Both stations read *test* and the variables that they intend to update. Suppose that the value of *test* is 10. Both send back *sets* including the value 10 for *test* along with the other variable updates. The first *set* that arrives will succeed, changing the value of *test* to 11, and setting the other variables. The second will fail, which is just what we wanted to happen. The loser should perform a fresh read and try again.

Now consider the second use for *TestAndIncr*. A single manager might have a series of *sets* that will be sent in separate messages, must all be performed, and must be executed in strict order. But SNMP messages may be lost or might arrive out of order! By including a *set* of a variable like *test* in each message, the manager can be sure that any message received out of order will fail.

The SNMPv2 MIB includes a *TestAndIncr* variable, *snmpSetSerialNo,* that is used to coordinate *sets*. Its OBJECT IDENTIFIER is:

```
iso.org.dod.internet.snmpV2.snmpModules.snmpMIB.
snmpMIBObjects.snmpSet.snmpSetSerialNo
```

That is,

```
1 . 3 . 6 . 1 . 6 . 3 . 1 . 1 . 6 . 1
```

## 31.5  MANAGING ROWS IN A TABLE

SNMP version 1 did not solve all of the problems that arise when multiple managers add, modify, and delete table rows. SNMP version 2 introduces a new textual convention that promotes MIB data integrity. Any table that can be updated by a management station will include a status column with type *RowStatus*. The definition of the *RowStatus* textual convention is:

- *RowStatus.* Used to manage the creation and deletion of rows in a table. Every table that can be updated by a network manager must contain a column of type *RowStatus*. The *RowStatus* is expressed as an INTEGER with values:

  1. active
  2. notInService

3. notReady

4. createAndGo

5. createAndWait

6. destroy

A similar convention called *EntryStatus* was introduced in RFC 1271. *RowStatus* expands on the original idea. Here's how it goes.

### 31.5.1   *createAndGo*

In the simplest scenario, the manager creates a new row by sending a *set* message that provides values for each column. The message *sets* the value of the table's status variable to *createAndGo*. If the *set* succeeds, a new row is created—and the status value automatically becomes *active*. Later, if we want to delete the row, we *set* the status to *destroy*.

### 31.5.2   *createAndWait*

A *set* that creates a row might alternatively specify a *createAndWait* status. This is appropriate when:

- The manager does not want the row to be used yet.

or

- There are some required columns that have not yet had their values *set*.

If all variables are present, the status after a successful *createAndWait* is *notInService*. If some values still need to be filled in, the status will be *notReady*.

If you want to create a good row, why not fill in all of the columns at once? Some tables have a lot of columns. SNMP messages usually have a modest size limit, so it just may not be possible to cram all of the columns into one *set*.

Sometimes an agent can provide an assist in creating new table rows. There may be columns for which an agent can provide perfectly good defaults, so that the manager would not have to fill them in.

On the other hand, there also may be some columns that a particular agent does not support. An attempt to *set* one of these will cause the entire *set-request* to fail.

It is a good idea for a manager to be methodical when creating a new row:

- Create a skeleton row with *createAndWait* status.
- Read through the row with *get-nexts*. Check what default values have been filled in, and find out whether some variables are not supported.
- Then *set* only the columns whose values need to be provided.

### 31.5.3   Use of *notInService*

During the life of a table entry, the entry can be switched between *active* and *notInService* (i.e., standby) several times. When would this be done? It sometimes is a good idea to switch a row to *notInService* before applying an update. Or, a *notInService* row can be used to indicate that some function for a device is temporarily unavailable.

## 31.6   TRANSPORT MAPPINGS

The transport requirements for SNMP are very simple. We need to move messages between agents and managers, managers and managers, or agents and agents (for proxy relationships).

UDP has been selected as the preferred transport. The designer of a simple piece of networking equipment—such as a modem or a CSU—benefits from a single, easy-to-build industry standard transport. The alternative is to license, build, and support half a dozen protocols, most of them proprietary.

On the other hand, there will be organizations whose networks are totally based on another protocol—for example, NetWare IPX, Appletalk DDP, or the ISO connectionless or connection-oriented service. A requirement to support IP and UDP—and perhaps more costly and complex multiprotocol routers—may impose an unreasonable hardship. Fortunately, where vendors of workstation software, servers, and routers find that they can better meet customer needs by supporting SNMP over a different protocol stack, SNMPv2 provides the flexibility to do this. As we shall see, SNMPv2 configuration information includes transport choices.

## 31.7   ADDITIONS TO THE OBJECT-TYPE MACRO

The OBJECT-TYPE template has been growing steadily in power. See Chapter 35 for a summary of its evolution. The major enhancements are discussed in the sections that follow.

### 31.7.1   Changing ACCESS to MAX-ACCESS

The ACCESS clause was renamed to MAX-ACCESS, which more correctly indicates what this clause should be about—namely, indicating the highest level of privilege at which a management station can access a variable value.

The ACCESS values changed slightly. In addition to *not-accessible, read-only,* and *read-write,* a new *read-create* selection indicates whether a manager can create an instance of an object. The *read-create* designation is actually short for *read-write-create. Read-create* is used to add entries to a table.

### 31.7.2   The UNITS Clause

The UNITS clause helps a MIB writer to be precise. For example, *snmp-AlarmInterval* is a 32-bit integer that is configured to set the number of *seconds* in a sampling interval. Note that the access is *read-create.*

```
snmpAlarmInterval OBJECT-TYPE
    SYNTAX          Integer32
    UNITS           "seconds"
    MAX-ACCESS read-create
    STATUS          current
    DESCRIPTION
    "The interval in seconds over which the data is
    sampled and compared with the rising and falling
    thresholds. . . . "[Some text omitted]
    ::= {snmpAlarmEntry 3 }
```

### 31.7.3   Changes to the STATUS Clause

In version 2, the STATUS clause expresses whether an object definition is *current, obsolete,* or *deprecated.* Recall that *deprecated* means still supported, but due to be dropped at some future date.

In version 1, the STATUS clause also could indicate whether support for an object was mandatory or optional. In version 2, conformance requirements have been removed from object definitions, and gathered together in separate MODULE-COMPLIANCE statements.

### 31.7.4   Using AUGMENTS
### to Add Columns to a Table

MIB writers have discovered that sometimes it is convenient to add columns to a table defined in another MIB module. The AUGMENTS clause was introduced to do this.

Whenever the extra columns are supported, they must behave exactly like an extension of the original table. That is,

- The new block of columns has the same index as the original table.

- For every row in the original table, there is a corresponding row in the new block of columns.

## 31.8    MODULE ENHANCEMENTS

A good MIB module is like a successful piece of software. Errors will be discovered, new features added, and old functions will be improved. Changes will be described in new releases of a MIB. How does a vendor identify which release is in a product? Where do you report a bug? Who is responsible for fixing it?

### 31.8.1    The MODULE-IDENTITY Macro

The new MODULE-IDENTITY macro contains clauses to identify:

- When a module was LAST-UPDATED
- The ORGANIZATION responsible for the module
- CONTACT-INFO identifying a contact person
- A DESCRIPTION of the module
- The module's revision history

The MODULE-IDENTITY macro also assigns an OBJECT IDENTI-FIER to a module. Previously, modules were identified only by a text name. Formal assignment of an OBJECT-IDENTIFIER is a far more stable method. The following example is taken from RFC 1450:

```
snmpMIB MODULE-IDENTITY
   LAST-UPDATED"9304010000Z"
   ORGANIZATION"IETF SNMPv2 Working Group"
   CONTACT-INFO
   "        Marshall T. Rose
   Postal:   Dover Beach Consulting, Inc.
             420 Whisman Court
             Mountain View, CA 94043-2186
             US

   Tel: +1 415 968 1052
   Fax: +1 416 968 2510

   E-mail:mrose@dbc.mtview.ca.us"
   DESCRIPTION
             "The MIB module for SNMPv2 entities."
   ::= { snmpModules1 }
```

### 31.8.2   Updating a Module

When you update a module, what are you allowed to do?

- You can add new objects, including new table columns.
- Some of the old objects may have turned out to be useless. You can mark them as deprecated or obsolete, or just delete them completely.
- You can revise an existing definition by:
  - —Adding a UNITS, REFERENCE, or DEFVAL clause
  - —Updating the SYNTAX—e.g., by adding new choices to an enumerated INTEGER, or by changing some labels

You cannot change the meaning or the descriptor of an existing object or reuse an old OBJECT IDENTIFIER for a new variable.

### 31.8.3   Maximum, Minimum, and Actual Levels of Support

The main concerns for SNMP version 1 were getting the protocol defined and implemented, getting definitions for needed variables in place, and collecting usage experience in real networks.

Even though there are many successful implementations of SNMP and they interwork reasonably well, it has become clear that a number of issues should be clarified. Which MIB variables must a *compliant* system provide? Can vendors omit variables at will? Can vendors offer products which don't allow a management station to *set* any values?

In SNMPv2:

- MIB definitions establish a maximum requirement level.
- The minimum or baseline level that *ought* to be provided is set forth in a MODULE-COMPLIANCE statement.
- A vendor describes the behavior of a particular implementation in an AGENT-CAPABILITIES statement.

### 31.8.4   Compliance Statements

A MODULE-COMPLIANCE statement lists one or more MIB modules. For each module, a MANDATORY-GROUPS clause identifies one or more groups that *must* be supported. On the other hand, a plain GROUP clause identifies a group which may or may not be appropriate for a specific system. Each MODULE-COMPLIANCE statement is assigned an OBJECT IDENTIFIER, so that it can be accurately referenced.

The following example, taken from RFC 1450, shows the compliance statements for the SNMPv2 MIB:

```
snmpMIBComplianceMODULE-COMPLIANCE
    STATUS current
    DESCRIPTION
        "The compliance statement for SNMPv2 entities
        which implement the SNMPv2MIB."
    MODULE RFC1213-MIB
        MANDATORY-GROUPS{ system }

    MODULE—this module
        MANDATORY-GROUPS{ snmpStatusGroup,ORGroup,
        snmpTrapGroup,snmpSetGroup}

        GROUP snmpV1Group
        DESCRIPTION
            "The snmpV1 group is mandatory only for those
            SNMPv2 entities which also implement SNMPv1."
    ::= {snmpMIBCompliances1 }
```

### 31.8.5  Capabilities Statements

The AGENT-CAPABILITIES statement enables a vendor to identify a product and its release level, and to describe precisely what management features are implemented within that product's agent. Implementation details include:

- A list of MIB modules that are supported
- For each module, the groups within the module that are supported
- Variations within the module, e.g.,
    - —Specific variables that are not implemented
    - —Variables whose access is restricted (e.g., to read-only)
    - —Variables whose values are restricted to a smaller range than defined in the MIB

The product identifier is either the *sysObjectID* or the new *snmpORID*. The *snmpORID* was introduced so that systems that were the home of several devices, each with its own MIB, could provide OBJECT IDENTIFIERs for each of these components.

Groups need to be dealt with a little differently in a capabilities module. Perhaps all variables *ought* to be supported, but in fact some are not. A group of supported variables is announced by means of a separate OBJECT-GROUP macro. Variations from MIB definitions are described in VARIATION clauses.

### 31.8.6    Example of an OBJECT-GROUP
Macro Definition

The definition that follows was taken from RFC 1444, and defines an OBJECT-GROUP called *systemGroup*.

```
systemGroupOBJECT-GROUP
    OBJECTS { sysDescr,sysObjectID,sysUpTime,
              sysContact,sysName,sysLocation,
              sysServices}
    STATUS current
    DESCRIPTION
            "The system group defines objects which are common
            to all managed systems."
    ::= { mibIIGroups1 }
```

### 31.8.7    Example of an AGENT-
CAPABILITIES Macro Definition

The following example is an abbreviated form of an example appearing in RFC 1444:

```
exampleAgentAGENT-CAPABILITIES
    PRODUCT-RELEASE     "ACME Agent release 1.1 for 4BSD"
    STATUS              current
    DESCRIPTION         "ACME agent for 4BSD"

    SUPPORTS                        RFC1213-MIB
      INCLUDES          { systemGroup,interfacesGroup,
                          atGroup,ipGroup,icmpGroup,
                          tcpGroup,udpGroup,snmpGroup}

      VARIATION         ifOperStatus
        SYNTAX          INTEGER{ up(1),down(2)}
        DESCRIPTION     "Information limited on 4BSD"

      VARIATION         ipDefaultTTL
        SYNTAX          INTEGER (255..255)
        DESCRIPTION     "Hard-wired on 4BSD"
    ::= { acmeAgents1 }
```

## 31.9    RECOMMENDED READING

The Structure of Management information for SNMP version 2 is described in RFC 1442. A complete set of textual conventions is presented in RFC 1443. RFC 1449 describes the methods of transporting SNMP messages over UDP, OSI, AppleTalk's DDP, and NetWare IPX.

# The SNMP Version 2 Protocol

## 32.1 INTRODUCTION

The biggest problems tackled by SNMP version 2 are authentication of the sources of messages, protecting messages from disclosure, and placing access controls on MIB databases. Solving these problems requires some significant changes to the format of SNMP Protocol Data Units.

Two new protocol operations have been added. One supports the efficient transfer of large amounts of MIB data. The other enables a manager to inform another manager of significant events.

## 32.2 UPDATING SNMP VERSION 1 OPERATIONS

The operations that were the workhorses of version 1 remain with us in version 2:

- *get-request.*
- *get-next-request*
- *set-request*
- *response*
- *snmpV2-trap*

Note that *"get-response"* has been shortened to the more appropriate name, *"response."*

### 32.2.1 Enhancements to "gets"

A very helpful change has been incorporated into *gets*. In version 1, if any variable on a list could not be retrieved, then the entire *get* would fail and no data would be returned. But in version 2, an agent can process the "*good*" variables in a request and return their values. The value field of a "bad" variable is filled with a special problem-reporting value. Specifically,

- If we ask for a variable that is not in the accessible database view, the value field for the variable is filled in with either the *noSuch-Object* or the *noSuchInstance* value.

- If a variable on the list in a *get-next-request* takes us beyond the end of a MIB view, the value field is filled in with the *endOfMibView* value.

In either case, a *response* message with an error status of 0 will be returned.

### 32.2.2   Improved Processing of "sets"

The processing of *set-requests* has been clarified. *Sets* are executed in a two-phase operation. First, each variable is validated. If any update would fail, then the entire operation fails. If the first phase succeeds, then actual updates are performed in a second phase.

### 32.2.3   Improved SNMPv2 *trap* Definition

In version 1, *traps* had a format that differed from the formats of all of the other PDUs. Version 2 actually simplifies *traps* by giving them the same format as *get* and *set* PDUs. The idea is simple:

- Get rid of the special fields and move all of the information that you need into the variable-bindings list.

Recall that version 1 *traps* had several special fields: enterprise, agent-addr, generic-trap, specific-trap, and timestamp. What information do we really need?

- We want to identify what type of trap this is.
- We want to provide an event timestamp.

In version 2, each type of *trap* is named by assigning it an OBJECT IDENTIFIER. The *sysUptime* timestamp and trap identifier are moved into the variable bindings list. The other special fields are discarded.

As in version 1, other variables that provide useful information about the condition of the sending system are included in the variable bindings list.

This simplifies life in two ways. First of all, we do not need the extra software that was used to parse a special message type. Second, *traps* become a lot easier to define. All that is needed to define a version 2 trap is to:

- Name the trap
- List the informational variables that must be included in the variable bindings list

The new NOTIFICATION-TYPE macro is a convenient template for defining traps. The macro is used to assign an OBJECT IDENTIFIER to a trap and list the objects that will be carried in the variable bindings list.* For example, using the macro, the classic *linkDown trap* type is redefined by

```
linkDown NOTIFICATION-TYPE
     OBJECTS { ifIndex }
     STATUS current
     DESCRIPTION
          "A linkDown trap signifies that the SNMPv2 entity,
          acting in an agent role, recognizes a failure in
          one of the communication links represented in its
          configuration."
     ::= { snmpTraps 3 }
```

The complete OBJECT IDENTIFIER for the *linkDown trap* type is

```
iso.org.dod.internet.snmpV2.
snmpModules.snmpMIB.snmpMIBObjects.snmpTraps.linkDown
```

That is,

```
1 . 3 . 6 . 1 . 6 . 3 . 1 . 1 . 5 . 3
```

The variable-bindings list in this *trap* includes:

- The current value of *sysUptime*
- The OBJECT IDENTIFIER for the trap, 1.3.6.1.6.3.1.1.5.3
- The *ifIndex* for the link that is down
- At the option of the agent, other variables that are considered informative

---

* The *sysUpTime* and trap identifier automatically are included in the variable-bindings list. The macro specifies additional variables.

In addition to the clauses shown in the example, a NOTIFICATION-TYPE macro optionally can include a REFERENCE clause which describes any relevant reference material.

## 32.3 NEW VERSION 2 OPERATIONS

There are two very useful additions to the family of protocol operations:

- *inform-request.* Enables a manager to report directly to another manager.
- *get-bulk-request.* Used to retrieve large chunks of MIB information efficiently.

## 32.4 THE *INFORM-REQUEST*

The *inform-request* enables a manager to send some information to another manager. The introduction of this message type helps organizations that want to set up a hierarchy of network management stations. As shown in Figure 32.1, local management stations can keep a Network Operations Center management station informed of changes of status or problems on their subnetworks.

The normal processing of an incoming *inform-request* is to pass its contents to an appropriate application and return a *response* message that echoes the original contents back to the sender.

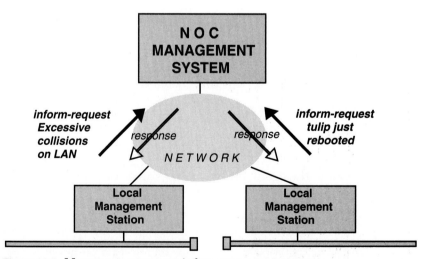

**Figure 32.1** Manager-to-manager *inform-request* messages.

There are strong similarities between an *inform-request* and an *snmp V2-trap* message:

- Both have the same PDU format. And just as in an *snmpV2-trap,* the variable list starts with a timestamp and an identifier.

- Both use the NOTIFICATION-TYPE macro to name and describe the information that will be sent.

- Both are sent spontaneously, not in response to a poll.

However, there also are some significant differences:

- A manager sending an *inform-request* wants to get a confirmation that it was received. The confirmation is a response message containing an identical variable-bindings list.

- Traps are triggered by very simple events. An agent residing in a low-level device will be capable of generating only very basic traps. In contrast, managers have intelligence and can generate an *inform-request* to report a complex event, such as the number of errors of a given type exceeding a threshold during an interval.

In fact, manager-to-manager communication via *inform-requests* has many points of resemblance to the monitor-to-manager communications described in Chapter 28 and defined in the RMON MIB. Various types of alarm conditions are configured. When an alarm condition occurs, it triggers an event which causes an *inform-request* to be transmitted to a remote manager.

To make this work, we will have to decide:

- Which variable will be monitored? What is the time interval? What is the high or low alarm threshold?

- What is the identifier of the notification that should be sent?

- To which manager(s) should the notification be sent?

The MIB tables that contain these choices are described in Chapter 34.

## 32.5   THE *GET-BULK-REQUEST*

Recall that message sizes are limited by the local capabilities of each agent. If I ask for too much data in an ordinary *get-request,* all that will come back is a "too big" error message and *no* data. If I err on the side of caution and ask for too little, I am not retrieving data efficiently.

The name of the new *get-bulk-request* operation reflects its purpose. If I have a lot of information to retrieve, I want to be able to say "cram as much of what I need as possible into your biggest response message."

A *get-bulk-request* can retrieve stand-alone scalar variables and/or columns from a table. The easiest way to understand how this works is to look at an example. Suppose that I think there is a problem with one or more of the interfaces at a system. I can send a *get-bulk-request* whose variable list asks for:

| | |
|---|---|
| sysDescr | 1.3.6.1.2.1.1.1 |
| sysUpTime | 1.3.6.1.2.1.1.3 |
| sysContact | 1.3.6.1.2.1.1.4 |
| ifNumber | 1.3.6.1.2.1.2.1 |
| ifType | 1.3.6.1.2.1.2.2.1.3 |
| ifOperStatus | 1.3.6.1.2.1.2.2.1.8 |
| ifLastChange | 1.3.6.1.2.1.2.2.1.9 |
| ifInErrors | 1.3.6.1.2.1.2.2.1.14 |
| ifInUnknownProtos | 1.3.6.1.2.1.2.2.1.15 |

The *get-bulk-request* behaves like a *get-next-request,* returning the OBJECT IDENTIFIER and value that lexicographically follows each requested variable. For example, for the first variable, the response returns the value of the unique instance of *sysDescr*—for example,

| | | |
|---|---|---|
| sysDescr | 1.3.6.1.2.1.1.1.0 | "An ABC router, software version 7.6.2" |

The response also will contain the unique instances for *sysUpTime, sysContact,* and *ifNumber.* It then will look into the *interfaces* table and fill in the first-row values for *ifType, ifOperStatus, ifLastChange, ifInErrors,* and *ifInUnknownProtos.*

What does a *get-bulk-request* do that a *get-next-request* does not do? The *get-bulk-request* can keep going. It can pull back several rows of selected interfaces table variables. Here's how it works. I include two fields in the message that structure my request:

- nonrepeaters
- max-repetitions

In my sample request, I will indicate that the first four variables on my list are nonrepeaters. That leaves five that are repeaters.

Setting max-repetitions to 4 asks the agent to return four row's worth of the five repeating table variables. Therefore, the total number of variables requested is

$$4 + 4 \times 5 = 24$$

If the 24 values can fit into the maximum message size, the agent will send back all of them. If not, the agent will send back as much as can be squeezed into a *response.*

To retrieve more values, I can send another *get-bulk-request* identifying variables in the last row that was successfully retrieved. The response will return variables starting at the *next* table entry.

Suppose that the *interfaces* table has only two rows? In this case the response will contain

- The four stand-alone variables
- The $2 \times 5 = 10$ values in the two rows
- The next 10 table values in lexicographic order (consisting of the five columns from *ifOutOctets* to *ifOutErrors*)

In other words, the bulk request continues onward from the last requested variable, marching through the table and getting variables in lexicographic order just like a *get-next*. Figure 32.2 illustrates how variables are selected for a bulk retrieval.

The *get-bulk* really behaves intelligently, deserving the epithet "awesome" bestowed upon it by Marshall Rose.

## 32.6  MESSAGE FORMAT

Recall that the overall message format for SNMP version 1 was

- Version of SNMP
- Community name
- Protocol Data Unit (i.e., get-request, get-next-request, etc.)

| sysDescr<br>sysUpTime<br>sysContact<br>ifNumber | Router<br>356991<br>J. Jones<br>4 | *Non-Repeaters = 4* |
|---|---|---|

| ifType | ifOper Status | ifLast Change | ifInErrors | ifInUnknown Protocols | |
|---|---|---|---|---|---|
| | | | | | *Repeaters* |
| 6 | 1 | 223226 | 143017 | 0 | *Max-Repetitions = 2* |
| 6 | 1 | 271004 | 156001 | 0 | |
| 22 | 1 | 312567 | 200451 | 0 | |
| 22 | 1 | 312550 | 100567 | 0 | |

**Figure 32.2** Data retrieved with a *get-bulk-request*.

We shall see that the simple version and community fields have been replaced with a more complicated framework. Before tackling this new framework, let's examine the simple enhancements to the Protocol Data Units.

### 32.6.1    Version 2 PDU

The format of the version 1 Protocol Data Unit part of the message has been retained in version 2, namely,

- The Protocol Data Unit is introduced with a numeric tag that indicates the type of PDU (*get-request, get-next-request,* etc.)
- *request-id.*  Identifier that allows a response to be matched with its request.
- *error-status.*  In a response, reports success or reason for failure.
- *error-index.*  In a response reporting failure, points to the variable that caused a problem.
- *variable-bindings:* A list of (OBJECT IDENTIFIER, value) pairs.

How do we fit the *get-bulk-request* into this format? It is easy. In an outgoing request, the *error-status* and *error-index* fields have no function, and normally are set to 0. For a *get-bulk-request,* we take over these fields and do the following:

- Put the number of nonrepeaters into the error-status position.
- Put the number of max-repetitions into the error-index position.

### 32.6.2    Good-bye Community, Hello Party

In version 1, the community name in a message determined

- Whether the message came from a valid source
- What operations could be performed
- What data could be accessed

Since anyone eavesdropping on a network could read the community names in the traffic, this was not exactly a bulletproof method. Version 2 takes a much more stringent approach:

- Sometimes the source of a message has to authenticate itself—that is, prove that it really is who it says it is.
- Sometimes information needs to be kept private, by encryption.

*The version 2 model handles these needs by defining roles called* parties.

Some parties are sociable and unconstrained. They talk openly. Other parties work with more sensitive information, and must provide proof that they are who they say they are. And some parties work with hush-hush data, and insist that everything that is sent to them must be encrypted.

Every party in the world will have a unique name. How will this be done? With OBJECT IDENTIFIERs, naturally.

### 32.6.3  Administration Using Parties

Parties are the basis of SNMPv2 administration. The purpose of network management administration is to control

- Which parties may talk to one another
- Whether a pair of parties talks in the clear, with authentication, or with *both* authentication and encryption
- The operations that can be performed by a pair of parties
- The scope of the MIB data that can be accessed by a pair of parties

The configuration tables that describe parties and their relationships will be presented in Chapter 34.

Manager entity A and agent entity B in Figure 32.3 each are made up of three parties. The first pair of parties is used for simple requests

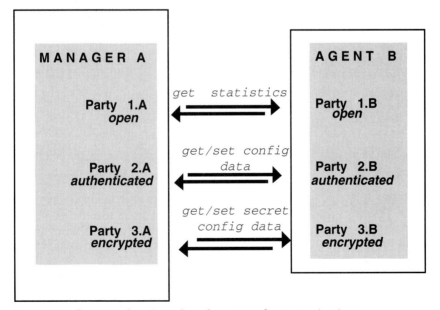

**Figure 32.3**  Open, authenticated, and encrypted communication.

to read management statistics. The second accesses configuration data, and must authenticate its requests. The third accesses very sensitive configuration information, and must protect its communications with encryption.

Instead of writing out full OBJECT IDENTIFIER names for the parties, we use nicknames 1.A, 1.B, 2.A, 2.B, 3.A, and 3.B.

### 32.6.4   The Version 2 Message Design

The message used in version 1 was very simple—the Protocol Data Unit was preceded by version and community fields. In version 2, the version and community fields are dropped, and a more complicated nested format is introduced that can support

- Open unprotected messages
- Authenticated messages
- Encrypted messages

The outermost "wrapper" of a version 2 message consists of

- *privDst.*   The party that is the destination for this message. The party is identified by an OBJECT IDENTIFIER. The identity of this party determines whether the rest of the message is encrypted or not.
- *privData.*   The rest of the message. For a hush-hush destination, it will be encrypted. Otherwise, it will be in the clear.

What is inside *privData?*

| | |
|---|---|
| *authInfo* | Authentication information |
| *dstParty* | The destination party, again |
| *srcParty* | The party that is the source of this message |
| *context* | An identifier that identifies a chunk of MIB data* |
| *PDU* | The protocol data unit, such as *get-request* or *get-next-request* |

What goes into the *authInfo?* That depends on the authentication protocol that the parties use. As usual, there is a lot of flexibility in the design.

---

\* This is a simplification. A context identifier alternatively might indicate that a proxy needs to be used for this communication.

Of course, with too much flexibility, systems will not be able to inter-work, so in this generation of products, the authentication information consists of the following:

- *authDigest.*   The result of a mathematical calculation performed on the message. The calculation is designed to detect whether anyone has changed the content of the message.
- *authDstTimestamp.*   The sender believes that this is the current value of a clock at the destination.
- *authSrcTimestamp.*   This is the current value of a clock at the source.

The digest prevents tampering with the message. The timestamps prevent a snooper from causing trouble by capturing and replaying a message. More details are provided in Chapter 33.

Of course, keep in mind that some pairs of parties will communicate without any authentication. In this case, the message contains place-holders for the authentication fields, but the values are empty.

## 32.7   RECOMMENDED READING

The SNMPv2 protocol Data Units are described in RFC 1448. The NOTIFICATION-TYPE macro is defined in RFC 1442.

# Version 2 Authentication, Security, and Control

## 33.1  INTRODUCTION

SNMP managers and agents communicate by means of messages, usually transmitted in UDP datagrams. The well-being of an entire network may depend on these messages. What are the security concerns in an environment like this?

1. When a party receives a message, how can that party be sure who sent it?

2. When a party receives a message, how can that party be sure no one has tampered with it, perhaps changing the value of some critical parameter?

3. We have to assume that a malicious eavesdropper may be able to capture copies of messages. How can a party be sure that this is a new message, not a nasty replay of a message that was sent yesterday which said "take this device out of service!"

4. How can we prevent eavesdroppers from reading messages that contain sensitive information?

5. How can we put restrictions on a MIB database so that some applications can view only part of the data?

6. How can we put limits on who can do what? For example, how could we allow many applications to read MIB data, but allow only one application to update MIB data?

## 33.2   THE SNMP VERSION 2
## SECURITY FRAMEWORK

The SNMP version 2 security framework addresses the first four of these concerns. The administrative framework deals with the last two issues. The security framework is very flexible.

- For some networks, or for specific devices, you may choose to operate without any security protection at all. That is your option.

- SNMPv2 supports the use of an authentication protocol to identify sources reliably, prevent message modification, and limit replays.

  A specific authentication protocol has been selected for immediate implementation. What happens if five years from now somebody "breaks" this protocol? A new protocol can replace the old one without disrupting the overall framework.

- SNMPv2 supports the use of encryption to keep some messages private. The source of a private, encrypted message must authenticate itself.

  A specific privacy protocol that encrypts data in order to deal with security issue number 4 has been selected for immediate implementation. Here again, there is no lockin. New privacy protocols can be introduced. All that is required is that the communicating parties both can execute the new privacy protocol.

To summarize, SNMPv2 lets you do nothing, support authentication, or support both authentication and privacy. To handle items 5 and 6,

- Database views define relevant pieces of a MIB. Access control lists control the rights to perform specific operations within a given view.

## 33.3   AUTHENTICATION AND INTEGRITY

In the days when terminals were directly cabled to a computer, or were connected via a leased line, we were content to accept a simple password to authenticate a userid. Today, when messages may pass through many intervening network devices and eavesdropping on a network is all too easy, more robust methods are needed.

Knowing who originally sent a message does not fully solve the authentication problem. We want to know that the message has not been changed along the way. An authentication strategy must validate both the identity of the sender and the integrity of the message.

The designers of SNMPv2 wanted to pick an authentication scheme that would work for messages exchanged via an unreliable protocol like UDP, and would not burden systems with excessive amounts of computing overhead. The current recommended authentication procedure is the *Digest Authentication Protocol.* This protocol relies on a *message-digest* to authenticate message sources and prevent message tampering.

### 33.3.1   Message-digests

What is a message-digest? A message is treated like a string of 32-bit numbers; a message-digest is just a mathematical calculation that is performed on these numbers and included with the message.

This notion is a first cousin to an idea we've already seen at the Data Link layer. Each Data Link frame includes a calculated Frame Check Sequence (FCS). The FCS is designed to catch most bit errors. A message-digest is designed to assure that different messages will almost always have different digests.

The message-digest protocol chops a message into bits, mixes up the bits with a secret ingredient, and selects a few bits here and there to assemble into its result. The result is sent to the partner along with the original message.

But if everybody knows how to calculate the message digest, how can this protect a message?

Remember that an extra ingredient is thrown into the calculation. This ingredient is a number—the source party's secret authentication key. The destination party also must know the source's secret key, and will recompute the message-digest by tossing the same secret into the calculation.

If both parties have hidden the secret key, no one but the source party could have come up with the right digest for the message.

### 33.3.2   The MD5 Message-digest Algorithm

The *MD5* message-digest has been chosen for SNMP v2 authentication. MD5 is described in RFC 1321, *The MD5 Message-Digest Algorithm,* which also includes source code for its implementation. MD5 produces a 16-octet (128-bit) message-digest that can be computed quickly, and the calculation does not even need much memory. The secret keys assigned to parties also are 16 bytes long.

MD5 message digests are hard to fake. It is believed that it would take $2^{128}$ operations just to come up with a message that has a given digest.

How does MD5 protect the integrity of a message? Suppose that somebody wanted to steal a message, change the contents, and send the forgery to the destination. If the thief does not know the source's secret MD5 key, then such an individual cannot produce the right digest for his or her message.

### 33.3.3   Authentication Clocks and Timestamps

Suppose that the thief is just content to steal a message and replay it later—e.g., to say "disable all of your ports!" The message contains a timestamp to prevent replay. The timestamp is taken from an *authentication clock* maintained by the source party.

If the source timestamp in an incoming message indicates that the message is stale, the message will be discarded. A *lifetime* variable sets a limit on how old a message can be and still be considered fresh.

A thief cannot simply *replace* a timestamp, because the message digest will reveal that the message has been altered. If the thief leaves in the timestamp, then the receiver will know that this is a stale message.

There is one problem: each computer keeps its own time—how can a receiver be sure that it knows the time at the source? The answer is that the receiver keeps its own copy of the sender's authentication clock. The sender also keeps a copy of the receiver's authentication clock. An authenticated message includes the following:

- Source party timestamp
- Destination party timestamp

When a fresh authentic message arrives, both timestamps are examined and used to keep both pairs of clocks in synch.

### 33.3.4   Keeping Clocks in Sync

Authentication clocks make SNMP more complicated. I need to keep track of my clock *and* of your clock. But my computer may run faster or slower than yours, and after a while, our values will start to drift. Several mechanisms are used to keep clocks in sync. Suppose that I am a party that has just received a message.

- If the source clock value is bigger than my value for that clock, then I advance my clock to that bigger value.
- If the message's value for my clock is bigger than my clock, I advance my clock to that bigger value.

If I am a manager and my clock is running slower than an agent's view of my clock, the agent will start turning down my authenticated requests, because they will look stale. I can read the agent's version of my clock with an unauthenticated request, reset my clock, and then read the agent's clock again with an authenticated request, to make sure that we are in sync and that the previous answer *really* was from my agent.

I also have the option of setting your clock to a new, smaller value, but I have to change your authentication key when I do this.

There is a lot of work that needs to be done to make SNMPv2 work in a secure environment!

### 33.3.5  Protecting Against a Patient Thief

Authentication clocks get reinitialized from time to time. A very patient thief might watch the traffic go by, and wait for an opportunity to use an old, captured message.

The patient thief is foiled by the requirement that whenever a clock is reinitialized, the secret authentication key must be changed. At that instant, all of the old captured messages become totally worthless.

### 33.3.6  Extra Protection for Sets

Replayed *gets* may be a nuisance, but replayed *sets* can cause a lot of damage. A robust way to guard against replays of *sets* is to use the *snmpSetSerialNo* variable to control *sets* performed on an agent's MIB. If this *TestAndIncr* variable is included within each *set-request,* duplicates are guaranteed to fail. Why? Recall that a *set* of a *TestAndIncr* variable fails unless the requested value is the same as the current value—and the value always is advanced by 1 when a set succeeds.

## 33.4  PRIVACY

Authentication only proves that a message is genuine. It does not prevent an eavesdropper from reading the message. We advance to a higher level of protection by encrypting messages.

For example, a network manager might not want an eavesdropper to view information that reveals the detailed configuration of network devices. Or, it might be judged important to protect *set-requests* which alter the configuration of a device or cause a system to change its state.

SNMP version 2 is structured so that any privacy protocol can be dropped in and used. The protocol of choice at this time is *symmetric* encryption using the *Data Encryption Standard* (DES) as defined by the National Institute of Standards and Technology (NIST) and the American National Standards Institute (ANSI).

Encryption is *symmetric* when the same secret key that is used to encrypt a message also is used to decrypt it.

Authentication is perceived from the *sender's* point of view: "I have a secret that I will use to prove that I am who I say I am." Encryption is perceived from the receiver's point of view: "You can encrypt traffic in my key before sending it to me. That way it will be safe."

## 33.5   CONFIGURING AUTHENTICATION AND PRIVACY

Let's pause for a minute and consider the minimum information that has to be preconfigured before we can exchange messages whose privacy is protected from prying eyes—and keep in mind that an encrypted message must also be authenticated. I need to know the following:

- My own party identifier.

- The authentication protocol that I will use in messages that I send. For initial implementations of SNMP v2, this will be *noAuth* or *v2md5AuthProtocol.*

- The private authentication secret (key) that I will use to calculate a message-digest for outgoing messages.

- The value of my authentication clock.

- A bound on the lifetime of my messages. If not delivered within this interval, a message will be considered stale and will be discarded by the receiver.

- The privacy protocol to be used in messages sent to me.

- My secret encryption key.

And, I will need to know the corresponding values belonging to each partner with whom I communicate. If I exchange messages with several partners, quite a lot of configuration information can pile up—and this is just the beginning!

The more partners there are who know my authentication secret and my encryption key, the bigger the possibility of a breach of security. I might want to use different secret keys when I communicate with different partners. Of course, this adds to the total amount of hush-hush information.

## 33.6   PRIVATE VERSUS PUBLIC KEYS

SNMP v2 initially will rely on traditional, symmetric private keys. Recently, there has been research into encryption that is *asymmetrical.* What this means is that the key used to decrypt a message is *not* the same as the key used to encrypt it.

This allows us to do something interesting. I can publish my encryption key to the whole world. I can decrypt the messages that anybody sends me—but nobody else can, because I am the only one who knows my secret decryption key, although everybody knows my public key!

As a matter of fact, the RSA* method, which is available under license today, supports public key encryption. RSA establishes a pair of distinct private and public keys that have the following characteristics:

- data → encrypted with my public key → decrypted with my private key → original data

- data → encrypted with my private key → decrypted with my public key → original data

RSA supports a very strong authentication signature as follows:

- I encrypt identity information with my secret key.
- I encrypt the result with my partner's public key.
- On receipt, my partner decrypts with his or her secret key.
- My partner then decrypts again with my public key. This ends the complete decryption of the identity information.

My partner and I are the only ones who can produce and decrypt the encoding of the identity information. This solves the problem of proof of identity.

## 33.7  PARTIES

Identifying a party is the way that you identify the voice for a message and decide what role that voice is playing. Recall that we name parties with OBJECT IDENTIFIERS. However, in the discussion that follows, we'll assign some nicknames like *Mary* and *Bill* to parties, because they are a little easier to read than "1.3.6.1.6.3.3.1.3.128.120.44.6.1."

## 33.8  ACCESS CONTROL

Suppose that a party receives a properly authenticated, uncorrupted, and encrypted message asking for some sensitive system information, or changing the status of the system to "down"—should the party do it?

Running a network management system requires administrative control over who can do what as well as authentication and protection of information. In other words,

- What operations can be performed?
- What information can be accessed?

---

\* Rivest, Shamir, and Adleman.

The notion of parties was introduced in order to make authentication and privacy work. The next job is to impose administrative control over what operations a party can request and what data a party can access.

### 33.8.1   The Access Control Table

SNMPv2 is very picky in its access control. A *subject* party sends management communications to a *target* party. What are the valid operations for this subject and this target? What body of information is valid for these operations?

For example, suppose that we have manager party Boss talking to agent party Mary, and that they do not use privacy or authentication in their messages. The following display shows a selection of access controls that could be applied.

| Subject | Target | Operations | Data |
|---------|--------|------------|------|
| Manager Boss | Agent Mary | get-request, get-next-request, get-bulk-request | system, interfaces, icmp |
| Agent Mary | Manager Boss | response | system, interfaces, icmp |

Manager Boss can ask agent Mary for *system, interfaces,* and *icmp* information. Agent Mary is allowed to respond. Unless more entries are added, manager Boss cannot view any other data, and cannot set any variables. Agent Mary will not send *traps* to manager Boss.

This display does not quite match the way that access information actually gets pulled together. In fact, the information is spread across three different tables. Indices within the tables tie their entries together. Let's begin at the beginning.

### 33.8.2   View Subtrees and MIB Views

A view subtree is the set of variables (object instances) with a common prefix in their names. The best way to visualize a view subtree is to look at a MIB tree, as shown in Figure 33.1. Pick a node, e.g., *icmp*. All of the leaf object instances reached below that node make up a view subtree.

A *MIB view* is a collection of view subtrees. For example, the set of leaf instances that lie below the *system, ipNetToMediaTable, icmp,* and *ethernet* nodes can make up a MIB view. The display following shows definitions of two MIB views. The first includes view subtrees under

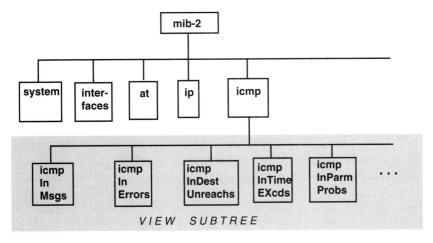

**Figure 33.1**  A view subtree.

*system* and *ifTable.* The second includes view subtrees under *system,*
*ipNetToMediaTable, icmp,* and *dot3* (ethernet).

| MIB view number | View subtree | Object identifier |
|---|---|---|
| 1 | system | 1.3.6.1.2.1.1 |
| 1 | ifTable | 1.3.6.1.2.1.2.2 |
| 2 | system | 1.3.6.1.2.1.1 |
| 2 | ipNetToMediaTable | 1.3.6.1.2.1.2.22 |
| 2 | icmp | 1.3.6.1.2.1.5 |
| 2 | dot3 | 1.3.6.1.2.1.10.7 |

Any MIB instance whose OBJECT IDENTIFIER starts with prefix
1.3.6.1.2.1.1 or 1.3.6.1.2.1.2.2 is in MIB view 1.

These are very simple MIB views. As the tree of objects sprouts more
and more branches, and as we get more specific and selective about
what goes into a MIB view, these enumerations will get very tedious.

For example, suppose that we want to change view subtree 1 so that
it includes all of the system information, except for the *sysLocation.*
And suppose that we don't want the entire *ifTable,* but only the information about interface number 3. We would have to write a lot of lines
into the table!

Fortunately, some shortcuts have been defined. First of all, we can
define subtrees as either included in the view or excluded from the
view. Now we can state our first condition succinctly as follows.

| MIB view number | View subtree | Object identifier | Type |
|---|---|---|---|
| 1 | system | 1.3.6.1.2.1.1 | included |
| 1 | sysLocation | 1.3.6.1.2.1.1.6 | excluded |

Next, we can use a *family mask* that says "Keep the numbers in the OBJECT IDENTIFIER that correspond to 1s in the mask, and match up the rest with wild cards." Matching 1.3.6.1.2.1.2.2.1.*.3 will give us all of the values in the interfaces table with index 3—that is, the row corresponding to the third interface. The correct mask is:

```
1 . 3 . 6 . 1 . 2 . 1 . 2 . 2 . 1 . * . 3
1   1   1   1   1   1   1   1   1   0   1 ( 0 0 0 0 0 )
```

We pad the mask with 0s to get complete octets, and then can express the mask as 'FFA0'H.

By convention, a mask that is shorter than the full length of an OBJECT IDENTIFIER is padded with 1s. The totally empty mask, "H, is interpreted as all 1s. Now we are ready to look at a complete set of entries for the new MIB view 1.

| MIB view index | View subtree | Object identifier | View mask | View type |
|---|---|---|---|---|
| 1 | system | 1.3.6.1.2.1.1 | "H | *included* |
| 1 | sysLocation | 1.3.6.1.2.1.1.6 | "H | *excluded* |
| 1 | ifEntry.0.3 | 1.3.6.1.2.1.2.2.1.0.3 | 'FFA0'H | *included* |

### 33.8.3  The Context Table

An agent party reads or updates MIB variables as a result of a request from a manager party. Sometimes a single agent is responsible for a very complex device—for example, a rack full of Ethernet bridges and Token-Ring bridges. In this case, there are many separate local MIBs that are accessed by the agent.

An entry in the SNMPv2 Context Table points an agent in the direction of the data that a manager wants to access. For local data at a simple device, all that is needed is a MIB view index. For a complex device, we could have entries for several different entities. For example,

| Context name | Entity | Index of MIB view |
|---|---|---|
| 1.3. . . 1 | Bridge_1 | 2 |
| 1.3. . . 2 | Bridge_1 | 5 |
| 1.3. . . 3 | Bridge_2 | 2 |

In the preceding sample entries, we have omitted the middle chunk of each OBJECT IDENTIFIER, writing " . . . " instead.

There are two contexts shown for Bridge_1 and one for Bridge_2. Each of these contexts corresponds to a MIB view belonging to one of the bridges. Each context is assigned an OBJECT IDENTIFIER, enabling a management station to name it unambiguously. Thus, the context name enables the manager to distinguish between MIB view 2 owned by Bridge_1 and MIB view 2 owned by Bridge_2.

### 33.8.4  Using Context Names in the Access Control Table

In Section 33.8.1, we saw a preview of the Access Control Table, which pulls together all of the information need to regulate what parties are allowed to do. In the preview, the scope of information was displayed as a list of MIB subtrees. A real Access Control entry uses a context name to define the scope of the information.

| Subject | Target | Operations | Context name |
| --- | --- | --- | --- |
| Manager<br>  Boss | Agent<br>  Mary | get-request,<br>get-next-request,<br>get-bulk-request | 1.3. . . 1 |
| Agent<br>  Mary | Manager<br>  Boss | response | 1.3. . . 1 |

As we saw in Chapter 32, every message identifies its subject (source) party, target (destination) party, context, and operation. The Access Control Table is used to screen each incoming message to see whether its operation can be performed by its subject and target parties within its context.

Chapter 34 contains detailed definitions of all of the tables used in the administrative framework.

## 33.9   PROXIES

A system may have some parties that act as agents, and others that act as managers. Figure 33.2 shows manager party *Bill* in a management station on a LAN interacting with SNMPv2 agents in systems on the LAN. The management station also contains proxy agent party *Mary* that communicates with party *Boss* in a primary management system at a Network Operations Center (NOC).

### 33.9.1   Native proxies

The local management station acts as a *native proxy* for devices on the LAN. The Network Operations Center (NOC) manager Boss will poll

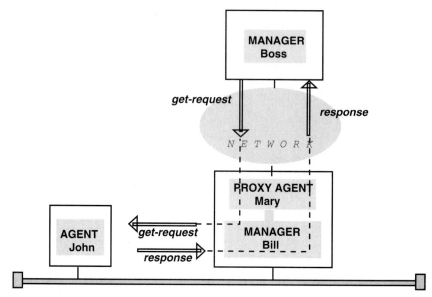

**Figure 33.2**  Managing by proxy.

*Mary* for device information. Mary passes the job to *Bill*. *Bill* will get the information, and then *Mary* will relay it back.

Boss does not want to know the details of how Mary does her work. How can we keep life simple for Boss? Boss is given a set of context names to use to get various pieces of information. Mary's context table includes these context names, along with everything needed to get the job done:

| | Context Table at the Mary's System | | |
|---|---|---|---|
| Context name known at initiator | Proxy source | Proxy destination | Context name known at destination |
| 1.3. . . 4 | Bill | John | 1.3. . . 2 |
| 1.3. . . 5 | Bill | Harry | 1.3. . . 1 |
| 1.3. . . 2 | Mary | Boss | 1.3. . . 4 |

Let's examine the first entry. If Boss sends a request to Mary for information in context, 1.3. . . 4, Mary passes the job to Bill. Bill satisfies the Boss's request by sending a request to John, identifying context 1.3. . . 2 at John's system. This corresponds to a MIB view within John's MIB.

The second entry works the same way. Boss sends a request to Mary for information in context 1.3. . . 5. Mary passes the job to Bill, and Bill asks Harry to satisfy the request, using a context that Harry knows about, 1.2. . . 1.

What happens when John sends Bill a response—or a trap—that must be relayed to Boss at the Network Operations Center? Now John is the initiator. He sends a message containing variables in his context 1.3. . . 2. When it arrives, Bill looks in the context table and sees that Mary must reformat the message and relay its contents to Boss. In the relayed message, the context name will be 1.3. . . 4, the name that Boss uses to discuss John's data.

The NOC system is aware of party *Boss,* party *Mary,* and suitable contexts that define the information at various devices. The context identifier is the tip-off that tells Mary that Bill will have to do the work. The context identifier also is used to look up which LAN agent Bill will have to talk to, and which MIB view should be accessed.

The proxy system has to be aware of *Boss, Mary, Bill,* all of the agents at local devices, and all of the context identifiers.

### 33.9.2 Dual Roles and Foreign Proxies

On request from the NOC manager, a LAN management station also can extract information from devices via some proprietary protocol, convert it to SNMPv2, and relay it to the NOC manager. The agent is said to support a *foreign proxy* relationship.

The NOC manager, Boss, can't tell the difference between an agent that accesses:

- Local MIB data
- A native proxy
- A foreign proxy

When data is retrieved via a foreign proxy, the NOC still is aware of party *Boss,* party *Mary,* and suitable context identifiers. The LAN management station uses a proprietary method of extracting information from devices.

### 33.9.3 Local Data, Proxies, and the Context Table

In the earlier sections, we provided two completely different sets of variables for the context table. How is this done? Each entry has placeholders for all of the variables.

- When a local context is accessed, the Context Table tells us the entity (e.g., Bridge_1) and the MIB view. Values are not filled in for the variables that describe a proxy relationship.

- For an entry that is used to identify how a proxy request will be carried out, the MIB view variable is zero, and the proxy source, destination, and context are filled in.

## 33.10   RECOVERING FROM A CRASH

We can see that a system might amass a large amount of information on party relationships, contexts, clocks, and keys. What happens if it crashes and forgets all of its current data?

An initialization configuration can be stored in nonvolatile memory. A system that behaves properly will send a cold-start trap to a manager, which can then reconfigure the system.

## 33.11   THOUGHTS ON SECURITY

SNMP version 1 was easy to implement and maintain. The introduction of authentication and privacy are essential to safe, centralized network management. But the price is a larger, more complex implementation, and far more maintenance effort.

The MD5 message digest and DES symmetric encryption require a system to know its own secrets and those of every party partner. If it is important for a particular system to be protected at all times, then its secrets and those of its partners will need to be kept in nonvolatile memory.

Movement to a public key system would reduce overhead. A system using public key security needs to know its own private key. Its public key, and those of any other systems, can be published anywhere. At initialization, the system could obtain the public keys of all of the parties with whom it needs to communicate from any convenient server. For example, these keys could be kept at a Domain Name Server.

### 33.11.1   A Secure Topology

Is the proposed system perfect? By no means. SNMPv2 software will be available on PCs, and a malicious attacker can still be a great nuisance. An attacker can do many annoying things. For example,

- Replay messages within the lifetime period. At minimum, this ties up agents and managers with a useless processing load.
- Capture and replay cold-start trap messages, forcing a manager to check the actual status of a system. A manager might prefer to reconfigure rather than check the whole agent database for validity.

However, networks can be made more secure by means of topology and technology changes. One of the most irksome security problems is the fact that standard LAN technologies such as Ethernet, Token-Ring, and FDDI enable any station to eavesdrop on anybody's traffic. A technology based on *switched* traffic would restrict a station to hearing only its own conversations.

Until recently, switching has not been used because of its failure to support appropriate LAN bandwidths, its inability to support enough stations, and its cost. The bandwidth problem has been solved by the ATM technology, as well as by a number of proprietary switching hub products. The next few years may see the introduction of products that overcome the number and price barriers.

## 33.12   RECOMMENDED READING

RFC 1445 discusses the SNMP version 2 administrative model, and presents a number of configuration examples. RFC 1510 describes version 5 of the Kerberos Network Authentication Service.

# 34

# Formal Definitions
# for SNMP Version 2

## 34.1 INTRODUCTION

In this chapter we are going to present the formal definitions that transform our concepts of parties, authentication, privacy, MIB views, contexts, and access control into MIB objects that we can configure and employ.

This chapter also includes MIB definitions for Manager-to-Manager communications. Finally, the MIB variables that track SNMP version 2 traffic and count problems of various sorts will be presented.

At the time of writing, the version of SNMPv2 presented in this chapter had the status of an elective protocol. Figure 34.1 shows how SNMP version 2 fits into the MIB tree, and the major subtrees under the *snmpV2* node.

## 34.2 PARTIES, AGENTS, AND MANAGERS

It is convenient to use the familiar language of "agents" and "managers," but in fact, roles are becoming less and less clear cut. The purpose of the set of administrative tables in this chapter is to spell out exactly when it is valid for one party (called a *subject*) to send a message to another party (called a *target*) containing a specific operation acting on a specific set of data.

This fine-grained level of control enables a party to act like an agent when talking to one partner, and act like a manager when talking to another partner.

Figure 34.2 illustrates party relationships. It shows managers talking to agents and to other managers. It shows agents talking to other

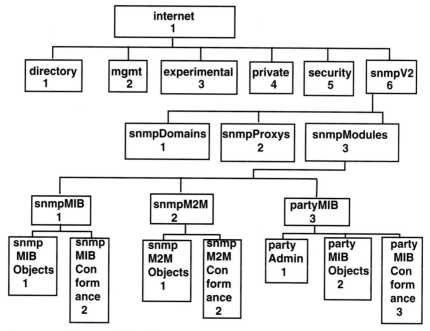

**Figure 34.1** The *snmpV2* subtree.

agents with which they have a proxy relationship. A proxy relationship is *native* if the agents communicate via SNMPv2. A proxy relationship is *foreign* if the agents use a different protocol—even SNMPv1.

### 34.2.1   Configuring Parties at a Manager

An SNMP manager will be configured with information about all of its local parties and all of the remote parties with whom the manager communicates. Most of these remote parties will be agent parties within managed devices. Some of these agents may be acting as proxies, extracting data from other agents.

SNMPv2 also supports direct Manager-to-Manager communications via *inform-request* Protocol Data Units. A manager's party database must identify any communicating peer managers that will exchange messages with the local manager.

### 34.2.2   Configuring Parties at an Agent

An SNMPv2 agent will be configured with all of its local parties and the manager parties with which it communicates. If the agent acts as a *native proxy,* it also will need information about its SNMPv2 agent partners. If the agent acts as a *foreign proxy,* it will need whatever information is needed to "talk" its partners' protocol. This information is outside the scope of SNMPv2.

## 34.3  IDENTIFYING PARTIES

Each party is named by an OBJECT IDENTIFIER which must be unique—in the entire world. Several conventional start-up parties are described in the Party MIB, RFC 1447. RFC 1447 assigns an OBJECT IDENTIFIER to each of these start-up parties; each identifier is made globally unique by including an IP address. A typical party identifier has the form:

```
initialPartyId.ipAddress.index
```

For example, typical party identifiers at an agent with IP address 128.1.1.5 would be:

```
initialPartyId.128.1.1.5.1
```

```
initialPartyId.128.1.1.5.2
```

A complete start-up configuration is presented later in this chapter.

Once the start-up parties are ready to get to work, new parties can by created by a manager. *Set* operations add the new definitions to the party table.

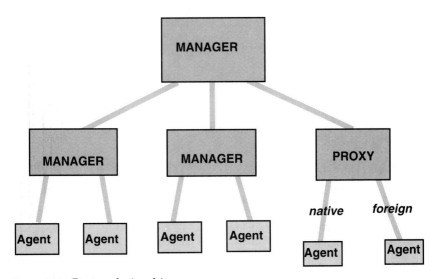

**Figure 34.2**  Party relationships.

Any organization running a network can obtain the authority to create its own unique party identifiers.

## 34.4  TEXTUAL CONVENTIONS

Several textual conventions make the tables that follow easier to read:

- *Party.*  A globally unique OBJECT IDENTIFIER that names a party.

- *TAddress.*  An OCTET STRING representing a transport address. For UDP, it is a 6-octet string representing an IP address and port number.

- *Clock.*  A 32-bit unsigned integer (UInteger32) that represents a party's authentication clock. This is a relative clock with 1-second granularity.

- *Context.*  An OBJECT IDENTIFIER that corresponds to information that will be accessed by some party or parties—less formally, a context identifies some chunk of MIB data at an agent.

- *StorageType.*  An integer indicating the storage stability of an entry:
  1. other
  2. volatile        Lost on reboot, e.g., in RAM
  3. nonVolatile    Can live through reboot, e.g., in nonvolatile RAM
  4. permanent     Cannot be changed or deleted, e.g., in ROM

- *Truth Value.*  An integer that represents true (1), or false (2).

- *RowStatus.*  An integer that represents the state of an entry, and also is used to assist in row creation and deletion. Values include:
  1. active
  2. notInService
  3. notReady
  4. createAndGo
  5. createAndWait
  6. destroy

- *InstancePointer.*  An OBJECT IDENTIFIER for a variable (instance). It can be used to point to a row in a table by identifying the variable in the first column of the row.

## 34.5  INTRODUCTION TO THE PARTY TABLE

Each entry in Table 34.2, the Party Table, contains configuration information for one party. Each party is assigned its identifier. The party's authentication and privacy protocols are declared and, where relevant, secret keys are assigned. Clock and lifetime values that protect an authenticated message against replay are included.

Several variables in the party table have default values of "H. This represents an empty OCTET STRING.

### 34.5.1   Authentication and Privacy

Each party is assigned the level of security at which it will operate by naming its authentication and privacy protocols. Some parties will operate in the open, without either authentication or privacy. Others will provide authentication, but no privacy. Parties that need to hide sensitive information will have both authentication and privacy.

In the first generation of SNMPv2 products, if authentication is supported at a system, it will be done by means of the MD5 message digest. Similarly, if privacy is supported, first-generation products will use DES encryption to support it.

The protocols selected for authentication and privacy are named by OBJECT IDENTIFIERS. The currently defined values are shown in Table 34.1.

A party's entry also contains space to hold private (secret) and public key variables if they are needed for authentication and encryption.

Private keys are protected and cannot be read. If a manager attempts to read a secret authentication key or secret encryption key, a 0-length octet string will be returned.

### 34.5.2   Changing Private Key Values

Suppose that a system supports authentication but not encryption. Can a manager *set* a new value of the private authentication key without giving it away to an eavesdropper? The answer is yes! The method is:

**TABLE 34.1   OBJECT IDENTIFIERs for Protocols**

| OBJECT IDENTIFIERs for Authentication and Privacy Protocols | |
| --- | --- |
| iso.org.dod.internet.snmpV2. snmpModules.partyMIB.partyAdmin.partyProtocols. | |
| Name | OBJECT IDENTIFIER |
| noAuth | 1.3.6.1.6.3.3.1.1.1 |
| nopriv | 1.3.6.1.6.3.3.1.1.2 |
| desPrivProtocol | 1.3.6.1.6.3.3.1.1.3 |
| v2md5AuthProtocol | 1.3.6.1.6.3.3.1.1.4 |

- Pick a new key. Compute its exclusive-OR with the old key.

- Send the result to the agent in a *set-request.*

- The agent performs an exclusive-OR of the current key with the value in the *set-request.* The answer is the new key.

An eavesdropper cannot extract the new key without knowing the old one.

The same trick could be used when *setting* a new value for the private encryption key. To be even safer, the whole message could be encrypted using the old key.

### 34.5.3   Making Sure That
### the Key Has Changed

A network may lose a message at any time. If a manager tries to change a key, it needs to know for sure whether the change is safely in place.

There is a clever way to do this using an unauthenticated read. Neither MD5 nor DES symmetric encryption makes any use of its public key, so these variables can be pressed into service. Suppose that the public key is *set* to a new value at the same time as the private key. According to the rules of SNMP, both *sets* will succeed together or fail together. The public key *can* be read with an unauthenticated *get-request.* If its value has changed, then the new private key also is in place and ready for use.

Even a manager cannot read an agent's secret keys. The keys must be stored in an encoded format. The previous key is kept, and the new key is stored as its exclusive-OR with the old key.

Note that any time that any key value is changed, it also has to be changed at *every* partner system. Trying to use the identical keys at lots of agents does not necessarily simplify life.

### 34.5.4   The Party Table

We finally are ready to look at Table 34.2, the Party Table. The *party-Local* variable indicates whether a party executes locally or is remote. For example, an agent will have entries for each of its remote managers in its party table.

The *partyMaxMessageSize* puts a realistic limit on the size of the messages that the party can handle.

Note that entries can be added and deleted dynamically. The *party-CloneFrom* variable provides for reuse of existing secret keys. When creating a new party, this variable is used to identify an existing party whose authentication and privacy keys should be copied into the new entry.

**TABLE 34.2    The Party Table**

iso.org.dod.internet.snmpV2.snmpModules.partyMIB.
partyMIBObjects.snmpParties.partyTable.partyEntry
1.3.6.1.6.3.3.2.1.1.1

| OBJECT IDENTIFIER | Syntax | Maxaccess | Description |
|---|---|---|---|
| partyIdentity<br>1.3.6.1.6.3.3.2.1.1.1.1<br>▶ Index | Party | not-<br>accessible | Globally unique<br>party identifier,<br>e.g., *initialPartyId.ipAddress.* |
| partyIndex<br>1.3.6.1.6.3.3.2.1.1.1.2 | INTEGER<br>(1.65535) | read-<br>only | Unique integer<br>index for each<br>table entry. |
| partyTDomain<br>1.3.6.1.6.3.3.2.1.1.1.3 | OBJECT<br>IDENTIFIER | read-<br>create | Party receives<br>management<br>traffic via this<br>transport. Default<br>*snmpUDPDomain.* |
| partyTAddress<br>1.3.6.1.6.3.3.2.1.1.1.4 | TAddress | read-<br>create | Transport address.<br>For UDP, it is the<br>IP address and<br>port number. |
| partyMax<br>MessageSize<br>1.3.6.1.6.3.3.2.1.1.1.5 | INTEGER<br>(484..65507) | read-<br>create | Maximum length<br>of SNMPv2<br>message that the<br>party will accept. |
| partyLocal<br>1.3.6.1.6.3.3.2.1.1.1.6 | Truth<br>Value | read-<br>create | If true, this is a<br>local party. If<br>false, this is a<br>remote party. |
| partyAuth<br>Protocol<br>1.3.6.1.6.3.3.2.1.1.1.7 | OBJECT<br>IDENTIFIER | read-<br>create | Authentication<br>protocol for this<br>party. |
| partyAuthClock<br>1.3.6.1.6.3.3.2.1.1.1.8 | Clock | read-<br>create | Authentication<br>clock. Default 0. |
| partyAuthPrivate<br>1.3.6.1.6.3.3.2.1.1.1.9 | OCTET<br>STRING<br>(for MD5,<br>SIZE (16)) | read-<br>create | The private<br>authentication key<br>(in a coded<br>format). Default<br>"H (empty). |
| partyAuthPublic<br>1.3.6.1.6.3.3.2.1.1.1.10 | OCTET<br>STRING<br>(for MD5,<br>SIZE (16)) | read-<br>create | A publicly<br>readable key.<br>Default "H. |
| partyAuth<br>Lifetime<br>1.3.6.1.6.3.3.2.1.1.1.11 | INTEGER<br>(0..2147483647) | read-<br>create | Upper limit in<br>seconds on the<br>acceptable delay<br>for messages<br>generated by this<br>party. Cannot be<br>changed after<br>creation of the<br>entry. Default 300<br>seconds. |

**TABLE 34.2    The Party Table (*Continued*)**

iso.org.dod.internet.snmpV2.snmpModules.partyMIB.
partyMIBObjects.snmpParties.partyTable.partyEntry
1.3.6.1.6.3.3.2.1.1.1

| OBJECT IDENTIFIER | Syntax | Maxaccess | Description |
|---|---|---|---|
| partyPrivProtocol 1.3.6.1.6.3.3.2.1.1.1.12 | OBJECT IDENTIFIER | read-create | The privacy protocol, used to decrypt all messages received by this agent. |
| partyPrivPrivate 1.3.6.1.6.3.3.2.1.1.1.13 | OCTET STRING (for DES encryption, SIZE (16)) | read-create | The private encryption key (in a coded format). Default "H. |
| partyPrivPublic 1.3.6.1.6.3.3.2.1.1.1.14 | OCTET STRING (for DES, SIZE (16)) | read-create | A publicly readable key. Default "H. |
| partyCloneFrom 1.3.6.1.6.3.3.2.1.1.1.15 | Party | read-create | At creation, authentication and privacy values are obtained using values from the named party. |
| partyStorageType 1.3.6.1.6.3.3.2.1.1.1.16 | Storage Type | read-create | Volatile, nonvolatile, or permanent. |
| partyStatus 1.3.6.1.6.3.3.2.1.1.1.17 | RowStatus | read-create | Status: under Creation, notReady, active, etc. |

## 34.6   DEFINING MIB VIEWS

From the start, SNMP has been modeled as a bunch of software applications that access MIB databases spread through a network. In the world of databases, it is common to create database *views*. A view limits the data that a user can access. The idea of database views has been incorporated into SNMPv2.

Recall that a MIB view formally is defined as the leaf instances for a specific collection of MIB subtrees. In Chapter 33, we described a shorthand for generating MIB views. The shorthand is based on using wild-card matches to pick out view subtree families, and also being able to *include* or *exclude* a particular family.

Each entry in Table 34.3, the View Table, describes a single family of view subtrees. Several entries in the table may be needed to define an entire MIB view. All of these related entries will have the same *viewIndex* value. Some of these entries indicate variables to be included, while others describe variables to be excluded from a MIB view.

Recall that a subtree can be selected very simply by means of an OBJECT IDENTIFIER. For example, 1.3.6.1.2.1.2, selects a subtree containing all *interfaces* variables.

Alternatively, masks containing wild-card positions may be used for pinpoint selections. For example,

| | |
|---|---|
| View Subtree | 1.3.6.1.2.1.2.2.1.0.1 |
| View Mask | 1.1.1.1.1.1.1.1.1.0.1 (Actually written 'FFA0'H) |

This combination chooses all of the variables in the first entry of the interfaces table. We might write this for ourselves informally as 1.3.6.1.2.1.2.2.1.*.1. Remember,

- If a mask is too short, it is padded out to the right with 1s until the length of the corresponding OBJECT IDENTIFIER is matched. Thus the mask "H means all 1s—i.e., there are no wild cards.
- If the length of the mask is not a multiple of 8, it will be padded to the right with 0s in order to fill its last octet.

**TABLE 34.3   The View Table**

iso.org.dod.internet.snmpV2.snmpModules.partyMIB.
partyMIBObjects.snmpViews.viewTable.viewEntry
1.3.6.1.6.3.3.2.4.1.1

| OBJECT IDENTIFIER | Syntax | Maxaccess | Description |
|---|---|---|---|
| viewIndex 1.3.6.1.6.3.3.2.4.1.1.1 ► Index | INTEGER (1..65535) | not-accessible | A unique number assigned to a MIB view. |
| viewSubtree 1.3.6.1.6.3.3.2.4.1.1.2 ► Index | OBJECT IDENTIFIER | not-accessible | OBJECT IDENTIFIER used to name a view subtree. |
| viewMask 1.3.6.1.6.3.3.2.4.1.1.3 | OCTET STRING (SIZE (0..16)) | read-create | A bit mask indicating which subidentifiers must match and which are wild cards. Default "H. |
| viewType 1.3.6.1.6.3.3.2.4.1.1.4 | INTEGER included(1), excluded(2) | read-create | Whether to include or exclude this family of subtrees. |
| viewStorageType 1.3.6.1.6.3.3.2.4.1.1.5 | Storage Type | read-create | Storage type for this row. Default is nonvolatile. |
| viewStatus 1.3.6.1.6.3.3.2.4.1.1.6 | RowStatus | read-create | Status of this row. |

## 34.7    THE CONTEXT TABLE

A message sent from one party to another identifies the *context* of the PDU operation. For example, if a manager wants to get some information from an agent's MIB, the request will name a context that corresponds to a MIB view. The response will name the same context.

Why not just name the MIB view directly? Why drag in something called a context, along with yet another table? Recall that an agent may be in charge of MIBs for several local entities. Or the agent may be acting as a proxy, extracting data from several remote systems.

Table 34.4, the Context Table, allows us to assign a unique name to each context, and to locate the right information, whether it is local to, or remote from, the agent. The *contextViewIndex* variable sorts out the two types of contexts. A value *greater* than 0 identifies a MIB view. A value of 0 means "check out the Proxy variables."

The *contextLocalEntity* variable identifies which entity's MIB data should be accessed. Once SNMP begins to be used for host management, the *contextLocalEntity* will truly be essential, since a host has so many hardware and software components, and there will be many MIBs involved.

### 34.7.1    Temporal Contexts

A system might want to remember more than one set of values for its MIB variables. For example, in addition to the current values, there might be a set of values that are used whenever the system is rebooted. Or, we might want to cache some recent (at most "N" seconds old) values.

The *contextLocalTime* variable is used to identify which of the various versions of the context this entry belongs to.

## 34.8    THE ACCESS PRIVILEGES TABLE

Table 34.5, the Access Privileges Table, imposes very tight control on the interactions between parties. The table says exactly who can perform which operations with which data.

Stated more precisely, when a destination (target) party receives a message, the table is consulted to see whether:

- The message is from an acceptable source (subject) party.
- The context in the message is permitted for this subject and target.
- The PDU operation is permitted for this subject, target, and context.

A message that does not pass these tests will be discarded.

**TABLE 34.4   The Context Table**

iso.org.dod.internet.snmpV2snmpModules.partyMIB.
partyMIBObjects.snmpContexts.contextTable.contextEntry
1.3.6.1.6.3.3.2.2.1.1

| OBJECT IDENTIFIER | Syntax | Maxaccess | Description |
|---|---|---|---|
| contextIdentity 1.3.6.1.6.3.3.2.2.1.1.1 ▶ Index | Context | not-accessible | OBJECT IDENTIFIER for this SNMPv2 context. |
| contextIndex 1.3.6.1.6.3.3.2.2.1.1.2 | INTEGER (1..65535) | read-only | Unique table index for this context. |
| contextLocal 1.3.6.1.6.3.3.2.2.1.1.3 | Truth Value | read-create | Indicates if this context corresponds to a local MIB view. |
| contextViewIndex 1.3.6.1.6.3.3.2.2.1.1.4 | INTEGER (0..65535) | read-create | If 0, see the proxy variables. If not 0, is the viewIndex of a local MIB view. |
| contextLocalEntity 1.3.6.1.6.3.3.2.2.1.1.5 | OCTET STRING | read-create | For a local context, identifies the component owning the MIB view. An empty string says that the information belongs to the SNMPv2 entity. |
| contextLocalTime 1.3.6.1.6.3.3.2.2.1.1.6 | OBJECT IDENTIFIER | read-create | The temporal context—current, used at boot time, or cached. |
| contextProxy DstParty 1.3.6.1.6.3.3.2.2.1.1.7 | Party | read-create | For a proxy context, identifies a SNMPv2 entity which is the proxy destination. |
| contextProxy SrcParty 1.3.6.1.6.3.3.2.2.1.1.8 | Party | read-create | For a proxy context, identifies a SNMPv2 entity which is a proxy source. |
| contextProxy Context 1.3.6.1.6.3.3.2.2.1.1.9 | OBJECT IDENTIFIER | read-create | For a proxy, identifies the context of the proxy relationship. |
| contextStorage Type 1.3.6.1.6.3.3.2.2.1.1.10 | Storage Type | read-create | Storage type for this row. |
| contextStatus 1.3.6.1.6.3.3.2.2.1.1.11 | RowStatus | read-create | Status of this row. |

**TABLE 34.5    Access Control Table**

iso.org.dod.internet.snmpV2snmpModules
partyMIB.partyMIBObjects.snmpAccess.aclTable.aclEntry
1.3.6.1.6.3.3.2.3.1.1

| OBJECT IDENTIFIER | Syntax | Maxaccess | Description |
|---|---|---|---|
| aclTarget<br>1.3.6.1.6.3.3.2.3.1.1.1<br>▶ Index | INTEGER<br>(1..65535) | not-<br>accessible | A *partyIndex*<br>identifying a party<br>that is the target of<br>an access control policy. |
| aclResources<br>1.3.6.1.6.3.3.2.3.1.1.3<br>▶ Index | INTEGER<br>(1..65535) | not-<br>accessible | A *contextIndex*<br>corresponding to an<br>SNMPv2 context. |
| aclPrivileges<br>1.3.6.1.6.3.3.2.3.1.1.4 | INTEGER<br>(0..255) | read-<br>create | The operations that a<br>target can perform for<br>a given subject within<br>the specified context. |
| aclStorageType<br>1.3.6.1.6.3.3.2.3.1.1.5 | Storage<br>Type | read-<br>create | Storage type for this<br>row. |
| aclStatus<br>1.3.6.1.6.3.3.2.3.1.1.6 | Row<br>Status | read-<br>create | Status of this row. |

The *aclPrivileges* variable packs all of the operations allowed for this subject, target, and context into a single integer. The integer is the sum of the following numbers that correspond to permitted operations:

| | |
|---|---|
| Get | 1 |
| GetNext | 2 |
| Response | 4 |
| Set | 8 |
| unused | 16 |
| GetBulk | 32 |
| Inform | 64 |
| SNMPv2-Trap | 128 |

For example, if *get, get-next,* and *get-bulk* are allowed, then the value of *aclPrivileges* is 35.

Note that the Access Control Table names a party by its integer index value in the Party Table, rather than its OBJECT IDENTIFIER. The context also is named by its integer index, rather than by its OBJECT IDENTIFIER.

## 34.9  STANDARD START-UP CONFIGURATION DATA

The sections that follow describe standard start-up data. This data includes configurations for:

- Agent start-up parties
- Two MIB views
- Two context identifiers
- Access control table entries that define operation privileges for a given subject party, target party, and context

### 34.9.1  Initial Agent Parties

In this section we describe six start-up parties for an agent's party table. The *noAuth/noPriv* agent and manager parties always will be supported. However, implementation of the *md5Auth/noPriv* parties depends on whether the agent supports authentication. Implementation of the *md5Auth/desPriv* parties depends on whether the agent supports both authentication and a privacy protocol.

In Table 34.6, the parties are presented in pairs, showing entries for an agent's local party and for its peer manager party. The OBJECT IDENTIFIERS for the standard parties are in subtree:

```
iso.org.dod.internet.snmpV2.snmpModules.partyMIB.
partyAdmin.initialPartyId
```

That is,

```
1 . 3 . 6 . 1 . 6 . 3 . 3 . 1 . 3
```

The *a.b.c.d* in the OBJECT IDENTIFIER for the agent party represents the IP address of the agent party. The *e.f.g.h* represents the IP address of the manager party. The IP addresses are included in the OBJECT IDENTIFIERs in order to make the identifiers globally unique.

It makes good sense to use permanent storage for parties at an agent. On the other hand, a manager will create dozens of parties on demand, and it makes sense to use volatile storage for parties defined at a manager.

**TABLE 34.6    (*a*) A noAuth/noPriv Agent and Manager**

Object Identifiers and Attributes for
Conventional SNMPv2 Parties

noAuth/noPriv Agent and Manager

| Party variables | noAuth/noPriv agent party | noAuth/noPriv manager party |
|---|---|---|
| partyIdentity | 1.3.6.1.6.3.3.1.3. a.b.c.d.1 | 1.3.6.1.6.3.3.1.3. e.f.g.h.2 |
| partyIndex | 1 | 2 |
| partyTDomain | snmpUDPDomain | snmpUDPDomain |
| partyTAddress | a.b.c.d, 161 | e.f.g.h, port number |
| partyMax MessageSize | According to local implementation | According to manager implementation |
| partyLocal | true | false |
| partyAuth Protocol | noAuth | noAuth |
| partyAuthClock | 0 | 0 |
| partyAuthPrivate | ”H | ”H |
| partyAuthPublic | ”H | ”H |
| partyAuth Lifetime | 0 | 0 |
| partyPrivProtocol | noPriv | noPriv |
| partyPrivPrivate | ”H | ”H |
| partyPrivPublic | ”H | ”H |

**TABLE 34.6    (*b*) A md5Auth/noPriv Agent and Manager**

Object Identifiers and Attributes for
Conventional SNMPv2 Parties

md5Auth/noPriv Agent and Manager

| Party variables | md5Auth/noPriv agent party | md5Auth/noPriv manager party |
|---|---|---|
| partyIdentity | 1.3.6.1.6.3.3.1.3. a.b.c.d.3 | 1.3.6.1.6.3.3.1.3. e.f.g.h.4 |
| partyIndex | 3 | 4 |
| partyTDomain | *snmpUDPDDomain* | *snmpUDPDomain* |
| partyTAddress | a.b.c.d, 161 | e.f.g.h, port number |
| partyMax MessageSize | According to local implementation | According to manager implementation |
| partyLocal | true | false |
| partyAuth Protocol | *v2md5AuthProtocol* | *v2md5AuthProtocol* |

**TABLE 34.6** (*b*) **A md5Auth/noPriv Agent and Manager (*Continued*)**

| | Object Identifiers and Attributes for Conventional SNMPv2 Parties | |
|---|---|---|
| | md5Auth/noPriv Agent and Manager | |
| Party variables | md5Auth/noPriv agent party | md5Auth/noPriv manager party |
| partyAuthClock | 0 | 0 |
| partyAuthPrivate | Assigned by administrator | Assigned by administrator |
| partyAuthPublic | ''H | ''H |
| partyAuth Lifetime | 300 | 300 |
| partyPrivProtocol | noPriv | noPriv |
| partyPrivPrivate | ''H | ''H |
| partyPrivPublic | ''H | ''H |

**TABLE 34.6** (*c*) **A md5Auth/desPriv Agent and Manager**

| | Object Identifiers and Attributes for Conventional SNMPv2 Parties | |
|---|---|---|
| | md5Auth/desPriv Agent and Manager | |
| Party variables | md5Auth/desPriv agent party | md5Auth/desPriv manager party |
| partyIdentity | 1.3.6.1.6.3.3.1.3. a.b.c.d.5 | 1.3.6.1.6.3.3.1.3. e.f.g.h.6 |
| partyIndex | 5 | 6 |
| partyTDomain | *snmpUDPDomain* | *snmpUDPDomain* |
| partyTAddress | a.b.c.d, 161 | e.f.g.h, port number |
| partyMax MessageSize | According to local implementation | According to manager implementation |
| partyLocal | true | false |
| partyAuth Protocol | *v2md5AuthProtocol* | *v2md5AuthProtocol* |
| partyAuthClock | 0 (initially) | 0 (initially) |
| partyAuthPrivate | Assigned by administrator. | Assigned by administrator. |
| partyAuthPublic | ''H | ''H |
| partyAuth Lifetime | 300 | 300 |
| partyPrivProtocol | *desPrivProtocol* | *desPrivProtocol* |
| partyPrivPrivate | Assigned by administrator | Assigned by administrator |
| partyPrivPublic | ''H | ''H |

TABLE 34.7  Standard MIB Views

| Definitions of Standard MIB Views | | | | |
|---|---|---|---|---|
| View index | View subtree | View object identifier | View mask | View type |
| 1 | system | 1.3.6.1.2.1.1 | "H | included |
| 1 | snmpStats | 1.3.6.1.6.3.1.1.1 | "H | included |
| 1 | snmpParties | 1.3.6.1.6.3.3.2.1 | "H | included |
| 2 | internet | 1.3.6.1 | "H | included |

### 34.9.2  Initial MIB Views

Table 34.7 shows the initial views to be created at a system by convention.

View number 1 permits access to system variables, statistics that count traffic and errors for SNMPv2 messages, and the party table. View number 2 provides access to everything under the *internet* node. In particular, this includes MIB-II and all of the *private enterprises* MIBs.

### 34.9.3  Initial SNMPv2 contexts

The two initial contexts correspond to the two standard MIB views defined in Table 34.8. Each of these standard contexts identifies a body

TABLE 34.8  Standard Contexts

| | Object Identifiers and Attributes for Conventional SNMPv2 Contexts | |
|---|---|---|
| Context variables | Context for MIB view 1 | Context for MIB view 2 |
| contextIdentity | 1.3.6.1.6.3.3.1.4. a.b.c.d.1 | 1.3.6.1.6.3.3.1.4. a.b.c.d.2 |
| contextIndex | 1 | 2 |
| contextLocal | true (local) | true (local) |
| contextViewIndex | 1 | 2 |
| contextLocalEntity | "H Owned by SNMPv2 entity | "H Owned by SNMPv2 entity |
| contextLocalTime | currentTime | currentTime |
| contextProxy DstParty | { 0 0 } | { 0 0 } |
| contextProxy SrcParty | { 0 0 } | { 0 0 } |
| contextProxy Context | { 0 0 } | { 0 0 } |

of variables managed by SNMPv2 in an agent's local database. The OBJECT IDENTIFIERS for the standard contexts are in subtree:

```
iso.org.dod.internet.snmpV2snmpModules.partyMIB.
partyAdmin.initialContextId
```

That is,

```
1 . 3 . 6 . 1 . 6 . 3 . 3 . 1 . 4
```

### 34.9.4   Initial Access Control Policy

The entries in Table 34.9 are recommended as conventional choices for access control policies for the initial parties defined earlier.

Party 1 plays the role of an agent, while party 2 is a manager. *Get, get-next,* and *get-bulk* requests sent from (subject) party 2 to (target) party 1 that reference context 1 will be honored. Note the use of the party table index, which is an integer, to identify the parties, instead of their formal OBJECT IDENTIFIERs. Similarly, the index of a context entry is used instead of its formal OBJECT IDENTIFIER.

## 34.10   MANAGERS TALKING TO MANAGERS

A large network will have more than one management station. Organizations need to be flexible in how they allocate work to each management station.

**TABLE 34.9   Recommended Initial Access Policies**

| | | Initial Access Control Policy | |
| --- | --- | --- | --- |
| Target | Subject | Resources: index of context | Privileges |
| 1 | 2 | 1 | 35 get, get-next, get-bulk |
| 2 | 1 | 1 | 132 response, SNMPv2-trap |
| 3 | 4 | 2 | 43 get, get-next, get-bulk, set |
| 4 | 3 | 2 | 4 response |
| 5 | 6 | 2 | 43 get, get-next, get-bulk, set |
| 6 | 5 | 2 | 4 response |

Work can be allocated in a hierarchical way—a local management station might be placed on each LAN and report to a management station at a Network Operations Center.

Or work may be allocated according to network function. One management station might be in charge of routers; another might watch bridges and telecom lines; another might be in charge of PCs; and another might watch large host servers.

SNMPv2 enables managers to report interesting events to other managers. SNMPv2 adopts some of the mechanisms of the RMON MIB to configure a manager to recognize an alarm condition, trigger an event, and send an appropriate *inform-request* to other managers.

The configuration information for alarms, events, and notifications is defined in the Manager-to-Manager (M2M) MIB. The definitions are in subtree:

```
iso.org.dod.internet.snmpV2snmpModules.snmpM2M.snmpM2MObjects
```

That is,

```
1 . 3 . 6 . 1 . 6 . 3 . 2 . 1
```

### 34.10.1   Alarms

As in the RMON MIB (see Chapter 28), alarms are based on examining a statistical sample of a value at regular intervals and comparing the result with threshold values.

Alarm information must not be used as a backdoor way for a manager to peek at information that the manager normally would be allowed to view. A manager will be restricted to creating and viewing alarms within one of its legitimate contexts. To impose this restriction, each alarm table entry is tied to a context. This is done by using the *contextIdentity* as one of the table indices.

Since several entries may refer to the same context, a second integer index variable, *snmpAlarmIndex,* is used to make the overall indexing unique. (See, for example, Table 34.10, the M2M Alarm Table.)

An alarm table probably will be implemented with a fixed size, and new entries will be slotted in wherever there is an unused row. The system maintains a stand-alone variable (*snmpAlarmNextIndex*) that points to an unused row. If the variable is 0, then the table is full. The object identifier for *snmpAlarmNextIndex* is

```
1 . 3 . 6 . 1 . 6 . 3 . 2 . 1 . 1 . 1
```

As in the RMON MIB, at the end of each time interval, a value is compared with a rising threshold and a falling threshold. Either a vari-

**TABLE 34.10  The M2M Alarm Table**

iso.org.dod.internet.snmpV2.snmpModules.snmpM2M.
snmpM2MObjects.snmpAlarm.snmpAlarmTable.snmpAlarmEntry
1.3.6.1.6.3.2.1.1.2.1

| OBJECT IDENTIFIER | Syntax | Maxaccess | Description |
|---|---|---|---|
| snmpAlarm Index 1.3.6.1.6.3.2.1.1.2.1.1 ▶ Index | INTEGER (1..65535) | not-accessible | An index that uniquely identifies an entry for some context. |
| snmpAlarm Variable 1.3.6.1.6.3.2.1.1.2.1.2 | Instance Pointer | read-create | The object identifier of a variable to be sampled. |
| snmpAlarm Interval 1.3.6.1.6.3.2.1.1.2.1.3 | Integer32 | read-create | The sampling interval in seconds. |
| snmpAlarm SampleType 1.3.6.1.6.3.2.1.1.2.1.4 | INTEGER absolute Value(1), delta Value(2) | read-create | The method used to compare the value at the end of the sampling interval with thresholds. Default is delta. |
| snmpAlarm Value 1.3.6.1.6.3.2.1.1.2.1.5 | Integer32 | read-only | Value of the statistic for the last complete measurement period. For delta measurements, the calculated difference is recorded here. |
| snmpAlarm StartupAlarm 1.3.6.1.6.3.2.1.1.2.1.6 | INTEGER rising Alarm(1), falling Alarm(2), risingOr Falling Alarm(3) | read-create | Type of alarm that may be sent as a result of the measurement for the first interval after the entry becomes active. |
| snmpAlarm RisingThreshold 1.3.6.1.6.3.2.1.1.2.1.7 | Integer32 | read-create | An event will be generated when the value changes from below to above this threshold. |
| snmpAlarm FallingThreshold 1.3.6.1.6.3.2.1.1.2.1.8 | Integer32 | read-create | An event will be generated when the value changes from above to below this threshold. |
| snmpAlarm RisingEventIndex 1.3.6.1.6.3.2.1.1.2.1.9 | INTEGER (0..65535) | read-create | Index of the event for a rising threshold. If 0, no event will be generated. |
| snmpAlarm FallingEventIndex 1.3.6.1.6.3.2.1.1.2.1.10 | INTEGER (0..65535) | read-create | Index for the event for a falling threshold. If 0, no event will be generated. |
| snmpAlarm UnavailableEvent Index 1.3.6.1.6.3.2.1.1.2.1.11 | INTEGER (0..65535) | read-create | Index for the event generated if the variable becomes unavailable. If 0, none. |
| snmpAlarm Status 1.3.6.1.6.3.2.1.1.2.1.12 | RowStatus | read-create | The status of this row (e.g., createAndWait or active). |

able's actual value (e.g., for a gauge variable) or else the delta amount of change (e.g., for a counter) is used in the comparisons. See Chapter 28 for a more detailed discussion of measurements and threshold comparisons.

### 34.10.2   Some Standard Alarm Notification Types

Several standard notifications are defined under the *snmpAlarm* subtree. These are displayed in Table 34.11. These notifications are suitable for use when a rising or falling threshold is crossed or when a variable becomes unavailable.

### 34.10.3   Events

If a value crosses a critical threshold, it should be reported. As we saw in the alarm table, an event number can be associated with crossing a threshold. This number is looked up in the Event Table. As shown in Table 34.13, the Event Table, an entry describes the inform-request that should be sent. Since there are quite a few steps involved, let's walk through the whole process.

- A threshold listed in the alarm table is crossed.

- The corresponding event index is not 0. We look up the event in the event table.

- We extract the OBJECT IDENTIFIER for this event.

**TABLE 34.11   Standard Alarm Notifications**

| iso.org.dod.internet.snmpV2.snmpModules.snmpM2M. snmpM2MObjects.snmpAlarm.snmpAlarmNotifications 1.3.6.1.6.3.2.1.1.3 | | |
|---|---|---|
| OBJECT IDENTIFIER | Varlist objects | Description |
| snmpRisingAlarm 1.3.6.1.6.3.2.1.1.3.1 | snmpAlarmVariable, snmpAlarmSampleType, snmpAlarmValue, snmpAlarmRisingThreshold | Appropriate when an alarm measurement has crossed its rising threshold. |
| snmpFallingAlarm 1.3.6.1.6.3.2.1.1.3.2 | snmpAlarmVariable, snmpAlarmSampleType, snmpAlarmValue, snmpAlarmFallingThreshold | Appropriate when an alarm measurement has crossed its falling threshold. |
| snmpObject UnavailableAlarm 1.3.6.1.6.3.2.1.1.3.3 | snmpAlarmVariable | Appropriate when a monitored variable becomes unavailable. |

- We prepare an inform-request message. The *sysUpTime* is placed in the first variable in the variable-bindings list. The OBJECT IDENTIFIER is copied into the *snmpEventID* position, which is the second variable in the variable-bindings list.

- We check to see if there is a NOTIFICATION-TYPE macro definition for this OBJECT IDENTIFIER. If there is, we copy any additional variables listed in the macro into the variable-bindings list.

- To whom should we send the *inform-request?* There is an Event Notify Table that will point the way to the correct recipient(s).

- We transmit the inform-request(s) and wait for the response(s).

- If a response does not arrive within its timeout period, we retransmit.

Several auxiliary variables are needed to make this work. How long should we wait before retransmitting? If we do not get a response, how many times should we retry before giving up? These values can be configured separately for each event using the SNMP Event Notify Table, which will be described later. However, the configured values will be honored only if they are consistent with overall bounds that are established for a minimum retransmission interval and a maximum number of retries.

As was the case for the Alarm Table, the Event Table also probably will be implemented with a fixed size, and new entries will be slotted in wherever there is an unused row. The system maintains a stand-alone variable (*snmpEventNextIndex*) that points to an unused row. If the variable is 0, then the table is full.

Variables providing the next index and the overall retransmission settings are displayed in Table 34.12. The variables in the Event table are described in Table 34.13.

### 34.10.4   Configuring Event Notifications

Table 34.14, the SNMPv2 Event Notify Table, determines which parties will receive *inform-requests* and contains some optional configuration parameters.

Choosing target parties for *inform-requests* is done rather subtly. The Event Notify Table is indexed by *snmpEventIndex* and *context-Identity*.

- For a given event, we look up all of the entries with that event index. This yields one or more contexts and their matching parameters.

- The Access Control Table is searched for entries with matching *contextIdentity* and with targets to whom *inform-requests* may be sent.

- An *inform-request* is sent to each of these target parties.

**TABLE 34.12     Some Event Variables**

<table>
<tr><td colspan="4" align="center">iso.org.dod.internet.snmpV2.snmpModules.snmpM2M.<br>snmpM2MObjects.snmpEvent<br>1.3.6.1.6.3.2.1.2</td></tr>
<tr><td>OBJECT<br>IDENTIFIER</td><td>Syntax</td><td>Maxaccess</td><td>Description</td></tr>
<tr><td>snmpEvent<br>NextIndex<br>1.3.6.1.6.3.2.1.2.1</td><td>INTEGER<br>(0..65535)</td><td>read-<br>only</td><td>Variable that points to next<br>free row in which to place a<br>new entry. 0 means no more<br>room.</td></tr>
<tr><td>snmpEventNotify<br>MinInterval<br>1.3.6.1.6.3.2.1.2.3</td><td>Integer32</td><td>read-<br>only</td><td>Absolute minimum interval in<br>seconds before retransmitting an<br>inform-request.</td></tr>
<tr><td>snmpEventNotify<br>Max<br>Retransmissions<br>1.3.6.1.6.3.2.1.2.4</td><td>Integer32</td><td>read-<br>only</td><td>Absolute maximum number of<br>times that the SNMPv2 entity<br>will retransmit a notify-request.</td></tr>
</table>

**TABLE 34.13     The Event Table**

<table>
<tr><td colspan="4" align="center">iso.org.dod.internet.snmpV2.snmpModules.snmpM2M.<br>snmpM2MObjects.snmpEvent.snmpEventTable.snmpEventEntry<br>1.3.6.1.6.3.2.1.2.2.1</td></tr>
<tr><td>OBJECT<br>IDENTIFIER</td><td>Syntax</td><td>Maxaccess</td><td>Description</td></tr>
<tr><td>snmpEventIndex<br>1.3.6.1.6.3.2.1.2.2.1.1<br>► Index</td><td>INTEGER<br>(1..65535)</td><td>not-<br>accessible</td><td>Unique index for event entry.</td></tr>
<tr><td>snmpEventID<br>1.3.6.1.6.3.2.1.2.2.1.2</td><td>OBJECT<br>IDENTIFIER</td><td>read-<br>create</td><td>Identifies the event type, and<br>will be included in the inform-<br>request that is sent. If there is<br>a matching NOTIFICATION-<br>TYPE macro, its objects will be<br>included in the inform-request.</td></tr>
<tr><td>snmpEvent<br>Description<br>1.3.6.1.6.3.2.1.2.2.1.3</td><td>Display<br>String<br>(SIZE<br>(0..127))</td><td>read-<br>create</td><td>A comment describing this<br>*snmpEvent* entry.</td></tr>
<tr><td>snmpEventEvents<br>1.3.6.1.6.3.2.1.2.2.1.4</td><td>Counter32</td><td>read-<br>only</td><td>Number of events of this type<br>that have been generated.</td></tr>
<tr><td>snmpEvent<br>LastTimeSent<br>1.3.6.1.6.3.2.1.2.2.1.5</td><td>Time<br>Stamp</td><td>read-<br>only</td><td>Value of *sysUpTime* the last<br>time that this entry generated<br>an event. (0 if none sent.)</td></tr>
<tr><td>snmpEventStatus<br>1.3.6.1.6.3.2.1.2.2.1.6</td><td>RowStatus</td><td>read-<br>create</td><td>Status of this entry (e.g., read-<br>create or active).</td></tr>
</table>

**TABLE 34.14    The SNMPv2 Event Notify Table**

iso.org.dod.internet.snmpV2.snmpModules.snmpM2M.
snmpM2MObjects.snmpEvent.snmpEventNotifyTable.
snmpEventNotifyEntry
1.3.6.1.6.3.2.1.2.5.1

| OBJECT IDENTIFIER | Syntax | Maxaccess | Description |
|---|---|---|---|
| snmpEventNotify IntervalRequested 1.3.6.1.6.3.2.1.2.5.1.1 | Integer32 | read-create | Requested interval in seconds for retransmission of inform-requests for this entry. Default 30 seconds. |
| snmpEventNotify Retransmissions Requested 1.3.6.1.6.3.2.1.2.5.1.2 | Integer32 | read-create | Requested number of retransmissions of inform-requests for this entry. Default 5. |
| snmpEventNotify Lifetime 1.3.6.1.6.3.2.1.2.5.1.3 | Integer32 | read-create | A timeout (in seconds) for the entry. The entry will be deleted automatically unless refreshed periodically. Default 86400 seconds. |
| snmpEventNotify Status 1.3.6.1.6.3.2.1.2.5.1.4 | Row Status | read-create | Status of this entry. |

The retransmission interval in Table 34.14 allows you to set a longer timeout interval than *snmpEventNotifyMinInterval*. The number of retransmissions in the table allows you to ask for fewer retransmissions than *snmpEventNotifyMaxRetransmissions*.

## 34.11    SNMPV2 STATISTICS

Table 34.15, SNMPv2 Statistics, contains counts of the total number of incoming SNMP messages, and then tallies the number of errors of various types. The mysteriously named *snmpStats30Something* variable actually counts the number of SNMP version 1 messages arriving at an entity that does not support SNMPv1. Version 1 messages start with '30'H.

As for counting errors, there are lots of things that can go wrong in SNMPv2. For example, the receiving party might not recognize the source party, or the message digest value in the *authDigest* field might be wrong, or the source timestamp might be stale (that is, earlier than the current source clock plus the source lifetime), or the context might be unrecognized, or the operation might be one that is not allowed.

**TABLE 34.15    SNMPv2 Statistics**

iso.org.dod.internet.snmpV2.snmpModules.snmpMIB.
snmpObjects.snmpStats
1.3.6.1.6.3.1.1.1

| OBJECT IDENTIFIER | Syntax | Maxaccess | Description |
|---|---|---|---|
| snmpStats Packets 1.3.6.1.6.3.1.1.1.1 | Counter32 | read-only | Total number of packets received by the SNMPv2 entity from the transport service. |
| snmpStats 30Something 1.3.6.1.6.3.1.1.1.2 | Counter32 | read-only | Number of messages starting with '30'H received by an SNMPv2 entity that does not support SNMPv1. |
| snmpStats EncodingErrors 1.3.6.1.6.3.1.1.1.3 | Counter32 | read-only | Number of messages received with bad encoding or invalid syntax. |
| snmpStats UnknownDst Parties 1.3.6.1.6.3.1.1.1.4 | Counter32 | read-only | Number of incoming messages for which the *privDst* field was not a known local party. |
| snmpStats DstParty Mismatches 1.3.6.1.6.3.1.1.1.5 | Counter32 | read-only | Number of incoming messages for which the *dstParty* field did not match the *privDst*. |
| snmpStats Unknown SrcParties 1.3.6.1.6.3.1.1.1.6 | Counter32 | read-only | Number of incoming for which the *srcParty* was not a known remote party. |
| snmpStats BadAuths 1.3.6.1.6.3.1.1.1.7 | Counter32 | read-only | Number of incoming messages whose authInfo field was inconsistent with the expected authentication protocol. |
| snmpStats NotIn Lifetimes 1.3.6.1.6.3.1.1.1.8 | Counter32 | read-only | Number of incoming messages judged inauthentic because the *authSrcTimestamp* was less than the source party's clock plus lifetime. |
| snmpStats Wrong DigestValues 1.3.6.1.6.3.1.1.1.9 | Counter32 | read-only | Number of incoming messages judged inauthentic because of an unexpected digest value. |
| snmpStats Unknown Contexts 1.3.6.1.6.3.1.1.1.10 | Counter32 | read-only | Number of incoming messages whose context field was an unknown context. |

**TABLE 34.15   SNMPv2 Statistics (*Continued*)**

iso.org.dod.internet.snmpV2.snmpModules.snmpMIB.
snmpObjects.snmpStats
1.3.6.1.6.3.1.1.1

| OBJECT IDENTIFIER | Syntax | Maxaccess | Description |
|---|---|---|---|
| snmpStatsBad Operations 1.3.6.1.6.3.1.1.1.11 | Counter32 | read-only | Number of incoming messages dropped because the operation was not allowed in the *aclTable*. |
| snmpStats SilentDrops 1.3.6.1.6.3.1.1.1.12 | Counter32 | read-only | Number of gets, get-nexts, get-bulks, sets, and informs silently dropped because even an alternate response with empty variable-bindings field was too big. |

## 34.12   PROPOSED SIMPLIFICATIONS

Steven Waldbusser of Carnegie Mellon University has proposed a number of conventions that will make it easier to implement and use the SNMPv2 administrative and security models. Waldbusser's proposal defines standard, automatic definitions for nonauthenticated parties. It reduces the configuration of authenticated or private parties to the assignment of a userid and password to the party. The major ideas include:

- By sticking to some simple conventions, all of the information about an unauthenticated party can be generated automatically.

- An identifier for an unauthenticated party can be assigned automatically by appending an IP address and port number to a standard introducer.

- Again, by using some simple conventions, party information for an unauthenticated or private party can be generated automatically, once a userid and password have been assigned to the party.

- A unique identifier for an authenticated or private party can be constructed by appending its userid after the IP address and port number.

- A party's keys can be generated from its assigned password.

- The clock values that are important are the ones stored at an agent. It must be possible to read the clock values without authentication.

- If a manager gets out of sync with an agent's clocks, the manager should read the agent's clocks and use these values when communicating with the agent. An agent's clocks should never be advanced artificially.

- Optionally, an agent can use a clock chip to initialize its clocks on start-up.

- Vendors are encouraged to preconfigure a set of useful MIB views and contexts.

## 34.13  RECOMMENDED READING

The party, MIB view, context, and access control tables are defined in RFC 1447, which also defines the initial configuration values. RFC 1445 explains how all of this information is used during the processing of an SNMPv2 message. RFC 1451 contains the Manager-to-Manager MIB, and SNMPv2 statistics are defined in RFC 1450.

The documents describing the Waldbusser simplifications are titled *Overview of SNMPv2 Simplified Security Conventions and Conventions for Simplified Usage of SNMPv2 Security.*

# 35

# ASN.1

## 35.1 INTRODUCTION

Traditionally, data communications protocol standards have described message formats 1 byte or even 1 bit at a time. This has made the standards difficult to write and incredibly tedious to read.

Furthermore, if a protocol was at all complex and allowed some optional choices, the specification became massive and the creation of correct, interworking implementations was extremely difficult.

End-user requirements change, and a protocol has to change with them. However, to add a new data item to a protocol message, a programmer had to do a lot of hard work to update the software that created and interpreted messages. Invariably, the new software was not backward-compatible with the old—or else backward compatibility was achieved by using twice as much software!

It was clear that protocols would remain costly to implement and hard to change unless some new, smart methodology could be discovered and adopted.

Another problem that plagued designers of communications protocols was the fact that every computer manufacturer chooses its own unique way to represent information. Was it possible to come up with a standard way to encode data that is sent across a network so that computers could comprehend what they were saying to one another?

## 35.2 MOVING TO A DATATYPE DEFINITION LANGUAGE

The breakthrough that changed the way protocols are defined and data is exchanged came out of the work of the CCITT committee that produced the X.400 electronic messaging standards.

A high-level *datatype definition language* was introduced in Recommendation X.409. This language allows standards writers to define datatypes *in a manner that is independent of the physical representation of data.* After some modifications, this language was adopted by ISO and named Abstract Syntax Notation 1 (ASN.1).

Using ASN.1, a standards author can define simple *primitive* data types, complex *constructed* data types, and entire message formats. Definitions written in the ASN.1 language are quite easy to read. The MIB definitions that have appeared in earlier chapters were written in ASN.1.

A set of *Basic Encoding Rules* (BER) was introduced along with ASN.1. The encoding rules define a way to translate data values into a string of octets for transmission across a network.

It is not the purpose of this chapter to turn the reader into an expert on ASN.1 and BER. Enough information is included to:

- Be able to read MIB definition documents
- Be able to read Internet network management standards
- Understand traces of SNMP traffic

### 35.3   SOME COMPUTER LANGUAGE CONVENTIONS

Before focusing in on ASN.1, let's take a look at how variables are declared in programming languages. A language such as *C* provides some basic built-in datatypes, such as *char, short int, long int,* and *float.* A *C* program contains declarations of variables that describe their datatypes:

```
short int n;
float x;
```

### 35.4   ASN.1 PRIMITIVE DATATYPES

Similar concepts are used in ASN.1, but they are expressed a bit differently. First of all, the ASN.1 built-in *primitive* types, which are always written in capital letters, include:

- INTEGER.   A whole number.
- ENUMERATED.   A limited set of integers is specified, each with an assigned meaning such as *red(1), white(2),* and *blue(3).*
- OCTET STRING.   Just what it says, a string of octets. When represented as a decimal number, an octet ranges from 0 to 255.

- OBJECT IDENTIFIER.   A string of numbers derived from a naming tree, used to identify an object.
- NULL.   An empty placeholder.
- BOOLEAN.   Takes the value *true* or *false.*
- BIT STRING.   Could be used, for example, for fax data, or can be used as *flags,* where setting a given bit to 1 is assigned a specific meaning.
- REAL.   A mantissa, base, and exponent, used to express a real number.

There are several primitive *character string* types, including *PrintableString* and *NumericString,* among others. In addition, there are types used to express time, such as GeneralizedTime and UTCTime.

## 35.5   ASN.1 CONSTRUCTOR DATATYPES

Compound structures can be defined by combining primitive types using the *constructors.*

- SEQUENCE.   An ordered list of datatypes. For example, a list of fields, such as (INTEGER, INTEGER, OCTET STRING, OBJECT IDENTIFIER), in a table entry.
- SEQUENCE OF.   An ordered list—but in this case, every item in the list has the same type. For example, a sequence of integers.
- SET.   An unordered list of datatypes.
- SET OF.   An unordered list, all of the same datatype.

Another useful language feature is:

- CHOICE.   An item must be picked from a given selection of datatypes.

## 35.6   SNMP PRIMITIVE DATATYPES

ASN.1 enables protocol designers to define rich, complex datatypes. However, the designers of SNMP version 1 wanted network management software to be simple enough to run in a bridge, hub, or even a repeater. Therefore, in defining the Structure of Management Information, the datatypes that could be used were limited to an *absolute minimum.* Why? Because fewer datatypes mean simpler messages and less software.

### 35.6.1 Types in Version 1

The basic or *primitive* built-in types used for version 1 are:

- INTEGER. Represents numeric measurements, such as the number of interfaces on a system. Also used for enumerations such as up(1), down(2), testing(3).

- OCTET STRING. Used to represent hexadecimal data such as the physical address of an interface. Also used for text strings. A description or textual convention indicates when an OCTET STRING is being used to hold a text string.

- OBJECT IDENTIFIER. Used to name an object by means of a string of numbers.

- NULL. Used as a placeholder. For example, a *get-request* contains a list of OBJECT IDENTIFIERS for variables, each paired with a NULL placeholder in a value field.

What about the other primitive ASN.1 datatypes? The designers of SNMP version 1 decided that they could do without them, and that the amount of software needed for an SNMP agent would be substantially reduced by working with fewer primitives. You can still get your meaning across if you need one of the other types by cheating.

- Turn any ENUMERATED type into an INTEGER, and describe what each number means.

- For a BOOLEAN, use an INTEGER with values *true(1)* and *false(2)*.

- For a bit string that is 32 bits or less, turn it into a 32-bit INTEGER by calculating the number represented by the bits. If there are more than 32 bits, turn it into an OCTET STRING.

- Any character string becomes an OCTET STRING. The *DisplayString* textual convention restricts an OCTET STRING to the Network Virtual Terminal (NVT) ASCII character set defined in the TCP/IP Telnet protocol.

- Just about anything else can be turned into an OCTET STRING too.

A few primitive types that are specific to SNMP application usage were added to the built-in primitives. These included *Counter, Gauge, TimeTicks, IpAddress, NetworkAddress,* and *Opaque.*

### 35.6.2 Types for Version 2

Version 2 added the BIT STRING datatype to hold enumerated lists of flags. To improve the precision of definitions, the following were defined:

- *Integer32.* Identical to INTEGER, range is −2147483648 to 2147483647.

- *Counter32.* Identical to Counter, range is 0 to 4294967295.

- *Gauge32.* Identical to Gauge, range is 0 to 4294967295.

- *NsapAddress.* For OSI addresses.

- *Counter64.* Range is 0 to 18446744073709551615.

- *UInteger32.* Unsigned integer, range is 0 to 4294967295.

## 35.7   SNMP CONSTRUCTOR DATATYPES

The only constructor types allowed are SEQUENCE and SEQUENCE OF. As we have seen in earlier chapters:

- A table entry is a SEQUENCE or list of variables.

- A table is a SEQUENCE OF table entries.

Thus, a table is a SEQUENCE OF SEQUENCES.

The CHOICE construct is occasionally used in the SNMP standards documents.

## 35.8   DATATYPE DEFINITIONS

The *C* language includes a *typedef* statement that is used to define new datatypes that can be used in declarations. For example, we can define a new type, *Length,* that is an integer:

```
typedef int Length;
```

We can then declare the two integral variables:

```
Length headLen;
Length textLen;
```

This may seem to be spectacularly useless, since we could just as easily have written:

```
int     headLen;
int     textLen;
```

However, it really pays off when you have a complex datatype. Suppose that a program needs to keep track of several dates. We can use the *C* *typedef* statement to define a new datatype called *Date.*

```
typedef struct Date {
    int day;
    int month;
    int year;
    };
```

Now we can declare as many variables with this structure as we need:

```
Date startDate;
Date endDate;
Date currentDate;
```

The variables startDate, endDate, and currentDate are *instances* of the *Date* datatype. It is important to make the distinction between the following:

- A *datatype* like *Date*—it provides a *template* (day, month, year) for declaring variables.

- A variable like *startDate*—it will be assigned *values* that have meaning for an application.

## 35.9   DATATYPE DEFINITIONS IN ASN.1

Similar ideas, but expressed very differently, are used to define ASN.1 datatypes. First of all, instead of typedef statements, ASN.1 datatype definitions are written in Backus-Naur form which looks like:

Name-of-Type-being-defined ::= definition

### 35.9.1   A Simple Datatype Definition

The name of a new datatype always starts with a capital letter. For example, every SNMP request contains an identification number. We define:

RequestID ::= INTEGER

By convention, descriptive multiword names are used for datatypes, and each word in the name starts with a capital letter.

We view a variable as an *instance* of a datatype. A variable is assigned values that have meaning for an application. A variable name always starts with a lowercase letter. In the language of ASN.1, a variable is called a *value reference*.

### 35.9.2   A More Complicated Datatype Definition

A more complex definition is used to describe an SNMP message. The definition that follows indicates that the Message datatype is made up of three fields: an INTEGER, an OCTET STRING, and a third type called PDUs. The *version, community,* and *pdu* labels convey the meaning of each field and also assign variable names to the fields. Here again, each variable name starts with a lowercase letter.

Note that ASN.1 turns the usual order used in *C* and other programming languages backward. In *C,* we would write *int version,* rather than *version INTEGER.*

```
Message ::=
  SEQUENCE {
    version      INTEGER { version-1(0) },
    community    OCTET STRING,
    pdu          PDUs
    }
```

Fields in a datatype definition are separated by commas, and the exact placement of words does not really matter. Braces after an INTEGER variable are used to enumerate valid values—in this case, the only possible value allowed is 0, used to indicate *version 1.*

## 35.10   ASSIGNING VALUES

Just to confuse things a little, Backus-Naur-form expressions also are used in ASN.1 to assign *specific values* to a variable. For example,

```
internet   OBJECT IDENTIFIER ::= { iso(1) org(3) dod(6) 1 }
```

Stated more formally, the *instance* named *internet* with datatype OBJECT IDENTIFIER has *value* 1.3.6.1.

## 35.11   THE MACRO CAPABILITY

ASN.1 includes a powerful capability that is important to standards authors. It is possible to create *macro* templates that actually extend the ASN.1 language in an extremely flexible way. A macro template can be designed to do whatever needs to be done.

For example, we need to pack quite a lot of information into the definition of a MIB *object,* such as:

1. What OBJECT IDENTIFIER and text label will be used to *name* the MIB object?
2. What datatype will the object hold (e.g., an integer or a string of octets)?
3. Are there any restrictions on the allowed *range* of values—for example, integers from 1 to 20 or octets that represent ASCII text characters only?

4. What *operations* are allowed on the object—namely, is it read-only, read-write, or not-accessible?

5. Is there any other *descriptive* information that a developer needs to know in order to implement this object correctly?

The MIB definitions that we have seen in earlier chapters were written using the ASN.1 *OBJECT-TYPE* macro template. The OBJECT-TYPE* macro provides all of the information described in items 1 to 5 above! For example,

```
ipAdEntReasmMaxSize OBJECT-TYPE
     SYNTAX INTEGER (0..65535)
     ACCESS read-only
     STATUS mandatory
     DESCRIPTION
             "The size of the largest IP datagram which this
             entity can re-assemble from incoming IP fragmented
             datagrams received on this interface."
     ::= { ipAddrEntry 5 }
```

This definition reveals the following:

1. The *OBJECT IDENTIFIER* for ipAdEntReasmMaxSize is { ipAddrEntry 5 }, which can be traced down the tree as 1.3.6.1.2.1.4.20.1.5.

2. The *SYNTAX,* or datatype, for the value of a *ipAdEntReasmMaxSize* variable is INTEGER.

3. The integer is limited to the range from 0 to 65535.

4. The *ACCESS* tells us the types of operations that can be performed. In this case, a management station can read this value, not update it.

5. The *STATUS* of mandatory informs an implementor that this variable must be supported.

6. The *DESCRIPTION* tells us that the value of this variable is the size of the largest datagram that can be reassembled from fragments at the interface.

## 35.12   CONSTRUCTING COMPLEX DATATYPES

It is common to reuse datatypes as piece parts of other datatypes. For example, *ipAdEntReasmMaxSize* appears inside a more complex data

---

* The ASN.1 language is used to define whatever MACROs are needed. Each template is assigned an identifier which, by convention, consists of uppercase letters. For example, "OBJECT-TYPE," "MODULE-IDENTITY," and "NOTIFICATION-TYPE" are macro identifiers.

structure—it is the last column in an IP address table. The complete table entry is defined as a sequence of five fields—an IP address, an integer, another IP address, and two more integers:

```
IpAddrEntry ::=
    SEQUENCE {
        ipAdEntAddr
            IpAddress,
        ipAdEntIfIndex
            INTEGER,
        ipAdEntNetMask
            IpAddress,
        ipAdEntBcastAddr
            INTEGER,
        ipAdEntReasmMaxSize
            INTEGER (0..65535)
    }
```

In spite of the fact that the ASN.1 language is not easy to describe, protocol specifications written with ASN.1 are fairly easy to read and write. As we've seen, once an object has been defined, its definition can be reused in the definition of other objects. In the sections that follow, we will go a little more deeply into the ASN.1 language and the way that SNMP datatypes are compiled into formatted messages.

## 35.13  TRANSLATING ABSTRACT SYNTAX NOTATION 1

A computer program written in a high-level programming language contains datatype declarations that must be translated (compiled) into machine-usable format before the program can be run. Similarly, ASN.1 statements must be translated into a serial stream of bytes before they can be transmitted across a network.

The compilation rules are known as a *Transfer Syntax*—that is, the Transfer Syntax determines the actual format of the stream of octets that will be transmitted. The designers of ASN.1 came up with a specific Transfer Syntax called the *Basic Encoding Rules for Abstract Syntax Notation 1* or *BER*.

Although the door was left open if anyone wanted to invent a new Transfer Syntax with a different set of rules, standards groups have chosen to stick with BER.* Since BER and ASN.1 were created at the same time by the same group of people, it is not surprising that BER and ASN.1 are closely linked.

---

* A simple example of the use of a different Transfer Syntax would be to incorporate data encryption into the compilation.

### 35.13.1   The Basic Encoding Rules (BER)

Let's take a look at an example of an old, pre-ASN.1 style for encoding the fields in a protocol data unit. Figure 35.1 shows a UDP header. The first field is 16 bits long and contains the binary encoding of an integer that represents the source port number. We know the data type (16-bit integer), its length (2 octets) and its meaning (port number) by the field's position in the header.

If we wanted to introduce a version number into the header and change the number of bits in the port fields, we would have to replace all of the UDP code in the world.

The idea behind the basic encoding rules is that every field is *self-defining*. A field has an *introducer* that tells you what it is and how long it is. This allows protocol data units to be defined in a far more flexible way. The basic pattern used to encode a value is:

[identifier] [length (of contents)]* [contents]

The identifier declares the datatype of the contents. The contents may be something very simple, such as a single integer. A type consisting of a single value is formally called a *primitive* type, fitting nicely with the primitive datatypes described earlier for ASN.1.

Alternatively, the contents may be one of the compound types—for example, a SEQUENCE of values. In this case, there is an introducer

---

* The length field is capable of expressing any length whatsoever. The details are omitted in this exposition.

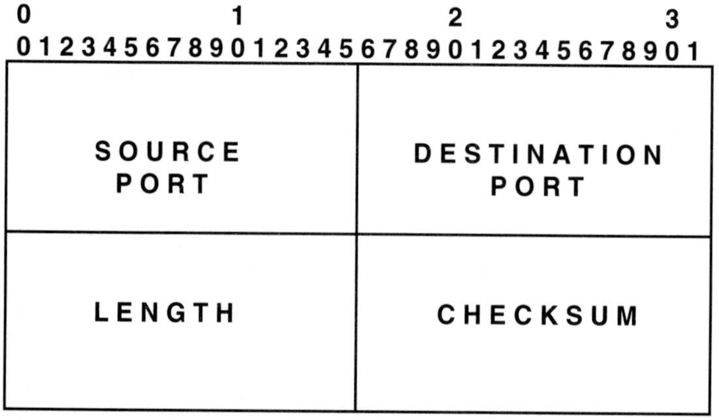

Figure 35.1  A UDP header.

that says a SEQUENCE follows in the contents field. Within the contents field, each variable within the SEQUENCE is introduced by its own identifier and length.

SNMP network management *messages* are constructed using the SEQUENCE datatype. Each MIB variable that is carried in an SNMP message is required to be a simple datatype.

### 35.13.2   BER Identifiers

A BER identifier number announces the datatype that will follow. Since ASN.1 will be used to write hundreds of protocols, each containing a multitude of datatypes, it could be quite a job to make sure that a unique number is assigned to each new datatype and to track all of the identifier numbers in the world. Furthermore, dozens or hundreds of BER identifiers will appear in a message. We want to keep these identifiers small, so that they do not introduce a lot of extra data communications overhead.

The method used to assign BER identifiers avoids these problems in the same way that we do in everyday life. Suppose that I am ordering items from a sporting goods catalog and a computer equipment catalog. My two order forms could appear as follows:

> Sporting Goods Application:
> Item #: 5 (Ice skates)
>     Feature #: 2 (All-leather boots)
>     Feature #: 5 (High-quality steel blades)
>
> Computer Equipment Application:
> Item #: 5 (Printer)
>     Feature #: 2 (Wide carriage)
>     Feature #: 5 (Envelope feeder)

The meaning of identifier number 5 is different for ice skates features and printer features. Note how we are able to use a small number as an identifier again and again.

Now let's look at how this is handled for BER. Datatypes are divided into four classes:

- *Universal.* Available for use within any protocol. The primitive datatypes—INTEGER, OCTET STRING, OBJECT IDENTIFIER, and NULL, are universal. The basic constructors, such as SEQUENCE, also are universal.

- *Application.* Available within a specific application. For example, the IpAddress datatype is available for use throughout the TCP/IP network management application.

- *Context-specific.*   This datatype is contained in a larger datatype. The identifier has a unique meaning within the context of the larger datatype (like features 2 and 5 above).

- *Private.*   Included so that ASN.1 could be used by private organizations to define proprietary datatypes.

The first 2 bits* of a BER identifier are used to sort out whether a datatype is universal, application, context-specific, or private. The bit assignments are:

| | |
|---|---|
| Universal | 0 0 |
| Application | 0 1 |
| Context-specific | 1 0 |
| Private | 1 1 |

The third bit indicates whether a datatype is primitive or constructed:

| | |
|---|---|
| Primitive | 0 |
| Constructed | 1 |

The remainder of the identifier is a numeric *tag* associated with a datatype. Tags ranging from 0 to 30 can be encoded in the remaining 5 bits of the octet. For larger tags, these 5 bits are set to 11111, and one or more subsequent octets are used to encode the tag. Because the use of context-specific tags allows low numbers to be reused again and again, tags bigger than 30 rarely (if ever) have to be used.

The ASN.1 definition of an APPLICATION datatype announces its class. For example,

        IPAddress ::= [APPLICATION 0]      --in network-byte order
                        IMPLICIT OCTET STRING (SIZE (4))

When no class is shown, then the class is CONTEXT-SPECIFIC. For example, a GetRequest-PDU is defined within the context of an SNMP message. A CONTEXT-SPECIFIC tag of 0 is assigned in:

        GetRequest-PDU ::= [0] IMPLICIT SEQUENCE {
            request-id          RequestID,
            error-status        ErrorStatus,    --always 0
            error-index         ErrorIndex,     --always 0
            variable-bindings   VarBindList
            }

---

* These are the leftmost, or highest-order bits.

### 35.13.3   Using IMPLICIT to Cut Down Overhead

New datatypes are defined by making a specialized use of an old datatype or by combining old ones. When we define a new type in terms of a specialized use of an old one, one of the things that tends to happen is a pileup of introducers:

[identifier] [length] [ [identifier] [length] [contents]]

For example, we define the application-specific datatype *IpAddress* for use in SNMP by:

- Giving it an APPLICATION tag number
- Defining the contents as an OCTET STRING with the special restriction that the string is 4 octets long

If we left it at that, the natural consequence would be that whenever an IpAddress was encoded, it would have two introducers:

[identifier-for-IpAddress] [length] [contents]

contents = [identifier-for-OCTET-STRING] [length] [string]

Identifier pileup is avoided—without damaging the ability to decode a value unambiguously—by using the term *IMPLICIT* in the datatype definition. IMPLICIT tells us that we can safely leave out the introducer for the type that follows. So, for the definition,

IpAddress ::= [APPLICATION 0] IMPLICIT OCTET STRING (SIZE (4))

the encoding becomes

[identifier-for-IpAddress] [length] [contents=OCTET STRING]

### 35.13.4   Identifiers for SNMP Versions 1 and 2

All of the identifiers that are needed for SNMP version 1 and version 2 are summarized in Table 35.1.

## 35.14   SAMPLE ENCODINGS

Let's look at some sample datatypes and their encodings to see how this gets put together.

**TABLE 35.1    Identifiers for ASN.1 Datatypes Used in SNMP**

| *Primitive ASN.1 Types* | Identifier in hex |
|---|---|
| INTEGER | 02 |
| BIT STRING | 03 |
| OCTET STRING | 04 |
| NULL | 05 |
| OBJECT IDENTIFIER | 06 |

| *Constructed ASN.1 type* | |
|---|---|
| SEQUENCE | 30 |

| *Primitive SNMP application types* | |
|---|---|
| IpAddress | 40 |
| Counter (Counter32 in version 2) | 41 |
| Gauge (Gauge32 in version 2) | 42 |
| TimeTicks | 43 |
| Opaque | 44 |
| NsapAddress | 45 |
| Counter64 | 46 |
| UInteger32 | 47 |

| *Context-specific types within an SNMP message* | |
|---|---|
| GetRequest-PDU | A0 |
| GetNextRequest-PDU | A1 |
| GetResponse-PDU (Response-PDU in version 2) | A2 |
| SetRequest-PDU | A3 |
| Trap-PDU (obsolete in version 2) | A4 |
| GetBulkRequest-PDU (added in version 2) | A5 |
| InformRequest-PDU (added in version 2) | A6 |
| SNMPv2-Trap-PDU (added in version 2) | A7 |

### 35.14.1    Encoding Simple Datatypes

An INTEGER is a Universal (00) Primitive (0) datatype with tag equal to 2 (00010). Thus, the identifier for INTEGER is 00000010 or, in hex, 02. The hexadecimal encoding of an integer with value 3 would be:

| Identifier | Length | Contents |
|---|---|---|
| 02 | 01 | 11 |

Next, let's look once more at the definition of the IpAddress datatype:

IpAddress ::= [APPLICATION 0]        – –in network-byte order
        IMPLICIT OCTET STRING (SIZE (4))

This definition tells us everything that we need to know in order to format an IP address. This is a single simple data item, so it is primitive. [APPLICATION 0] tells us that its class is APPLICATION and its *tag* is 0. Hence, the identifier is 0100 0000 or '40'H. According to the MIB definition, the length of the contents *must* be 4. The contents just consists of the 4 octets of the IP address. The hexadecimal encoding of IP address 128.1.1.1 is:

| Identifier | Length | Contents |
|:----------:|:------:|:--------:|
| 40 | 04 | 80 01 01 01 |

### 35.14.2   Encoding an OBJECT IDENTIFIER

The only primitive datatype whose encoding is not totally obvious and straightforward is the OBJECT IDENTIFIER. First of all, the rules say that the first two digits $x.y$ (1.3 for the identifiers of interest to us) must be collapsed to a single decimal number using the formula $40x+y$. Thus 1.3 translates to 43, which is written in hex as 2B.

The standards writers did not want to put any limit on the size of the remaining numeric labels. Therefore, they had to come up with a way to encode big numbers. This is done as follows:

- Use only the low-order 7 bits of each octet for data.
- Use the eighth bit as a *more* flag.

If a number is 127 or less, it will fit into 7 bits and the eighth bit is 0. Otherwise, an eighth bit of 1 signals that 2 or more octets must be combined to compute the number. For example, 1.3.6.1.1.4.134.129 is encoded

```
2B 06 01 01 04 81 02 81 01
```

### 35.14.3   A Complete SNMP Version 1
### Message Encoding

Constructed datatypes are used in the definition of the SNMP PDUs. The definition of a *get-request* protocol data unit is displayed below. The first three fields are INTEGERs.

```
GetRequest-PDU ::= [0] IMPLICIT SEQUENCE {
        request-id            RequestID,
        error-status          ErrorStatus,      --always 0
        error-index           ErrorIndex,       --always 0
        variable-bindings     VarBindList
            }
```

The variable-bindings part is a SEQUENCE of (*OBJECT IDENTIFIER, value*) pairs. Each pair is encoded as a sequence, so we have a sequence of sequences. The *value* in a pair is set to NULL. The *get-response* will replace NULL with the correct identifier, length, and contents for the requested object.

Figure 35.2 shows a Network General Sniffer trace of an SNMP *get-request* and its corresponding **get-response.** The hex expansion of each message includes a DIX Ethernet frame header, IP header, UDP header, and the SNMP contents. The SNMP part of the hex printout is in bold print.

```
Sniffer Network Analyzer data from 3-Aug-93 at 08:31:14,
SNMP: -----Simple Network Management Protocol -----
SNMP:
SNMP: Version = 0
SNMP: Community = public
SNMP: Command = Get request
SNMP: Request ID = 0
SNMP: Error status = 0 (No error)
SNMP: Error index = 0
SNMP:
SNMP: Object = {1.3.6.1.2.1.1.3.0} (sysUpTime.0)
SNMP: Value  = NULL
SNMP:
SNMP: Object = {1.3.6.1.2.1.2.1.0} (ifNumber.0)
SNMP: Value  = NULL
SNMP:
```

```
ADDR  HEX                                                ASCII
0000  00 00 C0 BF 45 5B 00 02  35 03 10 38 08 00 45 00   ....E[..5..8..E.
0010  00 52 56 BD 00 00 3C 11  25 D1 80 01 01 01 80 01   .RV...<.%.......
0020  01 0A 05 1C 00 A1 00 3E  00 00 30 34 02 01 00 04   .......>..04....
0030  06 70 75 62 6C 69 63 A0  27 02 01 00 02 01 00 02   .public.'.......
0040  01 00 30 1C 30 0C 06 08  2B 06 01 02 01 01 03 00   ..0.0...+.......
0050  05 00 30 0C 06 08 2B 06  01 02 01 02 01 00 05 00   ..0...+.........
```

```
SNMP: ----- Simple Network Management Protocol -----
SNMP:
SNMP: Version = 0
SNMP: Community = public
SNMP: Command = Get response
SNMP: Request ID = 0
SNMP: Error status = 0 (No error)
SNMP: Error index = 0
SNMP:
SNMP: Object = {1.3.6.1.2.1.1.3.0} (sysUpTime.0)
SNMP: Value  = 1135288 hundredths of a second
SNMP:
SNMP: Object = {1.3.6.1.2.1.2.1.0} (ifNumber.0)
SNMP: Value  = 1
SNMP:
```

```
ADDR  HEX                                                ASCII
0000  00 02 35 03 10 38 00 00  C0 BF 45 5B 08 00 45 00   ..5..8....E[..E.
0010  00 56 08 4C 00 00 40 11  70 3E 80 01 01 0A 80 01   .V.L..@.p>......
0020  01 01 00 A1 05 1C 00 42  87 81 30 38 02 01 00 04   .......B..08....
0030  06 70 75 62 6C 69 63 A2  2B 02 01 00 02 01 00 02   .public.+.......
0040  01 00 30 20 30 0F 06 08  2B 06 01 02 01 01 03 00   ..0 0...+.......
0050  43 03 11 52 B8 30 0D 06  08 2B 06 01 02 01 02 01   C..R.0...+......
0060  00 02 01 01                                        ....
```

**Figure 35.2** A Sniffer trace of a *get-request*.

Figures 35.3 and 35.4 show the correspondence between the fields in the *get-request* and *get-response* messages and the way that they are encoded.

## 35.15   DATA TRANSMISSION

The Basic Encoding Rules take a "big-endian" view of data. That is, the bits in an octet are numbered:

```
8 7 6 5 4 3 2 1
```

Bit 8 is the most significant bit, and is transmitted onto the network first. A multibyte nonnegative integer is represented with the most significant octet first, and the most significant octet is transmitted first.

## 35.16   USING MACROS TO DEFINE MIBS

The general, ASN.1 datatype definition mechanisms are used in the Simple Network Management Protocol specification. However, the use of *macros* predominates in the documents that define MIB objects.

### 35.16.1   The OBJECT-TYPE Macro Template

The *OBJECT-TYPE macro* that is the basic building block for MIB design has been steadily enlarged in successive enhancements of the network management specification. In the sections that follow, we will follow the development of the macro all the way to its newly proposed format for SNMP version 2.

### 35.16.2   Defining Objects in MIB-I

In the original MIB (as defined in RFC 1066), object types were first informally described in a text format, and then separately given brief macro definitions. For example, in RFC 1066, *sysDescr* is defined using a macro pattern:

```
sysDescr OBJECT-TYPE
        SYNTAX OCTET STRING
        ACCESS read-only
        STATUS mandatory
        ::= { system 1 }
```

## 35.17   OBJECTS IN MIB-II

In RFC 1212, *Concise MIB Definitions,* a DESCRIPTION clause was added to the macro. The new clause was used in the definition of

V E R S I O N   (0)
INTEGER     Length = 1    Value = 0
   02          01             00

C O M M U N I T Y
OCTETSTRING     Length = 6    Value= p   u   b   l   i   c
   04              06                70 75 62 6C 69 63

G E T   R E Q U E S T
getRequest   Length = 39
   A0            27

R E Q U E S T   I D
INTEGER     Length = 1    Value = 0
   02          01             00

E R R O R   S T A T U S         E R R O R   I N D E X
INTEGER   Length=1   Value=0     Integer   Length=1   Value=0
   02        01        00          02        01        00

S E Q U E N C E   (List of pairs of Object Identifiers and Valu
SEQUENCE     Length=28
   30          1C

   S E Q U E N C E (Pair: Object Identifier, Value)
   SEQUENCE     Length=12
      30          0C

   O B J E C T   I D E N T I F I E R for sysUpTime.0
   OBJECT IDENTIFIER     Length = 8          1.3.6.1.2.1.1.3.0
            06              08        2B 06 01 02 01 01 03 0(

   V A L U E   (Null Placeholder)
   NULL    Length=0
      05       00

   S E Q U E N C E (Pair: Object Identifier, Value)
   SEQUENCE     Length=12
      30          0C

   O B J E C T   I D E N T I F I E R for ifNumber.0
   OBJECT IDENTIFIER     Length = 8     1.3.6.1.2.1.2.1.0
            06              08        2B 06 01 02 01 02 01 00

   V A L U E   (Null Placeholder)
   NULL    Length=0
      05       00

**Figure 35.3** Detailed encoding of a *get-request* message.

```
Get-Response Message

S N M P   M E S S A G E
SEQUENCE    Length=56
  30          38


V E R S I O N  (0)
INTEGER    Length = 1   Value = 0
  02          01            00


C O M M U N I T Y
OCTETSTRING    Length = 6    Value= p  u  b  l  i  c
  04              06                 70 75 62 6C 69 63


G E T   R E Q U E S T
getResponse Length = 43
  A2          2B


    R E Q U E S T   I D
    INTEGER    Length = 1   Value = 0
      02          01            00


    E R R O R   S T A T U S       E R R O R   I N D E X
    INTEGER   Length=1 Value=0     Integer   Length=1  Value=0
      02        01      00           02        01       00


    S E Q U E N C E  (List of pairs of Object Identifiers and Values)
    SEQUENCE    Length=32
      30          20


        S E Q U E N C E (Pair: Object Identifier, Value)
        SEQUENCE    Length=15
          30          0F


            O B J E C T   I D E N T I F I E R  =  sysUpTime.0
            OBJECT IDENTIFIER    Length = 8       1.3.6.1.2.1.1.3.0
                  06                08           2B 06 01 02 01 01 03 00


                V A L U E            =  1135288 hundredths of a second
                TimeTicks    Length=3     Value
                  43          03        11 52 B8


        S E Q U E N C E (Pair: Object Identifier, Value)
        SEQUENCE    Length=13
          30          0D


            O B J E C T   I D E N T I F I E R for ifNumber.0
            OBJECT IDENTIFIER    Length = 8     1.3.6.1.2.1.2.1.0
                  06                08         2B 06 01 02 01 02 01 00


            V A L U E  (Null Placeholder)
            INTEGER    Length=1  Value=1
              02          01       01
```

**Figure 35.4**  Detailed encoding of a *response* message.

objects for the revised version of the MIB, MIB-II. Hence, in MIB-II we have:

```
sysDescr OBJECT-TYPE
        SYNTAX DisplayString (SIZE (0.255))
        ACCESS read-only
        STATUS mandatory
        DESCRIPTION
                "A textual description of the entity. This value should include
                the full name and version identification of the system's hard-
                ware type, software operating-system, and networking soft-
                ware. It is mandatory that this only contain printable ASCII
                characters."
        ::= { system 1 }
```

By the time that RFC 1212 was written, experience in implementing and using MIB definitions had made it clear that some additional optional clauses were needed. These clauses are described in the paragraphs that follow.

### 35.17.1   The REFERENCE Clause

The REFERENCE clause is used to provide a cross-reference to another document that contains background information or describes characteristics of an object type.

The example below is taken from RFC 1398, *Definitions of Managed Objects for the Ethernet-like Interface Types.*

```
dot3StatsAlignmentErrors OBJECT-TYPE
        SYNTAX Counter
        ACCESS read-only
        STATUS mandatory
        DESCRIPTION
                "A count of frames received on a particular interface that are
                not an integral number of octets in length and do not pass the
                FCS check. . . ."
        REFERENCE
                "IEEE 802.3 Layer Management"
        ::= { dot3StatsEntry 2 }
```

### 35.17.2   The INDEX Clause

The INDEX clause is used with definitions of *table entries*—that is, conceptual rows in a table. An index is used to select a unique row in a table. For example, the IP address table (*ipAddrTable*) is indexed (very naturally) by the IP address column (*ipAdEntAddr*):

```
ipAddrEntry OBJECT-TYPE
      SYNTAX IpAddrEntry
      ACCESS not-accessible
      STATUS mandatory
      DESCRIPTION
             "The addressing information for one of this
             entity's IP addresses."
      INDEX { ipAdEntAddr }
      ::= { ipAddrTable 1 }
```

What does this mean in practical terms? When we want to use a *get-request* to read the subnet mask for a particular IP address, we append the index—in this case, the *ipAdEntAddr*—to the OBJECT IDENTIFIER for *ipAdEntNetMask*.

An INTEGER, OCTET STRING, OBJECT IDENTIFIER, or IpAddress* can be used as an index. The most frequently used indices are INTEGERs and IpAddresses. Some tables need two or more indices in order to uniquely identify an entry.

### 35.17.3   OCTET STRING and OBJECT IDENTIFIER Indices

OBJECT IDENTIFIERs come in all sorts of lengths. Some OCTET STRINGs also have variable lengths. Suppose that we want to use one of these variable length quantities as an index.

To code a variable-length OCTET STRING index, the index is introduced by an octet that gives the length of the string that follows. Similarly, to code an OBJECT IDENTIFIER index, the index is introduced by an octet that gives the number of subidentifiers that will follow.

But suppose that a variable-length index is the only index or is the very last variable-length index. Then the extra octet giving the length is not really needed. We can tell that we've reached the end of the variable-length index because it is last, or else subsequent indices have fixed length. To flag the fact that the extra byte should be left out, the keyword IMPLIED is included in an INDEX statement. For example,

```
partyEntry OBJECT-TYPE
      SYNTAX          PartyEntry
      MAX-ACCESS not-accessible
      STATUS          current
      DESCRIPTION
             "Locally held information about a particular
             SNMPv2 party."
```

---

* More generally, a NetAddress, which might be an address used by a protocol other than IP, can be an index.

```
INDEX { IMPLIED partyIdentity }
::= { partyTable 1 }
```

### 35.17.4   The DEFVAL Clause

There are times when a network manager may need the ability to add a row to a table. However, there may be some variables that should not be *set* by the manager. There may be frequently used values for other elements that could be used as defaults. The DEFVAL clause enables a MIB writer to specify defaults that can be used.

For example, the following variable appears in RFC 1354, which proposes a more sophisticated version of an IP routing table. When a new entry is created, the default value of 0 is assigned to the age of the entry.

```
ipForwardAge OBJECT-TYPE
    SYNTAX INTEGER
    ACCESS read-only
    STATUS mandatory
    DESCRIPTION
        "The number of seconds since this route was
        last updated or otherwise determined to be
        correct. Note that no semantics of 'too old'
        can be implied except through knowledge of the
        routing protocol by which the route was
        learned."
    DEFVAL { 0 }
    ::= { ipForwardEntry 8 }
```

## 35.18   MODULES

ASN.1 provides a convenient way to collect and identify related definitions—the *module*. The easiest way to understand a module is to look at an example. In outline, MIB-II was defined as follows:

```
RFC1213-MIBDEFINITIONS::= BEGIN

IMPORTS
    mgmt, NetworkAddress,IpAddress,Counter,Gauge,TimeTicks
        FROM RFC1155-SMI
    OBJECT-TYPE FROM RFC-1212;

    mib-2                   OBJECT IDENTIFIER::= { mgmt 1 }

    -- textual conventions
    DisplayString ::=       OCTET STRING    -- SIZE (0.255)
    PhysAddress ::=         OCTET STRING
```

```
– – groups in MIB-II
system              OBJECT IDENTIFIER::= { mib-2 1 }
interfaces          OBJECT IDENTIFIER::= { mib-2 2 }
at                  OBJECT IDENTIFIER::= { mib-2 3 }
ip                  OBJECT IDENTIFIER::= { mib-2 4 }
icmp                OBJECT IDENTIFIER::= { mib-2 5 }
tcp                 OBJECT IDENTIFIER::= { mib-2 6 }
udp                 OBJECT IDENTIFIER::= { mib-2 7 }
egp                 OBJECT IDENTIFIER::= { mib-2 8 }
– –historical (some say hysterical)
– –cmot              OBJECT IDENTIFIER::= { mib-2 9 }
transmission        OBJECT IDENTIFIER::= { mib-2 10 }
snmp                OBJECT IDENTIFIER::= { mib-2 11 }

– –the System group
. . .
(more definitions)
. . .

END
```

In version 1, every module has a text name. This one is called RFC1213-MIB. The IMPORTS statement brings in definitions that have appeared in other modules. The bulk of a module is made up of new datatype definitions.

In version 2, every module is assigned an OBJECT IDENTIFIER.

## 35.19   GROUPS

A module is organized into *groups* of definitions. A group is a set of related definitions.

A vendor implements the groups that make sense for the vendor's product. For example, a bridge vendor would not bother with the *egp* group.

## 35.20   VERSION 2 OBJECT-TYPE MACRO

In Chapter 31, we described several important features that will improve the precision and power of SNMP version 2 MIB modules. The OBJECT-TYPE macro also was enhanced in version 2. Its definition is given following. Consult the current RFC describing the Structure of Management Information* for version 2 of SNMP for a detailed description of each field.

---

* At the time of writing, RFC 1442.

```
OBJECT-TYPEMACRO::=
   BEGIN
      TYPE NOTATION::=
                        "SYNTAX"type(Syntax)
                        UnitsPart
                        "MAX-ACCESS"Access
                        "STATUS"Status
                        "DESCRIPTION"Text
                        ReferPart
                        IndexPart
                        DefValPart

      VALUE NOTATION::=
                        value(VALUEObjectName)

   UnitsPart::=

                        "UNITS"Text
                        | empty

   Access::=

                        "not-accessible"
                        | "read-only"
                        | "read-write"
                        | "read-create"

   Status::=

                        "current"
                        | "deprecated"
                        | "obsolete"

   ReferPart::=

                        "REFERENCE"Text
                        | empty

   IndexPart::=

                        "INDEX" "{" IndexTypes"}"
                        | "AUGMENTS""{" Entry "}"
                        | empty
   IndexTypes::=

                        IndexType
                        | IndexTypes"," IndexType

   IndexType::=

                        "IMPLIED"Index
                        | Index
   Index::=

                        --use the SYNTAX value of the
                        --correspondentOBJECT-TYPEinvocation
```

```
                              value(IndexobjectObjectName)
        Entry::=

                              – –use the INDEX value of the
                              – –correspondentOBJECT-TYPEinvocation
                              value(EntryobjectObjectName)


        DefValPart::=

                              "DEFVAL""{" value(DefvalSyntax)"}"
                              | empty


        – –uses the NVT ASCII character set
        Text::="""""string""
        END
```

## 35.21  MIB COMPILERS

One of the big benefits of using a formal ASN.1-based language to define MIBs is that compilers can be built to automatically assist in MIB implementation.*

Many management station products allow a user to copy a MIB into a local file, and then load its variables by selecting an option from a menu. Generic management station protocol capabilities are then used to poll for any of the variables, tabulate or graph results, set thresholds, and handle alerts. For example, products discussed in this text—IBM's *NetView/6000,* Hewlett-Packard's *Openview Network Node Manager,* and SunConnects's *SunNet Manager*—all provide MIB compilers that can be used to import MIBs into the management environment.

Even agent implementations can be based on automatic MIB compilation. There are compilers that create C-code versions of all of the data declarations that are needed, and even generate skeletal outlines for the local code that will be needed to access values within a device.

In earlier sections, we saw how the OBJECT-TYPE macro has been steadily extended and improved. Although the steady enhancement of the OBJECT-TYPE macro has led to more focused and more accurate MIB definitions, the price has been that the MIB compilers needed to be revised every time the macro was revised!

## 35.22  RECOMMENDED READING

RFC 1212 describes how version 1 MIB Modules should be written. RFC 1442 describes the Structure of Management Information for version 2, and contains the updated macro definitions.

---

* Probably the best-known MIB compiler is *mosy,* which stands for "Managed Object Syntax-compiler (Yacc-based)." This compiler was created as part of the ISODE ("ISO Development Environment") toolkit.

Abstract Syntax Notation 1 is defined in ISO standard 8824, which was published in 1987, along with an addendum defining extensions. The Basic Encoding Rules were defined in ISO standard 8825, which was published in 1987, along with an addendum containing extensions corresponding to the ASN.1 extensions.

The July 1993 issue of *ConneXions* contained an excellent article on MIB compilers. *The Simple Book* by Marshall Rose contains a fairly detailed description of the MOSY compiler, and much useful implementation lore.

# Abbreviations and Acronyms

| | |
|---|---|
| AARP | AppleTalk Address Resolution Protocol |
| ACCM | Asyncronous-Control-Character Map |
| ACK | Acknowledgment |
| AIS | Alarm Indication Signal |
| AMI | Alternate Mark Inversion |
| ANSI | American National Standards Institute |
| API | Application Programming Interface |
| ARP | Address Resolution Protocol |
| ARPA | Advanced Research Projects Agency |
| AS | Autonomous System |
| ASA | American Standards Association |
| ASCII | American National Standard Code for Information Interchange |
| ASN.1 | Abstract Syntax Notation 1 |
| ATM | Asynchronous Transfer Mode |
| AUI | Attachment Unit Interface |
| B3ZS | Binary 3-Zero Substitution |
| B8ZS | Bipolar with 8-Zero Substitution |
| BBN | Bolt, Beranek, and Newman, Incorporated |
| BECN | Backward Explicit Congestion Notification |
| BER | Basic Encoding Rules |
| BES | Bursty Errored Seconds |
| BGP | Border Gateway Protocol |
| BPDU | Bridge Protocol Data Unit |

| | |
|---|---|
| BPV | Bipolar Violation |
| BSD | Berkeley Software Distribution |
| CAU | Communications Access Unit |
| CCITT | International Telegraph and Telephone Consultative Committee |
| CCV | C-bit Coding Violation |
| CEPT | Conference of European Postal and Telecommunications Associations |
| CES | C-bit Errored Second |
| CHAP | Challenge-Handshake Authentication Protocol |
| CIR | Committed Information Rate |
| CMIP | Common Management Information Protocol |
| CMIS | Common Management Information Services |
| CMOT | Common Management Information Services and Protocol over TCP/IP |
| CMT | Connection Management |
| CR | Carriage Return |
| C/R | Command/Response |
| CRC | Cyclic Redundancy Code |
| CS | Controlled Slip |
| CSES | C-bit Severely Errored Second |
| CSMA/CD | Carrier Sense Multiple Access with Collision Detection |
| CSS | Controlled Slip Seconds |
| CSU | Channel Service Unit |
| CTS | Clear to Send |
| CUG | Closed User Group |
| DARPA | Defense Advanced Research Projects Agency |
| DAS | Dual-Attachment Station |
| DCD | Data Carrier Detect |
| DCE | Data Circuit-terminating Equipment |
| DDN | Defense Data Network |
| DDP | Datagram Delivery Protocol |
| DE | Discard Eligibility |
| DEC | Digital Equipment Corporation |
| DES | Data Encryption Standard |
| DEV | Deviation |
| DISA | Defense Information Systems Agency |

| | |
|---|---|
| DISC | Disconnect |
| DIX | Digital, Intel, and Xerox Ethernet protocol |
| DLCI | Data Link Connection Identifier |
| DM | Disconnected Mode |
| DME | Distributed Management Environment |
| DNS | Domain Name System |
| DOD | Department of Defense |
| DQDB | Distributed Queue Dual Bus |
| DS0 | Digital Signaling level 0 |
| DS1 | Digital Signaling level 1 |
| DS3 | Digital Signaling level 3 |
| DSA | Directory System Agent |
| DSAP | Destination Service Access Point |
| DSR | Data Set Ready |
| DSU | Data Service Unit |
| DTE | Data Terminal Equipment |
| DTR | Data Terminal Ready |
| DXE | DTE or DCE |
| DUA | Directory User Agent |
| EA | Extended Address |
| EBCDIC | Extended Binary-Coded Decimal Interchange Code |
| EGP | Exterior Gateway Protocol |
| EIA | Electronic Industries Association |
| EOF | End of File |
| EOR | End of Record |
| ES | Errored Seconds |
| ESF | Extended SuperFrame |
| EXZ | Excessive Zeros |
| FCS | Frame Check Sequence |
| FDDI | Fiber Distributed Data Interface |
| FDL | Facility Data Link |
| FEAC | Far-End Alarm and Control |
| FECN | Forward Explicit Congestion Notification |
| FIN | Final Segment |
| FRMR | Frame Reject |
| FTAM | File Transfer, Access, and Management |

| | |
|---|---|
| FTP | File Transfer Protocol |
| FYI | For Your Information |
| GGP | Gateway-to-Gateway Protocol |
| GMT | Greenwich Mean Time |
| GOSIP | Government Open Systems Interconnection Profile |
| HDB3 | High-Density Bipolar 3-Zero Maximum Coding |
| HDLC | High-Level Data Link Control Protocol |
| IAB | Internet Architecture Board (formerly Internet Activities Board) |
| IAC | Interpret As Command |
| IANA | Internet Assigned Numbers Authority |
| IBM | International Business Machines |
| ICMP | Internet Control Message Protocol |
| ID | Identifier |
| IDPR | Inter Domain Policy Routing |
| IEEE | Institute of Electrical and Electronics Engineers |
| IEN | Internet Engineering Notes |
| IESG | Internet Engineering Steering Group |
| IETF | Internet Engineering Task Force |
| IGMP | Internet Group Management Protocol |
| IGP | Interior Gateway Protocol |
| IGRP | Interior Gateway Routing Protocol |
| IP | Internet Protocol |
| IPX | Internetwork Packet Exchange |
| IRTF | Internet Research Task Force |
| ISDN | Integrated Services Digital Network |
| ISN | Initial Sequence Number |
| ISO | International Organization for Standardization |
| ISODE | ISO Development Environment |
| ITU-T | International Telecommunication Union–Telecommunications Standardization Sector |
| JBZS | Jammed Bit Zero Suppression |
| KIP | Kinetics Internet Protocol |
| LAN | Local Area Network |
| LAPB | Link Access Procedures Balanced |
| LAPD | Link Access Procedures on the D-channel |
| LCP | Link Control Protocol |

| | |
|---|---|
| LCT | Link Confidence Test |
| LCV | Line Coding Violation |
| LES | Line Errored Seconds |
| LF | Line Feed |
| LLAP | LocalTalk Link Access Protocol |
| LLC | Logical Link Control |
| LMI | Local Management Interface |
| LOMF | Loss of Multiframe Failure |
| LOF | Loss of Frame Failure |
| LOS | Loss of Signal Failure |
| LQMP | Link Quality Monitoring Protocol |
| LQR | Link Quality Report |
| MAC | Media Access Control |
| MAN | Metropolitan Area Network |
| MAU | Multiple Access Unit |
| Mbps | Megabit per second |
| MD5 | Message Digest, version 5 |
| MF | Multiframing |
| MIB | Management Information Base |
| MOSY | Managed Object Syntax-compiler (Yacc-based) |
| MRU | Maximum Receive Unit |
| MS | Millisecond |
| MSS | Maximum Segment Size |
| MTA | Message Transfer Agent |
| MTU | Maximum Transmission Unit |
| MX | Mail Exchanger |
| NBP | Name Binding Protocol |
| NCP | Network Control Protocol |
| NCP | NetWare Core Protocol |
| NETBIOS | Network Basic Input Output System |
| NFS | Network File System |
| NIC | Network Interface Card |
| NIC | Network Information Center |
| NIS | Network Information System |
| NOC | Network Operations Center |
| NREN | National Research and Education Network |

| | |
|---|---|
| NSAP | Network Service Access Point |
| NSFNET | National Science Foundation Network |
| NUI | Network User Identification |
| NVT | Network Virtual Terminal |
| OOF | Out of Frame defect |
| OSF | Open Software Foundation |
| OSI | Open Systems Interconnect |
| OSPF | Open Shortest Path First |
| PAD | Packet Assembler/Disassembler |
| PAP | Password Authentication Protocol |
| PC | Personal Computer |
| PC | Port Connector |
| PCM | Physical Connection Management |
| PCV | Path Coding Violation |
| PDU | Protocol Data Unit |
| PES | P-bit Errored Second |
| PHY | Physical Layer Protocol |
| PI | Protocol Interpreter |
| PLCP | Physical Layer Convergence Procedure |
| PLE | Packet Layer Entity |
| PMD | Physical Layer Medium Dependent |
| POP | Post Office Protocol |
| PPP | Point-to-Point Protocol |
| PROM | Programmable Read-Only Memory |
| PSES | P-bit Severely Errored Second |
| PVC | Permanent Virtual Circuit |
| RAI | Remote Alarm Indication |
| RAM | Random Access Memory |
| RARP | Reverse Address Resolution Protocol |
| REJ | Reject |
| RFC | Request for Comments |
| RI | Ring Indicator |
| RIF | Routing Information Field |
| RIP | Routing Information Protocol |
| RMON | Remote Network Monitor |
| RMT | Ring Management |

| RNR | Receive Not Ready |
|---|---|
| ROM | Read-Only Memory |
| RPC | Remote Procedure Call |
| RR | Receive Ready |
| RSA | Rivest, Shamir, and Adleman |
| RST | Reset |
| RTMP | Routing Table Maintenance Protocol |
| RTS | Request to Send |
| RTT | Round-Trip Time |
| SABM | Set Asynchronous Balanced Mode |
| SABME | Set Asynchronous Balanced Mode Extended |
| SAP | Service Advertising Protocol |
| SCTS | Secondary Clear to Send |
| SDCD | Secondary Received Line Signal Detector |
| SDEV | Smoothed Deviation |
| SDLC | Synchronous Data Link Communications |
| SEFS | Severely Errored Framing Second |
| SES | Severely Errored Seconds |
| SGMP | Simple Gateway Monitoring Protocol |
| SAS | Single-Attachment Station |
| SIP | SMDS Interface Protocol |
| SLIP | Serial Line Interface Protocol |
| SMDS | Switched Multimegabit Data Service |
| SMI | Structure and Identification of Management Information |
| SMTP | Simple Mail Transfer Protocol |
| SMT | Station Management |
| SNA | Systems Network Architecture |
| SNAP | Subnetwork Access Protocol |
| SNI | Subscriber Network Interface |
| SNMP | Simple Network Management Protocol |
| SNMPv2 | Simple Network Management Protocol version 2 |
| SONET | Synchronous Optical Network |
| SPF | Shortest Path First |
| SPX | Sequenced Packet Exchange |
| SQ | Signal Quality detector |
| SQE | Signal Quality Error |

| | |
|---|---|
| SRTS | Secondary Request to Send |
| SRTT | Smoothed Round-Trip Time |
| SSAP | Source Service Access Point |
| STE | Spanning Tree Explorer |
| STP | Spanning Tree Protocol |
| SVC | Switched Virtual Circuit |
| SYN | Synchronizing Segment |
| T16AIS | Time Slot 16 Alarm Indication Signal Failure |
| TCB | Transmission Control Block |
| TCP | Transmission Control Protocol |
| TCU | Trunk Coupling Unit |
| TDR | Time-Domain Reflectometry (test) |
| TELNET | Terminal Networking |
| TFTP | Trivial File Transfer Protocol |
| TLI | Transport Layer Interface |
| TP4 | OSI Transport class 4 |
| TRR | Return-to-Repeat Timer |
| TRT | Token Rotation Timer |
| TS16 | Time Slot 16 |
| TTL | Time-to-Live |
| TTRT | Target Token Rotation Timer |
| TR | Token-Ring |
| UA | Unnumbered Acknowledgment |
| UAS | Unavailable Seconds |
| UDP | User Datagram Protocol |
| ULP | Upper-Layer Protocol |
| US | Unavailable Seconds |
| VC | Virtual Circuit |
| WAN | Wide Area Network |
| XDR | External Data Representation |
| XID | Exchange ID |
| XNS | Xerox Network Systems |
| ZBTSI | Zero-Byte Time Slot Interchange |

# RFCs Relating to Network Management

At the time of writing, the authoritative source of RFC documents was the directory */rfc* at *ds.internic.net*. Draft documents could be found in directory */internet-drafts*. An up-to-date index of all RFC documents is in file *rfc-index.txt* in directory */rfc*.

The most current version of the RFC document entitled *IAB Official Protocol Standards* establishes which RFCs define current standards, and the requirement level of each.

## SIMPLE NETWORK MANAGEMENT STANDARDS AND PROPOSED OR DRAFT STANDARDS

rfc1449   Transport Mappings for version 2 of the Simple Network Management Protocol (SNMPv2). J. Case; K. McCloghrie; M. Rose; S. Waldbusser; 05/03/1993

rfc1448   Protocol Operations for version 2 of the Simple Network Management Protocol (SNMPv2). J. Case; K. McCloghrie; M. Rose; S. Waldbusser; 05/03/1993

rfc1446   Security Protocols for version 2 of the Simple Network Management Protocol (SNMPv2). J. Galvin; K. McCloghrie; 05/03/1993

rfc1445   Administrative Model for version 2 of the Simple Network Management Protocol (SNMPv2). J. Davin; K. McCloghrie; 05/03/1993

rfc1444   Conformance Statements for version 2 of the Simple Network Management Protocol (SNMPv2). J. Case; K. McCloghrie; M. Rose; S. Waldbusser; 05/03/1993 rfc1443    Textual Conventions for version 2 of the Simple Network Management Protocol (SNMPv2). J. Case; K. McCloghrie; M. Rose; S. Waldbusser; 05/03/1993

rfc1442    Structure of Management Information for version 2 of the Simple Network Management Protocol (SNMPv2). J. Case; K. McCloghrie; M. Rose; S. Waldbusser; 05/03/1993

rfc1441    Introduction to version 2 of the Internet-standard Network Management Framework. J. Case; K. McCloghrie; M. Rose; S. Waldbusser; 05/03/1993

rfc1420    SNMP over IPX. S. Bostock; 03/03/1993

rfc1419    SNMP over AppleTalk. G. Minshall; M. Ritter; 03/03/1993

rfc1418    SNMP over OSI. M. Rose; 03/03/1993

rfc1212    Concise MIB Definitions. K. McCloghrie; M. Rose; 03/26/1991

rfc1157    A Simple Network Management Protocol (SNMP). M. Schoffstall; M. Fedor; J. Davin; J. Case; 05/10/1990

rfc1155    Structure and Identification of Management Information for TCP/IP-based Internets. K. McCloghrie; M. Rose; 05/10/1990

## RFCS DEFINING MANAGEMENT INFORMATION BASES

rfc1573    Evolution of the Interfaces Group of MIB-II. K. McCloghrie; F. Kastenholz; 01/20/1994

rfc1567    X.500 Directory Monitoring MIB. G. Mansfield; S. Kille; 01/11/1994

rfc1566    Mail Monitoring MIB. N. Freed; S. Kille; 01/11/1994

rfc1565    Network Services Monitoring MIB. N. Freed; S. Kille; 01/11/1994

rfc1559    DECnet Phase IV MIB Extensions. J. Saperia; 12/27/1993

rfc1525    Definitions of Managed Objects for Source Routing Bridges. E. Decker; K. McCloghrie; P. Langille; A. Rijsinghani; 09/30/1993

rfc1516    Definitions of Managed Objects for IEEE 802.3 Repeater Devices. D. McMaster; K. McCloghrie; 09/10/1993

rfc1515    Definitions of Managed Objects for IEEE 802.3 Medium Attachment Units (MAUs). D. McMaster; K. McCloghrie; S. Roberts; 09/10/1993

rfc1514    Host Resources MIB. P. Grillo; S. Waldbusser; 09/23/1993

rfc1513    Token Ring Extensions to the Remote Network Monitoring MIB. S. Waldbusser; 09/23/1993

rfc1512    FDDI Management Information Base. J. Case; A. Rijsinghani; 09/10/1993

rfc1493      Definitions of Managed Objects for Bridges. E. Decker;
             P. Langille; A. Rijsinghani; K. McCloghrie; 07/28/1993

rfc1474      The Definitions of Managed Objects for the Bridge Network
             Control Protocol of the Point-to-Point Protocol. F. Kastenholz;
             06/08/1993

rfc1473      The Definitions of Managed Objects for the IP Network Control
             Protocol of the Point-to-Point Protocol. F. Kastenholz;
             06/08/1993

rfc1472      The Definitions of Managed Objects for the Security Protocols
             of the Point-to-Point Protocol. F. Kastenholz; 06/08/1993

rfc1471      The Definitions of Managed Objects for the Link Control Proto-
             col of the Point-to-Point Protocol. F. Kastenholz; 06/08/1993

rfc1461      SNMP MIB extension for MultiProtocol Interconnect over X.25.
             D. Throop; 05/27/1993

rfc1451      Manager to Manager Management Information Base. J. Case;
             K. McCloghrie; M. Rose; S. Waldbusser; 05/03/1993

rfc1450      Management Information Base for version 2 of the Simple Net-
             work Management Protocol (SNMPv2). J. Case; K. McCloghrie;
             M. Rose; S. Waldbusser; 05/03/1993

rfc1447      Party MIB for version 2 of the Simple Network Management
             Protocol (SNMPv2). K. McCloghrie; J. Galvin; 05/03/1993

rfc1414      Ident MIB. M. St. Johns; M. Rose; 02/04/1993

rfc1407      Definitions of Managed Objects for the DS3/E3 Interface Type

rfc1406      Definitions of Managed Objects for the DS1 and E1 Interface
             Types. F. Baker; J. Watt; 01/26/1993

rfc1398      Definitions of Managed Objects for the Ethernet-like Interface
             Types. F. Kastenholz; 01/14/1993

rfc1382      SNMP MIB Extension for the X.25 Packet Layer. D. Throop;
             11/10/1992

rfc1381      SNMP MIB Extension for X.25 LAPB. D. Throop; F. Baker;
             11/10/1992

rfc1354      IP Forwarding Table MIB. F. Baker; 07/06/1992

rfc1318      Definitions of Managed Objects for Parallel-printer-like Hard-
             ware Devices. B. Stewart; 04/16/1992

rfc1317      Definitions of Managed Objects for RS-232-like Hardware
             Devices. B. Stewart; 04/16/1992

rfc1316      Definitions of Managed Objects for Character Stream Devices.
             B. Stewart; 04/16/1992

rfc1315      Management Information Base for Frame Relay DTEs.
             C. Brown; F. Baker; C. Carvalho; 04/09/1992

rfc1304      Definitions of Managed Objects for the SIP Interface Type.
             T. Cox; K. Tesink; 02/28/1992

rfc1285    FDDI Management Information Base. J. Case; 01/24/1992

rfc1271    Remote Network Monitoring Management Information Base.
S. Waldbusser; 11/12/1991

rfc1269    Definitions of Managed Objects for the Border Gateway Protocol (Version 3). J. Burruss; S. Willis; 10/26/1991

rfc1253    OSPF Version 2 Management Information Base. F. Baker;
R. Coltun; 08/30/1991

rfc1243    AppleTalk Management Information Base. S. Waldbusser;
07/08/1991

rfc1238    CLNS MIB—for use with Connectionless Network Protocol
(ISO 8473) and End System to Intermediate System (ISO
9542). G. Satz; 06/25/1991 (Experimental)

rfc1231    IEEE 802.5 Token Ring MIB. E. Decker; R. Fox;
K. McCloghrie; 02/11/1993

rfc1229    Extensions to the Generic-Interface MIB. K. McCloghrie;
08/03/1992 (Historic)

rfc1214    OSI Internet Management: Management Information Base.
L. Labarre; 04/05/1991

rfc1213    Management Information Base for Network Management
of TCP/IP-based internets: MIB-II. K. McCloghrie; M. Rose;
CP/IP-base

## RELATED RFC DOCUMENTS

rfc1390    Transmission of IP and ARP over FDDI Networks. D. Katz;
01/05/1993

rfc1378    The PPP AppleTalk Control Protocol (ATCP). B. Parker;
11/05/1992

rfc1377    The PPP OSI Network Layer Control Protocol (OSINLCP).
D. Katz; 11/05/1992

rfc1376    The PPP DECnet Phase IV Control Protocol (DNCP).
S. Senum; 11/05/1992

rfc1369    Implementation Notes and Experience for The Internet Ethernet MIB. F. Kastenholz; 10/23/1992

rfc1356    Multiprotocol Interconnect on X.25 and ISDN in the Packet
Mode. A. Malis; D. Robinson; R. Ullmann; 08/06/1992

rfc1321    The MD5 Message-Digest Algorithm. R. Rivest; 04/16/1992

rfc1294    Multiprotocol Interconnect over Frame Relay. T. Bradley;
C. Brown; A. Malis; 01/17/1992

rfc1239    Reassignment of Experimental MIBs to Standard MIBs.
J. Reynolds; 06/25/1991

rfc1236    IP to X.121 Address Mapping for DDN. L. Morales; P. Hasse;
06/25/1991

rfc1234    Tunneling IPX Traffic through IP Networks. D. Provan; 06/20/1991

rfc1228    SNMP-DPI—Simple Network Management Protocol Distributed Program Interface. G. Carpenter; B. Wijnen; 05/23/1991 (Experimental)

rfc1215    A Convention for Defining Traps for use with the SNMP. M. Rose; 03/27/1991

rfc1209    The Transmission of IP Datagrams over the SMDS Service. J. Lawrence; D. Piscitello; 03/06/1991

rfc1201    Transmitting IP Traffic over ARCNET Networks. D. Provan; 02/01/1991

rfc1170    Public Key Standards and Licenses. R. Fougner; 01/11/1991

# Private Enterprise Codes

Prefix: 1.3.6.1.4.1.

| | |
|---|---|
| 0 | Reserved |
| 1 | Proteon |
| 2 | IBM |
| 3 | CMU |
| 4 | Unix |
| 5 | ACC |
| 6 | TWG |
| 7 | CAYMAN |
| 8 | PSI |
| 9 | cisco |
| 10 | NSC |
| 11 | HP |
| 12 | Epilogue |
| 13 | U |
| 14 | BBN |
| 15 | Xylogics |
| 16 | Timeplex |
| 17 | Canstar |
| 18 | Wellfleet |
| 19 | TRW |
| 20 | MIT |
| 21 | EON |
| 22 | Spartacus |
| 23 | Novell |
| 24 | Spider |
| 25 | NSFNET |
| 26 | Hughes |
| 27 | Intergraph |
| 28 | Interlan |
| 29 | Vitalink |
| 30 | Ulana |

| | |
|---|---|
| 31 | NSWC |
| 32 | Santa Cruz Operation |
| 33 | Xyplex |
| 34 | Cray |
| 35 | Bell Northern Research |
| 36 | DEC |
| 37 | Touch |
| 38 | Network Research Corp. |
| 39 | Baylor College of Medicine |
| 40 | NMFECC-LLNL |
| 41 | SRI |
| 42 | Sun Microsystems |
| 43 | 3Com |
| 44 | Rockwell/CMC |
| 45 | SynOptics |
| 46 | Cheyenne Software |
| 47 | Prime Computer |
| 48 | MCNC/North Carolina Data Network |
| 49 | Chipcom |
| 50 | Optical Data Systems |
| 51 | gated |
| 52 | Cabletron Systems |
| 53 | Apollo Computers |
| 54 | DeskTalk Systems |
| 55 | SSDS |
| 56 | Castle Rock Computing |
| 57 | MIPS Computer Systems |
| 58 | TGV, Inc. |
| 59 | Silicon Graphics, Inc. |
| 60 | University of British Columbia |
| 61 | Merit |
| 62 | FiberCom |
| 63 | Apple Computer |
| 64 | Gandalf |
| 65 | Dartmouth |
| 66 | David Systems |
| 67 | Reuter |
| 68 | Cornell |
| 69 | LMS |
| 70 | Locus Computing Corp. |
| 71 | NASA |
| 72 | Retix |
| 73 | Boeing |
| 74 | AT&T |
| 75 | Ungermann-Bass |
| 76 | Digital Analysis Corp. |
| 77 | LAN Manager |
| 78 | Netlabs |
| 79 | ICL |
| 80 | Auspex Systems |

| | |
|---|---|
| 81 | Lannet Company |
| 82 | Network Computing Devices |
| 83 | Raycom Systems |
| 84 | Pirelli Focom Ltd. |
| 85 | Datability Software Systems |
| 86 | Network Application Technology |
| 87 | LINK |
| 88 | NYU |
| 89 | RND |
| 90 | InterCon |
| 91 | Coral Network Corporation |
| 92 | Webster Computer Corp. |
| 93 | Frontier Technologies Corp. |
| 94 | Nokia Data Communications |
| 95 | Allen-Bradley Company, Inc. |
| 96 | CERN |
| 97 | Sigma Network Systems, Inc. |
| 98 | Emerging Technologies, |
| 99 | SNMP Research |
| 100 | Ohio State University |
| 101 | Ultra Network Technologies |
| 102 | Microcom |
| 103 | Martin Marietta Astronautic Group |
| 104 | Micro Technology |
| 105 | Process Software Corporation |
| 106 | Data General Corporation |
| 107 | Bull Company |
| 108 | Emulex Corporation |
| 109 | Warwick University Computing Services |
| 110 | Network General Corporation |
| 111 | Oracle |
| 112 | Control Data Corporation |
| 113 | Hughes Aircraft |
| 114 | Synernetics, Inc. |
| 115 | Mitre |
| 116 | Hitachi, Ltd. |
| 117 | Telebit |
| 118 | Salomon Technology Services |
| 119 | NEC Corporation |
| 120 | Fibermux |
| 121 | FTP Software, Inc. |
| 122 | Sony |
| 123 | Newbridge Networks Corporation |
| 124 | Racal-Milgo Information Systems |
| 125 | CR SYSTEMS |
| 126 | DSET Corporation |
| 127 | Computone |
| 128 | Tektronix, Inc. |
| 129 | Interactive Systems Corporation |
| 130 | Banyan Systems Inc. |

| | |
|---|---|
| 131 | Sintrom Datanet Limited |
| 132 | Bell Canada |
| 133 | Crosscomm Corporation |
| 134 | Rice University |
| 135 | T3Plus Networking, Inc. |
| 136 | Concurrent Computer Corp. |
| 137 | Basser |
| 138 | Luxcom |
| 139 | Artel |
| 140 | Independence Technologies, Inc. (ITI) |
| 141 | Frontier Software Development |
| 142 | Digital Computer Limited |
| 143 | Eyring, Inc. |
| 144 | Case Communications |
| 145 | Penril DataComm, Inc. |
| 146 | American Airlines |
| 147 | Sequent Computer Systems |
| 148 | Bellcore |
| 149 | Konkord Communications |
| 150 | University of Washington |
| 151 | Develcon |
| 152 | Solarix Systems |
| 153 | Unifi Communications Corp. |
| 154 | Roadnet |
| 155 | Network Systems Corp. |
| 156 | ENE (European Network Engineering) |
| 157 | Dansk Data Elektronik A/S |
| 158 | Morning Star Technologies |
| 159 | Dupont EOP |
| 160 | Legato Systems, Inc. |
| 161 | Motorola SPS |
| 162 | European Space Agency (ESA) |
| 163 | BIM |
| 164 | Rad Data Communications Ltd. |
| 165 | Intellicom |
| 166 | Shiva Corporation |
| 167 | Fujikura America |
| 168 | Xlnt Designs INC (XDI) |
| 169 | Tandem Computers |
| 170 | BICC |
| 171 | D-Link Systems, Inc. |
| 172 | AMP, Inc. |
| 173 | Netlink |
| 174 | C. Itoh Electronics |
| 175 | Sumitomo Electric Industries (SEI) |
| 176 | DHL Systems, Inc. |
| 177 | Network Equipment Technologies |
| 178 | APTEC Computer Systems |
| 179 | Schneider & Koch & Co. |
| 180 | Hill Air Force Base |

| | |
|---|---|
| 181 | ADC Kentrox |
| 182 | Japan Radio Co. |
| 183 | Versitron |
| 184 | Telecommunication Systems |
| 185 | Interphase |
| 186 | Toshiba Corporation |
| 187 | Clearpoint Research Corp. |
| 188 | Ascom |
| 189 | Fujitsu America |
| 190 | NetCom Solutions, Inc. |
| 191 | NCR |
| 192 | Dr. Materna GmbH |
| 193 | LM Ericsson AB |
| 194 | Metaphor Computer Systems |
| 195 | Patriot Partners |
| 196 | The Software Group Limited |
| 197 | Kalpana, Inc. |
| 198 | University of Waterloo |
| 199 | CCL/ITRI |
| 200 | Coeur Postel |
| 201 | Mitsubishi Cable Industries, Ltd. |
| 202 | SMC |
| 203 | Crescendo Communication, Inc. |
| 204 | Goodall Software Engineering |
| 205 | Intecom |
| 206 | Victoria University of Wellington |
| 207 | Allied Telesis, Inc. |
| 208 | Dowty Network Systems A/S |
| 209 | Protools |
| 210 | Nippon Telegraph and Telephone Corp. |
| 211 | Fujitsu Limited |
| 212 | Network Peripherals Inc. |
| 213 | Netronix, Inc. Jacques Roth |
| 214 | University of Wisconsin—Madison |
| 216 | Tandberg Data A/S Harald Hoeg |
| 217 | Technically Elite Concepts, Inc. |
| 218 | Labtam Australia Pty. Ltd. |
| 219 | Republic Telcom Systems, Inc. |
| 220 | ADI Systems, Inc. |
| 221 | Microwave Bypass Systems, Inc. |
| 222 | Pyramid Technology Corp. |
| 223 | Unisys Corp |
| 224 | LANOPTICS LTD. Israel |
| 225 | NKK Corporation |
| 226 | MTrade UK Ltd. |
| 227 | Acals |
| 228 | ASTEC, Inc. |
| 229 | Delmarva Power |
| 230 | Telematics International, Inc. |
| 231 | Siemens Nixdorf |

| | |
|---|---|
| 232 | Compaq |
| 233 | NetManage, Inc. |
| 234 | NCSU Computing Center |
| 235 | Empirical Tools and Technologies |
| 236 | Samsung Group |
| 237 | Takaoka Electric Mfg. Co., Ltd. |
| 238 | Netrix Systems Corporation |
| 239 | WINDATA |
| 240 | RC International A/S |
| 241 | Netexp Research |
| 242 | Internode Systems Pty Ltd. |
| 243 | netCS Informationstechnik GmbH |
| 244 | Lantronix |
| 245 | Avatar Consultants |
| 246 | Furukawa Electoric Co. Ltd. |
| 247 | AEG Electrocom |
| 248 | Richard Hirschmann GmbH & Co. |
| 249 | G2R Inc. |
| 250 | University of Michigan |
| 251 | Netcomm, Ltd. |
| 252 | Sable Technology Corporation |
| 253 | Xerox |
| 254 | Conware Computer Consulting GmbH |
| 255 | Compatible Systems Corp. |
| 256 | Scitec Communications Systems Ltd. |
| 257 | Transarc Corporation |
| 258 | Matsushita Electric Industrial Co., Ltd. |
| 259 | ACCTON |
| 260 | Star-Tek, Inc. |
| 261 | Codenoll Tech. Corp. |
| 262 | Formation, Inc. |
| 263 | Seiko Instruments, Inc. (SII) |
| 264 | RCE (Reseaux de Communication d'Enterprise S.A.) |
| 265 | Xenocom, Inc. |
| 266 | KABELRHEYDT |
| 267 | Systech Computer Corporation |
| 268 | Visual |
| 269 | SDD (Scandinavian Airlines Data Denmark A/S) |
| 270 | Zenith Electronics Corporation |
| 271 | TELECOM FINLAND |
| 272 | BinTec Computersystems |
| 273 | EUnet Germany |
| 274 | PictureTel Corporation |
| 275 | Michigan State University |
| 276 | GTE Telecom Incorporated |
| 277 | Cascade Communications Corp. |
| 278 | Hitachi Cable, Ltd. |
| 279 | Olivetti |
| 280 | Vitacom Corporation |
| 281 | INMOS |

| | |
|---|---|
| 282 | AIC Systems Laboratories Ltd. |
| 283 | Cameo Communications, Inc. |
| 284 | Diab Data AB |
| 285 | Olicom A/S |
| 286 | Digital-Kienzle Computersystems |
| 287 | CSELT (Centro Studi E Laboratori Telecomunicazioni) |
| 288 | Electronic Data Systems |
| 289 | McData Corporation |
| 290 | Harris Corporation |
| 291 | Technology Dynamics, Inc. |
| 292 | DATAHOUSE Information Systems Ltd. |
| 293 | DSIR Network Group |
| 294 | Texas Instruments |
| 295 | PlainTree Systems Inc. |
| 296 | Hedemann Software Development |
| 297 | Fuji Xerox Co., Ltd. |
| 298 | Asante Technology |
| 299 | Stanford University |
| 300 | Digital Link |
| 301 | Raylan Corporation |
| 302 | Datacraft |
| 303 | Hughes |
| 304 | Farallon Computing, Inc. |
| 305 | GE Information Services |
| 306 | Gambit Computer Communications |
| 307 | Livingston Enterprises, Inc. |
| 308 | Star Technologies |
| 309 | Micronics Computers Inc. |
| 310 | Basis, Inc. |
| 311 | Microsoft |
| 312 | US West Advance Technologies |
| 313 | University College London |
| 314 | Eastman Kodak Company |
| 315 | Network Resources Corporation |
| 316 | Atlas Telecom |
| 317 | Bridgeway |
| 318 | American Power Conversion Corp |
| 319 | DOE Atmospheric Radiation Measurement Project |
| 320 | VerSteeg CodeWorks |
| 321 | Verilink Corp |
| 322 | Sybus Corporation |
| 323 | Tekelec |
| 324 | NASA Ames Research Center |
| 325 | Simon Fraser University |
| 326 | Fore Systems, Inc. |
| 327 | Centrum Communications, Inc. |
| 328 | NeXT Computer, Inc. |
| 329 | Netcore, Inc. |
| 330 | Northwest Digital Systems |
| 331 | Andrew Corporation |

332    DigiBoard
333    Computer Network Technology Corp.
334    Lotus Development Corp.
335    MICOM Communication Corporation
336    ASCII Corporation
337    PUREDATA Research/USA
338    NTT DATA
339    Empros Systems International
340    Kendall Square Research (KSR)
341    Martin Marietta Energy Systems
342    Network Innovations
343    Intel Corporation
344    Proxar
345    Epson Research Center
346    Fibernet
347    Box Hill Systems Corporation
348    American Express Travel Related Services
349    Compu-Shack
350    Parallan Computer, Inc.
351    Stratacom
352    Open Networks Engineering, Inc.
353    ATM Forum
354    SSD Management, Inc.
355    Automated Network Management, Inc.
356    Magnalink Communications Corporation
357    TIL Systems, Ltd.
358    Skyline Technology, Inc.
359    Nu-Mega Technologies, Inc.
360    Morgan Stanley & Co. Inc.
361    Integrated Business Network
362    L & N Technologies, Ltd.
363    Cincinnati Bell Information Systems, Inc.
364    OSCOM International
365    MICROGNOSIS
366    Datapoint Corporation
367    RICOH Co. Ltd.
368    Axis Communications AB
369    Pacer Software
370    Axon Networks Inc.
371    Brixton Systems, Inc.
372    GSI
373    Tatung Co., Ltd.
374    DIS Research LTD
375    Quotron Systems, Inc.
376    DASSAULT ELECTRONIQUE
377    Corollary, Inc.
378    SEEL, Ltd.
379    Lexcel
380    Sophisticated Technologies, Inc.
381    OST

| | |
|---|---|
| 382 | Megadata Pty Ltd. |
| 383 | LLNL Livermore Computer Center |
| 384 | Dynatech Communications |
| 385 | Symplex Communications Corp. |
| 386 | Tribe Computer Works |
| 387 | Taligent, Inc. |
| 388 | Symbol Technologies, Inc. |
| 389 | Lancert |
| 390 | Alantec |
| 391 | Ridgeback Solutions |
| 392 | Metrix, Inc. |
| 393 | Central Point Software |
| 394 | Naval Research Laboratory Communication Systems Branch |
| 395 | I.D.E. Corporation |
| 396 | Matsushita Electric Works, Ltd. |
| 397 | MegaPAC |
| 398 | Kinmel Park |
| 399 | Hitachi Computer Products (America), Inc. |
| 400 | METEO FRANCE |
| 401 | PRC Inc. |
| 402 | Wal*Mart Stores, Inc. |
| 403 | Nissin Electric Company, Ltd. |
| 404 | Distributed Support Information Standard |
| 405 | SMDS Interest Group (SIG) |
| 406 | SolCom Systems Ltd. |
| 407 | Bell Atlantic |
| 408 | Advanced Multiuser Technologies Corporation |
| 409 | Mitsubishi Electric Corporation |
| 410 | C.O.L. Systems, Inc. |
| 411 | University of Auckland |
| 412 | Desktop Management Task Force (DMTF) |
| 413 | Klever Computers, Inc. |
| 414 | Amdahl Corporation |
| 415 | JTEC Pty, Ltd. |
| 416 | Matra Communication |
| 417 | HAL Computer Systems |
| 418 | Lawrence Berkeley Laboratory |
| 419 | Dale Computer Corporation |
| 420 | IPTC, Universitaet of Tuebingen |
| 421 | Bytex Corporation |
| 422 | Cogwheel, Inc. Brian Ellis |
| 423 | Lanwan Technologies |
| 424 | Thomas-Conrad Corporation |
| 425 | TxPort |
| 426 | Compex, Inc. |
| 427 | Evergreen Systems, Inc. |
| 428 | HNV, Inc. |
| 429 | U.S. Robotics, Inc. |
| 430 | Canada Post Corporation |
| 431 | Open Systems Solutions, Inc. |

432    Toronto Stock Exchange
433    Mamakos/TransSys Consulting
434    EICON
435    Jupiter Systems
436    SSTI
437    Grand Junction Networks
438    Anasazi, Inc.
439    Edward D. Jones and Company
440    Amnet, Inc.
441    Kevin Gage
442    PEER Networks
443    Gateway Communications, Inc.
444    Peregrine Systems
445    Daewoo Telecom
446    Norwegian Telecom Research
447    WilTel
448    Ericsson-Camtec
449    Codex
450    Basis
451    AGE Logic
452    INDE Electronics
453    ISODE Consortium
454    J.I. Case
455    Trillium
456    Bacchus Inc.
457    MCC
458    Stratus Computer
459    Quotron
460    Beame & Whiteside
461    Cellular Technical Services
462    Shore Microsystems, Inc.
463    Telecommunications Techniques Corp.
464    DNPAP (Technical University Delft)
465    Plexcom, Inc.
466    Tylink
467    Brookhaven National Laboratory
468    Computer Communication Systems Gerard Laborde
469    Norand Corporation
470    MUX-LAB
471    Premisys Communications, Inc.
472    Bell South Telecommunications
473    J. Stainsbury PLC
474    Ki Research Inc.
475    Wandel and Goltermann Technologies
476    Emerson Computer Power
477    Network Software Associates
478    Procter and Gamble
479    Meridian Technology Corporation
480    QMS, Inc.
481    Network Express

| | |
|---|---|
| 482 | LANcity Corporation |
| 483 | Dayna Communications, Inc. |
| 484 | kn-X Ltd. |
| 485 | Sync Research, Inc. |
| 486 | PremNet |
| 487 | SIAC |
| 488 | New York Stock Exchange |
| 489 | American Stock Exchange |
| 490 | FCR Software, Inc. |
| 491 | National Medical Care, Inc. |
| 492 | Dialogue Communication Systemes, S.A. |
| 493 | NorTele |
| 494 | Madge Networks, Inc. |
| 495 | Teleglobe Communications |
| 496 | CTON |
| 497 | Leap Technology, Inc. |
| 498 | General DataComm, Inc. |
| 499 | ACE Communications, Ltd. |
| 500 | Automatic Data Processing (ADP) |
| 501 | Programa SPRITEL |
| 502 | Adacom |
| 503 | Metrodata Ltd |
| 504 | Ellemtel Telecommunication Systems Laboratories |
| 505 | Arizona Public Service |
| 506 | NETWIZ, Ltd., |
| 507 | Science and Engineering Research Council (SERC) |
| 508 | The First Boston Corporation |
| 509 | Hadax Electronics Inc. |
| 510 | VTKK |
| 511 | North Hills Israel Ltd. |
| 512 | TECSIEL |
| 513 | Bayerische Motoren Werke (BMW) AG |
| 514 | CNET Technologies |
| 515 | MCI |
| 516 | Human Engineering AG (HEAG) Urs Brunner |
| 517 | FileNet Corporation |
| 518 | NFT-Ericsson |
| 519 | Dun & Bradstreet |
| 520 | Intercomputer Communications |
| 521 | Defense Intelligence Agency |
| 522 | Telesystems SLW Inc |
| 523 | APT Communications |
| 524 | Delta Airlines |
| 525 | California Microwave |
| 526 | Avid Technology Inc |
| 527 | Integro Advanced Computer Systems |
| 528 | RPTI |
| 529 | Ascend Communications Inc |
| 530 | Eden Computer Systems Inc |
| 531 | Kawasaki-Steel Corp |

| | |
|---|---|
| 532 | Barclays |
| 533 | B.U.G., Inc. |
| 534 | Exide Electronics |
| 535 | Superconducting Supercollider Lab. |
| 536 | Triticom |
| 537 | Universal Instruments Corp. |
| 538 | Information Resources, Inc. |
| 539 | Applied Innovation, Inc. |
| 540 | Crypto AG |
| 541 | Infinite Networks, Ltd, Sean Harding |
| 542 | Rabbit Software |
| 543 | Apertus Technologies |
| 544 | Equinox Systems, Inc. |
| 545 | Hayes Microcomputer Products |
| 546 | Empire Technologies Inc. |
| 547 | Glaxochem, Ltd. |
| 548 | KPY Network Partners, Corp. |
| 549 | Agent Technology, Inc. |
| 550 | Dornier GMBH |
| 551 | Telxon Corporation |
| 552 | Entergy Corporation |
| 553 | Garrett Communications Inc. |
| 554 | Agile Networks, Inc. |
| 555 | Larscom |
| 556 | Stock Equipment |
| 557 | ITT Corporation |
| 558 | Universal Data Systems, Inc. |
| 559 | Sonix Communications, Ltd. |
| 560 | Paul Freeman Associates, Inc. |
| 561 | John S. Barnes, Corp. |
| 562 | Northern Telecom |
| 563 | CAP Debris |
| 564 | Telco Systems NAC |
| 565 | Tosco Refining Co |
| 566 | Russell Info Sys |
| 567 | University of Salford |
| 568 | NetQuest Corp. |
| 569 | Armon Networking Ltd. |
| 570 | IA Corporation |
| 571 | AU-System Communication AB |
| 572 | GoldStar Information & Communications, Ltd. |
| 573 | SECTRA AB |
| 574 | ONEAC Corporation |
| 575 | Tree Technologies |
| 576 | GTE Government Systems |
| 577 | Denmac Systems, Inc. |
| 578 | Interlink Computer Sciences, Inc. |
| 579 | Bridge Information Systems, Inc. |
| 580 | Leeds and Northrup Australia (LNA) |
| 581 | BHA Computer |

| | |
|---|---|
| 582 | Newport Systems Solutions, Inc. |
| 583 | Atrium Technologies |
| 584 | ROBOTIKER |
| 585 | PeerLogic Inc. |
| 586 | Digital Transmittion Systems Bill VerSteeg |
| 587 | Far Point Communications Bill VerSteeg |
| 588 | Xircom Bill VerSteeg |
| 589 | Mead Data Central |
| 590 | Royal Bank of Canada |
| 591 | Advantis, Inc. |
| 592 | Chemical Banking Corp. |
| 593 | Eagle Technology |
| 594 | British Telecom |
| 595 | Radix BV |
| 596 | TAINET Communication System Corp. |
| 597 | Comtek Services Inc. |
| 598 | Fair Issac |
| 599 | AST Research Inc. |
| 600 | Soft*Star s.r.l. |
| 601 | Bancomm |
| 602 | Trusted Information Systems, Inc. |
| 603 | Harris & Jeffries, Inc. |
| 604 | Axel Technology Corp. |
| 605 | GN Navtel, Inc. |
| 606 | CAP debis |
| 607 | Lachman Technology, Inc. |
| 608 | Galcom Networking Ltd. |
| 609 | BAZIS |
| 610 | SYNAPTEL |
| 611 | Investment Management Services, Inc. |
| 612 | Taiwan Telecommunication Lab Dennis Tseng |
| 613 | Anagram Corporation |
| 614 | Univel |
| 615 | University of California, San Diego |
| 616 | CompuServe |
| 617 | Telstra—OTC Australia |
| 618 | Westinghouse Electric Corp. |
| 619 | DGA Ltd. |
| 620 | Elegant Communications Inc. |
| 621 | Experdata |
| 622 | Unisource Business Networks Sweden AB |
| 623 | Molex, Inc. |
| 624 | Quay Financial Software |
| 625 | VMX Inc. |
| 626 | Hypercom, Inc. |
| 627 | University of Guelph |
| 628 | DIaLOGIKa |
| 629 | NBASE Switch Communication Sergiu Rotenstein |
| 630 | Anchor Datacomm B.V. |
| 631 | PACDATA |

| | |
|---|---|
| 632 | University of Colorado |
| 633 | Tricom Communications Limited |
| 634 | santix software GmbH |
| 635 | FastComm Communications Corp |
| 636 | The Georgia Institute of Technology |
| 637 | Alcatel Data Networks |
| 638 | GTECH Corporation |
| 639 | UNOCAL Corporation |
| 640 | First Pacific Network |
| 641 | Lexmark International |
| 642 | Qnix Computer |
| 643 | Jigsaw Software Concepts (Pty) Ltd. |
| 644 | VIR, Inc. |
| 645 | SFA Datacomm Inc. |
| 646 | SEIKO Telecommunication Systems, Inc. |
| 647 | Unified Management |
| 648 | RADLINX Ltd. |
| 649 | Microplex Systems Ltd. |
| 650 | Objecta Elektronik & Data AB |
| 651 | Phoenix Microsystems |
| 652 | Distributed Systems International, Incorporated |
| 653 | Evolving Systems, Inc. |
| 654 | SAT GmbH |
| 655 | CeLAN Technology, Inc. |
| 656 | Landmark Systems Corp. |
| 657 | Netone Systems Co., Ltd. |
| 658 | Loral Data Systems |
| 659 | Cellware Broadband Technology |
| 660 | ccmail, Inc. |
| 661 | IMC Networks Corp. |
| 662 | Octel Communications Corp. |
| 663 | RIT Technologies LTD. |
| 664 | Adtran |
| 665 | PowerPlay Technologies, Inc. |
| 666 | Oki Electric Industry Co., Ltd. |
| 667 | Specialix International |
| 668 | INESC (Instituto de Engenharia de Sistemas e Computadores) |
| 669 | Globalnet Communications |
| 670 | Product Line Engineer SVEC Computer Corp. |
| 671 | Printer Systems Corp. |
| 672 | Contec Micro Electronics USA |
| 673 | Unix Integration Services |
| 674 | Dell Computer Corporation |
| 675 | Whittaker Electronic Systems |
| 676 | QPSX Communications |
| 677 | Loral WD1 |
| 678 | Federal Express Corp. |
| 679 | E-COMMS Inc. |
| 680 | Software Clearing House |
| 681 | Antlow Computers LTD. |

| | |
|---|---|
| 682 | Emcom Corp. |
| 683 | Extended Systems, Inc. Al Youngwerth |
| 684 | Sola Electric |
| 685 | Esix Systems, Inc. |
| 686 | 3M/MMM |
| 687 | Cylink Corp. |
| 688 | Znyx Advanced Systems Division, Inc. Alan Deikman |
| 689 | Texaco, Inc. |
| 690 | McCaw Cellular Communication Corp. |
| 691 | ASP Computer Product Inc. |
| 692 | HiPerformance Systems Mike Brien |
| 693 | Regionales Rechenzentrum Sibylle Schweizer |
| 694 | SAP AG |
| 695 | ElectroSpace System Inc. |
| 696 | (NEEDS TO BE REASSIGNED) |
| 697 | MultiPort Software |
| 698 | Combinet, Inc. Samir Sawhney |
| 699 | TSCC |
| 700 | Teleos Communications Inc. |
| 701 | Alta Research |
| 702 | Independence Blue Cross |
| 703 | ADACOM Station Interconnectivity LTD. |
| 704 | MIROR Systems |
| 705 | Merlin Gerin |
| 706 | Owen-Corning Fiberglas |
| 707 | Talking Networks Inc. |
| 708 | Cubix Corporation |
| 709 | Formation Inc. |
| 710 | Lannair Ltd. |
| 711 | LightStream Corp |
| 712 | LANart Corp |
| 713 | University of Stellenbosch |
| 714 | Wyse Technology |
| 715 | DSC Communications Corp. |
| 716 | NetEc |
| 717 | Breltenbach Software Engineering |
| 718 | Victor Company Of Japan, Limited |
| 719 | Japan Direx Corporation |
| 720 | NECSY Network Control Systems S.p.A. |
| 721 | ISDN Systems Corp. |
| 722 | Zero-One Technologies, LTD |
| 723 | Radix Technologies, Inc. |
| 724 | National Institute of Standards and Technology Jim West |
| 725 | Digital Technology Inc. |
| 726 | Castelle Corp. |
| 727 | Presticom Inc. |
| 728 | Showa Electric Wire & Cable Co., Ltd. Robert O'Grady |
| 729 | SpectraGraphics |
| 730 | ACSYS Inc. |
| 731 | Wind River Systems |

| 732 | RADWAY International Ltd. |
| 733 | System Management ARTS, Inc. |
| 734 | Persoft, Inc. |
| 735 | Xnet Technology Inc. |
| 736 | Unison-Tymlabs |
| 737 | Micro-Matic Research |
| 738 | B.A.T.M. Advance Technologies |
| 739 | University of Copenhagen |
| 740 | Network Security Systems, Inc. |
| 741 | JNA Telecommunications |
| 742 | Encore Computer Corporation |
| 743 | Central Intelligent Agency |
| 744 | ISC (GB) Limited |
| 745 | Digital Communication Associates |
| 746 | CyberMedia Inc. |
| 747 | Distributed Systems International, Inc. |
| 748 | Peter Radig EDP-Consulting |
| 749 | Vicorp Interactive Systems |
| 750 | Inet Inc. |
| 751 | Argonne National Laboratory |
| 752 | Tek Logix |
| 753 | North Western University |
| 754 | Astarte Fiber Networks |
| 755 | Diederich & Associates, Inc. |
| 756 | Florida Power Corporation |
| 757 | ASK/INGRES |
| 758 | Open Network Enterprise |
| 759 | The Home Depot |
| 760 | Pan Dacom Telekommunikations Jens Andresen |
| 761 | NetTek |
| 762 | Karlnet Corp. |
| 763 | Efficient Networks, Inc. |
| 764 | Fiberdata Jan Fernquist +46 828 8383 |
| 765 | Lanser |
| 766 | Telebit Communications A/S |
| 767 | HILAN GmbH |
| 768 | Network Computing Inc. |
| 769 | Walgreens Company |
| 770 | Internet Initiative Japan Inc. |
| 771 | GP van Niekerk Ondernemings |
| 772 | Northern Telecom, Ltd. |
| 773 | Securities Industry Automation Corporation Chiu Szeto |
| 774 | SYNaPTICS |
| 775 | Data Switch Corporation |
| 776 | Telindus Distribution |
| 777 | MAXM Systems Corporation |
| 778 | Fraunhofer Gesellschaft |
| 779 | EQS Business Services |
| 780 | CNet Technology Inc. |
| 781 | Datentechnik GmbH |

| 782 | Network Solutions Inc. |
| 783 | Viaman Software |
| 784 | Schweizerische Bankgesellschaft Zuerich |
| 785 | University of Twente—TIOS |
| 786 | Simplesoft Inc. |
| 787 | Stony Brook, Inc. |
| 788 | Unified Systems Solutions, Inc. |
| 789 | Network Appliance Corporation |
| 790 | Ornet Data Communication Technologies Ltd. |
| 791 | Computer Associates International |
| 792 | Multipoint Network Inc. |
| 793 | NYNEX Science & Technology |
| 794 | Commercial Link Systems |
| 795 | Adaptec Inc. |
| 796 | Softswitch |
| 797 | Link Technologies, Inc. |
| 798 | IIS |
| 799 | Mobile Solutions Inc. |
| 800 | Xylan Corp. |
| 801 | Airtech Software Forge Limited |
| 802 | National Semiconductor |
| 803 | Video Lottery Technologies |
| 804 | National Semiconductor Corp |
| 805 | Applications Management Corp |
| 806 | Travelers Insurance Company |
| 807 | Taiwan International Standard Electronics Ltd. |
| 808 | US Patent and Trademark Office |
| 809 | Hynet, LTD |
| 810 | Aydin, Corp. |
| 811 | ADDTRON Technology Co., LTD |
| 812 | Fannie Mae |
| 813 | MultiNET Services |
| 814 | GECKO mbH |
| 815 | Memorex Telex |
| 816 | Advanced Communications Networks (ACN) SA |
| 817 | Telekurs AG |
| 818 | Victron bv |
| 819 | CF6 Company |
| 820 | Walker Richer and Quinn INC. |
| 821 | Saturn Systems |
| 822 | Mitsui Marine and Fire Insurance Co., LTD |
| 823 | Loop Telecommunication International, Inc. |
| 824 | Telenex Corporation |
| 825 | Bus-Tech, Inc. |
| 826 | ATRIE |
| 827 | Gallagher & Robertson A/S |
| 828 | Networks Northwest, Inc. |
| 829 | Conner Peripherials |
| 830 | Elf Antar France |
| 831 | Lloyd Internetworking |

# MIB-II Summary and MIB Reference

## MIB-II

```
iso.org.dod.internet.mgmt.mib-2.
1.3.6.1.2.1.

        1 system
          1 sysDescr
          2 sysObjectID
          3 sysUpTime
          4 sysContact
          5 sysName
          6 sysLocation
          7 sysServices

        2 interfaces
          1 ifNumber
          2 ifTable
              1 ifEntry
                    1 ifIndex
                    2 ifDescr
                    3 ifType
                    4 ifMtu
                    5 ifSpeed
                    6 ifPhysAddress
                    7 ifAdminStatus
                    8 ifOperStatus
                    9 ifLastChange
                   10 ifInOctets
                   11 ifInUcastPkts
```

```
                       12 ifInNUcastPkts
                       13 ifInDiscards
                       14 ifInErrors
                       15 ifInUnknownProtos
                       16 ifOutOctets
                       17 ifOutUcastPkts
                       18 ifOutNUcastPkts
                       19 ifOutDiscards
                       20 ifOutErrors
                       21 ifOutQLen
                       22 ifSpecific


     3 at
        1 atTable
             1 atEntry
                        1 atIfIndex
                        2 atPhysAddress
                        3 atNetAddress


     4 ip
        1 ipForwarding
        2 ipDefaultTTL
        3 ipInReceives
        4 ipInHdrErrors
        5 ipInAddrErrors
        6 ipForwDatagrams
        7 ipInUnknownProtos
        8 ipInDiscards
        9 ipInDelivers
       10 ipOutRequests
       11 ipOutDiscards
       12 ipOutNoRoutes
       13 ipReasmTimeout
       14 ipReasmReqds
       15 ipReasmOKs
       16 ipReasmFails
       17 FragOKs
       18 ipFragFails
       19 ipFragCreates

       20 ipAddrTable
             1 ipAddrEntry
                        1 ipAdEntAddr
                        2 ipAdEntIfIndex
                        3 ipAdEntNetMask
                        4 ipAdEntBcastAddr
                        5 ipAdEntReasmMaxSize
```

```
21 ipRouteTable
      1 ipRouteEntry
                1 ipRouteDest
                2 ipRouteIfIndex
                3 ipRouteMetric1
                4 ipRouteMetric2
                5 ipRouteMetric3
                6 ipRouteMetric4
                7 ipRouteNextHop
                8 ipRouteType
                9 ipRouteProto
               10 ipRouteAge
               11 ipRouteMask
               12 ipRouteMetric5
               13 ipRouteInfo

22 ipNetToMediaTable
      1 ipNetToMediaEntry
                1 ipNetToMediaIfIndex
                2 ipNetToMediaPhysAddress
                3 ipNetToMediaNetAddress
                4 ipNetToMediaType

23 ipRoutingDiscards

5 icmp
   1 icmpInMsgs
   2 icmpInErrors
   3 icmpInDestUnreachs
   4 icmpInTimeExcds
   5 icmpInParmProbs
   6 icmpInSrcQuenchs
   7 icmpInRedirects
   8 icmpInEchos
   9 icmpInEchoReps
  10 icmpInTimestamps
  11 icmpInTimestampReps
  12 icmpInAddrMasks
  13 icmpInAddrMaskReps
  14 icmpOutMsgs
  15 icmpOutErrors
  16 icmpOutDestUnreachs
  17 icmpOutTimeExcds
  18 icmpOutParmProbs
  19 icmpOutSrcQuenchs
  20 icmpOutRedirects
  21 icmpOutEchos
```

```
        22 icmpOutEchoReps
        23 icmpOutTimestamps
        24 icmpOutTimestampReps
        25 icmpOutAddrMasks
        26 icmpOutAddrMaskReps

    6 tcp
        1 tcpRtoAlgorithm
        2 tcpRtoMin
        3 tcpRtoMax
        4 tcpMaxConn
        5 tcpActiveOpens
        6 tcpPassiveOpens
        7 tcpAttemptFails
        8 tcpEstabResets
        9 tcpCurrEstab
       10 tcpInSegs
       11 tcpOutSegs
       12 tcpRetransSegs
       13 tcpConnTable
               1 tcpConnEntry
                       1 tcpConnState
                       2 tcpConnLocalAddress
                       3 tcpConnLocalPort
                       4 tcpConnRemAddress
                       5 tcpConnRemPort
       14 tcpInErrs
       15 tcpOutRsts

    7 udp
        1 udpInDatagrams
        2 udpNoPorts
        3 udpInErrors
        4 udpOutDatagrams

        5 udpTable
               1 udpEntry
                       1 udpLocalAddress
                       2 udpLocalPort

    8 egp
        1 egpInMsgs
        2 egpInErrors
        3 egpOutMsgs
        4 egpOutErrors

        5 egpNeighTable
               1 egpNeighEntry
```

```
                      1 egpNeighState
                      2 egpNeighAddr
                      3 egpNeighAs
                      4 egpNeighInMsgs
                      5 egpNeighInErrs
                      6 egpNeighOutMsgs
                      7 egpNeighOutErrs
                      8 egpNeighInErrMsgs
                      9 egpNeighOutErrMsgs
                     10 egpNeighStateUps
                     11 egpNeighStateDowns
                     12 egpNeighIntervalHello
                     13 egpNeighIntervalPoll
                     14 egpNeighMode
                     15 egpNeighEventTrigger
          6 egpAs


10 transmission


11 snmp
     1 snmpInPkts
     2 snmpOutPkts
     3 snmpInBadVersions
     4 snmpInBadCommunityNames
     5 snmpInBadCommunityUses
     6 snmpInASNParseErrs
     8 snmpInTooBigs
     9 snmpInNoSuchNames
    10 snmpInBadValues
    11 snmpInReadOnlys
    12 snmpInGenErrs
    13 snmpInTotalReqVars
    14 snmpInTotalSetVars
    15 snmpInGetRequests
    16 snmpInGetNexts
    17 snmpInSetRequests
    18 snmpInGetResponses
    19 snmpInTraps
    20 snmpOutTooBigs
    21 snmpOutNoSuchNames
    22 snmpOutBadValues
    24 snmpOutGenErrs
    25 snmpOutGetRequests
    26 snmpOutGetNexts
    27 snmpOutSetRequests
    28 snmpOutGetResponses
    29 snmpOutTraps
    30 snmpEnableAuthenTraps
```

# MIB-II MIBS

**TABLE D.1    Chapters for MIB-II MIBs**

mib-2 MIBS
iso.org.dod.internet.mgmt.mib-2.
1.3.6.1.2.1.

| Subtree name | Subtree number | Description | Chapter |
|---|---|---|---|
| system | 1 | System | 9 |
| interfaces | 2 | Interfaces | 10 |
| at | 3 | Address Translation | 11 |
| ip | 4 | IP | 12 |
| icmp | 5 | ICMP | 13 |
| tcp | 6 | TCP | 14 |
| udp | 7 | UDP | 15 |
| egp | 8 | Exterior Gateway Protocol | 16 |
| snmp | 11 | SNMP | 17 |

# ADDITIONAL MIBS

**TABLE D.2    Chapters for Additional MIBs**

Technology MIBS
iso.org.dod.internet.mgmt.mib-2.
1.3.6.1.2.1.

| Subtree name | Subtree number | Description | Chapter |
|---|---|---|---|
| transmission.dot3 | 10.7 | Ethernet | 18 |
| transmission.dot5 | 10.9 | Token-Ring | 19 |
| transmission.fddi | 10.15 | FDDI | 20 |
| transmission.rs232 | 10.33 | RS-232 | 21 |
| transmission.ppp | 10.23 | PPP | 22 |
| transmission.ds1 | 10.18 | DS1 | 23 |
| transmission.ds3 | 10.30 | DS3 | 24 |
| transmission.lapb | 10.16 | LAPB | 25 |
| transmission.x25 | 10.5 | X.25 | 25 |
| transmission.frame-relay | 10.32 | Frame Relay | 26 |
| dot1dBridge | 17 | Bridge | 27 |
| rmon | 16 | Remote Monitor | 28 |
| appleTalk | 13 | AppleTalk | 29 |

enterprises MIBs
iso.org.dod.internet.private.enterprises.
1.3.6.1.4.1.

| Subtree name | Subtree number | Description | Chapter |
|---|---|---|---|
| novell | 23 | Novell MIB | 30 |

snmpV2
iso.org.dod.internet.
1.3.6.1.

| Subtree name | Subtree number | Description | Chapter |
|---|---|---|---|
| snmpV2 | 6 | SNMP V2 MIBs | 34 |

# Glossary

**Abstract Syntax Notation 1 (ASN.1)**   A language used for defining datatypes. ASN.1 is used in OSI standards and in TCP/IP network management specifications.

**access control**   A facility that defines each user's privileges to access computer data.

**Access Control (SNMP)**   Restriction of the operations that may be performed for a party and of the data that the party may access.

**access mode**   A MIB access level of READ-ONLY, READ-WRITE, or NONE.

**Access Policy**   (version 1) The combination of a MIB view and an access mode applied to the MIB view.

**acknowledgment**   Receiving an acknowledgment indicates that data has been transmitted safely.

**Active Monitor**   In the Token-Ring protocol, a station that checks that a token is available, and that data is being removed from the ring. In case of trouble, the Active Monitor initiates recovery procedures.

**Active Open**   Action taken by an application to initiate a TCP connection.

**address mask**   A 32-bit binary number used to identify the parts of an IP address that are used for network and subnet numbers. Every bit in the network and subnet fields is set to 1.

**Address Resolution Protocol (ARP)**   A protocol that dynamically discovers the physical address of a system, given its IP address.

**address translation**   The process of translating a Network Layer address to a corresponding physical address for a device.

**agent**   Software that enables a device to respond to manager requests to view or update MIB data, and send traps reporting problems or significant events.

**Agent Capabilities Statement**   (version 2) Vendor's statement of support for MIB objects, including any variations from the MIB definitions.

**alarm**   A variable, sampling interval, and a Rising and Falling threshold. When a threshold is crossed, an event may be triggered.

**Alarm Indication Signal (AIS)**   Used in digital telephony. A source that is unable to send its normal, framed payload sends an Alarm Indication Signal pattern instead.

**Alternate Mark Inversion (AMI)**  A method of encoding 0s and 1s on a digital telephone link. AMI represents "1s" as alternatively positive (+) and negative (−) voltage pulses.

**American National Standards Institute (ANSI)**  Organization responsible for coordinating United States standardization activities. ANSI is a member of ISO.

**AppleTalk Address Resolution Protocol (AARP)**  A protocol similar to ARP, used to map Appletalk network addresses to physical addresses.

**application**  (telephony) Rules for multiplexing channels and protocols for extra channels used for maintenance functions, such as signaling errors.

**Application Programming Interface (API)**  A set of routines that enable a programmer to use computer facilities. The socket programming interface and the transport layer interface are both APIs used for TCP/IP programming.

**Advanced Research Projects Agency (ARPA)**  U.S. government agency initially sponsoring work on packet switching and TCP/IP protocols.

**ARPANET**  The world's first packet switching network, which for many years functioned as an Internet backbone.

**ASCII**  American National Standard Code for Information Interchange. Seven of the eight bits in an octet are required to define a ASCII character.

**asynchronous communication**  Character-oriented communication, in which characters are delimited by start and stop bits.

**Asyncronous-Control-Character map (ACC)**  A bit map that indicates which characters between '00'H and '1F'H need to be translated into 2-octet codes before transmission across an asynchronous link.

**Asynchronous Transfer Mode (ATM)**  A method of packaging and switching information within 53-octet cells that will be deployed for both local area network use and wide area networking.

**atomic update**  A series of updates that occurs as if it had been done in a single operation.

**Attachment Unit Interface (AUI)**  A cable attaching a station's Ethernet NIC to a transceiver that clamps onto a coaxial cable.

**augments**  Addition of columns to an existing table.

**authentication**  Proof of the identity of the sender of a message.

**authentication clock**  A clock used as the source of timestamps used to validate that a message is not a stale replay.

**Autonomous System (AS)**  A collection of routers under the control of a single administrative authority, and using a common Interior Gateway Protocol.

**Backward Explicit Congestion Notification (BECN)**  A flag in a Frame Relay message header that signals that there is congestion on the path from the receiver.

**Basic Encoding Rules (BER)**  A set of rules for translating ASN.1 values into a stream of octets to be transmitted across a network.

**baud**  A unit of signaling speed equal to the number of times per second that a signal changes state. If there are exactly two states, the baud rate equals the bit rate.

**Berkeley Software Distribution (BSD)**  UNIX software that included TCP/IP support.

**big endian**  A format for the storage or transmission of data that places the most significant byte (or bit) first.

**Binary 3-Zero Substitution (B3ZS)**  Telephony technique for avoiding strings of 0s by replacing 3 0s with a pattern containing a bipolar code violation.

**Bipolar Violation (BPV)**  See **Alternate Mark Inversion.** A failure to change from high-positive to low-negative voltage polarity, or from low-negative to high-positive polarity.

**Bipolar with 8-Zero Substitution (B8ZS)**  Telephony technique for avoiding long strings of 0s by replacing eight 0s with a pattern containing a specific bipolar violation pattern.

**Border Gateway Protocol (BGP)**  A protocol used to advertise the set of networks that can be reached within an Autonomous System. BGP enables this information to be shared with other Autonomous Systems. BGP is newer than EGP, and offers a number of improvements.

**bridge**  A device that connects two or more physical network components and forwards frames which have source and destination addresses on different network components.

**Bridge Protocol Data Unit (BPDU)**  Bridges exchange BPDUs in order to obtain information needed for the Spanning Tree algorithm.

**broadcast**  Transmission of a Protocol Data Unit to all nodes on a particular part of a network.

**brouter**  A device that performs both bridging and routing functions. Some traffic is selected for routing, while the rest is bridged.

**buffer**  An area of storage used to hold input or output data.

**C-bit parity application**  (telephony) Multiplexes signals in a two-step procedure, just as M23 does, but is able to use "C-bits" in maintenance channels used for error detection, error reporting, and initiating loopback tests.

**Carrier Sense Multiple Access with Collision Detection (CSMA/CD)**  A simple media access control protocol. All stations listen to the medium. A station wanting to send may do so if there is no signal on the medium. When two stations transmit simultaneously, both back off and retry after a random time period.

**Case diagram**  A figure that tracks the flow of incoming and outgoing Protocol Data Units.

**Challenge-Handshake Authentication Protocol (CHAP)**  PPP authentication protocol in which the receiver is challenged to use a secret key to produce the correct answer to a calculation performed against a specified number. The protocol does not send passwords across the link.

**Channel Service Unit (CSU)**   Telephony equipment that physically terminates the network's digital line to a customer's premise.

**Common Management Information Protocol (CMIP)**   A central OSI network management protocol.

**Common Management Information Services and Protocol over TCP/IP (CMOT)**   A specification for using OSI management protocols on a TCP/IP network.

**Communications Access Unit (CAU)**   For a Token-Ring, a concentrator used to connect multiple stations to the ring.

**Community**   (version 1) Formally, a pairing of an agent with a set of application entities. Its purpose is to identify valid sources for requests and limit the cope of data that can be accessed.

**Community Name**   (version 1) Used like a password in message, validating the right of the sender to access MIB data with a requested operation.

**Community Profile**   (version 1) The combination of a MIB view and an access mode which is applied to the whole MIB view.

**connection**   A logical communication path between TCP users.

**Connection Management (CMT)**   FDDI component responsible for establishing and maintaining physical connections with neighboring stations and maintaining the logical topology of the network.

**constructed type**   A composite datatype, such as a SEQUENCE.

**context**   An OBJECT IDENTIFIER that corresponds to information that will be accessed by some party or parties. A context corresponds to a collection of view subtrees or a proxy relationship.

**Cyclic Redundancy Code (CRC)**   A mathematical function applied to the bits in a frame, and appended to the frame. The CRC is recalculated when the frame is received. If the result differs from the appended value, then the frame is discarded.

**Data Circuit-terminating Equipment (DCE)**   Equipment required to connect a DTE to a line or to a network.

**Data Encryption Standard (DES)**   A U.S. government approved method of encryption. It is symmetric—that is, the same key is used to encrypt and decrypt data.

**Data Link Connection Identifier (DLCI)**   In frame relay, a local numeric identifier used to name a virtual circuit.

**Data Service Unit (DSU)**   Telephony equipment that connects a CSU to premise equipment, handling functions such as matching local clocking to network clocking.

**Data Terminal Equipment (DTE)**   A source or destination for data. Often used to denote terminals or computers attached to a wide area network.

**datagram**   The IP Protocol Data Unit. More generally, a layer 3 stand-alone message.

**Datagram Delivery Protocol (DDP)** Network Layer protocol used with AppleTalk.

**Defense Advanced Research Projects Agency (DARPA)** Department of Defense Agency that sponsored work on TCP/IP.

**deprecated** Status of a MIB variable, meaning that it still is supported, but is being phased out.

**Destination Service Access Point (DSAP)** An identifier for a frame's destination protocol entity.

**digital hierarchy** Within the digital telephone system, a sequence of levels of multiplexing of concurrent telephone circuits. In the United States, the levels are DS0 (1 circuit), DS1 (24 circuits), DS2 (96 channels), and DS3 (672 channels).

**digital signaling levels** The levels, DS0, DS1, DS2, or DS3, in the digital telephone hierarchy.

**Directory System Agent (DSA)** A facility that accepts queries from Directory User Agents and extracts information from a database. A DSA interacts with a Directory User Agent by means of X.500 protocols.

**Directory User Agent (DUA)** A facility enabling a user to send queries to an X.500 directory server. A DUA interacts with a Directory Service Agent (DSA).

**DisplayString** An OCTET STRING restricted to the Network Virtual Terminal (NVT) ASCII character set defined in the TCP/IP Telnet protocol.

**Distributed Computing Environment (DCE)** A set of technologies selected by the Open Software Foundation to support distributed computing.

**Distributed File Service (DFS)** A file server technology adopted by the Open Software Foundation.

**Distributed Management Environment (DME)** A set of technologies selected for network and system management by the Open Software Foundation.

**Distributed Queue Dual Bus (DQDB)** 802.6 Media Access Protocol, used in SMDS.

**Domain Name System (DNS)** A set of distributed databases providing information such as the IP addresses corresponding to system names, and the location of mail exchangers.

**Dual-Attachment Station (DAS)** In FDDI, a station that is attached to both the primary and secondary rings of a dual ring.

**Electronic Industries Association (EIA)** A standards organization, notably responsible for RS-232.

**Entry Status** (version 1) A table variable used to control row creation and deletion.

**Ethertype** An identifier originally used in DIX Ethernet that indicated the protocol to which a frame should be delivered.

**event** A table entry that identifies a notification message to be sent (in an inform-request) as a result of an alarm.

**explorer frame**   Message used in the Token-Ring Source Route protocol to discover a route between two stations.

**extended superframe (telephony)**   A unit made up of 24 T1 frames. Some of the framing bits are used for error detection and problem reporting.

**Exterior Gateway Protocol (EGP)**   A protocol used to advertise the set of networks that can be reached within an autonomous system. EGP enables this information to be shared with other autonomous systems. See **Border Gateway Protocol.**

**eXternal Data Representation (XDR)**   A standard developed by Sun Microsystems to define datatypes used as parameters, and to encode these parameters for transmission.

**facility data link (telephony)**   A channel formed of extra bits added to a telephony signal. The channel is used to notify the remote end of local errors, carry control information, or initiate a loopback test.

**Fiber Distributed Data Interface (FDDI)**   A standard for high-speed data transfer across a dual ring.

**File Transfer, Access, and Management (FTAM)**   The OSI file transfer and management protocol. FTAM allows users to copy whole files or part of a file, such as an individual record.

**File Transfer Protocol (FTP)**   The TCP/IP protocol that enables users to copy files between systems and perform file management functions, such as renaming or deleting files.

**flow control**   A mechanism that allows a receiver to limit the amount of data that a sender may transmit at any time. Flow control prevents a sender from exhausting the receiver's memory buffers.

**foreign proxy**   Proxy agent that communicates with its agents via a protocol other than SNMPv2.

**Forward Explicit Congestion Notification (FECN)**   A flag in a frame relay header that tells the receiver that there is congestion along the path to the receiver.

**forwarding database**   In a bridge, each entry contains a physical address along with the identity of the bridge port that is used to reach that address.

**fractional T1**   (telephony) Access to less than the full 24 circuits that make up a T1 carrier.

**fractional T3**   (telephony) Access to less than the full 28 T1s that make up a T3 carrier.

**fragmentation**   Partitioning of a datagram into pieces. This is done when a datagram is too large for a network technology that must be traversed to reach the destination.

**frame (data network)**   A layer 2 protocol data unit consisting of a header, (optionally) some information, and a trailer that usually includes a Frame Check Sequence.

**Frame Check Sequence (FCS)**   A mathematical function applied to the bits in a frame, and appended to the frame. The FCS is recalculated when the frame is received. If the result differs from the appended value, then the frame is discarded.

**functional address**   A MAC-layer address associated with a specific role in the network.

**gauge**   A datatype that measures a quantity that increases and decreases, such as a queue length.

**gateway**   An IP router. Many RFC documents use the term *gateway* rather than *router*.

**Gateway-to-Gateway Protocol (GGP)**   A protocol formerly used to exchange routing information between Internet core routers.

**get-bulk-request**   (version 2) A request for a mixture of individual and repeated (usually tabular) values.

**get-request**   A message that requests the value of one or more MIB variables.

**get-next-request**   Enables a manager to retrieve values sequentially. One popular use of the get-next-request is to read through the rows of a table.

**get-response**   Version 1 response to a get-request, get-next-request, or set-request.

**group**   A named set of closely related MIB definitions within a module.

**Hello**   Protocol message used to periodically check that some neighboring system is active.

**High-Level Data Link Control protocol (HDLC)**   A standard that is the basis for several link layer protocols.

**inform-request**   Manager-to-Manager message containing a notification.

**interface**   A sublayer between the Network Layer and access to a physical medium.

**International Telecommunication Union–Telecommunications Standardization Sector (ITU-TS)**   Organization that creates recommendations for international voice and data communications protocols and regulations.

**International Telegraph and Telephone Consultative Committee (CCITT)**   Original name for the ITU-TS (see above).

**internet**   A network made up of subnetworks connected by one or more routers.

**Internet**   A worldwide collection of interconnected computer networks.

**Internet Architecture Board (IAB)**   Board that oversees the Internet protocol development and standardization process.

**Internet Assigned Numbers Authority (IANA)**   The authority responsible for controlling the assignment of a variety of parameters, such as well-known ports, multicast addresses, terminal identifiers, and system identifiers.

**Internet Control Message Protocol (ICMP)**   Protocol used to report problems in delivering IP datagrams, and also supporting several information messages, including the echo message that is the basis of the ping function.

**Internet Engineering Steering Group (IESG)**   A group that coordinates the activities of the IETF working groups.

**Internet Engineering Task Force (IETF)**   A group directed by the IAB, charged with solving immediate Internet problems.

**Internet Gateway Routing Protocol (IGRP)**   Cisco System's proprietary routing protocol.

**Internetwork Packet Exchange (IPX)**   Novell NetWare layer 3 protocol.

**Initial Sequence Number (ISN)**   A sequence number defined during TCP connection setup. Data octets sent over the connection will be numbered starting from this point.

**Integrated Services Digital Network (ISDN)**   A set of CCITT standards aimed at integrating voice and data services. ISDN provides end-to-end digital services.

**interface**   Software and hardware that enables a protocol's Network Layer to transmit Protocol Data Units onto a transmission medium. An interface may be made up of several sublayers.

**Interior Gateway Protocol (IGP)**   Any routing protocol used within an autonomous system.

**Intermediate-System-to-Intermediate-System protocol (IS-IS)**   A protocol that can be used to route both OSI and IP traffic.

**International Organization for Standardization (ISO)**   An international body founded to promote international trade and cooperative progress in science and technology.

**International Telegraph and Telephone Consultative Committee (CCITT)**   An organization formed to coordinate the connection of telephony and data communications facilities into international networks.

**internet**   A set of networks connected by IP routers and appearing to its users as a single network.

**Internet**   The world's largest network, the Internet is based on the TCP/IP protocol suite.

**Internet Architecture Board (IAB)**   Formerly the Internet Activities Board. An independent group responsible for promoting protocol development, selecting protocols for Internet use, and assigning state and status to protocols.

**Internet Assigned Numbers Authority (IANA)**   The authority responsible for controlling the assignment of a variety of parameters, such as well-known ports, multicast addresses, terminal identifiers, and system identifiers.

**Internet Control Message Protocol (ICMP)**   A protocol that is required for implementation with IP. ICMP specifies error messages to be sent when datagrams are discarded or systems experience congestion. ICMP also provides several useful query services.

**Internet Engineering Steering Group (IESG)**   A group that coordinates the activities of the IETF working groups.

**Internet Engineering Task Force (IETF)**   A group directed by the IAB, charged with solving short-term Internet problems.

**Internet Group Management Protocol (IGMP)**   A protocol that is part of the multicast specification. IGMP is used to carry group membership information.

**Internet Protocol (IP)**   The TCP/IP layer 3 protocol responsible for transporting datagrams across an internet.

**Internet Research Task Force (IRTF)**   A group directed by the IAB, charged with long-term research on Internet protocols.

**IP address**   A 32-bit quantity that identifies a network interface.

**IP datagram**   The unit of data routed by IP.

**jabber**   In Ethernet, frames that are too long—that is, greater than 1518 octets in length.

**Kerberos**   An authentication service developed at the Massachusetts Institute of Technology. Kerberos uses encryption to prevent intruders from discovering passwords and gaining unauthorized access to files or services.

**Kinetics Internet Protocol (KIP)**   Protocol used to tunnel AppleTalk datagrams across an IP backbone.

**lexicographic order**   Order of variables in the MIB tree, based on comparing OBJECT IDENTIFIERs from left to right until the numbers differ in a position. For example, 1.3.6.1.2.1.1.6 is smaller that 1.3.6.1.2.1.1.7.

**Link Access Procedures Balanced (LAPB)**   Data Link protocol used with X.25.

**Link Access Procedures on the D-channel (LAPD)**   Data Link protocol used with ISDN.

**Link Control Protocol (LCP)**   Protocol that is used to negotiate PPP link options and open a PPP link.

**Link Quality Monitoring Protocol (LQMP)**   Protocol in the PPP family that enables each end of the link to find out what percentage of its data is being successfully transmitted.

**little endian**   A format for the storage or transmission of data that places the least significant byte (or bit) first.

**Local Management Interface (LMI)**   Network management interface between customer premise equipment and a service provider. In frame relay, it is used to obtain periodic performance and error statistics from the service network.

**logical byte**   A logical byte is a specified number of bits in length. In a file transfer, it is sometimes necessary to specify a logical byte size in order to preserve the integrity of data that is transferred.

**Logical Link Control (LLC)**   A layer 2 (data link layer) protocol that governs the exchange of data between two systems connected to a single physical medium, or connected via a sequence of bridged media.

**loopback**   A test signal sent to a device that is then returned to the source.

**M13 Multiplex Application**   (telephony) Often called the SYNTRAN application, an interleaving method that fills 28 DS1s into a DS3 signal.

**M23 Multiplex Application**   (telephony) An interleaving method that fills seven DS2s into a DS3 signal. "Stuff" bits can be inserted to make up for timing differences between the input and output signals.

**macro**   A facility for defining templates that expand the ASN.1 language.

**magic number**   A number unique to the source, included in some PPP messages to check that local messages are not being looped back from the remote end.

**mail exchanger**   A system used to relay mail into an locally administered internet.

**managed object**   An object holding network management information, characterized by an identifier, a value, implementation requirements, and valid operations.

**Management Information Base (MIB)**   A logical database made up of the configuration, status, and statistical information stored at a device.

**Manager**   Software in a network management station that enables the station to send requests to view or update MIB variables, and to receive traps from an agent. In version 2, also supports sending and receiving inform-requests.

**Manager-to-Manager protocol**   Enables one manager to report to another manager concerning events that result from statistics that cross a danger threshold.

**Maximum Receive Unit (MRU)**   Largest allowed size of the information field in a frame. (The information field may contain one or more sublayer headers as well as a datagram.)

**Maximum Transmission Unit (MTU)**   Size of the largest datagram that can be delivered across a particular path.

**maximum segment size**   The maximum permissible size for the data part of any TCP segment sent on a particular connection.

**Maximum Transmission Unit (MTU)**   The largest datagram that can be sent across a particular network technology, such as an Ethernet or Token-Ring.

**Media Access Control (MAC)**   A protocol governing a station's access to a network. For example, CSMA/CD provides a set of MAC rules for sending and receiving data across a local area network.

**message digest**   The result of a calculation on data that treats the information as binary numbers. A message digest is used to authenticate a message by including a secret key in the calculation.

**Message Transfer Agent (MTA)**   An entity that moves messages (such as electronic mail) between computers.

**Metropolitan Area Network (MAN)**   A technology supporting high-speed networking across a metropolitan area. IEEE 802.6 defines a MAN protocol.

**MIB-II**  A set of managed object definitions aimed at managing TCP/IP-based internets.

**MIB compiler**  A program that creates MIB data structures and translates values of MIB objects into a stream of bytes for transmission.

**MIB group**  A collection of closely related objects.

**MIB subtree**  The set of nodes that are children of a node in the tree of OBJECT IDENTIFIERS.

**MIB view**  A selected subset of the variables in a device's MIB.

**microsecond**  One millionth of a second.

**millisecond**  One thousandth of a second.

**module**  A named collection of MIB datatype definitions, e.g., for managing a specific technology such as Ethernet, a specific protocol family such as Net-Ware product protocols, or a specific application such as electronic mail.

**Module Compliance Statement**  (version 2) Identifies the conformance requirements for support of objects in a module.

**Module Identity Macro**  (version 2) Used to assign an OBJECT IDENTIFIER name to a module.

**monitor**  A device that listens to all traffic on a LAN or on a wide area link, gathering statistics, and capturing traffic that matches some specific criteria.

**multicast**  Transmission of a Protocol Data Unit to a selected set of nodes in a network.

**multiframes**  (telephony) A grouping unit holding multiple frames.

**multihomed host**  A host attached to two or more networks, and therefore requiring multiple IP addresses.

**Multilink Procedure (MLP)**  A procedure which makes several serial lines look like a single logical link.

**Multiple Access Unit (MAU)**  For a Token-Ring, a concentrator used to connect multiple stations to the ring.

**nanosecond**  One billionth of a second.

**native proxy**  Proxy that communicates with its agents via SNMPv2.

**NETBIOS**  A network programming interface and protocol developed for IBM-compatible personal computers.

**network address**  The 32-bit IP address of a system.

**Network Control Protocol (NCP)**  Protocol in the PPP family used to negotiate options for a particular protocol to be carried across the link, such as IP, IPX, or AppleTalk.

**Network File System (NFS)**  A set of protocols introduced by Sun Microsystems, enabling clients to mount remote directories onto their local file systems, and use remote files as if they were local.

**Network Information Center (NIC)**   A central administration facility for the Internet. The NIC supervises network names and network addresses, and provides several information services.

**Network Information Service (NIS)**   A set of protocols introduced by Sun Microsystems, used to provide a directory service for network information.

**Network Service Access Point (NSAP)**   An identifier used to distinguish the identity of an OSI host, and to point to the transport layer entity at that host to which traffic is directed.

**Network User Identification (NUI)**   Used somewhat like a computer account identifier, the NUI identifies an X.25 DTE to the service provider.

**Network Virtual Terminal (NVT)**   A set of rules defining a very simple virtual terminal interaction. The NVT is used at the start of a Telnet session, but a more complex type of terminal interaction can be negotiated.

**Network Virtual Terminal ASCII**   An ASCII character set defined in the TCP/IP Telnet protocol.

**notification**   A list of object values to be sent in a trap or inform-request message. A notification is named by means of an assigned OBJECT IDENTIFIER.

**OBJECT IDENTIFIER**   A string of numbers derived from a global naming tree, used to identify an object.

**Open Shortest Path First (OSPF)**   An internet routing protocol that scales well, can route traffic along multiple paths, and uses knowledge of an internet's topology to make accurate routing decisions.

**Open Systems Interconnection (OSI)**   A set of ISO standards relating to data communications.

**packet**   Originally, a unit of data sent across a packet switching network. Currently, the term may refer to a protocol data unit at any layer.

**parity bit**   An extra bit added to a character for the purpose of error checking.

**party**   A network management agent or manager role. Some parties communicate without authentication, others use authentication, and some use both authentication and encryption in order to protect the privacy of data.

**passive open**   Action taken by a TCP/IP server to prepare to receive requests from clients.

**Password Authentication Protocol (PAP)**   A simple exchange of identity and password across a PPP link.

**pathname**   The character string which must be input to a file system by a user in order to identify a file.

**Permanent Virtual Circuit (PVC)**   The packet switched network equivalent of a leased line.

**Physical Layer protocol (PHY)**   In FDDI, the protocol that deals with all physical layer issues that are independent of the medium, such as clocking and buffering.

**Physical Layer Medium Dependent (PMD)** In FDDI, a protocol that is defined for a specific medium type, dealing with issues such as cables, connectors, signals, acceptable bit error rates, and bypass management.

**Point-to-Point Protocol (PPP)** A protocol for data transfer across serial links. PPP supports extensive link configuration capabilities, and allows traffic for several protocols to be multiplexed across the link.

**port** For a bridge, an interface to a LAN or point-to-point link, or to a virtual circuit across a packet network.

**port number (TCP)** A 2-octet binary number identifying an upper-level user of TCP.

**primary ring** In FDDI, the normal path used by traffic.

**Primitive Type (ASN.1)** A basic datatype such as an INTEGER or OCTET STRING.

**privacy** Protection of the contents of a message by means of encryption.

**private key** A secret key used for authentication or encryption.

**promiscuous interface** An interface that absorbs all traffic on a broadcast medium. For example, a transparent bridge must examine every frame in order to determine whether it should be retransmitted out of a different bridge port.

**Protocol Data Unit (PDU)** A generic term for the protocol unit (e.g., a header and data) used at any layer.

**Protocol Interpreter (PI)** An entity that carries out FTP functions. FTP defines two PI roles: user and server.

**proxy agent** An agent that responds to requests from one or more managers by polling remote devices. A proxy also relays traps generated by devices under its supervision to other managers.

**proxy ARP** Use of a router to answer ARP requests. This will be done when the originating host believes that a destination is local, when in fact it lies beyond a router.

**reassembly** Process of connecting the pieces of a fragmented IP datagram in order to restore the original, entire datagram.

**receive window** The valid range of sequence numbers that a sender may transmit at a given time during the connection.

**refinement** Restriction of a datatype to a subset of values. For example, restricting an OCTET STRING to printable ASCII characters.

**Remote Network Monitor (RMON)** A device that collects information about network traffic.

**Remote Procedure Call (RPC)** A protocol that enables an application to call a routine that executes at a server. The server returns output variables and a return code to the caller.

**Requests for Comments (RFCs)** A set of documents containing Internet protocols and discussions of related topics. These documents are available online at the Network Information Center.

**resolver**   Software that enables a client to access the Domain Name System databases.

**Response**   (version 2) A message responding to a get-request, get-next-request, get-bulk-request, set-request, or inform-request.

**retransmission timeout (TCP)**   If a segment is not ACKed within the period defined by the retransmission timeout, then TCP will retransmit the segment.

**Reverse Address Resolution Protocol (RARP)**   A protocol that enables a computer to discover its IP address by broadcasting a request on a network.

**Ring Management (RMT)**   FDDI component that makes sure that ring activity is normal, and that there is a valid token.

**ring wiring concentrator**   A device that connects multiple stations to an FDDI network.

**RMON MIB**   A MIB that enables a manager to configure a monitor to report statistics, history, host activities, and events, and initiate or end packet capture.

**Round-Trip Time (RTT)**   The time elapsed between sending a TCP segment and receiving its ACK.

**router**   A system used to connect separate LANs and WANs into an internet, and to route traffic between the constituent networks.

**Routing Information Field (RIF)**   Field in a Token-Ring frame that holds a route to be followed, traversing segments and bridges.

**Routing Information Protocol (RIP)**   A simple protocol used to exchange information between routers. The original version was part of the XNS protocol suite.

**routing mask**   A 32-bit quantity with 1s covering the part of the address that is to be matched to a routing table entry, and 0s in the remaining positions.

**Row status**   (version 2) A table variable used to control row creation and deletion.

**runt**   In Ethernet, a frame that is too short—that is, less than 64 octets in length.

**secondary ring**   In FDDI, a ring normally used as a backup path or for wrapping a broken ring. Occasionally used as a concurrent path for transmission, along with the primary ring.

**segment**   (for TCP) A TCP header and (optionally) some enclosed application data.

**segment**   (for bridges) A portion of a LAN; a bridge is said to join LAN segments.

**send window**   The range of sequence numbers between the last octet of data that already has been sent and the right edge of the receive window.

**sequence number**   A 32-bit field of a TCP header. If the segment contains data, the sequence number is associated with the first octet of the data.

**Serial Line Interface Protocol (SLIP)**   A very simple protocol used for transmission of IP datagrams across a serial line.

**set-request**   A message that updates MIB variables.

**shortest path first**   A routing algorithm that uses knowledge of a network's topology in making routing decisions.

**Signal Quality Error (SQE)**   In Ethernet, a signal that reports improper signals on the medium, or responds to an "output idle" signal from the station.

**Simple Gateway Monitoring Protocol (SGMP)**   A predecessor of SNMP.

**Simple Mail Transfer Protocol (SMTP)**   A TCP/IP protocol used to transfer mail between systems.

**Simple Network Management Protocol (SNMP)**   A protocol that enables a management station to configure, monitor, and receive trap (alarm) messages from network devices. Refers to version 1.

**Simple Network Management Protocol version 2 (SNMPv2)**   A proposed update of version 1 that provides additional administrative structure, authentication, and privacy.

**Single-Attachment Station (SAS)**   In FDDI, a station that is attached to a single ring, or has a single attachment to a concentrator.

**socket address**   The full address of a communicating TCP/IP entity, made up of a 32-bit network address and a 16-bit port number.

**source quench**   An ICMP message sent by a congested system to the sources of its traffic.

**source route**   In a Token-Ring, a sequence of ring-number/bridge-number pairs that appear in a special frame Routing Information Field, that indicates the path between two communicating stations.

**source route**   In IP (layer 3), a sequence of IP addresses identifying the route a datagram must follow. A source route may optionally be included in an IP datagram header.

**Source Service Access Point (SSAP)**   An identifier for a frame's source protocol entity.

**Spanning Tree Protocol (STP)**   Protocol used to eliminate loops from a configuration of segments joined by bridges. Bridges exchange Bridge PDU messages, and based on the information, choose a root bridge and determine the best (unique) path from the root to each segment.

**Standby Monitor**   On a Token-Ring, stations perform Standby Monitor protocols which identify neighbors, and initiate recovery if the Active Monitor has failed.

**station**   Any node on a LAN that participates in the LAN's Media Access Control protocol.

**Station Management (SMT)**   An FDDI entity that supervises all of the components of an FDDI station.

**Structure and Identification of Management Information (SMI)**   Includes the definition of the global naming tree used to assign identifiers to managed objects, and the macros used to define object types.

**subnet**   A logical piece of an IP internet. Usually a related set of nodes on a LAN, an entire LAN, a point-to-point line, or some other wide area facility, such as a set of systems on an SMDS network that share a common subnet address.

**subnet address**   A selected number of bits from the local part of an IP address, used to identify a specific local area network or wide area network.

**subnet mask**   A 32-bit quantity, with 1s placed in positions covering the network and subnet part of an IP address.

**Subnetwork Access Protocol (SNAP)**   Implemented as a header that provides some required protocol information—usually a simple identifier that indicates the protocol (such as IP or IPX) to which a frame should be delivered.

**superframe**   (telephony) A unit made up of 12 T1 frames.

**Switched Multimegabit Data Service (SMDS)**   A data transfer service based on the IEEE 802.6 Metropolitan Area Network protocol.

**Switched Virtual Circuit (SVC)**   The packet switched network equivalent of a dial-up line.

**SYN**   A segment used at the start of a TCP connection. Each partner sends a SYN containing the starting point for its sequence numbering, and, optionally, the size of the largest segment that it is willing to accept.

**synchronous communication**   Bit-oriented communication based on clocked timing, and usually encapsulating messages in frames.

**Synchronous Data Link Communications (SDLC)**   A protocol similar to HDLC that is part of IBM's SNA communications protocol suite. SDLC is used for point-to-point and multipoint communications.

**Synchronous Optical Network (SONET)**   A telephony standard for the transmission of information over fiber-optic channels.

**SYNTRAN**   (telephony) See **M13 Multiplex Application.**

**Systems Network Architecture (SNA)**   The protocol suite developed and used by IBM.

**T1 frame**   (telephony) A framing bit followed by 24 8-bit slots carrying information for 24 8-bit slots carrying information for 24 telephone circuits.

**T2 frame**   (telephony) Formed by interleaving four T1 frames.

**T3 frame**   (telephony) Formed by interleaving 28 T1s or 7 T2s, along with some additional framing bits.

**table (logical table)**   A logical structuring of MIB variables into rows and columns.

**Target Token Rotation Timer (TTRT)**   The target maximum elapsed time between token arrivals at each FDDI station.

**Telnet**   The TCP/IP protocol that enables a terminal attached to one host to log in to other hosts and interact with their applications.

**temporal context**   An indication of whether a context is the current context, an initialization context, or a context that corresponds to data that has been cached for a short period of time.

**test and increment**   A variable used that can be used to control sets so that they occur atomically or in a specified order.

**textual convention**   A definition that does not add a new datatype but assigns a convenient name to an existing datatype, and possible imposes some restrictions on the range of values that may be encoded (e.g., restricting an INTEGER to a particular range of values).

**time-domain reflectometry test (TDR)**   A test used to locate an Ethernet co-axial cable fault.

**TimeTicks**   Time measurement in hundredths of a second.

**Time-to-Live (TTL)**   A limit on the length of time that a datagram can remain within an internet. The Time-to-Live usually is specified as the maximum number of hops that a datagram can traverse before it must be discarded.

**tinygram compression**   Ethernet requires that small information fields be padded to a minimum size. Tinygram compression removes the padding before sending the frames across a serial link between bridges.

**Token-Ring**   A local area network technology based on a ring topology. Stations on the ring pass a special message, called a token, around the ring. The current token holder has the right to transmit data for a limited period of time.

**Token Rotation Timer (TRT)**   Measures the time since a station last saw an FDDI token.

**transceiver**   In Ethernet, a device that transmits and receives Ethernet signals.

**transfer syntax**   A set of rules for translating data values into a stream of octets for transmission. See **Basic Encoding Rules.**

**Transmission Control Block (TCB)**   A TCP/IP data structure that contains all of the information about a TCP connection or a UDP communication endpoint.

**Transmission Control Protocol (TCP)**   The TCP/IP protocol that provides reliable, connection-oriented data transmission between a pair of applications.

**transport address**   Address at which a party can be reached. It may be an IP address, or an address based on another protocol.

**Transport Layer Interface (TLI)**   An application programming interface introduced by AT&T that interfaces to both TCP/IP and OSI protocols.

**trap**   A message that reports a problem or a significant event.

**Trivial File Transfer Protocol (TFTP)**   A very basic TCP/IP protocol used to upload or download files. Typical uses include initializing diskless workstations or downloading software from a controller to a robot.

**Trunk Coupling Unit (TCU)**   A hardware element connecting a Token-Ring station to the backbone of a ring.

**trunk ring**   In FDDI, the central, dual ring that forms the core of an FDDI network.

**unicast**   Transmission of a Protocol Data Unit to a unique destination.

**User Datagram Protocol (UDP)**   A simple protocol enabling an application to send individual messages to other applications. Delivery is not guaranteed, and messages need not be delivered in the same order as they were sent.

**variable-bindings list**   A list of (OBJECT IDENTIFIER, value) pairs.

**virtual circuit**   A term derived from packet switching networks. A virtual circuit is supported by facilities which are shared between many users, although each circuit appears to its users as a dedicated end-to-end connection.

**Wide Area Network (WAN)**   A network that covers a large geographical area. Typical WAN technologies include point-to-point, X.25, and frame relay.

**well-known port**   A TCP or UDP port whose use is published by the Internet Assigned Numbers Authority.

**X.121**   A CCITT standard describing the assignment of numbers to systems attached to an X.25 network. These numbers are used to identify a remote system so that a data call can be set up over a virtual circuit.

**X.25**   A CCITT standard for connecting computers to a network that provides reliable, virtual-circuit-based data transmission.

**X.400**   A series of protocols defined by the CCITT for message transfer and interpersonal messaging. These protocols were later adopted by ISO.

**Xerox Network System (XNS)**   A suite of networking protocols developed at Xerox Corporation.

**X-Window System**   A set of protocols developed at MIT that enable a user to interact with applications which may be located at several different computers. The input and output for each application occurs in a window at the user's display. Window placement and size are controlled by the user.

# Bibliography

American National Standards Institute, Carrier-to-Customer Installation—DS1 Metallic Interface, T1.403, February 1989.

———, ANSI X3.4-1977, American National Standard Code for Information Interchange, 1977.

———, ANSI/IEEE802.—Local and Metropolitan Area Networks—Overview and Architecture, 1990.

———, ANSI/IEEE802.1D—Local and Metropolitan Area Networks—Media Access Control (MAC) Bridges, 1990.

———, ANSI/IEEE802.1i—Local and Metropolitan Area Networks—Media Access Control (MAC) Bridges, Fiber Distributed Data Network (FDDI) Supplement, 1992.

———, ANSI/IEEE802.1y, Source Routing Tutorial for End System Operation, September 1990.

———, ANSI/IEEE802.5M-Draft 7, Source Routing Transparent Bridge Operation, 1991.

———, Carrier-to-Customer Installation-DS3 Metallic Interface, ANSI T1.404-1989.

———, Digital Hierarchy—Electrical Interfaces, ANSI T1.102-1987.

———, Digital Hierarchy—Formats Specification, ANSI T1.107-1988.

———, FDDI Station Management (SMT), Draft Proposed American National Standard, X3T9/92-067,X3T9.5/84-49, Rev. 7.2, 1992

———, Fiber Distributed Data Interface (FDDI)—Token Ring Physical Layer Protocol (PHY), ANS X3.148-1988, (also ISO 9314-1, 1989).

———, Fiber Distributed Data Interface (FDDI)—Token Ring Media Access Control (MAC), ANS X3.139-1987, (also ISO 9314-2, 1989).

———, Layer 1 In-Service Digital Transmission Performance Monitoring T1M1/92-0xx, T1M1.3/92-005R1, April 1992.

———, T1.105-1990, Digital Hierarchy—Optical Interface Rates and Formats Specification (SONET), 1990.

———, T1.107, Digital Hierarchy—Format Specifications, 1988.

———, T1.602—Telecommunications—ISDN—Data Link Layer Signalling Specification for Application at the Network Interface, 1990.

———, T1.606—Frame Relaying Bearer Service—Architectural Framework and Service Description, 1990.

———, ANSI T1.617-1991, ISDN—DSS1—Signaling Specification for Frame Relay Bearer Service, 1991.

———, ANSI T1.617 Annex D, Additional Procedures for PVCs Using Unnumbered Information Frames, May 1991.

———, ANSI T1.618, DSS1—Core Aspects of Frame Relay Protocol for Use with Frame Relay Bearer Service, November 1990.

———, T1S1/90-175—Addendum to T1.606—Frame Relaying Bearer Service—Architectural Framework and Service Description, 1990.

———, T1S1/90-214—DSS1—Core Aspects of Frame Protocol for Use with Frame Relay Bearer Service—Architectural Framework and Service Description, 1990.

———, T1S1/90-213—DSS1—Signalling Specification for Frame Relay Bearer Service, 1990.

AT&T, Publication 62411—High Capacity Digital Service Channel Interface Specifications, Compatibility Bulletin 142—The Extended Framing Format Interface Specification.

————, Publication 54016, Requirements for Interfacing Digital Terminal Equipment to Services Employing the Extended Superframe Format, May 1988.

Bellcore TA-TSV-001059, Inter-Switching System Interface Generic Requirements in Support of SMDS Service, December 1990.

————, TA-TSV-001060, Exchange Access SMDS Service Generic Requirements, December 1990.

————, TA-TSV-001062, Generic Requirements for SMDS Customer Network Management Service, February 1991 plus supplement April 1991.

————, TR-TSV-000773, Local Access System Generic Requirements, Objectives, and Interface in Support of Switched Multi-megabit Data Service, June 1991.

Bellovin, S., and M. Merritt, Limitations of the Kerberos Authentication System, Computer Communications Review, October 1990.

Black, Uyless D., Data Communications, Networks, and Distributed Processing, Reston, 1983.

Bolt, Beranek, and Newman, A History of the ARPANET: The First Decade, Technical Report, 1981.

Brand, R., Coping with the Threat of Computer Security Incidents: A Primer from Prevention through Recovery, at cert.sei.cmu.eduin/pub/info/primer, June 1990.

Callon, Ross, An Overview of OSI NSAP Addressing in the Internet, ConneXions, The Interoperability Report, December 1991.

Case, Jeffrey D., Partridge, Craig, Case Diagrams: A First Step to Diagrammed Management Information Bases, Computer Communication Review, May 1990.

CCITT Recommendation I.22, Framework for providing additional packet mode bearer services, Blue Book, ITU, Geneva, 1988

CCITT Recommendation I.122, Framework for providing additional packet mode bearer services, Blue Book, ITU, Geneva, 1988.

CCITT Recommendation I.361, B-ISDN ATM Layer Specification, 1992.

CCITT Recommendation I.362, B-ISDN ATM Adaptation Layer (AAL) Functional Description, 1992.

CCITT Recommendation I.363, B-ISDN ATM Adaptation Layer (AAL) Specification, 1992.

CCITT Recommendation I.413, B-ISDN User-Network Interface.

CCITT Recommendation Q.921, ISDN User-Network Interface Data Link Layer Specification.

CCITT Recommendation Q.922, ISDN Data Link Layer Specification for Frame Mode Bearer Services, April 1991.

CCITT Recommendation X.25, Interface between data terminal equipment (DTE) and data-circuit-terminating equipment (DCE) for terminals operating in the packet mode on public data networks, 1980 and 1984.

CCITT Recommendation X.400, Message Handling System, 1984 and 1988.

CCITT Recommendation X.500, The Directory, 1988.

Cerf, V., A History of the ARPANET, *ConneXions,* The Interoperability Report, October 1989.

CCITT Recommendation G.703, Physical/Electrical Characteristics of Hierarchical Digital Interfaces, July 1988.

CCITT Recommendation G.704, Synchronous frame structures used at primary and secondary hierarchical levels, July 1988.

CCITT Recommendation G.706, Frame Alignment and Cyclic Redundancy Check (CRC) Procedures Relating to Basic Frame Structures Defined in Recommendation G.704, July 1988.

CCITT Recommendation G.732, Characteristics Of Primary PCM Multiplex Equipment Operating at 2048 kbit/s, July 1988.

CCITT Recommendation G.821, Error Performance Of An International Digital Connection Forming Part Of An Integrated Services Digital Network, July 1988.

Cerf, V., and R. Kahn, A Protocol for Packet Network Intercommunication, IEEE Transactions on Communication, May 1974.

Cheswick, B., The Design of a Secure Internet Gateway, *Proceedings of the Summer Usenix Conference,* Anaheim, Ca., June 1990.

cisco, StrataCom, Digital Equipment Corporation, Frame Relay Specification with Extensions, Draft, 1990.

cisco Systems, *Gateway System Manual,* 1991.

Coltun, Rob, OSPF: An internet routing protocol, *ConneXions,* August 1989.

Comer, Douglas E., *Internetworking with TCP/IP,* volume I, *Principles, Protocols, and Architecture,* second edition, Prentice-Hall, 1991.

Comer, Douglas E., and Stevens, David L., *Internetworking with TCP/IP,* volume II, *Design, Implementation, and Internals,* Prentice-Hall, 1991.

Cooper, J., *Computer and Communications Security: Strategies for the 1990s,* McGraw-Hill, 1989.

Datapoint Corporation, Document 50694, Concepts of ARC Local Networking.

Deering, S., IP Multicasting, *ConneXions,* February 1991.

Dern, Daniel P., *The Internet Guide for New Users,* McGraw-Hill, 1994.

———, Standards for Interior Gateway Routing Protocols, *ConneXions,* July 1990.

Digital Equipment Corporation, Northern Telecom, Inc., Stratacom, Inc., Frame Relay Specification with Extensions, Based on Proposed T1S1 Standards, 1990.

Digital Equipment Corporation, Intel Corporation, and XEROX Corporation, The Ethernet: A Local Area Network Data Link Layer and Physical Layer Specification, September 1980.

Electronic Industries Association, EIA Standard RS-232-C, Interface Between Data Communications Equipment Employing Serial Binary Data Interchange, August 1969.

European Telecommunications Standards Institute—ETS"34M"—Metropolitan Area Network Physical Convergence Layer Procedure for 34.368 Megabits per Second, T/NA(91)18, May 1991.

Feit, Sidnie, *TCP/IP: Architecture, Protocols, and Implementation,* McGraw-Hill, 1992.

FTP Software, PC/TCP Kernel Installation and Reference Guide, Version 2.05 for DOS, 1990.

———, *PC/TCP User's Guide,* Version 2.05 for DOS, 1990.

GOSIP, U.S. Government Open Systems Interconnection Profile Version 2.0, Advanced Requirements Group, National Institute of Standards and Technology (NIST), April 1989.

Green, James Harry, *The Dow Jones-Irwin Handbook of Telecommunications,* Dow Jones-Irwin, 1986.

Hedrick, Charles L., Introduction to Administration of an Internet-based Local Network, Rutgers, The State University of New Jersey, 1988, at cs.rutgers.edu, in /runet/tcp-ip-admin.doc.

———, Introduction to the Internet Protocols, Rutgers, The State University of New Jersey, 1987, host cs.rutgers.edu,/runet/tcp-ip-intro.doc.

Hoffman, L., *Rogue Programs: Viruses, Worms, and Trojan Horses,* Van Nostrand Reinhold, 1990.

IBM GA27-3732, IBM Token-Ring Network Technology.

IBM GG24-3442, IBM AS/400 TCP/IP Configuration and Operation, 1991.

IBM GG24-3696, Managing TCP/IP Networks Using NetView and the SNMP Interface, 1991.

IBM SC31-6081, TCP/IP Version 2 Release 2 for VM: User's Guide, 1991.

IBM SC31-6084, TCP/IP Version 2 Release 2 for VM: Programmer's Reference, 1991.

IBM, Vocabulary for Data processing, Telecommunications, and Office Systems, 1981.

Institute of Electrical and Electronics Engineers, Draft Standard P802.1A—Overview and Architecture, 1989.

———, Local Area Networks—CSMA/CD Access Method, ANSI/IEEE 802.3, (ISO 8802-3).

———, Local Area Networks—Distributed Queue Dual Bus (DQDB) Subnetwork of a Metropolitan Area Network (MAN), ANSI/IEEE 802.6 (ISO DIS 8802-6, 1991).

———, Local Area Networks—Higher Layers and Interworking, ANSI/IEEE802.1, 1990 (ISO DIS 8802-1D, 1990).

———, Local Area Networks—Logical Link Control, ANSI/IEEE 802.2, 1989 (ISO 8802-2, 1989).

————, Local Area Networks—Network Management. Draft IEEE 802.1B, 1990.

————, Local Area Networks—Network Management—IEEE 802.3 Layer Management, November 1988.

————, Local Area Networks—Token-Bus Access Method, ANSI/IEEE 802.4, (ISO 8802-3).

————, Local Area Networks—Token Ring Access Method, ANSI/IEEE 802.5, 1989 (ISO 8802-5, 1989).

International Organization for Standardization, Information Processing Systems—Common Management information Protocol (CMIP), ISO 9596, 1990.

————, Information Processing Systems—Common Management information Service (CMIS), ISO 9595, 1990.

————, Information Processing Systems—Data Communications—Addendum to the Network Service Definition, ISO 8348 AD1.

————, Information Processing Systems—Data Communications—High-Level Data Link Control Procedures—Consolidation of Classes of Procedures, ISO 7809.

————, Information Processing Systems—Data Communications—High-Level Data Link Control Procedures—Consolidation of Elements of Procedures, ISO 4335.

————, Information Processing Systems—Data Communications—High-Level Data Link Control Procedures—Description of the X.25 LAPB-compatible DTE data link procedures, ISO 7776, December, 1986.

————, Information Processing Systems—Data Communications—High-Level Data Link Control Procedures—Frame Structure, ISO 3309, 1979.

————, Information Processing Systems—Data Communications—High-Level Data Link Control Procedures—Frame Structure—Addendum 1: Start/stop transmission, 1991.

————, Information Processing Systems—Data Communications—High-Level Data Link Control Procedures—General purpose XID frame information field contents and format, ISO 8885.

————, Information Processing Systems—Data Communications—Network Service Definition, ISO 8348.

————, Information Processing Systems—Data Communications—Protocol for Providing the Connectionless-Mode Network Service, ISO 8473.

————, Information Processing Systems—Data Communications—X.25 Packet layer Protocol for Data Terminal Equipment, ISO 8208, March 1990.

————, Information Processing Systems—Fibre Distributed Data Interface (FDDI)-Part 3: Token Ring Physical Layer, Medium Dependent (PMD)

————, Information Processing Systems—Open Systems Interconnection—Basic Connection Oriented Session Protocol Specification, ISO 8327.

————, Information Processing Systems—Open Systems Interconnection—Basic Connection Oriented Session Service Definition, ISO 8326.

————, Information Processing Systems—Open Systems Interconnection—Connection Oriented Presentation Protocol Specification, ISO 8823.

————, Information Processing Systems—Open Systems Interconnection—Connection Oriented Presentation Service Definition, ISO 8822.

————, Information Processing Systems—Open Systems Interconnection—Connection Oriented Transport Protocol, ISO 8073.

————, Information Processing Systems—Open Systems Interconnection—Intermediate System to Intermediate System Intra-Domain Routing Exchange Protocol for use in Conjunction with the Protocol for Providing the Connectionless-Mode Network service, ISO DIS 10589.

————, Information Processing Systems—Open Systems Interconnection—Message Handling System, ISO 10021/CCITTX.400.

————, Information Processing Systems—Open Systems Interconnection—Protocol Specification for the Association Control Service Element, ISO 8650.

————, Information Processing Systems—Open Systems Interconnection—Remote Operations: Model, Notation, and Service Definition, ISO 9072-1.

————, Information Processing Systems—Open Systems Interconnection—Remote Operations: Protocol Specification, ISO 9066-2.

————, Information Processing Systems—Open Systems Interconnection—Service Definition for the Association Control Service Element, ISO 8649.

————, Information Processing Systems—Open Systems Interconnection—Specification of Abstract Syntax Notation One (ASN.1), ISO 8824, December 1987.

————, Information Processing Systems—Open Systems Interconnection—Specification of Basic Encoding Rules for Abstract Syntax Notation One (ASN.1), ISO 8825, December, 1987.

————, Information Processing Systems—Open Systems Interconnection—Transport Service Definition, ISO 8072.

————, Information Processing Systems—OSI Reference Model—Part 4: Management Framework, ISO 7498-4.

————, OSI Routing Framework, ISO TC97/SC6/N4616, June 1987.

Jacobson, V., Congestion Avoidance and Control, ACM SIGCOMM-88, August 1988.

Jain, R., and K. Ramakrishnan, and D-M Chiu, Congestion Avoidance in Computer Networks With a Connectionless Network Layer, Technical Report, DEC-TR-506, Digital Equipment Corporation, 1987.

Kapoor, Atul, *SNA, Architecture, Protocols, and Implementation,* McGraw-Hill, 1992.

Karn, P. and C. Partridge, Improving Round Trip Time Estimates in Reliable Transport Protocols, *Proceedings of the ACM SIGCOMM,* 1987.

Kehoe, Brendan, *Zen and the Art of the Internet: A Beginner's Guide to the Internet,* Prentice-Hall, 1992.

Kernighan, Brian W., and Dennis M. Ritchie, *The C Programming Language,* second edition, Prentice-Hall, 1988.

Kessler, Gary C., and Train, David A., *Metropolitan Area Networks,* McGraw-Hill, 1992.

Kessler, Gary C., *ISDN,* McGraw-Hill, 1990.

Kochan, Stephen G. and Wood, Patrick H., consulting editors, *UNIX Networking,* 1989.

Krol, Ed, *Whole Internet Users Guide and Catalog,* O'Reilly and Associates, 1992.

Laquey, T. L., *User's Directory of Computer Networks,* Digital Press, 1989.

Lippis, Nick, and James Herman, Widening Your Internet Horizons, *ConneXions,* October 1991.

Malamud, Carl, *DEC Networks and Architectures,* McGraw-Hill, 1989.

————, *STACKS-The INTEROP Book,* Prentice-Hall, 1991.

McKenney, P., Congestion Avoidance, *ConneXions,* February 1991.

McNamara, John, Technical Aspects of Data Communication.

Mogul, Jeffrey C., Efficient Use of Workstations for Passive Monitoring of Local Area Networks, Proc. SIGCOMM '90 *Symposium on Communications Architectures and Protocols,* September 1990.

Narten, T., Internet Routing, *Proceedings of the ACM SIGCOMM,* 1989.

National Institute of Standards and Technology (NIST), Federal Information Processing Standard (FIPS) Publication 46-1, Data Encryption Standard, January, 1977; reaffirmed January, 1988.

Nemeth, Evi, Garth Snyder, and Scott Seebass, *UNIX System Administration Handbook,* Prentice-Hall, 1989.

Network General Corporation, Sniffer Network Analyzer Network And Protocol Reference, 1992.

Network General Corporation, Sniffer Network Analyzer Operations, 1993.

Pfleeger, C., *Security in Computing,* Prentice-Hall, 1989.

Postel, J. B., C. A. Sunshine, and D. Chen, The ARPA Internet Protocol, *Computer Networks,* 1981.

Postel, J. B., C. A. Sunshine, and D. Cohen, The ARPA Internet protocol, *Computer Networks,* vol. 5, no. 4, July 1981.

Postel, J. B., Internetwork Protocol Approaches, *IEEE Transactions on Communications,* 1980.

Quarterman, John S., and Hoskins, J. C., Notable Computer Networks, *Communications of the ACM,* October, 1986.

Quarterman, John S., The Matrix, *Computer Networks and Conferencing Systems Worldwide,* Digital Press, 1990.

Romkey, John, The Packet Driver, *ConneXions,* July 1990.

Rose, Charles G., *Programmer's Guide to NetWare,* LAN Times Book Series, 1990.

Rose, Marshall T., *The Little Black Book: Mail Bonding with OSI Directory Services,* Prentice-Hall, 1990.

————, *The Open Book: A Practical Perspective on OSI,* Prentice-Hall, 1990.

————, *The Simple Book: An Introduction to Management of TCP/IP-based Internets,* Prentice-Hall, 1990.

————, *The Simple Book: An Introduction to Management of TCP/IP-based Internets,* Prentice-Hall, second edition, 1994.

St. Amand, Joseph V., *A Guide to Packet-Switched, Value-Added Networks,* Macmillan, 1986.

Schwartz, Michael F., Resource Discovery and Related Research at the University of Colorado, *ConneXions,* May 1991.

Seyer, Martin, RS-232 Made Easy.

Sidhu, Gursharan S., Richard F. Andrews and Alan B. Oppenheimer, *Inside Apple Talk,* Addision-Wesley Publishing Company, 1989.

Stallings, William, *Data and Computer Communications,* Macmillan, 1984.

————, *Handbook of Computer Communications Standards,* Department of Defense Protocol Standards, 1988.

Stevens, W. Richard, *UNIX Network Programming,* Prentice-Hall, 1990.

Tannenbaum, Andrew S., *Computer Networks,* Prentice-Hall, 1981.

Tsuchiya, Paul F., Inter-domain Routing in the Internet, *ConneXions,* January 1991.

Vitalink, Building and Managing Multivendor Networks Using Bridge and Router Technologies, 1990.

Wiggins, Richard, *The Internet for Everyone: A Guide for Users and Providers,* McGraw-Hill, 1994.

XEROX, Internet Transport Protocols, Report XSIS 028112, Xerox Corporation, 1981.

# Index